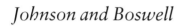

Johnson and Boswell

JOHN B. RADNER

Johnson and Boswell

A BIOGRAPHY OF FRIENDSHIP

Yale

UNIVERSITY PRESS
New Haven &
London

Published with assistance from the Annie Burr Lewis Fund, and from the foundation established in memory of Calvin Chapin of the Class of 1788, Yale College.

The author is grateful to the publishers of the following essays, where portions of this work originally appeared, for permission to reprint: "Boswell's and Johnson's Sexual Rivalry," *Age of Johnson* 5 (1992): 201–46; "Pilgrimage and Autonomy: The Visit to Ashbourne," in *Boswell: Citizen of the World, Man of Letters,* ed. Irma S. Lustig (Lexington: Univ. of Kentucky Press, 1995), 203–27; "From Paralysis to Power: Boswell with Johnson in 1775–1778," in *James Boswell: Psychological Interpretations,* ed. Donald J. Newman (New York: St. Martin's, 1995), 127–48; "'A Very Exact Picture of His Life': Johnson's Role in Writing *The Life of Johnson,*" *Age of Johnson* 7 (1996): 299–342; "Johnson and Boswell in the Hebrides: Constructing an Adventure, Negotiating for Narrative Control," in *Literary Couplings,* ed. Marjorie Stone and Judith Thompson (Madison: Univ. of Wisconsin Press, 2006), 59–78. In addition, the following materials from the Yale Boswell Collections are quoted by kind permission of the Yale Boswell Editions: vols. 1–9 of the *Correspondence* series, vols. 1–3 of the *Life of Johnson* Manuscript Edition, the unpublished volume of the *Life of Johnson* Manuscript Edition, *The Private Papers of James Boswell from Malahide Castle, in the Collection of Lt.-Colonel Ralph Heyward Isham* (18 vols., pub. 1928–1934), Boswell's published journals (1762–1795), and unpublished correspondence to and from Boswell.

Yale University Press books may be purchased in quantity for educational, business, or promotional use. For information, please e-mail sales.press@yale.edu (U.S. office) or sales@yaleup.co.uk (U.K. office).

Set in Sabon type by Keystone Typesetting, Inc.
Printed in the United States of America.

Library of Congress Cataloging-in-Publication Data
Radner, John B.
    Johnson and Boswell : a biography of friendship / John B. Radner.
        p. cm.
    Includes bibliographical references and index.
    ISBN 978-0-300-17875-3 (cloth : alk. paper)
1. Johnson, Samuel, 1709-1784 — Friends and associates. 2. Boswell, James, 1740–1795 — Friends and associates. 3. Authors, English — 18th century — Biography. 4. Authors, American — 19th century — Biography. I. Title.
PR3533.R24 2012
828'.609 — dc23
[B]
2012019520

A catalogue record for this book is available from the British Library.

This paper meets the requirements of ANSI/NISO Z39.48–1992 (Permanence of Paper).

10 9 8 7 6 5 4 3 2 1

To
Josh and Jack
&
to Elly

Contents

Preface

I would not have begun this evolving study of friendship and collaboration without the inspiration and encouragement of key mentors and friends,
and would not have completed it without ample assistance, guidance, and
support.

I was first introduced to Johnson by the late Walter Jackson Bate's engaging,
challenging lectures, which — along with the capaciousness, energy, and com-
passion of Johnson's prose — prompted me to write my honors thesis on Johnson's religion. My experiencing a few years later how Bate's presence inspired
all the students in a graduate seminar on Johnson to surpass ourselves, and
then my reading his masterly *Samuel Johnson* (1977), confirmed his role as a
key reader of anything I would write about Johnson. Throughout this project,
I have been collaborating with Bate, and also competing: seeking originality
without rejecting his hard-earned, brilliant, movingly expressed insights concerning Johnson's character and life.

Irma S. Lustig facilitated the early stages of this study, and my engagement
with Boswell. Her invitation to write a conference paper on the texts Johnson
and Boswell wrote during and after the long Hebrides trip led me to wonder
for the first time how traveling together — and regularly sharing journals —
fundamentally changed the structure of a friendship I then only sketchily
understood. She also accepted a paper, for a later conference, on Johnson's

and Boswell's "sexual rivalry", suggested I explore the Ashbourne visit for a collection of essays she was editing to mark the bicentennial of Boswell's death, introduced me to the rich collection of manuscripts at Yale, and challengingly assessed all the writing I showed her.

Deborah Kaplan thoughtfully annotated my unwieldy expansion of the original Hebrides paper, a draft that led me to realize I needed to write a book about this friendship, and singled out a long footnote on "sexual rivalry" for immediate development. Later she — along with Hans Bergmann and Lorna Irvine — helped improve "Johnson's and Boswell's Sexual Rivalry," which the late Paul J. Korshin then accepted for publication in *The Age of Johnson.* (Paul also accepted a second long article: "'A Very Exact Picture of His Life': Johnson's Role in Writing *The Life of Johnson.*")

As I began exploring this friendship, I learned much from students in several graduate and undergraduate classes on Johnson and Boswell. In addition, Amy Fulton-Stout, a student in the first of these graduate seminars, later spent a year as my research assistant, helping me chart the varied, shifting transactions described in Boswell's journals.

I used conference papers at the American Society for Eighteenth-Century Studies and the wonderful East-Central ASECS to probe key aspects of the Johnson-Boswell friendship, test ideas and connections, and discover what would be the shaping features of my book. Questions and comments during sessions and afterward helped clarify my thinking, and showed I was telling an engaging story. I am grateful to the chairs who accepted my papers and to all those who responded, especially Lisa Berglund, Mark Booth, Ted Braun, Peter Briggs, William Edinger, Isobel Grundy, Raymond Hilliard, Jim May, Philip Smallwood, Linda Troost, and Myron Yeager.

Drafts of some conference papers and other sections of the book were annotated and discussed by members of the long-lived Folger Colloquium on Eighteenth-Century Women Writers, established by Susan Lanser and eventually coadministered by Paula McDowell: a diverse group representing significant parts of the audience I hoped my book might interest. I learned much from these discussions, and without them my work would have been much lonelier.

From the start, I have also been indebted to generations of scholars and critics who edited the texts Johnson and Boswell published; edited their letters, diaries, and journals, and the manuscript of the *Life of Johnson;* wrote biographies of Johnson and Boswell; and illuminatingly examined their published and unpublished texts, especially their Hebrides texts and the *Life.* As the endnotes suggest, this study would have been impossible without their work.

I am grateful to George Mason University for two essential faculty study leaves, and to Irma Lustig, Patricia Meyer Spacks, and my two chairs (Hans Bergmann and Chris Thaiss) for supporting my applications. A Beinecke Fellowship supported my initial study of Boswell's manuscript of the *Life of Johnson*, and I again thank Gordon Turnbull and Howard Weinbrot for recommending me. I also thank Hans and Harriet Bergmann for hosting me during follow-up visits to Yale.

Living in Washington, D.C., I have easy access to the Folger Library, the Library of Congress, and the rare book room at Georgetown University; and through George Mason I have recently had access to Eighteenth Century Collections Online. But my book also draws on material in the Houghton Library at Harvard and heavily depends on material in the Beinecke Rare Book and Manuscript Library at Yale; and I thank the helpful staffs at both libraries. Also from near the start I have benefited from the resources in the Boswell Editions office at Yale and from the knowledgeable and extraordinarily responsive people working there: initially, the late Rachel McClellan and the late Irene Adams; more recently, Nadine Honigberg, James Caudle, and Gordon Turnbull.

Donald J. Newman solicited — and then helped deepen and clarify — "From Paralysis to Power: Boswell with Johnson in 1775–1778," an article complementing "Pilgrimage and Autonomy: The Visit to Ashbourne," which I had written for Irma Lustig's book. Marjorie Stone's and Judith Thompson's comments and questions pushed me to think more concretely and suggestively about collaboration as I wrote and revised "Constructing an Adventure and Negotiating for Narrative Control: Johnson and Boswell in the Hebrides" for their stimulating collection *Literary Couplings: Writing Couples, Collaborators, and the Construction of Authorship.*

Once I began drafting chapters, a number of friends offered to read portions: each added perspectives from his or her own interest and expertise, all collectively helped me better address a diverse audience. Henry Fulton, whom I met at the conference where I first talked about the Hebrides trip, agreed to read the whole of my text in its fullest, wordiest, clumsiest form in exchange for my reading his meticulously grounded and wide-ranging biography of the Scottish physician and author John Moore. Elizabeth Lambert generously read much of the draft at various stages, and Eileen Sypher read most of the revised version. All three consistently helped me see what I had overlooked or failed to make clear. Thomas Bonnell, William Granitir, Ann Kelly, Linda Merians, Jeffrey Nason, Lance Wilcox, and Margaret Yocom each gave shrewd, informed attention to several chapters, including some I had found particularly difficult to write. Paul D'Andrea, Jerry Gans, Nancy Gans, Patrick Henry, Audrey Kelaher, Peter Klappert, Roger Lathbury, George Mattingly, Barbara Melosh, Ellen

Moody, the late Paul Myron, Judith Plotz, Charlotte Smokler, Mary Margaret Stewart, and William Yarrow each helpfully read some. Collectively, they saved me from many ambiguities and infelicities, called for fewer details and a foregrounding of the central drama, and encouraged me to press forward. I hope they are as pleased with what has now been published as I was by their earlier attention.

I thank Richard Sher for urging me to submit the manuscript to Yale University Press, and Vadim Staklo for managing the process that led to the manuscript's being accepted for publication. I am grateful to two anonymous readers for many useful suggestions and corrections, and to Kip Keller for remarkably alert, knowledgeable, and resourceful copyediting. I also thank Margaret Otzel for skillfully and cheerfully overseeing the production of this book.

My creative and self-reliant sons, Josh and Jack, have helped me experience and understand much that lies at the core of this study: the shifts in power and responsibility, in authority and independence, as parents and children, teachers and students, become grown-up friends. My energetic, resilient wife, Elly Greene, read many of these chapters, astutely calling for clarity and relevance, and throughout this long project helped me stay focused and positive. It is with enormous gratitude that I dedicate this book to all three.

Introduction

Their first meeting was fortuitous. Having read with admiration some of Samuel Johnson's many publications, and having heard accounts of his brilliant conversation, James Boswell in 1762 accepted an invitation from the actor and bookseller Tom Davies to Christmas dinner, where Johnson was expected. But Johnson had gone to Oxford, having just learned that his dear friend Richard Bathurst had died in the siege of Havana. Then, five months later, while Boswell was having tea in Davies's back room on Russell Street, Johnson unexpectedly stopped by, "a Man of a most dreadful appearance," as Boswell noted in his journal, though his "great knowledge and strength of expression command vast respect and render him very excellent company." After a few hours, Boswell had to leave this feast of impressive talk, but later filled several journal pages with Johnson's authoritative analyses and forceful, decisive assessments.[1]

Over the next six weeks, Boswell and Johnson edged toward connecting. Boswell visited Johnson at his lodgings eight days after they first met, then waited twenty days before returning. But twelve days later they spent an evening at the Mitre Tavern in Fleet Street, where Boswell told the "history" of his religious doubts and the "Story" of his troubled relationship with his father, and Johnson offered reassuring, encouraging responses based on his own experience. In answering Boswell's doubts about Christianity, Johnson confessed "that he himself was once a talker against Religion; for he did not think against it, but had an absence of thought." Johnson also endorsed Boswell's plan to study abroad, insisting, "A Father & a Son should part at a certain time of life." When Boswell told how he had lapsed from Christianity to infidelity and then regained his faith, "tho' I might not be clear in many particulars," Johnson cried, "Give me your hand. I have taken a liking to you." When Boswell mentioned his need to study, Johnson promised to "put [him] upon a plan," and Boswell put out *his* hand, asking, "Will you realy take a charge of me?" When they finally parted after 1 A.M., having talked over port for four or five hours, they clearly were becoming friends.

Having seen each other on only five of the previous forty days, they were together on five of the next twenty-four, then on twelve of the final nineteen before Boswell sailed to Holland, including a full-day trip down the Thames to Greenwich and an overnight trip to Harwich on the coast. "It must be something curious for the people in the Turk's-head Coffee-house to see this great Man and poor Me so often together by ourselves," Boswell wrote near the end of his London journal. Certainly when they walked "arm in arm" along the Strand after each tavern evening, there was a striking contrast between the short, relatively plump, and youthful Boswell and the towering, ungainly, and clearly much older Johnson, especially if Boswell was wearing the silver-hilted sword that marked him as a fashionable gentleman. On 14 July, Boswell showed Johnson some of his current journal, in which he labored to capture Johnson's remarkable "strength of Sentiment and Perspicuity of expression," and Johnson said, "My Dear Boswell! I do love you very much." Johnson imagined traveling with Boswell to the Hebrides once his new friend returned from abroad, and seeing Boswell's family estate in Ayrshire. But as Boswell boarded the ship to Holland on 6 August, both worried what would become of their friendship.[2]

When he met Boswell in 1763, the fifty-three-year-old Johnson was a major figure in literary London, where he had lived since 1737, three years before Boswell was born. But his rise in stature had been slow. When *London* was published in 1738, the chief poet at the time, Alexander Pope, declared that the anonymous author of this powerful imitation of Juvenal's biting attack on Rome would "soon be *deterré*" (unearthed). But Johnson's verse tragedy *Irene,* finished shortly after he came to London, was performed only in 1749, when David Garrick, who had ventured to London with Johnson and soon become a leading actor and eventually the manager of the Drury Lane Theatre, arranged for it to be performed. Meanwhile, Johnson worked as an anonymous hack, writing poetry, translations, topical biographies, reviews, and other pieces mainly for the *Gentleman's Magazine,* including the substantial *Parliamentary*

Debates (from 1740 to 1743). In 1744, Johnson wrote a psychologically pen-etrating *Life* of the poet and celebrity Richard Savage, with whom he had often spent nights walking the streets of what was already the largest city in Europe, and still growing. Two years later, a group of booksellers commissioned John-son to produce a definitive English dictionary, and after nine years — years dur-ing which Johnson also wrote an imitation of Juvenal's Satire X (*The Vanity of Human Wishes* [1749]) and about two hundred and thirty substantial moral and critical essays (the *Rambler,* also the *Adventurer*) — the massive *Dictionary of the English Language* was published. For two years starting in April 1758, he wrote weekly *Idler* essays for the *Universal Chronicle,* and early in 1759 he quickly composed *Rasselas,* a philosophical tale set in Abyssinia and Egypt, to pay for his mother's funeral. (Johnson's wife, Elizabeth, had died in 1752, shortly after Johnson wrote the final *Rambler* essays; and despite a plan to "seek a new wife" the following year, Johnson had not married again.) But in 1760, Johnson began to sink into a general lassitude. In 1756, he had collected subscriptions for a new edition of Shakespeare, initially scheduled for publica-tion in 1758; but this was still not completed in 1763, a year after a royal pension of £300 a year had freed Johnson from the financial need to write.[3]

The twenty-two-year-old Scot who met Johnson in 1763 was in line to head an Ayrshire family that proudly traced its roots to the early sixteenth century. He had been in London once before, in spring 1760, when he fled the univer-sity at Glasgow, where he had been studying rhetoric and moral philosophy with Adam Smith, to become a Roman Catholic in London and then head toward France, where he hoped to become a monk or a priest. He had quickly been seduced by the glamour and dissipation of the capital, however, abetted by Alexander Montgomerie, the able but indolent tenth Earl of Eglinton. After three months, James was escorted home by his father, Alexander, eighth laird of Auchinleck, who in 1754 had become Lord Auchinleck, one of the fifteen judges of the Court of Session, the supreme court of Scotland for civil cases, and the following year had been named one of the six members of the High Court of Justiciary, the supreme criminal court.

Back in Edinburgh, Boswell reluctantly studied civil law with his father while also publishing theatre criticism and exchanging exuberant, self-consciously clever letters with a young officer and poet, Andrew Erskine — a correspondence that Boswell had published just five weeks before he met Johnson. Having in July 1762 passed his examinations in civil law, Boswell returned to London in November with an annual allowance of £200, hoping that well-connected patrons like the Duke of Queensberry, the Duchess of Northumberland, and the Earl of Eglinton would help him secure a commis-sion in the Foot Guards so he could live genteelly in the stimulating metropolis. He also hoped to refashion himself as someone more serious and reserved — "to attain constancy & dignity, without which I can never be satisfied" — a process he charted in journal entries sent in weekly installments to a friend from college, John Johnston, of Grange. In March 1763, he learned that he could get a commission only in a regular regiment, just when many were being disbanded in the aftermath of the Seven Years' War. So by June, when Boswell asked Johnson to "take a charge" of him, he was negotiating with his father for permission to spend two years studying and traveling abroad before returning home.[4]

Boswell's *Life of Johnson* (1791) makes it easy to imagine continuity and coherence in their friendship. But this was not how it seemed from within. Neither man suspected what would happen — and what would *not* happen — after Johnson agreed to "take a charge" of Boswell in 1763, but wrote only twice before again seeing him early in 1766, and sent only five more letters during the next six years. Neither knew how their friendship would change once Boswell decided to become Johnson's biographer, and Johnson then began systematically describing his early years, invited his biographer to share his usually private Good Friday devotions, and finally ventured to Scotland for the long-anticipated trip to the Hebrides. Traveling together for twelve weeks while regularly exchanging travel journals further transformed their friendship in ways neither had anticipated. After Johnson published an account of their richly collaborative journey, Boswell hoped to publish a version of the journal that Johnson had earlier praised and encouraged, but was angered and paralyzed by Johnson's resistance. Meanwhile, Johnson was disappointed that Boswell mostly no longer shared his current journal, and later refused to agree to another life-affirming "adventure." In its final years, the friendship was further challenged by the death of Henry Thrale, whose family for sixteen years had provided Johnson a second home; by Boswell's anxieties and ambitions when he finally became laird of Auchinleck; and by Johnson's physical decline.

This book charts the friendship from the moment Johnson and Boswell met on 16 May 1763 to the publication of Boswell's *Life* exactly twenty-eight years later. It analyzes the key interactions, seeking to understand what each friend experienced at every stage of their long-term attachment. It examines how Johnson and Boswell challenged and confirmed each other, and provided perspectives that became internalized. It explores how their friendship deepened and evolved, how and why it endured, and how each perceived his "rivals."

Sustained attention to the dynamics of this richly documented friendship risks exaggerating its significance to both men, especially Johnson, as Boswell deliberately did in the *Life*. But with the key exceptions of Johnson himself and perhaps Hester Thrale, no one invested more time and energy than Boswell in imagining and reimagining Johnson, in understanding and assessing him. Boswell had many other important friendships, but none as radically grounding as this one. Even after Johnson's death, no one else's opinion mattered more.

For Johnson, the situation was different. Many other friendships were at least as important, though not so fully documented, and some scholars have pointedly rejected Boswell's account of his significance, regarding him as essentially a parasite. But Johnson's letters as well as Boswell's journal suggest that from the start—long before Boswell decided to write the *Life*—Johnson found this friendship unusually promising and demanding. Then the biographical project, and especially their sharing of journals during a trip that occurred mainly because of that project, enhanced Johnson's ability to see how he appeared to others. This encouraged Johnson to modify his behavior in response to what his biographer said, what he saw in Boswell's journal, or what he imagined Boswell might eventually write. Engagement with Boswell also challenged Johnson to reconcile the many different self-images he helped construct. Hester Thrale remained more central than Boswell, and several others were more respected. But especially during and after the Hebrides trip, Johnson's friendship with Boswell was uniquely significant.

Part of the appeal of this friendship has been its archetypal, almost mythic quality, based largely on Boswell's texts. An insecure young man with a cold, judgmental father finds a wise and decisive older man who warmly endorses him, a childless widower who zestfully "adopts" him. A famous writer who excels in witty and instructive conversation finds someone eager to record much that he said and did. The story is especially engaging because Johnson was so enthusiastic and decisive, and Boswell had the persistence and skill to produce and then record much of Johnson's experience.

But the story of this friendship involves two particular persons who, when they met, had certain needs, expectations, and clearly developed patterns of interacting. Johnson differed in key ways from the others whom Boswell had asked to guide him, and Boswell differed from those Johnson was already mentoring. Boswell's account of what happened in 1763 suggests that from the start, this new friendship expanded each man's sense of what was possible and modified his sense of himself. Nine years later, when Johnson accepted Boswell's plan to become his biographer, they entered uncharted territory. There were many literary examples of mentor-mentee relationships, including those Johnson had created in *Rasselas*. But only after Boswell published the *Life* was there a model for the relationship between a writer and his or her "Boswell."[5]

This friendship is fascinating because of the energy and imagination of these articulate, passionate men, who produced most of the material that allows us to glimpse what they experienced and to empathize. In conversation and letters, in journals, and eventually in books — Johnson's *Journey to the Western Islands of Scotland* (1775), Boswell's *Journal of a Tour to the Hebrides* (1785) and *The Life of Samuel Johnson* (1791) — each used their friendship to define and assess himself. In this book, I challenge both, especially Boswell, as I describe a friendship that was much more volatile, contentious, and troubled than what is pictured in the *Journey,* the *Tour,* and especially the *Life.* I emphasize worry and fear and guilt as well as intimacy, and call attention to regular renegotiations. I chart the persistent neediness that drove Boswell to seek tangible links to Johnson, to publish their friendship in his book on Corsica, and to write himself into Johnson's life by becoming his biographer, as well his defiant and collaborative efforts to achieve autonomy in anticipation of living in a world without Johnson. I describe Johnson's engagement and empathy but also his envy and aggression; his delight with Boswell's exuberance, but also his worry that Boswell would never achieve self-control; his pleasure in telling his story through Boswell, but also his fierce desire to control what remained of his life, to narrate himself apart from as well as through Boswell, and to keep parts of his experience hidden.

I see this friendship as an evolving, multifaceted collaboration. Boswell's journal shows that he and Johnson quickly developed modes of interacting that satisfied their complementary needs. From the start, their friendship was what Boswell, in his shared Hebrides journal, called "a co-partnery," in which "each was to do all he could to promote its success." Boswell's requests for information, assessments, and clarifying arguments elicited energizing analyses, revealing anecdotes, and occasionally surprising fantasies. Johnson's "immense fund of knowledge and wit" had been locked up until Boswell set him in motion; and Johnson's vigorous talk grounded and enlivened Boswell. They soon added traveling together to tavern suppers, and eventually they shared Good Friday devotions and Easter dinner whenever Boswell was in London. As they zestfully imagined founding a college or exploring the Baltic, or spent Good Friday calmly reflecting on the "vanity of human wishes," or discussed Johnson's college memories while visiting Oxford, or judiciously recalled what Johnson had said the day before at events often arranged by Boswell to let his friend perform, they reaffirmed their close connection while they brought each other to life.[6]

They also worked together as writers or wrote with the other clearly in mind. Starting in spring 1772, Johnson regularly helped Boswell construct legal briefs and also began self-consciously preparing his friend to write the

Life. In fall 1773, they collaboratively constructed Boswell's Hebrides journal, with Johnson — its main subject and also its initial reader — helping his traveling companion produce and correct this fullest account of their collaborative tour. Johnson then wrote the *Journey* with minimal direct input from Boswell; but in significant ways, Johnson was responding to the journal he had read, privately addressing the friend best equipped to confirm or challenge his version of events. In addition, much that Boswell published during this friendship — especially his *Account of Corsica* (1768) and monthly *Hypochondriack* essays (1777–1783) — explicitly built on what Johnson had written and said, even though Johnson became aware of his role only when he later saw these works in print. And of course the *Life* was Boswell's sustained, final collaboration with his mentor and friend.[7]

In May 1763, Boswell wrote his father that he was "struggling for independency," while Lord Auchinleck was "struggling for authority." Six weeks later, Boswell reported Johnson saying that "there must always be a Struggle between a Father and Son, while the one aims at power, and the other at Independency." (In Johnson's *Dictionary,* "independence" and "independency" are equivalents, and the definitions of "power" and "authority" overlap.) If a tension between "authority" and "independence" aptly describes the relationship between Boswell and his father, at least as Boswell experienced and described it, it applies even more suggestively to the evolving, richly collaborative Johnson-Boswell friendship, from the moment Boswell got Johnson to agree to "take a charge" of him to the moment when Boswell, by publishing the *Life,* confirmed his authority to tell Johnson's story. As Johnson and Boswell scripted and directed their time together, questioned and advised and challenged, confided and held back, each at times serving as the other's conscience and guide — as they negotiated and renegotiated their deepening friendship — they richly experienced and articulated the shifts in authority and (in)dependence that occur in all long-term friendships, especially those between friends more than thirty years apart in age.[8]

The biographical project augmented the usual tensions. Preparing Boswell for the *Life* repeatedly confirmed Johnson's authority concerning what he had done and thought and felt, while allowing him to decide what experiences to reveal, what to keep secret. But charting Johnson's experiences for a work to be written only after Johnson's death linked Boswell with God's inscrutable assessment of how Johnson had used his time and talents, and thereby enhanced his control. Still, Boswell never outgrew a need for Johnson's approval and support. Even when he asserted his independence by rejecting some of Johnson's judgments and by modifying or defying some of his restraints. In fact, he wrote the *Life* in part to win the final blessing that his failure to write to his dying friend had cost him.

The evidence concerning this friendship is substantial but incomplete. It usually provides Boswell's perspective more clearly than Johnson's. And numerous gaps and silences call for interpretation.

We have most of Boswell's extensive journal describing time with Johnson from 1763 onward. But he sometimes wrote nothing about what he and Johnson said and did, and even in his fullest entries could never report all that had happened, all that Boswell thought and felt. Also entries for certain days were later removed by Boswell's scandalized descendants.

What survives of Johnson's much more limited diary includes a few telling references to Boswell, starting in 1772; and though we lack the notebook Johnson shared during the Hebrides trip, we have his long narrative letters to Hester Thrale. But Johnson never wrote anything about most of his time with Boswell. Also, aside from his letters to Boswell, there is little evidence of how Johnson thought and felt about the young Scot in his absence.

We have complete texts of seventy-six of these letters, but cannot see most of what Boswell did not print in the *Life* from twenty-four others. Boswell printed some of his many letters to Johnson, and described several others in the *Life* or in his Register of letters; but for most of what he wrote Johnson, we lack even descriptions. Some of their surviving letters to others, however, contain suggestive comments on this friendship; and comparing how they wrote to each other with how they wrote to other friends helps clarify how this friendship was special.

Though few friendships are so fully documented, especially at the start, the evidence is much fuller concerning Boswell than Johnson — except during the Hebrides trip. For all their encounters until 1772 and for most of them afterward, we have only what Boswell remembered and reported in memoranda, journal entries, letters, and the *Life* manuscript: words and gestures originally prompted by Boswell's questions, perhaps constricted by his presence, and filtered through Boswell's "reading" of Johnson. Because of this material, we know a great deal about Johnson's specific activities on many otherwise undocumented days. But we encounter Johnson as an actor in scenes that Boswell produced and described, following Boswell's lead or improvising in ways that delighted or puzzled his new friend.

Boswell did not express all his impressions of this evolving friendship, just as he surely kept secret some details when, on 25 June, he described his religious doubts and his troubles with Lord Auchinleck. But his letters and journal entries allow us to speak with assurance about much that he thought and felt. Writing decisively about Johnson is much trickier, since until his letter of 8 December 1763, we have only what Boswell reported. Concerning their six hours at the Mitre on 14 July, for instance, we can read what Boswell wrote in letters to three different friends and in his journal. But there is no way to know how Johnson would have described this evening, which of the items Boswell reported mattered to him, and what else he might have emphasized. We know much that Boswell experienced both before and after each encounter with Johnson, as well as how he discussed Johnson with others. But once Johnson left Boswell's sight, we usually no longer know what he did and saw except when he wrote letters, none of which mention Boswell until 1772; nor can we see what Johnson thought and felt about his new friend. It almost seems as if Johnson is waiting for Boswell to set him in motion.

Despite ample evidence of how little we generally remember of what we have seen and heard, and despite doubts some have raised about specific material Boswell added much later, I generally assume he and Johnson did and said what Boswell reported — even in entries written later from skimpy notes. Johnson himself called Boswell's Hebrides journal "a very exact picture" of this portion of his life, and comparing this journal both with letters that Johnson sent Hester Thrale from Scotland and with the *Journey* turns up only a few factual discrepancies, all of which can easily be resolved. What others occasionally wrote about Johnson and Boswell's interactions mostly confirm what Boswell reported. But these accounts usually include material Boswell did not mention, calling attention to the selectivity of even his richest entries, something Boswell himself sometimes highlighted. Also, since Johnson and Boswell differed significantly in what they chose to report while traveling together, in how they described their interactions, and in their images of "Johnson" and "Boswell," I regret having few comments by Johnson on their other days together. So I try to use Boswell's often-full entries without being seduced by them. I try to read behind the words Boswell assigns to Johnson. In particular, I keep in mind that Boswell often planned to share with others what he was writing, and also that what he wrote in a specific entry might chiefly reflect what happened between the day being described and the moment he was writing.[9]

Because even their fullest letters and journal entries cannot report all that was said and done, or all that Johnson and Boswell thought and felt, key parts of the story are elusive and enigmatic. Much must be constructed by zooming in on suggestive interactions and statements, or by filling in gaps and silences. "By conjecture only can one man judge of another's motives or sentiments," as Johnson wrote while praising the value of autobiography. Only by conjecture, for instance, can one suggest how — if at all — Boswell mattered to Johnson from August 1763 through March 1772, when they were seldom together and Johnson hardly wrote, or why Boswell decided to become Johnson's biographer, or how Johnson initially felt about this project. By immersing myself in all the available data, and by consistently trying sympathetically to construct both men's perspectives, I hope to illuminate key features of this fascinating friendship.[10]

But "what we collect by conjecture," Johnson added, "is easily modified by fancy or by desire." Given the enthusiasms and longings that drew me to explore this friendship, I risk misinterpreting. Like any biographer — and any reader of biography — I am guided and limited by my own experiences, and connect most deeply with what resonates personally. Attentive insistence on evidence can guard against outright projection and ensure that what I emphasize truly deserves attention. But there are undoubtedly aspects of this friendship that warrant more attention than I have given them, features others will need to highlight.

Taking Charge of Boswell (1763)

What did Johnson and Boswell each make of the other when they met on 16 May 1763, and what did each get from their time together during the next twelve weeks? What did their new friendship mean to each when they parted on 6 August? How did this change in the four months before Johnson finally replied to Boswell's August and October letters?

Keeping in mind that much is elusive about why people become friends, I want to begin answering these questions by charting the twenty-two days in 1763 when Johnson and Boswell were with each other, in each case noting where they met, whether they were in company or alone (or both), and whether they were together for just a few minutes (short), for a more substantial conversation (long), for several hours (hours), or for the whole day (all day). I have also included 25 December 1762, the first day Boswell attempted to meet Johnson, and have noted their letters during the final months of 1763.

25 December	JB dines at Tom Davies's expressly to meet SJ; instead meets Oliver Goldsmith		
16 May	SJ arrives while JB at tea with Davies	company/alone	hours
24 May	JB visits SJ's house, stays when others leave	company/alone	long

13 June	JB visits SJ's house	alone	long
15/16 June	JB & SJ meet by chance on street at 1 A.M.	alone	short
25 June	JB & SJ meet by chance at Clifton's chophouse;	alone	short
	sup together by arrangement at Mitre	alone	hours
1 July	JB & SJ sup with Goldsmith at Mitre	company	hours
5 July	JB stops by SJ's	alone	long
6 July	JB consults SJ about his landlord's rudeness;	alone	short
	JB invites SJ and four others to sup at Mitre	company	hours
9 July	JB finds others with SJ, later recalls nothing said	company	short
14 July	SJ and JB sup at Mitre	alone	hours
19 July	JB finds others with SJ, stays, sees SJ's "library"	company	long
20 July	SJ, Dr. Boswell & George Dempster sup at JB's	company	hours
22 July	JB to SJ's, then sup at Turk's Head Coffee House	alone	hours
26 July	JB to SJ's	alone	long
28 July	SJ and JB sup at Turk's Head Coffee House	alone	hours
30 July	daytrip to Greenwich, then sup at Turk's Head	alone	all day
31 July	JB to SJ's	alone	short?
2 August	SJ to JB's; tea with Mrs. Williams; sup at TH	company/alone	hours
3 August	final supper at Turk's Head	alone	hours
4 August	JB stops by SJ's to confirm Harwich trip	alone	short
5 August	SJ and JB in coach to Colchester; alone at night	company/alone	all day
6 August	coach to Harwich; dinner there; JB to ship	company/alone	all day
? 15 August	Boswell posts a troubled letter to Johnson		
7 October	Boswell sends a more positive letter		
8 December	Johnson writes a long letter (received 14 December)		
20 December	Boswell replies with a "noble letter"		

Even apart from Boswell's reports of what he and Johnson said and did while together, this chart clearly indicates a developing friendship. There was a steady progression in the frequency of contact: from six meetings (three by chance) on five days during the first six weeks — through 26 June — to eighteen meetings on seventeen days during the next six weeks. In the first six weeks, they were only twice together for hours; but in the next three weeks, they spent three evenings together; and they had considerable time together, mostly alone, on eight occasions during the final three weeks. Boswell wrote soon after reaching Holland and again about seven weeks later. But curiously, Johnson responded only in December, four months after the two friends had parted.

Later I argue that what Johnson and Boswell experienced before Boswell left, combined with what happened — and what did *not* happen — afterward, created the longings that eventually led Boswell to become Johnson's biographer and that inclined Johnson to accept this transforming adjustment. So I want to be as clear as possible about what each experienced in 1763.

Boswell (16 May to 6 August): "Will you really take a charge of me?"

During his first months in London, Boswell delighted in his diverse moods, his whims and openness to new experience, even as he worked at constructing a unified, dignified self. He relished his "sensibility," his "romantic imagination," his capacity to be moved by music and literature and landscape. But he hoped to acquire sufficient resolution and firmness of mind to bear up under disappointments. Early in 1763, he agreed with the flattering declaration by the actor and playwright David Garrick, whom Boswell had met in 1760, that Boswell would "be a very great man," for, as Boswell described himself, "There is a blossom about me of something more distinguished than the generality of Mankind." But he worried that this blossom "will never swell into fruit": "I sometimes indulge noble Reveries of having a Regiment, of getting into parliament, making a figure, and becoming a man of consequence in the state. But these are checked by dispiriting reflections on my melancholy temper and imbecility of mind." Seeing himself as a work in process, Boswell hoped to "become sounder & stronger as I grow up."[1]

To facilitate his progress Boswell had repeatedly sought authority and guidance from older men such as West Digges, a Scottish actor; Lord Kames, a Scottish philosopher and judge; and Sir John Pringle, a Scottish physician and Lord Auchinleck's oldest friend, though he also tried to maintain some "independency." Thomas Sheridan, an Irish actor and teacher of elocution, had been Boswell's mentor — "My Socrates" — from the summer of 1761 up through

January 1763, when he rejected Boswell's prologue for his wife's play, at which point Boswell approached Sir David Dalrymple, a lawyer and scholar respected by both Boswell and his father, who in 1762 had witnessed the agreement to let his father appoint trustees should Boswell inherit Auchinleck before he had proved capable of self-control. On 10 February 1763, Boswell asked Dalrymple to "take a charge" of him: to "let me know what books to read, & what company to keep, and how to conduct myself." His "precepts might do me good," Boswell added, and "I might follow them just as far as I thought them right," since Dalrymple in Scotland would not see any deviations. At Dalrymple's suggestion, they wrote every week for the next six months.[2]

In May, realizing he had no chance for a commission in the Foot Guards, Boswell asked Dalrymple to help negotiate a peace with his father. Partly because of Dalrymple's intercession, but chiefly because of Boswell's conciliatory letter, which suggested he was "a little settled from [his] reelings," Lord Auchinleck agreed to allow his heir two years of study and travel abroad before returning home for further study and the practice of law. (Lord Auchinleck had studied law at Leyden, but Dalrymple suggested Utrecht, where he had studied.) At the end of this letter, Lord Auchinleck urged Boswell to "find out some person of worth who may be a friend, not one who will say as you say when with you, and when he is away will make a jest of you as much as any other." Two months before Boswell read these words, William Temple, a close friend from college in Edinburgh, had come to London, and was with Boswell on about half the days from 2 April through 7 July. Though more "liberal" than five years before, Temple still encouraged Boswell's "fixing on some plan of life." He advised Boswell to "force [himself] to be reserved & grave" and provided occasions to be "rational & composed, yet lively & entertaining." On 9 June, a day after his father's letter arrived, Temple endorsed Boswell's decision to study law and assured his friend he "might live like Sir David Dalrymple at Edinburgh; be at London three months in the year, and live more comfortably than if [he] pushed the scheme of the Guards."[3]

Temple was a sobering, calming influence, just the sort of friend Lord Auchinleck had hoped Boswell would find. Before Temple left for Cambridge early in July, Samuel Johnson had also begun to assume this role.

At first, Boswell seems not to have been especially eager to reconnect with Johnson. He reported being "sorry" on 16 May at having to leave the lively conversation; but he delayed visiting Johnson for more than a week. On 24 May, Johnson received Boswell "very courteously" into his "very solemn and very slovenly" chambers, and spoke with such authority about the "very strong evidences" for Christianity that Boswell "listened to this great Oracle with much satisfaction," and resolved in the entry for 24 May to "cultivate this acquaintance." But they next met twenty days later, when Boswell once again stopped by Johnson's. When they then parted, Boswell reported that Johnson "shook me by the hand at parting, & asked me why I did not call oftener." But despite this explicit encouragement, and Boswell's awareness of the benefit of their connection — "I am never with this man without feeling myself bettered & rendered happier" — twelve days passed before their next sustained conversation.[4]

About this time, however, Boswell began seeking extended time alone with Johnson. According to the *Life,* as they parted on 13 June, Johnson promised to spend an evening with Boswell at the Mitre tavern, without designating a date. When they met by chance at 1 A.M. on 16 June, Boswell suggested their going then, but Johnson knew they would not be admitted so late. He offered to go "another night with all my heart," but nothing was scheduled. Two days later, Boswell planned to call on Johnson: "Be fine & appoint him to sup with you next week. Think of telling him your imbecility — your disposition to ridicule &c. & take his advice." Having initially sought Johnson as a London celebrity, and then as a reassuring authority, an energizing intellect, Boswell now wished to recast him as a mentor, complementing Dalrymple in the role once played by Sheridan. Having agreed with his father to abandon the Guards scheme and to practice law in Scotland after study and travel abroad, Boswell hoped Johnson would provide a plan for the time he had been given.[5]

If Boswell stopped by on 18 June, Johnson must have been out. But there is no record of Boswell's trying to connect until he saw Johnson a week later at Clifton's chophouse and arranged to meet him that evening. Then, as they talked from nine until after one, Boswell confessed much more than his "imbecility" and "disposition to ridicule," asked for more than a plan of study, and heard much more than advice. During these hours, their relationship significantly deepened, and Boswell "went home in high exultation."[6]

Until 28 July, Boswell continued to initiate their contacts, stopping by for visits and arranging tavern suppers. Boswell invited others to join them at their next two suppers: Johnson's friend Goldsmith on 1 July, and Goldsmith again on 6 July, along with Davies and two others — though, curiously, not Temple, who would return the next day to Cambridge. On 11 July, however, Boswell's memorandum reads, "see Johnson soon & consult on Plan fully and be as oft wt. him as you can"; and on 14 July, Boswell and Johnson spent a second long evening alone at the Mitre. They solidified their friendship by returning to all the topics raised on 25 June, confirmed that they were "very good Companions," and self-consciously agreed that two bottles of port "would seem to be the quantity for us." On 20 July, their next evening together, Boswell invited his eccentric uncle, John Boswell, M.D., and his friend George Dempster, a Scottish lawyer and member of Parliament. But from that point on, the two new friends were mostly alone, spending six additional evenings together before they parted on the beach at Harwich.[7]

When with others, they discussed a range of literary and political topics, on which Johnson spoke with authority and rebutted challenges. When alone, their talk regularly returned to the topics that Boswell had raised when they were first alone — his doubts about religion, his relationship with Lord Auchinleck, and his "plan of study" — on all of which Johnson offered advice and arguments grounded in his own experience. They also discussed their friendship, hoping it would survive the coming separation.

From the start, Boswell was impressed with Johnson's energy and power of mind, his "great Knowledge," and "that strength of Sentiment & perspicuity of expression for which he is remarkable." No one else had such range and forcefulness. Johnson established his authority by seeking fundamental explanations, general principles, springs of actions, as when he offered "strong reasons" to justify Boswell's "strong monarchical Inclinations." He also drew significant conclusions from "the most trivial matters," as when Boswell's report of a man (also named Johnson) riding at full gallop while standing first on one horse and then on two showed what could be achieved through "industry and application" and should inspire everyone to become "equally expert in whatever profession he chose to pursue." Even "lively enough" talk appeared "very trifling after being with Mr. Johnson," and the entries reporting their conversations — conversations also described in letters to Temple, Dalrymple, and Lieutenant Andrew Erskine — were generally much fuller than others.[8]

Johnson was all that Sheridan and Kames and Dalrymple had been — and more. He was wiser — or at least deeper delving — than anyone Boswell had met, and more consistently alert and lively. Boswell described Johnson as a "great Oracle," a "great man." But he was facetious, too, and exuberant, as when he imagined all the outrageous things Boswell might do if his surly landlord tried to hold him to the lease on rooms he now wished to vacate. Also Johnson clearly identified with Boswell, which none of his other mentors seem to have done, and Johnson's autobiographical revelations made him a heartening example. Johnson, too, had not always been an assured Christian, but now was a firm believer; and Boswell echoed Johnson when he wrote Dalrymple that his own past "skepticism was not owing to thinking wrong, but to not thinking at all." Johnson also knew from experience that struggle between a son and a father was unavoidable, but he confidently anticipated harmony once Boswell — "at thirty" — had become what Lord Auchinleck wanted him to be now.[9]

Johnson also reassuringly emphasized his indolence. Having initially promised to devise a plan of study for Boswell, he later reported having never followed a plan for more than two days. Instead, he advised Boswell simply "to read just as inclination prompted," to set aside "five hours a day for study, and in these hours gratify whatever literary desires may spring up." When Boswell worried he had been away from books so long that he had lost all interest in reading, Johnson reported that he, too, "allways felt an inclination to do nothing." ("He says he has led but an idle life," Boswell wrote Temple; "think . . . of that.") When Boswell marveled that "the most indolent man in Britain had written the most laborious work, *The English Dictionary,*" Johnson said that "if he had applied properly," he might have done it in three years rather than ten.[10]

Johnson also encouraged Boswell to "keep a journal of [his] life, fair and undisguised," something he himself had often unsuccessfully resolved to do. According to Boswell, Johnson "said it would be a very good exercise, and would yield me infinite Satisfaction, when the ideas were faded from my Remembrance." Lord Auchinleck was baffled that "a lad of sense and come to age should be so childish as to keep a register of his follies and communicate it to others as if proud of them," and Temple initially feared that writing a journal would make Boswell "hunt about for adventures to adorn it with" instead of being "calm & studious and regular in [his] conduct." But Johnson endorsed the reflective, self-defining writing Boswell been doing for more than ten months. And when Boswell "gave him a specimen" to read — probably the entry for 6 July, which reports their morning discussion of Boswell's rude landlord, then some of the wide-ranging talk that night, when "Mr. Johnson was exceeding good company" and Boswell "gently assisted conversation by those little arts which serve to make people throw out their sentiments with ease and freedom" — Johnson "laughed placid, and said very well." Boswell reported this sharing only to Erskine, who earlier had approved the journal. But he wrote Dalrymple that Johnson encouraged keeping a journal, assuming he would tell his father.[11]

Boswell also learned that Johnson had achieved so much despite suffering, like Boswell, from debilitating depression. On the same day he first told Johnson of his religious doubts and his troubles with Lord Auchinleck, Boswell wrote Dalrymple that he had "at bottom a melancholy cast, which dissipation relieves by making me thoughtless, and therefore an easier, tho' a more contemptible, animal." Four weeks later, when he finally told Johnson he was "much afflicted with Melancholy which was hereditary" — his grandfather, but not his father, had been prone to depression — Boswell was heartened to hear that Johnson, too, "had been greatly distressed with it, & for that reason had been obliged to fly from Study and Meditation to the dissipating variety of life." Unlike Lord Auchinleck and all his previous mentors, Johnson was a fellow depressive. Based on his experience, Johnson urged Boswell "to have constant Occupation of mind, to take a great deal of exercise, and to live moderately; especially to shun drinking at night." Boswell had recently given similar advice to his melancholy friend Johnston of Grange, and he had resolved to avoid taverns—except with Johnson, and the poet Charles Churchill. But it gave him "great relief" to discuss his melancholy with Johnson, "that strange satisfaction which human Nature feels at the idea of participating distress with others." Johnson's suffering from melancholy was especially reassuring because he had nevertheless written so much and so well, and had achieved such coherence of character.[12]

Boswell also reported with delight how Johnson repeatedly declared his affectionate regard, moving beyond "tak[ing] a charge" of Boswell to hugging him close. In the journal entry for 13 June, after reporting Johnson's assurance that "he was very glad to see me," Boswell added, "Can I help being vain of this?" On 25 June, when Boswell told the history of his religious life, Boswell saw Johnson "was much pleased with my ingenuous open way, & he cried, 'Give me your hand, I have taken a liking to you.'" At some point on 14 July, Johnson said, "My dear Boswell! I love you very much"—words Boswell reported the next day to Temple, a day later to Dalrymple, soon to Erskine, and eventually in the entry he posted to Grange, each time adding a version of "Can I help indulging Vanity?" Eight days later, Johnson "said (with an affection that almost made me cry) My dear Boswell! I should be very unhappy at parting, did I think we were not to meet again," and declared he would go with Boswell to the Hebrides once his new friend returned home—words Boswell again reported in letters before writing this part of his journal. "I am bound by the ties of nature to love you," Boswell's father had somewhat coldly written. Johnson's love was spontaneous and enthusiastic.[13]

The entry for 28 July recorded Johnson's fullest endorsement of Boswell's progress: "He said that I was very forward in knowledge for my age; that a man had no reason to complain who held a middle place and had many below him; and that perhaps I had not six above me. Perhaps not one. He did not know one." ("This was very high," Boswell noted.) Two months earlier, Lord Auchinleck had written that when Boswell applied himself to law, he "showed as much genius for it . . . as any ever I knew." Now Boswell explicitly cast Johnson as his father, asking "if he was my Father, and if I did well at the law, if he would be pleased with me." Johnson accepted the role with pleasure: "'Sir,' said he, 'I should be pleased with you whatever way of life you followed, since you are now in so good a way. Time will do all that is wanting.'" ("When you was in the irreligious way," Johnson added, "I should not have been pleased with you," prompting Boswell to thank him "for having established my Principles.") After they returned from Greenwich two days later, Johnson at supper offered to accompany Boswell to Harwich, which Boswell saw as a "prodigious mark of his affection."[14]

Boswell in response held tight to Johnson as a loving, approving, liberating mentor or substitute father. He marveled at how being with Johnson brought him to life in ways quite different from writing Erskine the letters they had recently published, or singing catches with Lord Eglinton, or fancying himself Captain Macheath (from John Gay's *The Beggar's Opera*) while enjoying "high debauchery" with "two pretty little Girls" in a tavern. "I think better of myself when in his company than at any other time," he wrote Dalrymple. "His conversation rouses every generous principle."[15]

Boswell saw limits in Johnson's sensibility and sometimes rejected his claims. But as Boswell began internalizing Johnson's perspective, he modified some initial objections, as when he reported Johnson's complaint that John Ogilvie's poetry lacked "novelty," or suggested eventually burning his journal, or criticized Dempster's lack of principles. He laughed at how Johnson urged him to "perambulate" Spain, but he still planned to go there. "I learn more from him than from any Man I ever was with," he wrote Temple on 23 July, after which he was with Johnson on three of the next seven days and six of the following seven.[16]

Johnson (16 May to 6 August): *"There are few people whom I take so much to, as to you"*

The Johnson presented in Boswell's journal and letters is a consistent character whose conversations with Boswell show strong affection for the young man and growing regard. But it is not wholly clear how Johnson experienced this developing friendship. What first attracted him to Boswell, and how did this attraction develop? What did he value in Boswell? In what ways—if any—did Boswell surprise him? In answering these questions, we can draw on Johnson's documented interactions with other young friends as well as on all he wrote about friendship. But we need to keep in mind the limitations of the evidence.

I suspect that Johnson in 1763 saw a Boswell very much like the Boswell presented in the London journal: someone curious and bright and full of potential, but self-absorbed and insecure; someone respectful and flattering, but also challenging; someone socially adept but radically needy, willing, after 9 June, to please his father but unwilling to admit defeat by returning at once to Edinburgh, and worried about managing abroad. Boswell's journal and letters suggest several different aspects to Johnson's response, distinct strands of what eventually constituted a rich and complex attachment. Some were present from the start, some not until 25 June, but all are evident from 14 July onward as Johnson anticipated Boswell's departure and arranged to spend more and more time with him.

In 1763 as throughout his life, Johnson delighted in company and feared solitude, and his need for distraction was greater now that the pension freed him from having to write regularly. Though it was not until 1769 that Boswell began to sense just why Johnson so disliked being alone, the gestures and words he reported make clear that Johnson enjoyed having the young Scot's companionship. Boswell initiated their early contacts, but Johnson prolonged and encouraged them. When Boswell rose to leave on his first visit, Johnson twice urged him to stay, saying that "he was obliged to any Man who visited him." When Boswell next visited, twenty days later, Johnson asked why he did not come more often; and when Boswell said he feared being "troublesome," Johnson replied he "was not; & he was very glad to see [Boswell]." When Boswell mentioned in their next conversation his need to study, Johnson offered to "put [him] upon a plan," but added, "It will require some time to talk of that," hence more conversations. "I hope we shall pass many evenings and mornings too together." When Boswell a month later asked again about his "method of Study at Utrecht," Johnson proposed that they "make a day of it": "Let us go down to Greenwich, and dine."[17]

There is ample evidence that Boswell was a charming companion who combined diffidence with zest and had a range of knowledge and interests. On 1 July, Goldsmith praised Boswell's "method of making people speak," prompting Boswell in his journal to add, "if I excel in anything, it is in address and making myself easily agreeable." Besides his own pressing issues, which he brought up regularly, Boswell introduced numerous other topics. At Davies's on 16 May, it was almost surely Boswell who asked about Kames's *Elements of Criticism* and Sheridan's lectures in Bath. On 13 June, he described the skillful rider he had seen perform three days earlier, and on 14 July he told "what a strange mortal" James Macpherson, the author of the celebrated prose epic *Fingal,* "was, or affected to be." Boswell also arranged for Johnson to connect with others: twice in the first week of July and once two weeks later. But Johnson seemed chiefly to prize their time alone, which is mainly what they had in the final month.[18]

The Johnson whom Boswell described appreciated Boswell's flattering gratitude. He was "pleased" on 24 May when Boswell said, "It is benevolent to allow me to sit and hear you," and "very complacent" on 25 June when Boswell said, "It is very good in you, Mr. Johnson, to allow me to sit with you thus." Similarly, when Boswell told Johnson on 14 July "that the *Rambler* shall accompany me round Europe, and so shall be a *Rambler* indeed," Johnson "gave me a smile of complacency." Boswell also passed along praise from others. On 14 July, he "introduced" Johnson to Sir David Dalrymple and read Sir David's praise of Johnson as "one of the best Moral Writers which England has produced"; and on 22 July, Boswell told Johnson that Sir James Macdonald "had a great respect, though at the same time a great terror, for him."[19]

This direct and reported flattery was especially effective, since Boswell did not simply flatter. On 24 May Boswell wondered whether it was right for Johnson to rise at noon, dine abroad at four, and generally return home at two, instead of better using "his talents." Johnson agreed this "was a bad habit," and seven weeks later told Boswell he intended to produce "more imitations of Juvenal." The journal entry Boswell probably shared on 14 July praised Johnson's "amazing universality" as a writer, lamenting, "It requires more parts than I am master of even to retain that strength of sentiment and perspicuity of expression for which he is remarkable." But it also criticized Johnson's "want of taste in laughing at the wild grandeur of Nature, which to a mind undebauched by Art conveys the most pleasing, awfull, sublime ideas." In addition, Boswell's sharing of this entry showed that anything Johnson said or did when with Boswell might be reported and assessed.[20]

Besides companionship, flattery, and a promise of having his words recorded, Boswell also offered Johnson a chance to be useful. In the conversations Boswell described, as in those Hester Thrale, Frances Burney, and others later reported, Johnson delighted in speaking with authority on religion and morality, on study and self-management. Like the wise poet Imlac in *Rasselas,* Johnson enjoyed guiding young men and women, and Boswell's eagerness for instruction allowed Johnson to transform long tavern evenings and a day in Greenwich into exercises of benevolence.

Johnson also strongly and explicitly identified with Boswell, finding or forging links with his new friend's religious doubts, his troubles with his father, his indolence, and his depression: connections that helped him instruct and, in the process, perhaps make up for past deficiencies. When Boswell's anxiety about Utrecht increased, Johnson established another link by suggesting they discuss Boswell's "plan of study" in the same place (Greenwich) where Johnson had taken "country lodgings" after first venturing to London, "and used to compose in the Park; particularly, his *Irene.*"[21]

To further deepen his intimacy with Boswell, Johnson shared other parts of his story, other ways he regarded himself. At least twice he remarked that were it not for his idleness, he would have finished the dictionary much sooner, without detailing the interrupted progress that scholars have recently begun to chart. On 25 June, he made clear that a sense of himself as "a very wicked fellow" who "will certainly be punished" unless he repents was "deeply impressed upon [his] mind." Four weeks later he told Boswell—and also Dempster and Dr. Boswell—that when he was a boy he "used allways to choose the wrong side of a debate, because most ingenious things[,] that is to say, most New things could be advanced upon it." Two days later he told Boswell that everything the skeptical Scottish philosopher David Hume "has advanced against Christianity had passed through his own mind long before Hume wrote."

Boswell told at length the "history" of his religious life and the "story" of his conflict with Lord Auchinleck, because he wanted advice and reassurance. Johnson instead did what people generally do when forming new friendships: he told anecdotes that incrementally revealed some of who he was and what he valued. Boswell's companionship offered Johnson a chance to define himself in a relatively free, noncompetitive, nonjudgmental arena. By asking why he got along so well with Johnson but not with his own father, Boswell gave his new friend a chance to flatter himself as "a man of the world" who takes on "the colour of the world as it moves along," in contrast to Lord Auchinleck, "a judge in a remote part of the country," all of whose "notions are taken from the old world." Six days later Johnson boasted "that no man who lived by literature had lived more independent than he had done." Each of these stories and boasts, especially those told to Boswell alone, was an affectionate gesture, comparable to Johnson's cordially taking his new friend's hand. Presumably, Johnson had told many of these stories when he first met other friends, just as he would do twenty years later while visiting the family of another new young friend, William Bowles.[22]

Johnson also lived vicariously through this young man whose prospects were so much richer than his had been, a usual practice of his. By imagining what he would do were he in Boswell's circumstances, he could advise with specificity while transforming potential envy into sympathetic delight. His advice on traveling was particularly exuberant: "I would go where there are courts of learned men"; "be as much as possible with men of learning, especially the Professors in the Universities, and the Clergy." "He is not very fond of the notion of spending a whole winter in a Dutch town," Boswell wrote Dalrymple on 16 July: "He also advises me to visit the northern kingdoms, where more that is new is to be seen than in France and Italy. But he is not against my seeing these warmer regions." Johnson repeatedly urged Boswell to explore Spain, about which so little was known that "a Man of inferior parts to [him] might give us useful observations on that Country." He also looked ahead to the time when Boswell would inherit the family estate, relishing his prospects as "a Scotch landlord" with many "families dependent upon, & attached to [him]," which "is perhaps as high a Situation as Humanity can arrive at."[23]

Boswell clearly was available, entertaining, and flattering, and his neediness gave Johnson a chance to use his time and talents well while also living vicariously. But Boswell's narrative also shows Johnson frequently affirming his liking and regard, his friendship and his love, for Boswell. Johnson accepted the role of "father" because he saw Boswell's insecurity, but also because he delighted in this adopted "son," who was "very forward in knowledge for [his] age" and now was "in so good a way."

On 22 July, Johnson gave three reasons why he "loved the acquaintance of young People": first, "I don't like to think of myself turning old"; second, "Young Acquaintances must last longest, if they do last"; and finally, "young Men have more virtue than old Men," and "the young dogs of this Age . . . have more wit & humour & knowledge of life, than we had." As he spoke these words, and when he later told Boswell, "There are few people whom I take so much to, as you," Johnson surely was thinking of the best known of these "young dogs": Robert Chambers (1737–1803), soon to become Vinerian Professor of Law at Oxford, and two just returned from Italy, Bennet Langton (1737–1801) and Topham Beauclerk (1739–1780) — all three slightly older than Boswell, all of whom Johnson had known for years. Six days later, Johnson must again have thought of these men when he declared that Boswell "had not six above [him]," adding, "Perhaps, not one." Johnson might also have been thinking of George Strahan (1744–1824), the son of his publisher and longtime friend, William Strahan, to whom he had written, "I love you, and hope to love you long," just hours before he took Boswell by the hand on 14 July and said, "My dear Boswell! I do love you very much."[24]

In the *Rambler*, Johnson eloquently described our deep longing for friendship "at once fond and lasting," and throughout *Rasselas* he highlighted the importance of friends. But he had also charted the many reasons why friendships fail to endure. In particular, he noted how "Friendship, like love, is destroyed by long absence, though it may be encreased by short intermissions." He therefore feared what would happen during Boswell's years abroad. So on 22 July, shortly before Boswell was to leave, Johnson proposed their eventually traveling together to the Hebrides, as a way of affirming that they would "meet again" after Boswell returned. Meanwhile, he devoted time to this engaging, seemingly uncompetitive attachment. When they returned from Greenwich on 30 July, Johnson offered to accompany Boswell to his ship. When Boswell that same evening described his family and Auchinleck, Johnson declared, "I must be there, and we will live in the Old Castle; and if there is no room remaining, we will build one." Eight days later, a day before they parted on the coast, Johnson said he might come to Holland the following summer "and accompany [Boswell] in a tour through the Netherlands."[25]

These spontaneous fantasies of shared, possibly adventurous travel, of do-

Fig. 1: Sir Joshua Reynolds, portrait of Samuel Johnson, 1769, studio variant, Houghton Library, Harvard University, MS Eng 1411.

mestic intimacy and collaborative room building, were not merely responses to Boswell's anxiety, and expressed more than delight in Boswell's flattering company. In Johnson's imaginings, each scenario involved the sort of isolation with Boswell that Johnson was enjoying when he proposed them. Johnson would be so fully connected with Boswell that he would momentarily forget all others — but not his duties, since time with Boswell always entailed teaching, guiding.

Fig 2: George Willison, portrait of James Boswell, 1765 (in Rome), reproduced by permission of the Scottish National Portrait Gallery, Edinburgh.

Johnson knew this exclusiveness was impossible — except at moments. But this did not block him from expressing his deep longings when comfortably engaged, as he seems to have been in those first weeks with Boswell, as he perhaps had been in when first connecting with the other "young dogs" he loved. Ten years later, when he and Boswell finally traveled together to the Hebrides, Johnson would come closer to satisfying these longings than he did during any other sustained period. But this was only after their friendship had been strained, reconfigured, and significantly deepened.[26]

First Tensions (3 August to 6 August 1763)

On 3 August, a day after Johnson introduced Boswell to Anna Williams — the former companion of Elizabeth Johnson who had lived with or near Johnson since his wife's death, a woman blinded by cataracts who sat up every night till Johnson stopped by for tea — an unexpected misunderstanding at their final Turk's Head supper probably heightened each friend's anxiety about their friendship. When Boswell, "laughing heartily" and expecting Johnson to join in, repeated David Hume's report that Johnson had said he "would stand before a battery of cannon, to restore the Convocation to its full powers," Johnson exploded with "high-church zeal": "And would I not, Sir? Shall the Presbyterian Kirk of Scotland have its General Assembly, and the Church of England be denied its Convocation?" As Johnson came close to Boswell, "his eyes flash[ing] with indignation," Boswell glimpsed an unexpected dimension in his new mentor and perhaps wondered what else he had not seen. Boswell did not report his misunderstanding and Johnson's passion in the brief entry he posted to Grange. But he had both vividly in mind twenty-four years later when he described this day in the *Life*.

Meanwhile, Johnson saw that his new friend had completely failed to grasp his perspective. The young Scot, who had earlier sought Johnson's help in refuting doubts raised by Hume's texts, had joined Hume in laughing at his settled position. Johnson perhaps suspected Boswell of having kept a strong connection with his nemesis, though he did not know that nine months earlier, Boswell had called Hume "the greatest writer in Brittain," and recently had been steadily reading his multivolume *History of England*.[27]

Two days later they started on their first overnight trip, during which Boswell for the first time reported Johnson teasing him in public and criticizing him in private. When all the passengers dined the first day, Johnson first confessed to having been "an idle fellow" all his life, then shifted attention to Boswell's idleness: "He was idle in Edinburgh. His Father sent him to Glasgow, where he continued to be idle. He then came to London, where he has been very idle, and now he is going to Utrecht, where he will be as idle as ever." Later, when Boswell pestered Johnson "with fanciful apprehensions of unhappiness," Johnson took advantage of a moth's burning itself on their candle to comment — "with a sly look, and in a solemn but quiet tone" — "That creature was its own tormentor, and I believe its name was Boswell." Then shortly before they parted the next day, Johnson rebuked Boswell for unthinkingly saying it would be "*terrible*" if Johnson were confined for long in so dull a place as Harwich: "Don't, Sir, accustom yourself to use big words for little matters."[28]

This teasing, scolding, and admonishing suggest Johnson's distress at Boswell's departure, but also apprehension. After praising Boswell eight days earlier for all he had accomplished, Johnson had added, "Time will do all that is wanting." Now he seemed worried. Boswell's "principles" were established, and he could easily learn to speak more carefully. But could he overcome his idleness and his self-tormenting worries? No notes survive for the trip to Harwich. But either Boswell had some when he narrated these days for the *Life,* or he remembered in detail the unexpected exchanges that raised doubts about Johnson's attitude, doubts Boswell had trouble silencing in Utrecht as he waited for Johnson to write.

On the beach at Harwich, they "embraced and parted with tenderness." Once Johnson turned toward town, the two friends were emphatically separate, with no clear sense of what would come next, no immediate way of knowing what the other was thinking and feeling. They had known each other for less than three months, but they had been together on twelve of the last nineteen days. According to the *Life,* when Boswell said, "I hope Sir you will not forget me in my absence," Johnson replied, "Nay Sir, it is more likely you should forget me than that I should forget you." They promised to write, as Boswell did within two weeks, and again six weeks later. Johnson, however, delayed his response for more than three months, and what he then wrote seemed to redefine his role in this friendship.[29]

Internalizing Johnson (7 August to 31 December)

Once Boswell reached Utrecht on 13 August, he lost control. "A deep melancholy seised upon me," he wrote Grange later: "I groaned with the idea of living all winter in so shocking a place. I thought myself old and wretched and forlorn. I was worse and worse next day. . . . I sunk quite into despair. I thought that at length the time was come that I should grow mad. I actually beleived myself so. I went out to the streets, and even in publick could not refrain from groaning and weeping bitterly. I said allways 'Poor Boswell! is it come to this? Miserable wretch that I am! What shall I do?'" Boswell returned to Rotterdam and told his troubles to Archibald Stewart, a merchant whom he had stayed with earlier and who "did every thing in his power to amuse" him. "But alas," Boswell lamented, "how could I be amused?"

Uncertain what to do next, Boswell on 14 August urged Dempster, then in Paris, to meet him in Brussels. Two days later, he wrote a long self-pitying letter to Temple. "O Good God! what have I endured! O my friend how much was I to be pitied! . . . All my resolutions of attaining a consistent character are blown to the winds. All my hopes of being a Man of respect are gone. . . . Is it possible that I can ever be well again?" Recalling his brother John's mental derangement — "I can now feel how my poor brother was afflicted" — Boswell repeatedly asked, "What can I do?" "O my friend! What shall I do?" Boswell did not share his distress with Grange or Dalrymple or his father. But he did write Johnson, whose company on 2 August had filled Boswell "with so many noble and just sentiments that the Daemon of despondency was driven away."[30]

Dempster rushed to Brussels, only to find that his "melancholy" friend had left on a "tour of Holland." Temple replied immediately, urging Boswell to "act a part more becoming yourself," to "remember your resolutions before we parted, allow reason to reassume her dominion, think of Johnson, and be again a man." But Johnson, whose name Temple invoked and whose advice he repeated, did nothing.[31]

Temple's advice to "think of Johnson" and to conquer the "disease" of idleness by reading prompted Boswell to start rereading the *Rambler,* now hearing Johnson's familiar voice as he read his prose. On 2 September, he announced he would return to Utrecht for a week and force himself "to study six hours a day," as Temple had recommended. Writing from Utrecht to Temple three weeks later, Boswell marveled at how Johnson's *Rambler* essays had cured him: "Several papers seem to have been just written for me. . . . He is the ablest mental physician that I have ever applied to. He insists much on preserving a manly fortitude of mind, and maintains that every distress may be supported." Writing to Grange for the first time on the same day as this second letter to Temple, Boswell charted in more detail what he had learned from the *Rambler:* "I met with several papers . . . describing the wretchedness of a mind unemployed, a peevish and gloomy fancy indulged. I began to think that I had no title to shelter myself from blame under the excuse of Madness, which was perhaps but a suggestion of idle Imagination." (As Thomas Crawford notes, Boswell seems to refer to *Rambler* nos. 29, 32, 47, 74, 85, and 134.) Inspired by Johnson's encouraging analyses of the heroic challenges of everyday moral life, Boswell made the "noble discovery . . . that melancholy can be got the better of. I dont say entirely. But by vigorously opposing it, I have a conscious satisfaction even in my dark hours and when I have the sunshine of the soul then I am doubly blest."[32]

Seven weeks earlier, as he anxiously prepared to leave Britain, Boswell had pictured Johnson chiefly as a source of precepts and grounded resistance to skepticism, as a mentor to whom he should "be grateful" and with whom he should "correspond": "Go abroad with a manly resolution to improve, and correspond with Johnson. Be grateful to him. Seek to attain a fixed and consistent character, to have dignity. Never despair. Remember Johnson's precepts on experience of mankind. Consider there *is* truth. . . . Study [to be] like Lord Chesterfield, manly." Now Johnson had also become Boswell's mental physician, his general in the battle against despondency, replacing the statesman and man of letters Philip Dormer Stanhope, the fourth Earl of Chesterfield, as the embodiment of manliness. But Johnson still had not written. Dempster had rushed to Brussels, and Temple had sent a rousing reply. What did Johnson's silence mean?[33]

Whatever Boswell wrote about Johnson's silence in the journal that was lost when later posted to Temple, he probably imagined various explanations, as he later did when Grange's reply to Boswell's first letter from Holland failed to arrive. I suspect he chiefly feared having offended Johnson with his unmanly loss of control. "Luckily," he had not written his father when first overwhelmed. But he *had* written Johnson, who, on their last evening together, had teased Boswell as a "self-tormentor." When he wrote Grange on 23 September that "Mr. Samuel Johnson honoured me with his company to Harwich," then added, "I was sick and filled with a crowd of different ideas," did Boswell fear that Johnson was now angry that he had so soon deserted his post in what reading the *Rambler* led him to see as "the warfare of life"? ("We should both take our Posts in the warfare of life," Boswell wrote Temple on 25 September.)[34]

Serious worries clearly underlay the remarkable memorandum Boswell wrote on 6 October after he had drafted a second letter to Johnson: "This letter to Mr. Johnson is a terrible affair. Don't take any more time to it. But either send him a short substantial one or copy out the large one; 'tis natural, though rude. He will like it, and you can correct your copy and make it very pretty, for there are fine, strong, lively passages in it. Copy out today the first business you do. . . . You'll never have such a task again." Writing to Johnson was "a terrible affair," the sort of "task" he would never have again, because Boswell was deeply insecure. He tried to assure himself that Johnson would like the "natural, though rude," letter, with its "fine, strong, lively passages." But could he be sure of Johnson's response? Dalrymple, in a letter Boswell received a day before writing this memorandum, had suggested that he ask his "good friend the Christian philosopher, Mr. Johnson," whether he should tell Lord Auchinleck about his initial breakdown: "He has studied the human mind so much and so well that your case will not seem extraordinary to him." After weeks of taking *Rambler* essays to heart, Boswell undoubtedly agreed.

But Boswell surely feared that Johnson now judged him hopeless. He was also probably angry.[35]

On 7 October, a day after brooding on this "terrible affair," Boswell posted a letter to Johnson. According to the *Life,* he "express[ed] much anxiety to hear from him," and Johnson's eventual reply indicates that Boswell had complained of his silence. Boswell also surely told Johnson some of what he had written to others about his recent progress, as he did the same day in his third letter from Utrecht to Lord Auchinleck. He would certainly have thanked Johnson for all he had learned from the *Rambler.* He probably also asked Johnson to endorse his current plan and to help him persist, the same support he had requested from his other correspondents. Whatever he wrote, Boswell had to wait more than two months — even longer than he had already waited — before getting a response.[36]

Throughout this long period, Johnson was regularly on Boswell's mind. "Mr. Johnson is ever in my thoughts when I can think with any manliness," he wrote Temple on 2 September. Later letters and memoranda spell out how often this was. The central lesson Boswell derived from the *Rambler* was evoked whenever he urged himself to "return to the charge" and "never to relax in your warfare." Johnson also featured significantly in the "Inviolable Plan" that Boswell wrote eight days after sending his second letter to Johnson. This text, which Boswell resolved to read every day, compensated for Johnson's silence by transforming the *Rambler* into a person in direct communication: "You believed you had a real distemper. On your first coming to Utrecht you yielded to that idea. You endured severe torment. You was pitiful and wretched. You was in danger of utter ruin. . . . Your friend Temple showed you that idleness was your sole disease. The Rambler showed you that vacuity, gloom, and fretfulness were the causes of your woe, and that you was only afflicted as others are. He furnished you with principles of philosophy and piety to support the soul at all times. You returned to Utrecht determined. You studied with diligence. You grew quite well." Boswell clearly had not forgotten Johnson. But he feared Johnson had forgotten him.[37]

On 14 December, a few days after Boswell had received his fourth letter from Temple, the same day he received his second letter from David Dalrymple and his fourth from Lord Auchinleck, Boswell finally heard from Johnson.

Johnson's "Boswell" (7 August to 8 December)

Johnson probably received Boswell's first letter late in August and his second in mid-October, after which both lay on a cluttered desk waiting to be answered. When he finally wrote, four months after parting from Boswell at

Harwich, Johnson hinted that he occasionally drank Boswell's health "in the Room in which we sat last together" and sometimes talked about Boswell with their common "acquaintances." But he was intentionally unspecific. Apart from this letter there is no evidence of what Johnson thought and felt about Boswell, or of how often he had Boswell in mind. But his long silence—his failure to respond at all to Boswell's cry for help or to answer his second letter in a timely manner—is suggestive.

Johnson's initial silence was not simply due to the "inclination to do nothing" that he had confessed to Boswell. For soon after receiving Boswell's August letter, he wrote three times to John Taylor, a friend from the Lichfield grammar school and Oxford, whose wife had just left him. (Johnson had written Taylor twice before hearing from Boswell.) Also, on 5 September, Johnson wrote Thomas Percy about a possible visit during which he hoped for his scholarly friend's "kind help" with his Shakespeare edition—a visit Johnson finally made a year later. On 20 September, when he wrote George Strahan, explaining why he had not written in seven weeks, Johnson may have recalled how anxious Strahan had been at his silence two months earlier. But he wrote nothing to Boswell.[38]

Later Johnson justified his initial delay by declaring that Boswell's August letter gave "an account so hopeless of the state of your mind that it hardly admitted or deserved an answer." Despite all his advice and encouragement, Boswell was totally adrift. In contrast to Taylor's marital problems, Boswell's distress in such enviable circumstances seemed fanciful and wholly self-inflicted. Also, instead of taking charge, Boswell was simply complaining. Boswell had been heartened to learn that Johnson was a fellow depressive, but Johnson was alarmed that Boswell was so helpless. So in response to Boswell's anguish, he wrote nothing—not even a brief note asking his friend to take control, consider how richly privileged he was, and write again once in motion. In mid-October, Johnson was "better pleased" by the letter Boswell had found so hard to produce, with its account of the "equal and rational application of [his] mind to . . . useful enquiry." But still he did not respond for almost eight weeks. Then, on 8 December, Johnson wrote a more critical and judgmental letter than he had ever sent to any of the other "young dogs" he loved. Boswell's irresolution and depression were like Johnson's own, so in this letter Johnson was also addressing himself.[39]

As the only document from 1763 that gives us the exact words Johnson addressed to Boswell—and all these words—this unusually long letter deserves special attention. Overall, it is generously helpful, but guarded. Johnson's first words—"You are not to think yourself forgotten or criminally neglected that you have had yet no letter from me"—respond to Boswell's anxiety in October, which would have deepened. "I love to see my friends," Johnson explained, "to hear them to talk to them and to talk of them, but it is not without a considerable effort of resolution that I prevail upon myself to write." Then Johnson twice claimed he would write — or at least would *intend* to write — whenever a letter was really needed: "I would not however gratify my own indolence by the omission of any important duty or any office of real kindness"; "If I can have it in my power to calm any harassing disquiet or fortify any generous resolution you need not doubt but I shall at least wish to prefer the pleasure of gratifying a friend much less esteemed than yourself before the gloomy calm of idle Vacancy." In August, however, Johnson had not responded to Boswell's "harassing disquiet," and only now was he writing to fortify the "generous resolution" Boswell had described two months earlier. So to brace Boswell for further disappointment, and if possible to avoid augmenting his own guilt, Johnson added, "Whether I shall easily arrive at an exact punctuality of correspondence I cannot tell."

The core of the letter was a *Rambler* essay written expressly to Boswell. Johnson explained that Boswell's "dissipation of thought" was "nothing more than the Vacillation of a mind suspended between different motives and changing its direction as any motive gains or loses Strength." As a cure, Johnson urged Boswell to "keep predominant any Wish for some particular excellence or attainment." Then, after also warning that desires might "tyrannize over" those who first encouraged them, Johnson again called Boswell to action by offering a comic version of his story: not a story about religious doubts or struggles with a father, but about "a gentleman who, when first he set his foot into the gay world as he prepared himself to whirl in the Vortex of pleasure imagined a total indifference and universal negligence to be the most agreeable concomitants of Youth and the strongest indication of any airy temper and quick apprehension" — a man who "thought that all appearance of diligence would deduct something from the reputation of Genius," and who has been led by "long habits of idleness and pleasure" erroneously to conclude "that Nature had originally formed him incapable of rational employment."

Having coaxed Boswell to laugh at his own fatuity, Johnson then roused him to action with short, imperative sentences: "Resolve and keep your resolution. Chuse and pursue your choice." He encouraged the initial effort by noting that the task would grow easier: "If you spend this day in Study you will find yourself still more able to study tomorrow." He also warned against overconfidence: "Depravity is not easily overcome. Resolution will sometimes relax and diligence will sometimes be interrupted." As an antidote to despair, Johnson added, "Let no accidental surprise or deviation whether short or long dispose you to despondency. Consider these failings as incident to all Mankind, begin again where you left off and endeavour to avoid the Seducements that prevailed over you before."

Johnson ended this personalized *Rambler*—an essay clearly addressed to himself as well as to Boswell—with a long sentence that blends affection, exasperation, and earnest hope: "This my Dear Boswell is advice which perhaps has been often given you, and given you without effect, but this advice if you will not take from others you must take from your own reflections, if you propose to do the dutys of the station to which the Bounty of providence has called you." In closing, though he was answering letters he had had for months, Johnson urged Boswell to "Let me have a long letter from you as soon as you can."

This letter demonstrated a shrewd concern with Boswell's welfare and eventually became cordial. But in two ways it suggests that Johnson remained deeply troubled by what Boswell had initially written. First, though he referred to Boswell's more pleasing second letter, and hoped his next one would contain "such a narrative of the progress of your studys as may evince the continuance of an equal and rational application of your mind to some useful enquiry," Johnson did not seem fully to credit what Boswell had reported. In urging Boswell to resolve "to spend a certain numbers of hours every day amongst your Books," he ignored his friend's success at reading five or six hours each day. In fact, his final appeal seems to be responding to the desperate August letter rather than to the more positive October report. Disappointment and distress at what Boswell had first written remained strong.

Second, Johnson's opening suggests an eagerness to redefine their friendship because of what had happened in August. Having earlier reached out physically and verbally to connect, Johnson now pulled back. While reassuringly hinting that Boswell remained part of his everyday life, he set clear limits on how he would write: "To tell you that I am or am not well, that I have or have not been in the country, that I drank your health in the Room in which we sat last together and that your acquaintance continue to speak of you with their former kindness topics with which those letters are commonly filled which are written only for the sake of writing I seldom shall think worth communication." Though Johnson had spent many hours talking about himself as well as about his young friend's hopes and fears, had suggested a trip to Greenwich to discuss Boswell's future and his own early experiences, and had accompanied Boswell to Harwich, he would not write just to keep in touch. He would not gossip or write about himself, as he did in letters to Chambers and especially to Langton. Instead of Boswell's "companion," regularly walking "arm in arm" along the Strand after hours of tavern conversation, Johnson would simply be his guide and judge. Now that Boswell was edging toward embodying some of Johnson's characteristic failings, Johnson no longer wanted so fully to invest himself in this friendship.

Johnson still regarded Boswell as an emissary who would fill his journal "with many observations upon the country in which you reside" and send him "books in the Frisick Language" (that is, Frisian, the language of northern Holland) and whatever he could discover about "how the poor are maintained" there. But not until 1771 would Johnson begin to write as he had imagined doing when they parted and as he had written other young friends from the start, combining advice and encouragement with news of common friends and other personal reflections. Not until 1772 would he include reports on his health. Not until 1773 — after he had accepted Boswell as his biographer — would he write a letter as relaxed and comfortable as those he regularly sent Langton.

On the surface, Boswell was delighted to get Johnson's letter. In his memorandum for 15 December, recalling his initial attempt to meet Johnson through the Irish poet Samuel Derrick, he wrote: "You was indeed a great man yesterday. You received letters from Lord Auchinleck, Mr. Samuel Johnson, Sir David Dalrymple. Mr. Johnson's correspondence is the greatest honour you could ever imagine you could attain to. Look back only three years when you was first in London with Derrick. Consider. He is the first author in England. Let his counsel give you new vigour. Return still to the charge." The next day, Boswell added a note about this "long letter from Mr. Johnson" to an unfinished letter to the Protestant clergyman Charles de Guiffardière. Pleased that his friend had finally written — and at such length — Boswell also surely appreciated how Johnson's analysis meshed with his own and how his energetic call to action echoed the tone of the "Inviolable Plan." But Boswell's reassuring himself that a letter from Johnson was "the greatest honour" he could imagine — "Consider. He is the first author in England" — suggests he was also addressing some disappointment.[40]

There were several reasons for Boswell to be upset. Johnson had finally written, but formally, uncompanionably. Also, unlike Dempster and Temple, and later Dalrymple, Johnson wholly refused to sympathize with Boswell's initial distress. The length of Johnson's letter showed concern, but his "esteem" was expressed only in passing. Inspired by the *Rambler,* Boswell for months had rigorously struggled for self-control. But Johnson wrote as if he had accomplished little during these months of strenuous effort.

Boswell could contrast the tone and substance of Johnson's letter with what he heard the same day from Dalrymple and Lord Auchinleck, both of whom had already applauded the promising start at self-construction that Johnson barely acknowledged. In fact Lord Auchinleck, replying to what Boswell had written when he also posted his second letter to Johnson, was unqualified in his approval: "I now bless god that I have the prospect of having comfort in you & support from you and that you will tread in the Steps of the former James who in this family have been remarkably usefull." His father's letters to Utrecht were uniformly supportive and praiseful. But Johnson seemed unimpressed.[41]

Boswell saw himself continually struggling against vanity and intemperance, and against his tendency to let his "general plan yield to the present moment." He repeatedly admonished himself, seeing Johnson's letter as another call to action. But it seems unlikely that he agreed with Johnson's implicit assumption that he had achieved little by 7 October, especially since for two additional months he had uncharacteristically "stood upon my guard and . . . repelled dissipation," as he wrote Guiffardière two days after first reading Johnson's letter. (Boswell had already urged this "vivacious" friend to remember his own resolution to acquire "intellectual dignity.") After struggling so hard for so long, guided by the insights and encouragement of the *Rambler* and with Johnson always in mind, Boswell surely deserved more credit from the man who had emphatically praised him in July. Also, where was the comfortable affection and camaraderie of their final weeks together?

Boswell advised himself to "Write to Johnson easy," and on 20 December wrote "cleverly to Mr. Johnson." He surely expressed joy that Johnson had written, and probably tried to win Johnson's full respect. The long "extract" on the "Frisick" language Boswell later printed in the *Life* may have been part of this letter, as Marshall Waingrow suggests. Boswell's hopes for a response to this "noble letter" were greatly disappointed, however. For he next heard from Johnson in January 1766, twenty-five months later.[42]

2

"Perpetual Friendship"? (1764–1767)

Between Boswell's sailing to Holland in 1763 and his traveling to see Johnson at Oxford in March 1768, the two friends saw each other on only a few days in February 1766. In the following four years (through March 1772), they were in the same place only twice: for about six weeks in the spring of 1768 and almost five in the fall of 1769. There were intimate moments each time they reconnected. But Boswell's accounts indicate that their time together was generally more tense and contentious than in 1763: Boswell grew increasingly feisty and defiant, challenging Johnson's assertions and eventually probing his secrets, and Johnson responded with dismissive putdowns and demeaning ad hominem retorts, refusing to let his friend win arguments even when they were alone, and toward the end growing seriously angry.

More importantly, when they were not near each other, they often were completely out of touch. Despite Boswell's efforts to coax replies, Johnson wrote no letters at all in 1764 and 1765, or during three other periods ranging from fifteen to nineteen months. Three times Boswell, too, stopped writing; and after leaving London in November 1769, Boswell waited seventeen months before finally sending what Johnson had expected soon after his friend returned home to be married. Clearly, neither was as central to the other as they had been in the weeks before they parted at Harwich.

During each of these four long silences, their friendship might easily have atrophied. Boswell, however, refused to let this happen. Johnson was on his mind even when he stopped writing or posting letters, and eventually he ended each sustained silence by writing something that got Johnson's attention. In contrast, there is little evidence that Johnson had Boswell in mind when they were not in touch. But his response each time Boswell reconnected showed that this friendship mattered, though Johnson sometimes resisted Boswell's control. Johnson saw Boswell as more deeply needy than the other "young dogs" he mentored, more challenging and defiant. He still longed for all that the Hebrides trip signified. But his friendship with Boswell was much more dominated by guilt than his other friendships: guilt at not writing, exacerbated by Boswell's worried complaints, and eventually additional guilt at his own passive-aggressiveness.

In November 1765, after Boswell ended the first silence by writing from Corsica, Johnson compensated for more than two years of not writing by praising his having visited this remote island and by insisting he was still Boswell's "unaltered" friend. Two years later, when Boswell ended the second silence by sending Johnson a copy of *An Account of Corsica,* which publicly wrote Johnson into Boswell's life by publishing this declaration of "unalterable" friendship, Johnson augmented his guilt at not having written by aggressively refusing to discuss the book when Boswell sought him out at Oxford. When Johnson returned to London five weeks later, he quickly gave *Corsica* the praise Boswell wanted. But sixteen months later — months when Johnson, as usual, wrote no letters, and Boswell again stopped writing — Johnson still regretted his initial silence about *Corsica.*[1]

Two months later, their roles shifted. Having left for Scotland soon after Johnson angrily threatened to end the friendship if Boswell continued asking about his fear of death, Boswell for seventeen months failed to write, although it was clearly his turn. Then, in April 1771, he explicitly absolved Johnson for having written so infrequently. Because Boswell retroactively forgave what he had so often lamented, removing this source of Johnson's guilt, Johnson finally wrote as he had imagined doing when they parted at Harwich almost eight years earlier. He dropped his sustained restrictions on news and gossip. More importantly, in response to mention of the Hebrides trip, which Johnson had first proposed as a guarantee that their friendship would endure, and later had threatened never to make if Boswell kept asking about death, Johnson warmly endorsed this collaborative adventure within their shared Christian framework.[2]

Boswell's forgiving letter suggests that he had decided to become Johnson's biographer, a role that would allow him to probe with impunity his friend's unexpected inner struggles and would guarantee him a close, ongoing connection, an inside track with Johnson, despite his many rivals. In the spring of

1772, Johnson accepted this unprecedented and transforming arrangement. But in January 1764, as Johnson read Boswell's "noble letter" and Boswell began waiting for a response, neither anticipated that eight years later Boswell would propose writing Johnson's life.

Boswell Abroad (January 1764 to January 1766)

Boswell stayed in Holland until 18 June 1764, continuing to study, to write essays in French (and eventually in Dutch, too) and verse in English, and to keep his journal. (Entries through 23 May 1764 were posted to Temple but never arrived.) In February, while again wondering at Johnson's silence, Boswell used some of his French themes to plan a Scots dictionary that would "give only the bare English word for a Scots one, and . . . send . . . readers to Mr. Johnson's *Dictionary* to get the definition"; and he probably described this first plan to collaborate with Johnson in the letter he resolved to finish on 5 March 1764, when he again had difficulty writing his silent mentor.[3]

A few days later, deeply troubled by news that Charles Boswell, the son Boswell had conceived with Peggy Doig early in 1762, had died, Boswell discovered that he had not completely conquered depression. "Black melancholy again took dominion over me," he wrote Grange, who had helped Boswell provide for his "little boy": "All the old dreary and fretful feelings recurred." "I have no friend," he wrote Temple, "to whom I can disclose my Anxieties and receive immediate relief." Johnson was both remote and silent. So on 30 March, Boswell used his ten lines of verse to address him:

> Illustrious Johnson! When of thee I think
> Into my little self I timid shrink.
> With all my soul thy genius I admire:
> Thy vig'rous judgment, thy poetic fire,
> Thy knowledge vast, thy excellence of mirth
> And all thy moral and religious worth.
> The noble dignity of man I see,
> But fear it cannot be attain'd by me.
> Yet I resolve the gen'rous path to try:
> Though less than thee, I may be very high.

Throughout his final weeks in Utrecht, Boswell repeatedly rallied himself by recalling the image of Johnson: "This day [Easter] rouse. Be Johnson" (22 April); "Be upon honour to continue Christian, as Johnson" (7 May).[4]

On 20 July, however, a month into travels that would last much longer than his father had anticipated or approved, Boswell realized he would never be happy by trying to be Johnson, Temple, or anyone else, and so began to relax the restraints he had imposed. "God would not have formed such a diversity of men if he had intended that they should all come up to a certain standard," he wrote in his entry for 20 July. "Let me then be Boswell and render him as fine a fellow as possible." As Frederick A. Pottle notes, these words mark the "crucial" moment when "Boswell turned from his usual pattern of anxious admonition to be West Digges, or Sir David Dalrymple, or Samuel Johnson, and contemplated with complacency the idea of being himself."

Boswell's memorandum the next day charted a course that in various ways would defy both Johnson and his father: "Be self. Be original. Be happy. You *was* so, certainly. Add to this learning and taste and devotion and *retenue*. Marry not, but think to have fine Saxon girls, &c., and to be with Temple. Continue journal. Keep firm, abroad another year—or marry Zelide. Go home, with design to *try* [the law], and if bad, Spain or France." Two days later, in a long philosophical letter to Temple, Boswell elaborated further, listing, along with Johnson, William Pitt, prime minister during most of the recently concluded Seven Years' War, and the poet Thomas Gray, Temple's mentor, as men to be admired but not imitated: "To be sure if we were all Pitts and Johnsons and Grays, we should be much nobler beings. But if, by studying to be great when We are intended for being agreeable, we become sowr and discontented, in that case, I think the vivacious and happy french & Italians may with some justice laugh at us." After a year of curbing his inclinations, Boswell now encouraged Temple—and himself—"to mix as much of the *dulce* in our cup as to render it neither too harsh, nor too luscious."[5]

The major issue was sex. Two months after meeting Johnson, Boswell explained in his journal that this new friend had shown him "that promiscuous concubinage is certainly wrong." It transgresses the commands of God, "who has ordained marriage for the mutual comfort of the sexes, and the procreation and right educating of children"; "much more misery than happiness, upon the whole, is produced by irregular love"; and "if all the men & women in Britain were merely to consult Animal gratification[,] Society would . . . soon cease altogether." Despite these principled arguments against "illicit love," so different from Boswell's earlier aesthetic disgust or his fear of gonorrhea, he "could not resist indulging" while still in London. But he had lived "chaste as an Anchorite" since leaving England, as he wrote Temple on 23 July 1764. "I have not yet had an opportunity of indulging my amorous genius," he added, "But I have hopes." He also had spelled out the fears in an earlier memorandum: "Concubinage is no dire sin, but never do it unless some very extraordinary opportunity of fresh girl that can do no harm; and such a case is impossible." Venereal disease was a risk, yet seducing the innocent could not be justified. Ten days after affirming his "hopes," while describing Lord Baltimore's "strange, wild life" in Constantinople, where he lived "as a Turk, with his seraglio around him," Boswell "trembled to think of [his] wild schemes."[6]

The entry for 9 August 1764 dramatizes Boswell's conflicting longings as he sought something between total restraint and "Turkish" excess, hoping to combine self-affirming indulgence with allegiance to the demanding friend who had written just once in the previous year. First he described a happy moment when he "sat in the Duke's *loge* [in Brunswick] and was fine with the ladies of the Court": "My mind was clear and firm and fertile. It contained in itself both male and female powers: brilliant fancies were begotten, and brilliant fancies were brought forth. I saw my error in suffering so much from the contemplation of others. I can never be them, therefore let me not vainly attempt it in imagination. . . . I must be Mr. Boswell of Auchinleck, and no other. Let me make him as perfect as possible. I think, were I such a one, I should be happy indeed. . . . I have but one existence. If it is a mad one, I cannot help it. I must do my best."

"Amidst all this brilliance," Boswell added, "I sent forth my imagination to the Inner Temple, to the chambers of Mr. Samuel Johnson. I glowed with reverence and affection, and a romantic idea filled my mind. To have a certain support at all times, I determined to write this great man, and beg that he might give me a 'solemn assurance of perpetual friendship,' so that I might march under his protection while he lived, and after his death, imagine that his shade beckoned me to the skies. Grand, yet enthusiastic, idea!" While reveling in his imaginative prowess, and in gallantry he assumed would have no appeal for Johnson, and without directly challenging Johnson's position on "promiscuous concubinage," Boswell imagined reaffirming his "reverence and affection," hoping to march under Johnson's protection — if Johnson would give a "solemn assurance of perpetual friendship." He wanted leeway to be himself, but feared being cut off.[7]

Every day for a week Boswell attempted to write Johnson, but was not "able to please" himself. Troubled by Johnson's long silence, uncertain whether to "beg" or "demand" his perpetual friendship, Boswell may also have worried how Johnson would react to his current "wild . . . fancies." (A few months later Boswell's mother's silence prompted "dreary ideas of her being . . . offended with me.") So after a week of trying, Boswell abandoned the project for more than a month.[8]

From the Schlosskirche in Wittenberg on 30 September 1764, his paper resting on the tomb of the Protestant reformer Philipp Melanchthon, Boswell finally wrote his silent friend. Because this letter reveals how Boswell now wanted to script this friendship, it deserves to be quoted in full:

My ever dear and much respected Sir: — You know my solemn enthusiasm of mind. You love me for it, and I respect myself for it, because in so far I resemble Mr. Johnson. You will be agreeably surprised when you learn the reason of my writing this letter. I am at Wittenberg in Saxony. I am in the old church where the Reformation was first preached and where some of the Reformers lie interred. I cannot resist the serious pleasure of writing to Mr. Johnson from the tomb of Melanchthon. My paper rests upon the gravestone of that great and good man, who was undoubtedly the worthiest of all the Reformers. He wished to reform abuses which had been introduced into the Church, but had no private resentment to gratify. So mild was he that when his aged mother consulted him with anxiety on the perplexing disputes of the times, he advised her to keep to the old religion. At this tomb, then, my ever dear and respected friend, I vow to thee an eternal attachment. It shall be my study to do what I can to render your life happy, and if you die before me, I shall endeavour to do honour to your memory and, elevated by the remembrance of you, persist in noble piety. May God, the Father of all beings, ever bless you! And may you continue to love your most affectionate friend and devoted servant,

James Boswell[9]

Instead of begging or demanding that Johnson reaffirm his friendship — what if he refused? — Boswell affirmed his own. At both ends of the letter, he asserted what he surely doubted after Johnson's long silence: that his friend loved his "solemn enthusiasm of mind." By warmly praising this early companion of Luther, Boswell demonstrated his piety, aligning himself with Johnson's Anglican zeal. Taking Johnson's love for granted, Boswell vowed his own "eternal attachment." Having fifteen months earlier asked Johnson to "take a charge of" him, and having a few weeks earlier imagined Johnson protecting him while he lived and then beckoning him to heaven, Boswell now resolved "to render your life happy, and if you die before me . . . to do honour to your memory and . . . persist in noble piety." The two fantasies were complementary, since Johnson and Boswell were connected in both. But by assuming the active role, Boswell emphasized his strength. Also, he wrote nothing about his plan to be "agreeable" rather than "great," implying that he still was as he had described himself in October, December, and March.

Boswell was proud of his letter — "It is really an excellent thought" — and felt it "must surely give [Johnson] satisfaction." But he did not post it. Thirteen years later, when he finally did send it, he said had been afraid of "appear[ing] at once too superstitious and too enthusiastick." But Boswell's entry for 30 September suggests he kept the letter because he was angry at Johnson's long silence and uncertain of how Johnson now regarded him. Boswell was experiencing what he initially described in the *Life* as "the long series of impatience" or "disappointment" that Johnson's silence made him "suffer." Having had the "serious pleasure" of writing what he knew would please his friend, Boswell decided to wait "till I see if he gives me a favourable answer to my two last letters." Nor did he write again until he had visited Corsica, fourteen months later.[10]

During this long silence, Johnson was regularly on Boswell's mind. In mid-December 1764, having secured time with Jean-Jacques Rousseau, Boswell fully described "the character of Mr. Johnson" to this controversial social theorist. Nine days later, when he visited the even more famous Voltaire, Boswell reported that "Mr. Johnson and I intended to make a tour through the Hebrides." The following March, he defended Johnson's "respectable charac-ter in the world of literature" against attacks by the notorious writer and politician John Wilkes, who had fled to Naples to escape prosecution for libel. Four months later, he boasted to Wilkes that his "veneration and love" of Johnson was "so great that I cannot promise to be always free from some imitation of him," and exhorted this "gay, learned, and . . . thoughtless infidel" to "let Johnson teach thee the road to rational virtue and noble felicity."[11]

But Boswell had no evidence of how Johnson currently regarded him. His anxiety that there was no real connection, however much he wanted one, prob-ably intensified in July 1765, when he read three letters Johnson had sent Giu-seppe Baretti in 1761 and 1762, after the Italian writer had returned home from London — wise, comfortable, and respectful letters full of news and confes-sional self-reflections. At Boswell's urging, Baretti wrote Johnson, and copied for Boswell, what he called "a joint Letter from two of your distant Friends," which complained of Johnson's silence.[12]

Meanwhile, Boswell was occasionally narrating his adventures in Italy, a land of ease and happiness, not to Johnson but to Rousseau, whom he de-scribed as the first person he had met in Europe "to whom I could lay open entirely my mind." During their five interviews in December, Boswell formed a bond with him that for a while rivaled his connection with the man he described to Rousseau as a "famous scholar who proved to me the truth of the Christian religion, though his variety of Christianity was a little severe." On all the topics closest to Boswell's heart, even the sexual conduct and fantasies he had not reported discussing with Johnson, Rousseau was comfortable and reassuring, not harsh and judgmental; and he offered Boswell the "beautiful" image of a God who would not punish. Instead of trying to inspire awe, Rousseau high-lighted his own limitations. He refused to "assume direction" of Boswell, de-claring, "I can be responsible only for myself." But in parting on 15 December 1764, after telling Boswell, "You are a fine fellow. . . . You are malicious; but 'tis a pleasant malice, a malice I don't dislike," Rousseau delighted Boswell by saying, "Remember always that there are points at which our souls are bound."

BOSWELL. "It is enough. I, with my melancholy, I, who often look on myself as a despicable being, as a good-for-nothing creature who should make his exit from life, — I shall be upheld for ever by the thought that I am bound to Monsieur Rousseau. Good-bye. Bravo! I shall live to the end of my days." ROUSSEAU. "That is undoubtedly a thing one must do. Good-bye."[13]

Five months later Boswell, from Rome, confessed to Rousseau, in French, his sexual lapses in Italy: "Dare I admit to you that my conduct has not been as virtuous as I expected when you gave me directions for my life?" Although since his excessive passion, "the fever," was now over, he was again "as [Rousseau] would wish to see" him. Then on 3 October 1765, shortly before he sailed to Corsica, Boswell wrote three drafts of a long letter "entirely about myself," describing in some detail for this sympathetic, tolerant confessor his "truly libertine" behavior in Naples, where he "ran after girls without restraint," and his shamefully servile conduct toward Lord Mountstuart, the eldest son of the former prime minister Lord Bute. He dwelt at length on his "perfect felicity" in Siena, where his "life slipped away in a delicious dream," while his "principles of systematic morality were melted down by the fire of a heated imagination" — where he was "utterly happy" with a married woman who shrewdly told him, "You are yourself precisely that Rousseau. Just like him. You talk a great deal about virtue, and yet you do wrong." Boswell reframed this point as he directly addressed his current mentor: "Yes, my soul is bound to yours. I have loved like you, I am pious like you. If we have committed crimes, we have also expiated them." Boswell mentioned this "very long letter" in a note he sent Rousseau as he sailed to Corsica on 11 October. But for some reason, he never finished it; nor did he post what he had written.[14]

It was friendship with Rousseau that chiefly prompted Boswell to visit Corsica rather than Spain, as Johnson had recommended. While struggling for independence from Genoa, the Corsicans had asked Rousseau to provide them a set of laws; and on 15 December 1764, shortly after receiving Dalrymple's request that he "circumscribe" his travels and not visit Spain the following summer, Boswell facetiously asked Rousseau, "Give me credentials as your ambassador to the Corsicans." When he sailed from Leghorn (Livorno) the following October, he carried a letter Rousseau had written to introduce him to Mateo Buttafoco, the captain of the Royal Italian Regiment on Corsica, or to General Pasquale de Paoli, the head of the revolutionary army. It was from Corsica, a country even less well known than Spain, a land with a true Roman hero leading its struggle for independence, that Boswell wrote Johnson for the first time in more than a year.[15]

Boswell never indicated why he wrote Johnson at this point in his travels. But several explanations seem plausible, including his not wanting to return to

London after almost two years of silence. Also, on 21 September, when he sent Baretti an announcement that Johnson's long-delayed edition of Shakespeare would soon be published — "He has now silenced all his foes, and added to his reputation a superior degree of luster" — Boswell added, "I can now no longer slumber in the shade of Indolence. I will rouse all my spirit, and try to be worthy of his friendship." Two months earlier, when Baretti had seconded Johnson's recommendation that he write "an exact Journal of his rambles," Boswell might have winced to think of Johnson reading entries describing witty conversations with Wilkes; quarrels with Mountstuart's tutor, Paul Henri Mallet; and various sexual intrigues. But by early November, after Boswell had climbed to the mountainous center of Corsica and interviewed Paoli, a man who fully embodied "manly virtue" and "generous ardour" for his people, a living example of the "highest idea" Boswell could imagine, he had finally produced a journal he would be proud to share uncensored not only with Rousseau but also with Johnson. So he gave Johnson "a sketch of the great things" he had seen on this remote island, and promised "a more ample relation" when they reconnected.[16]

As he contemplated finally returning home, Boswell may also have sensed the need for help with his depression: "I am afflicted by a malady which can make me see all things as either insipid or sad, which can take away all desire for enjoyment, which can make me lose taste even for virtue; and what is the darkest and most inexplicable of all, . . . which can so destroy my spirit that I scarcely even wish to be cured." Rousseau was free of constitutional melancholy; Paoli, too, because he held "always firm one great object," never felt "a moment of despondency." But Johnson, having heroically struggled with constitutional melancholy, had helped Boswell in his struggles. Acutely conscious that he lacked the "noble force which Johnson has," an energy of mind that would allow him to "embrace life firmly" even when all seemed vain, Boswell reached out for this friend's bracing support as he contemplated finally returning home. Having resolved early in 1765 to reread the *Rambler*, Boswell started doing this after posting his letter, and again "felt all the force and fancy of illustrious Johnson."[17]

The two short sentences that survive from the first letter Boswell sent to Johnson in almost twenty months — "I dare to call this a spirited tour. I dare to challenge your approbation" — suggest that instead of vowing perpetual friendship, Boswell simply demanded Johnson's attention. In return, Boswell seven weeks later not only got his first letter from Johnson in twenty-five months, but also heard something close to a vow of eternal attachment: "When you return you will return to an unaltered, and I hope unalterable, friend."[18]

Johnson's Silence

The opening of what Johnson wrote on 14 January 1766 — "Apologies are seldom of any use" — might suggest that he had occasionally thought about writing in the years between his first two letters, and felt guilty at not having done so. But nothing in Johnson's surviving diary entries or letters shows him thinking about Boswell. Instead, his writing records extended visits to Bennet Langton's family estate in Lincolnshire early in 1764, to Thomas Percy's residence in Northamptonshire in the summer, and a shorter trip to Cambridge with Topham Beauclerk the following spring. In February 1764, Johnson and the painter Joshua Reynolds, soon to become the first president of the Royal Academy, founded the famous Club, which met weekly at the Turk's Head, with Goldsmith, Langton, and Beauclerk among the original nine members, along with Edmund Burke, not yet a member of Parliament but already a notable writer. Early in 1765, when Boswell was exploring Turin, Johnson met Henry Thrale, a wealthy brewer and MP, and his sprightly wife, Hester, at whose estate near London, Streatham, Johnson soon was spending much of his time. The long-delayed edition of Shakespeare was published in October 1765, including the recently written preface, which displayed the masterly assurance and discrimination that had always impressed Boswell. But Johnson seems to have felt guiltier than usual during a period marked by sporadic activity and growing depression.

On Easter 1764, Boswell in Holland exhorted himself to "Be Johnson." But a day earlier, Johnson reflected gloomily on the previous year, which had begun shortly before he first met Boswell: "A kind of strange oblivion has overspread me, so that I know not what has become of the last year, and perceive that incidents and intelligence pass over me without leaving any impression. This is not the life to which Heaven is promised." On Johnson's fifty-fifth birthday five months later (18 September), when Boswell was lamenting having to part from Madame de Brandt in Berlin, whose "gallantries have been notorious," and "who might have greatly formed me," Johnson wrote in his diary, "I have now spent fifty five years in resolving, having from the earliest time almost that I can remember been forming schemes of a better life. I have done nothing; the need of doing therefore is pressing, since the time of doing is short." On Easter 1765, when Boswell in Rome was "nobly happy" while attending high mass at St. Peter's and momentarily felt certain there was no everlasting damnation, Johnson again reflected that his "time has been unprofitably spent, and seems as a dream that has left nothing behind." Four months later, just before Boswell arrived in "sweet Siena," Johnson explained in his earliest surviving letter to Hester Thrale that work on *Shakespeare* would postpone his enjoying Brighton with her family.[19]

On 14 January 1766, seizing the chance to expiate offered by Boswell's letter from Corsica, Johnson posted a letter to Paris. Writing the same day to his stepdaughter, Lucy Porter, Johnson explained why he had not written to her for a year. But he put off till Boswell's return discussing "the reasons good or bad" that had made him "such a sparing and ungrateful correspondent." Since Boswell had worried that Johnson no longer cared, Johnson "assured" him, "Nothing has lessened either the esteem or love with which I dismissed you at Harwich." Rather both had been "encreased" by what Johnson had heard from Boswell and from Baretti.[20]

Unlike Johnson's first letter, a *Rambler* essay personalized for Boswell, this was a masterful reflection — for both friends — on the dynamics of expectation. In the third paragraph, Johnson expressed eagerness to connect with his well-traveled friend: "Come home and expect such a welcome as is due to him whom a wise and noble curiosity has led where perhaps no native of this Country ever was before." But in the more guarded second and fourth paragraphs, Johnson warned against excessive hopes: "All you have to fear from me, is the vexation of disappointing me," of "frustrat[ing] expectations which have been formed in [your] favour." Johnson might have fostered this fear by noting, "The pleasure I promise myself from your journals and remarks is so great that perhaps no degree of attention or discernment will be sufficient to afford it." Boswell would almost surely disappoint, and therefore be disappointed. But Johnson insisted on taking the risk, urging Boswell to "Come . . . and take your chance." Johnson feared those in London would "find it difficult to keep among us a mind which has been so long feasted with variety," but he resolved to "try what esteem and kindness can effect."

Only at the end did Johnson edge toward admonition. Having heard from Boswell that Lord Auchinleck was ill and eager to see his heir, Johnson aligned himself with the man whose "liberality has indulged [Boswell] with so long a ramble," and urged his friend to hasten his return. "The longer we live and the more we think, the higher value we learn to put on the friendship and tenderness of Parents."[21]

Boswell in London (11 February to 29 February 1766)

Ten days after he reached Paris on 11 January 1766, Boswell was "nobly elated" by Johnson's letter, which treated him "with esteem and kindness." Five days later, he learned his mother had died, and on 31 January he wrote Johnson that he would soon be in London, where he arrived on 11 February, accompanied by Thérèse le Vasseur, Rousseau's common-law wife. The next day, Boswell took Thérèse from Hume's house in London to Cheswick, where he handed her to Rousseau, who "seemed so oldish and weak" that Boswell had no "enthusiasm for him." Then Boswell "immediately" went to Johnson's for the first time in thirty months.[22]

Johnson received Boswell "with open arms." Boswell "kneeled, and asked his blessing," and once Anna Williams left, Johnson hugged his friend "like a sack, and grumbled, 'I hope we shall pass many years of regard.'" For "some minutes," Boswell noted the next day, "You . . . saw him not so immense as before, but it came back." Boswell was viewing Johnson with the eyes of someone who "felt by comparison with former days in London how superior [he] was," and was also comparing the friend who greeted him with the heroic "Johnson" he had constructed while reading the *Rambler* in Holland.[23]

Boswell's incomplete journal for twelve of his nineteen days in London describes only three additional meetings with Johnson: supper alone at the Mitre on 12 February, supper at the Mitre with Johnson and Temple three days later, and a visit with Goldsmith on 22 February. The first Mitre supper resembled those from 1763 and seems fully to have pleased both friends. The other meetings were significantly tenser, leaving neither satisfied,

Johnson was keeping his New Year's resolution to "drink little wine," but otherwise their first evening at the Mitre seemed a sequel to those they had shared earlier. Johnson decisively and reassuringly addressed his young friend's pressing concerns and applauded Boswell's general progress: "You have five and twenty years, and you have employed 'em well." When Boswell repeated the still-galling criticism of Lord Mountstuart's tutor — "Do I know history, mathematics, law, &c." — Johnson offered a new perspective: "Why, Sir, though you may know no science so well as to be able to teach it, and no profession so well as to be able to follow it, yet your general mass of knowledge of books and men renders you very capable to study any science or follow any profession." Johnson rejected, too, Wilkes's recent warning that as a lawyer, Boswell would "be excelled by plodding blockheads," noting that "in the formal and statutory practice of law, a plodding blockhead may succeed, but in the equitable part of it, a plodding blockhead can never succeed." But Johnson's encouragement was nonetheless restrained: "Why, Sir, to be sure you will not be a good advocate at first . . . and perhaps in seven years you will not so good a lawyer as your father, perhaps never. But it is better to be a tolerable lawyer than no lawyer, and, Sir, you will always see multitudes below you."[24]

At various moments throughout the evening Johnson spoke energetically and authoritatively about religion. ("He was as great as ever," Boswell wrote the next day.) Boswell also reported mentioning his hope to publish something about Corsica, concerning which he had already written a series of paragraphs in the *London Chronicle*. He almost surely showed portions of his Corsica journal to Johnson, as he did when he saw Temple the following day, and Johnson urged him to focus on what he had seen. "You cannot go to the bottom [of the subject] but all you tell us is what we don't know. Give us as many anecdotes as you can."[25]

The other two meetings were different in part because the friends were not alone. Also, instead of being primarily inquisitive and needy, Boswell was aggressive, pushy, and insensitive, and Johnson, instead of being supportive and wise, was testy and dismissive, or troubled and self-protective.

The supper on 15 February was more consistently contentious than any meeting Boswell had yet described, except for the evening in 1763 when Johnson delighted Boswell by refuting his friend Dempster's arguments against subordination. Without openly presenting any of his truly heterodox ideas about religion and sexual morality, Boswell repeatedly challenged Johnson — perhaps so Temple could witness Johnson's mental agility and power, perhaps so Boswell could demonstrate his ability to argue forcefully — and Johnson curtly dismissed each of Boswell's claims.

The tone and some of the initial content were produced by Johnson's having discovered his friend's involvement with Rousseau, perhaps from the *London Chronicle* of 13 February, which described Boswell as "a friend of the celebrated John James Rousseau, who is an enthusiast for the Corsicans." Three days earlier, Boswell had reported several potentially objectionable things Baretti had said — "As a man dies like a dog, let him lie like dog"; "I hate mankind, for I think myself one of the best of 'em, and [I] know how bad I am" — finally getting Johnson to criticize this rival. Now it was Johnson, who seventeen years earlier had described how Rasselas told his mentor and guide Imlac that he had finally found "a man who can teach all that is necessary to be known," who saw Rousseau — and Wilkes and Hume — as rivals. When Boswell told Johnson "he looked ten years younger, and that [Tom] Davies had said he now got up at eight," Johnson, though pleased at having for more than six weeks kept his resolve to rise early, replied, "Why, Sir, if I were a friend of John James Rousseau then everything that concerned me would be of importance. As it is, Sir, it concerns nobody but myself." Later, when Boswell quoted Wilkes, whose name three days earlier had provoked no comment, Johnson snorted, "It seems you have kept very good company abroad — Wilkes and Rousseau!" Then, when Boswell asked, "Do you really think [Rousseau] a bad man?" Johnson replied, "Sir, if you are to talk jestingly of this, I don't talk with you. If you would be serious, I think him one of the worst of men." Though Boswell conceded that *La Nouvelle Heloise* "may do harm," he could not "think [Rousseau's] intention was bad." But Johnson retorted, "The want of intention, when evil is committed, will not be sustained in a court of justice," and he pointedly added, "If you are no better a lawyer than that, Bos., we must send you back to Utrecht."[26]

When Boswell then mentioned Hume's notion "that all were equally happy, who were happy," Johnson rejected this claim with the clarity and vigor that always delighted Boswell: "A peasant and a philosopher may be equally satisfied, but not equally happy. Happiness consists in the multiplicity of consciousness. A peasant has not capacity for having equal happiness with the philosopher." (In the *Life*, the key phrase became "the multiplicity of *agreeable* consciousness.") When Boswell began to respond, hoping to be more fully confirmed, Johnson dismissively said, "My dear Bozzy, let us have no more of this. It is extremely disagreeable to me. You are making nothing of this argument. I had rather you'd whistle me a Scotch tune."

Later, Boswell tried to corner Johnson by arguing that since "the vulgar are the children of the state and must be taken care of," then "a poor Turk must be a Mohammedan just as a poor man in Europe must be a Christian." Johnson described this as "just such stuff as I used to talk to my mother when I first began to think myself a clever fellow, and she ought to have whipped me for it." Boswell "took this in perfect good humour, and said, 'You ought then to whip me.'" But Johnson had been verbally whipping Boswell all evening, making clear that the self-confident companion of Rousseau, Wilkes, and Hume was only as clever at twenty-five as Johnson had been when much younger. Johnson's teasing was no longer playful and therapeutic, but aggressive and insulting.[27]

The final documented meeting that month was also tense and unsatisfactory. On 22 February, when Boswell and Goldsmith found Johnson too ill to sup at the Mitre, they stayed to nag their depressed friend to write more. Johnson rebuffed them: at first somewhat harshly — "The lad does not care for the child's rattle, and the old man does not care for the young man's whore" — then more reflectively — "as we advance in the journey of life, we drop some of the things which have pleased us; whether it be that we are fatigued and don't choose to carry so many things any farther, or that we find other things which we like better." Boswell suggested that Johnson might "give us something in some other way," and Goldsmith added, "Ay, Sir, we have a claim upon you." Were he alone with Boswell, Johnson might have acknowledged needing to use his time and talents, as he had in May 1763. Six weeks earlier, he had imagined writing "*the History of Memory,*" and a week later he thought of "writing a small book to teach the use of the Common Prayer." But when badgered by both these friends, Johnson insisted, "No man is obliged to do as much as he can. A man is to have part of his life to himself." When Boswell wondered why Johnson did not have "more pleasure in writing than not," Johnson acidly replied, "Sir, you *may* wonder."[28]

Neither Boswell nor Goldsmith understood or sympathized with what Johnson was experiencing. For more than seven weeks, he had kept his resolve to rise early — if not by eight at least by nine — an unprecedented "superiority over my habits" that by the end of March had given him "comfort and hope." "When I was up I have indeed done but little," he wrote Langton a few weeks after Boswell left for Edinburgh, "yet it is no slight advancement to obtain for so many hours more the consciousness of being." But having finally completed the Shakespeare edition, Johnson had no project. As Boswell would learn only in 1784, Johnson's depression had become so paralyzing by 1766 that he told Dr. William Adams, the master of Pembroke, Johnson's college at Oxford, "I would suffer a limb to be amputated to recover my spirits."[29]

Boswell and Johnson almost surely connected at least once during Boswell's final week in London, for which there are neither entries nor notes, and perhaps on other occasions as well. But they were together far less often than when Boswell was last in the city. As they parted for another long separation, both probably promised to write more regularly. But it is impossible to know what each expected.

March 1766 to February 1768

Having passed the examination in civil law in 1762, Boswell now resumed his studies, receiving special attention from his father. On 26 July, he defended his dissertation, which was published early in August. When he asked Lord Mountstuart about dedicating this text to him, his companion in Italy suggested giving this testimony of regard to one of the "many great men" who were Boswell's friends: "a Statesman Mr. Pitt. a great Warriour, Genl. Paoli. a great Genius Rousseau. a larn'd man Johnson. a Compound of them all, L'abbatè Baretti." But Boswell hoped by flattering Lord Bute's heir to gain substantial benefits.[30]

During his first months in Scotland, Boswell sent two letters to Johnson, and in August wrote again with a copy of his thesis. According to the *Life*, the first letter "complained of irresolution, and mentioned having made a vow as a security for good conduct." Johnson's eventual response suggests the second letter complained of Johnson's silence and discussed the book on Corsica. But only the dissertation finally produced a response, perhaps helped by a nudge from Tom Davies, who promised to "chide [Johnson] for his neglect."[31]

Between Boswell's departure and the arrival of his dissertation, Johnson reached the state of psychological collapse that led Henry and Hester Thrale, when they found him in June on his knees before a clergyman, John Delap, "beseeching God to continue to him the use of his understanding," to take "the helpless and broken Johnson" to Streatham for his first extended stay. But Johnson was back in the city on 21 August to receive Boswell's dissertation, perhaps hear Davies's chiding, and promptly write his third letter.[32]

"The reception of your Thesis put me in mind of my debt to you," Johnson began. But instead of apologizing, he aggressively asked why Boswell had dedicated this text "to a man whom I know you do not love." Unwilling to imagine a reason for paying court to the son of the former prime minister, even though he had told Boswell in February that "if you can get a shilling's worth of good for sixpence worth of court, you are a fool not to pay court," Johnson determined to "punish" Boswell by pointing out errors in the dedication's Latin. Only after a paragraph of playful vexation did Johnson turn to his friend's major concerns: pleasing his father, studying law, and writing about Corsica.

On the first two topics, Johnson wrote as a fellow melancholic and resolver, blending encouragement with the kind of hard-earned warnings he never found necessary when writing Langton or Chambers. He "sincerely approve[d]" Boswell's "resolution to obey [his] father," later adding, "You ought to think it no small inducement to diligence and perseverance [in studying law] that they will please your father." He also noted that by following this profession, "You have done exactly what I always wished when I wished you best." But drawing on his own experience with resolutions, Johnson warned Boswell not to "accustom yourself to enchain your volatility by vows": "They will sometime leave a thorn in your mind which you will perhaps never be able to extract or eject. Take this warning it is of great importance."

Johnson agreed that the study of the law was "copious and generous," and echoing what he had written in his very first letter — and also in many *Rambler* essays — he pointed to the key gain for anyone prone to depression: "security from those troublesome and wearysome discontents which are always obtruding themselves upon a mind vacant unemployed and undetermined." Two paragraphs later, in response to whatever Boswell had written about the "unexpected inconveniencies" of law, Johnson insisted "that all the importunities and perplexities of Business are softness and Luxury compared with the incessant cravings of Vacancy and the unsatisfactory expedients of idleness." Vicariously delighting in how Boswell's continued progress would please his father, Johnson also hoped sustained activity would preserve his friend from what he himself was experiencing.

Having encouraged study of the law as an antidote to melancholy, Johnson curiously ended his letter by asking Boswell to abandon the book on Corsica: "Mind your own affairs and leave the Corsicans to theirs." He sensibly noted Boswell had no special materials for a "history." But he knew Boswell had kept a journal while exploring this remote, rarely visited island. When supporting the project in February, Johnson had urged Boswell to highlight his "anecdotes." Why did he now see the book simply as a history and picture Boswell's interest in Corsica as a kind of madness, the idea having "obtained an unreasonable and irregular possession" of his mind?[33]

It is difficult to answer these questions, especially since we cannot see how Boswell described his plans. Perhaps, as Temple suspected, Johnson was opposed to Corsican independence, or perhaps, like Sir John Pringle six months later, he thought it imprudent to champion the Corsicans' struggle while the British government was uncommitted. But if these were his major objections, Johnson would surely have stated them. It seems unlikely that he feared the book would be too great a distraction from the law, since he later encouraged other writing projects precisely to fill otherwise idle moments. Though Sanford Radner suggests that Johnson was motivated by "professional jealousy" of Boswell's "hot topic" at a time when his own "career had hit a comparatively dry period," Johnson had warmed to the project when he first saw Boswell's journal. But perhaps Johnson shared the fear of David Dalrymple — known as Lord Hailes since joining Boswell's father as a judge on the Court of Session — that a book based heavily on his journal would dangerously encourage self-promotion, and doubted that Boswell could restrain himself. Also, Johnson surely associated Corsica with Rousseau and perhaps feared that writing the book would more fully attach his friend to Rousseau's unorthodox but seductive ideas. Whatever led Johnson to shift from being an encouraging to a blocking mentor, his discouragement turned the book into what Boswell seventeen years later recalled as a decisive act of defiance and self-assertion.[34]

Boswell's waiting more than two months before replying suggests that writing had again become a challenge — perhaps because Johnson opposed the book, as Boswell quickly reported to Temple. Boswell's November letter to Johnson is notable for its feistiness. He defended his Latin at length against Johnson's criticisms, a defense that Pottle found "sophistical on some points but clearly proved Johnson captious on others." He also rejected Johnson's earnest warning against vows, declaring his need for every possible help to stay "tolerably steady in the paths of rectitude," and citing for support what Johnson had written Baretti about the value of monastic vows for those unable to control themselves. Remarkably, however, Boswell seems to have said nothing about Corsica. (The material cut from the end of the letter probably involved Lord Auchinleck.) Boswell was reluctant openly to oppose Johnson. But he knew his friend would hear of his plans.[35]

When Johnson did not respond to this spirited letter, Boswell wrote several more. He probably wrote in January, when he also asked Baretti and Davies about Johnson; probably in April, when he again complained to Davies; and at least once — probably several times — in the long stretch from 10 May and 20 October 1767, when Johnson was away in Oxford or Lichfield. In these letters, none of which is mentioned in the *Life*, Boswell might have reported his purchase of Dalblair, a farm bordering Auchinleck, and how busy he was as a lawyer, since (as he wrote Temple) "nineteen out of twenty employ the Son of the judge before whom their Cause is heard." He would surely have described getting his brother David to swear to be faithful to "the ancient family of Auchinleck" before departing for Spain. Boswell probably reported his curious courtship of Catherine Blair, who frankly confessed loving the Auchinleck estate more than she loved its heir, and perhaps his continuing interest in Belle de Zuylen (Zélide), whose intellectual boldness both fascinated and frightened him. He might also have described his eager literary involvement in the notorious legal battle involving the inheritance of the Duke of Douglas's estate. But much that was central to his life would have been off-limits, including his work on the book both Hume and Hailes strongly supported.[36]

Besides writing Johnson frequently, Boswell asked two common friends to nudge him. Since Tom Davies had passed along "compliments" from Johnson in November 1766, Boswell included flattering comments on Johnson when he wrote Davies two months later. Also in January, replying to Baretti's announcement that he had returned to England, Boswell praised Johnson at length and copied the lines he had written on 30 March 1764, correctly assuming that Baretti would show this to Johnson; as a result, Baretti heard Johnson praise Boswell as "a clever fellow" who "will one day or other cut a good figure in this Kingdom," and later reported Johnson's thanks "for the continuation of [Boswell's] love to him." At Boswell's urging in yet another letter, Davies talked with Johnson about Boswell, and reported that before leaving for Oxford in May 1767, Johnson had "promised faithfully to write." Later, by enclosing a letter to Baretti in one he posted to Johnson, Boswell ensured that Johnson and Baretti would once more talk about him. But this letter with its enclosure, along with any others Boswell sent that summer, lay in London until Johnson returned on 20 October. Then Baretti quickly responded. But Johnson still failed to keep the promise Davies presumably had again mentioned.[37]

Given Boswell's persistence, Johnson's long silence seems almost willful. He received his friend's letter of 7 November 1766 shortly after he returned from Oxford, where for a month he "rose regularly to early prayers," and saw Chambers's need for help in composing his Vinerian lectures on the English law. After receiving whatever Boswell wrote early in 1767, Johnson was again at Oxford, then spent four months in Lichfield. But even after he returned to

London and Streatham in late October and received Boswell's additional letters, he still did not respond.[38]

When he finally did write in March 1768, after receiving a copy of *An Account of Corsica, the Journal of a Tour to That Island, and Memoirs of Pascal
Paoli,* instead of explaining his long silence, as he had seven months earlier to
the essayist and playwright George Colman, Johnson simply said, "I have omitted a long time to write to you, without knowing very well why." It seems
inadequate simply to say that Johnson was habitually indolent or to note his
having told Chambers that during the summer of 1767, "My old melancholy
has laid hold upon me to a degree sometimes not easily supportable," and that
his "spirits seem[ed] still very low" in early November, when Baretti passed a
whole day with Johnson "and could scarcely make him speak." For Johnson
occasionally did write others, often at length, clearly owed Boswell a letter, and
was regularly reminded of this debt.[39]

In November 1766 and again in January 1767, Johnson might have regarded
Davies and Baretti as proxy correspondents, supplying Boswell with news and
clear expressions of his regard. But afterward, as he repeatedly promised to
write and then was reminded of this promise, why did Johnson remain silent?
Whatever Johnson's thoughts and feelings as he read the feisty letter we have
and those that have not survived, and saw how Boswell described him to Baretti
and Davies, he continued to put off writing, even though he knew Boswell
might worry that he was angry or had ceased to care. I know of no other
example of such delay. Though Johnson claimed in 1763 that Boswell's very
first letter from Utrecht "hardly admitted or deserved an answer," Boswell now
was writing more carefully. But Boswell's concerted efforts to elicit a letter may
have fostered a stubborn resistance, even if Johnson also felt guilty at not playing his part. Perhaps, too, Johnson was upset by reports that Boswell was steadily working on the book he had had initially encouraged, but then had urged
his friend to abandon. Whatever the explanation, Johnson did not write until
March 1768, after receiving a copy of *Corsica.*[40]

Meanwhile, Boswell, after a year of trying to elicit a response, seems for a
second time to have stopped writing. Also, as he worked on his book and
heard nothing from Johnson, Boswell, who in March 1766 had described
himself to Temple as "the freind [*sic*] of Johnson & of Paoli," now chiefly
pictured himself simply as the friend of Paoli. In February 1767, for instance,
while trying to justify keeping a mistress, Boswell interrupted his self-serving
argument to write, "This is unworthy of Paoli's Friend." Seven months later,
when he sent Temple a letter from Lord Auchinleck that had made him furious, he wrote, "How galling it is to the friend of Paoli to be treated so!" In this
second letter, Boswell immediately added that he was no longer "depressed"

by what his father had written, but was "firm": "As my revered Friend Mr Samuel Johnson used to say, I feel the privileges of an independent human Being." But "used to say" called attention to Boswell's having heard nothing directly from Johnson for more than a year. There was no reassuring evidence of this friend's loving support.[41]

So Boswell used his book to write Johnson into his life. His preliminary sketch of materials to be included lists Johnson's praise of Sallust in *Rambler* 60, Johnson's talk about philosophers who milk the bull, Boswell's letter to Johnson from Corte (in Corsica), and Johnson's "come home." By featuring this material in a text constructed in defiance of Johnson's advice that he "Mind [his] own affairs and leave the Corsicans to theirs," and while Johnson once again was frustratingly silent, Boswell reaffirmed his respect, proclaimed their friendship, and tried to secure Johnson's attention.[42]

The hero of the book was General Paoli, to whom Boswell listened with his "whole attention" and whose ideas about government, religion, and morality fill the core of the *Journal.* But early in the book, instead of simply quoting Johnson's *Rambler* on biography, Boswell remarked how Johnson's "comprehensive and vigorous understanding, has by long observation, attained to a perfect knowledge of human nature." Boswell also referred to "the wisdom of the Rambler"; and after reporting his promise to send some English books for Paoli's library, he added in a footnote that that he sent "some of our best books of morality and entertainment, in particular the works of Mr. Samuel Johnson."[43]

Boswell also reported having given Paoli "the character of my revered friend Mr. Samuel Johnson," expressed his regret "that illustrious men, such as humanity produces a few times in a revolution of many ages, should not see each other," and imagined "an interview between such a scholar and philosopher as Mr Johnson and such a legislator and general as Paoli." Boswell had approximated such an interview on Corsica by repeating to Paoli some of Johnson's comments, "so remarkable for strong sense and original humour." Now he inserted these into the text in which both Johnson and Paoli were "introduced" to his readers. Boswell asked readers to pardon this "digression" from Corsica and Paoli: "I pay a just tribute of veneration and gratitude to one from whose writings and conversation I have received instructions of which I experience the value in every scene of my life." When Temple suggested cutting some of the material involving Johnson, probably these anecdotes, Boswell replied, "I must have my great Preceptour Mr Johnson introduced. Lord Hailes has approved of it."[44]

Finally, toward the end of the book, Boswell told of walking from the Franciscan convent to Corte "purposely to write a letter to Mr. Samuel Johnson": "I told my revered friend that from a kind of superstition agreeable in a certain degree to him as well as to myself, I had during my travels written to him from LOCA SOLENNIA, places in some measure sacred. That as I had written to him from the Tomb of Melanchthon, sacred to learning and piety, I now wrote to him from the palace of Pascal Paoli, sacred to wisdom and liberty, knowing that however his political principles may have been represented, he had always a generous zeal for the common rights of humanity. I gave him a sketch of the great things I had seen in Corsica, and promised him a more ample relation." Boswell then reported, "Mr. Johnson was pleased with what I wrote here, for I received at Paris an answer from him, which I keep as a valuable charter." Without having asked permission, Boswell then quoted much of this letter, beginning with Johnson's description of himself as Boswell's "unaltered, and I hope unalterable friend." He also quoted the whole second and third paragraphs, where Johnson praised him emphatically in order to offset two years of silence.[45]

The book reports Boswell's discussing Corsica with Rousseau both before and after he ventured there, and calls attention to Rousseau's letter of introduction. But Boswell made up for having styled himself "a friend of the celebrated John James Rousseau" by describing Rousseau as "the wild philosopher" whose "singular eloquence filled our minds with high ideas" while he lived "in romantic retirement," ideas that suffered much "when he came into the walks of men." Also Boswell aligned himself throughout the narrative with Johnson's sanity, wisdom, and perfect knowledge of human nature, which so richly complemented Paoli's. He demonstrated his attention and skill in recording conversation, voiced respect for Johnson's "own peculiar forcible language," and defended this language against "prejudiced or little critics" by quoting from *Idler* 70: "He that thinks with more extent than another will want words of larger meaning."[46]

Boswell was publicly writing into his life a man he had hardly seen in more than four years when his book was published, a man from whom he had heard nothing directly for eighteen months. His telling of how he repeated "Mr. Johnson's sayings" to Paoli "as nearly as I could in his own peculiar forcible language" suggested that he was Johnson's regular companion. His alluding to letters he had written Johnson while abroad, and quoting Johnson's prompt reply to the letter from Corsica, misleadingly suggested a regular correspondence. Shown Boswell declaring his "veneration and gratitude" and Johnson affirming his friendship, readers would naturally see the two as significantly linked. By making their mutual regard a matter of public record, Boswell hoped to secure a "perpetual" connection.

By collaborating with a wholly cooperative Paoli, Boswell connected himself with the unfolding history of Europe. By collaborating with his unsuspecting "great preceptour," Boswell tried to achieve narrative authority within their friendship. He was not constructing and publishing his book to supplant or destroy Johnson, but to bond with him, though on somewhat new terms. He was not directly seeking to rival any text Johnson had produced, but showing what he could achieve. His not asking permission to use Johnson's sayings and letter may have expressed anger at Johnson's attempt to block the project, and at his silence. But Boswell was not directly voicing disappointment or irritation. Instead, he broadcast his admiration while demonstrating how fully he had incorporated Johnson. By publishing his friend's declaration of "unaltered and . . . unalterable" friendship, he challenged Johnson to live up to this affirmation.

Jostling for Control (1768–1771)

In March 1768, Boswell arrived in London to relish his celebrity as the author of *Corsica*. Four years later, he arrived to defend in an appellate case before the House of Lords and also to get Johnson to begin formally preparing him to write the *Life*. For most of the time in between, the key drama in the life of each friend did not involve the other. But they spent time together in the spring of 1768 and the fall of 1769, experiencing more fully than before how commitments to others challenged their friendship. The surviving records suggest that neither was simply or fully satisfied with their time together. During new struggles for control, each discovered unexpected limitations or deficiencies in his friend. What happened during these visits — especially at the start of the first and near the end of the second — significantly reconfigured their friendship. Then, during his long silence after he left London on 10 November 1769, Boswell decided to assume the role of Johnson's biographer, a move that would fundamentally modify the dynamics of power.

Letters and Conversations (23 March through 8 June 1768)

When *Corsica* was published on 18 February 1768, Boswell sent Johnson a copy, with word he would soon be in London. There is no way to know how Johnson reacted to the book's flattery or to Boswell's skillfully prompting

anyone who knew Johnson to ask about the young Scot he had praised so enthusiastically. But judging from the short letter Johnson sent from Oxford on 23 March, he was angry that Boswell had published much of his letter without permission, even suggesting that this violation of privacy might retro-actively justify his own long silence: "I have omitted a long time to write to you, without knowing very well why. I could now tell why I should not write, for who would write to men who publish the letters of their friends without their leave? Yet I write to you in spite of my caution, to tell you that I shall be glad to see you, and that I wish you would empty your head of Corsica, which I think has filled it rather too long. But, at all events, I shall be glad, very glad to see you."[1]

A day before Johnson posted this letter to Edinburgh, Boswell reached Lon-don and heard from someone — perhaps Davies or his publishers, Edward and Charles Dilly — that Johnson was "displeased" with Boswell's having printed his letter. So after three days of being celebrated for his briskly selling book, Boswell went to Oxford. He looked for Johnson at New College, where he met the Vinerian Professor of Law, Robert Chambers, "a lively, easy, agreeable Newcastle man," and learned that Johnson had just written Boswell for the first time in nineteen months. Johnson then arrived and, as Boswell recorded the reunion, "He took me all in his arms and kissed me on both sides of the head, and was as cordial as ever I saw him." Boswell told Johnson "all [his] perplexity on his account," and that he "had come determined to fight him, or do anything he pleased." He saw it gave Johnson "high satisfaction" that he had come to Oxford "on purpose" to see him. But Boswell's substantial entry suggests that Johnson's displeasure was dropped without further comment as they began discussing Boswell's success during his first year as a lawyer. "What, Bozzy! Two hundred pounds! A great deal." Boswell wanted Johnson's opinion of *Corsica*, too. But Johnson soon remarked, "When an author asks me if I like his book and I give him something like praise, it must not be taken as my real opinion," and Boswell decided not to pursue the matter: "I thought within myself I should not ask him about my book."[2]

Boswell spent three nights in Oxford, sharing supper with Johnson and Chambers each evening, and on 28 March joining them for morning tea, too. (Boswell brought the Earl of Eglinton's nephew, Francis Stewart, to the last three meetings, having made him "promise to be very quiet and submissive.") During these fully documented conversations, Johnson strongly praised sev-eral books, promised to read Boswell's *Essence of the Douglas Cause,* and said "the severest thing about [William] Robertson's *History of Scotland* without intending it": "I love Robertson and I won't talk of his book." But Boswell heard nothing about *Corsica,* and surely wondered whether Johnson's silence expressed a similar judgment: *I love Boswell and I won't talk of his book.* Blocked by what the journal suggests had been said precisely to keep him from asking, Boswell was uncharacteristically reticent. And Johnson, notorious for directly expressing irritation and anger, maintained an aggressive silence.[3]

Postponing talk about *Corsica* for a day might have seemed an appropriate "punishment" for Boswell's publishing Johnson's letter without permission. But saying nothing for three days suggests that more was at stake, especially since Boswell had clearly realigned himself with Johnson by criticizing Rousseau in his book, and on his first night in Oxford had told a story critical of Wilkes's supporters. Once Johnson returned to London, having in the meantime received Boswell's reply to what Johnson had posted shortly before Boswell appeared, he immediately told his friend how highly he valued *Corsica*. At Oxford, however, Johnson had not been ready, even though the deliberate withholding of well-earned praise from a friend he had regularly complimented and encouraged left him enduringly guilty.[4]

I suspect Johnson was chiefly reacting to how skillfully Boswell had asserted control over their friendship, control Johnson had earlier evaded by not writing letters, despite reminders from Davies and Baretti. By publishing Johnson's fondness and praise, Boswell publicly held him to his word. Johnson's sustained silence in Oxford reestablished control. This speculation seems supported by an exchange at the end of the first evening when Johnson "put [Boswell] in mind" of their "journey to Harwich," and they "recalled many a circumstance" in which Boswell had been especially needy and Johnson unusually critical. Instead of discussing the book that publicized their friendship, Johnson turned to a time when he had been mostly in charge. He also revived the fantasy of traveling together to the remote Hebrides, a trip he could imagine being as free of competition and rivalry as were their first weeks as friends, five years earlier.[5]

Because of Johnson's aggressive silence and because they were seldom alone, the conversations Boswell recorded at Oxford differ in some respects from most of those in 1763 and from those on their first day together in 1766. There were two moments — one long anticipated and the other more spontaneous — when Boswell asked Johnson to resolve vexing concerns with clear, principled argument or boldly asserted prejudices. But many other reported exchanges, especially those on the second and third days, were more contentious.

Boswell "longed much" to have his "great preceptor" resolve his fear that practicing law "hurt[s] the principles of honesty," and with "wonderful force and fancy," Johnson satisfied Boswell concerning what "had often and often perplexed" him. "What do you think of pleading a cause which you know to be bad?" Boswell asked on his first evening in Oxford. "Does not the putting on a warmth when you have no warmth, and appearing to be clearly of one opinion when you are in reality of another . . . hurt one's honesty? Is there not some danger that one may put upon the same mask in common life, in the intercourse with one's friends?" "Sir," Johnson decisively replied, "you don't know [a cause] to be bad till the judge determines it. . . . An argument which does not convince you yourself may convince the judge before whom you plead it; and if it does convince him, why, then, Sir, you are wrong and he is right. . . . Everybody knows you are paid for putting on a warmth for your client, and it is properly no dissimulation. . . . Sir, a man will no more carry the artifice of the bar into the common intercourse of society than a man who is paid for tumbling upon his hands will continue tumbling upon his hands when he ought to be walking on his feet." Boswell was also delighted two days later when, after confessing to being afraid to marry Belle de Zuylen, a woman with "superior talents," he heard Johnson reply that there was nothing to fear: "before a year goes about you'll find that reason much weaker, and that wit not near so bright"—a reassuring comment that prompted Boswell to exclaim, "O admirable master of human nature!" (When Boswell argued that "virtue might be found even in a common street-walker," Johnson, aggressively replied, "Why . . . I shall have the Dutch lady; you can get a wife in the streets.")[6]

Boswell as usual raised numerous other topics. But now, without rejecting Johnson's fundamental positions, he was more willing to challenge some of his friend's assertions, discovering in the process that "having been two years a lawyer in real business had given me great force." They debated the value of Scottish writers and the virtue of prostitutes, whether scorpions commit suicide and whether animals might have immortal souls—each repeatedly measuring himself against the other, testing his knowledge and ingenuity. Johnson always won. This was Boswell's first sustained experience of Johnson's fierce need to win every argument, and Boswell both described and analyzed his friend's stratagems. Johnson no longer simply dismissed Boswell's challenges, as he had when they supped with Temple two years earlier. But he refused to acknowledge any strength in his friend's positions, and at times even refused to credit Boswell's evidence.

The most interesting tussle occurred at supper on the second day when Boswell tried to defend the unorthodox but "pleasing" idea that animals might have souls. Johnson resisted. And when Boswell, "with a serious, metaphysical, pensive face, ventured to say, 'But really, Sir, when we see a very sensible dog, we do not know what to think of him,'" Johnson "turned about, and growling with joy, replied, 'No, Sir; and when we see a very foolish fellow, we don't know what to think of him.' Then up he got, bounced along, and stood by the fire, laughing and exulting over" Boswell. Johnson's retort showed Chambers and Stewart he had no high regard for Boswell's intellect, even though his praise of Boswell's "wise and noble curiosity" had been published. But Johnson's triumph was superficial. For as Boswell later noted in his journal, he could easily have retorted, "Well, but you do not know what to think of a very sensible dog."[7]

Boswell returned to London early on 29 March. Johnson remained in Oxford throughout April, working with Chambers and also suffering what he referred to fifteen years later as "That dreadful ilness which seized me at New Inn Hall," severe bronchitis; because of it, Johnson "never since cared much to walk." Having probably received Johnson's letter early in April, Boswell responded on 26 April. Misrepresenting how much of Johnson's letter he had published, Boswell turned his defiance into a compliment: "Surely you have no reason to complain of my publishing a single paragraph of one of your letters; the temptation to it was so strong. An irrevocable grant of your friendship, and your dignifying my desire of visiting Corsica with the epithet of 'a wise and noble curiosity,' are to me more valuable than many of the grants of kings."

Then Boswell flatly rejected Johnson's wish that he "empty [his] head of Corsica." In fact, he asked his "noble-minded friend," whose "generous zeal for the common rights of humanity" he had applauded, "Do you not feel for an oppressed nation bravely struggling to be free?" Johnson's suggestion that Boswell abandon Corsica, following his sustained silence about the book, provoked a firmer self-assertion than exists in any earlier journal entries or surviving letters: "Empty my head of Corsica! . . . No! While I live, Corsica and the cause of the brave Islanders shall ever employ much of my attention, shall ever interest me in the sincerest manner."[8]

Soon after receiving this defiant letter, Johnson returned to London, and on 2 May he visited his friend, who was confined to cure gonorrhea. Only fragmentary notes survive for this unusual meeting. Boswell "jumped [up] and embraced" Johnson, crying "Thou great man!" and Johnson said, "Don't call names." But Boswell's flattery, combined with his letter, worked. For as soon as Boswell mentioned "the praise of my book," Johnson finally offered his own comments: "Sir, your book is very well. The *Account* may be had more from other books. But the *Tour* is extremely well. It entertains everybody. Sir, everybody who wishes you well [is] pleased." None of Johnson's other young friends had done anything comparable to this book.

Boswell's notes suggest that for the first time Johnson addressed him as a fellow writer, a peer. When Boswell asked him to review *Corsica*, Johnson replied, "No, one ass [should not] scratch [another]." Later, in arguing about "liberty," Boswell reported the following exchange:

JOHNSON. . . . "Liberty of press not much. Suppose you and I and two hundred more restrained, what then? What proportion?" BOSWELL. "Ay, but [suppose] ten thousand [restrained] from reading us?" JOHNSON. "Yes, they are the wretches [to be pitied]."[9]

After this easy, comfortable talk, their interactions were almost surely less tense than at Oxford. But there is little describing their being together before Boswell left town five weeks later. Boswell was confined through mid-May, but was sought out by a range of distinguished visitors, including Benjamin Franklin, then the agent for several American colonies, and General James Oglethorpe, the founder of the colony of Georgia. "Sir John Pringle, Dr. Franklin & some more company dined with me today," he wrote Temple on 14 May, "& Mr Johnson & General Oglethorpe one day Mr Garrick alone another & David Hume & some more Literati dine with me next week." Much of the time, Johnson was with the Thrales at Streatham, six miles south of the city, recovering from bronchitis and depression. Though Boswell wrote Temple that Johnson dined with him sometime in the first half of May, this dinner is not noted in Boswell's skimpy notes for 3–14 May, and no additional meetings are mentioned in surviving notes or letters, which tell little about Boswell's final three weeks in London. Writing to Hester Thrale years later, however, Boswell recalled how on one of these days, having heard Baretti describe this "fine and learned Lady" whose "liveliness and beauty [might] well revive [Johnson] a little, and recruit his mind with chearful ideas," he "sprang uninvited" into her coach as she waited for Johnson, and talked enough "to shew her that [he] was as Johnsonian as herself."[10]

In the *Life,* drawing on memories and perhaps undated notes, Boswell also described a supper with Johnson and several others at the Crown and Anchor, and his comfortable chat with Johnson the next morning. Besides Tom Davies, the company included two of the Scottish writers Boswell and Johnson had discussed six weeks earlier, Hugh Blair and William Robertson, and two long-time friends of Johnson's whom Boswell had just met, Thomas Percy and Bennet Langton. Despite Boswell's efforts, Robertson and Blair would not hazard speaking before Johnson, who was "in remarkable vigour of mind and eager to exert himself in conversation." The talk Boswell reported consisted chiefly of Johnson's attacks: on an Oxford don accused of swearing and talking bawdy, on Percy for misleadingly trying to defend this don, and on anyone who praised Jonathan Swift's *Conduct of the Allies* (1711). Nothing about this event was unusual. But what Boswell reported happening the next morning was unprecedented. When Johnson, "highly satisfied with his colloquial prowess the preceding evening," said, "We had good talk," Boswell replied, "Yes, Sir, you tossed and gored several persons."

Johnson's wanting Boswell's knowing admiration seems entirely new, as does Boswell's conspiratorial stance: both critical and praiseful, and confident that Johnson would not protest. Johnson was a bull, and Boswell his handler, whose job was first to provide an occasion and then to assess his performance. This might have been a natural extension of Boswell's new "peer" status, which Johnson had conceded five weeks earlier and perhaps had confirmed on other, unreported occasions. Certainly, Boswell eventually played this role. But no surviving entries before 1773 describe this sort of camaraderie. So I suspect the comfortable, intimate tone of this "morning after" exchange was achieved only later, though it was introduced at this point of the *Life*.[11]

Corsica had clearly gotten Johnson's attention, prompting his first letter since 1766. It also firmly linked Johnson and Boswell—a linkage soon reinforced when William Kenrick attacked Boswell for sending to Corsica the moral writings of Johnson, which "would pervert and corrode the native simplicity of Corsican virtue with Johnsonian sophistry." Even before Boswell jumped into her coach, Hester Thrale had probably asked Johnson about the young Scot he so warmly praised. But Boswell was not a major player in Johnson's life. Chambers was more significant in Oxford, and Thrale in town. Nor was it clear what would happen next. Boswell had dropped his demand that Lord Auchinleck approve an annual London visit, so there was no telling when he would next see Johnson. The trip to the Hebrides remained on the horizon. But they seem not to have discussed traveling there anytime soon. When they parted—and as in 1766, their parting was not reported—they probably once again promised to write. But no letters survive until after Boswell returned to London fifteen months later.[12]

9 June 1768 to 9 September 1769: Johnson

During these months, Boswell wrote several letters to Johnson, surely including one after Davies's alarming report about Johnson in July 1768: "His health is very precarious and I much fear we shall not have him long." On 14 November, Johnson recorded a resolve to write Boswell—but he did not write. Boswell, too, seems once again to have stopped writing, since otherwise Johnson would have acknowledged his failure to respond when he finally did write in September 1769.[13]

Johnson's major concern was his physical and mental health. On 12 July 1768, a day before Davies described Johnson's precarious condition, Johnson wrote Lucy Porter that he had "been too much disordered" in his health to keep track of whether he owed her a letter. "How the last year has past I am unwilling to terrify myself with thinking," he wrote on his birthday two months later. At the start of 1769, he again wrote, "How the last [year] has past, it would be in my state of weakness perhaps not prudent too solicitously to recollect"; and on his next birthday, nine months later, Johnson echoed this, then detailed his "slow progress of recovery."[14]

While struggling to regain health, Johnson continued to help Chambers finish the Vinerian lectures, visiting Oxford in December 1768, February 1769, and again May and June. In August 1769, he paid a short visit to Lichfield. Otherwise, he was with the Thrales, mostly at Streatham but also in Kent (September 1768) and Brighton (August–September 1769). It was from Brighton that he finally wrote Boswell 9 September 1769, responding promptly to the letter his young friend had just posted from Oxford.

Aside from Johnson's resolve to write, there is no evidence Boswell was on his mind. But since several people Johnson saw regularly had met Boswell, it is easy to imagine them occasionally asking about this young Scot, especially since *Corsica* was still being reviewed and discussed. Boswell's collection *British Essays in Favour of the Brave Corsicans* was published in December 1768, and a third edition of *Corsica* was published in May 1769, with an introduction by the politician and writer Lord Lyttelton. Johnson's reminding himself to write suggests he felt guilty at continuing to be "such a sparing and ungrateful correspondent." (From August 1763 through September 1769 there had been only four brief periods when Johnson did not owe Boswell a letter.) But Johnson's response on 9 September 1769, after Boswell charged him with "unkindness," indicates that he chiefly felt guilty for something Boswell surely did not have in mind: his having initially withheld his opinion of *Corsica*.[15]

That Johnson in September 1769 was still brooding on his sustained silence at Oxford, and had forgotten that he praised the book once he reached London, shows how conscious he was of aggressively saying nothing about this defiant and controlling text. Once again he tried to atone, praising Boswell's "curious and delightful" journal: "You express images which operated strongly upon yourself and you have impressed them with great force upon your readers. I know not whether I could name any narrative by which curiosity is better excited or better gratified." Because of Johnson's repeated failures to write and also — perhaps especially — because of his initial silence about *Corsica*, Johnson's friendship with Boswell was deeply connected with guilt even before the biographical project linked Boswell to God's judgment on how Johnson had used his time and talents.[16]

Whatever Boswell made of Johnson's forgetting that he had already praised *Corsica* — and in the *Life*, he avoided having to consider this by omitting their earlier talk about the book — the "unkindness" he had in mind in September 1769 probably combined Johnson's usual silence with his not being in London when Boswell wanted advice about his coming marriage and his father's plan to remarry.[17]

9 June 1768 to 9 September 1769: Boswell

After establishing himself as a lawyer and an author, Boswell's chief task was to find a suitable wife. His letters to Johnson might have chronicled his changeable affections for various eligible women, as did some of his letters to others. But it was chiefly to Temple — and also to his cousin Margaret Montgomerie — that Boswell worried whether his "wonderful inconstancy" would permit him to fix his love on any woman. It was only in his journal — and perhaps in unreported conversations — that he wondered whether, after a history of "vicious profligacy" and "feverish gallantry," he could settle into marriage.

Boswell had almost surely stopped writing Johnson by 3–4 May 1769, when he described to Temple and Dempster his growing love for Margaret, "the best companion I ever saw," and asked advice about marrying a woman who lacked a substantial dowry as well as social and political connections, and whom his father thought a poor prospect for his heir. Then Boswell was shocked to discover Lord Auchinleck planned to remarry.[18]

Early in 1767, Boswell had written Temple that unless Lord Auchinleck married again, he would be forced to live with him as his health failed. Ten months later Sir John Pringle, responding to Boswell's wish to live apart from his father, had concluded that it might be best if both father and son found good wives. So Boswell should not have been surprised in June 1769 that his father was thinking of marrying. But he was appalled. Nor would he admit that his father might be justified. In fact, when he described his initial suspicion in the entry for 30 June, and reported later conversations with his father and others, Boswell distanced himself from the very idea of a second marriage by expressing it in French.[19]

By 16 July 1769, Boswell was in such a rage against his father — "Damn him. Curse him" — that he was "absolutely mad," and imagined having been tempted and tormented by "evil spirits." He was "so furious and black-minded and uttered such horrid ideas" that his friend Grange, who had calmed Boswell's initial outrage, delivered an ultimatum: "If I talked so he would never see me again." Boswell saw Lord Auchinleck's remarrying as "an insult on the memory of my valuable mother" and "as the most ungrateful return to me for my having submitted so much to please him." It also showed that his respectable father was subject to "libidinous" passion and "wretched appetite," to use the language of "On Second Marriages: A True Story," the cautionary tale in which Boswell expressed his horror and disgust.

Like the "truly dutiful" eldest son in this story, Boswell determined to go abroad, leaving his father to sink into "folly and dotage." On 20 July, he asked Margaret whether she would marry him even if he abandoned all hope of inheriting the family estate: "Will you, . . . knowing me fully, accept of me for your husband as I now am; — not as the heir of Auchinleck, but one who has had his time of the world, and is henceforth to expect no more than £100 a year?" Two days later Margaret calmly accepted.[20]

Meanwhile, Lord Monboddo, a judge on the Court of Session best known for published speculation about human evolution, offered to mediate. Like Temple and Dempster, Monboddo was "clear and irresistible" in favor of Margaret, and like the physician Sir Alexander Dick, he thought Lord Auchinleck's remarrying "would be very foolish at his time of life — a terrible thing — a burthen on his family." On 4 August, when Lord Auchinleck grudgingly agreed to his heir's marrying Margaret, though "he thought [Boswell's] scheme of marriage improper and that Margaret and [he] would part in half a year," Boswell mistakenly assumed he had also abandoned his own marriage plan, especially since Lord Auchinleck was reluctant to reintroduce a subject that so disturbed his oldest son.[21]

Soon after Boswell and Margaret had confirmed they would marry, he declared his need to see Johnson. His ostensible reason for going to London was to be cured of all traces of gonorrhea after ten separate infections. Dr. John Gregory, a professor of medicine at the University of Edinburgh, assured him on 9 August that he was "in no bad way" and "might be cured very well" in Edinburgh; and Margaret tried to dissuade him: "If your health is not in question, you could see Mr. Johnson some other time." On 12 August, however, Boswell persuaded his father that only in London could he "clear [his] constitution." Then he prepared to depart. His letters to Margaret — especially what he wrote on 21 August to coach her for an interview with his father — were supportive and affectionate, even self-effacing. But despite her distress, Boswell insisted on going. Then he stayed away for almost eleven weeks, though the cure required only six, thus guaranteeing that Margaret would see Johnson as a major rival.[22]

Though Boswell's visit involved a range of activities, the chance to spend time with Johnson was what mainly drew him south. He looked for his friend early on 1 September, but waited till the next day before consulting Pringle about the cure. Starting on 22 September, Boswell was often with Paoli, whose arrival in exile Boswell had not anticipated; and at the end of October, he further delayed his return so he could visit Temple in Devon. But connecting with Johnson was always his chief goal.

As Boswell wrote Hester Thrale on 5 September, he wanted the author of the *Rambler* and *Rasselas* to speak wisely and decisively about love and marriage: "Before entering on that important state to happiness or misery, I am anxious to hear the Oracle." Having heard David Hume's "philosophical opinion that

[his] marriage [to Margaret] must be a happy one," Boswell wanted Johnson to be just as emphatic, especially since his father so clearly disapproved. In particular he wanted Johnson's reassurance that it was wise to marry someone who was already his "old friend," that "our friendship will not be lessened because we enjoy happiness together," and that Margaret "will make me the man I wish to be." He also hoped Johnson would share his outrage that Lord Auchinleck still planned to remarry. But though Boswell alerted others of his coming to London, he curiously did not write Johnson. Instead, he just walked to Johnson's house soon after arriving, learned from Anna Williams that he was at Brighton with the Thrales, and four days later from Oxford complained of Johnson's "neglect." He also wrote Hester Thrale, asking his "generous rival" to encourage Johnson to write, and offering to come to Brighton if they would not soon return home.[23]

When Boswell returned from Garrick's Shakespeare Jubilee in Stratford, he found Johnson's unusually prompt reply, praising *Corsica* and wishing Boswell well "in this crisis of your life." "What I can contribute to your happiness I should be very unwilling to withhold," Johnson added, "for I have always loved and valued you and shall love you and value you still more as you become more regular and useful[,] effects which a happy Marriage will hardly fail to produce." But instead of eagerly hoping to reconnect, as he had in 1766 and 1768, Johnson teased Boswell for traveling to the jubilee and then waiting to see him while the woman he planned to marry was far away. "I shall perhaps stay a fortnight longer, and a fortnight is a long time to a lover absent from his Mistress. Would a fortnight ever have an end?"[24]

The same day Boswell read these words, he began the cure, and on 14 September he wrote Johnson again, presumably urging haste. On 22 September, a day after he heard from Benjamin Franklin that Paoli was in town, Boswell called on the hero of *Corsica,* who "ran to me, took me all in his arms, and held me there for some time. . . . and instantly [we] were just as when we parted." Paoli's presence revived Boswell's celebrity, and Paoli's conversation was engaging. But his companionship clarified Boswell's need for Johnson. Not until 28 September, however, did Boswell and Johnson begin their fullest visit since 1763, their most ambivalent visit ever.[25]

Reconnecting (28 September to 10 November 1769)

Over the next six weeks, the two friends were much more frequently together than in 1768 or 1766, and were more often alone. They saw each other on five of the ten days from 28 September through 7 October, on at most one of the next eight (8–15 October), but then on at least eight of the next sixteen (16–31 October), and finally on 10 November, after Boswell returned from visiting Temple. Having earlier "introduced" Paoli to Margaret by sharing "her *most valuable letter*," in which she agreed to live with Boswell in exile, Boswell probably did the same when first with Johnson. Three weeks later he read his friend what Margaret had written concerning several *Rambler* essays, then relayed Johnson's praise of her "very pretty" comments. On 6 October, Boswell dined at Streatham with his chief rival for Johnson's time and attention, Hester Thrale, and spent the night. Later in the month—probably on 30 October—he arranged to have Johnson meet Paoli, his other moral hero, picturing himself as "an isthmus which joins two great continents." Whatever Johnson and Boswell had anticipated or hoped when the visit began, what happened during these weeks led directly to the key transformation of their friendship.[26]

As in 1766 after the first day of Boswell's visit to London, and as at Oxford in 1768, both men seem to have been somewhat uncomfortable much of the time as they renegotiated their roles. On only two days do they seem to have been wholly at ease, 10 October and 10 November, for both of which we have only what Boswell eventually wrote in the *Life*. Boswell was more deeply needy than at any time since 1763, and Johnson, having promised assistance, addressed his friend's pressing and practical questions. But only at the very end did Boswell report extensive talk about marriage. Also, Johnson refused to grapple with "the perplexed question of fate and free will," which would be a recurring topic from this time onward.

Johnson firmly endorsed Boswell's notion that a married man "ought to have his own house, and cannot possibly be happy under his father's roof." Having suggested in 1763 that Boswell would eventually become just what his father wanted, and having repeatedly urged his friend to work at pleasing his father, Johnson now accepted that the two were essentially different: "The disputes between you and him are matters of sensation not of judgment. . . . He grumbles because you come to London. He cannot understand why it is very right you should from time to time enjoy London. There is no help for it. Let him grumble." Johnson also agreed with Lord Monboddo that it would be "much better" if Lord Auchinleck did not remarry, and imagined that if James and Margaret lived nearby and saw him often, this would "be as effectual in preventing his marrying again as living with him would be."

But Johnson refused to share Boswell's "warm resentment" at his father's plan for marriage. Though Johnson did not describe his own hopes to find a second wife, and also seems not to have cited his own experience when he finally talked at length about marriage, he firmly denied that Lord Auchinleck's hoping to marry showed "disregard" of Boswell's mother. In fact, "by taking a second wife he pays the highest compliment to the first, by proving that she made him so happy as a married man that he has a mind to be so a second time." Johnson also insisted that Boswell "would be *a fool*" to give up "*everything and everybody*" if his father remarried. Seventeen days later, when Boswell lamented to Johnson and Mrs. Williams that he lacked sympathy with the distresses of others, Johnson recommended that he "read melancholy stories as how a man's father married again, and how he was driven into foreign parts with his wife," facetiously alluding to Boswell's morbid "On Second Marriages." Having earlier tried reason, Johnson now turned to therapeutic laughter.[27]

During this visit, Johnson regularly teased or insulted Boswell when others were present, perhaps because he knew those who saw them together would have read his letter in *Corsica*. When Boswell dined at Streatham, for instance, and boasted that most good gardeners came from Scotland, Johnson wittily replied: "Why, Sir, that is because gardening is much more necessary amongst you than with us. . . . Things which grow wild here must be cultivated with great care in Scotland." Later, when Boswell praised the heroism of the Corsicans, Johnson "burst out into a violent declamation" that seemed particularly inappropriate after Paoli's recent defeat: "What is all this rout about the Corsicans? They have been at war with the Genoese for upwards of twenty years, and have never yet taken their fortified towns. They might have battered down the walls and reduced them to powder in twenty years. They might have pulled the walls in pieces, and cracked the stones with their teeth in twenty years." By forcefully rejecting Boswell's claims, and disparaging Paoli's revolutionary struggle, Johnson showed Hester Thrale how he treated *her* "rival," while he much more gently dismissed her defense of Matthew Prior's love poetry — "My dear lady, talk no more of this. Nonsense can be defended but by nonsense" — and her praise of Garrick's light verse — "Nay, my dear lady, this will never do."[28]

More significantly, when Boswell on 16 October arranged a dinner for Johnson and several members of his circle, including three who were seeing the two friends together for the first time — Garrick, the playwright and actor Arthur Murphy, and Sir Joshua Reynolds — Johnson mocked Boswell's intellect. After Johnson quoted the conclusion of Pope's *Dunciad* and others praised the lines, Boswell "ventured to say, 'Too fine for such a poem: a poem on what?'" Johnson, "with a disdainful look," replied, "Why, on *dunces*. It was worth while being a dunce then. Ah, Sir, hadst *thou* lived in those days! It is not worth while being a dunce now, when there are no wits." At other points in this conversation, Johnson teased Goldsmith and chided Garrick. But only Boswell was gratuitously ridiculed. Johnson let everyone Boswell had invited see how he treated the man whose "wise and noble curiosity" he had applauded; and since Boswell did not complain, Johnson saw no need to apologize.[29]

In response to these teases and insults, Boswell became more focused and sustained in questioning Johnson. When he stopped by Johnson's the morning after having been mocked as a "dunce," for instance, he raised a number of hypothetical possibilities to demonstrate his non-dunce-like skills. After Johnson declared that suicide was "a crime," Boswell asked, "But may it not be done to save many lives, if you can't bear torture and would discover?" Then he recorded a series of questions about whether one was obliged to keep promises made under duress: "If you promise a highwayman £100, should you keep it?" "But, sir, if £10,000?" "But he has perhaps a wife and family." Johnson played his part, patiently answering Boswell's questions before finally declaring, "Rules cannot be given for improbable cases. One must judge when they happen."

Two days later, when Boswell stayed with Johnson and Mrs. Williams until two in the morning, the conversation he later reported consisted of Johnson's responses to several series of questions, the most extended involving "our feeling for the distresses of others." Boswell wanted to discover whether Johnson cared more for him than for Baretti, at whose murder trial he would testify the next day, so he asked what Johnson would do if Boswell "were in danger of being hanged?" But he was also reasserting himself after Johnson had laughed at his "melancholy" story. (Earlier in the evening Johnson encouraged his friend to complete his "Dictionary of words peculiar to Scotland.")[30]

On 26 October, too, a demeaning comment was followed by Boswell's controlling questions. When Johnson insisted to those assembled at his house that medicated baths, like those currently provided by Bartholomew de Dominiceti, "can be no better than warm water: their only effect can be that of tepid moisture," Boswell opposed this and suggested he might try the experiment. This prompted Johnson to reply, "Well, Sir, go to Dominiceti, and get thyself fumigated; and let the steam be directed to thy *head,* for *there's* the *peccant part*"—a retort that "produced a triumphant roar of laughter" from those whom Boswell in the *Life* described as a "motley assembly of philosophers, printers, and dependents, male and female." But Boswell soon demonstrated his intellectual poise by getting Johnson systematically to respond to a series of questions concerning political economy and Roman Catholic practices. When Johnson mocked his intelligence, Boswell now reestablished his control.[31]

Three other exchanges on 26 October, the only day Johnson and Boswell were together from midday dinner until late at night, also deserve attention as both new and significant. Two seem to have been mutually satisfying, anticipating modes of interacting that later would become increasingly central. The third was more troubling than anything the two friends had thus far experienced together.

The initial new transaction was their first sustained, collaborative argument. When Johnson, while dining with Boswell at the Mitre, asserted that trade produces "a considerable profit in pleasure, as it gives to one nation the productions of another," Boswell amplified by noting that trade also pleases by "procuring occupation to mankind." Boswell was echoing what Johnson had written in 1766 about how practicing the law would secure him from the discontents of a mind "unemployed and undetermined." But now Johnson argued against this:

> JOHNSON. "Why, Sir, you cannot call that pleasure to which all are averse, and which none begin but with the hopes to be idle; a thing which men dislike before they have tried it, and when they have tried it." BOSWELL. "But, Sir, the mind must be employed, and we grow weary if idle." JOHNSON. "That is, Sir, because others are busy, and we want company; but if we were all idle, there would be no wearying; we should all entertain one another. . . . No man loves labour for itself." BOSWELL. "Yes, Sir, my father does. He is a very laborious judge, and he loves the labour." JOHNSON. Sir, that is because he loves respect and distinction. Could he have them without labour, he would like it better." BOSWELL. "He tells me he likes it for itself." JOHNSON. "Why, Sir, he fancies so, because he is not accustomed to abstract."

Johnson "won" by insisting Lord Auchinleck did not understand himself and faulting Boswell for accepting his father's testimony. But without an audience to laugh with him, Johnson did not directly insult Boswell. Instead, he seems to have enjoyed sparring with his eager disciple, deftly countering each argument the young Scot offered, including those Johnson had earlier supplied. Boswell, too, seems to have been pleased with this mostly respectful tussle.[32]

The second new transaction involved their first fully collaborative fantasy. Soon after the "triumphant roar of laughter" at Johnson's insulting retort ("peccant part"), and before Boswell questioned Johnson about political economy and Catholicism, he regained control by asking his friend to accept a "wild . . . supposition": "If, Sir, you were shut up in a castle, and a new-born child with you, what should you do?" Johnson replied, "Why, Sir, I should not much like my company," and seemed uninterested in explaining how he would raise this infant. But Boswell's persistent questioning, plus the presence of those who had just laughed at the joke about Boswell's diseased head, eventually coaxed Johnson to engage:

> "Why yes, Sir, I would; but I must have all the conveniencies. If I had no garden, I would make a shed on the roof, and take [the child] there for fresh

air. I should feed it, and wash it much, and with warm water to please it, not with cold water to give it pain." BOSWELL. "But, Sir, does not heat relax?" JOHNSON. Sir, you are not to suppose the water is to be very hot. I would not *coddle* the child. No, Sir, the hardy method of breeding up children does no good. I'll take you five children from London, who shall cuff five Highland children. Sir, a man bred in London will carry a burthen or run or wrestle as well as one brought up in the hardiest manner in the country."

After another exchange on what made Londoners so strong, Boswell pulled Johnson back into the initial scene by asking, "Would you teach your child anything?"

> JOHNSON. "No, I should not be apt to teach it." BOSWELL. "Would not you have a pleasure in teaching it?" JOHNSON. "No, Sir, I should *not* have a pleasure in teaching it." BOSWELL. "Have you not a pleasure in teaching men?—*there* I have you. You have the same pleasure in teaching men that I should have in teaching children." JOHNSON. "Why, something about that."

W. J. Bate shrewdly suggests that Boswell was trying to discover just what enticed Johnson to stay with the Thrales and their young children, including Johnson's four-month-old goddaughter, Lucy, when he might be with more grown-up company in town. An erotic attraction to Hester Thrale was Boswell's main suspicion, especially now that the upright, seemingly unemotional Lord Auchinleck was planning to remarry. But while testing this other possibility, Boswell got Johnson to help construct the first of many collaborative fantasies. Boswell did the initial imagining, then coaxed a reluctant Johnson to inhabit the scene, and continued to push even after Johnson became fully involved—a mode of collaboration they would later perfect in the Hebrides.[33]

The third new interaction eventually made 26 October the most significant day since Johnson first agreed to "take a charge of" Boswell, but it initially threatened to end the friendship. When they were alone or almost alone late that night, Boswell tried to probe something else that seemed strangely at odds with the heroic image of Johnson he had formed in Utrecht, his fear of death, and Johnson responded by threatening never to come to Scotland.

A week before, when Boswell told Johnson and Mrs. Williams that none of the criminals he had recently seen executed had seemed to be afraid, he asked, "Is not the fear of death natural to us all?" Johnson had replied, "So much so, Sir, that the whole of life is but keeping away the thoughts of it." Johnson probably spoke with suggestive intensity, prompting Boswell a few days later to raise the topic with Langton, who reported whatever Boswell had alluded to when he noted, "Johnson—deeply struck with death." Langton presumably knew what Boswell would learn only eight years later: that death terrified

Johnson because he feared damnation. But Boswell was puzzled. Johnson had confirmed Boswell's belief in personal immortality rather than annihilation, and clearly lived a worthy life. So why did he fear death, as Boswell at times no longer did?

On 26 October, therefore, when next alone with Johnson — or with Johnson and Mrs. Williams — Boswell reintroduced this topic. Drawing on his own experience in March 1768, when he had witnessed a public execution "with great composure" — an experience he had just repeated — and hoping to test whatever Langton had recently told him, Boswell "maintain[ed] that the fear of [death] might be got over." Boswell may have expected a "manly" reflection on how to approach this dreadful moment. Instead, he heard an angry threat to end their friendship.[34]

There are two complementary accounts of what happened: full journal notes written soon afterward on sheets that have disintegrated, though the pieces have been patiently reassembled, with suggestions for some of the missing letters or words; and a fuller narrative written later and eventually revised as the manuscript for this portion of the *Life*. (The journal has Mrs. Williams present during most of the conversation, but in the *Life* Boswell removed her.) Neither tells the whole story.

At the start of both accounts, Johnson denied suggestions that death was not always frightening, such as David Hume's claim that "he was no more uneasy to think he should *not be* after this life than that he *had not been* before he began to exist," and the mimic Samuel Foote's report that when very ill, he had not feared dying. "Hume knows he lies," Johnson insisted. "He may tell you he holds his finger in the flame of a candle without feeling pain. Would you believe him? . . . Hold a pistol to Foote's breast or to Hume's breast and threaten to kill them, and you'll see how they behave." When Boswell then asked, "But may we not fortify our minds for the approach of death?" Johnson replied, "No, Sir — let it alone. It matters not how a man dies, but how he lives. The act of dying is not of importance, it lasts so short a time." He added — with "an earnest look" — "A man knows it must be, and submits. It will do him no good to whine." (At this point, the journal reports Mrs. Williams leaving.)

When Boswell persisted, hoping to understand his friend's puzzling weakness, Johnson said, "Give us no more of this," and "was thrown into such a state of agitation that he expressed himself in a way that alarmed and distressed me": Johnson "shewed an impatience" to have Boswell leave him, and, when the latter "was going away, said, 'Don't let us meet tomorrow.'" The journal reported some of what alarmed Boswell: "One may a⟨t?⟩ a time discuss ⟨?such⟩ a question gravely. But you ⟨tease⟩ me with question after question very idly without seeming to care about the matter. (This was terrible) Sir

⟨sa⟩id I ⟨you⟩ have settled ⟨?so⟩ man⟨y⟩ of my doubts ⟨th⟩at ⟨I⟩ must apply to you. Don't ⟨yo⟩u lo⟨ve⟩ to instruct? Dont I ⟨lov⟩e to instruct? Why what sort of a question is that? Sir I wont come & see you in Scotland if you teise ⟨me⟩ so — Sir I tell you t⟨his is⟩ ⟨un⟩supportable." (At this point, the journal reports that Mrs. Williams returned, then started to leave, prompting Johnson "angrily" to cry, "Don't go away.")[35]

Boswell voiced puzzlement at Johnson's agitation, and neither acknowledged his aggression nor analyzed its roots. But his veneration and love of Johnson clearly coexisted with some hostility. He seems to have been fascinated that his friend was weaker, more vulnerable than he had imagined. He had found a way to make Johnson wince, to push against the authority he both needed and resented. This "great man [ha]s a gl[o]omy horrour for dea[th] and cannot bear the subject — . So I was wrong — & he became very sower and angry."

Deeply angered by his friend's insensitivity, Johnson asked him *not* to stop by the next day, one of the few mornings he would be in town. He even shockingly threatened to end or radically constrict their friendship, saying he would *not* to come to Scotland if Boswell did not stop "teising" him. The next morning, therefore, Boswell sent a note "acknowledging that I might have been in the wrong, but it was not intentionally," and announcing that he would stop by briefly — "five minutes by my watch": "You are . . . in my mind since last night surrounded with cloud and storm. Let me have a glimpse of sunshine and go about my affairs in serenity and cheerfulness." Johnson was talking with the Shakespeare editor George Steevens and the author Thomas Tyers, both strangers to Boswell. But Johnson received his friend "complacently," and Boswell "unexpectedly found [him]self at ease and joined in the conversation." After a certain amount of talk, Boswell whispered to Johnson — creating intimacy in the presence of two others — "Well, Sir, you are now in good humour." Later, as he started to leave, Johnson stopped him at the staircase "and smiling said, 'Get you gone — *in*,'" after which Boswell stayed longer. Perhaps Johnson forgave Boswell as someone lacking in judgment but not deliberately offensive. Perhaps, too, he simply found it hard to deny himself Boswell's company, despite the ambivalence suggested by "Get you gone — *in*."[36]

What occurred at the end of 26 October and the next morning had more impact on their friendship than anything else since 1763. Boswell glimpsed Johnson's inner turmoil. Johnson discovered that Boswell's persistent questioning could be unsympathetic, even menacing. And both saw that Johnson, though antagonized, still forgave. This tense exchange about the fear of death was so disturbing that they waited eight years before again directly discussing the topic. But both friends kept this episode in mind. It helped produce an unusual silence once Boswell returned to Scotland. It also seems to have influenced Boswell's decision to become Johnson's biographer, and Johnson's eventual acceptance of this project.[37]

Johnson saw Boswell on 31 October, when he and Paoli witnessed their young friend signing his marriage contract, and perhaps also on the day before. When Boswell returned on 9 November from a long visit with Temple, he wrote Johnson, "begging" to see him to town before he left for Scotland, and in return received another invitation from Hester Thrale. Boswell spent the night in town, but went early the next day to Streatham, where Johnson finally talked wisely about marriage: "You may often find yourself out of humour, and you may often think your wife not studious enough to please you, and yet you may have reason enough to consider yourself as upon the whole very happily married." Then Johnson surprised Boswell by accompanying him to his post chaise, once again wanting as much of Boswell's company as possible.

After this seemingly harmonious parting, however, there was no communication for seventeen months, "a total cessation of all correspondence . . . without any coldness on either side," as Boswell later explained in the *Life*. This was the first long silence when it was Boswell's turn to write.[38]

November 1769 through December 1771

There is little indication of how Johnson or Boswell regarded each other or their friendship during what would be the final long period without letters. Johnson wrote more surviving letters and diary entries than usual. In *The False Alarm* (January 1770), he supported the expulsion of John Wilkes from the House of Commons; and in *Thoughts on the Late Transactions Respecting Falkland Islands* (March 1771), he opposed a war with Spain. Also, in January 1770 he probably helped Chambers compose his final lectures. But there is no evidence that Boswell was on Johnson's mind, though at times he surely wondered about the friend whose marriage contract he had witnessed shortly before they parted.

There is less information than usual concerning Boswell after he married Margaret Montgomerie on the same day Lord Auchinleck set for his own marriage: no journal or memoranda until September 1771, only a few surviving letters, only a little evidence that he thought of Johnson. In September 1770, Boswell's essay "On the Profession of a Player" quoted what he had heard from Johnson, "the most illustrious author of this age, whose conversation is thought by many even to excel his writings," perhaps hoping Johnson might see this in the *London Magazine*. Writing Garrick six months later, Boswell praised the "vigour" of Johnson's *Falkland Islands* and corrected the line

Johnson had criticized in a witty song about marriage that Boswell had earlier shown Garrick. Then on 18 April 1771, Boswell wrote a letter that redefined his friendship with Johnson as decisively as Johnson's first letter had.[39]

The labored first sentence, which is all Boswell printed in the *Life*, clearly marked a significant shift in tone and substance. In the past, Boswell had regularly complained about Johnson's disturbing silence, prompting Johnson in three of his first five letters to reaffirm his abiding love and esteem. In contrast, Boswell now accepted Johnson's professions, since he had had the same experience: "I can now fully understand those intervals of silence in your correspondence with me, which have often given me anxiety and uneasiness; for although I am conscious that my veneration and love for Mr. Johnson have never in the least abated, yet I have deferred for almost a year and a half to write to him." In forgiving himself for having long failed to write, Boswell finally forgave Johnson for years of sustained silence.[40]

Boswell's strategy resembled what he had done in *Corsica* and in the still-unposted Wittenberg letter — but with a key difference. As in both these earlier texts, Boswell declared his enduring "love and veneration" for Johnson, and also assumed Johnson's for him. But now Boswell acknowledged Johnson's troubling lack of letters and his own disappointment and anger. Boswell's failure to write for seventeen months allowed him to reinterpret Johnson's long silences, so he confidently refused to see these as legitimate causes for concern. He and Johnson had both been neglectful, but their friendship was strong. Their love was constant even when they were not in touch.

According to the *Life*, the rest of Boswell's letter gave "an account of my comfortable life as a married man and a lawyer in practice at the scotch bar — invited [Johnson] to Scotland and promised to attend him to the highlands and Hebrides." Judging from Johnson's reply, Boswell also presented himself as free from melancholy and irresolution. Having grown "more regular" after his marriage, as Johnson had predicted, he was ready to enter a new stage in their friendship.[41]

This letter worked. Having experienced the only long stretch since August 1763 when he did not owe Boswell a letter, and the longest period when he had heard nothing directly or indirectly from Boswell, Johnson replied two months later, just before he left London for Lichfield and Ashbourne. Though pleased that Boswell had tried to reduce the guilt his earlier letters had helped produce, Johnson reprimanded his friend for only *now* accepting what Johnson had repeatedly claimed, and he modeled an alternative response: "If you are now able to comprehend that I might neglect to write without diminution of affection you have taught me, likewise, how that neglect may be uneasily felt without resentment." Because Boswell's retroactive forgiveness absolved some of the guilt Johnson had experienced throughout this friendship, Johnson forgave his friend's current neglect and comfortably offered praise and encouragement: "I never was so much pleased as now with your account of yourself, and sincerely hope, that between publick business, improving studies, and domestick pleasures, neither melancholy nor caprice will find any place for entrance."

Johnson still worried about "melancholy" and "caprice," as he never did when writing Chambers and Langton. But he no longer imagined his friend experiencing "the incessant cravings of Vacancy," as he had five years earlier. More significantly, Johnson responded to Boswell's invitation to Scotland: "If we perform our duty, we shall be safe and steady . . . whether we climb the Highlands, or are tost among the Hebrides; and I hope the time will come when we may try our powers both with cliffs and water." In other words, he imagined them adventurously traveling together in the eye of Providence: "safe and steady" because dutiful and free of guilt, alone together despite Hester Thrale and Margaret Boswell, collaborating without rivalry or competition despite their recent struggles for control.[42]

Langton and Chambers were still more central to Johnson than Boswell. But this open-ended, life-affirming fantasy of adventurous travel is much richer than Johnson's anticipation two months earlier of spending time with Chambers in London — "We can live together in town, and dine in chambers or at the mitre, and do as well as at New inn hall." It is also more challenging and all-encompassing than his hope years earlier to visit Langton's family estate in Lincolnshire: "I shall delight to hear the ocean roar or see the stars twinkle, in the company of men to whom nature does not spread her volumes or utter her voice in vain." Also, as Johnson closed what was only his seventh letter to Boswell in eight years, he edged toward writing as he regularly wrote these other friends and as he probably would have written Boswell in 1763 had the young Scot not lost his bearings in Utrecht. Dropping the restrictions he had defensively established, Johnson offered some news and even a hint of a confession: "I see but little of Lord Elibank" — an accomplished and learned writer, whom Johnson had known at least since 1765 and Boswell at least since 1768 — "I know not why; perhaps by my own fault. I am going this day into Staffordshire and Derbyshire for six weeks." Johnson's letters to others regularly contained much more news and much fuller confessions, and not until he next wrote nine months later would he mention his health. But a shift was occurring.[43]

I suspect Boswell was able to produce this change, inspiring Johnson to revive and expand the long-standing Hebrides fantasy, because he had imagined a new framework for their friendship. Having tried in *Corsica* to write Johnson into his life, despite long gaps between contact and Johnson's silence, Boswell now had determined to eliminate the silence and reduce the gaps by becoming his friend's biographer.

"I have a constant plan to write the Life of Mr. Johnson," Boswell wrote in his entry for 31 March 1772, his first formal statement of this project. Kevin Hart may be correct in assuming that Boswell had something like a biography in mind as early as September 1764, when he declared in the Wittenberg letter his intention "to do honour to [Johnson's] memory" if he died before Boswell. If so, Boswell may have been thinking of a biography ten months later when he wrote Wilkes, "Could my feeble mind preserve but a faint impression of Johnson, it would be a glory to myself and a benefit to mankind." But in those earlier moments, Boswell seemed mainly to imagine preserving some of Johnson's conversation, as he would do in *Corsica*, and following Johnson's precepts. The *Life* reports his asking Johnson on 2 May 1768 about publishing his letters after his death; but there is no mention of this in Boswell's notes for that date. Boswell's "Strictures on the Genius and Writings of Dr. Johnson" (March 1769), besides praise for each of Johnson's publications, also contains some biographical material concerning Johnson's friendship with Richard Savage. Boswell's notes on the talk with Langton seven months later — "Johnson educated at Litchfield — But youll get these things from Johns." — show that he then imagined gathering information about Johnson's childhood, though he did not report asking Johnson about "these things" until 1772. But I see the seventeen months between Boswell's marriage in November 1769 and his writing Johnson in April 1771 — months when Margaret Boswell became pregnant with a child who died shortly after birth and Boswell brooded on his recent preconception-jostling visit with Johnson — as the key gestation or consolidation period for this project, which Boswell seems to have had clearly in mind when he finally wrote.[44]

Married, hoping soon to help produce a male heir, and wishing in time to move to London and perhaps become a member of Parliament, Boswell was also eager to connect firmly with the man who had initially hugged him close but had recently become more remote. If Johnson approved, the biographical project would secure Boswell's connection with this intellectually energetic, decisive, grounded authority, this mental giant whose experience in key ways paralleled Boswell's own. As Johnson's biographer, Boswell would have guaranteed access to his subject, despite rivals for Johnson's attention and regard. He would have a special place no matter how close Johnson was to Baretti or Chambers, Langton or Hester Thrale, a status like that which he enjoyed with Paoli after the hero of *Corsica* came to London. Johnson would be as available as he had been in 1763, a closeness unrepeated since then. Boswell would continue to coproduce parts of Johnson's life: scripting conversations and drawing out Johnson's opinions on various topics, arranging suppers and dinners and recording what transpired. But he would have a respected role, would not be dismissed as "dunce." He would be an integral part of Johnson's world. Even when not together they would be firmly linked. And when Johnson died, Boswell would write his *Life,* having in a sense become his heir, no matter how strong the claims of others.

The biographical project would also provide an outlet for aggression that Boswell refused to examine or even admit, authorizing him to probe Johnson's newly discovered secret spaces. At the same time, it might also allow Boswell to protect the heroic, manly "Johnson" from what seemed like radical weaknesses, such as his need to win every argument, his acceptance of second marriages, and his puzzling fear of death. Instead of trying to be Johnson, Boswell would seek to understand and assess him, while still striving firmly to connect.[45]

Until the *Life* was published, in 1791, Boswell would not know everything that writing it would entail. He knew it could be written only after Johnson's death, unlike the projects he had discussed with Johnson in 1769 and those he had described to Temple in March 1771. But Boswell probably anticipated doing what he clearly had in mind during and after the Hebrides trip: immediately publishing accounts of his travels with Johnson, as he did when Paoli came to Scotland in the fall of 1771. In fact, it was only when Boswell discovered in 1775 that this would be impossible — that he would have to wait until Johnson died before he could publish their intimacy — that he fully realized the need to prepare himself to live in a world without Johnson.[46]

Though Boswell obviously could not have anticipated in 1771 all the ways this project would transform their relationship, he surely hoped for some changes. And significant changes occurred. In large part because of the biography, the friendship in 1772 and especially in 1773 became almost all that Boswell and Johnson had desired when they first bonded, and the eight years from 1772 through 1779 differed remarkably from the previous eight. Instead of being in the same place during just four brief periods totaling about fourteen weeks, as in 1764–1771, Johnson and Boswell would be in the same place during nine different periods, totaling about sixty weeks. They spent time together on at least 275 different days, including Johnson's long visit to Scotland, in contrast to fewer than thirty in 1764–1771. Even more importantly, when Johnson and Boswell were apart, as they were more than four-fifths of the time, they much more regularly exchanged letters. Starting in 1772, Johnson wrote an average of eight a year through 1779, and Boswell an average of ten. Only twice in 1772–1779 did the gaps between visits last longer than ten months. In the first of these, between November 1773 and March 1775, Johnson sent

Boswell seventeen letters, more than in all ten previous years, and Boswell sent at least seventeen, more than in the previous five. In the long gap between May 1776 and September 1777, Boswell sent seventeen letters and Johnson fifteen. During these eight years—especially from April 1773 through May 1778—they were clearly connected, each a central actor in the other's life. Not until 1780 was there another period of more than three months when neither wrote, and not until 1781 did six months pass without a letter from Johnson.

4

New Collaborations (1772)

In the spring of 1772, both friends were in better shape than when last together. Having not published anything for years after finally completing the Shakespeare edition, Johnson had recently written two widely debated pamphlets, texts he discussed when first with Boswell; and he was busy with what he half-mockingly called the "very great work" of revising the *Dictionary*. Also, four weeks after he first reconnected with Boswell on 20 March, Johnson fulfilled the resolution he had made the previous Easter, but then had forgotten until the beginning of Lent, to read the whole Bible by Easter.

Meanwhile Boswell, having come to London to represent a client whose exoneration by the Court of Session had been appealed to the House of Lords, contrasted the poise he had achieved with his "sickly state of mind" when he had first met Johnson, lacked "any fixed rational purpose," and was "hardly able to observe common decency of conduct." He was happy to have made Lord Auchinleck "amends for what he had suffered from my former folly and bad conduct," and was delighted to hear two older Scots confirm that he seemed just "like [his] father" — "very steady and very composed." Dining with Johnson and Goldsmith at General Oglethorpe's on 10 April, Boswell "had a full relish of life": "I just sat and hugged myself in my own mind. . . . Words cannot describe our feelings. The finer parts are lost, as the down upon a plum." So Boswell renewed his hope that "Parliament or the English bar" would let him be in London regularly.[1]

Even before Boswell arrived, he and Johnson had begun working together on the appeal, and by the end of the visit, Johnson had begun explicitly preparing Boswell to write his *Life*. Largely because of these mutually satisfying collaborations, their interactions were generally less contentious than in the recent past, and there was a key shift in their friendship—a shift that would become more complete the following year when Johnson agreed to Boswell's being with him during much of Good Friday, and three weeks later got his biographer elected to the exclusive Club.

March Letters

Since Boswell's letter of 3 March 1772 and Johnson's reply of 15 March have both survived, we can observe the two friends preparing to reconnect after more than two years. In July 1771, Boswell had sent the young poet and philosopher James Beattie a letter of introduction to Johnson, and in October had thanked Johnson for his June letter and also for his "obliging reception of Mr. Beattie." Now instead of complaining of Johnson's silence since June or urging him to write with "regularity," Boswell accepted that Johnson was "a fountain of wisdom from whence few rills are communicated to a distance, and which must be approached at its source to partake fully of its virtues." During Boswell's most recent visits to London, Johnson had been away, but now Boswell hoped to find him home, "and at length to fix our voyage to the Hebrides, or at least our journey through the Highlands of Scotland."

Boswell then described the case he was appealing, that of a schoolmaster, John Hastie, who had been dismissed "for being somewhat severe in the chastisement of his scholars." Boswell had successfully contested this dismissal in the Court of Session, but the schoolmaster's "enemies" had appealed, and Boswell asked Johnson's assistance. In closing, he noted that if Johnson could "without much trouble" write him "a few lines" when he received this letter, it would make Boswell "very happy."[2]

This combination of flattery, invited collaboration, and nonpressing exhortation worked, and within a week Johnson sent a cordial response. Delighted that Boswell was coming soon, and "coming as an advocate," he offered to help, adding that what had been done to the schoolmaster "appears very cruel, unreasonable, and oppressive." Because Boswell had mentioned their proposed trip, Johnson reported having not yet fully recovered from rheumatism and bronchitis. He still hoped to see Beattie's college in Aberdeen and had "not given up the western voyage." But he suggested they "try to make each other happy" when they met, and not refer their "pleasure to distant times or distant places."

Early in this letter, however, while agreeing to help with the appeal, Johnson for some reason wondered about his love for Boswell: "My kindness for you has neither the merit of singular virtue, nor the reproach of singular prejudice. Whether to love you be right or wrong, I have many on my side: Mrs. Thrale loves you, and Mrs. Williams loves you, and what would have inclined me to love you, if I had been neutral before, You are a great favourite of Dr. Beattie." Johnson had teased Boswell in four of his first five letters, and his tone here is playful. But asking whether it was "right or wrong" to love Boswell was curious, since Johnson had repeatedly reaffirmed both his love and his esteem, suggesting that the two were connected. The question suggested ambivalence about the young friend with whom he was about to be reunited.

I suspect that some of Johnson's friends, especially Chambers, had wondered what Johnson saw in this young Scot, as Johnson recalled when he agreed to help with the appeal. In fact, on 11 April, when he was about to confer on the case, Johnson wrote Chambers that he was expecting Boswell, "with his noisy benevolence." Having pointedly labeled Boswell a "dunce" in 1769, Johnson may have regarded this attachment as the equivalent of intellectual slumming: indulging in the seductive delights of Boswell's excessive flattery and deferential good humor. So he wondered whether loving Boswell was "right or wrong" and suggested that a definitive answer was unavailable. All he could do was note those who "sided" with him.[3]

Reconnecting

Johnson's letter was posted a day after Boswell left for London, so was read only after the two friends had been together before dinner on 21 March and then from 9:30 onward. Boswell's remarkably full account of what he and Johnson did and said that day serves as a rich gloss on both their letters. (Since Boswell now was self-consciously preparing to write the *Life,* he spent several evenings writing journal entries instead of socializing; so the first month of this visit is described in much more detail than their recent time together.) Before Boswell read the sentence in which Johnson wondered whether his love was "right or wrong," Johnson had "embraced [him] with a robust sincerity of friendship, saying, 'I am glad to see thee, I am glad to see thee.'" Also, at some point that first day, Johnson said, "I do love thee, I do love thee," emphatically responding to what Boswell had not yet read.[4]

But as Boswell reported this at the end of a remarkably full entry, he surely realized that other parts of their conversation showed Johnson's feelings to be more conflicted than they had seemed nine years earlier, when he first declared, "My dear Boswell! I do love you very much." At two key moments, Johnson responded to what Boswell asked or said with zestful fantasies that revealed strong but opposing desires: a longing for intimacy and collaborative adventure, but also an aggressive wish to torment — at least momentarily.

Sometime before dinner, when Boswell asked about possibly buying the island of St. Kilda in the Outer Hebrides, Johnson urged him to do so: "We shall go and pass a winter amid the blasts there. We shall have fine fish, and we shall take some dried tongues with us and some books. We shall have a strong-built vessel and some Orkney men to navigate her. We must build a tolerable house. But we may carry with us a wooden house ready made and nothing to do but to put it up. . . . We must give them a clergyman, and he shall be one of Beattie's choosing. I'll be your Lord Chancellor or what you please." Puzzled by Johnson's zest and specificity, Boswell asked whether he was serious, and heard, "Why yes, I am serious." Five days later, however, Boswell learned the island was not for sale.

This spontaneous fantasy combined both goals Johnson had earlier linked to travel with Boswell: domestic intimacy and shared adventure. He now added social improvement: "you may keep the people from falling into worse hands." Boswell's modest wealth offered Johnson a chance to imagine using his talents as Boswell's lord chancellor. His detailed picture of emphatic cooperation — "We shall . . . We shall . . . We shall . . . We shall . . . We must . . . We may . . . We must" — also resolved any potential power struggle, while expressing Johnson's wish for a sustained, collaborative connection.[5]

The other fantasy differed strikingly in tone, suggesting both embarrassment at Boswell's folly and envy of his inheritance. At the end of the evening, presumably after Mrs. Williams had left them, Boswell for the first time mentioned a document he had signed in 1762 empowering Lord Auchinleck to appoint trustees over the family estate. He also described how, having recently had this paper in his hands, he had been tempted to burn it, but "had a scruple, and so laid it back again into its place." Johnson first rebuked his friend for having foolishly renounced his right, but then gleefully identified with the forces of authority as he imagined what might have happened had Boswell burned the document: "We should have had you hanged, ha! ha! ha! No. You would not have been hanged, but you might have been whipped or transported, ha! ha! ha!"

Boswell did not speculate about Johnson's feelings, wrote nothing about what he thought and felt, and omitted this entire exchange from the *Life*. But Johnson's unplanned and seemingly gratuitous aggression — his initial refusal to sympathize with his friend's frustration that Lord Auchinleck could still limit his inheritance, and his heady laughter at the thought of Boswell's being hanged or whipped — hardly meshes with the longing for collaborative intimacy on St. Kilda. After briefly tormenting Boswell, however, Johnson pulled back, probably sympathizing with Boswell's evident discomfort: "Sir, your father did wrong to take it from you, and he ought to give it up to you. If you do not tease him, he will make no use of it and it can do you no harm." Ten days later, Johnson further reassured Boswell by explaining what he should do once he became laird.[6]

Together in London

After this richly documented first day, Johnson and Boswell were together on only three of the next fourteen, though always at great length, but then on nineteen of the thirty-seven days from 5 April through 11 May, usually for a considerable time. Having sat up late on three of their first four days together — and they would have done this on 23 March, too, if it had not been Johnson's "Club night" — they spent nine additional evenings together, mostly at Johnson's, often till two or three in the morning, when Boswell, having discovered that "sitting up late hurt [his] health," reluctantly pulled himself away. They had never been together on so many days in a single year.[7]

Especially at the start, Boswell was self-consciously solicitous to please. When he asked whether Johnson were serious in urging him to buy St. Kilda, for instance, he added, "For if you should advise me to go to Japan, I believe I should do it." A week later, having heard Johnson say he would like to meet Sir Alexander Macdonald of Skye, Boswell arranged the introduction, noting in his journal, "Every wish of Mr. Johnson's is watched by me." Also, Boswell was mostly careful not to provoke, dropping topics Johnson seemed unwilling to consider. When Johnson "avoided" discussing "the particular state of souls after death" on 21 March, Boswell shifted focus, noting in his journal, "I must try at another time." A week later, finding Johnson "in excellent good humour," he reframed the question. Unsatisfied with what Johnson said on 9 April concerning the efficacy of prayer, and again frustrated that Johnson seemed unwilling to grapple with how we can be free if God knows exactly what we will do, Boswell postponed further questioning until a later visit.[8]

But Boswell also presented himself as someone with his own resources. When he found Johnson working on the *Dictionary,* he provided "a meaning of side which he had omitted; viz., father's or mother's side," which Johnson "said he would put it in" — and did. And despite whatever had led Johnson to wonder whether loving Boswell was "right or wrong," Johnson generally seemed comfortable publicly affirming him. At supper with Langton and several others on 15 April, for instance, when Boswell "ventured to say" that Tacitus was not a good historian — "that he had admirable sense and elegant sentences, but was too compact, had not sufficient fullness" — Johnson fully endorsed this assessment. Unlike the newly arrived Langton, who was "afraid to venture forth," Boswell "risked boldly" to engage Johnson. Unlike Goldsmith, whose foolish talk Boswell regularly encouraged Johnson to criticize, Boswell mostly made sense. So on 19 April, when Paoli urged Johnson "to come often to see him, without waiting for an invitation," Johnson replied, "I will come with my friend Boswell, and so I'll get a habit of coming." Boswell was a friend Johnson was proud to acknowledge.[9]

There were tussles, with each friend on occasion challenging the other. But Johnson no longer denied Boswell's intelligence, even when momentarily exasperated by what he saw as obtuseness. When Boswell questioned Johnson's dismissal of Henry Fielding as "a blockhead," and "boldly blamed" his "neglecting" Garrick in the preface to Shakespeare, and when Johnson defended a preacher who had been denied a position because of fornication, and insisted that what kept Boswell's brother in Spain was not the "fine climate" but "some woman," Johnson always had the last word. But he won with agility and ingenuity rather than ad hominem retorts. They had learned to contend without harshness and without high-handedness, though it was outrageous for Johnson to assume he understood better than Boswell this brother he had never met.[10]

The only exception occurred on 15 April, when Boswell aggressively defended drinking, even though Johnson "looked very awful and cloudy upon [him] for doing so." The topic was provocative, since Johnson was now abstaining. In his entry, Boswell simply wrote, "I would needs defend drinking." But Boswell probably chose the topic because he was angry that Johnson had not heard him defend the schoolmaster the day before and had not asked about his success. When Boswell quoted the maxim "in vino veritas," asserting that "a man who is warmed with wine will speak truth," Johnson handily retorted, "Why, Sir, that may be an argument for drinking if you suppose men liars; but, Sir, I would not keep company with a fellow who lies as long as he is sober and whom you must fill drunk before you can get a word of truth out of him." Then Boswell shifted to an argument calculated to disturb a melancholic who had resolved not to drink: "But, Sir, you know all mankind have agreed in esteeming wine as a thing that can cheer the heart, can drive away care. . . . Would you not, Sir, now, allow a man oppressed with care to drink and make himself merry?" "Yes," Johnson replied, "if he sat next you," using a personal attack to end this debate. Boswell was momentarily silenced. But he was "not at all hurt" by this "great broadside." For he knew that Johnson relished his company. In fact, when the others left, Boswell went with Johnson to have tea with Mrs. Williams, where he told what had happened at the House of Lords.[11]

Defending the Schoolmaster

Collaboration on the appeal had begun in the March letters and continued on 21 March, when Johnson assured his friend that as long as the schoolmaster neither broke bones nor fractured skulls, "he is safe enough." Boswell wanted Johnson's solidly grounded arguments to complement those that had already prevailed in the Court of Session; and Johnson set aside two days for this work, 23 March and 11 April.

On 23 March, Boswell offered to read aloud the account of the original trial, but Johnson declined, saying, "I can read quicker than I can hear." As he finished the Court of Session papers and began reading the call for an appeal, Johnson fully identified with Boswell's side: "This is a bloody charge against us." Once Johnson had read everything, he responded at the Mitre to Boswell's wish for additional perspectives: "The government of a schoolmaster is somewhat of the nature of a military government; that is to say, it must be arbitrary according to particular circumstances. You must show some learning upon this occasion. You must show that a schoolmaster has a prescriptive right to beat, and that an action of assault and battery cannot be admitted against him unless there is some great excess, some barbarity. This man has maimed none of his boys. They are all left the full exercise of their corporeal faculties." This conversation ended the first phase of collaboration, though Johnson promised to assist Boswell further "by putting down some thoughts upon the subject."[12]

The next phase occurred almost three weeks later, after Boswell learned that Johnson would be "at leisure" late on 11 April. While observing appellate hearings at the House of Lords on seven different days during those weeks, Boswell had postponed getting his arguments printed, probably hoping Johnson would write something. But early on 11 April, he went to the shop of William Strahan (the son of Johnson's publisher) and "made several additions" to his case based on "Mr. Johnson's Corpus Juris" — presumably what Johnson had said about a master's "prescriptive right to beat," provided he does not maim. Late that night, after exchanging this freshly printed argument for the case for the appellant, Boswell brought both to his friend. (Several copies of both cases, printed and bound at the expense of the appellant, would eventually be lodged in the office of the House of Lords; but those representing Hastie insisted on seeing Boswell's case before releasing theirs.)

Once Johnson had read the two cases, he and Boswell negotiated the next step. Boswell hoped Johnson would now write down his thoughts; Johnson preferred just to talk. As a compromise, Boswell proposed that Johnson "should dictate and [he] would write." When Johnson agreed, Boswell "sat with most assiduous care and eagerness, and [Johnson] dictated . . . a noble Defence." He learnedly argued that "children, being not reasonable, can be governed only by fear": "Locke, in his treatise of Education, mentions a mother, with applause, who whipped an infant eight times before she had subdued it; for had she stopped at the seventh act of correction, her daughter, says he, would have been ruined." Then Johnson analyzed the motives of parents who opposed having the schoolmaster reinstated, and rebutted the argument that he should not retain his school, since he has lost the confidence of the townspeople. The brief contained the breadth and clarity that had always impressed Boswell, though he thought what Johnson "threw . . . out in conversation was stronger and had more fire than what he dictated."

Their negotiation led to a collaboration neither friend had imagined ahead of time or initially saw as ideal. All the words in the brief were Johnson's. But Boswell had created the occasion and provided a copy of what he and his colleague Andrew Crosbie, a brilliant Edinburgh advocate well known for defending the rights of poor prisoners, needed to rebut. He also acted as scribe, preserving everything Johnson said, as he could not have done had they simply talked. The resulting brief was more sustained than anything Boswell had ever quoted Johnson as saying, and significantly longer than Johnson's substantial first letter. In the *Life,* Boswell even listed this as one of only two texts Johnson produced in 1772, when otherwise he "was altogether quiescent as an author."[13]

As often in conversation with Boswell, Johnson had the satisfaction of thinking clearly and decisively about topics he had not previously considered. The give-and-take of talk was usually livelier, especially when Boswell challenged Johnson's claims or pressed for clarification. But in dictating this brief, as in writing essays or letters, Johnson had space to expatiate on topics like the need to proportion "correction" to each degree of "obstinacy." Also, Johnson was spared the drudgery of writing, though he must often have had to wait for his scribe to catch up.

Anticipating this collaboration with Boswell seems to have reminded Johnson of his sustained work on the Vinerian Lectures, since he wrote Chambers while waiting for Boswell. His dictated brief was slight compared to Chambers's magisterial lectures on the English law. But this collaboration was more adversarial. In advising Boswell earlier about how to behave as laird, Johnson had zestfully imagined himself in his friend's circumstances: "If I were a man of great estate, I would drive all the rascals whom I did not like out of the country at an election"; "I would propagate all kinds of trees that will grow in the open air. . . . I would introduce foreign animals into the country; for instance, the reindeer." As he developed arguments Boswell could use in court, Johnson might have imagined actually addressing Lord Mansfield, the chief justice, who presided over the assembled lords. He was connecting with Boswell in a new way.

Though neither friend knew in advance what would happen when Boswell returned late on 11 April, both clearly enjoyed the process, since four weeks later they spent time on two different days producing a second brief, twice as long as the first, this time against relaxing the strict punishment of anyone found guilty of "vicious intromission," or meddling in the effects of someone deceased, a case on which Boswell earlier "had exhausted all [his] powers of reasoning in vain." Also, from this point onward, Johnson's dictating of texts — usually briefs, but occasionally reflections on religion and politics — became a regular activity.[14]

In the schoolmaster's case, both knew there would be another stage of collaboration, when Boswell would combine what he had transcribed with the printed brief. In the *Life*, Boswell reported Johnson saying, as he finished dictating, "This, Sir, . . . you are to turn in your mind, and make the best use of it you can in your speech." Circumstances had forced Boswell to take down Johnson's dictation in the early hours of Sunday, but he piously postponed further work until Monday, a day before the hearing. Having conferred with Crosbie about their plan, Boswell went home and reworked his speech, "introducing into it the great thoughts and masterly expressions which Mr. Johnson had given" him. Wholly in charge, Boswell "did not take all" that Johnson had suggested, but "interwove a good deal" as he wrote his oration, in the process producing an even more richly collaborative text.[15]

Early Tuesday morning, the aged General Oglethorpe, "with the activity of a young soldier and the zeal of a warm friend," came to Boswell's with encouraging advice. Sir Alexander Macdonald brought Boswell to Crosbie's, where he put on his gown and special neckband. More lords than usual were present at the hearing, including Lord Lyttelton and Lord Mountstuart, who attended at Boswell's request. Oglethorpe was there, too, as was Garrick, whom Boswell had seen only once that spring, and a large number of others who, as Boswell observed, "would hardly attend a Scotch appeal" had he not been involved. But not Johnson. So when writing the entry for 13 April, Boswell made up for Johnson's absence by twice describing the brief as his friend's gift.[16]

As Crosbie presented the case, Lord Mansfield's questions showed that he favored the appeal, "which was discouraging." Boswell was "a flutter till it was [his] turn to speak," and "felt much palpitation" when called. But he was careful to avoid "appearing anyhow bold or even easy," spoke "slowly and distinctly, and, as [he] was told afterwards, very well." Mainly, he used the collaborative text he had constructed the night before. But he was most pleased with his opening "sally of wit," when he explained that he warmly defended this schoolmaster "from gratitude": "For [I] am sensible that if I had not been very severely beat by my master, I should not have been able to make even the weak defence which I now make."

The schoolmaster lost, but Lyttelton later reported that Lord Mansfield had said Boswell "spoke very well." Boswell won applause less for what he had from Johnson than for his clever introduction and for his uncharacteristic restraint. Lyttelton also told those dining at the home of Elizabeth Montagu, "Queen of the Bluestockings," that Boswell "has been pleading for tyranny, a thing he never did before, nor never will do again." When Boswell supped at the home of his kinsman Godfrey Bosville, Sir Alexander, too, "sounded [Boswell's] praises," and at breakfast the next morning, Garrick confirmed that Boswell "had done very well in the House of Lords." When Boswell went home with Johnson at midnight a day later and reported — seemingly without having been asked — what people had said about the performance his friend had helped script, Johnson declared, "That was worth coming to London for."[17]

Embarking on the Biography

Unlike collaboration on the appeal, which mainly occurred on two days, collaboration to prepare Boswell to write Johnson's biography occurred whenever the two friends were together as well as when Boswell wrote his entries or notes describing their conversations or when he talked with others about Johnson. In fact, once Boswell determined to become Johnson's biographer, he saw that work on this project had begun as soon as they met, especially when Johnson told key parts of his story, explained what he was like, and expressed his deep longings. After Johnson became aware of Boswell's plan, he, too, realized that everything he had said and done with this young Scot had been preparing him to write his *Life*.

From the start of this visit, Boswell's work on the biography was more thorough and self-conscious. On 21 March, for instance, he asked Johnson about newspaper reports claiming that after the appearance of Johnson's recent pamphlets, Lord North had increased his pension, which Johnson denied, and whether he had wanted to sail on Captain James Cook's second voyage of discovery, which he affirmed. More interestingly, when Johnson noted a similarity between the schoolmaster Boswell was defending and John Hunter, his master in Lichfield, who used to beat his students "unmercifully," Boswell triumphantly declared that since the schoolmaster who beat Johnson was named Hunter, "a Scotch name," he could "now account for [Johnson's] prejudice against Scotsmen." But Johnson, insisting that Hunter "was not Scotch," rejected this conclusion. Two days later, however, when Boswell read in Johnson's library the dedication to John Kennedy's *Complete System of Astronomical Chronology* (1763) and recognized the style as Johnson's — "You cannot deny it" — Johnson acknowledged his authorship.[18]

Boswell also was more persistent than usual in getting stories about Johnson from others, or at least in recording these, especially after work on the appeal had ended. On 2 April, he heard Samuel Foote claim that "Mr. Johnson had once a great inclination to become a Methodist," and two weeks later he heard Garrick defend himself against Johnson's insinuation in the Shakespeare preface that he had not let his friend use his early editions of the plays — both stories Boswell got Johnson to address before he recorded them. Having heard Johnson talk suggestively about Burke, Boswell got Davies to describe how Burke keeps to Johnson "like a man fishing salmon with a single hair: lets him flounce, then draws." At supper on 7 May, he heard "Much of Johnson" from Goldsmith, Reynolds, and Langton; two days later, he saw Garrick perform what he had seen and heard at the school Johnson had run early in his marriage; and on 11 May, he talked "Much of Johnson" with Hester Thrale.[19]

In addition, Boswell used his journal more often than before to analyze and assess Johnson. Instead of just disagreeing on matters of taste, as he had from the start, or faulting Johnson's mode of winning arguments, as he had from 1766, Boswell now pointed to certain intellectual limitations and defects in character. In the entry for 9 April 1772, for instance, after reporting Johnson's comment on the efficacy of prayer, Boswell lamented that "the greatest powers may be enfeebled and cramped when confined by a system of orthodoxy" — for the first time substituting his understanding for Johnson's on a question of religion. Boswell also critically analyzed Johnson's character. In the entry for 15 April, after noting how differently Johnson and Garrick recalled what had happened when Johnson asked to use Garrick's early Shakespeare editions, Boswell suggested that Johnson's behavior then, like his persistent denigration of actors, was motivated by envy: "Mr. Johnson may perhaps be insensibly fretted a little that Davy Garrick, who was his pupil and came up to London at the same time with him to try the chance of life, should be so very general a favourite and should have fourscore thousand pounds, an immense sum, when he has so little." Then in the entry for 17 April — after Johnson had failed to attend Boswell's hearing or even to ask about it — Boswell reported having heard Langton agree that Johnson "was deficient in active benevolence," and add that Topham Beauclerk, "another of Mr. Johnson's great friends," had also complained. Boswell was aligning himself with those who loved and revered Johnson but also saw his faults.[20]

Johnson had become aware of Boswell's project at least by 31 March, their fourth day together, when, after hearing Johnson insist that "nobody could furnish the life of a man but those who had eat and drank and lived in social intercourse with him," Boswell asked his friend to tell "all the little circumstances of his life, what schools he attended, when he came to Oxford, when he came to London, etc., etc." While "not disapprov[ing] of [Boswell's] curiosity as to these particulars," Johnson said, "They'll come out by degrees." Johnson explicitly helped prepare Boswell for this task on two days toward the end of the visit. On 24 April, thirteen days after dictating the first brief, Johnson provided some of the information he had imagined coming out "by degrees," describing in sequence his six teachers from Dame Oliver in Lichfield to Dr. Adams at Oxford. Two weeks later, Boswell got Johnson to confirm (or reject) his authorship of each of the forty-four anonymous publications on a list that Robert Levet, who had lived with Johnson for years while providing medical help to some of the London poor, had recently dictated to Thomas Percy. But since Johnson had seen some of Boswell's journal nine years earlier, he knew — as soon as he discovered Boswell's plan — that anything Boswell heard him say might be recorded.[21]

Initially, Boswell worried about how Johnson would react to this project. In his entry for 31 March, after writing, "I have a constant plan to write the life of Mr. Johnson," he added: "I have not told him of it yet, nor do I know if I should tell him." It seems strange that he wondered whether he should tell Johnson, since Boswell would regularly need Johnson's assistance. The implication that Johnson had not already guessed his plan also seems odd, since Boswell added that Johnson "did not disapprove" of his asking about early experiences. But Boswell had heard Johnson declare that the whole of life is spent avoiding the thought of death, and then had witnessed Johnson's fury when pressed to explain. Since in eighteenth-century Britain, biographies of any scope were published only after the subject had died, Boswell sensibly worried about how his friend would react to a project that inevitably pointed ahead to his death. In asking Johnson about his early life, Boswell was not suggesting that death was imminent, as newspaper obituary writers do. Whatever Boswell thought and felt about inheriting Auchinleck — a topic the two friends discussed right after Boswell asked about Johnson's early life — Boswell was not eager to live in a world without Johnson. In fact, he hoped the biographical project would firmly connect him with Johnson for years. But Boswell's preparing to write Johnson's life invited both friends to anticipate the moment when Boswell would use whatever he was now hearing. So his apprehension was reasonable.

Johnson's initial response to Boswell's questions — saying that the information would emerge incrementally — made clear there was no hurry. He was not about to die. In fact, in July 1773, while discussing with Hester Thrale just who might write his biography, Johnson declared a hope to "outlive" all the would-be biographers they mentioned. And that November when Boswell said he intended to erect a monument to Johnson at Auchinleck, "If I survived him," the sixty-four-year-old Johnson defiantly told his young friend, whose only child was just six months old, "Sir, I hope to see your grandchildren." But aside from wanting to assume that the *Life* would not be needed for years, what was Johnson's response to this new collaboration?[22]

On 5 April, their first day together after Johnson learned of the biography, when he told Boswell "he went more frequently to prayers than to sermon, as the people required more example to go to prayers than to sermon; hearing sermon being easier to them than to fix their minds on prayer," Johnson might have wanted to get this explanation "on record." But he might well have said this even if he did not know of Boswell's project. In fact, knowing of Boswell's plan might have led Johnson not to share personal anecdotes. On two of their first three days together that spring, Johnson had told stories from his past. But after learning of Boswell's plan, he seems to have told such stories on none of his next ten days with Boswell, since Boswell would surely have reported any he heard.[23]

Johnson was used to being a celebrity, was interested in his image, and helped make available many of the anecdotes that were widely circulated, including the full account of his conversation with George III in 1767. But being a biographical subject was new, and narrating his years in sequence was different. On 24 April, however, the same day he faulted Boswell for not realizing why his brother stayed in Spain, Johnson began answering Boswell's questions about the schools he attended, and seemed to savor the experience.[24]

Johnson's Autobiographical Narratives

Boswell's notes on what Johnson said in this first narrative session, with blanks where Boswell did not remember names, suggest some of the ways the process was significant. (During their third and fourth sessions in the fall of 1773, Boswell avoided blanks by writing as Johnson talked.) "He said learnt to read of Dame ——, a Widow. When he went to College at 19, brought Gingerbread and gave, saying best scholar ever had. Then Thomas Brown. He died. Then with Usher ——; then Hunter, severe. Then at —— in Worcestershire with Wentworth. Very good Master, but did not agree. Was idle, mischievous, and stole. 'I was too good a scholar. He could get no honour by me. Saw I would ascribe all to my own labour or former Master.' Dr. Adams of

Shrewsbury Tutor at Oxford. Was idle as a boy considering could not see duert [?] as they shoot, etc." These notes give little sense of Johnson's tone or what he might have felt as he began to narrate his life in sequence. But his steady movement from teacher to teacher, probably prompted at times by Boswell, indicates at least a willingness to review systematically this portion of his life, perhaps including episodes he seldom thought about.[25]

Telling his past experiences in some detail to an admiring but not uncritical biographer differed strikingly from what Johnson did each year on his birthday and before Easter, when he produced narratives that usually stressed what he had failed to do in the previous year. On his last birthday, for instance, after describing his inching toward health, Johnson lamented having "neither conquered nor opposed" indolence and indifference: "I have neither attempted nor formed any scheme of Life by which I may do good, and please God." Similarly, six days before telling Boswell about his early schools, when Johnson had begun to review what he had done since the previous Easter, he was "able to recollect so little done, that shame and sorrow, though perhaps too weakly, come upon" him: "By sleepless or unquiet nights and short days, made short by late rising, the time passes away uncounted and unheeded. Life so spent is useless."[26]

In substance and tone, what Johnson told Boswell about his teachers most closely resembles what survives of his "Annals," a text describing his first ten years, in which Johnson started to do what in the *Idler* he recommended for everyone, especially writers: "calmly and voluntarily to review his life for the admonition of posterity or to amuse himself." Without a deadline and with no hope of an immediate response, Johnson wrote roughly 5,000–7,000 words about his life from 1709 through 1719. One of the two sections rescued by Francis Barber, the former slave who for years was Johnson's servant, describes Johnson's first three years; the other describes years nine and ten. Just as Johnson seems to have enjoyed sharing with Boswell the memory of Dame Oliver's gingerbread—an anecdote he repeated in 1773 when he resumed narrating his early life—he clearly savored reporting here his mother's saying, "We often . . . come off best, when we are most afraid," and "I was proud that I had a boy who was forming verbs." "These little memorials sooth my mind," Johnson wrote. He also lingered wistfully on a moment of unusual concentration: "I was writing at the kitchen windows, as I thought, alone, and turning my head saw Sally dancing. I went on without notice, and had finished almost without perceiving that any time had elapsed. This close attention I have seldom in my whole life obtained." Earlier, in recalling his mother's purchases when she took him to London at two and a half—the "speckled linen frock" he knew as his "London frock," the small silver cup that "was one of the last pieces of plate which dear Tetty sold in our distress," and the spoon he still had — Johnson linked together at least five discrete moments from 1712 to the time he was writing.[27]

Internal evidence suggests that Johnson might have written some of the "Annals" as late as 1772 — perhaps even after describing his early teachers for Boswell. He might have seen writing this text as a way to retain control over his story now that Boswell — and also Percy — were preparing to write his *Life*. ("I intend to . . . write my Life myself," he would tell Hester Thale in July 1773.) Whether or not Johnson wrote some or all of this text after he learned of Boswell's project, he certainly kept what he had written as he actively prepared Boswell to tell his story, though in the end he tried to burn it.

It seems that Johnson intended to continue this narrative, to produce a full autobiography. But for some reason, he did not move beyond 1719. Besides Johnson's notorious indolence, I can imagine two complementary explanations for his not finishing the project. First, pushing forward would eventually have been disturbing. On his birthday in 1768, Johnson imagined writing "the history of my melancholy," but he was hesitant: "On this I purpose to deliberate. I know not whether it may not too much disturb me." According to Edmond Hector, Johnson's schoolmate from Lichfield, "nothing gave him greater pleasure than calling to mind [the] days of our innocence." But narrating himself through college and beyond, including his eventually troubled marriage, his unsuccessful school, and the hard first years in London, would have led to moments charged with anger and envy and guilt, periods when his options were limited by poverty, times when he might have written more or finished tasks more expeditiously, and eventually to years like 1768 and 1769, which he was "unwilling to terrify [him]self" by reviewing. He might have wanted to stop before reaching these troubling times. In fact, when he and Boswell resumed talking about his early experiences in April 1773, Johnson still lingered on the years before Oxford, though he surely pushed further forward — selectively — during two longer sessions during the Hebrides trip, perhaps moving through his years at Oxford, his marriage, and his many years in London before meeting Boswell.[28]

Perhaps, too, once Johnson saw in Scotland how fully and judiciously Boswell was recording this portion of his life, he was willing to tell his story through Boswell, as General Paoli had deliberately done when Boswell came to Corsica, and as Richard Savage had unwittingly done by telling the stories Johnson later used in his *Life of Savage*. Johnson could emphasize whatever he wished, like his idleness as a schoolboy, while keeping secret whatever he did not want known, and he could turn parts of his future life into a sustained collaboration with his biographer — a collaboration more wide-ranging and open-ended than Johnson's work with Chambers and, of course, much less detached from the rest of his experience.[29]

Moving systematically through Johnson's early schools was Boswell's idea, but Johnson was in full control. Since six days earlier—eighteen days after Boswell had first asked for "all the little circumstances" of his life—Johnson had written in his diary that his memory was "confused," though he had "of late" turned his thoughts "with a very useless earnestness upon past incidents," he surely relished his ability to recall so much. There is also evidence that Johnson enjoyed the process of autobiographical remembering. For two days after telling Boswell about his teachers, Johnson completed his narrative of the previous Sunday (Easter) with some unusual autobiographical musings. After somewhat tentatively describing what he had done seven days earlier— "What devotions I used after my return I do not distinctly remember. I went to prayers in the evening, and, I think, entered late"—and after noting again his satisfaction at having "attained to know, even thus hastily, confusedly, and imperfectly, what the Bible contains," Johnson added this paragraph: "I have never yet read the apocrypha. When I was a boy I have read or heard Bel and the dragon, Susannah, some of Tobit, perhaps all. Some at least of Judith and some of Ecclesiasticus; and, I suppose, the Benedicite. I have some time looked into the Maccabees, and read a chapter containing the question Which is the Strongest, I think, in Esdras." In focus and tone, this differs from the bulk of Johnson's surviving Holy Week reflections and resembles what he had been doing with Boswell two days earlier. Working with Boswell seems to have hooked Johnson on the process of recalling past episodes.[30]

Looking Ahead

Between 24 April and Boswell's departure on 11 May, there were no additional discussions of Johnson's early life or of how Boswell might act as laird. There was no hurry. The brief defending the schoolmaster needed to be done before the scheduled hearing. But Johnson was not about to die, so the narrative could be continued during later visits.

On 7 May, however, Boswell got the list of texts from Percy that he needed to check. So on 8 May, after Johnson began dictating a brief for the "vicious intromission" case and before Boswell left for dinner, he got his friend to confirm or deny each of the anonymous publications Levet had listed. Johnson flagged two erroneous attributions, which led Percy later to assign Boswell "all the rights of an Author" over the corrected list. But Boswell noted that Johnson was "angry" at his "asking as to works," the first hint of friction from the biographical project.

Johnson boasted to Boswell that he had put Levet and Percy "right only sometimes as the inclination took him," and the following year he told Hester Thrale that he "purposely suffered [Percy] to be misled, and he has accordingly gleaned up many Things that are not true." But clearly, Boswell checked more carefully than the scholarly Percy. Also, Boswell's rigorously compiling a complete and accurate list of Johnson's anonymously published works for a book to be written only after Johnson had died might troublingly have called to mind God's eventual judgment of how Johnson had used his time and talents. The biographical project was turning Boswell into Johnson's judge.[31]

Notes for their conversation on the night before Boswell left for Scotland (11 May) — notes Boswell never fleshed out — suggest that Johnson acknowledged the biography with curious detachment: "Sir Joshua says Percy's writing life. They'll be 50. I hope you'll write all their lives. Farewell. God bless. I wish you as well." Having just discussed Percy's plan with Reynolds, Johnson seemed intrigued that there was such interest in writing his life. But by telling Boswell, "I hope you'll write all their lives," rather than "all our lives," Johnson seemed to imagine his friend writing not the "life" of Johnson but the "lives" of all fifty of all those planning to write his "life." Whatever Johnson thought and felt as he and Boswell parted, these notes suggest he still held himself somewhat aloof from his friend's project. Nor did he or Boswell yet realize how radically the biography would reshape their friendship.[32]

5

Embracing the Biographer (1772–1773)

Back in Scotland after the heady, self-affirming London visit, his first in more than two years, Boswell became dejected. After the ebullience of dining at Oglethorpe's with Johnson and Goldsmith, or at Reynolds's with Goldsmith, Beauclerk, and Burke, he found Edinburgh dull. He kept only sketchy journal notes from 16 May through 17 June, then none for almost seven weeks. Having written Temple five letters between 24 March and 2 May, he next wrote on 4 August.

Boswell assumed Johnson would come north for the long-anticipated Hebrides trip. Early in the London visit — probably before Johnson met the beautiful Lady Macdonald on 6 April and said, "I will go to Skye with this lady. I'll go anywhere under this lady's protection" — the two friends confirmed they would travel during the fall court recess. On 16 July, Boswell wrote to remind Johnson; and when the session ended on 11 August, he refused to accompany his father to Auchinleck, partly because Lord Auchinleck still held tight to the document empowering him to appoint trustees when Boswell inherited the family estate, but mainly because Boswell expected Johnson. Only on 4 September did Boswell learn that his friend would not be coming.[1]

The Hebrides Postponed (May 1772 to March 1773)

Whatever Johnson had earlier felt about traveling to Scotland, by mid-August he had replaced this adventurous journey with a trip to Lichfield and Ashbourne. But he waited until 31 August before informing Boswell, though he remained "very sincere in [his] design to pay the visit, and take the ramble." Knowing he was disappointing his friend, Johnson first emphasized his "regret": "I have missed a journey so pregnant with pleasing expectations, as that in which I could promise myself not only the gratification of curiosity, both rational and fanciful, but the delight of seeing those whom I love and esteem." Then, after a passage Boswell cut when printing this letter in the *Life,* Johnson made his absence seem virtually inevitable: "Such has been the course of things, that I could not come." The major obstacle was the *Dictionary,* which Johnson finished revising only on 8 October. "My work will, I am afraid, hold me here to the end of September," he wrote Taylor on 15 August. To Boswell, Johnson was less explicit, perhaps not wishing to focus on what he might have finished sooner. Also although Johnson wrote Taylor that his health was better than it had been in "many years," to Boswell he further diminished his responsibility: "Such has been, I am afraid, the state of my body, that it would not well have seconded my inclination." But his body was growing better, he added; "I refer my hopes to another year."[2]

Johnson praised Beattie's *Essay on Truth,* which he was regularly using in revising the *Dictionary,* and continued to identify with Boswell's appeal on behalf of the schoolmaster, writing that he was "yet of opinion, that *our cause* was good" (emphasis added). He concluded with a paragraph urging his friend to use the time they had hoped to spend in travel to research "the antiquities of the feudal establishment," a project they had discussed in 1769 and perhaps in 1772: "The whole system of ancient tenures is gradually passing away; and I wish to have the knowledge of it preserved adequate and complete." Significantly, Johnson addressed Boswell not as a melancholic needing to escape "troublesome and wearisome discontents," but as "a scholar who studies the laws of his country," a gentleman "naturally . . . curious to know the condition of his own ancestors."[3]

Having explained why he was postponing the trip to Scotland, and having assigned Boswell tasks, Johnson completed his revision, took the coach to Lichfield on 15 October, and two weeks later arrived in Ashbourne for a five-week visit. While away, he wrote thirteen letters to Hester Thrale. But there is no indication that he thought at all about Boswell until he returned to London, where he was disappointed not to find a response from Boswell and feared that he had been "forgotten." "To be forgotten by you," he eventually wrote Boswell, "would give me great uneasiness."[4]

There is ample evidence that Boswell had not forgotten Johnson. On 10 September, he wrote Garrick that though Johnson could not come to Scotland that fall, "he says, 'I refer my hopes to another year; for I am very sincere in my design to pay the visit and take the ramble.'" Boswell quoted the same sentence to Temple on 24 September, and to Beattie on 29 October, when he also relayed Johnson's praise of the *Essay*. To Garrick, Boswell confirmed his connection with Johnson by revealing that "If I survive Mr. Johnson, I shall publish a *Life* of him, for which I have a store of materials," including "many of his expressions to your honour"; and he assured Garrick that he could "explain with truth, and at the same time with delicacy, the coldness with which he has treated your Publick Merit." On 5 October, Langton and his wife, Lady Rothes, arrived in Edinburgh, and over the next ten weeks Boswell "got many *Johnsoniana* from him," as Boswell wrote Garrick on the same day he finally wrote Johnson (25 December). If he had not already told Langton about his biographical project, he surely did now.[5]

But Boswell had waited almost four months before writing Johnson, suggesting he was hurt and angry at his friend's disorienting failure to come. In the first part of what he printed in the *Life* from his response, Boswell reported having been "much disappointed that [Johnson] did not come to Scotland last autumn." But then he argued against feelings that had long delayed his answer: "I must own that your letter prevents me from complaining; not only because I am sensible that the state of your health was but too good an excuse, but because you write in a strain which shews that you have agreeable views of the scheme which we have so long proposed." Later, Boswell quoted Beattie's emphatic praise of Johnson, and Beattie's deep gratitude for "the extraordinary civilities," "the paternal attentions," and "the many instructions" he had received from the man to whom Boswell had introduced him."[6]

After receiving Boswell's letter, Johnson seems to have thought about responding at various times. In fact, although he wrote on 24 February 1773, he was not entirely sure he had; and when Boswell's reply arrived a month later, he wrote Hester Thrale, "Did not I tell you that I thought, I had written to Boswel?"—Johnson's usual spelling of his friend's name.

Johnson's February letter to his prospective biographer was his most balanced yet. He thanked Boswell for "the elegant Pindar," sent at Johnson's request, and even more for his "kind letter," with its news of Boswell's activities and inclusion of Beattie's praise, the latest of many "testimonies of affection" that Boswell had passed along. He encouraged Boswell to "endeavour to consolidate in [his] mind a firm and regular system of law, instead of picking up occasional fragments." But in response to a published account of a masquerade in Edinburgh hosted by Sir Alexander Macdonald and his lovely wife, Johnson gently admonished Boswell for having attended what he considered "a very licentious relaxation of manners." He reported that Baretti and Davies had had "a furious quarrel," enticingly described the "quick and gay" dialogue of Goldsmith's new comedy (not yet titled *She Stoops to Conquer*), announced publication of the revised *Dictionary,* and gave a reassuring update on his health.[7]

Johnson remained a bit detached, however. When he reported that Goldsmith's new play would be performed "in the spring," he did not wonder whether Boswell might be able to see it. More importantly, when he hoped that "brighter days and softer air" would free him of "a vexatious catarrh," Johnson said nothing about the trip that had been mentioned in all their recent letters. He urged Boswell to write "now and then," but seemed to assume their lives would not soon intersect.

There is no indication of how Boswell reacted on 3 March when he received Johnson's letter. His two March letters to Johnson are neither described nor mentioned in the *Life.* The first—one of seventeen Boswell wrote announcing the birth of Veronica Boswell on 15 March—probably mentioned that he would soon be in London. On 29 March, he probably reported that he was about to leave. Then late on Friday, 2 April, soon after this second letter was delivered, Boswell himself arrived.

Boswell in London (2 April 1773 to 11 May 1773)

In contrast to Boswell's visit in 1772, this time he had no professional excuse for an expensive trip when he might have stayed with Margaret and their first child. But he had a full agenda. He wished to consolidate his place in Johnson's life, so was with him on sixteen of the thirty-five days when they were both in London. (When not at his own house, Johnson now stayed with the Thrales close by in Southwark, while Hester spent half of each week caring for her dying mother at Streatham.) Boswell continued gathering stories and impressions of Johnson from those who had known him before 1763, including several who now knew he planned to write Johnson's life. He also spent considerable time with Lord Mountstuart, from whom he hoped for help in securing a position that would supplement his income if he decided to practice law in London. In addition, Boswell reveled in the enlivening variety of London, where "every thing smiles upon you, every thing contends to make you gay & chearful," as Temple wrote in reply to Boswell's first letter from town.

Johnson was the chief attraction, and Mountstuart needed to be courted. But London contained much, much more, including the "great feast" of hearing Burke for the first time at the House of Commons, "like a man in an orchard where boughs loaded with fruit hung around him, and he pulled apples as fast as he pleased and pelted the ministry."[8]

Boswell was so busy that he began writing his journal for 3 April only on 20 April, wrote the entry for 7 April on 30 April, and produced full entries for only his first eleven days, in contrast to 1772, when he wrote much fuller entries for his first thirty-three days in town. But notes for all his days with Johnson are substantial. In particular, Boswell fully documented two key, collaboratively produced events that confirmed Johnson's deepening friendship, making his future biographer a full participant in both his private and his public life. A week after Boswell arrived, Johnson allowed his biographer to share his usually private Good Friday devotions, and then invited him to Easter dinner, after which Johnson resumed narrating his early life. Then, three weeks later, Johnson got Boswell elected to the exclusive Club. From that point on, whenever Boswell was in London for Holy Week, he would not feel like an unwelcome intruder, as he had on Good Friday in 1772, but would be Johnson's companion during this annual ritual of prayer and spiritual reorientation. Also, he would be included in the evenings Johnson weekly spent with his most distinguished friends.

Sharing Good Friday and Easter (9 and 11 April 1773)

Ever since his wife died, in 1752, Johnson had used the final days of Holy Week to prepare for Easter communion. Starting on Good Friday, a day of fasting and reflection, he reviewed the past year and perhaps the whole of his life, usually finding little done, much time wasted. Then he formed resolutions to redeem the time misspent, hoping to make his review of the year just beginning less depressing. He composed a prayer to be used before receiving communion, "to commemorate the sufferings and the merits of our Lord and Saviour Jesus Christ" and to mark the beginning of "a new course" of life. Generally, Johnson also narrated in detail what he did, thought, felt, and said on each of these days, especially on Easter. Then Johnson often forgot his resolutions, turning his thoughts away from death and judgment until he happened to come upon what he had written.[9]

Judging from his surviving meditations and letters, Johnson preferred to spend Good Friday alone when not at St. Clement's Church in the Strand; then on Easter, after going to church, he usually dined with Mrs. Williams and others. In 1770, for instance, he reported coming "home [from Streatham] on Fryday morning" to "pass the day unobserved," though he was with the Thrales that night, before returning to the city on Saturday. In 1772, when Boswell stopped by on Good Friday, he found Johnson with a large folio Greek New Testament open on his table; "and sometimes he would read a little with a solemn hum, and sometimes talk to himself, either as meditating or praying." Johnson was so absorbed that Boswell simply left. When Boswell stopped by after tea the next day, Johnson again was "in solemn mood, with the great New Testament open"; but Boswell got him briefly to address two topics. Writing in his diary after Boswell left, Johnson found "little done" in the previous year, and hoped "to cast my time into some stated method," to "let no hour pass unemployed," to "rise by degrees more early in the morning," and to "keep a journal." On Easter, Johnson reformulated these hopes and wrote a prayer, then went to church, where he prayed, meditated, and received communion. Then he "came home, and found Paoli and Boswel waiting"; and when he resumed narrating this day a week later, he could not "distinctly remember" what he had done once they left.[10]

In 1773, Johnson and Boswell together modified the routine Boswell had already somewhat disrupted. Having spent Wednesday night (7 April) at the Thrales' house in Southwark, with Boswell visiting till one, Johnson returned home the next day. When Boswell stopped by after tea, Johnson "hardly spoke at all." But when Boswell eventually noted it was midnight, Johnson said, "What's that to you and me?" and asked Frank to tell Mrs. Williams they were coming. Later, Boswell reported telling Johnson that he "would come and go to church with him tomorrow" (Good Friday), and "He allowed me." So the next day, Boswell joined Johnson and Levet for breakfast: "tea and good cakes" for Boswell, "one cup of tea without milk" for Johnson. The two friends then went to St. Clement's, and afterward returned to Johnson's, where they read and talked until the afternoon service. Then Boswell walked Johnson home and continued to Dilly's, but not before Johnson surprisingly invited him to Easter dinner.

When Johnson returned from church two days later, he privately repeated the prayer he had composed the day before and the collect for Easter, then joined Boswell for some devotional reading and dinner. Afterward, when Boswell again asked for the specifics concerning Johnson's early life — "when he was born, when he came to London and such things" — Johnson said, "You shall have them (or 'I'll give you them') all for twopence. I hope you shall know a great deal more of me before you write my Life." Then Johnson added to what he had already said about his early teachers: emphasizing that Dame Oliver's giving him gingerbread when he went to Oxford "was as high a proof of merit as he could conceive," describing how Tom Brown "wrote an English spelling-book and dedicated it to the Universe," and also explaining that his father "knew Latin pretty well, but no Greek; did not read so much as he might have done, and was rather a wrong-headed man."[11]

Together they had devised a new ritual, one they would repeat in six of the next ten years, altering the tone of Johnson's Good Fridays and enhancing Boswell's perception of Johnson. Why did they add what both soon came to see as a key feature of their friendship?

At least some of Boswell's motives seem clear, though he simply wrote, "I was very desirous of seeing Mr. Johnson at church." He picked Good Friday because he "could not get a better opportunity than the Holy Week." Having in 1769 glimpsed Johnson's acute distress when asked about death, and having been rebuffed on the previous Good Friday by Johnson's self-absorption, Boswell surely hoped that being with Johnson at church and afterward would help him better understand his friend's inner turmoil.

Judging from Boswell's journal, spending Good Friday with Johnson was special. After morning services, they eventually talked about various topics. But at first there was no conversation. Johnson read the Greek New Testament while Boswell looked at several books. Their earlier silence as correspondents, especially Johnson's, had often been worrisome, and on Good Friday in 1772, Johnson's meditative reading had turned Boswell away. But now they were connected by shared silence. Also, their hours at Johnson's — first reading and then talking, fasting rather than dining on this day set apart for prayer and meditation — were preceded and followed by silent time at St. Clement's.

What seemed most remarkable to Boswell about this day involved seeing Johnson in church. Early in the entry, Boswell noted that Johnson "was solemn and devout," though Boswell did not know just what his friend was experiencing, as he would a few years later after surreptitiously reading and copying Johnson's private meditations. Having noted later that he could not recall what the different clergymen preached at morning and evening services, Boswell added, "They must indeed have been remarkable discourses that the very shadow of the great mind of Johnson would not have obscured; that the very idea of his power would not have annihilated." Boswell did not explain his experience further. But clearly his sense of Johnson's "power" was augmented.

Exactly a year earlier, Johnson's remarks on prayer had suggested to Boswell that his great "powers" were "cramped" by "orthodoxy"; and when Johnson insisted two days before this shared Good Friday that a public speaker's gestures have no effect on reasonable listeners, Boswell concluded that he suffered "some defect in the finer parts of capacity — in the powers of delicate perception." But there is no hint of Johnson's deficiencies or limitations in the entry for Good Friday. In their talk between services, Johnson astutely explained how a statement attributed to Charles I — that he could not be a lawyer because he could not "defend a bad, nor yield in a good cause" — was "false reasoning." He insisted that "if he were Langton he would go resolutely to France and live on £100 a year rather than sell a mass of land which his family could never get back," and he "observed strikingly" that if Boswell settled in London, his children would be "English, and quite strangers to his estate." When Boswell slyly reported that Goldsmith had said, "As I take my shoes from the shoemaker, and my coat from the tailor, so I take my religion from the priest," Johnson decisively declared, "He knows nothing. He has made up his mind about nothing." Johnson remained the shrewd and assured advisor, the vigorous defender of Christianity that Boswell had always valued. His "great mind" now seemed larger than before, the proper object of veneration and reverential awe. Yet he was also Boswell's companion. Unlike Goldsmith, Boswell took religion seriously. Unlike Langton, Boswell was not noticeably living beyond his means. And unlike both — and all Johnson's other friends — Boswell was spending Good Friday with Johnson.[12]

When Boswell in 1772 had tried to get Johnson to share his "pleasing" fantasy that in heaven "we shall see our friends again," Johnson had surprised him by noting "that when we are become purely rational, many of our friendships will be cut off": "We form many friendships by mistake, imagining people to be different from what they really are. After death we shall see every one in a just light." But now Johnson had shared this solemn day of fasting and reflection. Also, he invited Boswell to Easter dinner, where Boswell, having "never supposed [Johnson] had a dinner at home," and imagining he would "hardly see knives and forks, and only have the pie which he mentioned," was surprised to find everything was "in very good order": "We had a very good soup, a boiled leg of lamb and spinach, a veal pie, an excellent rice pudding, pickled walnuts and onions, porter and port wine." Afterward, they resumed collaboration on the biography.[13]

While Boswell's motives are clear, it is harder to say why Johnson abandoned his policy of keeping to himself on Good Friday. I suspect two main motives combined: his wanting to have on record his observance of Holy Week, when the liturgy helped him directly confront the fear of death he had angrily refused to discuss in 1769; and his sense that Boswell's diverting company, authorized by the biographical project, would ease the burden of this annual review. Having told Boswell in 1772 that he went to public prayers more often than to sermons because "people required [an] example," Johnson now allowed his biographer to chart his Good Friday fasting, reflection, and church attendance, presenting himself as a fervent Christian. "On this day I went twice to Church," Johnson wrote at the start of his Good Friday narrative, "and Boswel was with me."

Boswell's biographical project pointed ahead to Johnson's death, after which further reform would be impossible. But the day Johnson set aside for fasting and prayer was already an "awful day." Also, Johnson almost certainly sensed that the companionship of this earnest, compliant young friend, who had already sat up late with him on three of the previous six days and shared his longing to reaffirm Christian faith despite skeptical doubts, and who was not yet perceived as a censor or a judge, would in fact diminish or domesticate his fear of death, or at least momentarily distract him from self-lacerating thoughts. Fasting with Boswell was not really fasting, as Langton remarked five years later. Twice in subsequent years, Johnson and Boswell talked so long at breakfast that they arrived late for morning services, and midday conversations often made them late in the afternoon. In 1775 and again in 1778, Johnson also invited Boswell home after evening services, further postponing the time he was left alone with his thoughts.

On this first shared Good Friday, possibly because of Boswell's companionship, Johnson "found the service not burthensome nor tedious, though I could not hear the lessons." On Easter Sunday, after praying three times for delivery from "evil and vexatious thoughts" and for "light to discover my duty, and Grace to perform it," Johnson resumed telling Boswell about his early life, lingering on the time before Oxford, boastfully distinguishing himself from his father. So in spring 1782, on hearing that Boswell could not afford a London visit, Johnson shared his friend's regret at having to miss the "pleasure" they had learned to "receive from each other on Good-Friday and Easter-day."[14]

There is no way to know what Johnson made of the discrepancy between how he described himself in his Holy Week meditations, in which he lamented the time misspent and resolved to narrate himself into a different future, and how he described his life to Boswell for a work that would be written only when God would already have judged him. But it is clear that Johnson sought to control the biographical process. He welcomed Boswell from breakfast through evening services on Good Friday, but did not share his assessment of the previous year and the whole of his life, and only in 1777 would he explain the fear of damnation that made Holy Week so grim. (In contrast, two weeks later Johnson wrote Hester Thrale, whose mother was dying, "You, or I, or both, may be called into the presence of the Supreme Judge before her," then added, "I have lived a life of which I do not like the review. Surely I shall in time live better.") Johnson invited Boswell to Easter dinner, but not to church beforehand.[15]

Johnson also continued to determine just what to tell Boswell and what to conceal. Before communion on Easter, he had prayed for Richard Bathurst and Hill Boothby, both special friends, and for his wife. But he seems not yet to have talked about any of these with his biographer. When Boswell said he hoped to interview Dr. William Adams, "Johnson's tutor at Oxford," Johnson misleadingly said this was "not worth while," because "you know more of me than he does" — even though three months later, Johnson would tell Hester Thrale that "little Doctor Adams" was one of three men who could "give a better Account of my early Days than most Folks." Johnson seems to have wanted to remain Boswell's sole source of information. (Johnson also kept secrets from Hester Thrale. When he asked her in July 1773, "Who will be my biographer . . .?" he did not reveal that he had begun preparing Boswell for this task — something she learned only in 1775 when she read Boswell's Hebrides journal.)

Although he kept some of his experiences secret from Boswell, Johnson was interested in seeing how his biographer was describing their current time together. Having on the day before Easter resolved "from this time to keep a Journal," he told Boswell the next day that "he had twelve or fourteen times attempted to keep a Journal, but never could persevere." Then he explained how in keeping a journal, "The great thing . . . is the state of your own mind; and you ought to write down everything that you can" and "write immediately while the impression is fresh, for it will not be the same a week later." Ten years earlier, when Johnson had similarly urged Boswell to keep a journal, he immediately saw some of what his new friend had just written. So I suspect he now hoped to see how his biographer had described their recent time together. But Boswell had no fresh entries to share, and instead told his distress at having lost those he had written in Utrecht.[16]

Getting Boswell Elected (April 1773)

A week after privately sharing Good Friday with Boswell, Johnson publicly proclaimed him a valued friend by nominating him for membership in the Club (sometimes known as the Literary Club). Founded in 1764 with nine original members, the Club had expanded in 1768 to twelve, including Chambers and Percy, and since the start of 1773 had added four new members, including Garrick. Early in his visit, Boswell had probably heard from Garrick or Beauclerk or Percy or Goldsmith that the Club was expanding. Since he had met ten of the current fifteen members and corresponded with five, Boswell may have asked Johnson about proposing him. Or the idea may have been Johnson's after they shared Holy Week. Despite his earlier reservations about Boswell, Johnson was supporting his membership by 16 April. A week later, he wrote Goldsmith to explain that he would miss that night's meeting because of a trip to Oxford, and formally proposed "Mr. Boswel for a candidate of our Society." A week later Boswell was voted in.[17]

Once Johnson agreed or decided to nominate him, Boswell "assiduously and earnestly recommended [him]self to some of the members, as in a canvass for an election into Parliament." On 16 April — by which point he had spent some time with Garrick, Beauclerk, and Percy, much time with Goldsmith, and had seen Johnson on seven different days — Boswell wrote Percy, hoping he would "remember [Boswell] at the Club tonight," where "Sir Joshuah, Mr. Johnson and Dr. Goldsmith have obligingly engaged to be for" him. On 24 April, he invited Percy, Reynolds, Goldsmith, and perhaps others to dine with him in his lodgings. He stopped by Langton's and Percy's on 27 April, spent much time with Beauclerk, and on 29 April dined with Johnson, Reynolds, Goldsmith, Langton, and Henry Thrale at Oglethorpe's. (Neither Thrale nor Oglethorpe was a member.)[18]

On Friday, 30 April, Beauclerk arranged for Boswell to dine with Johnson, "Lord Charlemont, Sir Joshua Reynolds, and some more members of the Literary Club, whom he had obligingly invited to meet me." Afterward, the members left Boswell with Lady Diana Beauclerk to wait anxiously for the outcome, knowing that a single negative vote would exclude him. In less than half an hour, however, Beauclerk's coach returned to bring Boswell to his first meeting. Having secured Boswell's admission into a select society that included many friends Johnson had known for years before he first met Boswell, four of whom had heard him call Boswell a "dunce" in 1769, "Johnson placed himself behind a chair on which he leant as on a desk or pulpit, and with humourous formality gave [Boswell] a Charge, pointing out the conduct expected from . . . a good member of this Club." He also agreed to dine with Boswell at the Mitre the next day.[19]

Johnson's nominating Boswell for the Club did not signal his unqualified respect. When Boswell on 19 April naively wondered that "two good men" like the printer William Strahan and the author and educator James Elphinston "could not agree," Johnson was exasperated: "Don't talk . . . like one just hatched on this earth." Also, a day before the election, when Boswell defended actors with what he thought was an unanswerable argument based on Johnson's consistent claims about lawyers, Johnson delighted in outwitting him. But by nominating Boswell to the Club, Johnson openly acknowledged his friendship, though not Boswell's status as authorized biographer.

Boswell's election also confirmed his ability to impress distinguished men like Reynolds, Burke, and Beauclerk. (In August, however, Johnson would jostle Boswell's assurance by revealing that several had wished to keep him out.) After spending his first evening as a member of this distinguished company, Boswell spent the whole night writing journal entries, ending with a sustained account of his dining at General Oglethorpe's on 13 April with

Goldsmith and Johnson. Feeling ill the next day, Boswell was too fatigued at the Mitre to draw Johnson out. But though little was said, they were "comfortable"; and after tea with Mrs. Williams, Boswell got Johnson to dictate another brief.[20]

Six days later (7 May), because Boswell was now a member of the Club, he and Johnson spent more time together than on any day since 1763, starting with a "good breakfast" at Southwark and ending with tea after supper at the Club. (Before dinner, Boswell spent a few hours with Temple and his wife, Anne, who would soon accompany him most of the way to Scotland.) At breakfast Johnson grew angry when Boswell tried to defend Lady Diana, whose adulterous affair with Topham Beauclerk had ended her first marriage ("Go to Scotland! Go to Scotland! I never heard you talk so foolishly"). So Boswell afterward took pains not to oppose Johnson on a day when he seemed quick to take offense.

At dinner Boswell sided with Johnson in a sustained debate concerning toleration, during which Goldsmith angered Johnson by accusing him of interrupting one of the two dissenting ministers who were opposing him. ("Sir, I was not interrupting the Gentleman. I was only giving him a signal of my attention. Sir, you're very impertinent to me.") Langton also unintentionally outraged Johnson by suggesting "the doctrine of the Trinity" as an example of an opinion "merely speculative." ("Sir, I'm surprised that a man of your piety [can introduce this subject in a mixed company].") Later, on the way to the Club, Johnson confided to Boswell and Langton his plan to placate Goldsmith, as he then did. When Johnson momentarily stepped out, Goldsmith reported what Johnson had said to Langton, and Boswell later recorded his pleasure at having finally seen Langton "tossed." At the end of the day, Boswell alone accompanied Johnson to drink tea with Mrs. Williams.[21]

In his final hours in London three days later, Boswell again deliberately took Johnson's side as he laughed at one longtime friend and discomforted another. When they met at Chambers's apartment in the Temple, Johnson criticized Langton for having his sisters inherit his family estate ahead of remote male relatives, and "laughed immoderately" as the fastidious Chambers walked him and Boswell to the gate: "Chambers, you helped him. Did you put in 'being of sound understanding'? Ha, Ha, Ha. I hope he has left me a legacy. He should leave hatbands and gloves to all the Club." Unlike Chambers, Boswell "cherished" Johnson's manic laughter, though he did not understand it, and even joined in, crying, "Langton the Testator, Langton Longshanks," after which Johnson said of this remarkably tall friend, "I wonder to whom he'll leave his legs? Ha, ha, ha." At his door, Johnson "embraced" and "blessed" Boswell, who left for home a few hours later, trusting that Johnson would join him in August, after which they would finally tour the Hebrides.[22]

Getting Johnson to Scotland (May–August 1773)

Early in Boswell's visit, Johnson had confirmed his "serious resolution to visit Scotland this year," as Boswell wrote William Robertson on 15 April, requesting a response to strengthen this resolve. Two weeks later, Johnson asked Boswell to read the reply to those gathered at Oglethorpe's, and was pleased by Robertson's flattering account of "the grand features of nature" he might experience and the "many person here who respect him," some whom Johnson would "think not unworthy of his esteem." Having recovered from the violent cold that had harassed him in January and February, Johnson was again interested in this adventure. By making the plan public, Boswell hoped to confirm Johnson's commitment.[23]

Less than three weeks after he left London, Boswell wrote Johnson to urge him "to persevere in his resolution." (About the same time, Hester Thrale wrote a distressed Johnson that "Dissipation is to you a glorious Medicine, and I believe Mr Boswell will be at last your best physician.") Johnson waited five weeks before responding, chiefly because from the middle of May his good eye "was so darkened by an inflammation" that he could not read. But he reported on 5 July that his eye was "gradually growing stronger," and asked just when Boswell would be free. Then, in his last three paragraphs, Johnson was comfortably playful in ways new to this correspondence. After describing how he saw little of Beattie, who was "so caressed, and invited, and treated, and liked, and flattered, by the great," Johnson imagined their friend so "well provided for" with his newly awarded pension that he and Boswell would be able to "live upon him at the Marischal College, without pity or modesty." He told how Langton had left town "in deep dudgeon" and without taking leave: "Where is now my legacy?" About to meet his friend's "dear lady," he wrote, "I have that opinion of your choice, as to suspect that when I have seen Mrs. Boswell, I shall be less willing to go away." As the trip drew closer, Johnson's letter warmly embraced Boswell.[24]

Boswell wrote a day after Johnson's letter arrived, presumably to say that his vacation would begin on 12 August. Then on 29 July, concerned that Johnson had not responded, Boswell wrote again, "expressing perhaps in too extravagant terms [his] admiration of" Johnson, and his "expectation of pleasure from [their] intended tour." He enclosed this letter in one to Henry Thrale, counting on Thrales to set Johnson in motion.

Before receiving Boswell's second letter, Johnson had written a note, dated 3 August, saying he would leave London with Chambers in three days and reach Edinburgh as soon as convenient. Boswell's letter arrived before this was posted, prompting Johnson to worry that his friend was anticipating too much. "To disappoint a friend is unpleasing," Johnson added, "and he that forms expectations like yours, must be disappointed." Then dropping the role of moralist, Johnson wrote, "Think only when you see me, that you see a man who loves you, and is proud and glad that you love him." About to begin their long-planned trip, a journey they were finally making because the biographical project had significantly strengthened their connection, Johnson no longer wondered whether loving Boswell was "right or wrong," but simply affirmed both his delight that Boswell was his friend and his eagerness to reconnect. Eleven days later, ten years after they had first parted at Harwich and less than three months after Boswell had left Johnson at his door in London, the two friends were walking arm in arm through the odiferous streets of Edinburgh, eager for the intimate adventure they had long anticipated.[25]

6

Cooperation and Rivalry in Scotland (14 August to 22 November 1773)

Whatever the two friends expected as they together entered Boswell's house on 14 August 1773, with the "very handsome and spacious rooms" Johnson described to Hester Thrale a few days later, both would be surprised by much that occurred during the ensuing three months of constant contact. Traveling together for twelve weeks, and sharing their journals describing the trip, both deepened and transformed their friendship.[1]

Until August 1773, their shared travel had consisted of a day trip to Greenwich soon after Johnson first proposed the Hebrides adventure, and an overnight trip to Harwich. On a number of days, they had spent many hours together; on several occasions they had seen each other on two or three consecutive days, and once on five. But almost always they had spent hours — often days — with others before reconnecting. From the time they left Edinburgh on 18 August, however, until they returned on 9 November, whether alone or with others, they were seldom apart except when sleeping, or when they separated to write letters or journal entries, or when one — usually Boswell — stayed up later than the other or woke first, or on the few occasions when one made short excursions without the other. It was as if their overnight trip to Harwich were being extended for almost three months.

In the previous ten years, Johnson and Boswell had been together on, at most, about ninety days, never more than twenty-three in a single year. When

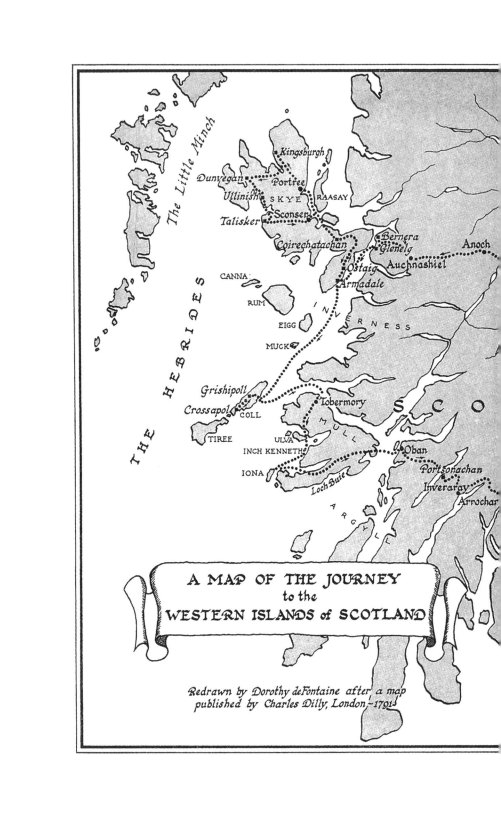

A MAP OF THE JOURNEY
to the
WESTERN ISLANDS of SCOTLAND

Redrawn by Dorothy deFontaine after a map
published by Charles Dilly, London ~1791

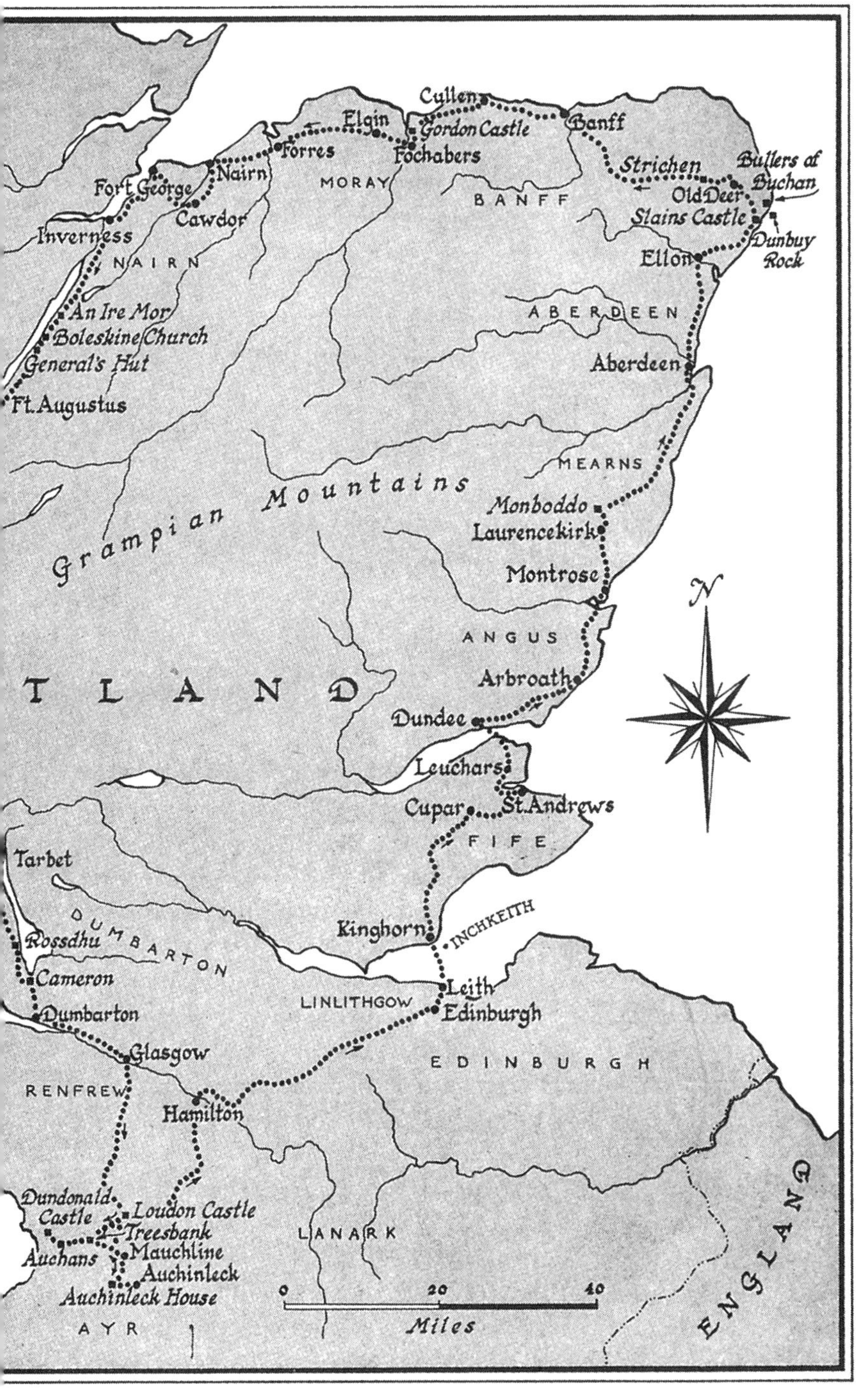

Cullen
Elgin
Gordon Castle
Banff
Forres
Fochabers
Nairn
MORAY
Strichen
Bullers of Buchan
Fort George
BANFF
Old Deer
Cawdor
Slains Castle
Inverness
Dunbuy Rock
Ellon
NAIRN
ABERDEEN
An Ire Mor
Boleskine Church
General's Hut
Aberdeen
Ft. Augustus
MEARNS
Grampian Mountains
Monboddo
Laurencekirk
Montrose
N
ANGUS
Arbroath
TLAND
Dundee
Leuchars
St. Andrews
Cupar
FIFE
Tarbet
Kinghorn
INCHKEITH
DUMBARTON
Rossdhu
Cameron
Leith
LINLITHGOW
Edinburgh
Dumbarton
Glasgow
EDINBURGH
RENFREW
Hamilton
Dundonald Castle
Loudon Castle
Treesbank
LANARK
Mauchline
Auchans
Auchinleck
Auchinleck House
0
20
40
Miles
AYR
ENGLAND

Johnson boarded the coach for England on 22 November, the two friends had been together for 101 consecutive days. For much of this time, Boswell was almost as cut off from Margaret—and Johnson from the Thrales—as they would have been had they spent a winter on St. Kilda, as Johnson had imagined them doing. They posted letters when they could, but seldom received any. Boswell heard from Margaret and others at Dunvegan (14 September), at Sconsor (25 September), and four weeks later at Inveraray (23 October). Johnson found a letter from Hester Thrale at Aberdeen on 21 August, but then heard nothing for more than ten weeks. (Dorothy de Fontaine's map shows their route.)

Meanwhile they collaborated and competed in narrating the trip. As soon as Boswell awoke on their first morning away from Edinburgh, Johnson shared his notes about the previous day. Soon Boswell was sharing *his* account of what they had seen and done; and they continued this exchange. Starting on 20 August, Boswell also wrote a series of private letters to his wife, and on 25 August, a week into the trip, Johnson wrote what Boswell described as "a long letter to Mrs. Thrale"—"I wondered to see him write so much so easily" —the first of eleven narrative letters Johnson did not share. The following year, Johnson wrote *A Journey to the Western Islands of Scotland* (published early in 1775), and in 1785, the year after Johnson's death, Boswell finally completed, revised, and published *The Journal of a Tour to the Hebrides with Samuel Johnson, LL.D.*[2]

Most of Boswell's original journal survives, as do Johnson's letters, though Johnson's notebook and most of Boswell's letters do not. Johnson's *Journey* and Boswell's *Tour* provide additional material. So there is a much fuller, much more balanced and complementary record of what both friends experienced during this significant trip than for any other portion of their friendship. We can read, day by day, what each later reported having seen and done, thought and felt during this long adventure, and can track the various ways that traveling together affected their friendship. We can also speculate about the impact of each friend's reading (or not reading) what his companion had written, and suggest the possible effect of what had happened in the meantime on each report. (I argue, for instance, that Boswell's entry for 12 September was colored by what had occurred on 16 September, and that what Johnson wrote Hester Thrale about 1 September was affected by what had happened on 18 September.) Ideally, for each day in August and September, we would read the sources in the following order: Boswell's original entry, noting when possible when it was written, and later taking this into account; what Johnson wrote to Hester Thrale, usually after having read Boswell's account of that day and after experiencing much that had happened since; then what Johnson eventually wrote in the *Journey*, looking back on the entire trip. For 1–21 October, we would read Johnson's letters first, since for most of that period he described those days before Boswell wrote his entries. From that point onward, we would read Boswell's entries last of all, since he wrote them only after reading the *Journey* and wrote those for 26 October onward only after Johnson's death.[3]

I encourage readers with sufficient time to do this, taking several days to follow the two friends through their long journey. Here, however, I must be more selective. This chapter, after making some general points about how traveling together for twelve weeks — as distinct from writing texts to be shared or not — enriched and reconfigured the Johnson-Boswell friendship, briefly sketches the texture and tone of the entire trip while focusing on a few key interactions. The next chapter explores how each friend narrated the trip and speculates about the significance of their sharing — and in the case of Johnson's letters, not sharing — what they were writing. Chapter 8 examines Johnson's *Journey* as a response to Boswell's journal, and also as part of Johnson's effort to keep this journal out of circulation. Finally, Chapter 16 charts how Boswell, after Johnson's death in 1784, completed and modified the journal he was finally free to publish, changing it in key ways from what Johnson had earlier read.

A Transforming Adventure

As they toured Edinburgh, traveled through the Highlands, and explored some of the Hebrides, Johnson and Boswell continued to cooperate and collaborate as in the past, but in wholly new ways, too. The core of their friendship had always been talk, and they continued to construct and sustain conversations. But now they often talked in situations new to both: riding side by side along Loch Ness, for instance, or on a boat while crossing from island to island, or in a castle or a cave, or at the edge of the sea. They also amused themselves by noting how they were actually doing what earlier had seemed "distant and improbable": "contending with seas," "cross[ing] the Atlantic in an open boat." They also collaboratively constructed new, self-consciously zany fantasies. On the way to Banff, for instance, after Boswell suggested staffing a college at St. Andrews with members of "our club" — a college "to teach all that each of us can in the several departments of learning and taste" — he and Johnson together assigned areas to each of the sixteen current members. Boswell emphasized their enjoyment in elaborating the daydream: "It was really a high entertainment. Mr. Johnson said we only wanted a mathematician, since Dyer died, who was a very good one. But as to everything else, we would have a very capital university." (Johnson bonded further with Boswell and underscored how far-fetched the idea was: "We'd persuade Langton" — despite his wife and family — "to lodge in the garret, as best for him, and if he should take a fancy of making his Will, we'd get him to leave his estate to the college.") Two weeks later, as they were passing the small island of Scalpay on their way to Raasay, Johnson revived part of his St. Kilda fantasy, suggesting that he and Boswell should buy it and have "a good school and an Episcopal church . . . and a printing-press where we should print all the Erse [Scottish Gaelic] that could be found."[4]

Jointly reacting to the landscape, exploring caves and ruins, daily discussing the people they had just been with and what had been said, sharing delights and irritations while reflecting on where they had been and where they were going, reaffirmed and strengthened their sense of being tightly connected, a team. So did their regular talk about common friends like Goldsmith, Beauclerk, Langton, Burke, and Reynolds, and frequent references to "our Club."[5]

Johnson and Boswell mainly lodged with families, so had only a few evenings alone. But during this long holiday adventure there were more frequent moments of intimate sharing than at any time since the summer when Johnson had first proposed the trip: moments when Boswell came to Johnson's room before breakfast, or after they shared "a good gallop" on Coll (9 October), or as they gathered shells together on Inch Kenneth (18 October). At Aberdeen four days into the trip (22 August), and eight weeks later at Tobermory (14 October), Johnson resumed answering Boswell's questions about "several particulars of his life from his early years." Certain moments of explicit, self-conscious openness and intimacy seem especially freighted with significance, as when Boswell, eight weeks into the trip, told Johnson how diverted he was "to hear all the people with whom we were . . . say, 'Honest man! He's pleased with everything. He's always content!'" — after which Boswell knowingly added, "Little do they know," and Johnson "laughed and said, 'You rogue.'"

But there was more — or more obvious — guardedness, too, especially in Johnson, who shared his journal with Boswell, but kept his letters to Hester Thrale private. In addition, each friend occasionally sought to free himself from the enlivening, reassuring, but also confining and controlling presence of the other in order to escape his companion's defining expectations. So, over time, they learned to build in time apart, even on days when they could not easily separate even to read or write letters.[6]

The sustained proximity that deepened their affection and strengthened their reliance on each other also fostered wide-ranging competition, made their aggression more evident, and intensified their rivalry.

Boswell had disputed with Johnson from the start, especially after he published *Corsica,* but seemed to be more persistent and effective than usual on the journey, forcing Johnson to revert to ad hominem insults. When Boswell and John MacLeod of Talisker asserted that the Scottish clergy "excelled the English" in "visiting and privately instructing their people," for instance, Johnson, besides claiming that the Scottish clergy were too ignorant to instruct, having produced no valuable books "since [they] sunk into Presbyterianism," thundered, "I see you have not been well taught, for you have not charity." At times, Johnson also challenged Boswell's descriptions of what they were seeing as well as his responses to the landscape.[7]

There were other contests, too, that tapped into aggression that in the past had more often been evident in Johnson than in Boswell. When they stopped for refreshment on 1 September, for instance, Johnson imagined that Boswell's dish of milk "was better than his" — until he tasted both "and was convinced that [Boswell] had no advantage over him." Five weeks later when they shared an "excellent bedroom" on Coll, both friends childishly disputed which bed had "the best curtains" and "the best posts." (Boswell quickly conceded that Johnson's linen curtains were better; but when he insisted that his posts were better, "which was undeniable," Johnson replied, "If you have the best posts, we'll have you tied to 'em and whipped.")

Also, because travel was often arduous and sometimes dangerous — whether by horse or pony, on foot or in small or large boats — the trip invited them to compare their physical strength, their ability to bear hardships, and their fearlessness. After only three days of travel, most of it in carriages, Johnson declared, "If we must *ride* much, we shall not go; and there's an end on't." So Boswell the next day taunted his friend as a fop — "You're a delicate Londoner — you're a macaroni! You can't ride!" — prompting Johnson, who two weeks earlier had described Boswell to Taylor as "an active lively fellow," to reply, "Sir, I shall ride better than you. I was only afraid I should not find a horse able to carry me."[8]

On the larger islands, Boswell frequently walked while Johnson rode or took a boat. But on 24 September, as Boswell was about to walk off without Johnson to survey a number of waterfalls, Johnson boasted "that he rode harder at a fox chase than anybody." Four days later Johnson boasted that he had "more the spirit of adventure" than Boswell, since he was "for going to see as many islands as we could" in the six weeks before they were due in Edinburgh, "never minding the uncertainty of the season," while Boswell was eager to get to Mull, an easy hop to the mainland. As Pat Rogers has noted, Johnson seems to have seen the trip as "a prolonged effort to defeat the expectations of age, and a heroic demonstration of the adventurous and youthful spirit which survived in [his] corporeal frame." Certainly, he seems not to have mentioned to Boswell the poor health he regularly reported to Hester Thrale.[9]

A month into the journey, their contentiousness in arguments, observations, and assessments, and their steady competition concerning energy and fearlessness, took on an explicitly sexual dimension as Johnson and Boswell competed for the attentions of specific women, both real and imagined, and challenged or threatened each other's potency. For the first time, Johnson's sexual desire became a significant part of their shared experience: a challenge to Boswell, who came to see this special adopted father as a sexual rival; a weapon for Johnson, who came to associate Boswell's newly assertive independence and his control of the trip with his enviable sexual prowess. But after an aggressive exchange concerning Johnson's "seraglio," each sought ways to neutralize or reconfigure what he had just discovered.

Finally, because they were constantly together, noticing whatever the other said and did and reading some of what he wrote, Johnson and Boswell each began more actively to play a judgmental role in the other's struggle for self-control, asserting authority that was sometimes appreciated, sometimes resented. On the very first evening, when Boswell was "half abstracted" by a vivid "dream or vision" as they traveled toward St. Andrews, Johnson complained that he was not listening; and later Boswell wrote in his journal, "I must try to help this." Four days later, after their third session spent preparing Boswell to write the *Life,* Boswell urged Johnson to "write expressly in support of Christianity," as Hugo Grotius and Joseph Addison had done, and Johnson said, "I hope I shall." Later, however, especially after Boswell called attention to Johnson's birthday, Johnson pushed against Boswell's reminders of his responsibilities. Also, the last full entry Boswell completed while traveling with Johnson describes his resolving to ignore Johnson's request that he not stay up drinking.[10]

All these modes of interacting, both old and new, occurred to some extent throughout the trip, fostered by sustained contact, and both exacerbated and modulated by the exchange of travel journals. Brian Finney has suggestively argued that the trip transformed "a relationship based on false social role-playing into one of genuine love and mutual respect based on a fuller understanding of the true nature of one another." I agree that traveling together and sharing journals produced major changes. But I see these as part of a process that had begun as early as 1766, when Boswell returned from the Continent and for the first time provoked and critiqued Johnson's contentiousness, a process that culminated years later. The trip enriched the intimacy that Johnson had already deepened by sharing Good Friday with Boswell, and produced a much fuller mutual understanding and appreciation. All these persisted afterward. But so did their enhanced competition and rivalry, as did each man's ambivalence about his friend's moral control. Only the following year, in writing the *Journey,* did Johnson openly acknowledge some of the criticisms Boswell had included in his journal, thus edging toward accepting his young companion as moral censor. And only in the spring of 1778 was Boswell able directly to voice his discomfort with his friend's verbal excesses and demeaning insults, and to get Johnson to change his behavior.[11]

From Edinburgh to Glenelg (18 August to 1 September)

After Johnson spent three days in Edinburgh, breakfasting and dining with notable residents, some of whom helped guide him through parts of the city, he and Boswell left Margaret Boswell and five-month-old Veronica in Edinburgh. They traveled by carriage up the east coast of Scotland, stopping to tour the college and cathedral ruins at St. Andrews, what remained of Arbroath Abbey, and the two cities and colleges of Aberdeen, where Johnson had the "unexpected pleasure" of discovering that an old acquaintance was a professor. They spent additional nights at Stanes Castle, Banff, Forres, and Calder before reaching Inverness. Then, on 30 August, mounted on four horses — one each for Johnson, Boswell, and Boswell's servant Joseph Ritter, and one for their luggage — they set out with two guides for a day of smooth riding along the east side of Loch Ness to Fort Augustus. The next day, they took the mountainous road to the tiny village of Annoch, where they slept with some apprehension. The following day, after riding for hours through mountain valleys and climbing over "a very formidable hill named Rattiken," they finally arrived toward nightfall at a wretched inn on the coast, which had "neither wine, bread, eggs, nor any thing that we could eat or drink" (Johnson), "no spirits but whisky, no sugar but brown grown black" (Boswell), where, after a scanty meal, they spread hay over their dirty beds.

Boswell had arranged the overall itinerary, perhaps in part with an eye to the route Charles Edward Stuart (the Young Pretender) followed after his forces were defeated at Culloden (16 April 1746), as Rogers has argued. But early on the first day, Johnson "determined" they should land on the small island of Inchkeith, and six days later he alarmed Boswell by "poking his way" at the edge of a steep precipice near Stanes Castle, "built upon the margin of the sea," and then "insisted" they take a boat and pass through a narrow passage into the immense Buller of Buchan (a collapsed sea cave). So six days later, Boswell called to Johnson's attention a "wretched little hovel" near Loch Ness, hoping he would say, "Let's go in," as he did.[12]

Meanwhile, they worked in concert to explore and assess this land and its people and to enrich their experience. On Inchkeith, Johnson measured the ruins, and both men looked for wells. The next day at St. Andrews, Boswell questioned an old woman who spoke only Lowland Scots, then told Johnson what she had said. At a hut on Loch Ness, after Johnson asked Boswell—who asked the guides, who then asked the old woman in Scottish Gaelic—just where she slept, Boswell lit a piece of paper and explored what he later described. (Later on the rocky island of Raasay, where "there is no riding," Boswell walked ten miles to see the old castle, then described it for Johnson.) When they crossed the heath near Forres, where Macbeth met the witches, Johnson solemnly repeated lines from this scene; and at Inverness two days later, when they viewed "the ruins of what is called Macbeth's Castle," Boswell quoted from the play he had asked Garrick to perform the previous spring.[13]

The key day during this stretch was 1 September, their first long day on horseback, which ended with Johnson angrier at Boswell than ever before and Boswell both troubled and confused by his friend's persistent outrage.

At the start of the day, both friends shared their fears of being murdered in their sleep, then started toward the coast, initially accompanied by Mr. Macqueen, their host the night before, a Highlander about to emigrate, who told what he had done when Prince Charles rallied a Highland army. When they stopped midday for refreshments at a rural village, they cooperated and competed in distributing tobacco, bread, and coins to the curious Highlanders gathered around them. Having regretted a day earlier that he "was not head of a clan," Boswell now invited his friend to embrace this fantasy, saying Johnson "would make a good chief." Johnson accepted and told how "he would dress his servants better than himself, and knock a fellow down if he looked saucy to a Macdonald in rags." But Johnson also planned to elevate the tone of clan life: "He would not treat men as brutes. He would let them know why all of his clan were to have attention paid to them. He would tell his upper servants why, and make them tell the others."

Earlier, however, after stopping to rest their horses, Johnson had sat "on a green bank" to take notes rather than conversing with Boswell. Then at dusk, as they rode silently toward the coast after the difficult climb over Rattiken, Boswell suddenly rode ahead to make arrangements without any interference from Johnson and also to free himself from his weary and silent companion. But Johnson, having been frightened when his horse slipped on the descent, called Boswell back with a "tremendous shout" and later said that had Boswell not stopped, "I was thinking that I should have returned with you to Edinburgh and then parted, and never spoke to you more." The next morning, when Boswell told how "uneasy" he had been, Johnson apologized for what he had spoken "in passion." But Johnson did not explain the source of his "passion": his earlier fear, his dependence on Boswell, and his discomfort with this neediness. Though Johnson seemed to accept Boswell's request to give "fair warning in case of any quarrel," his outrage and threat colored the rest of the trip and were clearly on Johnson's mind when he described this day in the *Journey.*[14]

Skye and Raasay (2 September to 2 October)

On 2 September, they were taken by boat to the island of Skye, where they would spend the next month, apart from a short visit to nearby Raasay (8–12 September). Having been delighted when they dined in London with Sir Alexander Macdonald and his wife, who said "*Rasselas* was the finest novel she had ever read," they were surprised by "the meanness and unsuitable appearance of everything" at Armadale, where the Macdonalds hosted them when they first reached Skye. Both friends failed to "inspirit" Sir Alexander to live as a true laird. (Johnson declared that if he were laird, "in seven years he would make this an independent island; that he'd roast oxen whole and hang out a flag as a signal to the Macdonalds to come and get beef and whisky.") On Raasay, however, they found what Johnson called "truly the patriarchal life": "I rose and found the Dining room full of company, we feasted and talked and when the Evening [came] it brought musick and dancing." (On Raasay, Boswell saw Johnson's "horror at dead men's bones," two weeks after Johnson had discovered Boswell's fear of ghosts.)[15]

Back on Skye, Flora Macdonald described how in 1746 she had helped Charles Edward escape after Culloden, and she arranged for Johnson to sleep in the very bed Charles had used. Then after "a very long and tedious expedition," traveling "partly on horseback where we could not row, and partly on foot where we could not ride," they arrived at Dunvegan, where Norman MacLeod, who had "the full spirit of a feudal Chief," and Lady MacLeod, "a sensible clever woman" Johnson had met in London, entertained them so hospitably that Johnson was reluctant to leave. But eight days later (21 September) they rode south to Ullinish, on the west coast of Skye, where Johnson crept "wonderfully" into "a subterraneous house" and for the first time saw "muscles and whelks in their natural state." Two days later they had a "fine sail" to Talisker, a cultivated spot in a lovely setting: "A place where the imagination is more amused cannot easily be found." Then, after riding east across Skye two days later (25 September), with "a full view of Raasay, just opposite," they spent a week "on the margin of the sea, waiting for a boat and a wind."[16]

Midway through the month there were two key interactions: the first involving sexual rivalry, the second indicating the growing impact of Boswell's biographical project.

Boswell's journal suggests that before this trip, he and Johnson seldom talked together about their sexual longings and activities. There are hints that Johnson envied Boswell's wide-ranging sexual potency, especially his seeming ability to satisfy his erotic desires without self-lacerating guilt. But Johnson seems mostly to have kept his sexuality private from Boswell. Meanwhile, Boswell, despite having heard that Johnson had told Garrick he would not return backstage at Drury Lane, "For the white bubbies and the silk stockings of your Actresses excite my Genitals," wanted to picture Johnson as essentially asexual. But early in the trip, Johnson's sexuality — and Boswell's — became part of their ongoing discourse.[17]

When their guides reported on 30 August that the old woman near Loch Ness had feared they "wanted to go to bed to her," Boswell facetiously said it was Johnson "who alarmed the poor woman's virtue," to which Johnson replied: "No, sir, . . . She'll say, 'There came a wicked young fellow, a wild young dog, who I believe would have ravished me had there not been with him a grave old gentleman who repressed him. But when he gets out of the sight of his tutor, I'll warrant you he'll spare no woman he meets, young or old.'" Boswell denied this, reversing their roles: "She'll say, 'There was a terrible ruffian who would have forced me, had it not been for a gentle, mild-looking youth, who, I take it, was an angel.'" (Neither empathized with the woman whose fears provided the occasion their playful, competitive fantasies.)[18]

Twelve days later, after Flora Macdonald reported having heard that Boswell was coming to Skye accompanied by "Mr. Johnson, a young English buck," Johnson and she facetiously played with this image. Describing the afternoon of 31 August, Johnson said, "I, being a *buck*, had Miss in to make tea," referring to Macqueen's daughter, a "very decent Girl" who (as Johnson later wrote in the *Journey*) "looked and talked not inelegantly" and "engaged me so much that I made her a present of Cocker's Arithmetick," hoping she would not "forget me." The next morning, when Boswell joked that Flora Macdonald had "contrived" with Johnson to have him sleep in the bed that had been used by Prince Charles, their fifty-one-year-old hostess replied, "You know young *bucks* are always favourites of the ladies."[19]

Three days later, in a debate about the advantages of wearing linen, Johnson surprised everyone by saying: "I have often thought that if I kept a seraglio, the ladies should all wear linen gowns, or cotton; I mean stuffs made of vegetable substances. I would have no silk; you cannot tell when it is clean. It will be very nasty before it is perceived to be so. Linen detects its own dirtiness." This was the only moment when sexual desire was introduced by Johnson, and the rough joking that followed was the clearest case of explicit conflict with Boswell.

Having recently been pictured as a "young buck," and having since then discussed female licentiousness and polygamy, what Johnson "often thought" was close to the surface, as he inadvertently revealed while explaining the superiority of linen. Donald Macqueen, who a few days earlier had been intrigued by the relationship between Boswell and his "governor" Johnson, noted Boswell's surprise at this "truly curious" revelation and asked whether Johnson would "admit" Boswell into his seraglio. Johnson, embarrassed at having let his biographer know he regularly imagined having what he had defined as "a house of women kept for debauchery," instead of adding further details about the place into which Boswell had already in effect been admitted, threatened his friend with one of his deepest fears, castration: "'Yes,' said he, 'if he were properly prepared; and he'd make a very good eunuch. He'd be a fine gay animal. He'd do his part well.'"

"I take it," Boswell replied, "better than you would do your part," a witty response he was still proud of when he described the exchange. "Though [Johnson] treats his friends with uncommon freedom," Boswell added, "he does not like a return. He seemed to me to be a little angry." In response to Boswell's challenging his ability fully to enjoy the women whose clothing he had so carefully imagined, Johnson said, "I have not told you what was to be my part," after which, instead of explaining his role in this recurrent fantasy, he "expatiated . . . with such fluency" on Boswell's "office as eunuch . . . that it really hurt [Boswell]."[20]

Boswell and Johnson both seem to have been troubled by this contentious exchange — "the old bull vs. the young bull," as Frank Brady described it, the only recorded instance of "overt sexual competitiveness." For each later tried to deny what he had experienced.

The clear evidence that Johnson had strong erotic desires — that he relished the role of "young English buck" and knew exactly what the women in his seraglio would wear — radically challenged Boswell's assumptions. Also, this evidence of Johnson's desire led directly to the suggestion of castration and to his own openly aggressive challenge. So in the entry for 13 September, written soon afterward, Boswell described how Johnson, having no space to dismount on the left side, in the usual way, "alighted on the other side, as if he had been a *young buck* indeed," and "fell at his length upon the ground." Boswell may have been "implicitly reproving Johnson," as Finney noted, "for his attempts to encroach on Boswell's territory."[21]

In the entry for 27 September, Boswell tried to reestablish his vision of an essentially asexual Johnson, willfully misreading what happened when Dr. Alexander Macdonald's wife, "a neat, pretty little girl . . . sat down on Mr. Johnson's knee, and upon being bid by some of the company, put her hands round his neck and kissed him." "Do it again," said Johnson, "and let us see who will tire first," seizing this chance to act the young buck, to turn potential embarrassment into sustained sexual play. But Boswell, even while writing that Johnson "was now like a *buck* indeed," refused to imagine that his friend really enjoyed being kissed by this desirable woman: "All the company laughed in great glee, and they were all pleased to see him have so much good humour. To me it was a very high scene. To see the grave philosopher — the Rambler — toying with a little Highland wench. There was a coincidence of opposed ideas. But what could he do? He must have been surly, and weak too, had he not behaved as he did. He would have been laughed at, and not more respected, though less loved." Instead of letting Johnson's imagination dominate and virtually exclude Boswell, or lead the company to laugh at Boswell, Boswell describes how he and the others collectively viewed Johnson with delight, complimenting his friend's good humor while not allowing him erotic pleasure.[22]

While Boswell tried to deny Johnson's erotic desires, Johnson edged toward picturing his athletic friend, whose clever and hostile retort — "better than you would do your part" — showed a new willingness openly to challenge and also wittily contrasted Boswell's youthful prowess with Johnson comparative impotence, as a child. When Boswell fell into a brook four weeks later, and then changed into dry clothes, including a short black coat with silver buttons, Johnson said that if Boswell "were to go a-courting, [he] should wear such a coat," curiously returning this new father to an earlier stage of his life. The next morning, Johnson scolded Boswell for "bustling and walking quickly up and down" while waiting for a ship, picturing him as preadolescent: "'All boys do it,' said he; 'and you are longer a boy than others.'" On 1 November, Johnson was therefore delighted when the image of Boswell as a "boy" — not a sexually wild youth needing restraint, but a schoolboy needing instruction — was suggested by the Countess of Eglinton, who was eighty-three but "in full vigour of mind, and not much impaired in form." Boswell reported how the countess, having learned that Johnson had been born a year after she had married, "adopted" her sixty-four year old visitor and in parting embraced him, saying, "My dear son, farewell!" Johnson was so pleased by what she said about Boswell that he uncharacteristically included the dialogue in his letter: "She called Boswell the boy. 'Yes, Madam' said I, 'we will send him to school.' 'He is already,' said she, 'in a good school'; and expressed her hope of his improvement."[23]

Johnson's reaction to what happened on 18 September, two days after he had revealed his longing to have a seraglio, shows that Boswell's plan to write the *Life* after Johnson's death was connecting him with the judgment that mattered most, especially now that Johnson was reading Boswell's journal. According to Boswell, "Before breakfast Mr. Johnson came up to my room to forbid me to mention that this was his birthday; but I told him I had done it already, at which he was displeased." Johnson, however, interrupted his narrative letter to Hester Thrale to announce that "Boswel, with some of his troublesome kindness, has informed this family and reminded me that the eighteenth of September is my birthday," and six days later he wrote in his diary that he "might perhaps have forgotten" his birthday "had not Boswel told me of it, and, what pleased me less, told the family at Dunvegan."

Birthdays generally filled Johnson with "thoughts which it seems to be the general care of humanity to escape." Another year had passed, usually with little accomplished, leaving him with more "misspent" time to be redeemed and less time to do this. As he wrote Thrale on this birthday, "I can now look back upon threescore and four years, in which little has been done, and little has been enjoyed, a life diversified by misery, spent part in the sluggishness of penury, and part under the violence of pain, in gloomy discontent, or importunate distress."

That year's birthday came a month into a sustained "off duty" adventure that was justified by the book Johnson planned to write, and four days after he had reached the ease and comfort of Dunvegan, where he publicly declared that "vile melancholy" inherited from his father had made him "mad all [his] life, at least not sober," began planning an adventurous trip with Boswell to Sweden, and would soon confess to regularly staying in bed till noon. Whether or not Johnson had wholly forgotten his birthday, he put off for six days the process of formally reviewing the year that had just been "added to those of which little use has been made," and planning — diffidently — to reform his life.

Also, it seems significant that Johnson credited Boswell with reminding him of the anniversary. Shortly before leaving for Scotland, Johnson had reported discovering his recent Holy Week resolutions, "some of which [he] had forgotten." But Boswell, having early in the trip gotten Johnson to agree to write in support of Christianity, and later to give a warning ahead of any quarrel, clearly would have reminded Johnson of his commitments. Five months earlier, Boswell had been with Johnson on Good Friday and Easter. Now he was connected with Johnson's other annual ritual of self-refashioning through review and resolutions. Also, the biographical project linked Boswell to God's judgment of how Johnson had used his time.[24]

While accepting Boswell's role as moral memory, Johnson kept his biographer from realizing how much power he held, and sought to resist his overall control. When Boswell suggested they leave Dunvegan on Monday 20 September, Johnson said, "I'll not go before Wednesday. I'll have more of this good." (Bad weather forced a compromise, delaying their departure until

Tuesday.) On 30 September, Johnson suggested he would leave for London soon after they returned to Edinburgh, but then agreed to "do what is fit." But when Boswell said, "All I desire is that you will let me tell you when it is fit," Johnson declared, "Sir, I shall not consult you." Seventeen days later, when Boswell asked for Johnson's help in deciding whether to visit Iona at the risk of not stopping at Auchinleck — "Be my council. I shall be king, and determine after I have heard you" — Johnson avoided responsibility by saying, "Do as you will," refusing to play the role he had assigned himself when he urged Boswell to buy St. Kilda.[25]

Coll (3 October to 13 October)

As they sailed toward Mull, passing the islands of Eigg and Muck, a fierce storm forced them to take refuge on the small, treeless island of Coll, where they were trapped for ten days, liberally entertained by the progressive young laird, who labored to improve the agriculture of the island, from which, in stark contrast to Skye, no one had departed for to America. Early in their stay, Johnson voiced two new criticisms of Boswell: one involving perception and especially assessment, the other involving self-control.[26]

On 1 September, Johnson had rejected Boswell's comment that one mountain near their path was "like a cone" and another was "immense," playfully insisting on linguistic precision. But five weeks later, when Boswell entered a small room in the old castle on Coll and reported it was "a circular closet," a description the young laird also endorsed, Johnson, having only glanced into the space, said, "How the plague is it circular?" The shape of this small room — and whether Johnson could rely on his one good eye — mattered. So Johnson squeezed through the narrow passage he had not attempted earlier and "confuted" both his companions, confirming his initial perception and establishing that he was the only one who saw the room clearly.[27]

On 5 October, a day before they explored this castle, there was a dispute of a different kind about how to respond to the sight of a vast stretch of the island — perhaps two miles square — where onetime plowed land or meadow had been buried under wind-blown sand dunes. Boswell, seeing "only dryness and cleanliness," was delighted. But "Johnson was like to be angry with [Boswell] for being pleased. . . . He said he never had had the image before. It was horrible, if barrenness and danger could be so." At stake here was not the ability to see or describe accurately, but the power to grasp the full significance of the natural process that had recently taken four square miles out of cultivation on an island where workable land was scarce, as well as to understand the potential danger of traveling here when the wind blew fiercely. The dunes that pleased Boswell recalled for Johnson the scene described in lines he quoted from Joseph Addison's famous play *Cato*:

> The helpless traveller, with wild surprise,
> Sees the Dry desart all around him rise,
> And smothered in the dusty whirlwind dies.[28]

Two days after rebuking Boswell for failing to see the implications of the dunes, Johnson grew alarmed by his friend's report that he was "really pleased" every morning to take "a *scalck*" (a dram of brandy), as was customary on these islands. Though Boswell had earlier worried that his getting drunk was "very inconsistent with that conduct which [he] ought to maintain while the companion of the Rambler," drinking—chiefly after Johnson had gone to bed—allowed him to escape the pressures of the trip. So he persisted, especially when Johnson said nothing. When Boswell woke at noon on 26 September "with a severe headache" after sharing four bowls of punch the night before, Johnson joked about his friend's condition. And when their host offered Boswell some brandy, Johnson said, "Ay . . . fill him drunk again. Do it in the morning, that we may laugh at him all day. It is a poor thing for a fellow to get drunk at night, and skulk to bed, and let his friends have no sport."

But Johnson also worried, and offered himself as an example. On 16 September, just days after Boswell first reported getting drunk, Johnson had explained how a long illness had broken his own habit of drinking, after which he had denied himself all fermented liquor, since he could not drink "in moderation." Now, on Coll, he "justly reproved" Boswell for coming to depend on a morning scalck and got him to desist—at least for two days.[29]

Mull and Iona (*14 October to 23 October*)

On 14 October, they finally reached Mull, the second largest of the Hebrides, and two days later the weather permitted them to make the "difficult and tedious" journey across the island, "over rocks naked and valleys untracked, through a country of barrenness and solitude," and spend the night in a "mean house." The next day (Sunday), they reached the small island of Inch Kenneth, where Sir Allan Maclean received them "with a Soldier's frankness, and a Gentleman's elegance": "One of the Ladies read, and read very well, the Evening service—And Paradise was open'd in the wild." Two days later, accompanied by Sir Allan, they reached Iona, (Icolmkill), a small island just off the southwest tip of Mull, where St. Columba, "the first great Preacher of Christianity to the Scots," had founded a monastery responsible for the conversion of Scotland and Northumbria, a "venerable place" Boswell had long imagined visiting with Johnson. Three days later they were back on the mainland.

The trip along the coast of Mull from Inch Kenneth to Iona, in a boat rowed by four of Sir Allan's men, was emblematic of the wide range of interactions that had now become standard. Early in the trip, they stopped to explore an enormous cave, which Johnson called "the greatest natural curiosity he had ever seen," and Boswell later described in detail in his journal. When they later went ashore to eat the provisions they carried, Boswell suggested keeping their feet warm by strewing the boat with the heath that surrounded them; he joined the crew in pulling up heath, and Johnson, too, "pulled very assiduously." When it grew dark before they had reached their destination, Boswell remembered the terrifying crossing to Coll and begged to go safely ashore until morning. But Johnson, who had lain asleep below deck during the earlier storm, dismissed his friend's timidity: "Sir Allan, who knows, thinks there is no danger." They therefore persisted; and when their boat eventually got close to rocky Iona, Boswell and Sir Allan Maclean were "carried on men's shoulders from the boat to the shore." But Johnson, who "could not bear to be treated like an old or infirm man," as Boswell wrote in a later entry completed only after Johnson's death, "sprang into the sea and waded vigorously out." The two friends then "cordially" shook hands and "manfully" made their beds in a barn: Johnson sleeping fully dressed on hay, as at Glenelg, and Boswell once again sleeping in sheets.

The next day the two companions explored together before breakfast, with Johnson measuring the surviving structures and both discussing what matched or failed to meet their expectations. But after breakfast, Boswell "slipped away . . . to perform some pleasing serious exercises of piety." Johnson entered the cathedral as Boswell was writing to his friend Grange, as promised, and he did not protest when Boswell left to take "a pleasant ride over some fertile land" and to offer more private devotions on the shore. After nine weeks of shared travel, they enjoyed experiencing Iona together but also separately.[30]

The following night, however, their last on the islands, as Johnson headed to bed while Boswell and others finished a bowl of punch, he "admonished" his friend, "Don't drink any more *poonch*." Boswell, despite having vowed a day earlier to "maintain an exemplary conduct," describes having had such "an avidity for drinking" that he defiantly "slunk away" from Johnson, "resolved to drink more." But in the next-to-last paragraph of the journal written before the return to Edinburgh, Boswell reported that before more punch was ready, he "grew very sick," vomited, then fell asleep. The next morning, he was contrite and Johnson was cordial. After suggesting that "none of our Club would get drunk," Johnson reconsidered: "Burke would get drunk and be

ashamed of it; Goldsmith would get drunk and boast of it, if it had been with a little whore or so, who had allowed him to go in a coach with her." Johnson worried about Boswell's drinking, however, as he did not about Burke's or Goldsmith's, and Boswell knew this.[31]

Journey's End (23 October to 22 November)

On 22 October, they returned to the mainland, where the Duke of Argyll provided Johnson with a good horse, and soon both were traveling in carriages. In Glasgow (28–29 October), as in Aberdeen, the professors "did not venture" to contend with Johnson, and Johnson sought Boswell as a "refuge" when pressed with questions by the publishers Robert and Andrew Foulis. In Auchinleck (2–8 November), Johnson later reported having been "less delighted with the elegance of the modern mansion, than with the sullen dignity of the old castle," where he "clambered with Mr. Boswell among the ruins," as he had imagined doing ten years before, when he first heard about his new friend's family estate. In Edinburgh, the two friends were applauded for having accomplished an extraordinary feat, and Johnson stayed through the first ten days of the winter court session, dining abroad every day and sometimes supping abroad as well, meeting all the Edinburgh notables except David Hume. Then, early on 22 November, Johnson and Boswell finally parted, after constant contact for more than three months had changed their friendship in ways neither had anticipated.[32]

7

Negotiating and Competing for Narrative Control (14 August to 22 November 1773)

It seems likely that simply traveling together for eighty-four days would have modified the Johnson-Boswell friendship in many of the ways described in the last chapter. But these changes were augmented by their collaborating and competing to narrate their adventure and especially by their sharing some — but not all — of their travel narratives. Having used Boswell's journal and Johnson's letters, and occasionally the *Journey* and the *Tour*, to describe key interactions during their long trip, I will now focus directly on what they wrote while traveling: especially on Boswell's writing his journal for Johnson to read, on Johnson's response to this journal, and on Johnson's withdrawing from his layered conversations with Boswell to write the Thrales.

From the start, Johnson and Boswell exchanged journals while keeping their letters private. (For clarity, I will refer to what Johnson called his "book of remarks," which Boswell described as the "notes or hints" Johnson "put down," as Johnson's notebook, to distinguish it from Boswell's "regular" or "very particular & diffuse" journal.) Every day, they observed scenery and examined ruins, played their respective roles in public conversations, and privately talked over what they had experienced while planning what to do next. On most days, each spent some time recording in notebook or journal, and often in letters, what he had seen and done. On many days, each also read some of what the other had written. At some point on 15 September, for instance, Johnson wrote notes concerning 14 September, their first full day at Dunvegan, and either then or soon afterward read what Boswell had written the day before about the day they reached Raasay (8 September). On the 15th, Johnson also began the long letter to Hester Thrale he would post a week later, first sketching the wild but elegant spot where they were being graciously entertained, then resuming the travel narrative that in previous letters had reached the afternoon of 31 August. Meanwhile, Boswell, having probably posted a letter to Margaret the day before, and having perhaps read Johnson's notes concerning 14 September, pressed ahead with the journal he would bring up to the moment five days later, at which point Johnson's notebook would also be current, though the narrative in his letter would have reached only 7 September.

Each process of writing added another chance for retrospection, and reading what the other had written allowed each to see what had happened from another perspective. Seeing how his friend perceived himself and his companion, and noticing what his friend was not perceiving, clarified each man's sense of how they differed while helping him see what had happened as his friend did. Each might soon have begun to imagine how his friend would eventually describe what had just happened, or what was about to happen, and he might have responded in conversation — or in the text he would later share — to what he just read. Both also realized more fully the implications of Boswell's biographical project.

The whole process surely deepened each friend's understanding of how the self presented or constructed in conversations or in written narratives depended on audience, and sharpened the conflicts over privacy and self-ownership that were already part of their evolving friendship, especially after Johnson accepted Boswell as his biographer. Nowhere more clearly and suggestively than in the texts that survive from this trip do we get a sense of Johnson and Boswell as separate subjectivities continually interacting: seeking and often achieving intimacy yet also setting up boundaries and maintaining a sense of separation; sharing memories and fantasies as well as some of the texts they were producing, but striving to control the trip, the friendship, and the representation of all they experienced.

Though Johnson's notebook, Boswell's journal, and Johnson's (and Boswell's) letters were produced concurrently throughout this long journey, I will discuss them in the order just listed, the order in which they generally described what had happened, as I try to determine what each man expected and experienced as a writer, as a reader, and — for Johnson's letters — as someone not permitted to read particular material.

Johnson's Notebook

In format and tone, the now-lost notebook probably resembled what Johnson wrote when he traveled through Wales in 1774 and to Paris in 1775.

Like these later texts, it probably included a fair amount of narrative, much precise description, and discriminating analyses of landscapes, buildings, manufacturing processes, and curious animals. As in Wales and France, there were probably days without entries, when nothing new was seen or heard. Johnson might have recorded more purposefully once he decided on 1 September to write a book about the trip; but he might have included less narrative once he began writing the unusually long letters to the Thrales. Though he may occasionally have fallen a bit behind, Johnson's notebook was generally more current than his letters or Boswell's journal.[1]

Johnson sometimes wrote notes while observing: describing the scene and his impressions during their first stop on 1 September, for instance, and taking notes while examining the ruins at Iona seven weeks later. We can also infer that something in the notebook lay behind those passages in the *Journey* that have no parallel in the surviving letters. Though Pat Rogers doubts that Johnson's notes "exist[ed] in any sustained form for the entire journey," J. D. Fleeman suggests that Johnson was probably relying on the notebook whenever the arrangement of items in the *Journey* differs from that in the letters.[2]

Johnson's later travel journals include autobiographical memories, resolutions, and a few longings or regrets. But Johnson might have limited these here, knowing Boswell would see whatever he wrote. Pleased at having so quickly begun this journal, Johnson may have shown Boswell the first entry to keep himself on task with what would be his first sustained, detailed journal. He probably also saw his notes as extending the previous day's collaborative noticing and assessing, and invited Boswell to comment and perhaps augment or correct, as Boswell did when he described Johnson's initial "notes" as "Wonderfully minute, & exact except as to not seeing trees." (Later, Boswell contrasted Johnson's "notes or hints" with his own "very particular & diffuse Journal.") Johnson may also have sought to control the narration of a day during which he had clearly helped determine their itinerary. But I suspect Johnson shared what he had just written primarily in order to invite Boswell to reciprocate. There is no evidence that Boswell had earlier planned to show his journal to Johnson. But Johnson's intimate gesture when Boswell woke in St. Andrews led to a regular sharing that transformed their friendship.[3]

Boswell's Journal

In contrast to Johnson's notebook, a text about which we can only conjecture, the remarkably full journal Boswell began soon after reading Johnson's account of 18 August is almost entirely available. Because he had wonderful material, was relatively free from distractions on many nontravel days, was preparing for his own book, and had Johnson as a steady reader, Boswell wrote more about the first nine weeks of this trip than about any other nine-week period. Eleven days out of Edinburgh, he wrote Garrick that he already had "a rich Journal of [Johnson's] conversation"; and most of the trip was still to come.[4]

Boswell's journals were always collaborative, since he gave considerable space to what he heard others say and usually anticipated sharing entries with special friends. Here the dynamic was different, since Johnson — the major focus in each entry — would also be its first reader. Like the countryside they traveled through, the inns and houses where they slept, the college they imagined establishing at St. Andrews, and the island of Iona toward which they journeyed, this journal was shared space. The paper was Boswell's, though eventually he borrowed a third notebook from Johnson. The writing throughout was Boswell's. But Boswell's focus was mainly on Johnson. As Johnson wrote Hester Thrale on 30 September, Boswell's journal contained "as much of what" he said and did "as of all other occurrences together." Like the trip itself, Boswell's journal was self-consciously a joint production, with each friend having various kinds of input. Boswell produced material by maneuvering Johnson to various places, asking provocative questions, and challenging Johnson's opinions. Johnson provided material by speaking and acting as Boswell anticipated, by volunteering stories Boswell did not request, such as how he had "composed about forty sermons," and also by doing the unexpected, as when he told a little girl at Aberdeen "that he lived in a cave and had a bed in the rock, and she should have a little bed cut opposite it," or when he astonished Boswell two weeks later by mimicking Lady Macdonald, "leaning forward with a hand on each cheek and her mouth open." In Gordon Turnbull's words, Boswell's Hebrides journal was "a collaborative coproduction of Johnsonian utterance and Boswellian journalism."[5]

Also, because of Johnson's inviting example, the journal was shared. When Boswell revised it for publication in 1785, he described this sharing as an "ordeal": "A great part of [the journal's] value is its authenticity and its having passed the ordeal of Dr. Johnson himself." Knowing Johnson would read whatever he wrote, Boswell may have omitted some thoughts and feelings, especially sexual fantasies and longings, such as those expressed in an entry he added nine years later. But sharing the journal also allowed Boswell to pose questions, to communicate what he could not otherwise say, to present in full his vision of their friendship, and to establish his narrative authority.[6]

In a number of ways, Boswell regularly used the journal to ask Johnson's assistance. Most obvious and direct were occasional blanks when Boswell "was not quite sure" what Johnson had said — blanks that remain in one of the final entries, in which Johnson is reported to have said that the *Turkish Spy* "was written in London by —— and ——." Even when Boswell did not highlight uncertainty, he implicitly asked his friend to confirm that the words reported were accurate.

Boswell also frequently noted topics he wished to have Johnson discuss: "I must set him to inquire if evil has place in Raasay"; "I must have this more amply discussed with him" (whether "men knew that women were an overmatch for them"); "This too must be discussed" (whether "culture, which brings luxury and selfishness with it, may weaken the principle or passion of gratitude"); "I must hear Mr. Johnson upon this subject" (why "scenes through which a man has gone improve by lying in the memory"). Ostensibly memos to himself, these notes functioned as questions once Johnson read them. Similarly, Boswell's writing what he had heard from Langton and others about Johnson's letter rejecting Lord Chesterfield's belated assistance with the *Dictionary* invited Johnson to dictate this defiant, already-famous text.[7]

In less direct ways, too, Boswell asked for explanations. In the entry for 14 October, for instance, Boswell listed a number of Johnson's "particularities which it is impossible to explain," like never wearing a nightcap, always sleeping with a window open, and often "speaking to himself," hoping Johnson would clarify. And when he earlier described Johnson's imagining what he might do with the island Donald MacLeod had offered him near Dunvegan — "how he would build a house, how he would fortify it, how he would have cannon, how he would plant, how he would sally out and *take* the Isle of Muck; and then he laughed with a glee that was astonishing, and could hardly leave off" — Boswell was asking Johnson to comment on this wild laughter, and on his similarly manic response four months earlier when he heard about Langton's will: a scene Boswell had sketched in full notes for May and now described again for Johnson.[8]

Also, whenever Boswell speculated about Johnson's motives, as when he "suppose[d]" Johnson was "displeased" that the MacLeods had been told about his birthday — "from wishing to have nothing particular done on his account" — he was inviting Johnson to confirm or correct his interpretation. When he repeated anecdotes he had heard from others, like Beauclerk's story about Johnson's fearlessly stopping two large dogs from fiercely fighting, he was asking Johnson to affirm or modify what he reported while also demonstrating the store of materials he was gathering toward the *Life*. When he reported Percy's claim that "there was no more foundation" to suspect sexual impropriety between the poet Edward Young and the clergyman's widow who lived with him "than between Mr. Johnson and Mrs. Williams," he hoped Johnson would comment.[9]

Boswell also used the journal to explain behavior that seemed to bother Johnson. In his entry for 7 September, for instance, he wrote that the need to keep a full journal accounted for his occasional silence. Having spent much of the morning writing entries, he "did not exert [him]self to get Mr. Johnson to talk that [he] might not have the labour of writing down his conversation." Boswell's writing also kept the two men apart, as he said on 19 September, when Johnson asked "how we were so little together." After reporting this conversation the next day, Boswell noted, "It is curious that although I will run from one end of London to another to have an hour with him, I should omit to seize any spare time to be in his company when I am in the house with him. But my Journal is really a task of much time and labour, and Mr. Johnson forbids me to contract it." Similarly, in the entry for 2 October, Boswell explained at length why he spent some evenings dancing rather than conversing with his friend: "I do not like dancing. But I force myself to it, when it promotes social happiness. . . . I thought it was better that I should engage the people of Skye by taking a cheerful glass and dancing with them rather than play the abstract scholar."[10]

The effectiveness of these passages depended on Boswell's addressing not just Johnson but also all those who might someday read his text. The implied presence of other readers was especially important when Boswell used the journal to describe how Johnson had frightened and deeply troubled him and to ask for clarification and reassurance.

In the entry for 1 September, for instance, Boswell described Johnson's unexpected, relationship-threatening anger after he rode off toward Glenelg, and explained why his intentions in riding ahead were "not improper": "I wished . . . to see if Sir A. Macdonald had sent his boat; and if not, how we were to sail, and how we were to lodge, all which I thought I could best settle myself, without his having any trouble." By spelling out what he had been too flustered to say at the time, and by including a complimentary critique of Johnson's wish to decide everything — "To apply his great mind to minute particulars is wrong" — Boswell tried fully to justify himself while prompting Johnson to explain his "passion" and to reconfirm that he would "never . . . spring a mine upon me." (Boswell also tried to placate Johnson by praising his philosophical calm at the wretched inn: "It was a considerable satisfaction to me to see that the Rambler could practice what he nobly teaches.")[11]

Similarly in the entry for 16 September, after describing how "truly curious" it was to hear Johnson say that he had "*often* thought" of keeping a seraglio, Boswell described how he felt when Johnson said he would "admit" Boswell only "if he were properly prepared," and responded to Boswell's aggressive retort by expatiating "with such fluency" on Boswell's "office as eunuch . . .

that it really hurt me." Having shown the scene from his perspective — "He made me quite contemptible for the moment" — and having spelled out Johnson's unfairness — "Though he treats his friends with uncommon freedom, he does not like a return" — Boswell added: "Perhaps, too, I imagined him to be more serious in this extraordinary raillery than he really was." (What would Johnson's being "serious" mean?) Boswell hoped Johnson would confirm this suspicion or at least would acknowledge that Boswell was "of a firmer metal than Langton and can stand a rub better."[12]

Boswell might easily have asked directly about the things he noted as wanting Johnson to discuss. But the journal makes clear that when Boswell first tried to explain his riding ahead toward Glenelg, he "justified [him]self but lamely" in the face of Johnson's anger. When Boswell tried to defend himself later that night, "Johnson was still violent upon that subject," and he shockingly said he would have ended their friendship had Boswell not come back. The following morning, when an anxious Boswell told Johnson "how uneasy" this made him, Johnson admitted that he had spoken "in passion" and would have been "ten times worse" than Boswell had he acted on his threat. But he avoided further discussion. So it was only in the journal, narrating the scene for a reader who had not been there, that Boswell could explain at length just why his riding ahead had been reasonable, ask Johnson about his "passion," and confirm his promise to give "fair warning in case of any quarrel."

Also, it was only in this shared journal that Boswell dared to express discomfort at Johnson's aggressive teasing about having his biographer castrated, and edged toward asking his friend to change this behavior. When he reported Johnson's next gratuitous, demeaning insult four weeks later — "All boys do it . . . and you are longer a boy than others" — Boswell used the entry for 13 October to retort (with help from Horace): "He himself has no alertness, or whatever it may be called; so he may dislike it, as *Oderunt hilarem tristes* [Gloomy people hate a merry fellow]." When they saw "a mere black barren rock" two weeks later, Johnson said, " 'This shall be your island, and it shall be called Inch Boswell'; and then he laughed, with a strange appearance of triumph." But before reporting this, Boswell noted critically, "Mr. Johnson takes a kind of pleasure in laughing at his friends in trifles." Just before Johnson arrived in Edinburgh, Boswell had written Langton that he would "never murmur though [Johnson] should at times treat [him] with more roughness than ever." But his willingness to absorb insults clearly had limits. Not yet ready to challenge Johnson face to face, he used his journal to express his anger.[13]

More generally, Boswell used the journal to present a nuanced vision of himself, of Johnson, and of their friendship, a vision designed to muffle, defuse, or transform their aggressive competition by assigning each friend his proper role. By revealing his depression, his worries about his wife and daughter, and his other fears and insecurities, Boswell highlighted his need for Johnson, whose "firmness kept [him] steady." Boswell also used the journal to present himself as a mature Johnsonian who shared Johnson's "political notions," applauded his clarification concerning "the satisfaction of Christ," and valued his example of patience and fortitude.[14]

In two entries written not long after the seraglio exchange, Boswell pictured the balance and reciprocity he saw as essential to both the trip and their friendship. The first emphasized Boswell's "assiduous attention" to Johnson, "the happy art" he had "of contriving that he shall be easy wherever he goes," and especially his "admirable talent of leading the conversation": "Mr. Johnson appeared to me like a great mill, into which a subject is thrown to be ground. That is the test of a subject. But indeed it requires fertile minds to furnish materials for this mill." A few entries later, Boswell restated this point by picturing Johnson as a "fountain of wisdom" and by explaining how the trip (and the friendship) was a "co-partnery between Mr. Johnson" and him. Johnson's "immense fund of knowledge and wit was a wonderful source of admiration and delight." But as those they met realized, without Boswell's efforts they would hear little of Johnson's brilliance: "They observed that it was I who always 'set him a-going.' The fountain was locked up till I interfered." While applauding Johnson's intellectual resources, Boswell stressed his essential role.[15]

Boswell used the journal also to establish his ability fully to describe this trip. He repeatedly provided Johnson with glimpses of himself he would not otherwise have had: striding across Inchkeith "like a giant among the luxuriant thistles and nettles," sitting "high on the stern [of Raasay's boat] like a magnificent Triton," or creeping "wonderfully" into a cave near Ullinish. He carefully described the comic dimensions of certain interchanges, like the "double talking" that occurred on 5 October, when Johnson and Mr. Hector Maclean, both hard of hearing, each "talked in his own way, and at the same time," neither attending to what the other was saying. Boswell also regularly reported in the journal what their hosts and others had said about Johnson, like Martin Macpherson's calling him "an honour to mankind, and . . . an honour to religion," or Donald MacLeod's saying that when you see him, you are first "struck with awful reverence; then you admire him; and then you love him cordially." Besides flattering Johnson, these passages demonstrated Boswell's access to material only he could make available.[16]

Above all, Boswell filled his entries with Johnson's conversation. "I am vexed that I cannot take down his full strain of eloquence," he wrote at the end of the entry for 14 September. But he had just written hundreds of words Johnson had spoken about subjects as varied as the punishment of women for fornication, a book on the gout, and the naturalness of goodness. In the previous entry, after recording Johnson's explanation of why he always ate fish with his fingers — "It is because I am short-sighted, and afraid of bones; for which reason I'm not fond of eating many kinds of fish, because I must take my fingers" — Boswell worried that he might "put down too many things in this Journal," since he had "no fanners in [his] head, at least no good ones, to separate wheat from chaff." But he immediately shifted direction (and changed images), noting that no matter how much he put down, "what is written falls greatly short of the quantity of thought," so "a page of my Journal is like a cake of portable [dried] soup": "A little may be diffused into a considerable portion." By conveying the range and vigor of Johnson's talk, Boswell demonstrated his ability to narrate this portion of Johnson's life, and also the rest of it.[17]

Though there were moments when Johnson's behavior puzzled him, Boswell generally wrote confidently about his friend's motives and character. When, for instance, Lady MacLeod wondered at Johnson's saying, "I inherited a vile melancholy from my father, which has made me mad all my life, at least not sober," Boswell explained that Johnson "knows that with that madness he is superior to other men," and later recorded this comment for Johnson to confirm. "He is really generous," he had written seventeen entries earlier, "loves influence, and has the way of gaining it." Also, Boswell assessed Johnson with seeming impartiality and poise throughout the journal. He praised his intellectual and moral achievements, including his "minute observation" and amazing "variety of knowledge," his "proper pride" and "delicacy," and also his "intrepidity" and "Herculean strength." Moreover, he described Johnson with a detached, critical perspective. When he quoted Johnson's observations and arguments, Boswell regularly included an endorsement ("Mr. Johnson justly observed"), an objection ("Here, however, I think Mr. Johnson mistaken"; "Mr. Johnson here was too severe, as usual, on Garrick"), or some additions ("I would illustrate this by saying"). Boswell also criticized Johnson's "copious exaggeration" and "robust sophistry" concerning Scotland before the Union, his argumentative roughness and aggression, and his petulant resistance to Boswell's efforts at collaborative trip management. Instead of just recording, Boswell appraised.[18]

Ideally, after reading these entries, Johnson would answer Boswell's questions, explain what was puzzling or disturbing, and open himself up more fully. He would applaud Boswell's full and judicious narrative of their adventurous trip, confirm Boswell's ability to understand and assess him, accept Boswell's criticisms, and change his behavior.

Reading Boswell's Journal

Boswell first reported Johnson reading the journal in the entry for 19 September, when Johnson "came to [his] room this morning before breakfast to read [his] Journal." But he had done this "all along," Boswell added. So Johnson probably began reading soon after Boswell started writing. Johnson read the journal not in a few sessions, as a reader today might, but bit by bit as Boswell wrote it. On 20 September, for instance, a day when Boswell brought the journal up to the moment and the second time he reported Johnson reading, Johnson probably read the 2,000–3,000 words Boswell had just written, including the passage just quoted about his reading the journal on 19 September. Each time — at least until the entry for 12 October, when Boswell started writing on loose sheets of paper — Johnson would eventually get to the remaining blank pages and perhaps wonder how Boswell might describe what had happened in the meantime or what was about to happen.[19]

It is impossible to know all that reading this journal meant to Johnson or to determine how reading the journal — as distinct from traveling with Boswell — affected Johnson's sense of himself, of Boswell, and of their friendship. But there are hints in the journal itself, in Johnson's letters from Scotland, and in his *Journey.* We can also notice what Johnson said in March 1775 when Boswell mentioned publishing his journal as a companion volume to the *Journey,* and what he wrote two months later, after learning that Hester Thrale had read the journal.

Midway through the trip, Johnson called this journal "a very exact picture of his life," a substantial and judicious narrative of his main activities, especially the wide-ranging, energetic talk that had initially drawn Boswell to Johnson, along with what Boswell heard about Johnson as they traveled and what he had earlier heard from others. Johnson glimpsed what he could not otherwise have seen, such as how he looked when asleep "with a coloured handkerchief tied round his head." He may also have read "observations which he himself [did] not remember" having made, as Boswell wrote Langton a year later concerning his journal. He experienced what it meant to have a biographer in residence: a man who sometimes failed to notice or understand, but in some ways knew Johnson better than Johnson himself did; who connected events in Scotland with what he had seen elsewhere and with stories others had earlier told him; who described both public and intimate moments in a text potentially available to others. The friendship that earlier had been primarily a collaboration to plan Boswell's studies and shape his character became a collaboration to write Johnson: to record his past, to describe him in the present, and even to chart his future.[20]

Johnson's copying part of the journal into his notebook showed he valued its accuracy. More significantly, Johnson's frequently reading it with "great delight," his providing Boswell with extra paper and urging him to beg for more rather than "contract" the journal, and his wishing Boswell's notebooks "were twice as big" indicate his fascination with this remarkably full text, even though he sometimes resented how it robbed him of Boswell's company. Johnson even seems to have deferred writing to Hester Thrale during their long, unplanned stay on Coll, letting Boswell use their limited stock of paper for what had become the official record of the trip.

Johnson's explicit praise — "You improve. It grows better and better" (19 September); "This will be a great treasure for us some years hence" (2 October) — suggests that his regularly reading these entries was one reason he wrote Thrale that Boswell "has better faculties, than [he] had imagined, more justness of discernment, and more fecundity of images" (3 November). The young man Johnson had befriended ten years earlier had become the "chronicler" who would help guarantee that he would not be forgotten. With its remarkable fullness and narrative energy, its blend of flattery and critique, Boswell's journal gave Johnson a preview of the *Life*.[21]

Reading the journal made Johnson a more self-conscious participant in the collaborative production of his experience, deliberately helping shape the biography Boswell eventually would write. Though Wilkes, once he heard that Boswell regularly reported conversations in his journal, claimed to be "restrained" in his company, there is no evidence that reading the journal inhibited what Johnson did or said. Throughout the trip he shared autobiographical memories and private fantasies to an unprecedented extent, knowing these would likely be recorded. Pleased to see how much of what he said and did was being preserved, Johnson conferred narrative authority on the journal by reading it with minimal protest and by encouraging Boswell to continue writing full entries even when paper was scarce.[22]

But Johnson's behavior during the trip suggests that he was not simply delighted with this seductively full narrative, perhaps because it confirmed Boswell's control. Though they collaborated on potential input, Boswell alone determined what to record. Boswell also decided how to frame what he reported, when and how to analyze and assess, to comment and criticize. Johnson could later call attention to material Boswell had left out, correct his mistakes, and address or ignore Boswell's questions and provocations. But Boswell then would decide whether and how to include anything Johnson said. When Johnson found fault with Boswell's "expatiating too much on the luxury of the little-house [outhouse] at Talisker," for instance, it was Boswell who chose to report this, adding a note about Johnson's tone: "He mentioned

[this] as if he liked it — as if my expatiating had been congenial with his own feelings."[23]

So Johnson often refused to cooperate, resisting the power of the journal to pin him down. Johnson almost aggressively failed to respond, contrary to what Boswell "hoped he would have done," to the many hints, queries, and intentionally provocative statements, leaving his biographer uninformed. He concealed what caused his unexpected anger when Boswell began to ride ahead, refused to explain his uneasiness at being reminded of his birthday, and repeatedly withheld other information Boswell requested, though he shared many memories and fantasies. If Boswell's understanding of Johnson was shrewder than Johnson had realized, it was clearly limited; and Johnson continued to keep parts of himself private.[24]

Johnson's complex reaction to the journal, and to the biographical project for which it was preparing, is suggested by an exchange on 27 September. After Johnson said, "The more I read of this, I think the more highly of you," Boswell asked, "Are you in earnest?" According to the journal, Johnson replied, "It is true, whether I am in earnest or no" — an enigmatic response that Johnson failed to correct or clarify when he later read this entry. (Boswell cut both his question and Johnson's answer when he revised the journal.) At a minimum, Johnson's response suggests irritation that Boswell was fishing for further compliments. But admiration for Boswell as journal writer seems to have been combined with other feelings.

Perhaps Johnson competitively resented how much more fully Boswell was chronicling their trip, since a few days later he would contrast his own "book of remarks" with Boswell's "regular journal," the difference being length and completeness. On 19 August, before Boswell had written any new entries, Johnson boasted as usual of his speed of composition, including his writing "forty-eight of the printed octavo pages of the *Life of Savage* at a sitting, but then [he] sat up all night." But four weeks later (16 September), when Boswell had written enough to fill at least 130 printed pages and was steadily bringing his journal up to the moment while Johnson was still telling Hester Thrale about events more than two weeks old, Johnson imagined having his friend castrated. During the next eleven days, Johnson wrote close to 4,000 words to Hester Thrale and perhaps 1,000–2,000 in his notebook. But he had seen Boswell write five times as much. So his "earnest or no" may have been intended to throw his chronicler off balance.[25]

In addition, Johnson's reaction in March 1775 when Boswell asked about turning this journal into a book, along with statements in Johnson's letters to Hester Thrale a few months later, after she had read Boswell's journal, shows that he worried about losing control of his image. More powerfully, it suggests that this full and occasionally critical journal, by giving Johnson a foretaste of the text Boswell would write only after Johnson's death, helped link his biographer with Johnson's deep and abiding anxiety about God's final judgment, and ironically transformed Johnson's fearful and needy chronicler into his judge.

Johnson asked to "look over" whatever Boswell thought "might be published" from the journal he had already praised, and "advised" him in the meantime "not to show [the] journal to anybody." When Johnson later heard that Boswell had defiantly left the journal with Hester Thrale, his frequent questions indicate that he was worried about its impact: "I am not sorry that you read Boswel's Journal. Is it not a merry piece? There is much in it about poor me" (22 May 1775). "You never told me, and I omitted to enquire how you were entertained by ⟨Boswell's Journal⟩. One would think the Man had been hired to be a spy upon me. He was very diligent and caught opportunities of writing from time to time. You may now conceive yourself tolerably well acquainted with the expedition" (11 June). "Do you read Boswel's Journals? He moralised, and found my faults, and laid them up to reproach me. Boswel's narrative is very natural, and therefore very entertaining, he never made any scruple of showing it to me. He is a very fine fellow" (19 June).

Boswell's "merry piece" added significant information to what Thrale had read in Johnson's letters and the *Journey*. But it also isolated Johnson's "faults": those Johnson had long acknowledged, like indolence, but also his domineering pushiness and occasional pettiness, his "impetuosity of manner" that "spare[d] neither sex nor age," his persistent, aggressive teasing. If Johnson alone could say with assurance why he had erupted when Boswell rode ahead to Glenelg, or what he felt when reminded of his birthday, Boswell was the authority on how Johnson's words and actions had affected him, and by sharing the journal had become as intimidating as Langton seems to have been from the start. (Thrale's response to Johnson's questions has not survived.)[26]

Even in the Hebrides, Johnson may have worried about others seeing this full account of his off-duty journey. He seems to have regarded it as his and Boswell's shared secret, like their knowledge that Johnson was not really "pleased with everything," as some of their hosts imagined. He assumed Boswell would eventually use some of this material, along with the other entries he had written or would write, when he finally composed the *Life*. But while still alive, Johnson hoped to limit the journal's circulation.[27]

Letters Home

Besides talking steadily with Boswell, writing notes he shared, and regularly reading his companion's full journal, Johnson throughout the trip tried to sustain a conversation with Hester Thrale and her family. Instead of writing short letters every two or three days, as during earlier trips, Johnson posted longer letters about once a week. "Though I am perpetually thinking on you," he wrote a week after leaving Edinburgh, "I could seldom find opportunity to write. . . . You just consider the fatigues of travel, and the difficulties encountered in a strange Country." After posting a short note on 14 September, only his third letter in three weeks, Johnson's one-sided conversation with Thrale became remarkably regular for the rest of the month: he wrote something on at least ten of the next nineteen days, including eight of the first ten, probably putting more energy into these long journal letters than into his book of remarks. From early on 3 October, however, when Johnson added a postscript to the unusually long letter he had begun on 30 September, there was a long break until late on 14 October, when he finally got more paper at Tobermory. Then the conversation resumed, with Johnson writing two relatively short and two substantial letters to Hester — plus three short letters to Henry — in the four weeks before he reached Edinburgh, and two additional letters before he started home.[28]

Boswell mentioned Johnson's August letters in his journal, inviting Johnson to share these, too. But these letters, unlike his notebook and Boswell's journal, were private spaces. Johnson excluded his companion from his conversation with the woman Boswell had long seen as a rival. So on 16 September, when Boswell remarked to Lady MacLeod that they were "feasting upon [Johnson] undisturbed at Dunvegan," whereas in London "Reynolds, Beauclerk, and all of them are contending who shall have" him, he pointedly did not mention the major contender for Johnson's time. For even in Scotland she had Johnson's attention. On 14 October, when a fresh supply of paper finally allowed Johnson to resume this conversation, he grew irritated at Boswell's request that he not stay up late to "expatiate": "What must be done, must be done; the thing is past a joke." By the time Johnson boarded the London coach, Boswell had seen him send Hester Thrale almost as many substantial letters in fifteen weeks as he had sent Boswell in the previous ten years, underscoring her significance and his exclusion.[29]

By turning away from his layered conversation with Boswell to correspond with Thrale, Johnson actively resisted the confining power of Boswell's narrative, momentarily escaped Boswell's judgmental scrutiny, and told his own story without interference. The sheets of paper used for letters were open to the Thrales alone. (The sheet Johnson used for his birthday meditation was entirely private.)

Johnson's letters differ strikingly from the journal in focus and emphasis and in their overall account of the journey and of the Johnson-Boswell friendship. Boswell focused mainly on Johnson and his interactions with Boswell and others. Regarding himself as "a very imperfect topographer," Boswell usually avoided describing scenery, though he was fuller than Johnson on dimly lit interiors like the "raw and dirty" bedroom at Glenelg. In contrast, Johnson tried to help those unfamiliar with the landscape to visualize it. Also, he was fascinated with sublime scenery, whether seen or imagined, noting that the shallow streams they crossed "must be tremendous torrents" after heavy rains. In addition, Johnson generally was more attentive than Boswell to how things were managed and produced.

Whereas Boswell showed Johnson being physically and mentally set in motion and guided, Johnson represented himself as very much in charge. He wrote one letter without even mentioning Boswell (6 September), and another without assigning him any specific role (24 September). In addition, several references to Boswell—especially those written right after Boswell had informed the MacLeods of Johnson's birthday—are unflattering: "Boswel blustered" at Glenelg, "but nothing could he get." And Johnson contrasted Boswell's agitation at Sir Alexander Macdonald's skimpy hospitality—"Boswel was very angry, and reproached him with his improper parsimony"—with his own reflective poise: "I did not much reflect upon the conduct of a man with whom I was not likely to converse as long at any other time."[30]

Instead of emphasizing how pleasant it was traveling with Boswell, Johnson longed for the Thrales. He suggested that Boswell lacked the ability to get him thinking, but that if the Thrales had been there, they "should have produced some reflections among [them] either poetical or philosophical"—"We should have excited the attention, and enlarged the observations of each other." Johnson told Boswell and others how he would fortify MacLeod's island and take the Isle of Muck. But for Hester Thrale, he developed a more domestic fantasy, suggesting that this island "would be pleasanter than Bright[on], if [she] and Master could come to it."[31]

For most of the trip, Johnson's conversation with the Thrales, unlike his many-layered conversation with Boswell, was one-sided. He received no letters between 21 August and 28 October, a ten-week period during which he regularly added to nine mostly long letters. A few days into the letter he began on 15 September and planned to continue "every day," Johnson compensated for not having heard from Hester in almost a month by musing at length that she was "possibly imagining" that he was "withdrawn from the gay and the busy world into regions of peace and pastoral felicity, and enjoying the reliques of the golden age." On 30 September, he imagined that "Mr. Thrale, probably, wonder[ed] how" he was living "all this time without sending to him for money." On 23 October, having still heard nothing from Streatham, Johnson described at length a scene on Inch Kenneth that he "wish[ed] You and my Master and Queeney [Hester Maria Thrale, the eldest daughter] had partaken," and in closing asked, "Do not You wish to have been with us?" Then, after repeatedly urging both Hester and Henry Thrale to inform him "how all things are at home" (15 October) — "I long . . . to hear from you and from my Mistress" (23 October), "I have now not heard from London for more than two months" (26 October) — Johnson spent part of his first day at Auchinleck responding to each of the six letters he had found at Glasgow a week before. Though he remained with his young friend for another eighteen days, Johnson now felt fully reconnected with the Thrales, and on 18 November he anticipated that before Mrs. Thrale read what he was then writing, he would "be coming home."[32]

Journey's End

When Boswell and Johnson returned to Edinburgh on 9 November, they were delighted at having accomplished what for ten years had been a shared fantasy, what had already begun to be a treasured memory. They had explored many of the destinations on their itinerary as well as some unplanned islands, and they had reached Iona. They had also transformed their friendship.[33]

Johnson had never traveled that long or far, or to a place so unfamiliar. In Newcastle on 12 August, he had worried that the trip would not fulfill expectations: "One town, one country is very like another. Civilized nations have the same customs, and barbarous nations have the same nature." Also, as one might expect from a moralist who brooded on "the hunger of the imagination which preys incessantly upon life," enabling people to imagine being in better circumstances and thereby leaving them discontented with their present state, Johnson at times wished he were traveling with the Thrales instead of Boswell, just as when the Thrales later took him to France, he lamented the absence of his long-dead wife. In addition, when bad weather confined him for weeks on Skye and then on Coll, Johnson feared not getting home before Chambers sailed to "far off" India.

The trip, however, was surprisingly fulfilling. Johnson had come too late to find what Martin Martin described in the book that first inspired Johnson to want to see the Hebrides: "a people of peculiar appearance, and a system of antiquated life." But he heard stories of ancient, bloody feuds, including a fierce battle fought just before his birth, as well as firsthand accounts of the events of 1745–1746 told by some of the principal participants. The landscape was often bleak and the weather seldom helpful. But the people were hospitable, energetic, and interesting. There was much that mentally engaged Johnson, and he finally reached St. Columba's island at the edge of European civilization. Also, he was delighted to have done so much at his age. Four years later, when Johnson longed for another journey that could "fill the hunger of ignorance, or quench the thirst of curiosity," it was this trip with Boswell he had in mind, not those he and the Thrales had in the meantime taken to Wales (1774) and France (1775).[34]

For the well-traveled Boswell, the chief novelty was journeying with Johnson. Eight weeks into the journey, when Johnson asked "if [their] jaunt had answered expectations," Boswell replied, "It had much exceeded it." He had "expected much difficulty with [Johnson], and had not found it." But Boswell seems to have been uncomfortable with their persistent competition and with Johnson's—and his own—aggression. Also, except when he explored on his own or stayed up drinking, he was always on duty: adjusting to Johnson's moods, sustaining conversation, planning their itinerary, and finding time to write the substantial entries Johnson urged him to keep producing. At Auchinleck, despite all Boswell's precautions, his father and Johnson had angrily quarreled about "Whiggism and Presbyterianism, Toryism and Episcopacy." Then, in Edinburgh, Margaret made clear her eagerness to be rid of this disruptive guest with his late hours, endless cups of tea, and excessive influence over her husband.[35]

After three months of sustained cooperating, competing, and wrestling for control, each more fully appreciated his friend's strengths and vulnerabilities—and his own. Johnson had discovered more mental resources in Boswell than he had imagined, though he kept his friend from realizing just how much power the biographical project gave him; and Boswell remarked Johnson's persistence and stamina. But both friends had also noted Johnson's moodiness, unpredictability, and quickness to attack, and Boswell's timidity, feistiness, and tendency to drink excessively. Both had also discovered that deepened affection and admiration could coexist with intensified aggression and anger.

On 20 November, two days before Johnson's would start for London, the two friends rode south, partly so Johnson could board the coach later in the day, but mainly so they could pass by Hawthornden, where Boswell would have "the pleasure of seeing . . . *Sam. Johnson* at the very spot where *Ben Jonson* visited the learned and poetical Drummond." Then, after breakfast on 22 November, the long-anticipated visit, with all its intimacy and rivalry, all its jostling for control, all its collaborative and competitive reporting of what they done and seen, said and heard, ended. Competition to narrate the journey now entered its final phase. Having decided to write a book on 1 September, Johnson revealed his plan seven weeks later, perhaps because Boswell expressed a wish to publish an account of their travels, as he had done after General Paoli visited Scotland in 1771. But after months of daily conversations and regular communication through shared journals, these friends would be able to negotiate only through letters.[36]

Collaboration Manqué
(November 1773 to May 1775)

As Johnson and Boswell parted in November 1773, they expected to reconnect in March, when they would once again share Holy Week, attend meetings of the Club, and work together on Johnson's book about their trip. Boswell would also bring his journal, which he hoped would be the basis for his own book.

Boswell, however, did not come to London until March 1775, two months after Johnson's *Journey to the Western Islands of Scotland* had been published. There is no evidence that he directly expressed a wish to review what Johnson was writing, and Johnson made no effort to send Boswell the manuscript or page proofs. Johnson did not decisively say no to Boswell's hope to publish a companion volume. But sensing his friend's reluctance, Boswell was paralyzed, unable to produce anything for Johnson to review before returning home, and likewise showed Johnson no new journal entries. So in May 1775, the saga that had begun in August 1773, when the two friends started exchanging travel journals, ended with Boswell angry and apprehensive and Johnson disappointed.

Getting Johnson to Write

On 27 November 1773, five days after leaving Scotland, Johnson wrote he had reached London the night before, "without any incommodity, danger, or weariness," and urged Boswell to send the box of materials gathered during the trip, to check "the order of the Clans," and to prompt the Reverend Alexander Webster to send information he had promised. Then, for two months Johnson wrote nothing to the friend he had seen daily for more than three months. Meanwhile, Boswell, having "exhausted all [his] powers" through managing, entertaining, and chronicling Johnson, sank into a state of "languor & indolence," as he wrote seven months later, when he finally resumed his journal: "I was like a man who drinks hard and is kept in high glee by what is wasting his constitution, but perceives its enfeebling effects as soon as he lives without it." But Boswell wrote law papers, pleaded causes, and worked at getting Johnson to produce his book.[1]

On the same day Johnson left, Boswell urged Henry Thrale to keep Johnson "in mind of the expectations which he has raised." On 2 December, he answered Johnson's question about the clans, promised to "quicken" Webster, and reported that the box of materials would be "sent next week by sea." The following day, he wrote General Oglethorpe "not to fail in exhorting [Johnson] to communicate the entertainment to the press." Two weeks later Boswell again wrote Johnson, reminding him of a promise to provide a suitable inscription for his painting of Mary, Queen of Scots, and almost surely saying something to keep him on task.

In addition, having already written the publisher Charles Dilly from Auchinleck, Boswell wrote twice in December, presumably discussing what he had described to Oglethorpe as his own "very particular & diffuse Journal." Late in January 1774, having still not heard from Johnson, Boswell asked Sir John Pringle about publishing his own book immediately, and was advised to let Johnson, as "the older man," go first. Boswell also sent the *St. James's Chronicle* an eight-paragraph excerpt titled "Extract from Notes of Mr. Samuel Johnson's tour to Scotland and the Western Isles," whetting readers' appetites for a book based on his journal.[2]

When Johnson finally replied on 29 January, he apologized, explaining that work on his book had "been hindered by a cough": "At least I flatter myself, that if the cough had not come I should have been further advanced." But he also complained to his taskmaster that no information had arrived: "I have had no intelligence from Dr. W[ebster,] nor from the excise-office, nor from you. No account of the little borough. Nothing of the Erse language. I have yet heard nothing of my box." He urged Boswell to "make haste and gather . . . all" he could, "and do it quickly," or Johnson would "do without it." Nine days later, Johnson reported that the "very welcome" box arrived soon after his "discontented letter," and that Oglethorpe had stopped by ("You know his errand. He was not unwelcome"). But Johnson again asked Boswell "to hasten

Dr. Webster, and continue to pick up what . . . may be useful." Johnson also asked for ways to benefit Mrs. Boswell, who had had "trouble enough" when he was her guest, requested news of his "Scottish friends," gave news of Chambers, and inquired "how fees come in," and when he was to see Boswell next.[3]

Boswell responded to both of Johnson's letters on 15 February, then wrote again four days later, though these letters were not mentioned in the *Life* or referred to when Johnson wrote on 5 March. Johnson's starting his book had produced their first sustained correspondence.

Johnson assumed Boswell would soon be in town to keep him on task, making the *Journey* almost as collaborative as the Hebrides journal. Boswell, however, wrote to explain that his finances were strained and that Margaret, pregnant with their second child, objected to his leaving again. But Boswell hoped Johnson would nevertheless endorse a visit, since London always provided both "pleasure and improvement," and attending St. Paul's at Easter "appeared like going up to Jerusalem at the feast of the Passover."[4]

Johnson did not reply immediately, for which he apologized. But then he argued decisively that Boswell's reasons for coming were "not of sufficient strength to answer the objections." Any "improvement" found in London could be supplied (or compensated for) at home. Any "pleasure" got "by unseasonable or unsuitable expence, must always end in pain"; and pleasure "enjoyed at the expence of another's pain, can never be such as a worthy mind can fully delight in." Eager to please Margaret, Johnson pointedly reminded his friend "how much [he] ought to study the happiness of her, who studies [his] with so much diligence": "She permitted you to ramble last year, you must permit her now to keep you at home."

Then Johnson responded at length to Boswell's notion that worshipping at St. Paul's each Easter was like the Jews celebrating Passover in Jerusalem: "We know, and ought to remember, that the Universal Lord is every where present; and that, therefore, to come to Iona, or to Jerusalem, though it may be useful, cannot be necessary." Johnson took Boswell's "fancy" seriously, but sided with the "sweet lady" who had been so glad when he left that he had facetiously imagined "com[ing] again, that she may again have the same pleasure." Then, in closing, Johnson hoped to be "very diligent next week about" what he called "our travels," which he had "too long neglected."[5]

Disappointed at not being there as Johnson began writing, Boswell now had no way to participate beyond providing additional materials and encouraging Johnson to press on. He wrote in April, asking about the death of Goldsmith, probably reporting that he was studying Scots law with Charles Hay, and almost surely mentioning the book. He also exhorted both Langton (10 April) and Garrick (11 April) to "quicken" Johnson, since "Posterity will be the more obliged to his friends the more than they can prevail with him to write." A month later (12 May), having heard nothing from Johnson, Boswell sent some printed sheets from Lord Hailes's *Annals of Scotland* for Johnson to review and return, in the process showing what Johnson might do later with his own text. Boswell may also have "beg'd to be permitted to read over the Manuscript before it went to the Press," as Sir William Forbes, Boswell's banker and friend, reported the following February. Boswell wrote Henry Thrale, too, apologizing for the many packets he had sent for Johnson (Thrale, as a member of Parliament, had free postage), and "rejoic[ing] to hear" — probably from Dilly — that Johnson's "*Northern Tour* is well advanced." Boswell asked for "a few lines" telling him how the Thrales were, "and how Mr. Johnson is," hoping to nudge Johnson himself to write. A week later, Boswell again wrote to Johnson, probably inquiring about a short letter Johnson had written for a lady who wished to "make use of [Boswell's] skill and eloquence" as a lawyer, and then by mistake had posted to Boswell rather than the lady, and perhaps adding a postscript announcing the birth of his second daughter, Euphemia.[6]

The Journey *at the Press*

Despite Boswell's letters and indirect nudges, Johnson sent nothing for three months except the letter of introduction to the lady in need of a lawyer, though he regularly thought of Boswell while reliving their trip. Then on 21 June, about to leave for Wales on a journey required by property Hester Thrale had just inherited, Johnson reported that he had just "put the first sheets of the 'Journey to the Hebrides' to the press." "I have endeavoured to do you some justice in the first paragraph," Johnson added; and he asked Boswell to consider how best to distribute twenty-five gift copies. This short, businesslike letter contained no gossip, nothing about Johnson's health, and no response to most of what Boswell had recently written, though by sending "compliments to your lady and both the young ones," Johnson acknowledged having heard of Euphemia's birth.[7]

Boswell replied at once, probably expressing "lively joy" that the book was almost done, as he reported in his journal, and his being "much elated" by Johnson's promised praise. But the first paragraph of the reply as printed in the *Life* expresses exasperation at what Johnson had *not* said and suggests anger at what he had not done: "You do not acknowledge the receipt of the various packets which I have sent you. Neither can I prevail with you to *answer* my letters, though you honour me with *returns*. You have said nothing to me about poor Goldsmith, nothing about Langton."

Elsewhere in this letter, Boswell might have stated more directly his disappointment at having been virtually excluded from the process of composing "our travels." But I doubt this. Even in his journal, Boswell did not describe the feelings that led him—right after quoting the sentence about Johnson's doing him "some justice"—to add: "One must pause and think, to have a full feeling of the value of any praise from Mr. Johnson. His works and his majesty of mind must be kept in view." While traveling with Johnson, Boswell had used his journal to express what he could not say directly. Writing just for himself, he now was unwilling to explain what led him to emphasize the "full value" of praise he had not yet read in a book he had not directly helped his friend write.[8]

A few days after reading this letter, Johnson replied cordially to what Boswell had written and to what he sensed his friend was feeling. He provided an inscription for the painting of Mary, Queen of Scots, and thanked Boswell for all his pamphlets. He gave a deft account of Goldsmith, who "died of a fever, made, I am afraid, more violent by uneasiness of mind." He used the birth of Hester Thrale's second son, Ralph, after five daughters in a row, to reassure Boswell that as long as Margaret was well, he should "never doubt of a boy." Johnson wrote nothing about Langton, who had complained to Boswell of Johnson's silence; but the next day, Johnson finally replied to what Langton, at Boswell's urging, had written eight months earlier.[9]

More importantly, Johnson opened by addressing what was chiefly on Boswell's mind: "I wish you could have looked over my book before the printer, but it could not easily be. I suspect some mistakes; but as I deal, perhaps, more in notions than facts, the matter is not great, and the second edition will be mended, if any such there be." Johnson repeated this regret three months later, wishing that Boswell "could have read the book before it was printed, but . . . distance does not easily permit it." But what Johnson next mentioned in July —Lord Hailes's sheets, which he was returning with annotations—pointed to how he might have arranged for the person best equipped to catch errors and omissions to review the text before it was published. Strahan, who posted printed sheets to Johnson in Wales, might have sent these to Boswell, too.

Johnson's failure to consider how he might more fully have involved Boswell, especially after he sensed his friend's distress and had Hailes's *Annals* as an example, suggests a deliberate choice to limit his traveling companion's involvement. But Boswell, curiously, seems not to have asked directly to see the sheets. Instead, Boswell drank heavily and at times was "domineering and ill-bred." Also, he waited three weeks before responding to Johnson's "more than ordinarily good" letter, which Margaret had given him only after he had recovered from "a complete riot" on the day it arrived.[10]

By then had begun another three-month period with no letters from Johnson, who had written the Thrales so often while in Scotland. Boswell wrote again on 3 September, asking whether Johnson might interpose to get his client John Reid's sentence commuted from hanging to transportation—an urgent matter that would have guaranteed a reply were Johnson in London. On 16 September, realizing that "Wales has probably detained you longer than I supposed," Boswell wrote again, asking Johnson to post a copy of the *Journey* "as soon as it is printed"[11]

While waiting to hear from Johnson, most of Boswell's time and sober energy was absorbed by the trial of John Reid, who had been his very first criminal client, eight years earlier, and who was again accused of stealing sheep. The grim drama of defending Reid at a trial where Lord Auchinleck took the lead in examining witnesses, trying to have the death sentence either rescinded or commuted, briefly exploring the possibility of resuscitating Reid's body after he was hanged, and all along seeking to determine whether Reid was really innocent fully engaged Boswell until the execution on 21 September. Also, as Gordon Turnbull has brilliantly argued, defending Reid greatly strengthened Boswell's longing to relocate to London: to escape from the language of law, which "fixes character and destroys it," to the language of biography, which "resurrects character and immortalizes it."[12]

Johnson wrote Boswell on 1 October, right after he returned, lest Boswell suspect him of "negligence" in the pressing business with which he had asked for help. In other ways, too, Johnson tried to please his neglected friend, starting with a comment that Wales, unlike Scotland, "is so little different from England, that it offers nothing to the speculation of the traveler." He apologized for having long left his work "suspended," but promised "now to drive the book forward."[13]

This letter was "a cordial" when it arrived, and Boswell's entry for the following day (6 October) reveals a longing to connect more directly. A threatened duel was the occasion. When the son of a man Boswell had attacked anonymously in the *London Chronicle* challenged him, if he was the author, Margaret suggested James go "quite privately" to London, retrieve his manuscript, and then deny having written it. Initially, Boswell liked the proposal because in such an important matter, he "would have the advice of Mr. Samuel Johnson, with whom [he] would hold secret and solemn interviews," reviving their special intimacy. But Boswell soon adopted a less duplicitous strategy and so put off writing Johnson until late October, when he included the sad news that the enterprising young laird of Coll had drowned.

Before receiving Boswell's letter, Johnson had written again, hoping what he had just read about Coll was incorrect. ("We, you know, were once drowned," he wrote, referring to newspaper reports of the "remarkable storm" that drove them to Coll.) He also reported that 240 pages of the *Journey* had been printed. A month later (26 November), Johnson announced that he had "corrected the last page of our 'Journey to the Hebrides'" and asked his collaborator manqué for his frank opinion: "Tell me, and tell me honestly, what you think and others say of our travels." Seven weeks later (14 January 1775), while posting the book in franked packets as Boswell had requested, Johnson again asked the same favor of his special reader: "Let me know, as fast as you read it, how you like it."[14]

"Our Travels"

Johnson's first major work since his edition of Shakespeare (1765) was a combination of travel narrative, social geography, and speculation about how life in such remote, mountainous regions might be improved. It also contained numerous pointed arguments. Concerning those Scots who, despite the lack of evidence, believed James Macpherson's Ossian poems were translations of ancient Gaelic texts, Johnson wrote, "A Scotchman must be a very sturdy moralist, who does not love Scotland better than truth." Concerning those who supported the repressive laws passed after Culloden, despite their disastrous consequences, Johnson wrote: "To hinder insurrection, by driving away the people, and to govern peaceably, by having no subjects, is an expedient that argues no great profundity of politics. . . . It affords a legislator little self-applause to consider, that where there was formerly an insurrection, there is now a wilderness."

Johnson also mocked the "curiosity [that] pants for savage virtues and barbarous grandeur," which had led him to these regions. After describing his "generous and manly pleasure" in imagining the warlike past of these islands, when every man slept "securely with his sword beside him," ready to "engage the enemy," Johnson noted "that a man who places honour only in successful violence, is a very troublesome and pernicious animal in times of peace; and that the martial character cannot prevail in a whole people, but by the diminution of all other virtues." In addition, the book contained Johnson's sustained debate with himself about what progress was possible in this inhospitable landscape and how to judge those who emigrated from the Hebrides to America — questions concerning which his feelings were strong and conflicted.[15]

The *Journey* was also the final phase in Johnson's conversation with Hester Thrale about the trip she had supported. Whenever he focused on himself or Boswell, he knew she would see differences from the account given in his travel letters. She might also notice how Johnson replaced nostalgia for the Thrales with a wish not to be forgotten by those he had met in rural Scotland.[16]

Johnson's private communication with Boswell, the friend who had enabled and shared the journey, was even richer as Johnson negotiated how to represent himself, Boswell, and their friendship. Johnson carefully avoided material he knew might embarrass or offend, such as their dismay at Sir Alexander Macdonald's parsimony. He wrote nothing of his heated argument with Lord Auchinleck and took pains to describe shared experiences in ways likely to please. Though he mentions Boswell's journal only once, in key ways Johnson finally responded to that text. He publicly affirmed great respect for Boswell, acknowledged that his criticisms were on target, and even accepted Boswell's role as his conscience.[17]

For the most part, Johnson replaced the "Boswell" he had sometimes depicted for Hester Thrale with the "Boswell" he had seen in the journal. He included no references to his friend's troublesome kindness, his ineffectual anger, or his fear of ghosts. At Glenelg, when Johnson slept in his riding coat on a bundle of hay, "Mr. Boswell being more delicate, laid himself sheets with hay over and under him, and lay in linen like a gentleman." But weeks later, when a strong wind blew their ship to Coll, both travelers—not just Boswell— "were willing to call it a tempest." "I was sea-sick and lay down," Johnson added, but "Mr. Boswell kept the deck."[18]

Johnson also assigned Boswell positive qualities he knew would be appreciated, such as "gaiety of conversation and civility of manners," "acuteness of observation [which] would help my inquiry", and "inquisitiveness . . . seconded by great activity." He credited Boswell with sensible reflections on what they experienced, such as noting that the noise of the wind on Coll "was all its own, for there were no trees to increase it." Johnson privileged his friend's feelings, too, first reporting his being "much affected" by the ruins of Iona, then adding that their ride the next afternoon "was through a country of such gloomy desolation, that Mr. Boswell thought no part of the Highlands equally terrifick." Competition to see, describe, and analyze was replaced by praise of Boswell's mental powers and sensibility.[19]

By describing Boswell in ways that would surely please, Johnson invited his friend reciprocally to endorse his carefully constructed persona: a "Johnson" who was occasionally negligent but still decisive, compassionate but tough minded, nostalgic but sensible. Johnson further encouraged his future biographer to endorse this revised "Johnson" by acknowledging some of Boswell's criticisms. As though admitting that he had been excessively pushy, for instance, Johnson occasionally denied having been in charge, even when both surviving early accounts report his having taken the lead. Early in the *Journey,* Johnson also mocked his notorious anti-Scottish prejudice, as in reporting on their lodgings at Montrose: "We did not find a reception such as we thought proportionate to the commercial opulence of the place; but Mr. Boswell desired me to observe that the innkeeper was an Englishman, and I then defended him as well as I could."[20]

Johnson even edged toward explaining why he had erupted when Boswell rode off toward Glenelg, a reaction stemming from a scare he received on the climb over Rattiken : "My horse, weary with the steepness of the rise, staggered a little, and I called in haste to the Highlander to hold him. This was the only moment of my journey, in which I thought myself endangered." There was no need to tell readers of his fear. But this revelation might help Boswell understand the "passion" Johnson had resisted discussing. Having come to see this episode from Boswell's point of view — first when he and Boswell talked the next morning, then when he later read Boswell's entry — Johnson now helped Boswell view it from his perspective.[21]

Johnson also partially apologized for having resisted Boswell's necessary planning, while publicly complimenting his friend's energy and sense of purpose. After describing the "plenty and elegance, beauty and gaiety" of Raasay, Johnson wrote, "If I could have found an Ulysses, I had fancied a Phaeacia." A few pages later, he continued the Homeric allusions: "At Dunvegan, I had tasted lotus, and was in danger of forgetting that I was ever to depart, till Mr. Boswell sagely reproached me with my sluggishness and softness. I had no very forcible defence to make, and we agreed to pursue our journey." The rhetoric is self-consciously inflated. But Johnson transformed his young friend into the clearheaded, resolute leader whose guidance he needed. Writing of his dangerous attraction to ease and his need to have someone keep him on task, Johnson came close to stating what he had realized throughout the trip — that his young friend had become his moral censor.[22]

As he traveled with Boswell, Johnson's multilayered process of narrating himself in his notebook and letters, in two sessions spent answering Boswell's biographical questions, in two birthday reviews, as well as in daily conversations, surely heightened his sense of how variously he constructed himself, depending on audience and occasion. Each narrative was necessarily selective, in certain ways contradicted the others, and potentially stood in competition with the narratives of others, including Boswell's detailed descriptions of what Johnson had just said and done, and also with God's definitive assessment of Johnson's life. Building on his notebook and letters, and on what he remembered of Boswell's journal, to create a persona for his longest-surviving personal narrative must have deepened Johnson's understanding of the selectivity and artificiality of self-presentation. For he knew how many other "Johnsons" he had already independently and collaboratively produced, and how each of them differed in some ways from Boswell's "Johnson."

Johnson was constructing a rhetorically useful persona, as Edward Tomar-kan has carefully shown. But by reliving the trip with deeper understanding and sympathy, and more humility, Johnson was also making up for past deficien-cies, such as his failure to respond fully to the landscape when they first stopped early on 1 September, and his failure to explain himself to Boswell later that day. Instead of simply resolving to change, he was actually acting differently. He also tried to make amends for his petulance and insults. So as he posted the *Journey* to Edinburgh, Johnson asked Boswell to respond as soon as he had read it. A week later, he wrote again, longing "to hear how you like the book."[23]

Reading the Journey, *Anticipating Reconnecting*

The *Journey* reached Boswell on 18 January, the same day it was pub-lished in London, accompanied by the first of five letters Johnson sent in the six weeks between 14 January and 25 February 1775. Boswell finished the book that night, and the next day wrote the first of five letters he would send before 18 February. (He had already written on 3 January.) This was a much fuller conversation in letters than they had constructed the previous March, with each writing his third letter just two weeks after his first. Also because Boswell included in the *Life* hefty portions of four of his letters, we can see almost everything they said as they anticipated reconnecting for the first time since the trip.[24]

The main topic was the *Journey*. In each of his first three letters, Johnson asked how Boswell and others in Scotland had responded. On 19 January, besides noting that despite a bad cold, he had stayed up "the greatest part of the last night," delighted with what he read, Boswell recalled their first talking of the trip "many years ago, when sitting by [themselves] in the Mitre tavern, in London, . . . about the *witching time o'night*." He clearly was gratified that Johnson praised his "acuteness frankness & gaiety," as he wrote Oglethorpe five weeks later. Boswell also noted two errors and promised to list others.

In a short letter written on 28 January, perhaps five days after he had re-ceived Boswell's first letter and two or three days before he got his second, Johnson acknowledged Boswell's praise — "I am glad that you like the book so well" — and longed "to know what Lord Hailes says of it." adding, "Lend it him privately." Boswell's letter of 11 February probably reported what Lord Hailes had just written about the *Journey*, including an endorsement of John-son's complaints about the lack of trees, and possibly how Sir Alexander Dick had praised the book earlier that day. Two weeks later, after reporting that sales were "sufficiently quick," Johnson acknowledged Boswell's mention of errors and asked him bring his corrected copy to London.[25]

Johnson and Boswell also opened three new collaborations. After praising the *Journey* profusely on 19 January, Boswell asked for help defending the Aberdeen infirmary against charges brought by a physician, reminding Johnson he had been made a citizen of that city. Johnson, after complaining on 28 January that Boswell had "sent . . . a case to consider," but "no facts" except "what are against us, nor any principles on which to reason," soon got what he needed from Dr. Thomas Lawrence, the president of the London College of Physicians. On 21 January, Johnson invited Boswell to help with a "secret" pamphlet on the conflict with America. Boswell, after reporting his impression "that [the British] government has been precipitant and severe in the resolutions taken against the Bostonians"—an opinion he had earlier shared with Oglethorpe—deferentially asked Johnson to tell him "what to read" on this issue, and assumed that once Johnson wrote on the subject, he would "certainly understand it."[26]

In addition, each asked the other for help concerning James Macpherson, who was "furious" at Johnson's attacks on his widely read poems. A day after responding directly to Macpherson's "foolish and impudent note," Johnson requested additional "intelligence" concerning the author and also asked, "Is Lord Hailes on our side?" Eager to be an effective supporter, Boswell, before reporting on 2 February that Lord Hailes planned to "keep out" of the controversy, wrote that it was "confidently reported" in Edinburgh that Johnson had refused Macpherson's offer to confirm "the authenticity of Ossian's poems" by examining the original manuscripts. Boswell reassured Johnson that he was standing up for him against the imputation of intellectual cowardice: "You may believe it gives me pain to hear your conduct represented as unfavourable, while I can only deny what is said, on the ground that your character refutes it." But he wanted specifics.

Boswell was delighted when Johnson denied the rumor: "Macpherson never in his life offered me the sight of any original or of any evidence of any kind, but thought only of intimidating me by noise and threats." But Johnson attacked Boswell for even asking about it: "I am surprised that, knowing as you do the disposition of your countrymen to tell lies in favour of each other, you can be at all affected by any reports that circulate among them." Similarly, when Boswell, having heard several Highlanders insist "that in the Highlands and Islands Erse [Scottish Gaelic] was written long ago," speculated in his next letter that skilled "men of veracity" might be able to determine convincingly whether manuscripts "in the possession of families in the Highlands and isles are the works of a remote age," Johnson testily rejected what he called "going wild about Ossian": "Why do you think any part can be proved? . . . None of the old families had a single letter in Erse that we heard of. . . . Do not be credulous; you know how little a Highlander can be trusted. Macpherson is, so far as I know, very quiet. Is not that proof enough?"[27]

Another, much more significant transaction occurred in the context of their comfortable talk about the *Journey* and their edgy new collaborations: a troubling exchange after Boswell asked about showing others a poem Johnson had sent him. What each said is mostly obscured, since Boswell cut from the *Life* the relevant sections from his letter of 2 February and Johnson's letter of 7 February and printed nothing from his prompt reply. Boswell's journal, however, shows that both men were aroused.

Toward the end of his cordial letter of 21 January, after short paragraphs of intimate gossip, Johnson further connected with Boswell, who "love[d] verses," by sending those he had made about Inchkenneth ("Insula sancti Kennethi"), the small island off Mull where they had shared what Johnson described as "the most agreeable Sunday evening" he had ever experienced — verses that ended with Johnson's asking (in Latin), "Why should I wander any further? All that is required anywhere is here; here is serene repose, and here is honourable love." Johnson stipulated that Boswell was to show the lines to no one except Lord Hailes, "whom I love better than any man whom I know so little." If asked, Boswell might transcribe them, provided Hailes "promise[d] not to let them be copied again, nor to show them as mine."

Boswell's journal reports that he asked permission to read the verses to others, too, a request Lord Hailes supported. But Johnson, in the letter that first attacked Boswell for seriously imagining that Macpherson had offered to show his manuscripts, harshly denied this request, using words Boswell omitted from the *Life* but quoted in his journal: "Your love of publication is offensive and disgusting, and will end, if it be not reformed, in a general distrust among all your friends." I suspect this angry censure expressed Johnson's worry about what Boswell might do with his Hebrides journal, which he had already used for a newspaper article early in 1774.

Johnson's letter arrived at night on 11 February, and Boswell's entry for that day — written four days later, when he wrote all the entries for 2–15 February — contains a rare report of anger and also shows how he calmed himself. Johnson's rebuke of his "love of publication" was "too severe, as Lord Hailes had agreed . . . that the verses should be freely shown." Margaret, being "more touchy," was "really angry for a little." Boswell, too, "began first to be vexed, and then somewhat angry," but finally relented: "I soon recollected the authority which Mr. Johnson had over me as a preceptor, and his real kindness for me, and was satisfied." Boswell responded quickly, but printed none of this letter in the *Life*. So we cannot know whether he wrote while still "vexed" or "angry," or how he justified himself, or even whether he addressed this topic.

(Nothing in Johnson's next letter refers to the verses.) It seems likely, however, that Boswell wrote something about Margaret, perhaps letting her anger substitute for his own. For Johnson closed his letter of 25 February by writing, "Make my compliments to Mrs. Boswell; I suppose she is now just beginning to forgive me" — a striking contrast to the way he had mentioned Margaret in all his letters after he had supported her wish to have Boswell stay home the previous March.[28]

Boswell did not write again before he left Edinburgh on 15 March, carrying the journal he had shown Forbes and Hailes and had promised to show to others, a text he hoped now to publish. In Edinburgh sixteen months earlier, Boswell had let Johnson tell Lord Elibank about their trip, and two months later had accepted Pringle's advice to let Johnson publish first. Johnson's book was now in print. So it was Boswell's turn. His book would complement and at times correct the *Journey* while demonstrating how fully Boswell had produced and documented this significant adventure, how sagely he appreciated Johnson. Though the *Journey* firmly linked Boswell to Johnson, Boswell's book would do much more.[29]

But Johnson's eruption concerning the verses, like his anger in 1768 when Boswell published his letter in *Corsica,* highlighted the need to secure permission. So did a letter from Lord Hailes, to whom Boswell had sent the Hebrides journal while asking about publication. Though Hailes greatly enjoyed Boswell's text, he strongly argued against publishing while Johnson was alive. "Would you repeat what he has said, or contradict him, or supply what he has thought fit to pass over in silence?" Boswell's reply has not been found, and he did not comment in his journal. But he brought the Hebrides journal to London, where he enigmatically reported that Johnson received him "as kindly as he can receive anybody."[30]

What "might be published"?

Boswell was in London from 21 March through 18 April, then spent a few days with Paoli visiting the Earl of Pembroke at Wilton and a week with the Temples at Mamhead before returning for three final London weeks. As usual his days were busy. But he saw Johnson more frequently than during any previous London visit, especially in May. At the start, Boswell hoped to publish the first of a series of "travels with Johnson," and Johnson hoped to continue seeing what his biographer was writing about their current activities. Neither got what he wanted. When they parted at 2 A.M. on 22 May, Johnson had seen no new journal entries, and Boswell was carrying home those he had imagined publishing.[31]

Boswell reports just one conversation about his Hebrides journal. Riding in a coach from Johnson's to Sir Joshua Reynolds's on 27 March, Boswell mentioned Dilly's request for a book based on his journal, and Johnson told him to "draw out of it what [he] thought might be published," and Johnson would "look it over." In addition, Johnson asked Boswell "not to show the journal to anybody."

They might have discussed this project later, too, especially if they talked about the eleven pages of notes Boswell had written about the *Journey*. But no additional conversations are described. We can infer a great deal, however, concerning what each thought and felt about having something published, and some of what each assumed the other was thinking and feeling, from Boswell's account of what they said and did on 27 March. The significance of this project during the next eight weeks also seems evident in other transactions reported in Boswell's journal and letters and in Johnson's Holy Week diary and letters, including Johnson's seemingly not asking about Boswell's progress in selecting what "might be published," and Boswell's not showing Johnson any new entries.

Johnson had not seriously objected to anything in the Hebrides journal, which he assumed Boswell eventually would use in writing the *Life*. Nor had he asked to look over the biography Boswell would eventually publish, as Lord Kames had recently done when Boswell suggested writing *his* biography. But Johnson naturally wanted to control what would be published while he was alive from a text that included so much talk about living contemporaries, so many fantasies and confessions, so many potentially embarrassing scenes. Though he found it impossible simply to refuse Boswell's request, Johnson seems to have agreed reluctantly. At least Boswell sensed Johnson's unwillingness: "He did not seem desirous that my little bark should 'pursue the triumph and partake the gale,'" as he wrote in the entry for 27 March. If so, Johnson would hardly have been displeased when Boswell gave him nothing to look over. Nor would he have pressed him to revise—something Boswell later complained about to Temple.[32]

Boswell did not report directly expressing his feelings to Johnson. But he revealed some of his anger and frustration by defiantly sharing the journal with Reynolds immediately after Johnson asked him not to show it to anybody. He also read or showed the journal later to Langton and Oglethorpe, to Pembroke and Temple. However reasonable it was for Johnson to control what might soon be published from the text Bowell had earlier shared, Johnson could not legitimately prohibit Boswell from showing friends what Johnson had already been able to challenge and correct. Near the end of his visit, Boswell left his journal with Hester Thrale, too, hoping to encourage her to share Johnson's letters from Scotland, and also the text that Boswell had just heard about from Henry Thrale, a "book of Johnsoniana" in which "all Mr. Johnson's sayings and all that they can collect about him is put down."[33]

Meanwhile, on the night Johnson insisted on reviewing whatever Boswell wanted to print, Boswell got "as drunk as *muck*." The next night at the Thrales' house in Southwark, having noted that Johnson in the *Journey* had written that no man in the Hebrides "is so abstemious as to refuse the morning dram, which they call a *skalk*," Boswell declared that the morning drams Johnson had sternly warned him against on Coll helped him "get up in the morning when nothing else would." Four days later, he showed up drunk for his fourth meeting of the Club and made a "foolish attempt" to challenge Johnson about a benefit for the actress Frances Abington, which both had attended. Boswell had earlier thought Johnson "vain of a fine actress' solicitations," noting that "if she had not been a woman much in fashion, [Johnson] probably would have been less complying." Now he badgered Johnson for being too old to enjoy the performance:

> "Why, Sir, did you go to Mrs. Abington's benefit? Did you see?" JOHNSON. "No." BOSWELL. "Did you hear?" JOHNSON. "No." BOSWELL. "Why, then, did you go?" (roaring boisterously). JOHNSON. "Because she is a favourite of the public; and when the public cares the thousandth" (I think) "part about you that it does about her, I'll go to your benefit too."[34]

Boswell self-consciously highlighted his comic ineffectuality. But when he described this alcohol-fueled assault and his strenuous attacks on Johnson's positions during the following week, he did not reflect on the roots of his aggression. Similarly on Good Friday, when Johnson once again advised his friend to "keep a Journal fully and minutely," almost certainly hoping to see some of what Boswell had written since coming to London, Boswell did not remark on what had turned him against further sharing.[35]

Johnson, however, almost certainly realized why he was not seeing recent entries. He was posing for a portrait by Reynolds's sister Frances when Boswell read portions of the Hebrides journal to Sir Joshua, so may not have noticed Boswell's defiance right after being told not to share this journal. But it is hard to imagine that Johnson did not eventually hear Reynolds's opinion that Boswell's text was "more entertaining" than the *Journey*. Johnson seems not to have bristled at Boswell's aggression, however. When his intoxicated friend challenged him four days afterward, Johnson surely understood the frustration expressed in this attack. He was firm, but not inappropriately insulting. The next day, after reproving Boswell for showing up drunk, Johnson quickly shifted the topic. Soon they were playfully discussing what Johnson did with the orange peels he regularly pocketed, with Johnson emphasizing that only he could say for sure why he acted, but affirming his special attachment to Boswell.

> BOSWELL (laughing pretty heartily). "The world then must be left in the dark. 'He scraped them and let them dry, but what he did with them next, he never could be prevailed with to tell.'" JOHNSON. "Nay, Sir, you should say it more emphatically, — 'he could not be prevailed with even by his nearest'" (I think) "'friends to tell.'"

Later they quietly sat in Johnson's study, Johnson correcting sheets for Lord Hailes and Boswell writing his wife.[36]

In fact, throughout the visit, perhaps because he knew he was complicating, even thwarting, Boswell's plans to publish, perhaps because of what he had learned during the trip and while writing the *Journey,* Johnson was unusually genial and respectful. When Boswell challenged him in company, Johnson generally won, but without ad hominem insults or triumphant laughter. Also, after asking Boswell home following Good Friday evening services on 14 April, Johnson affirmed his biographer's special place in his life while also expressing a longing for something different from the vigorous, often combative talk for which Boswell's texts have since made him famous. Alluding to Boswell's hope to practice law in England, a venture Johnson had encouraged the same day he later asked to review whatever Boswell hoped to publish from his journal, Johnson declared: "If you come to settle here, we will have one day in the week on which we will meet by ourselves. That is the happiest conversation when there is no competition, no vanity, but a calm interchange of sentiments." Johnson also offered Boswell a room in his house for nights they stayed up late talking. On Easter, two days later, they comfortably collaborated in thinking about happiness. Johnson seconded Boswell's wish to have read more books, but he also praised his friend's "powers" of mind.[37]

Anticipating Johnson's Death

Meanwhile Boswell was trying without success to extract what might be published from his Hebrides journal, though no record survives of the process. "Mr Johnson has allowed me to write out a supplement to his Journey," Boswell wrote Temple on 4 April. So he could set aside Lord Hailes's objection to publication. But Johnson insisted on reviewing whatever Boswell selected, and Boswell had not been "able to settle to it." Trying to select material for Johnson's review while sensing Johnson's reluctance, Boswell was paralyzed. How would Johnson respond to episodes and conversations that challenged what he had presented in the *Journey?* Also, how could Boswell determine what to exclude, now that he had come to value what he called his "Flemish" style, which captured not just "the large features" but was "exact as to every hair, or even every spot on his countenance"?

Boswell had begun to experience the constraints of an eighteenth-century biographer. He knew, of course, that once Johnson died, he would be able to publish without getting approval. As he wrote Temple six months later, anything not published in the meantime would "be good materials for my *Life of Dr. Johnson.*" But if trying to revise his text for Johnson to "look . . . over" led Boswell to anticipate the time when he would be free to publish whatever he wished, the thought was hardly pleasant.[38]

In July 1774, when Boswell "thought of Mr. Samuel Johnson's death happening some time hence," his "mind was damped," though he comforted himself by reflecting "that worthy Langton and others, who were touched by that noble loadstone and whose souls would point to heaven like needles to the pole, would remain to console [him]." As he traveled toward London in March 1775, he imagined increasing his income by taking "a good employment abroad," but immediately realized he "could not give up being with Mr. Johnson on any account." Of course, Boswell had to survive Johnson in order to write the *Life*. But he had decided to become Johnson's biographer primarily to connect with him more fully. He found the thought of living in a world without Johnson deeply disturbing.[39]

A letter Boswell wrote on 22 April but did not post provides a glimpse of his frustration and anger, his anxiety and sadness, as he encountered Johnson's restrictions on the journal and realized how in time he would be free. Momentarily depressed at Wilton, despite the company of Paoli, the Earl of Pembroke, and others, and access to "the very walk where Sir Philip Sidney composed his *Arcadia,*" Boswell wrote the friend he had seen four days earlier and would soon see again. The first and last sentences of this short letter — "Every scene of my life confirms the truth of what you have told me, 'there is no certain happiness in this state of being'"; "In your *Vanity of Human Wishes,* and in Parnell's *Contentment,* I find the only sure means of enjoying happiness; or, at least, the hopes of happiness" — echo their talk on Good Friday evening. For Johnson, this recent conversation delayed the moment when he "look[ed] back upon resoluti[ons] of improvement and amendments, which have year after year been made and broken, either by negligence, forgetfulness, vicious idleness, casual interruptions, or morbid infirmity." But it had left Boswell "clouded and depressed," and seeking immediate relief in the presumably sexual "irregularity" he described in pages eventually removed from his journal. Eight days later, momentarily "weary and gloomy" during his "present absence" from Johnson, Boswell asked for "a few lines from you; a few lines merely of kindness, as a *viaticum* till I see you again." (Johnson's *Dictionary* defines "viaticum" as "provision for a journey" and "the last rites used to prepare the passing soul for its departure.")[40]

I suspect that after trying for several weeks to produce for Johnson's review a book based on his Hebrides journal, all the while realizing that he would have no constraints once Johnson had died, Boswell's "present absence" from Johnson suggested the permanent separation that would finally allow him to write the *Life* — an "absence" for which he felt radically unprepared. That Johnson's death was on Boswell's mind seems supported by his sending this letter two years later, accompanied by the letter he had written (but not posted) on 30 September 1764, the only early letter in which Boswell explicitly looked ahead to surviving Johnson. Boswell had then been away from Johnson for more than a year and had good reasons to feel cut off, having received no letter in more than nine months. But with his paper resting on Melanchthon's tomb, he looked ahead to Johnson's death, when he would endeavor "to do honour to [his] memory and, elevated by the remembrance of [him], persist in noble piety." In April 1775, Boswell was sure of Johnson's affectionate regard. In fact, he recalled Johnson's "cordiality" in promising weekly intimate conversations if Boswell moved to London. But he appreciated more feelingly than he had even a month earlier that Johnson would not always be available. About to travel to Temple's parsonage in Devonshire, where he would share his current journal and add to it, where he would show his Hebrides journal and try to revise it for Johnson's review, Boswell asked for a few kind words "as a *viaticum* till I see you again."[41]

For some reason, Boswell did not post this letter. Perhaps, as he claimed in June 1777, he feared "being reproved as indulging too much tenderness," or was guarding against disappointment if Johnson did not immediately reply. More likely, Boswell did not want to broach — even obliquely — the issue that seems to have underlain the letter. In 1777, recent experiences had made Boswell less uncomfortable imagining Johnson's death, but in April 1775, he preferred not to share his fearful anticipation of the long separation to come.

Also, Boswell was angry, as he continued to be when back in London. While at Mamhead on 23–30 April, he finally began reworking his journal, since on 10 May he wrote Temple that he had "not written another line," finding it "impossible to do" in London. Having recently heard Thomas Sheridan describe Johnson as "the vainest and the proudest man in the world," who "would have no other man praised but himself," Boswell now explicitly ascribed his paralysis to Johnson's envy: "Between ourselves, he is not apt to ⟨e⟩ncourage one to *share* reputation with himself." Just as Lord Auchinleck continued to block Boswell's moving to London, Johnson now thwarted his publishing the journal. So Boswell suggested to Temple an act of defiance that would surely have ended his friendship with Johnson: "I may write out my remarks in Scotland, and send them to be revised by you, and then they may be published freely." Boswell's bypassing Johnson altogether — though taken seriously by Temple, who was "afraid what to advise," and recalled six months later, when Boswell had fresh reasons for anger — was less a realistic plan than an indication of resentment at the constraints Boswell could escape only by losing Johnson.[42]

Meanwhile, Boswell and Johnson were often together. Johnson had planned to leave for Lichfield early in May, but Boswell asked him to delay while he was still in town, and Johnson complied. "Boswell would have thought my absence a loss," he explained to Hester Thrale, "and I know not who else would have considered my presence as profit." On both 6 and 8 May, Johnson dictated briefs, and on 12 May, two days after Boswell had defiantly imagined sending Temple what he hoped to publish from his journal, Boswell for the first time slept in the room Johnson set aside for him. (That May, as during his later London visits, Boswell stayed at Paoli's.) They saw each other on all but one of the next ten days, ending when they supped at Dilly's on Boswell's final night. Then they went to the inn where Boswell boarded the Newcastle Fly, carrying the letter he had not posted from Wilton and the journal he had recently retrieved from Hester Thrale and only now revealed he had shown her, leaving Johnson concerned about her reaction.[43]

For two years, each had played a larger than usual role in the life of the other. But what did they imagine would happen next — aside from Boswell's publishing in Edinburgh newspapers Johnson's apology for a mistake in the *Journey* concerning John MacLeod of Raasay, and Johnson's sending a chest of books from London bookstalls? Each time they had parted since Boswell's visit in the spring of 1772, when they formally began collaborating on the biography, they had anticipated reconnecting in three or four months: either to explore the Hebrides or to collaborate in describing that adventure. This time they would not be together for at least ten months, and they had no big project in mind. Boswell had just dined often enough at the Inner Temple to fulfill one term's residence, and both assumed he would do this two more times, qualifying him to practice law in England. But unless a patronage position provided additional income and Lord Auchinleck surprisingly acquiesced, this move would come only after Boswell inherited Auchinleck. When he announced having completed the *Journey,* Johnson had recalled their scheme of venturing to Sweden and Russia — "Shall we touch the continent?" But first he would accompany the Thrales and Baretti to Italy. Both friends assumed they would continue collaboratively documenting Johnson's past while producing and recording some of his fresh experiences. But neither was comfortable anticipating the moment when the *Life* could be written.[44]

They almost surely did not expect that within three years their friendship would be significantly modified. But Johnson had sensed the possibility for major enrichment on Good Friday, when confessional conversation with his biographer postponed his grim self-assessment. And Boswell, angry at not being able to publish his Hebrides book and anxious about living in a world without Johnson, felt that major changes were needed, without knowing how to produce them.

Renegotiating the Friendship,
Part 1 (1775–1777):
Depression, Defiance, and Dependency

When the two friends parted in the early hours of 22 May 1775, they had no idea that Boswell would soon experience the most intense and sustained depression since his marriage, or that in October he would become angrily (but secretly) defiant after learning Johnson had failed to report his trip to France. Nor did they anticipate that in April 1776, after Johnson had spent eleven days with his biographer narrating himself through the landscape of his youth, Boswell would edge toward open confrontation. Nor that in the summer Johnson would refuse to explain how David Hume could die peacefully, even cheerfully, while not believing in personal immortality, forcing Boswell to cope on his own with doubts that Johnson had formerly resolved. But by September 1777, when Johnson finally spoke about Hume and explained his own fear of death, Boswell had achieved sufficient autonomy openly to challenge Johnson's published arguments on America. Then by augmenting and modifying several of Johnson's positions in journal entries he did not share, Boswell prepared for when Johnson would no longer be there to ground his thinking and banish depression. By the spring of 1778 — after years of oscillating between neediness and defiance, years of oblique and direct negotiation and repositioning — Boswell finally managed to voice some of the anger and disappointment he had earlier communicated through his Hebrides journal. Their friendship had become significantly more balanced, helping make the

1778 London visit the best ever for both friends, their shared Good Friday the most richly satisfying. In May 1775, however, neither Johnson nor Boswell anticipated this transformation. Nor at the start did they deliberately seek the changes they together produced.

Melancholy and Defiance (Summer and Fall 1775)

Johnson wrote five days after seeing Boswell off, shortly before he himself left town. Two days after receiving this letter, Boswell reported that he had arranged for Johnson's correction to be published; and ten days later, he wrote that John MacLeod of Raasay was satisfied. Meanwhile, Boswell began to experience "a pretty severe return . . . of that melancholy or Hypochondria which is inherent in [his] constitution," but from which he had been "wonderfully free" in the previous six years. "I do not remember any portion of my existence flatter than these two months," he wrote after the Court of Session ended its summer term on 11 August. "While afflicted with melancholy, all the doubts which have ever disturbed thinking men, come upon me," he explained to Temple on 12 August. "I awake in the night dreading annihilation, or being thrown into some horrible state of being." Because Boswell kept no journal during this period, it is easy to imagine his experience as uniform. But there were probably variations, as there would be during later, more fully documented depressions.[1]

Boswell anticipated a grim summer as soon as he returned from London. "The unpleasing tone, the rude familiarity, [and] the barren conversation" of Edinburgh, so different from what he had just left in London, "really hurt [his] feelings," he wrote Temple early in June. Also, he approached "with aversion the dull labour of the court of Session," especially since moving to London seemed unlikely anytime soon. After he and Margaret dined with Lord Auchinleck on 17 June, Boswell described another source of depression: his father's general "dissatisfaction" with him, and his inability to assert himself in this relationship. It galled him that his father still held tight to the "renunciation of [his] birthright," which Boswell "*madly* granted to him, & which he has not the generosity to restore." In addition, no financial arrangements had been made for Margaret and his two daughters, should Boswell die and his younger brother David inherit Auchinleck.[2]

These features — "my father's coldness to me, the unsettled state of our family affairs, and the poor opinion which I had of the profession of a lawyer in Scotland, which consumed my life in the meantime" — collectively seem sufficient to account for the deep depression that lifted precisely when Lord Auchinleck left Edinburgh at the end of the session. But I suspect new aspects

of Boswell's relationship with Johnson contributed to its severity, just as anticipation of Johnson's arrival in 1773 had helped make that summer session
more bearable. I have in mind Boswell's disappointment at not being able to
publish his Hebrides journal, his mostly suppressed rage at what he saw as
Johnson's envious resistance, and his anxiety about how he would cope when
Johnson was no longer an energizing presence in his life. Certainly, Boswell's
depression heightened his need for Johnson's support. Having anticipated the
box of books that Johnson had promised in their "warmly affectionate" parting — "I am to read more & drink less," he explained to Temple as he traveled
home — Boswell felt neglected when nothing arrived and when Johnson then
failed to answer either the two letters sent to Lichfield early in June or his later
call for help. Meanwhile, Boswell had done his part. He was so "remarkably
busy" writing about sixty law papers that only Margaret and "worthy Grange
had the least notion of [his] being at all uneasy"; and he lapsed only once from
his solemn vow at Temple's to drink moderately.[3]

Later, Boswell wondered that he had not sent Temple a few lines, "merely as
firing guns of distress." But on 26 July, he wrote Johnson from within a depressive episode for the first time since Utrecht. He wrote again four weeks later,
lamenting the lack of his friend's "warming and vivifying rays" and reporting a
coming visit with his father. In at least one of these letters, Boswell also worried that Johnson had ceased to care.[4]

Johnson, having not replied to the letters he received in Lichfield, though on
19 June he wrote Hester Thrale that Boswell "is a very fine fellow," found two
additional letters when he returned home in August. His response to Boswell's
depression was supportive. In the second paragraph, he offered his usual rec-
ommendations: "honest business or innocent pleasure," and varied reading.
At the start, Johnson also modeled how to overcome their shared tendency to
discontent: "I was glad to go abroad, and, perhaps, glad to come home; which
is, in other words, I was, I am afraid, weary of being at home, and weary of
being abroad. Is not this the state of life? But, if we confess this weariness, let
us not lament it; for all the wise, and all the good say, that we may cure it."
Later in this friendly letter, Johnson finally thanked Boswell for his help concerning Raasay, and reported that Hester Thrale had "almost read herself
blind" over Boswell's journal. Then, in closing, Johnson reaffirmed his deep
feelings and high regard for Boswell: "You may settle yourself in full confidence both of my love and my esteem; I love you as a kind man, I value you as a
worthy man, and hope in time to reverence you as a man of exemplary piety. I
hold you as Hamlet has it, 'in my heart of heart.'"[5]

Three days later, Johnson returned three parcels containing Lord Hailes's
text, with a note asking to hear from Boswell: "Write to me soon, and write

often, and tell me all your honest heart." He wrote again two weeks later, responding — with comments not printed in the *Life* — to whatever Boswell had written after returning from Auchinleck, and reaffirming that his regard for Boswell was "so radicated and fixed that it is become part of [his] mind, and cannot be effaced but by some cause uncommonly violent." But Johnson prefaced this declaration by dismissing, as unmanly "freaks and humours," Boswell's fancying himself "neglected" whenever Johnson failed to respond to his letters. (In the *Life of Pope*, Johnson would refer to discord produced by "the freaks, and humours, and spleen, and vanity of women.") By adding that he would "not very soon write again," since he was "to set out to morrow on another journey," Johnson prepared Boswell for what might otherwise seem like neglect. But by saying nothing more, Johnson ensured that his friend would feel toyed with once he learned that this "journey" would be to France.[6]

On 24 October, when Boswell received a letter from Langton congratulating him on the birth of a son, Alexander, and mentioning "the Excursion to Paris with Mr. and Mrs. Thrale that our venerable Friend has been engaged in," Boswell immediately replied that Johnson had "very kindly" warned him "he was going to set out '*on another Journey*' but not a word did he say of a French expedition." Boswell wrote Johnson, too, since Langton assumed that "Mr. Thrale's duty in Parliament" would have called him home. At the same time, Boswell began fulfilling the resolution he had made two weeks earlier, at the birth of his first son, "to keep a journal of my life every day from this important era in my family."[7]

Boswell did not describe how he felt on learning he had not been told about Johnson's first trip abroad. But defiance of Johnson over America, the Hebrides journal, and Hume expressed some of his anger. Boswell also reported drinking and sexual indulgence, compulsive gambling and acts of violence — defiant gestures directed at Margaret and Lord Auchinleck, but also at Johnson.[8]

Though in January 1775 Boswell had imagined Johnson instructing him what to think about the conflict with America, he took the side of the son in what he pictured as a father-son conflict. Two months later, in an essay on "the American tea war," he anonymously published his "doubts about American Measures" and his "sincere Satisfaction that our Rulers are now disposed to be more calm and gentle." By August, he was "growing more & more an American": "I see the unreasonableness of taxing them without the consent of their Assemblies. I think our ministry are mad in undertaking this desperate war." Dining with guests four days after hearing about Johnson's trip to France, Boswell expressed anger at having been kept in the dark by warmly defending the colonists, "*notwithstanding Dr. Johnson's eloquence.*"[9]

Writing to Temple nine days later, Boswell imagined expanding his defiance.

After mentioning Johnson's trip to France and suggesting that he and Temple travel together to Europe, Boswell complained, "Dr. Johnson has said nothing to me of my *Remarks* during my journey with him, which I wish to write," and revived his plan of sending his text to Temple for review. He imagined posting weekly installments, suggesting this was a concrete proposal. But he immediately added that these remarks, if not published now, would be "good materials" for the *Life*; and Boswell never moved further with a scheme that surely would have ended his friendship with Johnson.[10]

Meanwhile, Boswell flirted in two ways with deepening his cordial relationship with David Hume, the only Scottish intellectual Johnson had made sure not to meet while in Edinburgh. A week after writing Temple about the Hebrides text, Boswell had the "strange thought" of talking to Hume about living without religious belief: "At present I [am] happy in having pious faith. But in case of its failing me by some unexpected revolution in my mind, it would be humane in him to furnish me with reflections by which a man of sense and feeling could support his spirit as an infidel." In other words, he imagined a mental "revolution" that would cut him off from the man who for twelve years had confirmed his Christian faith and who two months earlier had hoped "in time to reverence [him] as a man of exemplary piety." Five weeks later, having for days been "quite a sensualist, quite a being for the immediate time, without thought of future existence," and after reassuring himself "that eternity of punishment *could not be*, according to my notions of the Divinity" — a statement he later guiltily inked over — Boswell had "really a good chat" with Hume over a bottle of port and found "the Great Infidel" to be "such a civil, sensible, comfortable looking man" that he thought of writing his life.[11]

Boswell's entry for the next day (18 December) suggests that he saw this thought, and also his having supported the colonists at dinner seven weeks earlier, as affronts to Johnson and irrationally worried about his friend's reaction. "Uneasy" at not having heard from Johnson "for a long time," Boswell "feared that he was ill or had perhaps heard" of Boswell's "defending the Americans and was angry" with him. But Boswell had received a letter from Johnson just twenty-three days earlier, a letter he had waited ten days before answering. So there was no good reason to worry that Johnson had not immediately replied to what probably reached him only nine days before. This was hardly "a long time." Nor was it likely that Johnson, who was so quick to resent direct attacks, would put off writing because he had somehow heard that Boswell had defended the American colonists at his dinner table. Boswell's unrealistic worry shows how timid he was about defying Johnson — at least when not drunk. But the timing of this worry suggests that Boswell was chiefly anxious about his warm connection with Hume.[12]

In the *Life*, Boswell printed just two sentences from his anxious letter: one worrying that Johnson was ill, the other reporting his fear of rejection: "Sometimes my imagination which is upon occasions prolifick of evil hath figured that you may have some how taken offence at some part of my conduct." Concerned for Boswell's peace of mind, Johnson replied immediately, reporting that his health remained good, but first dismissing the possibility of "offence": "Never dream of any offence, how should you offend me? I consider your friendship as a possession, which I intend to hold till you take it from me, and to lament if ever by my fault I should lose it." Puzzled by his friend's worry, especially since Boswell seems not to have confessed any specific offenses, Johnson urged him to "hinder," if possible, the "first ingress" of any "morbid" fears. But instead of dismissing these as "freaks and humours," Johnson encouraged Boswell always to express any suspicions that "find their way into [his] mind," promising that he would then "make haste to disperse them."[13]

When Boswell got this "kind letter" late on 27 December, his need for Johnson's advice and support far outweighed any resentment. For after an "abominable altercation" with Lord Auchinleck, Boswell was more anxious about his inheritance than at any time since learning that his father planned to remarry.

Entailing Auchinleck (November 1775 to March 1776)

In November 1775, Boswell's relations with his father had become unusually good, despite Lord Auchinleck's having unexpectedly opposed the candidate his heir supported in the 1774 Ayrshire election, and despite Pringle's sense that his close friend would never approve Boswell's move to London. Initially "very guarded" at the birth of his first grandson, who had been given his name, Alexander, Lord Auchinleck four days later took Margaret "kindly by the hand, as if by stealth, and said, 'God bless you all.'" Eight days later, he agreed to pay off Boswell's debt (£1,245) on Dalblair, the small estate purchased in 1767. A week later, when they had "a quiet, comfortable chat together," Boswell felt "a real happiness in being well with him."[14]

But on the same day he promised to cover Boswell's debt (18 November), Lord Auchinleck announced that he had composed an entail, stipulating that the family estate would be inherited by "heirs whatsoever of his own body," including Boswell's daughters. Boswell, however, had long maintained that since the fifth laird had passed over his own four daughters to leave Auchinleck to a nephew, the estate should go only to male heirs—a position he felt Johnson supported. Since Boswell, as heir, needed to approve the entail before it could take effect, his father stipulated that if Boswell did not agree, he would forfeit the right to inherit the substantial properties Lord Auchinleck had added to the estate. Boswell calmly decided to accept a reduced inheritance "rather than let a female and her race by a stranger cut out the *sons of the Family*." Margaret complained violently that Boswell "would not only disinherit [his] own daughters, but deprive [his] own son of part of his inheritance." But Boswell felt the "principle" of male inheritance was not to be abandoned for any "bribe": "The idea of the Old Castle of Auchinleck going to a female in exclusion of *Boswells* was horrid."[15]

On 27 December, Lord Auchinleck reported that in deference to his son's strong feelings, he had modified the entail so that the estate would go to males descending from his own father, and to females only when no male heir was available. If Boswell refused to agree, however, his father would reduce his annual allowance from £300 to £100, and would not pay the debt due on Dalblair. Also, if Boswell attempted to challenge this entail, Lord Auchinleck threatened to sell the estate "and do with the money" what he pleased.

Boswell reported calmly expressing surprise at "such usage" after years of "pursu[ing] the very plan of life which [his father] was anxious" Boswell should follow, "though it was disagreeable"; and he condemned his father as "unjust and tyrannical." But Lord Auchinleck — like Margaret and others — was appalled that Boswell would insist on having his own children disinherited, and concluded he "had not natural affection."[16]

Boswell immediately got "very drunk," and at Grange's two days later made a "wild speech" concerning his father, which he recalled with regret six weeks later after dreaming his father had died. Then, on 31 December, when he attentively reread his grandfather's account of the family, he realized that what his great-grandfather had inherited from the laird who had passed over his four daughters was "little better than a bankrupt estate." Any precedent based on this action, therefore, applied to little of what was now Auchinleck. So Boswell saw — as in "a blaze of light" — that he had erred in thinking he was obliged "in *justice* to give the succession all along to heirs male." He was free to yield to his father's wishes.

Boswell feared he might simply be capitulating to Lord Auchinleck's threats, however. So on 2 January, he wrote Johnson "a long, serious, and earnest letter," laying out his "discovery," and two days later added a substantial postscript. Margaret, besides copying this twelve-page letter, wrote one of her own, urging Johnson to convince her husband to agree with his father.[17]

These letters initiated a steady exchange. Having already written just before receiving Boswell's long letter, which "much impressed" him, Johnson promised to do what he could with this question and recommended that Boswell also consult Lord Hailes, who was "both a Christian and a Lawyer" and would "not think the time lost in which he may quiet a disturbed, or settle a wavering mind." Then Johnson wrote four times in February and twice early in March; Boswell followed his initial letter with five others. Never before had their conversation in letters been so sustained and rich. Moreover, there seem to have been no insults or teases, no anger or guilt, but generous concern and constructive helpfulness from Johnson, earnest appeals and eventually some manipulation from Boswell. Also, as Boswell waited for Johnson's initial response, he began rereading the *Rambler,* wondering at "how long it was since [he] had read any of Dr. Johnson's works, though they are the food of [his] soul."[18]

At first, Johnson wondered whether he was "quite equal" to the task. But early in February, he embraced the challenge of delving to moral and legal bedrock. In addition to resolving "this troublesome and vexatious question" for the man he had just called his "dearest friend," Johnson hoped to gain "some ground" with Margaret. ("I know that she does not love me," he had written in November, "but I intend to persist in wishing her well till I get the better of her.") Early in February, Johnson thought through the issue at length, pushing beyond what either Boswell or his father took for granted in order to argue against any attempt to restrict inheritance, since "he who receives a fief unlimited by his ancestors, gives his heirs some reason to complain if he does not transmit it unlimited to posterity." Being fully engaged, Johnson added to these first thoughts in two additional letters, including in the second a response to what Lord Hailes had meanwhile written.[19]

Once he received this evidence of Johnson's grounding intellect and active helpfulness, Boswell became self-consciously manipulative. He decided to delay telling Lord Auchinleck that he no longer objected to the entail until after he returned from London, hoping his compliance then would help offset his father's anticipated displeasure at the trip. But Boswell told Johnson that he delayed because "it is better not to act too suddenly," and got an endorsement for "deliberation." When Johnson "hurt [Boswell] somewhat" by discouraging a London visit, perhaps because Margaret strongly opposed it, Boswell persisted. He justified the trip to himself—and perhaps to Johnson—by claiming he "could not resolve to come to a final agreement" with his father till he "had heard Dr. Johnson upon particulars." But he also complained to Johnson that grim and seemingly unpredictable depression had once again seized him, robbing his soul of all "vigour of piety," and he appealed to Johnson's "kindness," informed by his own "experience of dejection of mind."

Boswell's "dark gloom of melancholy" lifted two days after he wrote these words. Four days later, as Johnson's reply was on its way, Boswell responded to a display of weakness by his father—his speaking against a position in court but then voting for it—by revealing that he no longer objected to the entail;

and the next day he and Lord Auchinleck comfortably settled their "affairs." So by the time Boswell read Johnson's letter, the arguments that had convinced his friend to endorse what both knew would distress Margaret were no longer valid.

"Very sorry" that Boswell's melancholy had returned, and "sorry likewise if it could have no relief but from my company," Johnson offered time together before he left for Italy: "If you will come, you must come very quickly, and even then I know not but we may scour the country together, for I have a mind to see Oxford and Lichfield before I set out on this long journey." Boswell replied at once, "begging" Johnson not to leave town before he arrived. He lacked the "resolution," however, to counter his father's objections to an "idle and expensive" trip, so asked his stepmother to prepare Lord Auchinleck by explaining his "reasons." Then, instead of returning to speak with his father, Boswell got drunk, sent a note saying he "had had a return of melancholy and required relaxation," and was off to London, where Lord Auchinleck's angry report prompted Pringle to insist that Boswell write a proper apology.[20]

London, the Midlands, and Bath (15 March through 16 May 1776)

Boswell's goals for the visit included pressing Lord Mountstuart for a sinecure, as he did at dinner on his second full day in the city and repeatedly afterward, saying eventually: "I am indifferent as to how small an office it is, if you get me an independency from my father." (Johnson noted that "£200 a year would be of more advantage . . . now than much more some years hence.") But mainly Boswell wanted to connect with Johnson, with whom he spent much of 16 March, a bit of 18 March, then most of the next ten days. Having twice in the past ten months suffered deep, persistent depression, he wanted bracing advice and encouragement. But he seemed eager to express some of his anger, too, and assert his independence.[21]

Johnson hoped to resolve his friend's remaining doubts before the long-planned journey to Italy, for which the trip to France had been both prelude and preparation. He also probably anticipated recalling key moments from his early life while traveling with his biographer. Perhaps, too, he would see some of Boswell's journal. Then, when the trip to Italy was postponed following the sudden death of young Harry Thrale, Hester and Henry's only son (their younger son, Ralph, having died the previous July), Johnson continued to make time for Boswell: seeing him in London on nine of the sixteen days from 30 March through 14 April, on five or six days in Bath and Bristol at the end of April, and in London on ten of the twelve days from 5 through 16 May. But

Johnson at times grew angry at Boswell's biographical questions, was troubled by his wild behavior, and at the end was more apprehensive than ever before.

Though Boswell's depression had ended two weeks before he reached London, Johnson's talk completed the cure. When Boswell reached the Thrales' house in Southwark on the morning of 16 March, "Johnson was in full glow of conversation," and even before he affectionately greeted his newly arrived friend, Boswell "was elevated as if brought into another state of being." "This is *Hermippus Redivivus*," Boswell told Hester Thrale, alluding to a book he had discussed with Johnson in 1763, which argued that a man's life could be prolonged by the breath of young women: "I am quite restored by him, by transfusion of mind." (This was also a moment of unprecedented harmony with Hester Thrale, and at this point in the *Life*, Boswell has her say, "There are many who admire and respect Mr. Johnson; but you and I *love* him.")

Boswell also helped enliven Johnson. In conversations that began at Southwark, continued on their way back to the City, and concluded at the end of the day when Boswell came to the house in Bolt Court to which Johnson had just moved, Johnson spoke decisively about all the topics Boswell introduced, including the trip to France. He also confirmed that Boswell would accompany him on a "jaunt" through the Midlands.[22]

An (Auto)biographical Jaunt

On 19 March, the two experienced traveling companions set out for Oxford, Birmingham, and Lichfield, with Johnson guiding his biographer through these haunts of his early years, determining where they would go and how long they would stay, and introducing Boswell to many longtime friends, including William Adams, Edmund Hector, and John Taylor, and to his stepdaughter, Lucy Porter. On 22 March, Boswell wanted to stay the night in Birmingham, but Johnson insisted on reaching Lichfield, where the next day he had David Garrick's brother, Peter, give Boswell a tour of the city while he waited on Elizabeth Aston.[23]

For Johnson, the "jaunt" was a sustained exercise in autobiographical memory, prompted by the places and people they encountered, but now partly shared with his biographer. As they came to Oxford, Johnson described not attending his tutor, William Jorden, after the first day and telling him with "nonchalance" that he had been "sliding upon the ice in Christ-Church meadow," not realizing this was "irreverent." In the common room at Pembroke, he later remembered playing "at draughts" there with Philip Jones, who "loved beer & did not get much forward in the Church," and John Fludyer, who "turned out a scoundrel, a Whig and said he was ashamed of having been bred at Oxford." As they entered Birmingham two days later, Johnson told Boswell what he had told Hester Thrale

when they stopped there two years earlier: that Edmund Hector's sister, Mrs. Carless, was the first woman with whom he was in love. The presence of a company of players in Lichfield the next day reminded Johnson that forty years earlier "he had been in love with . . . Mrs. Emmet, who acted Flora in *Hob in the Well,*" an adaptation of a play by Colley Cibber.[24]

Johnson undoubtedly remembered anecdotes like these whenever he visited these familiar places, anecdotes different from those he regularly told to affirm his cleverness, good sense, and uncommon speed as a writer. But now he was spontaneously sharing more of these than at any earlier time, getting parts of his history on record while reaffirming his ability to remember. As usual, however, he decided what to reveal and what to keep secret. When Boswell at Lichfield said he was "now quite easy" with Johnson and would "have no difficulty to tell him of any folly" that he had committed, Johnson cautioned against too much openness: "A man . . . should never tell tales of himself." When he answered Boswell's questions, confirmed or corrected stories Boswell heard from others, or spontaneously shared information about his past, Johnson presumably exercised restraint, telling only some of what he remembered, revealing part but not all of what he thought and felt. He seems never to have confessed his religious doubts and "vain scruples," for instance; and he revealed only obliquely his fear of insanity—the "secret far dearer to him than his Life" that he had entrusted to Hester Thrale several years earlier.[25]

And for the first time, Johnson bristled at Boswell's inquiries. Before breakfast on their third day in Lichfield, he rebuked him "smartly" for "pressing [him] closely" with biographical questions, insisting "that questioning was not the conversation among gentlemen; that it was assuming a superiority; that a man might not wish to have parts of his former life brought under his view." Perhaps Boswell had asked about Johnson's teaching school at Market Bosworth, having not yet heard—as he soon would from both Lucy Porter and John Taylor—that Johnson did not like recalling that "very unhappy" period of his life. (The day before, Johnson had been "shocked" when Boswell asked Peter Garrick whether his brother, David, "was not bred to the wine trade.") Also, though Boswell usually regarded Johnson as the final authority on anecdotes he heard from others, Johnson initially could not convince his biographer that his father had written the epitaph for the duckling Johnson had stepped on as a toddler. For Lucy Porter reported having heard Johnson's mother claim that her precocious son had composed it.[26]

Boswell also continued to remind a somewhat resistant Johnson of his obligations. The previous year, when Boswell tried to refute Beauclerk's claim that "Johnson did not practice religion" by arranging for tea on Sunday, 2 April, to be served early so Johnson could attend afternoon services, Johnson had declared, "I shall not go to church this afternoon, and I'm in no haste for tea." Now when Boswell told Dr. Nathan Wetherell, the master of University College, that Johnson had never written in direct support of the British Constitution or Christianity and insisted "there was a claim upon him," Johnson asked, "Why should *I* be always writing?" But Johnson had shared his wish more frequently to attend public worship and had promised at Aberdeen to expressly support Christianity. The biographical project gave Boswell leverage.[27]

Boswell's power to enforce Johnson's resolutions was enhanced by his still not sharing his journal, as he had done when they last traveled together. Two years later, Johnson would write Hester Thrale from Ashbourne that Boswell "kept his journal very diligently," adding, "I should be glad to see what he says of ⟨the Duchess⟩ of Argyle." So it is easy to imagine him wanting to see what Boswell frequently snatched time to write as they traveled. But Johnson remained as ignorant of how his biographer was describing what he now did and said as he was of how God would assess this portion of his life. (As he steadily fell behind while writing his detailed entries, Boswell memorably reflected, "I should live no more than I can record, as one should not have more corn growing than one can get it. There is a waste of good, if it be not preserved.")[28]

"A Course of Concubinage"

While his unshared journal gave Boswell power he was not aware of, his recent bouts of depression left him needing support. Unable to predict when he would be in "a troubled, fretful state," or to explain how he was suddenly relieved, and fearing what he might do "in some sudden rage," Boswell turned to the man whose *Rambler* had been so helpful in Utrecht. Three times during their jaunt — on one of the first nights, early on the fourth day, and as they returned to town seven days later — Johnson earnestly advised Boswell on managing his mind. In reporting the first of these conversations, Boswell wrote he was "prepared by [his] revered friend for conducting [himself] through any future gloom." But after declaring that he "treasured up" Johnson's "sage counsel," Boswell left blank the first thing Johnson had urged him to "remember always." By the time he wrote this entry, fourteen days later, he had entirely forgotten. But Boswell remembered his puzzlement that Johnson did not call for resolute battle against depressing thoughts, the message he had earlier drawn from the *Rambler*. Instead, Johnson was "shocked" at Boswell's notion of "thinking down" melancholy. If this showed "spirit and resolution," as Boswell thought, it was "the spirit and resolution of a madman." Someone with "a very ticklish mind" — like Boswell or Johnson — must "divert distressing thoughts, and not combat with them." Johnson therefore urged his friend to "contrive to have as many retreats" for his mind as he could, "as many things to which it can fly from itself."[29]

So Boswell adjusted his assumptions. If Johnson would not rally him to battle against melancholy, perhaps he would license what Boswell often did for relief. When Johnson remarked that Richard Steele "practiced the *lighter* vices," Boswell "catched at this saying as a kind of indulgence to licentiousness in women and wine." (Boswell's recent "visits to an amorous lady in London gave [him] an interest in desiring such an indulgence.") And when Johnson two days later asked Boswell to "take a course of chemistry, or a course of rope-dancing, or a course of anything" to which he was "inclined at the time," Boswell "*thought* of a course of concubinage, but was afraid to mention it." The previous spring as he had traveled to London, Boswell had tested Temple's reaction to the notion that casual sexual relationships were permitted a man whose appetite was strong and whose wife was "averse to hymeneal rites," at least if she agreed that her husband could "go to whom [he] pleased." Now he imagined that Johnson might see depression as an excuse for sex. "I *must* venture to consult Dr. Johnson upon it," he added on 4 April, as he wrote the entry for 22 March, "for he can, by his noble counsel, make my judgement clear and my resolution vigorous."[30]

On 23 March, Boswell had edged toward doing this when he described how his uncle, whom Johnson had met in 1763, went to bawdy houses and talked "as if the Christian religion had not prescribed any fixed rule for intercourse between the sexes." Though "humbled" when Johnson said, "Sir, there is no trusting to that crazy piety," Boswell later that day warmly kissed the "beautiful, gentle, sweet maid" who showed him through the house where Johnson had been born. Six days later in the post chaise to London, when Johnson urged diverting melancholy "by every means but drinking," Boswell again thought of women. He assumed Johnson "no more thought of [his] indulging in licentious copulation than of [his] stealing." But he hoped for leniency from the man who three years earlier had revealed often fantasizing about keeping a seraglio, who at some point had told David Garrick that "the greatest pleasure" in life was "fucking," and who at Lichfield had just denied that "more evil than good" was produced by the sexual appetite. Instead of speaking up, however, Boswell in London engaged in what William Ober calls "a compulsively riotous outburst of sexual activity," drinking and whoring to excess. By the time he did broach this subject, ten days later, Boswell was about to begin treatment for his first case of gonorrhea since his marriage.[31]

After leaving Johnson on 29 March, Boswell got drunk at dinner, discovered that the lady with whom he had lately twice renewed an "amorous" connection was out, and went "in a kind of brutal fever" to St. James's Park, where he was "relieved by dalliance," as he was again after supper. Then he "was picked up by a strumpet," and in "drunken venturousness" lay with her—an act he repeated on each of the next three days. This risky behavior was unusual, and seems hard to explain. Between March 1760 and May 1769, Boswell had had at least ten bouts of gonorrhea. But since then, though he occasionally "toyed" with prostitutes, he always stopped short of intercourse. The previous April, for instance, he had met "a beautiful Devonshire wench" in the Strand, "was lasciviously fond of her," and "dallied for a while." But he "was restrained from completion by other considerations than religion," as he was again the next day. Now, however, having already defied his wife by coming to London, and his father by leaving without any conversation, he secretly defied both again, and also Johnson, whom he saw only once — briefly — in the four days between 29 March and 3 April.[32]

Boswell's language — "I was in a kind of brutal fever" (29 March); "the whoring rage came upon me" (31 March); "this fit of debauchery" (1 April) — suggests loss of control. Intoxication accounted for his initial "venturesome-ness" and fueled his "whoring rage" two days later. But Boswell seems to have been sober when he risked venereal infection with "a pretty, fresh-looking girl" on 30 March, and also two days later. Boswell later explained that his "moral principle as to chastity was absolutely eclipsed for a time," distinguish-ing his state of mind when he and Johnson returned to London from what he thought and felt on 9 April, when he wrote these entries: "I thought of my valuable spouse with the highest regard and warmest affection, but had a confused notion that my corporeal connexion with whores did not interfere with my love for her," even though he knew any injury to his health would affect her. The ferocity of the "fever" or "rage" astonished him: "This is an exact state of my mind at the time. It shocks me to review it." Boswell's mind was changed partly by the infection, which he began to suspect on 3 April, but mainly by Johnson's reaction when he finally spoke out.

After posing hypothetical questions about fornication and adultery on both Good Friday (5 April) and Easter (7 April), Boswell soon afterward said some-thing that outraged Johnson, prompting Boswell to write a letter defending himself, as he had in 1769 after pressing a troubled and eventually angry Johnson to explain his fear of death. When Boswell next saw Johnson, on 10 April, he initially "had an awful timidity lest he should be so much offended . . . as to treat me with distant coldness," and was delighted to be greeted as usual. The entries for 8 and 9 April, and perhaps the end of the entry for 7 Ap-ril, have been removed, so we cannot read what Boswell and Johnson said. Based on all the entries written that spring, especially those for 26 March through 3 April, which Boswell wrote on 9 April, and on Boswell's worry when he saw Johnson on 10 April, I suspect that he finally acknowledged thinking that amorous indulgences were minor offenses for someone in his circumstances, and perhaps confessed to having recently acted on the idea, and that Johnson was outraged. Boswell's reaction to the "severity" of Johnson's response to whatever he had said is evident when he reported being "shock[ed]" at having so recently imagined that intercourse with whores did not affect his love for Margaret, even though he knew this "might injure [his] health, which . . . was an injury to her," and called his mind "wild" in condoning "casual intercourse" with an amorous "lady," even when there was no risk of infection.[33]

Already on 10 April, however, Boswell had begun "again to imagine that irregularity of commerce between the sexes was a trivial offence." He continued to visit Margaret Stuart, the wife of Lord Mountstuart's brother and Margaret Boswell's good friend, and he flirted passionately with Lady Jean Eglinton, "la bella Contessa." Also, on 22 April, shortly before he joined Johnson at Bath, Boswell made the first of four visits to the notorious Margaret Caroline Rudd, who had recently been acquitted of forgery; he discovered why she was "reckoned quite a sorceress, possessed of enchantment," and concluded the evening with a kiss, after which he wondered "what she thought of" him. Boswell was proud of these elegant flirtations, which worried his friend Temple. But on 9 May, when Johnson warmly welcomed him to a bedroom in his house, Boswell thought it "not right to think of the Contessa" while sleeping "under the roof of the Rambler."[34]

Johnson, however, generally applauded Boswell's high spirits and exuberance. When he eventually heard a lady censure Boswell's visits to Margaret Caroline Rudd, he declared, "I envy him his acquaintance with Mrs. Rudd." On 15 May, when Boswell deceptively maneuvered his friend into dining at Dilly's with his longtime adversary, John Wilkes, Johnson bonded with Wilkes by telling how he had improved Boswell: "I turned him loose at Lichfield, my native city, that he might for once see real civility. For you know he lives among savages at home, and among rakes in London." Johnson lived more zestfully through Boswell than through most of his other young friends. "Boswel goes away on Thursday, very well satisfied with his journey," he wrote Hester Thrale a day before the dinner at Dilly's. "Several great men have promised to obtain him a place, and then a fig for *my father,* and his new wife" (emphasis added). Even when most critical, Johnson strongly identified with his young friend.[35]

But because of what had happened right after the March jaunt, Johnson at the end of Boswell's visit was also worried, especially about his friend's drinking. Two months earlier, he had said "he had no objection to a man's drinking wine if he could do it in moderation," while again explaining how his own tendency "to go to excess" had led him to stop altogether. But after hearing from Henry Thrale that Boswell had reported getting drunk on twelve of his first fifteen days in London, and from Paoli how he had made Boswell promise on 9 April to drink only water—a promise Boswell kept through 11 May, and modified only with Paoli's and Johnson's approval—Johnson now insisted on total abstinence: "Every man is to take existence on the terms on which it is given to him. Yours is given to you on condition of your not using liberties which other people may." To enforce this advice, Johnson added, "You may when drunk do what you deserve to be hanged for next day."[36]

Johnson also tried to distance himself from Boswell. At breakfast on 13 May, he stopped Boswell from asking Levet questions about Johnson's life, declaring —memorably but inaccurately—"You have but two topicks, yourself and me, and I'm sick of both." In parting three days later, Johnson exhorted Boswell, "Don't talk of yourself or of me. . . . Don't make yourself and me a proverb." After seeing Boswell off, he reported to Margaret that her husband "has led a wild life": "I have taken him to Lichfield, and he has followed Mr. Thrale to Bath. Pray take care of him, and tame him." Two days later, he wrote Hester Thrale what he had not told Margaret about Boswell's final day: "He paid another visit, I think, to Mrs. Rudd, before he went home to his own deary." Then he added, "He carries with him two or three good resolutions. I hope they do not mould upon the road."

Three days later, Johnson confessed having neither "practiced nor recollected" his own Easter resolutions. But he now fulfilled his year-old promise to send Boswell books. When Johnson then heard nothing from Boswell, he worried, as Hester Thrale reported when she wrote Boswell five weeks after he left.[37]

The Return of Melancholy, Hume's Troublingly Cheerful Death (June to August 1776)

It is not clear how Boswell felt about Johnson's stern parting advice. But soon after returning home, he again became deeply depressed. He was "not at all well" when the court session began on 12 June, finding everything "indifferent, or rather irksome." On 25 June, when he finally wrote Johnson that he was "afflicted with melancholy," he surely expected his friend to sympathize, as he had done in March and also the previous August. Perhaps, too, Johnson's response would revive him. When Johnson told him on 10 April that the trip to Italy had been postponed, Boswell had marveled at his "manly calmness in a situation in which *I* should have been very peevish, or at least discontented," adding, "All evils lose their force in your presence." Surely a letter from Johnson would help.[38]

Instead of sympathy and bracing advice, however, Johnson sent what Boswell later described as "a good deal of severity and reproof, as if [his depression] were owing to [his] own fault, or that [he] was, perhaps, affecting it from a desire of distinction." (Five months earlier, Boswell had, in fact, "felt a kind of pride in being melancholy and fretful like [his] grandfather," whose failing he saw as ennobling.) Johnson's conversation always lifted Boswell's spirits, so he had never seen his friend deeply depressed, and what Boswell later decided to print from this letter was petulant. Johnson complained of Boswell's "very long delay" in writing and worried that reading George Cheyne's *English Malady* (as Johnson had recommended) might reinforce the "foolish notion that melancholy is a proof of acuteness." He also found Boswell's report that he had not even opened the boxes of books "very offensive": "I am, I confess, very angry that you manage yourself so ill."[39]

Boswell was surprised by Johnson's tone. He knew that Johnson, too, was prone to "constitutional melancholy," and eight weeks earlier he had secretly read the diary in which Johnson on Easter reported having at times been "almost compelled" to "general sluggishness" by "morbid melancholy and disturbance of mind." Johnson's rebuke was especially disappointing because Boswell read it right after his unsettling deathbed interview with Hume.

Eight months earlier, soon after discovering that Johnson had gone to France without telling him, Boswell had defiantly imagined asking Hume how he might maintain his spirits were he no longer to believe in personal immortality. But witnessing Hume's cheerful acceptance that he would soon cease to exist — hearing him insist that "the thought of annihilation" gave him "not the least" pain — Boswell recoiled: "I . . . felt a degree of horror, mixed with a sort of wild, strange, hurrying recollection of my excellent mother's pious instructions, of Dr. Johnson's noble lessons, and of my religious sentiments and affections during the course of my life. I was like a man in sudden danger eagerly seeking his defensive arms; and I could not but be assailed by momentary doubts while I had actually before me a man of such strong abilities and extensive inquiry dying in the persuasion of being annihilated." Then, once home, Boswell got Johnson's letter of chastisement.[40]

Four days later, Boswell happily received a more sympathetic letter, in which Johnson wrote that if Boswell were "really oppressed with overpowering and involuntary melancholy, [he was] to be pitied rather than reproached." Boswell cut whatever came next, but not Johnson's attempt to jolly him into activity: "Now, my dear Bozzy, let us have done with quarrels and with censure. Let me know whether I have not sent you a pretty library. There are, perhaps, many books among them which you need never read through; but there are none which it is not proper for you to know, and sometimes to consult." Then Johnson shifted to other matters, especially the brief Boswell had sent supporting Joseph Knight, a slave who was petitioning for freedom after being brought to

Scotland. He also reported having been painfully "seized by the gout" and so urged his friend to "make use of youth and health" while he had them.

A week after receiving this second letter, Boswell replied to both. Pleased with Johnson's "spontaneous tenderness," he announced he was "much better." But he "was the worse of seeing David Hume dying in infidelity," and wondered whether he should see him again. (Hume died five weeks later.)[41]

From the start, Boswell had relied on the temperamentally skeptical Johnson to refute Hume's arguments against Christianity. Four months earlier, when Margaret Stuart confessed that Hume's essay "Of a particular Providence and of a future State" had almost made her "an infidel," Boswell was embarrassed not to have counterarguments ready. So at Oxford he got Johnson to join his complaint that Dr. William Adams, in responding to Hume's "Essay on Miracles," had treated with too much civility the man Boswell likened to "an abandoned profligate" seeking to "debauch [his] wife." Now Boswell wanted Johnson to explain how this nonbeliever could die so placidly. Six weeks later—five days after Hume's death on 25 August 1776, two days after Boswell got drunk and "madly" lay with "a comely, fresh-looking girl," and a day after he and Grange witnessed the funeral from a distance—Boswell "resolutely" wrote again. Since he still had not heard from Johnson, Boswell also wrote Langton and Hester Thrale, asking each what Johnson was saying about the shocking "firmness of so able a man in infidelity."[42]

Johnson, however, refused to play his part, just as he had failed in 1769 and 1772 to consider in depth how human freedom was compatible with divine omniscience. He wrote nothing to Boswell before going to Brighton late in September; and when he finally did write, on 16 November, he responded enthusiastically to Boswell's report about his recent visit to Auchinleck, asked Boswell's advice concerning Langton's puzzling "scheme of life," and used his own bad example to show the value of "throw[ing] life into a method, that every hour may have its employment, and every employment its hour," but said nothing about Hume. (In Boswell's register of letters, he noted Johnson's "not answering several particulars of which [he] had written him.") Nor did Johnson mention Hume in the letter that arrived as a particularly valuable "gift" on Christmas Day: congratulating Boswell on the birth of a second son, David, further encouraging him to cultivate his father's "paternal tenderness," trusting him to distribute copies of the *Journey,* and offering some news.

Since Johnson had written promptly about the entail in January and about melancholy six months later, his silence concerning Hume was puzzling, as was his failure in November to acknowledge his long delay. He seems to have been reluctant to grapple in writing with the challenge of Hume's calm, cheerful dying—an event he had earlier insisted was impossible. Boswell was therefore on his own.[43]

Coping Alone with Religious Doubts
(August 1776 through April 1777)

Boswell's telling Sir John Pringle and others in March that the debate about America "was the only great point upon which [he] had got from under Dr. Johnson" showed a desire for some intellectual independence. So did journal entries challenging some of Johnson's claims or insisting "there were no certain divine precepts as to intercourse between the sexes." Concerning Hume's comfortable acceptance of annihilation, however, Boswell wanted decisive assistance. Johnson's silence forced him to find his own answers.[44]

Right after seeing Hume buried, and a day before writing Johnson, Langton, and Thrale, Boswell was "somewhat dejected in mind" after reading some of Hume's essays, and for twenty-four days wrote no additional entries. Three days later, Boswell spent the morning reading Soame Jenyns's *View of the Internal Evidence of the Christian Religion*, a book Temple had recommended as "a very ingenious & masterly" antidote to Hume, and was "pleased with its neat perspicuity, and with the ease with which the subject, which is generally considered as so awful, is treated." Boswell continued to question and brood during the next several months, especially once he realized that Johnson was not going to comment on Hume. Prompted by Hume's inexplicably calm death, and by the deaths of several friends and relatives, eventually including his sickly newborn son, Boswell filled his journal from August 1776 through April 1777 with much more speculation than usual about death and what follows, frequently noted which strong-minded individuals believe in personal immortality, and occasionally reflected on happiness and the vanity of human wishes.[45]

With no direct help from Johnson and without rereading the *Rambler*, Boswell sought to reconfirm his Christian faith. "I could not . . . prevent imaginations of skepticism from springing out in my mind at times," he wrote on 12 October 1776, "But I checked them, and considered that there is a rational preponderation both for a future state and for Christianity." "I felt an acquiescence even in annihilation," he wrote a month later, eight days before finally hearing from Johnson, "but hoped as a Christian."

In October 1775, Boswell had published in the *London Magazine* a request for "A Cure" for "Occasional Impotence of Mind" — for the indolence that "seizes us we know not how, as a palsy sometimes seizes the body" — "a *cure,* which a man himself can have at command, when he wishes for it." In November 1776, Boswell constructed a reply drawn from advice he had received from the friend who had failed to comment on Hume's challenging example. He affirmed from his own experience "that the *impotence of mind* of which many are too ready to complain, is not a real affliction, but is only a cloudy picture in the imagination." He insisted on the importance of living "according to a plan," as he had in Holland; and he emphasized the value of strengthening one's resolution by engaging "on a course of study, or business, or exercises, under the direction of some person of known steadiness." At the start, Boswell also stressed that the "pious prospect of immortality" was a "noble resource," and urged those without it to "fervently ask it from our Father in Heaven, from whom cometh every good and every perfect gift." Responding a month later to a panegyric to David Hume in the *London Chronicle,* Boswell argued against erecting a "monument sacred to skepticism and infidelity" and insisted that morality could not "flourish in its full extent, where a state of retribution and all beyond the grave is disregarded as an idle dream."[46]

Hume's death and Johnson's silence concerning Hume also helped initiate a turbulent, sensual period. Boswell regularly drank too much, expressing only "faint hopes" of ever becoming sober and settled. He often sought out prostitutes and sometimes "madly ventured coition." He confessed some of this misconduct to Margaret; and after seeing his journal early in December, she resolved "never again to consider herself as [his] *wife;* though for the sake of her children and [his], as a *friend,* she would preserve appearances." (A week later, she was "quite reconciled" with Boswell, as she would repeatedly be in the future.) On 21 December, Boswell faulted himself for "having no elevated views, no great ambition" apart from moving to "a more enlarged sphere" in England — a plan that was on hold. A week later, Margaret scolded his "coarse, ill-bred, and abusive style of conversation," which was so "disagreeable and provoking" that he received hardly any invitations.[47]

After Johnson failed to comment on Hume's death, Boswell's correspondence dropped from at least sixteen letters a month in August–November 1776 to just six in December, then to just two in the first six weeks of 1777, after which he wrote eight in the last half of February, twenty-four in March, and thirty-one in April. Boswell's journal entries for December 1776 and January 1777 — on average about three times longer than those during his summer depression — document this emotionally and intellectually messy but formative period. On 24 January, for instance, he reported having for some time had "total indifference as to all objects of whatever kind, united with a melancholy dejection": "I saw death so staringly waiting for all the human race, and had such a cloudy and dark prospect beyond it, that I was miserable as far as I had animation." He found "immediate relief by instantaneously praying to God with earnestness"; but the thought that those he was most fond of would all die left him unable to "value them properly at present." Four days later, while seeing a churchyard "thick-crowded with people" at a funeral, Boswell thought of "the last day and resurrection," and "Death actually appeared to [his] mind without any horror"; and later at dinner he heard Monboddo talk "in a manly strain as to this world, and with firmness as to a future state."[48]

Given Johnson's parting advice, Boswell surely thought of this friend whenever he reported drinking excessively. He also had Johnson in mind whenever he picked up Cheyne's *On Health;* for when he reported starting it on 28 December and finishing it three weeks later, he both times noted having read it on "Dr. Johnson's recommendation." On 28 January, he read passages of Johnson's *Journey* to Lord Monboddo, who "applauded greatly." Then on 14 February — almost three months after he had last written — Boswell began the long letter to Johnson that he finished and posted three days later.

At the start, Boswell addressed issues he did not wish to acknowledge in the *Life,* perhaps including his doubts since Hume's death. At the end, on a sheet that has survived even though not printed in the *Life,* Boswell described his son David's poor health, reported his father's "very discouraging" — even "unnatural" — "inattention" to himself, his wife, and his children, which he blamed on his stepmother, and recalled the Hebrides trip and their "very agreeable" jaunt the previous March. The core of the letter concerned four litigations Johnson had asked about in December. Two had already been decided, including the one for which Johnson had dictated a brief, though Boswell thought the judges were wrong in determining for his (and Johnson's) client, the City of Aberdeen. A third was currently in court, but would surely be appealed, so Boswell asked Johnson to support his client, Sir Allan Maclean, and fully explained the issues. (He noted that Johnson had generously promised to help Sir Allan "when [they] were under his hospitable roof" on Inch Kenneth, even though his adversary, the Duke of Argyll, had later mounted Johnson on a fine horse.) The fourth — Joseph Knight's petition for freedom, which greatly interested Johnson — also had not yet been decided. In July, Johnson had judged John Maclaurin's plea for Knight "excellent," and Boswell promised to send what was now being prepared "on the side of slavery." After an unusually long silence, Boswell was collaboratively reconnecting.[49]

Meanwhile, Johnson, finding himself "not easy" at Boswell's silence since November, wrote for reassurance. He praised Blair's sermons, provided news of Beauclerk and Langton, reported on his poor but improving health, and requested two books not available in London. He promised that Boswell's room would be ready whenever needed and, in closing, formally affirmed his need for Boswell's friendship: "My dear Boswell, do not neglect to write to me, for your kindness is one of the pleasures of my life, which I should be very sorry to lose."[50]

On 22 February, five days after posting the letter that would just have reached London, Boswell was heartened by Johnson's "very affectionate letter." Two days later, he replied that he was "elated" to hear that his "kindness" was "of some consequence" to Johnson, and emphatically declared that his "affection and reverence" for the older man were "exalted and steady": "I do not believe that a more perfect attachment ever existed in the history of mankind. And it is a noble attachment; for the attractions are Genius, Learning, and Piety." Johnson's "valuable proof of . . . regard" was empowering. Though Johnson still had not commented on Hume's calm death, this letter helped Boswell process what had earlier shocked him. It also allowed him—uncharacteristically—to forgo a visit to London.[51]

On 27 February, three days after replying to Johnson, Boswell "picked up a big fat whore, and lay with her" in a shed "just by David Hume's house." Four days later, while plying his blood "pretty freely with wine," which Boswell thought would reveal as soon as possible whether he had been infected, Boswell finally wrote his "Last Interview with David Hume, Esq.," a full account of what had produced such "a degree of horror" eight months earlier that he only now described it at length. Eleven days later, Boswell had his "horror of death alleviated" when he read how Montaigne had been relieved from the terror of dying "by having been in a fainting fit, which he was persuaded was the same with death." On 16 March, Boswell felt he had "arrived at that philosophical calm, that *aisance du monde,* which [he] had formerly desired to have, but scarcely hoped to be so happy." Three days later, soon after getting Johnson's "kind" reply to his two February letters, Boswell "drank too much brandy punch . . . and fell from or rolled off [his] horse." But the following week he "was so free of melancholy that [he] could think long . . . without any gloom falling on [his] mind" and "viewed even death with tranquility and calm hope"—a perspective he developed further in the entry for 28 April 1777 (written on 25 May).[52]

Having clearly seen his importance to Johnson, Boswell was much less needy than he had been the previous year, when he had countered Margaret's strong objections and overcome Johnson's initial hesitation by claiming he required Johnson's conversation, then slipped away without confronting his father. Now, despite fresh grief at David's death, Margaret was willing that he should visit London as usual in the spring. Lord Auchinleck surprised Boswell by consenting to a London visit, "though he said it was nonsense"; and Johnson assumed his friend would come if his father approved. But once Boswell learned that the appeal concerning the inheritance of the Duke of Douglas's estate, with which he had been asked to assist, had been postponed, he judged it would be "very unkind" to leave Margaret unless required by "important business." He also hoped his not going would show his father he "could refrain from London." So he stayed home. And as he outlined his reasons, Boswell significantly said nothing about the friend he had been desperate to see a year before, the man who had recently declared how much he treasured Boswell's kindness.[53]

10

Renegotiating the Friendship,
Part 2 (1777–1778):
Confrontation, Collaboration, and Celebration

On 4 April 1777, a few days after his son David's funeral, Boswell wrote Johnson, explaining why he would not be coming to London and suggesting that they meet in the fall, perhaps in Carlisle, the only English cathedral town Johnson had not visited: "If you are to be with Dr. Taylor, at Ashbourne, it would not be a great journey to come thither. We may pass a few most agreeable days there by ourselves, and I will accompany you a good part of the way to the southward again." When Johnson on 3 May replied to this and another letter Boswell had written on 24 April, he said nothing about a fall meeting. So, in a long letter posted on 9 June, Boswell insisted that Johnson commit himself: "Tell me *where* you will fix for our passing a few days by ourselves." Anticipating resistance at being pressed, Boswell added, "Now don't cry 'foolish fellow,' or 'idle dog.' Chain your humour, and let your kindness play." None of Johnson's other friends wrote like this. Boswell also enclosed two earlier letters he had not posted: the one he wrote in 1775 at Wilton but did not send "for fear of being reproved as indulging too much tenderness," and the one he wrote in 1764 at the tomb of Melanchthon but "kept back, lest [he] should appear at once too superstitious and too enthusiastick."

This letter — with its enclosures — worked. Three weeks later, Johnson agreed to meet "somewhere towards the north," and on 22 July he suggested Taylor's in Ashbourne: "We shall have much time to ourselves, and our stay will be of no expense to us or him."[1]

The Ashbourne visit lasted about as long as the March 1776 jaunt and was much more richly and mutually satisfying. But it still left both friends disappointed. Also, Boswell was anxious after a fierce dispute on the final night. Their regrets and Boswell's anxiety helped produce changes that were evident in March 1778, when they reconnected for their best London visit ever. Because of what they had learned at Ashbourne and afterward, and especially because of the new self-assurance Boswell achieved by writing collaborative journal entries concerning the visit—entries in which he significantly augmented what Johnson had said when they were together—and by composing the first of his comparably collaborative, monthly *Hypochondriack* essays, there was an unusual degree of parity and directness. Boswell, temporarily heeding Johnson's call for total abstinence, played a fuller, more decisive role in their conversations, shared some of his journal for the first time since Scotland, and openly criticized Johnson's verbal excesses and insults. Johnson, while remaining contentious and at times petulant, internalized Boswell's rebukes and admonitions and worked at changing his behavior.

The Ashbourne Visit (14 September to 24 September 1777)

Soon after Boswell read Johnson's suggestion that they meet at Ashbourne, each man pulled back. "I know not whether I shall go forward without some regret," Johnson wrote Henry Thrale on 31 July, three days after reaching Oxford. "I cannot break my promise to Boswell and the rest, but I have a good mind to come back again." His health was poor. When he reached Lichfield a week later, he "could hardly walk." But Hester Thrale urged him on: "It would be better for *you* to go on now you are half way, or the People who expect to see you will think you whimsical. . . . I shall be sorry for Mr Boswell if you don't see him."

Before Johnson responded to this scolding, he heard that Boswell needed to be at Auchinleck whenever Godfrey Bosville visited, and that Margaret had spat up some blood, perhaps the first symptom of the "consumption" (pulmonary tuberculosis) that had afflicted others in her family. Johnson urged his friend not to worry about their meeting but to focus on Margaret's health and to "keep her mind as easy as is possible."[2]

Johnson did not reply to whatever Boswell wrote soon afterward, when he began to fear that Johnson would think him "unsettled as to [their] interview" and be "angry." Nor did Johnson respond immediately to Boswell's report on 12 August that Margaret "continued to grow better" and Godfrey Bosville might not be coming—a letter Boswell sent to Ashbourne and also to Henry Thrale, to be forwarded. But once Johnson reached Taylor's on 30 August, he urged Boswell to come—"Make haste to let me know when you may be expected"—and two days later he wrote at greater length. "Life admits not of delays," he wrote, having discovered at Birmingham and Lichfield that Elizabeth Roebuck, Harry Jackson, and Catherine Turton, all longtime acquaintances, had died since March 1776, and that Elizabeth Aston was seriously ill, as was Mrs. Williams in London. "When pleasure can be had it is fit to catch it: Every hour takes away part of the things that please us, and perhaps part of our disposition to be pleased."[3]

On 3 September, however, when Johnson's first letter from Ashbourne reached Edinburgh, Boswell was again reluctant. Only after Margaret and Grange urged him not to risk offending Johnson did Boswell write that he would arrive about the 13th. Then, on 9 September, Boswell responded to Johnson's "kind and philosophical" second letter with Johnsonian consolations concerning Mrs. Williams's incurable illness and the "gloomy circumstances" of Harry Jackson's death and Mrs. Aston's palsy. "When my mind is unclouded by melancholy," Boswell added, "I consider the temporary distresses of this state of being, as 'light afflictions,' by stretching my mental view into that glorious after-existence, when they will appear to be as nothing." He also reported having with "great satisfaction" just reread *Rasselas,* the book Johnson had written when his mother died.[4]

Late on Sunday, 14 September, shortly after this uncharacteristic letter reached Ashbourne, Boswell himself arrived. He described his visit in an unusually full journal, written partly at Ashbourne and partly afterward; and he also recorded biographical information and a few key conversations in the separate notebook he had begun using in 1776. Johnson mentioned Boswell's visit in nine letters to Hester Thrale as well as in a few brief journal entries. Then they exchanged letters after the visit. So it is easier than usual to say what each friend anticipated, how he experienced those days of steady contact, and what he thought and felt afterward.[5]

Johnson wanted—and got—diversion. Hester Thrale assumed Boswell would "make Ashbourne alive better than three Hautboys [oboes] & the Harpsichord"; and Johnson soon reported that his friend's "good humour" and "usual vivacity" disrupted the eternal sameness of Taylor's, where, "if you were to lay a pebble on his chimney-piece, you would find it there next year." Boswell was an audience whenever Johnson debated Taylor, and he regularly stayed up with Johnson after their host went to bed, introducing a wide range of topics and inviting Johnson to speak authoritatively on each of his current concerns. Johnson could also show Boswell local attractions such as Lord Scarsdale's fine house at Kedleston, the silk mills and china works at Derby, and the garden at Ilam Hall.[6]

Since Boswell had asked for "an exact list" of what Johnson had written to assist the Reverend William Dodd, the fashionable minister who had been executed for forgery, Johnson brought these texts with him, including the sermon Dodd had preached three weeks before he was hanged, and he let Boswell copy them. Johnson volunteered other biographical information as well. He gave a more complete account of his life as a reader, including how he once "imagined his brother had hid some apples in his Father's shop, & climbing up to look for them he had found Petrarch in which he read keenly" — an anecdote that provided Boswell a rare glimpse of the sibling rivalry Hester Thrale saw as responsible for Johnson's "severe reflections on family life in *Rasselas.*" Johnson convincingly corrected what Beauclerk had told Boswell and Hester Thrale about Johnson's shocking ingratitude to his friend and benefactor, the Honorable Thomas Hervey, speaking (as Irma Lustig put it) "like a man who knows himself to be a biographical subject, and wishes honestly to meet the obligations to his public." Boswell also recorded a fuller account than the one from 1763 of how Johnson had once been a "talker against religion," and of "the first occasion of his thinking earnestly of Religion, after he became capable of rational inquiry": his picking up William Law's *Serious Call* while at Oxford, "expecting to find it a dull book as such books generally are & perhaps to laugh at it," but instead finding "Law quite an Overmatch for him."[7]

Early in the visit, Boswell also got Johnson to explain how Hume had died "quite easy at the thought of annihilation." Dismissing this empirical evidence for what Hume had consistently claimed, Johnson bluntly declared Hume had "lied," having "a vanity in being thought easy" — a claim Johnson supported with an argument like the one Hume had used to deny miracles: "It is more probable that he lied than that so very improbable a thing should be as a man not afraid of death; of going into an unknown state and not being uneasy at leaving all that he knew." Johnson also noted that Hume "had been at no pains to inquire into the truth of religion, and had continually turned his mind the other way." In addition, Johnson now finally explained why, despite believing in personal immorality, "he never had a moment in which death was not terrible to him." For no one "can be sure that he is in a state of acceptance with God." In fact, "the better a man was, the more afraid he was of death, having a clearer view of infinite purity."

Without confessing in detail what he saw as his failings, Johnson confided some of his thoughts about dying: "I sometimes thought that I would wish to die quite alone, and have the whole matter transacted between God and myself; sometimes that I would have a friend with me." Whether or not Johnson imagined Boswell as such a friend, sharing his fears with his biographer seems to have been comforting. "There is not a man in the world to whom [Johnson] discloses his sentiments so freely as to you," Sir William Forbes wrote after reading the Ashbourne journal.[8]

In two ways, however, the visit left Johnson unsatisfied. He had the mostly pleasing consciousness that nothing he said that week would be "lost to Posterity," as Mrs. Thrale wrote midway through the visit. But once again Boswell did not share what he was writing. More importantly, Boswell would not agree to another major trip. As soon as Johnson finished writing the *Journey,* and especially after Italy was postponed indefinitely, his letters to Boswell repeatedly alluded to another journey — ideally, the trip to Sweden and Russia they had first dreamed of while on Skye, or even a return to the Hebrides. "It may not be amiss to contrive some other little adventure," he suggested when urging Boswell quickly to join him at Ashbourne. Johnson wanted Boswell to endorse travel that could momentarily push away thoughts of dying and would serve as a challenging diversion to anticipate as he began writing the *Lives of the Poets,* narrating more than fifty writers from birth to death. "What [this little adventure] can be I know not," he coyly added, noting that his new friend Margaret Boswell "must have some part in the consultation."[9]

"Let us, by all means, have another expedition," Boswell replied. But knowing what Johnson mainly had in mind, Boswell reported "shrink[ing] a little from [their] scheme of going up the Baltick." Lamenting that Johnson had already visited Wales, Boswell suggested Ireland, and added, "We shall try to strike out a plan when we are at Ashbourne." A day before Boswell arrived, Johnson wrote Thrale that Boswell "shrinks from the Baltick expedition," which he considered "the best scheme in [their] power," the one most likely to "fill the hunger of ignorance, or quench the thirst of curiosity." Boswell reports their frequently talking "with wonderful pleasure of mere trifles which happened during [their] Hebrides journey." But he did not report talk about future travel.

A comment by Johnson on 19 September, however, while he and Boswell were driving to Derby, suggests that Boswell again refused to endorse a major journey. "If I had no duties and no reference to futurity," Johnson said, "I would spend my life in driving briskly in a post-chaise with a pretty woman, one who could understand one, and would add something to the conversation." Modifying the "seraglio" fantasy he had inadvertently shared on the day they first imagined exploring the Baltic, Johnson pointedly substituted a pretty, intelligent woman like Hester Thrale, or Nekayah or Pekuah from *Rasselas,* for his current companion, who balked at traveling abroad. "We have not agreed upon any other expedition," Johnson wrote Hester Thrale once Boswell left. Having spent ten years anticipating the Hebrides trip and at least five anticipating Italy, Johnson now had rich memories but no concrete plans.[10]

Boswell, too, got much that he wanted from the visit, but not everything.

Johnson's agreeing to meet, and then his eagerness, confirmed that he valued Boswell's friendship. Johnson also answered all of Boswell's biographical questions, in contrast to his reticence in 1776. He still put off dictating his famous letter to Lord Chesterfield, mainly to assert that his death was not imminent, but left Boswell thinking he would soon send it. Boswell also got encouragement and practical advice about moving to London once he became laird; and Johnson affirmed that Boswell could indulge his love of London "without a violation or neglect of any duty."[11]

Johnson reassuringly condemned Lord Auchinleck's persistent "coldness" toward Boswell and his brothers and recommended that Boswell "expostulate" in a letter. (Boswell did this a week after returning home, "begging to be treated with less coldness," and in reply received "a tolerably descent letter.") Though Boswell had not cited depression as a reason to connect, Johnson's "conversation had an immediate cordial effect" on his friend's oppressed spirits, just as Boswell's company helped divert Johnson from depressing thoughts about aging and death.[12]

Boswell was delighted also when Johnson "philosophically" explained what Boswell had "often and often experienced": how "a madman loves to be with people whom he fears; not as a dog fears the lash, but of whom he stands in awe"; and how madmen, when very ill, seek pain rather than pleasure. "I was not now afraid of him," he told Johnson, "but I had an awe of him which made me happier in his company. . . . I should find no difficulty go to into a battle under his command while I heard him talk." But when Boswell reported his difficulty in rising in the morning, Johnson's account of the learned poet Elizabeth Carter's alarm was unhelpful. For Boswell did not need to be awakened, but to "rise without pain, which [he] never did." When Johnson later recommended having books of all sorts nearby, Boswell complained that Johnson assumed he "had keen desires for reading, but unluckily that is not the case."[13]

Boswell also found Johnson's claim that the best men most fear death "too gloomy." But he was not left "clouded and depressed," as he had been on Good Friday in 1775 when Johnson reflected on the vanity of human wishes. "I felt my own mind much firmer than formerly," he reported in an entry written six days later (22 September), "so that I was not depressed tonight; and even the gloom of uncertainty in solemn religious speculation, being mingled with hope, was much more consolatory than the emptiness of infidelity." On 23 September, in a conversation he recorded almost immediately in a separate notebook, Boswell got Johnson to agree that it was "not wrong to hope" that the wicked would not be "eternally punished." There are "strong" Biblical passages concerning "everlasting punishment"; but it is possible to "mitigate their interpretation."[14]

Finally, though Boswell had hoped that Johnson would "not say a single harsh thing" to him or of him, his own aggressive acts — announcing on 17 September that the next day was Johnson's birthday, and challenging Johnson's position on America six days later — guaranteed hostile reactions. In key ways, each exchange jostled what both friends had assumed about their friendship, and each had an enduring impact.

Boswell was "pretty sure that mentioning [Johnson's] birthday would offend him, and yet did it." Whatever he saw as his motives — a wish to produce and direct Johnson's life, to observe him in various situations, to protest his being "foiled by futurity" — Boswell knew his announcement was insensitive and aggressive, especially since Johnson had just confided his deep anxiety about how God would assess him. But Boswell did not anticipate Johnson's response, which revealed a shockingly low opinion of his biographer.

When Boswell noted that Taylor's lighting the crystal chandelier the next day would appropriately mark Johnson's birthday, Johnson insisted that it *not* be lighted; and at breakfast the next morning, he voiced the harshest rebuke Boswell ever recorded. Alluding to Boswell and the birthday, Johnson told Taylor, "I had a mind to have forbid him to mention it, but was in hopes he would have forgot it; and I thought he would do better from not knowing what was wrong than if he had been told to avoid it." This telling remark — the only recorded instance of Johnson launching an attack hours after a provocation — revealed not momentary anger but distress at having been betrayed. What Johnson had called "troublesome kindness" when his biographer announced his birthday in 1773, reminding Johnson that one less year remained to redeem the time he had wasted, now seemed meddlesome, even cruel. So Johnson spoke of Boswell as "a being of little judgement or conduct," as Boswell put it, perverse and willful, more likely deliberately to do what was wrong than what was right. But when Boswell finally reported this comment, twelve days later, he noted that when Johnson saw that Boswell had been "somewhat disconcerted, he retracted, or at least expressed himself in terms that showed he had been in jest."[15]

As in 1769, when Boswell had insisted that Johnson explain his fear of death, Johnson experienced his friend's lack of sympathy — and his own willingness to forgive. But Boswell realized that Johnson still had major reservations about their friendship, and so repeatedly sought assurances of his love and esteem — assurances Johnson gave while complaining of Boswell's constant need "for kind words." "My regard for you is greater than I can (almost) find words to express," he declared at the end of the visit. "But I do not chuse to be always repeating it. Write it down on the first leaf of your pocket-book & never doubt of it again."[16]

Boswell recorded these words soon after they were spoken, weeks before he wrote the entry for their final evening, when his fears about how Johnson regarded him were intensified. After Johnson offered to "sit up *all night*" with the friend who would leave the next morning, Boswell argued against what Johnson had published on America, then held his ground despite Johnson's "violent" reaction. When Boswell reported this exchange, he was still apprehensive about how Johnson felt, so he described the confrontation as more or less accidental: "I got, I know not how, upon the American controversy." Boswell also denied having had any wish to press the issue: "I would gladly have been off it again as soon as possible. For he was quite violent." But some of Boswell's motives for broaching this subject and persisting seem clear.

As hostilities in the colonies intensified, Boswell's opposition to the policies Johnson had supported strengthened; and by challenging Johnson's published defense of the British government, Boswell asserted *his* independence. He also channeled some of his long-term resentment at Johnson's overbearing behavior, including Johnson's refusal to let Boswell win disputes even when he used solid, "Johnsonian" arguments and directly asked his friend not to "ridicule" them. In his journal, Boswell presented himself as entirely calm, though fearful because he "dreaded offending" Johnson. But in the *Life,* Boswell acknowledged that he, too, "grew warm." Surprised at being challenged, and at first furious, Johnson also seems to have respected Boswell's persistence and skill, for they kept arguing until 3 A.M.

There was no clear winner. But for Boswell, this stalemate represented victory, or at least improvement, since Johnson had always triumphed in the past. The fuller account in the *Life* also makes clear that when Boswell shifted the focus to the British Parliament and the Roman Senate, Johnson moved from sarcastic outbursts to reasoned assertions, accepting his friend's right to be treated seriously. Johnson's respect also seems clear in Boswell's sketchy description of their parting the next morning. Midway through the visit, Johnson had again worried about Boswell's drinking. He shared Paoli's fear that drinking would make their friend "go mad, for madness was in [his] family." At the end, however, Johnson did not stress abstinence, as in May 1776, but instead urged his friend to cultivate the small estate he had purchased ten years earlier.[17]

Secret Collaboration
(25 September 1777 to 28 February 1778)

Six months later, Boswell and Johnson would discover that their heated, sustained dispute on America was a major breakthrough, a necessary rite of

passage as Boswell moved toward autonomy and Johnson toward fuller respect. But as Boswell left Ashbourne, he was worried. All his strong and varied
feelings about the visit, especially his anxiety about how his defending the
colonists had affected Johnson, were on his mind when he began a letter two
days after reaching Edinburgh, a letter he finished and posted only four days
later. Besides asking Johnson to explain why "lively and affectionate feelings"
are more satisfying when remembered than when first experienced — a question he had earlier asked in the Hebrides journal — Boswell had a specific
request. Before correcting the story about his alleged ingratitude to Hervey,
Johnson had insisted on knowing the source, and Boswell had reluctantly
named Beauclerk. Now Boswell asked Johnson not to discuss this before he
could see Beauclerk, since what he had done "might be interpreted as a breach
of confidence, and offend one whose society [he] valued." Boswell also asked
Johnson to respond "quickly," trusting that a letter would reveal Johnson's
current feelings after their contentious dispute.[18]

On 30 September, a day after momentarily setting this letter aside, Boswell
began completing his journal, starting from just before Johnson's birthday;
and he added material almost every day through 10 October. But once he
began describing the day he challenged Johnson on America, Boswell got
drunk for the first time since Ashbourne, resuming the journal only eleven
days later. Meanwhile, on 16 October, Boswell tried to coax a reassuring letter
from Johnson by writing Taylor that the innkeeper at Chatsworth had described Johnson as "the greatest writer in England," who "has a correspondence abroad, and lets them know what's going on" — an anecdote he assumed
Taylor would share.[19]

Boswell's hesitation in writing the entry for 23 September suggests anxiety
about his forceful and sustained challenge — anxiety that affected how he composed the entries for 18–22 September. Those that Boswell had written while
at Ashbourne were in various ways critical, even subversive. Now he continued to criticize and defy, and to emphasize how he differed from Johnson,
while also reporting his having surreptitiously copied some of Johnson's journal — out of "veneration and love of him." But as he resumed writing, Boswell
approached the birthday insult by formally aligning himself with Johnson.
After describing Johnson's argument with Taylor on the 17th about the British
monarchy, and before reporting what Johnson said the following morning,
Boswell wrote that his friend's "old Oxford eloquence" reawakened Boswell's
"venerable mysterious notions of the sacredness of monarchy and [his] gallant
affectionate feelings of loyalty." The following day, with Johnson's insult and
the heated dispute about America on his mind, and with his letter still not
posted, Boswell cultivated a less confrontational way of asserting his grown-

up status. He produced collaborative reflections. Instead of simply endorsing Johnson's opinions, while perhaps adding an example or an illustration, as he had in the past, or arguing against Johnson's claims, perhaps reinforcing what he had said in conversation, Boswell now substantially augmented Johnson's positions. He constructed analyses that affirmed his allegiance but also established his independence and intellectual self-sufficiency.[20]

This sort of collaboration was anticipated in some earlier journal entries, as well as in Boswell's adaptation of what Johnson had dictated before defending the schoolmaster in 1772. But it was nowhere so fully developed or so dense as in these entries. The frequency of such reflections in this portion of the Ashbourne journal might have arisen from Boswell's beginning to write the *Hypochondriack* essays, as the editors of *Boswell in Extremes* suggest. Boswell even read proofs for the first essay on the day he wrote a "collaboration" on the fear of death, which closely resembles the fifth paragraph of the essay Boswell would write twelve days later. But it seems more accurate to say that in these collaborative entries, and also in the monthly essays, Boswell was trying to establish his autonomy on large moral issues but without defying Johnson, as he had just done concerning America.[21]

The first example occurs right after Boswell reported that the ladies who had heard about Johnson's birthday "plagued him unknowingly by wishing him joy." Noting that Johnson's "dread of death has sometimes shocked me," Boswell contrasted his friend's constant fear with his own ability "at times" to view death with "no great horror." First, he presented the contrast in conventional images: "Perhaps such minds as his may be assailed with more violent terrors than feebler and more confined ones, as oaks are torn by blasts which shrubs escape by their lowliness." But Boswell "was now led to have a new state of reflection as to death" — "neither to be indifferent from insensibility nor cheerful from imagination, but to consider it as an awful event, which God intends should be awful, and which I must meet with as much pious hope as I can reasonably entertain." Citing "a collection of instances of men of different persuasions 'qui sont morts en plaisantant' ['who died with a jest'],'' quoting Alexander Pope, using an idea of Paoli's about the fear of death that Johnson had earlier endorsed while also assuming what Johnson consistently affirmed about life after death, Boswell filled almost an entire printed page with a thoughtful, balanced reflection that differed from Johnson's "too gloomy" position — and also from his own before he started writing.[22]

In the entry for 19 September, written on the day he posted his letter to Johnson, Boswell produced an even longer collaboration, beginning with the report that he had "learnt from Dr. Johnson during [their] interview not to think with a dejected indifference of the works of art and the pleasures of life, because it is uncertain and short"—as Boswell often had—"but to consider such indifference as a failure of reason, a morbidness of mind." Boswell then fully explained this new, Johnsonian perspective. Drawing throughout on Johnson's example of "contemplating a large mass of human existence," but citing or quoting the poets Edward Young, Gray, and Pope, and the philosopher George Berkeley, Boswell constructed something at once Johnsonian and Boswellian, original but not defiant, and in the process proved himself a mature, somewhat autonomous Johnsonian.[23]

Creative collaborations like these affirmed Boswell's intellectual maturity without defying Johnson, hence without risking his anger. But I think Boswell produced them when he did—before he got to the entry for 23 September—precisely because he had heatedly challenged Johnson and was worried. These collaborations assumed Boswell's distinct experiences and point of view, and those on death and happiness depended on Boswell's being temperamentally different from Johnson. But in these entries, as in the anonymous monthly *Hypochondriack* essays he wrote during the next six years—especially those on topics Johnson had treated—Boswell constructed reflections both he and Johnson could endorse.[24]

Unlike the Hebrides journal, these collaborative entries were not shown to Johnson and so could not win his praise. (Boswell showed some essays to Johnson only in 1784.) But writing these collaborative texts—realigning himself with Johnson while demonstrating his thoughtfulness and poise—prepared Boswell to describe their angry dispute, which he finally did on 22 October. Then he had to wait thirty-nine additional days before learning that Johnson had never considered doing what his "dear friend" had earnestly asked concerning Beauclerk.

Johnson stayed at Ashbourne until mid-October, writing the *Life* of Abraham Cowley on the 11th and finishing the *Life* of John Denham two days later. No longer concretely imagining a journey that would challenge his stamina and engage his intellect, he began tracking the lives and assessing the achievements of one poet after another, transforming what he had described to Boswell as "little Lives, and little Prefaces" into a major test of his abilities. Johnson also sent thirteen letters to Hester Thrale before joining her in mid-November. But he put off writing to Boswell until he had seen Beauclerk in Brighton, resolutely maintaining control of his life. Then he tried to justify of what he had done—and not done.[25]

Johnson acknowledged that his not writing sooner had probably both puzzled and pained Boswell. But he strained to defend his delay and his not complying with the request of the friend who had given him a chance to correct a shocking story and whom he had forced to reveal the source. He insulted Boswell's letter to explain why he had ignored it. Having earlier complained to Hester Thrale that Boswell "shrinks from the Baltick expedition," Johnson now wrote that Boswell's request "had in it such a strain of cowardly caution as gave me no pleasure." "I could not well do what you wished," Johnson added, meaning that he would not let Boswell script his behavior toward Beauclerk. So instead of "vexing" Boswell by refusing—and allowing his friend forcefully to restate his request—Johnson maintained a worrisome silence. Now he had seen Beauclerk and "set all right, without any inconvenience," as far as he knew, to Boswell. "It was pity to keep you so long in pain," Johnson added. "But, upon reviewing the matter, I do not see what I could have done better than as I did."

Having assumed the right to judge his own conduct in dismissing Boswell's "cowardly" request, Johnson tried to mollify his friend by thanking him again and again for having journeyed to Ashbourne, where he hoped Boswell "met nothing that displeased" him. Johnson also briefly described his recent activities, passed along other news, and concluded: "Well, now I hope all is well."

Boswell replied immediately. Instead of repressing his anger and disappointment, he politely but firmly rejected Johnson's assessment: "I cannot see that you are just in blaming my caution. But if you were ever so just in your disapprobation, might you not have dealt more tenderly with me?" Having challenged Johnson on America, weathered his violence, and collaboratively affirmed his own autonomy, Boswell now complained directly about Johnson's insulting insensitivity.

Johnson did not address his friend's complaint when he wrote affectionately on 27 December. But shortly after receiving Boswell's letter, he asked Hester Thrale to take his measure: "Draw up my Character your own Way, shew it me, that I may see what you will say of me when I am gone."[26]

When Boswell, early in January 1778, reported Margaret's "alarming" new symptoms, Johnson offered her his bedroom if she came to London in March. Also since Boswell "always seem[ed] to call for tenderness," Johnson added: "In the first month of the present year I very highly esteem and very cordially love you. I hope to tell you this at the beginning of every year as long as we live; and why should we trouble ourselves to tell or hear it oftener?"

On 26 February, Boswell reported that Margaret was "a good deal better" and planned to take their children to "some country place in Scotland." But he hoped to appear as one of Archibald Douglas's counsel "in the great and last competition between Duke Hamilton and him," and diffidently asked Johnson to tell him by return post whether he approved.

Two days later, Boswell wrote again, ostensibly to ask a question about the poet Thomas Parnell, but mainly to gloat that the ministry had abandoned the position on America that Johnson had supported: "What do you say to *Taxation no Tyranny*, now, after Lord North's declaration, or confession, or whatever else his conciliatory speech should be called?" Boswell had referred to Lord North's speech of 17 February when writing Pringle and Pembroke on 24–26 February. But he mentioned it to Johnson only after he had "wonderfully" completed a collaborative reflection on melancholy begun on the day he asked Johnson about the Douglas appeal.[27]

Three days after writing in triumph, Boswell resumed a regular journal after "a long interval" when he had written only notes. Twelve days later, he set off for London, where he surprisingly realized he could anticipate Johnson's death without anxiety and regard him without "reverential awe," where he publicly admonished Johnson for excessive violence in arguments, and where he finally told his friend how troubled he was by his gratuitous insults.[28]

"The best London I ever had" (17 March to 19 May 1778)

As usual, Boswell came to London in mid-March and left in mid-May. Johnson was mostly at Streatham in March, so Boswell saw him on only four of his first seventeen days. Early in May there was a five-day stretch when Boswell pulled back after an insult. But between 30 March and 2 May, Johnson and Boswell were together more frequently than during any other five-week period in London, and they saw each other on ten of the twelve days from 8 through 19 May. The day before leaving Edinburgh, Boswell noted being more "agitated" than he wished, so he resolved to "maintain a calm mastery" of himself in London and not grow "giddy" as usual. Helped by almost complete abstinence, he seems to have succeeded, making the visit "the best London [he] ever had, owing to no wine." His remarkably full journal was one consequence of this sustained sobriety.[29]

Soon after arriving, Boswell discovered he could calmly contemplate the prospect of living in a world without Johnson. In February 1777, when Johnson reported having "been so distressed by difficulty of breathing, that [he] lost, as was computed, six-and-thirty ounces of blood in a few days" (that is, by being bled by a surgeon, a standard medical procedure at the time), Boswell had replied, "Your difficulty of breathing alarms me, and brings into imagination an event, which although in the natural course of things, I must expect at some point, I cannot view with composure." But in the entry for his first day in London in 1778, when Boswell made up for Johnson's being at Streatham by reading the *Life of Denham* at Dilly's, the thought of Johnson's death was no longer distressing: "It was a feast to me, and my powers of admiration in every view were excited. His knowledge, his judgement, his expression filled me with wonder and delight. I thought of his having been ill. I thought of his death. I could not at this moment think gloomily even of that. I could not suppose a mind so extensive, so distinguishing, so luminous, but in a state of exalted felicity." Picturing Johnson securely in heaven decisively corrected Johnson's "gloomy" worries about salvation and benignly expressed any wish Boswell might have had for the moment when he would finally be able to write the biography of the man whose masterly *Denham* he had just finished.[30]

Three days later (20 March) — three days before he described this reading experience — Boswell's first evening with Johnson since their heated dispute in September also helped confirm his ability to survive and perhaps even thrive in a world without Johnson. Though Boswell had ended his second, triumphant February letter by writing, "But, enough of this subject; for your angry voice at Ashbourne . . . still sounds aweful 'in my mind's *ears*,'" his sending this feisty letter showed he no longer feared Johnson's anger concerning their dispute about America. Now he discovered with mixed feelings that he was "quite easy" with Johnson, "quite as companions," without the "awful reverence with which [he] used to contemplate *Mr. Samuel Johnson* in the complex magnitude of his literary, moral, and religious character."[31]

In his entry for 20 September 1777, Boswell had noted his own experience to confirm Johnson's claim that "a madman loves to be with people . . . of whom he stands in awe": "Awe composes the uneasy tumult of my spirits, and gives me the pleasure of contemplating something at least comparatively great." Now, six months later, Boswell was surprised that his awe of Johnson was gone. Having just feasted on *Denham* and the "still greater" *Cowley,* Boswell had fresh reasons to "worship" Johnson, "not *idolatrously,* but with profound reverence, in the ancient Jewish sense of the word." But his fear was gone. He was now so "advanced in [his] progress of being" that he could view Johnson "with a steadier and clearer eye." Boswell compared the difference between his former "awful reverence" for Johnson and his current view with St. Paul's distinction between now seeing "as in a glass, darkly" and seeing "face to face" in heaven; and two days before writing these words, Boswell had urged Temple to join him in London and "have a foretaste of Heaven."[32]

Though Boswell described himself as "anxious to see Dr. Johnson as soon as possible," he did not remark needing Johnson's conversation to elevate him "into another state of being" or to relieve his "wretched changefulness." After meeting Johnson unexpectedly on 18 March and spending an evening with him two days later, Boswell waited a week before asking about reconnecting, and three more days before going to Streatham. When Margaret Stuart told him on Easter that Edward Gibbon's "unanswerable objections" to the truth of Christianity had made her lose her faith, Boswell told Johnson he wished to have "the arguments for Christianity always in readiness." But he seems to have been much less troubled than in 1776, when he had learned that reading Hume made Mrs. Stuart "almost . . . an infidel."[33]

Boswell still wanted reassurance that Johnson loved and respected him, however, and mostly was satisfied. Johnson had given Boswell's room to two women he was supporting. But Boswell reported receiving more compliments than usual from his friend, partly because Johnson still hoped Boswell might agree to another major trip. On 7 April, while the two returned to London after Boswell's second dinner at Streatham, Johnson said, "You make yourself agreeable wherever you go. Whoever has seen you once wishes to see you again." A week later at Dilly's, Johnson told the learned Quaker Mary Knowles, "You have been flattering me all this night. I wish you'd now give Bozzy a little. If you knew his merit as well as I do, you'd say a great deal. He's the best travelling companion in the world." Two days later, when Boswell said, "There is none of your friends on whom you could depend more than on me," Johnson replied, "No, Sir, none who would do more for me of what I'd wish to have done." But then Johnson confirmed the significance of this friend who was always asking for reassurance by aggressively imagining outliving his would-be biographer: "Were you to die, it would be a limb lopped off."[34]

Johnson again got no promise of another trip, even though on 7 April, Boswell teasingly remarked how well they traveled together: "I love to be under some restraint, some awe, and you're as easy with me as with anybody." But in April and much of May, Johnson frequently had Boswell's companionship. Also, I suspect he saw some of Boswell's current journal. On 10 April, Johnson "refreshed [Boswell] as to yesterday's conversation" at Sir Joshua Reynolds's, which Boswell had already reported. (It fills about six printed pages.) As Boswell recounted it: "I wrote little additions. He said, 'Don't be scribbling.' But he was not displeased." Boswell did not report showing Johnson what he had just written, nor did he report discussing other entries. But this talk seems to have been the prelude to Boswell's sharing the impressively full entries he would soon write, including one describing a dramatic dinner at Dilly's on 15 April, at which Johnson debated with Mary Knowles whether a "rational man could die without apprehension," made clear that he feared annihilation even more than damnation, and finally tried to explain how there could be freedom when God knows exactly what we will do. Another detailed entry described their remarkable Good Friday two days later.[35]

This Good Friday was the best ever, the most mutually satisfying. In 1776, Boswell had missed breakfasting with Johnson, who complained that his friend had later "interrupted" his Good Friday "exercises of piety." Joining Johnson for breakfast two years later, Boswell was pleased that "a larger cup" was ready, as he had requested. Their conversation was so lively that "talk lost [their] time," as Johnson wrote later, and they were late for services, allowing Boswell to offer parental reassurance: "This being late vexes one a little, but these things are always happening." Then, as they returned home, Johnson was approached by Oliver Edwards, a man he had known at Oxford. Prompted by Edwards's questions, Johnson spent much of the day seeing his life as Boswell did, and postponed until Monday writing reflections on the "melancholy and shameful blank" of the previous year.

At first Johnson did not recognize Edwards, but gradually recollected, at which point he described exactly what they each had said while "drinking together at a house near Pembroke gate." Catching up as at a fiftieth reunion, Johnson movingly told of having had — and lost — a wife, and reported that he once drank "a great deal" of wine, "then had a severe illness and left it off." He proudly presented himself as a man unaffected by what he ate or by the weather, as one who could fast for two days "without any inconvenience," but also as "a straggling" who "may leave this town and go to Grand Cairo without being missed here or observed there." When Edwards said, "We are old men now," Johnson replied, "Don't let us discourage one another," and urged Edwards to "drink water and put in for a hundred."

Johnson's autobiographical narrative was less full than the one he had incrementally constructed for Boswell, but much more concrete and celebratory than his usual Holy Week reviews. Discussion after Edwards left was also radically reaffirming. When Boswell reported Edwards's suggestion that Johnson should have had a profession, like law, Johnson initially agreed. But he eventually sided with Boswell in endorsing all that had happened. Had Johnson been a lawyer, he might have become a judge, perhaps even the lord chancellor, and "delivered opinions with more extent of mind and in a more ornamental manner" than others. But "there would not have been another who could have done the *Dictionary.*"

Three days later — on the Monday after Easter — Johnson finally reviewed the past year and reported, as usual, so little done "that days and months are without any trace," even though he had written "a little of the lives of the poets . . . with all [his] usual vigour," and hoped "with the help of God to begin a new life." But on Good Friday, having focused on key experiences since Oxford and confirmed the value of what he had accomplished, Johnson did not recoil — as he had six years earlier and would six years later — when Boswell remarked how pleasing it was to anticipate seeing one's departed friends in heaven, even though embracing this fantasy meant assuming one's salvation. When Boswell then told how "a very accomplished woman" had once humored him by saying that the first thing he would find in the other world would be "an elegant copy of Shakespeare," Johnson simply smiled.[36]

Sobriety and Incivility

During this visit, for the first time since Johnson began to worry about Boswell's heavy drinking, Boswell almost wholly abstained from wine, doing on his own what Paoli had made him promise in April 1776, what Johnson had urged a month later. In February 1777, nine months after Johnson warned that Boswell, when drunk, might do something that deserved hanging, Boswell ended a long letter by noting that Cheyne approved of moderate drinking. Seven months after that, when Johnson at Ashbourne tried to shock Boswell into abstinence by worrying that drinking might make him "go mad," Boswell still "schemed to enjoy the satisfaction of drinking" — moderately. But Boswell also worried. His journal regularly reported his drinking to excess and described moments when he had acted "like a perverse madman" (31 May 1777), "terribly wild with rage" (2 June), "sadly intoxicated, even insane" (28 June). "Vexed a little" when he drank too much just before reaching London on this visit, Boswell afterward drank seldom, never more than two glasses. Johnson applauded and reinforced his friend's resolve, siding with him when first Garrick and later Reynolds argued that Boswell should drink to please his companions.[37]

In part because Boswell was so fully in control, so comfortably connected with Johnson in ways he was documenting in unusually full entries, he for the first time openly criticized Johnson's excessive conversational violence, getting Johnson secretly to pray for a change. Boswell still could be deeply hurt by Johnson's unexpected insensitivity and rudeness. But for the first time he managed to explain directly how troubling he found his friend's demeaning insults, prompting Johnson to apologize fully and to desist.

In his Hebrides journal, but not in reported conversations, Boswell had noted with mixed feelings Johnson's roughness and impetuosity in argument and had described his own discomfort at his friend's teasing. In 1775 and 1777, he had cited others as criticizing Johnson's argumentative excesses: repeating Temple's puzzlement that Boswell's "moral" friend could support such "barbarous measures" in America that the ministry "had not the face to ask even their infidel pensioner Hume to defend"; and noting that Lord Eglinton, because he had the same contempt for the English as Johnson had for Scots, would call Johnson a "damned rascal! To talk so of the Scotch." Now Boswell spoke for himself — at first genially and playfully, then with sober, parental judgment — in faulting Johnson's intemperate attacks on the rebellious colonists.[38]

At Dilly's on 15 April, after Johnson declared that "he was willing to love all mankind *except an American*," and called the colonists "rascals and robbers and pirates" who deserved to be burned and destroyed, he failed to see what the Lichfield poet Anna Seward meant in saying, "We are always most violent against those whom we have injured." Instead, he "roared again, till he was absolutely hoarse," until Boswell changed the topic. The next day, Boswell privately told Johnson that his conversation at Dilly's had been "like a warm southern climate," where the same heat that brings forth "luxurious foliage" and "luscious fruits" at times "produces violent thunder and lightning or a terrible earthquake."[39]

Boswell did not describe Johnson's reaction to this retrospective critique. But he remarked Johnson's exasperation at an immediate rebuke two days later. When Johnson once again "roared terribly" against the Americans to a small group at his house, Boswell, who that morning had finished his "best *Hypochondriack* yet," first spoke on the colonists' behalf, then calmly admonished Johnson for "his ungovernable violence," saying he "was always sorry when [Johnson] talked on that subject." Johnson said nothing immediately, but "the cloud was charged with sulphureous vapour, which was afterwards to burst in thunder." So when Boswell facetiously suggested that the best way to get Langton to leave London, which he could not afford, was to have all his friends quarrel with him, Johnson said, "Nay, Sir . . . we'll send you to him. If your company does not drive a man out of his house, nothing will."

Boswell described this as "a horrible blunt shock," which "stunned" him. But he had anticipated some outburst. Also, Johnson's insult was remarkably feeble, for he regularly praised Boswell's "agreeable" companionship. In addition, Boswell soon comfortably asked why Johnson had not immediately retaliated, and heard in reply, "I had nothing ready. A man cannot strike till he has his weapons."[40]

Only when he read Johnson's *Prayers and Meditations* seven years later would Boswell learn that Johnson took his admonishment to heart; for in the Easter prayer he composed that evening, Johnson asked God to make him "to love all men" — including, presumably, those Americans he had recently boasted of *not* loving. But a day after Easter, Johnson openly welcomed Boswell's help in placating a friend he had angrily insulted. In a dispute a week earlier about the accuracy of Thomas Pennant's descriptions of Northumberland and Scotland, Thomas Percy had noted that Johnson was "short-sighted," and Johnson eventually retorted that Percy's objections showed "the resentment of a narrow mind." Once Boswell learned that Percy remained "uneasy," he choreographed a dance of reconciliation, which Johnson agreed to perform, as he had done several times in the past. When Johnson five years later told his new friend William Bowles his pleasure with "the marks of respect and benignity which he had received from those whom he had made by his own behaviour his enemies," including John Wilkes, with whom he "had a very rough bout," he was partly acknowledging Boswell's success at helping him live up to his self-image as someone neither "uncandid" nor "severe," though he admitted, "I sometimes say more than I mean in jest, and people are apt to believe me serious."[41]

No matter how poised and self-assured Boswell had become, however, he remained vulnerable. On 2 May, a few days after Johnson and Percy had fully reconciled, something Johnson said — something seemingly unprovoked, hence unexpected — led Boswell to avoid Johnson for five days, and even to consider returning home without seeing him. When Langton thoughtfully brought the two friends together, Boswell finally was able to tell Johnson how his demeaning insults made him feel, and Johnson both apologized profusely and changed his behavior.

No journal entries survive for 1–11 May, so the only account of the provocation and the follow-up is in the *Life,* in which Boswell wrote this about dinner at Reynolds's on 2 May: "There were several people there by no means of the Johnsonian school, so that less attention was paid to him than usual, which fretted him; and upon some imaginary offence from me he attacked me with such rudeness that I was vexed and angry, because it gave those persons an opportunity of saying how ferocious he was, and how shockingly he treated his best friends." Boswell's not reporting Johnson's words indicates they still bothered him, as did all the insults he omitted from the *Tour* and the *Life.* Johnson, as usual, felt justified. But Boswell thought the attack gratuitous, since he learned of his "imaginary offence" only on 8 May, when Johnson "insisted that [Boswell] had interrupted him, which [Boswell] assured him was not the case."

Startled by Johnson's excessive rudeness, Boswell was angry. But he did not immediately protest, as he had done when he read Johnson's insulting letter five months earlier. Face-to-face, Johnson was too intimidating. So Boswell pulled back. Having seen Johnson on twenty-two of the previous thirty days, including five of the last seven, Boswell was "so much hurt and had [his] pride so much roused" that he avoided Johnson for five days, "and perhaps might have kept away much longer — nay, gone to Scotland without seeing him again — had not [they] fortunately met and been reconciled."[42]

Boswell confided in Langton, who five years earlier had left London without explaining how upset he was that Johnson had harshly rebuked him for suggesting there should be legal toleration for anyone preaching against "the doctrine of the Trinity," since such unorthodoxy was a "merely speculative" opinion that would not "lead to action," and who had been reconciled only twenty months later. In the fall of 1773, Boswell had urged Langton to write

Johnson, and later had nudged Johnson to respond. Now Langton recipro-cated by telling Johnson how hurt Boswell was, and inviting both to dinner on 8 May.

The day before, Boswell prepared for this encounter by writing entries for three earlier days spent partly with Johnson, entries that reveal some of what he thought and felt as he and Johnson were about to reconnect. He repeatedly emphasized his admiration and attentiveness, preparing for his claim on 8 May that "no man has a greater respect and affection" for him, "or would sooner go to the end of the world to serve" him. Boswell also provided a basis for forgiveness. After reporting Johnson's statement on 29 April that "a man's being in good or bad humour depends upon his own will," Boswell first re-marked, "If this be true, the Doctor is much to blame upon many occasions." But he immediately added, "A man's humour is often irresistible by his will."[43]

Once Langton left his two friends alone, Boswell explained how "very un-easy" he had been six days before. When Johnson justified his harsh words, Boswell assured him that he had not interrupted, and insisted that even had he done so, Johnson's reaction was excessive and insensitive. "Why treat me so before people who neither love you nor me?" Johnson instantly apologized and promised to "make it up to [him] twenty different ways," as he pleased. Boswell reported having told Reynolds, "I don't care how often or how high he tosses me when it is among friends, when I fall upon soft ground. But I do not like falling among stones, which is the case when enemies are present." When he asked whether this was not "a pretty good simile," his apologetic friend called it "one of the happiest thoughts I have heard." Boswell probably discounted this compliment, since he had recently seen Johnson overpraise Percy "from his instantaneous desire to make up." But Johnson clearly wished to placate, and the two friends joined in laughing heartily "at some ludicrous but innocent peculiarities" of the friend who had brought them together.[44]

They also arranged to dine the next day at the Mitre, their first dinner alone that spring. Once there, Johnson made up further by discussing a topic Bos-well had long wanted to hear him address: "the sensual intercourse between the sexes, the delight of which [Johnson] ascribed chiefly to imagination." No entry survives for 9 May, and in the *Life* Boswell primly determined "it would not be proper to record the particulars of such a conversation in moments of unreserved frankness." We are left to wonder, therefore, whether Boswell deferred to Johnson, talked as an equal, or drew on his presumably more extensive experience. After Johnson's outrage in April 1776, it seems unlikely that Boswell confessed his regular encounters with "No. 36," which he felt "did not weaken affection at home." I also doubt that Boswell directly in-quired whether Johnson ever "went to women" — something he had told Pringle in 1776 he "durst not ask." But there is no knowing what either friend revealed in this unique conversation.[45]

Just as Johnson stopped roaring against the Americans after Boswell's rebuke on 18 April, his gratuitous personal attacks on Boswell ended after 8 May. Johnson was sometimes angry or testy, and he occasionally rebuked and scolded, especially when Boswell eventually resumed drinking. At times there were tense struggles to control Johnson's life and heated debates in which Boswell now held his ground despite Johnson's roughness. But there were no demeaning attacks.

The effect became clear in two transactions on 12 May 1778, when Boswell dined with Johnson at Streatham and stayed the night. When Boswell announced he had just arranged for Lord Marchmont, Pope's friend and executor, to call on Johnson the next day and "communicate all he knows of Pope," Johnson surprisingly rejected this plan, saying, "I shall not be in town tomorrow." To resist Boswell's management, Johnson was willing even to appear foolish, declaring, "I don't care to know about Pope." When Mrs. Thrale said, "I suppose, Sir, he thought that as you are to write Pope's life, you'd wish to know about him," Johnson answered, "If it rained knowledge, I'd hold out my hand. But I would not trouble myself for it." Johnson would have been even angrier if he knew Boswell had promised Lord Marchmont he could look over whatever Johnson wrote. But Johnson eventually suggested a compromise — that "Lord Marchmont would call on him and then he'd call on Lord Marchmont"; and the following April, Johnson graciously let Boswell produce this interview, which Boswell later memorably described in the *Life*.[46]

Later, after Hester Thrale had gone to bed, Johnson, Boswell, and Henry Thrale returned to a topic Reynolds and Johnson had debated two days earlier, with Johnson again insisting "that vice did not hurt a man's character" in society. Johnson got "very hot" during what soon became a dispute about Beauclerk. "Who thinks the worse of Beauclerk for [debauching a friend's wife]?" Johnson asked. When Boswell persisted, Johnson angrily said, "Nay, Sir, there is no talking with a man who will dispute what everybody knows. . . . Don't you know this?" (Johnson at one point said, "Ask Mr. Thrale"; but their host would not challenge Johnson, though the next day he privately assured Boswell that Johnson had been wrong.) Having earlier been stubborn and petulant, Johnson now was rough and unyielding. But Boswell seemed self-assured rather than anxious, and he reported this heated dispute much more fully — and quickly — than he had done for their argument about America eight months earlier.[47]

Johnson had earlier learned to defeat Boswell mostly without ad hominem triumphs, and now Boswell could hold his ground even when Johnson was overbearing. On Good Friday, Boswell had even used Johnson's "own style" to dismiss his objections to publishing an account of his trip to France: "You had better have given us your travels in France. I am sure I am right, and there's an end on't." At the end of the visit, when Johnson and Boswell embraced "with great affection," Boswell was more secure and independent than ever before, and Johnson was correspondingly less worried. They had moved closer to the parity and mutual respect anticipated during Hebrides trip, with little competition and rivalry, though Boswell was troubled he could not get Johnson to criticize Beauclerk.[48]

But a change was about to occur. Having each been a central player in the other's life for the past five years, they were entering a period when their friendship would matter much less: when nothing significant happened while they were together, and when their correspondence — especially Johnson's — sharply declined.

11

"Strangers to Each Other"
(May 1778 to March 1781)

In the thirty-four months from 20 May 1778 through 19 March 1781, Boswell and Johnson were much less significantly in touch than in the previous six years. Aside from the seven weeks in the spring of 1779 when Boswell was in London, and three months that fall, when they exchanged letters both before and after a brief October visit, they were less connected than during the years since March 1772. Boswell skimpily documented these two visits, especially the first, suggesting they hardly mattered. Also, except in the fall of 1779, Johnson seldom wrote. Having sent on average a letter a month since the Hebrides trip, though with several long silences, Johnson wrote only two letters in the last seven months of 1778, five in 1779 (plus two notes during Boswell's spring visit), three in 1780, and one early in 1781.

The major dramas in their friendship during the previous three years had involved Boswell's moving from anxiety at living in a world without Johnson to more poised assurance, from repressed anger and secret defiance to more open self-assertion, and eventually Johnson's efforts to engage Boswell for another adventurous journey. Now a key drama involved Boswell's repeatedly seeking proofs of Johnson's love and esteem, even though he had no pressing need for Johnson's advice and knew that Johnson's "languor" — "a disease of which [Johnson] does not clearly know the cause or complications of causes," as Boswell wrote Hailes — often prevented him from writing when there was no urgency. In response, Johnson regularly tried to get his insecure friend to accept that his esteem and love were constant, though not unqualified, and also encouraged Boswell to manage more effectively the depression he reported regularly and at times seemed to nurture.[1]

Then, in 1780, the first year since 1774 when the two friends spent no time together, each separately — but with his friend very much in mind — reassessed all he had done and been as a grown-up: Boswell as he reread his early journals and letters and reconnected after thirteen years with his brother David; Johnson as he wrote biographies of many poets whose lives overlapped with his own.

Seeking Reassurance, Advising Self-control (May 1778 to March 1779)

Six days after leaving London early on 20 May 1778, Boswell wrote from Yorkshire, describing his visit to Lincoln and lamenting how little had been done to facilitate his move to London. (Pringle had "roused" him a week earlier by saying he "was *born* for England.") Three weeks later — a month after he last saw Johnson — Boswell wrote again, including more of Hailes's text and much information about the Scottish poet James Thomson. He quoted Thomson's claim that all his friends knew his reluctance to write letters, so they should "never impute the negligence of [his] hand to the coldness of [his] heart"; but Boswell still feared that Johnson's "neglect" indicated a lack of regard and concern.[2]

"You have all possible assurances of my affection and esteem," Johnson insisted about ten days after receiving Boswell's second letter; "but you must not think me criminal or cold if I say nothing, when I have nothing to say." Johnson was also troubled that Boswell, who earlier seemed to accept that he could move to London only if he got "a place or pension," was making himself miserable by longing for what he currently had no concrete way of achieving, instead of appreciating the many "ingredients of happiness" he already possessed: "good humour, prospect of a good estate, good wife and good children." So Johnson urged his friend to "correct or restrain [his] imagination, and imagine that happiness, such as life admits, may be had at other places as well as London."[3]

Boswell wrote three times in the next four months, including more complaints of neglect, before Johnson again replied. On 18 August, Boswell told of his "late dreary dejection." A month later, he reported the birth of a healthy son, James. Eight weeks later, he described a visit to Auchinleck, including news that the aged Countess of Eglinton, who had playfully adopted Johnson in November 1773, now said, "Tell Mr. Johnson I love him exceedingly." Also, since it was "very long" since he had heard from Johnson, Boswell reported being "a little uneasy."[4]

Soon after receiving Boswell's first letter, Johnson wrote Langton, whom he was about to visit, that Boswell "seems to be in his *old lunes,*" wanting to move to London — a comment indicating that he regularly talked with Langton about Boswell's "fits of lunacy or frenzy," just as he frequently talked with Boswell about Langton's need for economy. (The longest paragraph in Johnson's July letter to Boswell concerned Langton's "confused views.") But Johnson delayed writing Boswell for three months, at which point he acknowledged Boswell had "some reason to complain." Johnson congratulated Boswell on the birth of another son, hoped the pregnancy had restored Margaret's health, as it seemed to do, and delighted that his friend was "gaining ground at Auchinleck." Then, before giving news, Johnson offered some new advice on combating depression: "When any fit of anxiety, or gloominess, or perversion of mind, lays hold upon you, make it a rule not to publish it by complaints, but exert your whole care to hide it." Also, in response to something Boswell had written — perhaps a report that he had tried to cure "a swimming in [his] head" with strong wine — Johnson again urged "abstinence . . . from wine."[5]

Boswell waited eight weeks before replying, weeks during which he kept no journal at all, or only the briefest of notes. Then he quickly sent three letters. On 22 January 1779, he reported being "the better [because] of drinking wine sometimes," requested the famous letter to Lord Chesterfield as a "News Years gift," and told of having asked Francis Barber to collect the proof sheets for the *Lives,* which Johnson had agreed he could have. (In separate letters, Boswell reminded Barber of this task and asked Henry Thrale about Johnson's health.) When he learned of Garrick's death eleven days later, Boswell wrote at length about this shared friend. Three weeks later (23 February), Boswell reported being "uneasy" at Johnson's silence, though it had been just more than a month since he had first written.[6]

Johnson responded on 13 March, outraged at Boswell's manipulation: "Why should you take such delight to make a bustle, to write to Mr. Thrale that I am negligent, and to Francis to do what is very unnecessary." Three days before Johnson wrote these words, Boswell had left for London; and when he joined Johnson for breakfast the morning after he arrived, he was surprised that his friend had been angry. But Johnson looked better than ever, and Boswell was in fine health and spirits, so "all was gladness" as the two friends began another period of sustained contact.[7]

Together in London (16 March to 3 May 1779)

Boswell saw Johnson often during the next seven weeks, especially from 23 March through 18 April, when they were together on twenty-one of twenty-seven days. But Boswell "was unaccountably negligent in preserving Johnson's sayings," as he confessed in the *Life*. He recorded a fair number of Johnson's opinions and a few of his vivid, witty comments, and he collected many anecdotes from others. But he reported few of Johnson's sustained conversations, none as substantial as at least ten of those transcribed in 1778.[8]

Based on Boswell's notes, there were no major issues he needed Johnson to clarify or resolve. But after receiving only three letters in ten months, Boswell wanted reassurance that Johnson valued his friendship. On 24 April, when Boswell reported Wilkes's description of Garrick as a man "with no friend," Johnson agreed that Garrick "had no man to whom he wished to unbosom himself," and added that he, unlike Garrick, "would wish to have a friend with whom to compare mind[s] and cherish private virtues." Boswell hoped Johnson regarded him as such a friend. But the evidence from the previous six weeks was not conclusive.

At their first meeting, Johnson "embraced [Boswell] with cordial complacency"; but after "a few kind inquiries," Johnson returned to a translation he had been asked to assess. Two weeks later (31 March), when Boswell asked Johnson, whom he not seen since they had traveled to town in Thrale's coach two days earlier, "How have you been?" Johnson teasingly replied, "How could I be well when you have not seen me for a day and two nights?" Two days later, when Boswell came as usual to share Good Friday, Johnson gave him Pascal's *Pensées*—"that he might not interrupt me," as Johnson noted in his diary; and that year, in contrast to their last three shared Good Fridays, conversation did not make them late for afternoon service, though it had in the morning. (Not guessing Johnson's motives, Boswell regarded the *Pensées* as an assigned text, which he twice reported reading later in the visit.) Also, Johnson did not ask Boswell to return home with him after evening services on Good Friday.[9]

Five days later (7 April), in the most fully documented conversation since Boswell first reconnected with Johnson, there was a curious, possibly troubling exchange about the summer they first met, which Boswell later fleshed out in the *Life*. The context was Johnson's standard disquisition on different liquors, beginning with the assertion that claret is so weak that "a man would be drowned by it before he was made drunk": "No, Sir. Claret is the liquor for boys; port for men; but he who aspires to be a hero must drink brandy." As Johnson continued—"the flavor of brandy is most grateful to the palate, and then brandy will do soonest for a man what drinking *can* do for him"—Boswell "put him in mind how jollily" the two of them "used to drink wine together when [they] were first acquainted," as they had not done since, "and how [Boswell] used to have a headache after sitting up with him." "It was not the *wine* that made your head ache," Johnson noted, "but the *sense* I put into it." "BOSWELL. 'What, Sir, will sense make the head ache?' JOHNSON. 'Yes, Sir, when it is not used to it.'"

In the *Life,* Boswell suggested that Johnson "did not like to have this recalled," or perhaps thought Boswell "boasted improperly." In 1779, however, as he wrote his original—now missing—notes, Boswell also knew how strongly Johnson would disapprove of his current heavy drinking, which Paoli scolded a few days later. Instead of savoring the memory of "jollily" deciding with Boswell that two bottles of port was just the right amount, then walking arm in arm to the Temple Bar, Johnson stressed their radical disparity, teasing the man who planned to write his *Life.*[10]

At this point in the *Life,* Boswell called attention to Johnson's "repeated proofs that he valued him." But within nine days of this exchange at Reynolds's and a week before Johnson declared his wish for "a friend with whom to compare mind[s] and cherish private virtues," a private conversation with Beauclerk and Langton, followed by an angry dispute between Beauclerk and Johnson at the Club, left Boswell with an enhanced sense of how formidable a rival Beauclerk continued to be.

On 15 April, Boswell was so impressed with Beauclerk's clarity and force of mind in refuting Johnson's criticism of Langton's living beyond his means that he wrote exceptionally full notes. Beauclerk also complained of Johnson's "saying rough and severe things to people in company" and wished someone "violent" would teach him "how to behave": "At his age," Johnson "should be thinking of better things than to abuse people." Then at the club the next day, in arguing with Johnson about the Reverend James Hackman, who had recently shot the Earl of Sandwich's longtime mistress before trying to kill himself, Beauclerk responded angrily to Johnson's triumphant tone, politely but firmly answered Johnson's counterattack, and quickly produced a reconciliation. Beauclerk accomplished immediately and without help what Boswell a year before had achieved only days after Johnson's insults, and only with Langton's assistance. After dining at Beauclerk's eight days later (24 April), Boswell reported Johnson saying—I suspect with a prompt from Boswell—that "there was in Beauclerk a predominance over his company that one does not like." But Johnson added that Beauclerk "was a man who lived so much in the world that he had a short story for everything, was always ready to begin and never exhausted."[11]

On 29 April, Boswell explained in a note that he would be leaving sooner than planned because his father was "much indisposed." Having last seen Johnson three days earlier, when he and Reynolds stopped by after a dinner Boswell was unable to attend, Boswell hoped they might connect on each of his final four days. They managed two or three, starting on 1 May, when

Johnson met Boswell at Paoli's, "dressed in his best suit and Parisian wig," for the interview with Lord Marchmont, followed by dinner at Streatham. They probably dined at Paoli's next day, as Boswell had proposed. They certainly spent the afternoon and evening of 3 May at the home of Charles Dilly, with whom Boswell departed the next morning for a visit with the dying Edward Dilly on his way home.[12]

Loosely Connected (May 1779 to April 1780)

After returning to Scotland, Boswell adopted a new strategy to test Johnson's concern. He deliberately did not write. As he later explained to Johnson, "I was willing . . . to try whether your affection for me would . . . make you write first."

In June 1776, Johnson had begun worrying after only a few weeks of Boswell's silence, and in February 1777, after waiting more than eight weeks for an answer from Boswell, Johnson had sent an empowering confirmation of his affection. Now on 13 July, ten weeks after Boswell's departure and two weeks after Johnson had returned from Ashbourne and Lichfield, he first wrote Charles Dilly, to whom Boswell had recently written twice, and later that day wrote Boswell. "What can possibly have happened that keeps us two such strangers to each other?" he asked, while suspecting the truth. "No ill I hope has happened; and if ill should happen, why should it be concealed from him who loves you? Is it a fit of humour, that has disposed you to try who can hold out longest without writing? If it be, you have the victory. But I am afraid of something bad: set me free from my suspicions."[13]

Having reestablished that Johnson cared, Boswell by return post explained what he had done, and promised "never again [to] put you to any test." But he noted how often he had suffered from Johnson's long silences and how Johnson had chided him "for expressing [his] uneasiness." Two days later, Boswell wrote a much fuller letter, including an account of his final interview with Edward Dilly, some anecdotes from Lord Hailes concerning Matthew Prior, and "a variety of particulars" Boswell did not specify in his letter register. Then he waited for a reply.[14]

When Johnson finally responded seven weeks later (9 September), he was still angry about the earlier test. Though Boswell had written twice in mid-July, Johnson scolded him for "playing the same trick again, and trying who can keep silence longest": "Remember that all tricks are either knavish or childish; and that it is as foolish to make experiments upon the constancy of a friend, as upon the chastity of a wife." Boswell knew Johnson was wrong to be angry, for it was his turn to write. But he "*felt* even an unmerited reproof from

Him," as he wrote in his entry for 13 September — especially since Johnson referred to Boswell as "a man who, probably, acts only by caprice." A week later, Boswell quoted his entry — "written, upon my honour, without the least intention of your ever seeing it" — as he began to defend himself: "Indeed, My Dear Sir, I did not deserve to be suspected of a trick, or to speak more softly of making such another experiment as I did after I last left London. I wrote to you that I never would; and as you was a letter in my debt, the too long cessation of our correspondence was in strict law to be imputed to you." But after noting Johnson's error and reporting how his "unmerited reproof" nevertheless stung, Boswell deferentially refused to fault his friend for writing so seldom: "I am fully sensible of the honour and happiness of hearing from you so often as I do. But you will allow me to defend myself."

As a postscript, Boswell whimsically suggested a plan that would eliminate all possibility of anxiety and false accusation: "We should send off a sheet once a week, like a stage-coach, whether it be full or not; nay, though it should be empty. The very sight of your handwriting would comfort me; and were a sheet to be thus sent regularly, we should much oftener convey something, were it only a few kind words." If they always did this, there would be no question that each had the other in mind, with no opening for misunderstanding.[15]

A day after Boswell posted this letter, Colonel James Stuart invited him to travel with him to his regiment in Leeds and then to London, where his brother, Lord Mountstuart, was about to sail to the court of Sardinia. "You have a very good excuse to your father," Stuart said, "that you are going to see my brother before he goes abroad, which I think you should, and the journey up shall not cost you a farthing." Margaret was willing, provided Boswell "would not drink hard." So he left Edinburgh on 27 September, and three days later from Leeds wrote Johnson that he was coming.

When Boswell arrived early on 4 October, Johnson "expressed a satisfaction at this incidental meeting with as much vivacity as if he had been in the gaiety of youth," and asked Frank to "get some coffee and let us breakfast in splendour." Boswell saw Johnson again either later that day or the next morning, when he reported seeing no signs of the stroke Henry Thrale had suffered in June; and they connected on at least four additional days. Since the journal for this "jaunt" has not survived, this is the only London visit concerning which we have only what Boswell included in the *Life,* along with the letters Johnson sent Hester Thrale in Brighton. (Boswell must have written substantial entries, since his interactions with Johnson on five days fill about half as many pages in the *Life* as their meetings on twenty-eight days in the spring.)[16]

At the start of the visit, Boswell consulted Johnson about choosing a guardian for his children. At some point, he also tried to interest Johnson in a trip to Ireland, at least to Dublin, though Johnson insisted it was "the last place where

I should wish to travel." Since Boswell had earlier planned to ask Johnson about whether keeping a frank and detailed journal, including material he would be ashamed to have published, was "preserving evidence against oneself," I suspect he did so, but naturally did not report it in the *Life.*

Perhaps because Boswell kept a relatively full journal, Johnson seemed more intent than in the spring on speaking for the record. On Sunday, 10 October, for instance, when he decided not to go to evening prayers because of painful gout, he said, "Whenever I miss church on a Sunday, I resolve to go another day. But I do not always do it." Later that evening when Boswell suggested that when Johnson began the *Dictionary* he "did not know what [he] was undertaking," Johnson insisted, "Yes, Sir. I knew very well what I was undertaking, and very well how to do it, and have done it very well."[17]

Boswell left early on 18 October, and for the next five weeks there was the first brisk exchange of letters in years. On 22 October, Boswell wrote from Chester, requesting a quick response—even just "two lines"—while he was still there, and Johnson replied on 27 October. Eight days after receiving Johnson's letter, Boswell wrote from Carlisle, and again Johnson responded promptly, this time to Edinburgh. On 22 November, as soon as he had the information Johnson had requested for Lucy Porter, Boswell sent a third letter. Never before had they written so frequently without a compelling agenda such as the *Journey* or the entail. Also, since we have the complete texts of all these letters, we can compare their competing scripts for the friendship.[18]

Boswell wrote as an affectionate flatterer and a self-delighted performer, traveling with Johnson in mind while seeking his approving attention. His first letter was essentially a travel journal, detailing an energetic round of visits on a rainy morning in Lichfield, then more briefly describing his delight with Chester, which "pleases my fancy more than any town I ever saw." Three years earlier, Johnson had introduced Boswell to all the people who now greeted him in Johnson's hometown: "What a great key-stone of kindness, my dear Sir, were you that morning! For we were all held together by our common attachment to you." Boswell's welcome in Chester, which Johnson had visited five years earlier on the way to Wales, depended on the civility of Colonel Stuart and his officers, and the attentiveness of the bishop, whom Boswell had met before. But Johnson was still part of his conversation, for the bishop admired "very highly, [Johnson's] Prefaces to the Poets." Having played his roles with gusto, Boswell in closing asked Johnson "to add to the happiness of a happy friend" by responding quickly: "If you do not write directly, so as to catch me here, I shall be disappointed."

"Why should you importune me so earnestly to write?" Johnson asked, as he started doing so. "Of what importance can it be to hear of distant friends, to a man who finds himself welcome wherever he goes, and makes new friends faster than he can want them?" Johnson wrote mainly as moralist, insisting that Boswell look beyond his current jaunt and urging him to manage his mental health. After thanking Boswell for news from Lichfield, Johnson asked the friend who was so enjoying travel to consider how he would keep off the "black dog" of depression once back home. As possibilities, Johnson recalled two large projects they had often discussed: "enquir[ing] into the old tenures and old charters of Scotland," a challenging task that had intrigued Johnson for years, and narrating "the late insurrection in Scotland, with all its incidents," including those they had heard about while in the Hebrides. Boswell could "make collections for either of these projects, or for both, as opportunities occur, and digest [his] materials at leisure." Working on these would keep him busy, which was essential. Johnson concluded this exhortation by referring to the conclusion of Robert Burton's *Anatomy of Melancholy* (1621), a book he consistently praised: "The great direction which Burton has left to men disordered like you" —or like Johnson himself—"is this, *Be not solitary; be not idle:* which I would thus modify;—if you are idle, be not solitary; if you are solitary, be not idle."[19]

As soon as he reached Carlisle, Boswell thanked Johnson for his "polite kindness and masterly counsel, [which] came like a large treasure upon [him], while already glittering with riches." Instead of trying to summarize his extended stay in Chester, where he had been "quite enchanted"—"But the enchantment was the reverse of that of Circe; for so far was there from being any thing sensual in it, that I was *all mind*"—Boswell offered to send a copy of his journal, "which is truly a log-book of felicity." (He was also suggesting how travel to nearby places could be stimulating—Chester was on the way to Ireland—and demonstrating how much more Johnson might have seen there had he traveled with Boswell rather than the Thrales.) Instead of committing to the tasks Johnson had suggested to keep away "the black dog," Boswell requested another letter, using imagery he had associated with Johnson since Utrecht: "As I have been for some time in a military train, I trust I shall *repulse* him. To hear from you will animate me like the sound of a trumpet."

Again Johnson quickly replied, though I suspect he would not have written had Lucy Porter not requested information concerning a Scot who was courting David Garrick's niece. Describing Boswell's letter as "not only kind but fond"—a word linked in the *Dictionary* with folly—Johnson advised his friend "to get rid of all intellectual excesses, and neither exalt [his] pleasures, nor aggravate [his] vexations, beyond their real and natural state." Since Boswell ignored what Johnson had suggested for the depression he might experience at home, Johnson now simply wrote, "Why should you not be as happy at Edinburgh as at Chester? *In culpa est animus, qui se non effugit usquam* [what is at fault is the mind, which never escapes from itself]. Please yourself with your wife and children, and studies, and practice." Then Johnson commented on some specifics in Boswell's letter, asked for information about Lord Auchinleck, passed along secondhand accounts on the health of Beauclerk and Henry Thrale, and reported that among his own household at Bolt Court "there is much malignity, but of late little open hostility."[20]

Boswell replied from home on 22 November once he had a clear report for Lucy Porter. He refused to dispute why he should not be as happy at home as at Chester, but described being "better disposed to study than usual," as he demonstrated by commenting on an "ingenious and orthodox" Latin treatise he judged "worth translating." He also enclosed copies of Goldsmith's poems *The Traveller* and *The Deserted Village*, asking Johnson to mark those lines he had supplied for each. But now Johnson fell silent. He quickly sent Boswell's information to Lichfield. But he did not write Boswell until April 1780, after which he would write only three additional letters before he saw Boswell again in March 1781.[21]

Boswell wrote a month later (21 December), just after reporting that no period of his life had been "more sound and cheerful" than the preceding weeks, and tried to elicit a reply with news concerning the sister of Francis Stewart, who had worked for Johnson on the *Dictionary*, and again asked for the Chesterfield letter. A third letter, eleven days later, included Lord Marchmont's comments on Pope from the previous May and repeated the request for the Chesterfield letter. In a fourth letter, ten weeks later (13 March), Boswell reported that he could not afford a London visit and described his "bad spirits." But instead of worrying that Johnson had ceased to care, Boswell facetiously hoped his friend "had been in so much better company" — the poets whose *Lives* he was writing — "that he had not time to think of his distant friends": "for if that were the case, I should have some recompence for my uneasiness."[22]

On 8 April 1780, though writing for the first time in almost five months, Johnson did not apologize for being "a sluggish correspondent," as he did the same day to Lucy Porter. In fact, he faulted Boswell for requesting information about Goldsmith's poems before Johnson had provided the Chesterfield letter, though neither were onerous tasks. But for the most part Johnson was supportive and appreciative. He sympathized with Boswell's financial constraints and endorsed his decision "not to increase [his] own perplexity by a journey hither." He gave news about Beauclerk's death, a fire in Percy's apartment, and Henry Thrale's "apoplectic disorder." He also warmly thanked Boswell for finding and assisting the sister of Francis Stewart, "an ingenious and worthy man," and urged him not to "lose sight of her."

More importantly, since Boswell's recent letters repeatedly mentioned his melancholy, Johnson skillfully reworked his earlier advice that Boswell not "publish" his anxiety or gloominess:

Having told you what has happened to your friends, let me say something to you of yourself. You are always complaining of melancholy, and I conclude from those complaints that you are fond of it. No man talks of that which he is desirous to conceal, and every man desires to conceal that of which he is ashamed. Do not pretend to deny it; *manifestum habemus furem* [we have the unmistakable thief]; make it an invariable and obligatory law to yourself, never to mention your own mental diseases; if you are never to speak of them, you will think on them but little, and if you think little of them, they will molest you rarely. When you talk of them, it is plain that you want either praise or pity; for praise there is no room, and pity will do you no good; therefore, from this hour speak no more, think no more, about them.

Besides denying any lingering sense that melancholy was a sign of genius, and therefore the basis for "praise" — a position that still appealed to Boswell, though he had rejected it early in *Hypochondriack* 5 (January 1778) — Johnson insisted that pity would not help, whereas silence would. He was again asking Boswell to take full control, to become more like Johnson himself.[23]

When Boswell first read the *Life of Cowley,* two years earlier, he had singled out Johnson's comment that Cowley's *The Complaint* "had the usual effect of complaints: it made him be more despised than pitied." After praising Johnson's "noble manliness of mind," Boswell lamented his own tendency to complain and resolved to do so "only to a very intimate friend." But in *Hypochondriack* 6, the collaborative essay "On Hypochondria" he wrote at this time, Boswell expressed his longing for what he regularly received from Grange: "the comfort of a friend who will oppose him in nothing, nay will not trouble him with conversation but just as he appears to wish, watching him with soft attention, and as much as possible preserving an union with him." In February 1780, Boswell had returned to this topic in the essay "On Pity" (*Hypochondriack* 29), which concludes by quoting Johnson's remark on *The Complaint.* Since pity makes a person "more or less an object of disgust," Boswell urged readers to be "very cautious of complaining to people indiscriminately." But "affection" can "counterbalance- . . . disgust," he added, so it might be appropriate to complain to those who love us. In his entry for 12 April 1780, however, Boswell wrote that Johnson's advice not to talk to anyone about his melancholy "may perhaps be good": "I shall try to follow it."[24]

"Another Meeting . . . in the North of England"
(May through October 1780)

On 2 May 1780, three weeks after receiving Johnson's letter and three days after sending a letter of introduction for his brother David to give Johnson once he reached London, Boswell wrote directly to his friend. "To shew [his] mind was not languid," he enclosed a prepublication copy of his *Letter to Lord Braxfield,* Lord Auchinleck's successor in the Court of Session, praising the qualities his father had embodied as a judge, and "begged" Johnson to "review it for my private satisfaction." He also expressed a wish to meet "somewhere in the North of England" during the fall recess, as they had in 1777, declaring that Johnson, "as the richest at present[,] should take the largest part of the journey."

In the past, Johnson had always promptly acknowledged Boswell's publications. But now he did not reply, and Boswell also remained silent. Then, sixteen weeks later, almost simultaneously, both friends ended the longest mutual silence since they had begun formally working together on the *Life,* each independently recalling their richly collaborative Hebrides trip.[25]

Johnson's waiting till August was hardly unusual, especially since he knew Boswell's brother would report their having met in June. ("He is a very agreeable man, and speaks no Scotch," Johnson wrote Hester Thrale on 21 June.) Also, Johnson was stuck in London until he finished the remaining *Lives,* and even on 21 August did not know when he might be free. He did not admit to Boswell that he "ought to have written" sooner, as he did to Beattie on the same day; and he said nothing about *Braxfield.* Instead, since Boswell for the first time in years had waited months without writing a follow-up letter, Johnson accused him of having "taken one of [his] fits of taciturnity, and resolved not to write" until he was written to — a "peevish humour" he gruffly faulted. But Johnson then confessed having himself done less than necessary: "I have sate at home in Bolt-court, all the summer, thinking to write the Lives, and a great part of the time only thinking." If he had finished, he would have accompanied the Thrales to Bath and Brighton, or gone to Lichfield: "I might have had time, if I had been active; but I have missed much, and done little."

Johnson's writing Boswell suggests a longing for a diverting visit like their time together at Ashbourne. His health was much better than during the Hebrides trip, which he recalled had begun in August; and Johnson again expressed a wish that he and Boswell might one day "shew [them]selves on some part of Europe, Asia, or Africa." But the unfinished work still confined him, and he was not sure he would "get a ramble" that autumn.[26]

This letter, which Johnson gave Dr. James Dunbar to take to Edinburgh, reached Boswell at Auchinleck only on 4 September, eleven days after Boswell had finally written Johnson. In 1777, Boswell had followed his first request for a fall visit with another three weeks later, and then wrote two additional letters to pin Johnson down. His long silence in 1780 probably reflected his troubles that summer, plus an effort to follow Johnson's advice against complaining.

For various reasons—including Boswell's reunion with a brother who had challenged his assessments of their father, their stepmother, and himself—Boswell's "mind was rather sickly" until mid-August. He kept a journal, as he had the summer before. But significant portions have been removed, suggesting more wildness than usual. He wrote few letters; and on 1 September, a month after he winced for the second time that year at the "sickly weakness" documented in his journal for 1762–1763, the "most foolish time of [his] life," he burned most the letters he had written then to James Bruce, the overseer of Auchinleck.[27]

On 23 August, four weeks after reading Donald MacNicol's abusive *Remarks on Dr. Samuel Johnson's Journey to the Hebrides* (1779), and two days after Johnson—in the letter Boswell would see only ten days later—reported being in "better health" than when traveling in Scotland, Boswell began writing entries for their final days of travel, when he and Johnson had been tightly connected. The next day, he "easily" wrote to Johnson. Besides asking whether Johnson might meet him in York, Boswell probably noted that he was "easier" at Auchinleck than he had been for years and that he was completing his Hebrides journal. He might also have reported that David had helped him realize "that much of [his] unhappiness was *mouldy imagination*." Soon after he got Johnson's report that a fall visit was not certain, Boswell wrote again, pressing Johnson to come to York or Carlisle. Nine weeks later, Boswell sent a third letter, enclosing Sir Godfrey Bosville's invitation for them both to stay with him at York.[28]

Because Boswell on 6 September reported being "as happy at Auchinleck as in [his] earliest days," and on 1 October "was just as [he] could wish," he wrote nothing about needing Johnson's company. Building instead on Johnson's exhortation that they should "keep each other's kindness by all means in [their] power," Boswell suggested a plan: "To keep each other's kindness, we should every year have that free and intimate communication of mind which can be had only when we are together. We should have both our solemn and our pleasant talk." Boswell also appealed on behalf of posterity. Passing along Sir Godfrey's report that he never spent an evening in Johnson's company without hearing "something from him well worth remembering," Boswell wrote: "Let not the year 1780 be a blank . . . in that record of wisdom and wit, which I keep with so much diligence, to your honor, and the instruction and delight of others."[29]

In 1777, a combination of flattery and expressed need had secured the Ashbourne visit. Now Boswell's stronger flattery and the needs spelled out in his three letters were outweighed by a greater obligation. On 17 October, Johnson wrote that the "year must pass without an interview." His summer had been "foolishly lost," like many other summers and winters. He was finishing the *Life of Swift*, the major prose writer during his early life, leaving only the *Life of Pope* to write. So he might have spent a week in York. But Henry Thrale's "loss of health has lost him the election," Johnson explained. "He is now going to Bright[on], and expects me to go with him, and how long I shall stay I cannot tell." Knowing this decision would "not please," Johnson for the first time in three years wrote with no complaints, no criticism, and only the standard exhortation to "make your father as happy as you can." He also addressed what he knew was Boswell's deepest need, reaffirming that despite their limitations, their love was mutual, strong, and enduring: "We must . . . content ourselves with knowing what we know as well as man can know the mind of man, that we love one another, and that we wish each other's happiness, and that the lapse of a year cannot lessen our mutual kindness."

Unwilling as usual to embrace the hope expressed in Boswell's August letter that they would meet in heaven, "never to be separated," Johnson no longer hinted that their friendship might not endure once they became "purely rational." But his final paragraph was curiously detached. After again noting that his health was better than it had been in years, Johnson echoed what Swift had written Pope a month after he returned to Ireland for the last time—the words Johnson spoke in 1778 when Boswell remarked that "one of us must survive the other"—"Perhaps it may please God to give us some time together before we are parted." Having just tracked so many writers from birth to death, and conscious of Henry Thrale's precarious health, Johnson was reluctant to take the future for granted.[30]

Living without Johnson (October 1780 to March 1781)

Johnson's coming more than halfway for a visit would have reaffirmed Boswell's significance. His not coming demonstrated Boswell's secondary status. Having lived without direct contact for more than a year, and having received only three letters since November 1779, Boswell would not see Johnson before March, and might not hear from him before then.

Boswell eventually discovered a new way to write himself out of the depression partly triggered by Johnson's not coming to York, and learned early in 1781 that he could weather entirely on his own the "dreadful melancholy" produced by brooding on the arguments against free will. But the process was far from comfortable. Entries for almost half the days between 1 November and 31 December 1780 have been removed, presumably because they described Boswell's wild attempts to escape the depression described in the remaining entries. So has most of the sketch Boswell wrote of the first seven weeks of 1781. What remains hints at what living in a world without Johnson was like.

In the first three weeks of October, while still expecting to connect, Boswell was mostly in excellent spirits. He "never was sounder or more cheerful" than on 1 October, for instance, and on 17 October "was in high spirits," "wonderfully easy and gay." In the final days of October, Boswell's mood was flatter, his behavior less controlled. But on 3 November, after adding about 2,000 words to a letter he had begun writing Temple two months earlier, Boswell told his friend, "I am afraid a fit of Hypochondria is come, & that it may last some time." Entries for the first six days of November are missing. The short entries for 7–14 November seldom describe Boswell's feelings. On 17 November, after whatever occurred at the end of 14 November and during the next two days, Boswell's "spirits" were low, though he "was not deeply miserable." Finishing his third installment of "On Living in the Country" for the *London Magazine* gave him "some satisfaction." But after completing a letter to Langton and writing the entries for 9–16 November, Boswell reflected on the insignificance of his current life: "How little do I read! I am making no considerable figure in any way, and I am now forty years of age." Then, in ways Johnson would have applauded, Boswell shifted perspective: "But let me not despond. I am a man better known in the world than most of my countrymen. I am well at the bar for my standing. I lead a regular, sober life. I have a variety of knowledge and excellent talents for conversation. I have a good wife and promising children." Four days later, however, Boswell was "vexed" that at forty he had no government position, "sadly hurt" by his father's coldness, "depressed" at being kept in a "state of dependence," and angry at "Lord Mountstuart's neglect of [his] interest."[31]

Entries for the following ten days have been removed, and the next entry that survives reports that on 2 December, Boswell was "still in every bad spirits, but resolved to bear [his] distress," though he "had no *spirit,* no manly firmness." The next day, "while quite sunk, and in the state of everything seeming 'stale, flat, and unprofitable' " — part of a favorite passage from Hamlet's first soliloquy — Boswell "read some of Dr. Johnson's *Preface* to Milton, and was at once animated and ennobled." As when he read *Denham* in March 1778, Boswell was led to think of Johnson's death, and he "hoped to meet him in immortality."[32]

Reading *Milton* did not end Boswell's depression. In fact, after writing his wish to meet Johnson in heaven, Boswell did not resume writing journal entries for eight days. On 15 December, he was almost despondent: "Got up in sad hypochondria. Had several law papers and a *Hypochondriack* to be written without delay. Was quite in despair. Could not see any good purpose in human life." The next day, probably before beginning whatever prompted removal of entries for 16–26 December, Boswell wrote to Johnson. Though Boswell had been heeding Johnson's advice not to complain of melancholy to his correspondents, it is hard to imagine him sticking with that resolution now. But he may have described what he had just achieved in writing a third essay titled "On Hypochondria."[33]

In writing this essay, Boswell doggedly pushed through lethargy, proving once again he could rise to the challenge. But in a key way, he modified the procedure used in his two essays from early 1778, collaborations with Johnson in which Boswell functioned as both commentator and expert witness. For the first time, Boswell wrote at length about what he was currently experiencing. "The Hypochondriack is himself at this moment in a state of very dismal depression," he began, "so that he cannot be supposed capable of instructing or entertaining his readers." Johnson in *Rambler* 134 had rooted his reflection on procrastination in being forced to write what he put off till the end. But in his very first words—"I sat yesterday employed in deliberating on which, among the various subjects that occurred to my imagination, I should bestow the paper of to-day"—Johnson imagined himself in the moment ("today") when others would be reading what he had only begun to write. Boswell, in contrast, focused on what he was experiencing *as* he wrote. Sunk in "dismal depression," he turned to his readers, trusting that they would "make a kindly allowance for him" as he tried to see what he could "write in so wretched a state of mind."[34]

For the bulk of the essay, Boswell described "some of those thoughts, the multitude of which confounds and overwhelms the mind of a hypochondriack." Writing about his present condition while drawing on what he had experienced regularly, especially since 1775, he shifted from "the Hypochondriack" of the first paragraph and the "I" of the next three paragraphs to a generalized "he," representing anyone suffering depression. He was not complaining but analyzing.

> His opinion of himself is low and desponding. . . .
> He is distracted between indolence and shame. . . .
> Everything appears to him quite indifferent. . . .
> His distempered fancy darts sudden livid, glaring views athwart time and space. . . .
> An extreme degree of irritability makes him liable to be hurt by everything that approaches him in any respect. . . .
> He is either so weakly timid as to be afraid of everything in which there is a possibility of danger, or he starts into the extremes of rashness and desperation. . . .
> Though his reason be entire enough, and he knows that his mind is sick, his

gloomy imagination is so powerful that he cannot disentangle himself from its influence, and he is in effect persuaded that its hideous representations of life are true. . . .

   Could the hypochondriack see anything great or good or agreeable in the situation of others, he might by sympathy partake of their enjoyment. But his corrosive imagination destroys to his own view all that he contemplates. . . . Finding that his reason is not able to cope with his gloomy imagination, he doubts that he may have been under a delusion when he was cheerful; so that he does not even wish to be happy as formerly, since he cannot wish for what he apprehends is fallacious.

Having fully sketched the "helpless and hopeless wretchedness" of melancholy, Boswell then used three paragraphs to describe the "comforts" available to anyone who has "take[n] care to have the principles of our holy religion firmly established in his mind when it [was] sound and clear." By religion, and only by religion, could a hypochondriack's "troubled thoughts" be "calmed."[35]

   At the end of *Hypochondriack* 6, Boswell described the comfort a melancholic can receive from a wholly sympathetic friend. Now, at the end of *Hypochondriack* 39, written for friendly readers who would see it only days later, Boswell reported that he had "by some gracious influence been sensibly relieved from the distress under which [he] laboured when [he] began." Instead of whining about his melancholy, or trying to "think . . . down" distressing thoughts, or diverting himself while not talking about his melancholy, Boswell had written his way out of depression by analyzing what he was currently experiencing. The cure depended on Christian faith, for which Johnson remained Boswell's chief apologist. But it also depended on Boswell's strategy of directly writing his experience.

   It is unclear how long Boswell's relief lasted. The entry for 27 December 1780 — the first available after 15 December — reports his having been "in a dejected, uneasy state" on the night of 26 December. By the end of 27 December, however, Boswell "was in better spirits than [he] had been for many days." On 28–31 December, he was "wonderfully free from gloom," and his entries for these days — the last of which was written on 4 January — suggest considerable energy and poise. His mood was undoubtedly helped by a letter from Hugh Blair (dated 30 December), praising the three early *Hypochondriack* essays on death as "very well written" — "very Johnsonian" but also wholly original. Then, on 5 January 1781, Boswell read Lord Monboddo's argument that "every action of man was absolutely fixed and comprehended in a series of causes and effects from all eternity," and immediately "sunk into a dreadful melancholy."[36]

   Few of Boswell's bouts of melancholy began with such sudden intensity, and concerning none do we know so little. Unlike Johnson and Temple, Boswell took the arguments against free will seriously, and they lay "heavy upon [him]." Only on 17 February, after six weeks of darkness, did he report to Johnson and Temple in now-lost letters that he was no longer tormented. Ten days later, he wrote Paoli that he had "a full consciousness of Liberty," though he could not "explain" it.

Whatever the specifics — and most of Boswell's "Review" covering the first seven weeks of 1781 was later removed, presumably because of the means he used to escape depression — Boswell clearly received no direct help from Johnson, to whom he alluded in the *Hypochondriack* essays written in January and February, to whom he wrote as soon as he was free of depression, and from whom he still had not heard three weeks later (10 March), when he announced he would soon be in London. Whatever Boswell had gained by writing himself out of melancholy in a new way, and then surviving the depression produced by arguments against free will, he longed to end this sustained experience of life without Johnson.[37]

Had Boswell been in Edinburgh to receive Johnson's immediate response to his March letter, he would have been angry that his friend dismissed what he had just suffered as "all this hypocrisy of misery," an "affectation of distress." But long before Johnson's letter reached him, Boswell had "unexpectedly" met Johnson in Fleet Street and heard him say emphatically, "I love you better than ever I did."[38]

12

The Lives of the Poets *and*
Johnson's (Auto)biography (1777–1781)

While Boswell in December 1780 was finding a new way to write himself out of melancholy, and then weathering a bout of depression triggered by arguments against free will, Johnson was writing the *Life of Pope,* completing the assignment he had accepted four years earlier and greatly expanded. He had produced critical biographies of fifty-two writers, starting with those who had died before or shortly after he was born, but soon reaching those whose lives overlapped significantly with his own, some of whom he knew well. The first set of twenty-two, including *Milton* and *Dryden,* had been published early in 1779. Johnson wrote most of the longer second set in 1780, the first year since 1774 when he spent no time with Boswell, a year he refused to leave town until he was almost finished.[1]

Johnson wrote these *Lives* apart from Boswell, but with Boswell and Boswell's biographical project steadily in mind. From May 1777, when Johnson asked Boswell for information about James Thomson, his biographer had labored to involve himself. He quickly arranged for Thomson's sister to answer Johnson's questions, reported she had some of the poet's letters, and hoped she would "let *us* see them" (emphasis added). In later letters, Boswell passed along what Lord Hailes had told him about Matthew Prior and what Hugh Blair reported about Pope's *Essay on Man,* and summarized what Lord

Marchmont had said about Pope in the interview Boswell had ensured took place. Also, by January 1779, Johnson knew his biographer eventually would have all or most of his manuscript and proof sheets, and so would be able to chart his omissions and adjustments in what had already become a major endeavor. Johnson's health was surprisingly good from June 1779 through 1780. But he turned seventy-one before finishing, older than all but a few of his subject writers had been at death. So Johnson wrote in part to guide and constrain, to challenge and tease Boswell — and anyone else who eventually would write *his* biography.[2]

Addressing Boswell in the Lives

There are only a few passages in the *Lives,* like so many in the *Journey,* that were clearly written with Boswell as the intended primary audience. But Johnson often seems to be in private conversation with his biographer when alluding to aspects of his own experience.

He surely imagined Boswell would pay special attention when Johnson noted the reluctance of some biographers to allow Milton to "be degraded to a schoolmaster," and that Richard Blackmore's having been "compelled by poverty to teach school" was used to "reproach him, when he became conspicuous enough to excite malevolence," and would see the autobiographical significance of the comment "Every man that has ever undertaken to instruct others can tell what slow advances he has been able to make." I also imagine Johnson thinking of his biographer when he declared, early in the *Life of Addison,* that "not to name the school or the masters of men illustrious for literature, is a kind of historical fraud, by which honest fame is injuriously diminished," or when he remarked of Milton that "every house in which he resided is historically mentioned, as if it were an injury to neglect naming any place that he honoured by his presence." For he knew that Boswell had collected this information concerning him. When he described how Joseph Spence lived with Pope "in great familiarity, attended him in his last hours, and compiled memories of his conversation," Johnson must have been thinking of Boswell.[3]

I also imagine Johnson winking at Boswell while writing that "Pope, with all his labour in the praise of music, was ignorant of its principles and insensible of its effect," since just before writing the first of the *Lives,* he had told Boswell "that music made very little impression on him." When he wrote in *Shenstone* that Pembroke College was "a society which for half a century has been eminent for English poetry and elegant literature," he certainly anticipated Boswell's adding Johnson to this list. He knew also that Boswell would think of

Johnson when he read in *Akenside* that "by an acute observer, who had looked on the transactions of the medical world for half a century, a very curious book might be written on the Fortunes of Physicians."[4]

Boswell eventually supposed that in the "character" of Dryden, who appears "to have had a mind very comprehensive by nature, and much enriched with acquired knowledge," and whose "compositions are the effects of a vigorous genius operating upon large materials," Johnson had "unintentionally" given "some touches of his own." But I suspect Johnson was deliberately marking the resemblance, something he confirmed by later declaring his preference for Dryden over Pope. Certainly, when Johnson reported how Dryden boasted of his speed at composition, or how Edmund Smith "was remarkable for the power of reading with great rapidity, and of retaining with great fidelity what he so easily collected," or how Thomson "often felt the inconveniences of idleness, but never cured it," or how "the thoughts of death rushed upon [Swift] at this time with such incessant importunity, that they took possession of his mind when he waked for many years together," he knew Boswell could see how those statements applied to Johnson, too. He also knew that when Boswell and others read that "traditional memory retains no sallies of [Pope's] raillery, nor sentences of observation, nothing either pointed or solid, either wise or merry," they would note the striking contrast with Johnson, whose shrewd and witty remarks had been circulated for years.[5]

By including extended discussions of prose style in both *Addison* and *Swift*, Johnson challenged Boswell and others to assess his own self-consciously different prose. He might also have had Boswell specifically in mind as he demonstrated how a literary biographer needed fully to encompass his subject's mind. Johnson had no trouble assessing Addison's learning, and easily described the philosophical debate between Jean Pierre de Crousaz and William Warburton concerning Pope's *Essay on Man*. But given Boswell's repeated requests for grounding arguments and clarifications, and his limited familiarity with many of the books Johnson knew well, Johnson might well have wondered whether his biographer could claim to encompass him.

Johnson also flagged the need, when writing biographies of those whose relatives and friends were still living, "rather to say *nothing that is false, than all that is true*" — a degree of restraint he knew would be difficult for Boswell, who regularly distressed Garrick and Langton by repeating stories and comments he had heard. (This surely was one reason Johnson had insisted on looking over whatever Boswell hoped to publish from his Hebrides journal.) Finally, when Johnson in *Pope* challenged the common belief "that the true characters of men may be found in their letters, and that he who writes to his friend lays his heart open before him," and argued instead that there is "no transaction which offers stronger temptations to fallacy and sophistication than epistolary discourse," he was in effect warning Boswell and others to be cautious in assessing his own letters.[6]

The Lives *and Autobiographical Memory*

Johnson in the *Lives* also offered Boswell much biographical information not otherwise available. As Robert DeMaria, Jr., has noted, writing those texts involved a steady exercise of autobiographical memory, as Johnson recalled what he had thought and felt when he first read the works he was now reconsidering, recalled the people from whom he had heard stories about the poets and with whom he later discussed them, and remembered direct encounters with several of the writers. To glimpse what this process might have been like, spend fifteen minutes imagining how you might describe those contemporary writers you know best, including those you have heard read their works, seen or heard interviewed, perhaps studied in a course or discussed in a book group. Take enough time to recall specific episodes and notice what personal memories also come to mind.

Like traveling with Boswell in 1776 through a landscape dense with memories from his years before London, journeying through the life of each writer provided an organizing principle. In 1780, when Johnson made almost thirty such journeys, he was probably more diversely in touch with specific moments from throughout his life than at any other time. The result was not a narrative like the one he had begun in the "Annals," or the one he had constructed as he answered Boswell's questions about his early life. But the process of remembering was probably more extensive. It was certainly much more specific and thorough than what Johnson recorded in most of the surviving birthday or Holy Week reviews of his life. Some of the experiences Johnson remembered were probably as familiar as the anecdotes he repeatedly told Boswell and others. But many surely were not, since thinking about these writers brought to mind people and incidents that Johnson did not usually recall. Johnson did not tell or write most of these memories, but he had them in mind.[7]

A note to the printer and writer John Nichols in May 1780, while Johnson was writing the short *Life* of Elijah Fenton (1683–1730), shows how he drew on specific memories to clarify whether and when Fenton served as secretary to the fourth Earl of Orrery, and also whether Fenton had written *On the First-Fit of the Gout:* "When Lord Orrery was in an office Lewis was his Secretary. Lewis lived to my time. I knew him. The Gout verses were always given to Fenton, when I was young, and he was living. Lord Orrery told me that Fenton was his Tutor, but never that he was his father's secretary." Writing the *Lives* repeatedly called for this sort of focused recollection, though we get only glimpses of small portions of what Johnson recalled, little on how the experience affected him.[8]

Sometimes Johnson introduced personal memories to establish his authority. In *Butler,* for instance, he reported what "an old Puritan, who was alive in [Johnson's] childhood," had said when invited to a Christmas feast. He told how Addison had managed the "barring-out" of the schoolmaster at Lichfield (a form of rebellion in which pupils locked a teacher out of a schoolroom), based on what he had been told as a boy "by Andrew Corbet of Shropshire, who had heard it from Mr. Pigot his uncle." He described being in the theatre for the first performance of Thomson's *Agamemnon* and hearing how Thomson "accompanied the players by audible recitation, till a friendly hint frighted him to silence." He reported having "received from Mr. Locker, clerk of the Leatherseller's Company, who was eminent for curiosity and literature, a collection of examples selected from Tillotson's works, as Locker said, by Addison," who had also thought of making an English dictionary; but it "came too late to be of use, so I inspected it but slightly, and remember it indistinctly." More significantly, Johnson's close ties to William Collins informed his analysis of this poet's mental disorder, which "was not alienation of mind, but general laxity and feebleness, a deficiency rather of his vital than intellectual powers."[9]

On occasion, Johnson savored key relationships. The most extensive and memorable example comes in *Smith,* in which Johnson movingly sketched his early friendship with Gilbert Walmesley, at whose "table [he] enjoyed many chearful and instructive hours," while lamenting that David Garrick could not be "gratified with this character of our common friend," his recent death having "eclipsed the gaiety of nations, and impoverished the publick stock of harmless pleasure." At this point, Johnson mentioned as well his longtime friend Dr. Robert James, "whose skill in physick will be long remembered." In addition, Johnson reported discussing writers like Thomson and Pope with Richard Savage, fleshing out in these later texts what he had written about this formative early friendship in the relatively restrained *Life of Savage,* which Johnson now reprinted with only minor changes.

Cornelius Ford, the cousin whom Johnson had briefly described to Boswell in 1778, and about whom he would have written at length had his "Annals" reached 1725, was identified as the source of Johnson's description of William Broome, and also seems to be the clergyman referred to in the *Life of Fenton* "whose abilities, instead of furnishing convivial merriment to the voluptuous and dissolute, might have enabled him to excel among the virtuous and the wise." At the start of the *Life of Parnell,* Johnson lingered over a tribute to Goldsmith, "a man of such variety of powers, and such felicity of performance, that he always seemed to do best that which he was doing." After accounting for the enduring appeal of Nicholas Rowe's *Fair Penitent,* Johnson praised his friend Samuel Richardson, whose Lovelace excelled Rowe's Lothario "in the moral effect of fiction." Having given his "scheme" for writing the life of Swift to John Hawkesworth — "in the intimacy of our friendship" — Johnson now had little to add to what had been written by "a man capable of dignifying his narrative with so much elegance of language and force of sentiment."[10]

Other autobiographical allusions, though less full, are richly suggestive. In the early *Lives,* for instance, there are two interesting references to Johnson's father, Michael Johnson. In *Dryden,* Johnson wrote that the reception of *Absalom and Achitophel* "was eager, and the sale so large" that his father, "an old bookseller," told Johnson that "he had not known it equaled but by Sacheverell's trial." Then in *Sprat,* having reported in detail what happened when Thomas Sprat and Gilbert Burnet, "old rivals," preached before the House of Commons, Johnson added that he had been told this "in [his] youth by [his] father, an old man, who had been no careless observer of the passages of those times." At both these points, we overhear bits of conversation between the young Samuel and his father, in whose shop Johnson first encountered the works of many of these poets — anecdotes recalled when Johnson was about as "old" as his father was when he told them.[11]

Some autobiographical allusions are coyly incomplete, as if to tease future biographers. (In the first edition, Johnson did not identify his father as the "old man" who told about Sprat and Burnet, and clarified it only after the *Gentleman's Magazine* had guessed this man was Walmesley.) As he began assessing John Gay as a poet, for instance, Johnson wrote, "He was, as I once heard a female critick remark, 'of a lower order,'" encouraging readers to ask who this critic was. (The answer: Johnson's wife, Elizabeth, whom he met shortly after the death of Gay.) Later, commenting on Edward Young's "very ingenious, very subtle, and almost exact" comparison of Quicksilver with Pleasure in *Night Thoughts,* Johnson reported having heard this "repeated with approbation by a lady, of whose praise [Young] would have been justly proud." (This lady was Hester Thrale.) Finally, when Johnson appended to the *Life of Pope* his earlier essay on Pope's epitaphs, he kept his report of having "once heard a lady of great beauty and excellence object" that the fourth line of one "contained an unnatural and incredible panegyrick." (This lady was Molly Aston.) Since Boswell had asked in 1778 for the identity of the "lady" Johnson described as having first explained to him why "the interest of money is lower when the supply of money is plenty" — "Molly Aston, Sir, the sister of those ladies whom you saw at Lichfield" — he surely assumed Boswell would notice these autobiographical allusions, and perhaps ask questions.[12]

As happened whenever Johnson in conversation mentioned specific episodes from his life to illustrate a point or tell part of his story, he almost surely remembered much more than he described. When he reported what he had heard from Michael Johnson about Sprat and Burnet, or noted what Ford had told him about Broome and Fenton, or what Savage had said about Thomson or Pope, or how Tetty had described Gay, he recalled much about his relationships with each of these key figures and about how he regarded himself and the world at the time he was remembering. And the process continued, especially in 1780, when, having written about one writer whose life overlapped his own, he followed a somewhat different path through many of the same years as he wrote the next. After writing of Thomson (1700–1748), for instance, Johnson moved through much of this period — and in most cases even more of his life — as he wrote about Collins (1721–1759) and Akenside (1721–1770), Lyttelton (1709–1773) and Young (1683–1765), and finally Swift (1667–1745) and Pope (1688–1744). But Johnson did not include in the *Lives* most of what he remembered, nor did he later share these memories with his biographer.

Guilty Memories

Several diary entries and letters suggest that writing the *Lives,* especially the final set, may have focused or augmented Johnson's remorse concerning his mother, his wife, and his father, and certainly led him to wonder about his brother.

When Johnson described "Pope's filial piety" toward his mother, who died at ninety-three, and reflected that "Life has, among its soothing and quiet comforts, few things better to give than such a son," it seems likely that he thought of his own behavior toward a mother who was almost ninety when she died early in 1759. But Johnson's references to Sarah Johnson in surviving documents from the previous fifteen years — a few cryptic notes from 1766–1767 and 1777, and a letter in 1775 asking Edmund Hector to discover when she had been christened — do not indicate clearly whether Johnson felt satisfaction at having, like Pope, "lamented" his mother's death, or guilt at not having returned home during her final eighteen years.[13]

Besides recalling what Elizabeth Johnson had said about Gay, Johnson surely thought of his wife often as he repeatedly moved through the years of their marriage (1735–1752). In the *Life of Ambrose Philips,* for instance, he suggested that Garrick was his source for declaring that Addison wrote the impressive epilogue to *The Distrest Mother;* but he probably had his wife in mind, too, since he had earlier told Boswell that she had heard this from the bookseller Jacob Tonson's partner. More importantly, Johnson's diary entries suggest that as he again and again relived his years as a husband, he somewhat modified what Gay W. Brack describes as a "concerted if unconscious effort to forget the realty of his troubled marriage and to substitute a harmonious illusion."

On 20 April 1778, three days after he told Oliver Edwards that the death of his wife "almost broke [his] heart," Johnson wrote privately, "Poor Tetty, whatever were our faults and failings, we loved each other. I did not forget thee yesterday. Couldest thou have lived —." But Johnson's fuller comments four years later, a year after he finished the *Lives,* seem to draw on the experience of repeatedly reliving his seventeen years with Elizabeth: "On what we did amiss, and our faults were great, I have thought of late with more regret than at any former time. She was I think very penitent. May God have accepted her repentance: may he accept mine." Sustained attention to his marriage while writing the *Lives* fostered concrete repentance.[14]

Johnson's experience in 1780–1781 may also have prompted his famous visit to the Uttoxeter market, where he had defiantly refused to set up a book-stall six weeks before his father died. This act of resistance had "ever since lain heavy on [his] mind," though he seems not to have described it before October 1781, when he tried to expiate his guilt over the omission. "To do away with the sin of disobedience," Johnson explained to his hostess in Lichfield, "I this day went in a postchaise to Uttoxeter, and going into the market at the time of high business, uncovered by head, and stood with it bare an hour before the stall which my father had formerly used, exposed to the sneers of the standers-by and the inclemency of the weather; a penance by which I trust I have propitiated heaven for this only instance, I believe, of contumacy towards my father."

Johnson did not go to Uttoxeter in spring 1779, after he had compensated in *Dryden* and *Sprat* for having sometimes described his father as "wrong-headed." Instead, he waited until his first visit to Lichfield after finishing the final set, in which Michael Johnson is not mentioned. Johnson might have waited simply because 1781 was the fiftieth anniversary of his defiance. But it is also possible — and I think likely — that his experience in 1780 of returning again and again to 1731, the year of his refusal, prompted this act of expiation when he was next in Lichfield, where he also wrote a Latin poem describing how his "father with his calm voice" taught Johnson to swim. In the *Journey,* Johnson had atoned for the faults highlighted in Boswell's journal for the previous fall, and at Uttoxeter he atoned for an event he had repeatedly recalled the year before.[15]

The clearest example of how remorse was awakened by frequently moving through his own life while writing the *Lives* concerns Johnson's brother, Nathaniel, who died early in 1737 after having — in James Clifford's words —

"apparently [been] involved in something discreditable, perhaps dishonest, which shocked his mother and elder brother and led to some kind of family quarrel." (Bate suggests forgery.) Johnson barely included his brother in what survives of the "Annals" or in the stories he told Boswell, who seemed uninterested in Johnson's sibling rivalry. Nathaniel is seldom mentioned in Johnson's surviving diaries and is never referred to in the *Lives*. But it seems more than coincidental that late in 1780, after moving again and again through the years of his brother's short life — 1712–1737 — Johnson longed for anecdotes about his final days.

On 14 August 1780, when Johnson wrote Mary Prowse concerning the allowance her recently deceased mother had provided for the care of his deranged cousin, Elizabeth Herne, he also requested that she ask her servants, when next in the nearby town of Frome, to "collect any little tradition that may yet remain of one Johnson, who more than forty years ago was for a short time, a Bookbinder or Stationer in that town." Four months later Johnson wrote again, thanking Mary for her efforts, and explaining that the man he had asked about was a "near relation": "An adventurer who came from a distant part in quest of a livelihood, and did not stay a year. He came in 36 and went way in 37. He was likely enough to attract notice while he staid, as a lively noisy man, that loved company. His memory might probably continue for some time in some favourite alehouse. But after so many years perhaps there is no man left that remembers him." The brother whose life ended soon after Johnson reached London was clearly on Johnson's mind as he completed this project, which had repeatedly led him through the years of their rivalry.

Four years later, Johnson's writing epitaphs for Nathaniel, his mother, his father, and his wife, and his ordering "deep, massy, and hard" stones to "protect their bodies," clearly showed a desire to make up for past neglect. In 1780, too, Johnson seemed eager to atone by learning the specifics of Nathaniel's final months and by better understanding his brother's final days, though of course he did not share this wish with Boswell, whom he wrote a week after first asking Mary Prowse to inquire concerning Nathaniel.[16]

Self-Acceptance

If Johnson's moving again and again through his own life awakened remorse at specific failings, Johnson's Holy Week and birthday reflections and prayers suggest that writing the *Lives* also contributed to a significant reassessment of all he had done. In particular, the experience in 1780 of judging so many of his contemporaries with poise and generosity while producing such a substantial body of work seems momentarily to have lightened Johnson's enormous burden of guilt at having done less than he had hoped. Having firmly but compassionately judged the moral and intellectual characters of these writers — as he made clear, all men whose thoughts and feelings, motives and aspirations, he could not know as firmly as he knew his own, and whose failures to fulfill their potential he often attributed to extenuating circumstances — Johnson seemed more willing than usual to acknowledge privately the significance of what he had accomplished.[17]

"When I survey my past life," Johnson wrote on Easter 1777, a day after agreeing to take on the *Lives* project, "I discover nothing but a barren waste of time with some disorders of body, and disturbances of the mind very near to madness; which I hope he that made me will suffer to extenuate many faults, and excuse many deficiencies." Five months later, having not yet begun the first of the *Lives,* Johnson confessed to Hester Thrale to having "loitered with very little pleasure," then added: "To say this of a few weeks, though not pleasing, might be born, but what ought to be the regret of him who in a few days will have so nearly the same to say of sixty eight years." But once Johnson had completed the second set of *Lives,* including biographies of twenty writers who were alive when he came to London in 1737, it was harder to dismiss his life as "nothing but a barren waste of time." In particular, his writing so much in 1780, when he made up for having done little in 1779 by staying in London instead of traveling with the Thrales, or visiting old friends in Lichfield and Ashbourne, or meeting Boswell in York, seems to have allowed Johnson to set aside some of his guilt at having wasted so much of his time and to express some satisfaction in his private reviews. If standing bare headed in the Uttoxeter market eventually atoned for a refusal years earlier, his writing so many *Lives* so quickly helped redeem the "misspent" time he was reliving again and again. Writing so much and so well at such an advanced age helped justify his entire life.[18]

Some of Johnson's life between 6 April and 28 August 1780 is charted in the thirty-three surviving letters he wrote while the Thrales were in Bath and Brighton. While lamenting his confinement, Johnson accepted this consequence of his idleness and repeatedly resolved to stay put until finished. Here are some representative passages: "I am seeking for something to say about Men of whom I know nothing but their verses, and sometimes very little of them. Now that I have begun, however, I do not despair of making an end" (April 11, to Hester Thrale); "I have been so idle that I know not when I shall get either to You, or to any other place, for my resolution is to stay here till the work is finished" (30 May, to Henry Thrale); "I should like to move when every body is moving, and yet I purpose to stay till the work is done, which I take little care to do" (21 June, to Hester Thrale); "I have not yet persuaded myself to work, and therefore know not when my work will be done" (8 August, to Hester Thrale); "I am afraid that I shall not see Lichfield this year, yet it would please me to shew my friends how much better I am grown; but I am not grown, I am afraid, less idle; and of idleness I am now paying the fine by having no leisure" (25 August, to Hester Thrale).

In letter after letter, Johnson turned his correspondents — mainly Hester Thrale, but also Henry Thrale, and eventually Boswell — into parental figures to whom he reported delays but also some progress. As he balanced self-pity with playful self-castigation, noting how his present situation was emblematic of the whole of his life, Johnson repeatedly used the language of his private meditations. His "resolution" was to stay until he was finished. He would not "despair" of finishing, even though when he wrote those words, eighteen *Lives* were unwritten, including two that would be long. In fact, Johnson was wholly confident, as he rarely was when he formed resolutions during Holy Week or on his birthday. He had seldom risen early for long, or kept a journal, or avoided idleness. But he had never failed to complete a major piece of writing — eventually. Also, his resolution to stay in town until the work was done, unlike the "resolutions or purposes" he recorded privately and then forgot, could not slip his mind. For he repeatedly declared it.[19]

A week after first agreeing to produce the *Lives*, Johnson had written a grim report on his declining health, reflecting, "If I am decaying, it is time to make haste." Two years later, having published twenty-two *Lives*, Johnson initially failed to take advantage of a remarkable "remission of those convulsions in [his] breast which had distressed [him] for more than twenty years." But by 18 June 1780, when he thanked God for a full year of remarkable and continuing good health, he for months had been making up for time wasted. He was not always diligent, but he was no longer simply idle.[20]

On 21 August, when he finally answered Boswell's letter of 4 May, Johnson reported having stayed "at home in Bolt-court, all the summer, thinking to write the Lives, and a great part of the time only thinking." But several were done, and he still thought "to do the rest." (Here and throughout that August, as Roger Lonsdale notes, Johnson understated how much he had already written.) When he next wrote Boswell, eight weeks later, he had almost finished *Swift,* leaving only *Pope*. By the time he wrote again, almost five months later, he was done, having in a remarkably productive year written texts that fill hundreds of printed pages. On 14 March 1781, nine days after arranging for the second set to be sent to Margaret Boswell and Lord Hailes, Johnson triumphantly wrote Boswell, "I have at last finished my Lives, and have laid up for you a load of copy, all out of order, so that it will amuse you a long time to set it right."[21]

By frequently telling the Thrales and Boswell that he was confined to London because of prior idleness, and then doing what he had openly resolved to accomplish — constructing something more impressive than any of those fifty-two poets had written after turning seventy — Johnson seems even to have dissolved some of his guilt at having wasted so much of his past life. After this, though self-castigation remained constant, there seem to be small but significant changes in the rhetoric of his Holy Week reflections, and especially in what he wrote and did on his birthday.

On Easter Monday 1778, despite the momentary satisfaction he had experienced during and after the Good Friday encounter with Oliver Edwards, Johnson as usual reported "a melancholy and shameful blank" since the previous Easter, "so little has been done that days and months are without any trace," even though he added, "I have written a little of the lives of the poets, I think, with all my usual vigour. I have made sermons perhaps as readily as formerly." On Good Friday 1779, Johnson again saw "little but dismal vacuity" in the previous year, "neither business nor pleasure; much intended and little done." But again he added that he had just "published the lives of the poets, written," he hoped, "in such a manner, as may tend to the promotion of piety." He specified the next day that he had written "part of the life of Dryden, and the Life of Milton." But outside of that project, he saw no progress: "My mind has neither been improved nor enlarged. I have read little, almost nothing, and am not conscious that I have gained any good, or quitted any evil habit." After so many "resolutions" made "with so little effect," Johnson's lunge toward change was determined but desperate: "Good resolutions must be made and kept. I am almost seventy years old, and have no time to lose. The distressful restlessness of my nights makes it difficult to settle the course of my days. Something however let me do."[22]

No Holy Week diary entries survive for 1780. But in 1781, Johnson's assessment of the past year was more positive. After briefly reporting on Good Friday that he had forgotten the resolutions made at the start of the year, Johnson immediately added, "Sometime in March I finished the lives of the Poets, which I wrote in my usual way, dilatorily and hastily, unwilling to work, and working with vigour and haste." He was grieving the death of Henry Thrale nine days earlier. But having completed the *Lives of the Poets* was satisfying. "Little done" — the phrase twice repeated in 1779 — is not part of this assessment, for he had just written so much. "I have corrected no external habits," he added the next day, "nor have kept any of the resolutions made in the beginning of the year." But his "hope still to be reformed" seemed more confident, since he had "advanced by pious reflections in [his] submission to God, and [his] benevolence to Man." His wish "not to lose my whole life in idle purposes" seems merely formulaic, given how purposefully and productively he had spent the past year.[23]

The shift in Johnson's surviving birthday meditations is even more striking. For 1778, neither birthday prayer nor meditation has survived. Just before his birthday in 1779, midway through the long period when he put off working on the second set of *Lives*, Johnson left the servants at Streatham a guinea to drink his health, and "escape[d]" to Anthony Chamier's at Epsom, "a house where [his] Birthday not being known could not be mentioned." He stayed up till past midnight, when "a new year, a very awful day began," and prayed. He prayed again when he awoke, and spent the day partly with his friend, partly alone, but with no open acknowledgment of the birthday. His next birthday came at the end of Thrale's unsuccessful bid for reelection, and Johnson — after reporting having "more strength of body and greater vigour of mind than, I think, is common" at seventy-one, and applauding how he had "diminished the bulk of my body" — was sternly judgmental, mentioning the unwritten lives of Swift and Pope, not the many he had finished: "I have not at all studied, nor written diligently. . . . I have forgotten or neglected my resolutions or purposes [which] I now humbly and timorously renew. Surely I shall not spend my whole life with my own total disapprobation." He had not protested a day before when the Thrales celebrated Queeney's birthday — and his — by "fill[ing] the Summer House with Food, Fiddles, &c." But he was not ready to accept what Hester had written three weeks earlier: "Never compare yourself with perfection, but look as Boswell says at other people's Friends, and think not those Years wretched which have at least been spent on the Improvement of others, though you have perhaps left yourself unimproved."[24]

Johnson's narrative for 18 September 1781, the first birthday after he completed the *Lives*, was strikingly different: "I said a preparatory prayer last night, and waking early made use in the dark, as I sat up in bed of the prayer. . . . I rose, breakfasted and gave thanks at Church for my Creation, Preservation, and Redemption. As I came home I thought I had never begun any period of life so placidly. I read the second Epistle to the Thessalonians, and looked into Hammonds notes. I have always accustomed to let this day pass unnoticed, but it came this time into my [mind] that some little festivity was not improper. I had a Dinner and invited Allen and Levet."

Johnson's birthday remained "an awful day." But instead of going where no one knew its significance, Johnson decided to celebrate. In the now-lost "book K," in which Johnson wrote what "passed in [his] thoughts on this anniversary," he might still have regarded his life with "total disapprobation," as he had the year before. But I doubt it. For his narrative included nothing about forgotten resolutions or a failure to acquire knowledge or good habits.

Also, Johnson's birthday prayer for 1781 is much less graphically self-critical than usual. Instead of "Pardon me . . . all the offences, which in the course of seventy years I have committed against thy holy Laws, and all the negligences of those Duties which Thou has required" (1779), he wrote, "Let me at last repent and amend my life . . . assist my amendment, and accept my repentance." Instead of "Look with mercy upon my wretchedness and frailty, rectify my thoughts, relieve my perplexities, strengthen my purposes, and reform my doings" (1780), he wrote simply, "Relieve the diseases of my body, and compose the disquiet of my mind." For some reason or cluster of reasons, Johnson seems to have felt less guilty and desperate than usual, more confident and hopeful. At least momentarily, he was like the old man he described near the end of *Rasselas,* who recalled "many opportunities of good neglected, much time squandered upon trifles, and more lost in idleness and vacancy . . . many great designs unattempted, and many great attempts unfinished," but who, because his "mind [was] burthened with no heavy crime," still hoped "with serene humility" to possess after death "that happiness which here [he] could not find, and that virtue which here [he had] not attained."[25]

I attribute this difference to Johnson's having written so much during the previous eighteen months, and with such "vigour," and having so variously relived his life while comparing himself to each of the other writers he assessed. His completing such a substantial project made it difficult to see the past year as a blank. The steady comparison highlighted also how much he had accomplished as a writer. He had not been as precocious as Cowley or as assiduous as Pope. He had written nothing as sublime as Milton's *Paradise Lost* or as intellectually alive as Swift's *Tale of a Tub.* But he clearly excelled all these writers as a critic and biographer; and only he had compiled a dictionary. He was as impressive as any in conversation and more memorable than most. Clearly, he had used some of his time well.

Six months earlier, having finished the final autobiographical journey required in order to write the second set of *Lives,* Johnson had, in response to news that Boswell would soon be in London, expressed a deep longing to reconnect. After brusquely dismissing what had triggered Boswell's recent depression — "What have you to do with Liberty and Necessity? Or what more than to hold your tongue about it?" — Johnson addressed Boswell's chief worry after their longer than usual separation (seventeen months) and his own long silence (almost five months): "Do not doubt but I shall be most heartily glad to see you here again, for I love every part of you but your affectation of distress." Having finished the *Lives* and set aside "a load of copy, all out of order," to amuse his biographer, Johnson was eager to revive their friendship: "Come to me, my dear Bozzy, and let us be as happy as we can. We will go again to the Mitre, and talk old times over."[26]

Reconnecting (1781–1783)

When Boswell and Johnson "unexpectedly" met in Fleet Street a day after Boswell reached London, neither knew that the still remarkably healthy Johnson would die within four years. But by the end of the visit, Johnson's health was beginning to totter; and when they next met, in March 1783, Boswell was shocked by how close to death his friend seemed. By then, their friendship had also been challenged by the deaths of others. The death of Henry Thrale in April 1781 left Johnson uncertain about his connection with the family that for years had provided a second home, and alarmed Boswell that Johnson might marry Thrale's widow. The death of Lord Auchinleck in August 1782 left Boswell desperate for Johnson's encouragement and approval, while Johnson worried about Boswell's persistent neediness, his heavy drinking, and his continuing to imagine that only moving to London could make him happy. Except for the first days of the 1781 visit, therefore, there was always considerable anxiety as the two friends interacted, even in moments when they recaptured the magic of "old times."

Boswell in London (19 March through 2 June 1781)

In London for the first time in seventeen months, Boswell hoped to record some of the "wit and wisdom" he had missed in 1780; and Johnson anticipated continuing to live vicariously through this young friend, whose letter of 10 March probably mentioned his representing Archibald Montgomerie, 11th Earl of Eglinton, whose recent election to the Ayrshire seat in Parliament had been appealed by Sir Adam Fergusson to the Court of Session and would now be challenged before a select committee of the House of Commons. A day after they met by chance, Johnson surprised Boswell with the "load of copy" promised in the letter Boswell had not yet received. He dictated a paragraph to help with the appeal and advised Boswell how best to address the committee. He also told those gathered at the house Henry Thrale had rented in Grosvenor Square that "Mr. Boswell never was in anybody's company who did not wish to see him again."

Boswell encouraged Johnson's playful humor, which he then recorded. At Reynolds's on 30 March, for instance, he mentioned a "ludicrous" news story that Johnson was learning to dance from Gaetano Vestris, the leading dancer at the Paris Opera; and when asked if this were true, Johnson facetiously "kept up the joke," suggesting that if anyone wrote denying this, he would reply: "That he who contradicted it was no friend either to Vestris or me. For why should not Dr. Johnson add to his other powers a little corporeal agility? Socrates learnt to dance at an advanced age, and Cato learnt Greek at an advanced age." They were playing familiar roles.[1]

The death of Henry Thrale five days later decisively changed the tone of their interactions. Thrale had suffered a stroke in 1779, and in 1780 looked so ill that he lost his seat in Parliament. But he still talked of traveling to Italy and continued to entertain lavishly at the house he rented in town. His death on 4 April deeply affected Johnson, who "felt almost the last flutter of his pulse, and looked for the last time upon the face that for fifteen years had never been turned upon [Johnson] but with respect or benignity." Johnson grieved deeply. "No death since that of my Wife has ever oppressed me like this," he wrote Hester Thrale the following day. Six days later he felt "like a man beginning a new course of life": "I had interwoven myself with my dear friend." With Hester at Brighton through 21 April, Johnson had nobody nearby with whom to share his uneasiness. Two weeks after Henry's death, Johnson wrote Hester that he was finally regaining "that tranquility which irremediable misfortunes necessarily admit." But he wondered how his "mode of life" would be affected. With Thrale "were buried many of [his] hopes and pleasures."[2]

Besides mentioning Johnson's not attending the Club on the night of Thrale's death, Boswell wrote nothing about his friend's grief. Nor did he describe his own reaction. But while Johnson was sad and apprehensive, Boswell feared Johnson would marry the young widow, with whom he had lived so intimately. There is no evidence that either Hester Thrale or Johnson was interested in a marriage, though Johnson clearly desired sustained contact with this family. But Boswell, having secretly copied the diary entries in which, thirty years earlier, Johnson reported his wish to "seek a new wife," thought marriage possible, even likely. Nor was he alone. On Easter, Dr. William Scott, the distinguished young lawyer who had accompanied Johnson from Newcastle to Edinburgh in 1773, agreed with Boswell "that . . . Mrs. Thrale might marry Dr. Johnson." "We both wished it much," Boswell added. But Boswell's criticism of Johnson during Holy Week, his "Epithalamium on Dr. J. And Mrs. T.," his drunken challenge a day after Hester returned to town, and his seldom being with Johnson for the next six weeks all suggest anxiety.[3]

In talking with Dr. Scott, Boswell linked the likelihood of a marriage to Johnson's "love of great company and good dinners," which he had criticized on Good Friday, when he faulted his friend for having twice dined with bishops during Passion Week — a "laxity" that showed he had changed from when he wrote the solemn *Rambler* 7 at the start of Holy Week in 1750. Marrying Hester Thrale would demonstrate that Johnson lacked the high-mindedness and manly self-control that had made him truly great.[4]

The Good Friday conversation about dining with bishops seems as close as Boswell came to warning Johnson directly not to abandon his heroic stature by marrying the young widow. But at Reynolds's house the evening before, after he and Reynolds had dined with Johnson at the bishop of Chester's, Boswell more fully expressed his anxiety by composing the "Epithalamium," a gross and tasteless forty-four-line poem he shared with Reynolds as he wrote it, then recited two days later after dinner. To allay his fears that Johnson would be completely drawn away, Boswell presented him in the role of an eager lover, anticipating for Mrs. Thrale the sensual and intellectual joys of their marriage:

> Charming cognation! With delight
> In the keen aphrodisian spasm,
> Shall we reciprocate all night,
> While wit and learning leave no chasm?

Surely this was too grotesque, too out of character ever to have happened. But if it did, Boswell had already coaxed others to join him in laughing. Boswell's late condolence note once Hester Thrale had returned to town — "Mr. Boswell . . . hopes she will believe he feels all he ought to do, though his gaiety of fancy is not to be subdued" — might even suggest that he hoped his rival had heard of his poem, with its warning of the ridicule that would follow a marriage to Johnson.[5]

While Hester was at Brighton, Boswell saw Johnson almost as frequently as before Henry's death, culminating with what Boswell later called "one of the happiest days" that he remembered having enjoyed "in the whole course of [his] life," 20 April, when they shared dinner and then tea with those whom David Garrick's widow had invited for her first entertainment since her husband's death. When somebody said, "The life of a mere literary man could not be very entertaining," there was a moment of public intimacy when Johnson, who had just written many such lives, insisted that "as a literary life it could" and Boswell knowingly added that it would be better if the life had "some active variety": if the writer "goes to Jamaica, or . . . to the Hebrides." When they later stopped to look at the Thames, Boswell mentioned, "with tenderness," the "two friends [they] had lost who lived here, Garrick and Beauclerk," and Johnson replied, "Ay . . . and two such friends as cannot be supplied." Then Boswell walked with Johnson to Temple Bar, as he had done so often, "wished him good-night and came home."[6]

Hester Thrale returned to London the next day, and a day later Boswell showed up drunk at the house of a young and fashionable bluestocking, sat next to Johnson, and accosted him "in a loud and boisterous manner, desirous to show the company how [he] could contend with Ajax." Six years earlier, after Johnson had discouraged publication of the Hebrides journal, Boswell had vented some of his anger by forcing his friend to admit he could neither see nor hear at a benefit performance they had both just attended. Now, despite all the poise he had acquired in the meantime, Boswell expressed some of his anxiety at a possible marriage by asking Johnson whether he would not be "very happy" if he imagined the Duchess of Devonshire, "the loveliest duchess in His Majesty's dominions," were in love with him. The facetious story about Johnson's learning to dance had included a "rumour" that his first appearance in public would be at court, where "he [was] to be honoured with the fair hand of her Grace of Devonshire." Boswell now suggested that the beautiful duchess was much more likely to desire him. But since Hester Thrale seemed to find Johnson engaging, Boswell's anxiety persisted. Also, Boswell had seen his own father marry a much younger woman, and felt she had turned his father against him.[7]

Having seen Mrs. Thrale on nine of his first twelve days in London, Boswell made no effort to see her after she returned. He also saw much less of Johnson. They had been together on more than half of Boswell's first thirty-five days in London, often at length. But Boswell saw Johnson on just twelve of his final forty days, often briefly. He also spent much less time recording what Johnson said than he had earlier, sometimes because Johnson "said nothing and seemed dull" (30 April), but sometimes because Boswell focused on others, as he had in the spring of 1779.[8]

During these weeks, Johnson, as one of Henry Thrale's executors, was ener-getically helping manage Thrale's brewery while also trying to sell it. There is little indication of how he thought about the inwardly rebellious, essentially aloof Boswell. In the *Life,* after reporting his asking boisterously about the Duchess of Devonshire, Boswell added, "It may easily be conceived how [John-son] must have felt." But I find it hard to imagine all that might have gone through his mind. On 7 May, Johnson scolded Boswell for excessive drinking, saying, "I hope you don't intend to get drunk tomorrow as you did at Paoli's." But the next day, he again joined Wilkes in joking about Boswell and Scotland. Then on 21 May — only the second time he was with Boswell after 9 May — Johnson arranged for Boswell to join him the next day at the printer Edmund Allen's instead of going to the Club. Four days later, Johnson cheerfully prom-ised the letter to Chesterfield — "You shall make one copy for [your]self, one for me" — though he still postponed dictating it.[9]

Traveling Together Again (2 June to 5 June 1781)

Once the brewery had been sold, despite Johnson's delight in managing the business as one of Henry Thrale's executors, Johnson agreed to accom-pany Boswell on the first leg of his journey to Edinburgh, including a few days at Charles Dilly's estate in Welwyn, Bedfordshire. After six weeks of only sporadic contact, the two friends were steadily together from breakfast on 2 June through a second breakfast three days later. Whatever they expected from this first trip since March 1776, their first sustained time together since Ashbourne in 1777, the minitrip was notably successful. Away from Hester Thrale and the distractions of the city, alone much of the time, they experi-enced what they had, for the most part, missed since the death of Thrale: the blend of playful and serious conversation they associated with long evenings, shared Good Fridays, and travel.[10]

Boswell organized the trip. Johnson hesitated when he learned how Boswell had arranged his return to London — "If I had known there was to be such trouble, I would not have come" — then accepted what Boswell had planned. Boswell "slipped away" on the first afternoon to secure an invitation from the son of the poet Edward Young, which gave Johnson a chance to share stories about a writer whose *Life* had just been published, and prompted Boswell to wish he had seen the two together. Two days later, Boswell arranged a visit to Luton Hoo, Lord Bute's magnificent estate, where Johnson found the library "very splendid, the dignity of the rooms . . . very great, and the quantity of pictures . . . beyond expectation, beyond hope." Johnson was once again someone whose words were worth taking to heart, and Boswell both elicited his reflections and recorded them. Boswell also recorded as many autobiographical anecdotes as during the previous eleven weeks.[11]

On Sunday, 3 June, Johnson for the first time that spring played the role of Christian moralist. First, he applauded Boswell for having received Communion, which he "had not thought of," even though two years earlier he had resolved to do this "at least thrice a year." But when Boswell replied: "I'd fain be good, and I am very good just now. I fear God and honour the King; wish to do no ill, and to do good to all mankind," Johnson cautioned "against trusting impressions": He added that "there was a middle state of mind between conviction and hypocrisy, of which many were conscious (a fine remark), and that by being subject to impressions a man was not a free agent. If so, he should not be suffered to live. If he owns he cannot help acting in a particular way, there can be no confidence in him, no more than in a tiger."[12]

When they then discussed "Original Sin and the Sacrifice of Christ," Boswell got Johnson to dictate comments that complemented what he had said at Aberdeen, when he also promised to "write expressly in support of Christianity." Since Johnson could assume that what he now dictated would eventually be published, he was both instructing a friend and fulfilling his earlier promise. The next day, Johnson dictated an extended brief defending Thomas Robertson, the publisher of the *Edinburgh Gazette,* and finally dictated the Chesterfield letter.[13]

Having drifted apart during Boswell's last weeks in London, they momentarily revived their dynamic, collaborative friendship. But during the next six months, Johnson and Boswell were hardly in touch.

Silence and Worry (6 June 1781 through 9 January 1782)

There is some evidence that Boswell had Johnson in mind during these months, starting when he wrote detailed entries about their trip. A month later (5 July), he wrote a letter, not described in Boswell's letter register or later mentioned in the *Life,* which may have noted his usual summer depression. Seven weeks later, while Boswell was still experiencing "darkness and uncertainty," James Dunbar brought a "small parcel" of manuscripts for the *Lives,* which Johnson had earlier overlooked when he handed Boswell the promised "load of copy." Two days later, after rejecting "the horrible thought of suicide," Boswell somehow — "I know not how it happened" — experienced "a complete relief from melancholy for an hour or two," time he spent fully enjoying "some of Dr. Johnson's *Lives of the Poets.*" Probably early in September, Boswell wrote a letter of introduction for John Sinclair, a fellow student of Scottish English, who was again traveling to London. He also thought of

Johnson in November when, despite what Johnson had recently dictated concerning Robertson, the court reversed its earlier decision favoring Boswell's client.

Early in November, however, having heard nothing from Johnson in months, Boswell grew "anxious lest [his] Epithalamium in an hour of pleasantry [had] been maliciously told to Dr. Johnson," as Wilkes had threatened to do, and Johnson had been "offended." So on 6 November, Boswell wrote his brother — "Begging him in confidence to call on the Dr. & sound him about me & let me know what passes. But to give no hint of my fear."[14]

On the final day of 1781, after Boswell had ceased the riotous behavior that prompted later removal of entries for 16–29 December, and a day after he learned that Lord Auchinleck would restore £100 he had recently withheld from his heir's allowance, he once again wrote Johnson: wondering at his long silence, announcing his plan to visit London in March, and mainly reporting that Margaret was again coughing up blood.[15]

While Boswell clearly had Johnson in mind during the last half of 1781, Boswell seems to have dropped from Johnson's attention. He thought of Boswell at least momentarily when he received his letter in July, when he arranged in August for Dunbar to carry the manuscripts to Edinburgh, and perhaps in the fall, if Sinclair presented the letter of introduction before Johnson began an eight-week trip to Lichfield and Ashbourne. (Later, Johnson thought Sinclair had not come.) Then, a few weeks after returning from this "poor, sickly, comfortless journey," with "much gloom and little sunshine" — the trip during which he visited the Uttoxeter market and hoped for "serious conversation" with Hector and Taylor — Johnson read Boswell's account of Margaret's "alarming symptoms" and immediately responded. For the first time in three years, he apologized for not having written — "I have not satisfied myself with my long silence." He strongly hoped for Margaret's recovery, since "in losing her [Boswell] would lose [his] anchor, and be tost, without stability, by the waves of life." Johnson's own health had been "tottering," a decline he initially blamed on his own "negligence and indulgence"; and he confessed, "I can give no very laudable account of my time. I am always hoping to do better than I have ever hitherto done."[16]

From this point until they met in March 1783, they remained in touch, with Boswell writing at least nine substantial letters, and Johnson eight, as new fears arose concerning Boswell's finances and Johnson's health, and new longings for direct contact. Boswell initiated all four phases of the correspondence, as he had by writing at the end of 1781. But Johnson usually responded quickly. So there were only three periods when Johnson (once) or Boswell (twice) had to wait eight to ten weeks before hearing from his friend.

The first phase — two letters from Boswell in late February and March 1782 and one from Johnson — focused on whether Boswell could or should visit London. The second — Boswell in late May, Johnson early in June, and Boswell three weeks later — chiefly involved reports of Johnson's alarming health, and Margaret's. The third and longest — four letters from Boswell in mid-August through early October, four from Johnson from late August through early December, plus two letters from Margaret and Johnson's reply to the first — initially concerned whether and where they might meet for a visit both desired. Lord Auchinleck's death augmented Boswell's need to connect. But awareness of his friend's new duties impelled Johnson to postpone what each hoped would be diverting contact. The final phase — Boswell in January 1783 and Johnson in February — focused on Boswell's actions as laird, as he sought to gain the full endorsement of a mentor who lamented his friend's lack of perspective.

Visits Postponed and Discouraged: Mounting Debts, Tottering Health

Once Johnson's "kind letter" arrived on 9 January 1782, Boswell's "heart was comforted and [his] spirits raised," and he wrote his brother the following day that "he need take no notice of [Boswell's] apprehension" concerning the poem. But Boswell waited more than six weeks before responding. Then, on 23 February, Boswell reported that Margaret was better, explained he could not afford a visit, and asked whether Johnson might meet him in Cumberland.

Three weeks later, however, after Boswell heard there was a new ministry led by Lords Shelburne and Rockingham, with Burke as paymaster general, he was unwilling to let his debts keep him from pressing for a position, like the then-vacant office of judge advocate in Scotland. Since his best asset was to be "the pleasantest and best-tempered man in the world," as Burke eventually described him in his recommendation, Boswell felt he had to be "upon the spot." So he wrote Burke on 18 March for assistance and advice, and the same day asked Johnson to endorse the venture. To Burke, Boswell looked for justification: "Tell me . . . if my restlessness out of the great scene of exertion be not 'the divinity that stirs within me' and points out the line I should take." To Johnson, Boswell emphasized how pleasing it would be once again to share Holy Week. He also wrote Hester Thrale concerning Johnson's health, hoping she would secure a reply.[17]

Writing on 28 March, just five days after receiving Boswell's second letter, Johnson tried to restrain his friend's exuberance. He doubted that "this time of

bustle and confusion" would benefit him, since "every man has those to re-
ward and gratify who have contributed to his advancement." More importantly, "to come hither with such expectations at the expence of borrowed
money, which . . . you know not where to borrow, can hardly be considered as
prudent." Long troubled by Boswell's drinking and his tendency to make
himself miserable, Johnson now became alarmed that his friend, having "already gone the whole length of [his] credit," seemed willing to go even deeper
into debt. So with the balance and poise that always delighted Boswell, Johnson earnestly spelled out the folly of borrowing more on the slim chance of a
benefit: "If you anticipate your inheritance, you can at last inherit nothing; all
that you receive must pay for the past. You must get a place, or pine in penury,
with the empty name of a great estate. . . . Live on what you have, live if you
can on less; do not borrow either for vanity or pleasure; the vanity will end in
shame, and the pleasure in regret; stay therefore at home, till you have saved
money for your journey hither." Johnson repeated advice like this in five of his
next six letters to Boswell, suggesting deep distrust of Boswell's self-control.[18]

Boswell received Johnson's letter on 1 April. But he waited until he heard
from Burke, to whom he wrote again on 18 April, and Paoli, to whom he
complained the next day of Burke's "neglect," before deciding what to do.
Burke on 23 April recommended Boswell for judge advocate, but discouraged
his coming, whereas Paoli three days later urged him to come at once. Boswell
stayed in Edinburgh and waited another month before writing Johnson. But in
the meantime, he wove the financial advice of this "great judge of men and
things," "of whom more remarks deserve to be remembered, than of any
person [he] ever knew," into a collaborative *Hypochondriack* essay titled "On
Penuriousness & Wealth." When Johnson's next letter expanded on his earlier
advice, Boswell wrote a second essay on the same topic, further demonstrating
his mastery. Having finished this essay on 17 June, Boswell in his entry for 18
June reported having "as full satisfaction in [his] own existence as Mr. Burke
has, only that" Boswell wished "for greater objects." (With his extraordinary
abilities and success in Parliament, Burke had become someone Boswell hoped
to emulate.)[19]

Boswell began another exchange of letters on 25 May after receiving Hester
Thrale's report that Johnson had "lost no fewer than 50 ounces of Blood
within this last week, 100 since this Year began; & though the Symptoms are
relieved by this practice, the Disease — a Cough & difficulty of Breathing — is
not removed." Fearing that by not visiting in April he may have missed his last
chance to see Johnson alive, Boswell "resolved" to be with him in August —
"God willing" — and asked whether Hester might every week "let me know by
a single line how he recovers." Several days later he wrote Johnson directly.[20]

Johnson responded immediately with a full report of how for months he had "scarcely been well" for a whole week: "My respiration has been much impeded, and much blood has been taken away. I am now harassed by a catarrhous cough, from which my purpose is to seek relief by change of air; and I am, therefore, preparing to go to Oxford." But Johnson spent most of his letter further explaining the consequences of debt, concerning which he could be more decisive. In closing, Johnson hoped they would meet in the fall, "both well and both cheerful; and part each the better for the other's company."[21]

This letter, plus what Hester Thrale wrote then and a month later, reassured Boswell there was no immediate danger. Thrale's short letters also suggested she was not possessively attached to Johnson, but keenly anticipated Boswell's August visit. So Boswell in July wrote a glowing retrospective on their relationship, "starting from the day that I first had the pleasure to meet you, when I jumpt into your coach, not I hope from impudence, but from that agreeable kind of attraction which makes one forget ceremony."

On 22 June, however, Margaret "had a violent coughing between three and four, and spit up a great quantity of blood." Though for years she had shown signs of pulmonary tuberculosis ("consumption"), neither she nor James wanted to admit she had the disease that had killed so many in her family. But now her symptoms became so alarming that Boswell charted them in a separate journal, which for a while replaced his own. Fearing his wife might die before he became laird, an elevation that "would place her in a situation which she so well deserves," Boswell also allowed himself openly to regard his father's death "as a desirable event," especially since "he and his women" had consistently "treated [Margaret] with shameful coldness."[22]

On 27 June, Boswell reported Margaret's relapse, but reaffirmed that he would meet Johnson in London if she recovered. Since Johnson had quickly responded to earlier news of Margaret's illness, his failure to reply to this new alarm prompted R. W. Chapman to speculate that he may not have received Boswell's letter. But Johnson surely knew that Hester Thrale on 4 July expressed concern, and Boswell's report on 9 July that Margaret was better would have reassured Johnson, too. On 13 August, however, almost seven weeks after reporting Margaret's fresh symptoms, Boswell expressed uneasiness "at having no answer to [his] last letter," and declared that Margaret was so "much better" that he could meet Johnson "when & where he pleases." Soon after getting this letter, Johnson agreed to meet Boswell at Ashbourne or London—"you have your free choice." Though a fall meeting had been mentioned in all their recent letters, each of these August letters seems to have been prompted by a key conversation shortly before it was written.[23]

On 12 August, James Beattie told Boswell "a striking anecdote of Dr. Johnson, to account for his being often unwilling to go to church." Responding to Beattie's distress "with shocking impious thoughts, of which he could not get rid," Johnson had confessed that two-thirds of his own waking moments were filled with such thoughts. Since Boswell wrote the next day to arrange a meeting, it seems likely that this fascinating revelation, which showed Johnson to be as conflicted as Boswell himself, made Boswell eager to hear Johnson describe these "shocking" thoughts and to confirm that he had told his biographer everything significant about his life.[24]

Johnson's key conversation came a few days after he received Boswell's letter and two days before he responded. On 22 August, his "Recovery . . . from an Illness we all thought dangerous" gave Hester Thrale the "courage" to announce a plan to retrench expenses by renting Streatham and taking her daughters to Italy. The place that had been Johnson's second home since 1765 would soon not be available, and the woman who had been a stabilizing and cheering presence for as long as he had earlier been married was planning to travel to Italy with the musician Gabriel Piozzi, whom she would soon hope to marry.

Johnson's not protesting—his even telling Queeney Thrale that he would not accompany them to Italy if asked—startled Hester Thrale, leading her to the reassuring conclusion that Johnson "feels nothing in parting with [her], nothing in the least." But Johnson fully appreciated how much he was about to lose from a world already shrunk. His constant housemate, Robert Levet, a man he later told Langton he had planned always to "endeavour to retain . . . about [him]," had suddenly died in January. His physician and friend Thomas Lawrence had suffered a debilitating stroke in May. Others were seriously ill, including Mrs. Williams. So two days after hearing Mrs. Thrale's plan to lease Streatham and leave the country, Johnson urged Boswell to decide where they should meet. He offered to travel halfway and did not ask whether Boswell could afford a trip.[25]

Before Boswell could fix a time and place to meet, his father died, intensifying his need for Johnson's support and advice. Johnson's need for diversion also increased as plans to vacate Streatham advanced. But Johnson judged that Boswell's new responsibilities, combined with unexpected limits to the income from a heavily encumbered estate, ruled out any meeting before spring. Boswell reluctantly accepted this, but only after a precipitous trip to London was halted by Margaret's symptoms, then blocked by a letter from Johnson.

Possessing Auchinleck

On 20 August 1782, a week after he wrote Johnson and a few days before Johnson posted his response, Boswell took Margaret to Valleyfield, the country house of Sir George and Lady Preston in Fife. Six weeks earlier, while lamenting that Margaret lacked his "English juiciness of mind" and "warmth of imagination," and "instead of cherishing [his] genius" was "perpetually checking it," Boswell had acknowledged that his wife's "prudence has kept [him] out of many follies, and made [his] life much more decent and creditable than it would have been without her." Now he admired how "genteel" she looked on horseback, "was as much in love with her as a man could be," and on 23 August was "sadly alarmed" when she "spit some blood mixed with matter, coughed severely, and felt the pain between her shoulders very painful."

Starting on 22 August, Boswell spent part of each day reliving the end of the Hebrides trip. First he copied what he had written in 1780 onto "paper of the same size with the rest" of his journal. Then, on the first evening Margaret spat up blood, he pushed further with his narrative, fleshing out his skimpy notes, "recollect[ing] wonderfully": "It pleased me much to revive the scenes." His father had recently been remarkably harsh, Margaret was ill, and he had not heard from Johnson for more than two months. But Boswell could fully reexperience what had happened as he and Johnson traveled together to meet a cordial (though eventually belligerent) Lord Auchinleck, and then back to Edinburgh where a younger, healthier Margaret graciously endured days of disruption.[26]

A week after Boswell began adding to this journal, he was called home to his father's deathbed. Lord Auchinleck had been declining for years. His "death could not be considered as a matter of regret," Forbes wrote Langton soon afterward: "His faculties were much impaired, and he might be said in some measure to have survived himself." But partly because Boswell had never learned directly and calmly to express his anger and resentment, as he had with Johnson, Lord Auchinleck never modified how he treated his heir, and died without giving Boswell anything like a final blessing. Despite occasional hugs and smiles, his father continued to treat Boswell like a child, denigrated his connection with Johnson, and belittled his prospects in London. He never affirmed that his heir could function effectively.

It galled Boswell on 29 August that his stepmother kept him from his father's deathbed, saying, "It will confuse his head. Don't torture him in his last moments." Though stunned, Boswell did as she asked: "I was benumbed and stood off. Wept; for, alas! There was not affection between us." The next day Lord Auchinleck died.[27]

Boswell announced the death in numerous letters, including one to Johnson that complained of his father's enduring coldness and probably worried about his new challenges. Johnson immediately replied with what Boswell labeled "excellent counsel," though his letter assumed Boswell needed considerable instruction. Like Temple two days later, Johnson emphasized that Boswell was largely responsible for his father's coldness: "Kindness, at least actual, is in our power, but fondness is not; and if by negligence or imprudence you had extinguished his fondness, he could not at will rekindle it." Johnson then spent half his letter urging economy, prudence, and restraint: "Begin your new course of life with the least show, and the least expence possible; you may at pleasure encrease both, but you cannot easily diminish them. . . . Therefore, begin with timorous parsimony. Let it be your first care not to be in any man's debt." Johnson also longed to know the specifics of Lord Auchinleck's will.[28]

Boswell, having assumed since May that he would visit London in the fall, determined by 9 September to go there once he had been formally installed as laird. He announced this plan in his reply to Johnson's letter while also reporting that much more income than expected had been settled on his stepmother. He left Auchinleck early on 24 September, even though Margaret had again coughed up blood, and he would have boarded the fast coach to London the next day had Margaret not called him home after another "violent fit of spitting of blood." Then before Boswell could leave again, he got a surprisingly harsh letter from Johnson, insisting he stay put.[29]

Boswell wanted advice from Johnson on a number of issues, including what to do about the excessive jointure provided his stepmother. On this and other matters, "Dr. Johnson's wisdom was highly requisite." More importantly, having never received Lord Auchinleck's blessing, Boswell wanted Johnson once again to side with him against his father and stepmother and to reassure him he was fit to play the prestigious role of laird. As in August 1769 and February 1776, his deep need for Johnson trumped all other considerations. "I felt myself drawn irresistibly," he wrote on 1 October. However independent Boswell sometimes felt, he needed Johnson's authoritative support.[30]

Since his banker, Sir William Forbes, had not objected to the visit, and Johnson had just offered a "free choice" of London or Ashbourne, Boswell anticipated no objection. But for Johnson, despite his wish for diversion, Boswell's new duties and unanticipated financial constraints clearly ruled out a trip. Having accepted the coming loss of Streatham and the eventual loss of the Thrales, Johnson now resigned himself to not seeing Boswell until spring. He expected Boswell, too, to be a grown-up, and scolded his plan to leave Auchinleck.

Johnson's letter was so critical that Boswell later printed only the paragraph that urged him to spare no expense to "preserve" his wife, "the prop and stay of [his] life," even if "it should be necessary to transplant her for a time into a softer climate" — a paragraph that explained why Margaret then invited Johnson to Auchinleck, leading to an exchange of gracious letters that Boswell wanted to include. Because Johnson insisted that Boswell stay home and attend to her recovery, Margaret finally relinquished her resentment of his influence. The first words quoted — "One expence, however, I would not have you to spare" — show that Johnson opposed Boswell's coming to London as costly, especially since he now knew how much income had been settled on Lady Auchinleck. Boswell's response indicates also that Johnson had accused his friend of "deserting [his] station," neglecting what Johnson had earlier described as his "new cares, and new employments." The tone of what Boswell printed is not harsh. But it is easy to imagine Johnson scolding his friend's failure to act responsibly, especially if he regretted having earlier encouraged a trip he must have known Boswell could not afford.[31]

Because Johnson pushed him back to Auchinleck so sternly, Boswell's need for reassurance increased. So four days after getting Johnson's letter, Boswell set aside his pain and anger at what he later excluded from the *Life* and tried to lure Johnson north. If not direct contact, he hoped at least to get decisive answers to two vexing questions concerning his stepmother, along with clear evidence of Johnson's affectionate regard. Though not mentioned in the *Life*, this long letter of 1 October 1782 has survived, allowing us to see how Boswell combined confession and flattery with reports of dutiful behavior.

Without hinting that Johnson's letter had surprised and hurt him, Boswell spelled out his deep need for Johnson's company and counsel by telling how, despite Margaret's illness and her wish that he stay, he would have left again had his friend's "excellent letter" not arrived just in time to dissuade him: "I imagined I could neither act nor think in my new situation till I had talked with you." To flatter Johnson even more, Boswell quoted what he had written in his journal about this letter: "Well, he is a most wonderful man! He can drive me to the end of the world or confine me in a dungeon." Boswell's overlooking Margaret's alarming condition demonstrated a powerful longing to connect, and a lack of moral clarity. But Boswell imagined he would both please Johnson and reduce his own irresponsibility by writing, "I love and value [Margaret] as much as ever husband did wife; and I should upbraid myself for having resolved to leave her, had it been with any other purpose than to be with You."

Boswell also described how he was already following Johnson's earlier advice. He had begun "to look into the affairs of the estate" and was attending to those matters that required his presence, like the renting of several farms. Though "very ignorant . . . of country affairs," he had listened to diverse opinions and done as well as he could, hoping in time to become better informed. In addition, he assured Johnson that he had been "as sober as" his friend "could wish [him] to be": "It was my determination that I should maintain the decorum of the representative of Auchinleck; and I am doing so."

Boswell hoped for time with Johnson, either at Auchinleck or somewhere between there and London, where he and Johnson "could discuss more in an hours conversation than in a great deal of writing." He even used Margaret's condition to lure Johnson north, enclosing her invitation to Auchinleck and calling attention to her warning "that delays are dangerous in her complaining state of health." If he and Johnson could not meet, Boswell at least wanted a response that shared his outrage at how his stepmother had selfishly manipulated his father, and that explained whether he should challenge the will or acquiesce, and whether he should end "all intercourse with so bad a woman."[32]

Boswell had to wait almost ten weeks for the answer he had worked so artfully to elicit, and three additional months before seeing Johnson. He remained at Auchinleck until 11 November, consolidating his understanding of the estate. Waking early, he before breakfast read the Bible and Thomas à Kempis's *Imitation of Christ,* "by which my mind is calmed and sanctified." Delighted to be free "from the melancholy clouds which used to hang upon [his] mind" at the end of the year, he was again convinced that these were "mere *shadows*": "I am lost when I think intensely of the course of things, and especially of the operations of my own mind. But I avoid that kind of thinking, and have some notion of the kind of existence which my father had all his life till his faculties decayed."

Once back in Edinburgh, Boswell spent considerable time with the dying Lord Kames, who was remarkably alert at eighty-six. Having prepared Boswell to write his biography, Kames welcomed his companionship. Though Lord Auchinleck had never spoken with Boswell about his religious beliefs, Kames assured him that his "father had never doubted of Christianity, and . . . was sure he would be well in another world." Then, on 10 December, when Kames "seemed to be firm in his belief of future existence," Boswell saw something "that put [him] in mind of [his] father when in a calm, serious frame": "He quieted me somehow. I told him I frequently could not help thinking my father was alive and that I might go and consult him; and when I was taking care of his improvements at Auchinleck I thought I was doing what he approved; and I wished always to preserve the notion of his seeing what I was about." The following day, Boswell finally heard from Johnson, and so he had these three "fathers" in alignment.[33]

Leaving Streatham

On 5 October, two days after Boswell posted his long letter, Johnson went for a final weekend at Streatham, which had been leased for three years to Lord Shelburne, the new prime minister. On 6 October, he composed a prayer of thanksgiving for the "comforts" and "conveniences" he had enjoyed there since 1765, a prayer he recited after packing up the following morning. Then he read in the library he would never revisit. A "slight cold" Johnson had caught on 24 September hung on, leaving him so short of breath when he reached Brighton that he "stopped four times to rest between the inn and the lodging." By restricting his diet mainly to broth and fish, he grew strong enough in early November to take a three-day trip through western Sussex, accompanied by Philip Metcalfe, a wealthy London brewer and friend of Reynolds. On 29 November, he returned to London, where Hester Thrale had rented a house on Argyll Street. The next day he returned to Bolt Court, where, I think, he found the letters Boswell and Margaret had posted almost two months before. A week later (7 December) Johnson responded.[34]

His poor health and the start of winter ruled out a visit, as Johnson explained in a separate letter to Margaret. But his "excellent letter" satisfied many of Boswell's needs, providing both advice and a degree of blessing. With one exception, what Boswell included from this letter in the *Life* was intimate and supportive.

Johnson began by focusing on his health, describing, with poise that he knew Boswell would appreciate, his efforts to recover from the latest of "a succession of disorders": "By physick and abstinence I grew better, and am now reasonably easy, though at a great distance from health. I am afraid, however, that health begins, after seventy, to have a meaning different from that which it had at thirty. But it is culpable to murmur at the established order of the creation, as it is vain to oppose it. He that lives, must grow old; and he that would rather grow old than die, has God to thank for the infirmities of old age." Then Johnson addressed his friend's affairs.

He assumed Boswell had followed his repeated advice to economize. But to be sure, he included a short version: "Resolve not to be poor: whatever you have, spend less." To prepare himself better to assist with Auchinleck and to prompt Boswell to begin learning the specifics of his estate, Johnson asked for a full history of his activities as laird and for a detailed accounting: "How many houses, how many cows, and how much land in your own hand, and what bargains you make with your tenants." Then, after an unprinted section in which Johnson probably endorsed Boswell's decision not to contest Lord Auchinleck's settlements on his widow, and to behave toward her "with wonderful decorum," Johnson reported a new edition of the *Lives of the Poets* and asked what Boswell had done with the many pages Johnson had given him the previous year.

As he began this letter, however, Johnson was curiously aggressive. Though he was writing much later than Boswell had hoped, he did not explain why he had not answered sooner, nor did he apologize. Instead, he declared himself "rather angry" at Boswell's "long silence," scolding him — especially now that he had become "head of [his] house" — for testing which of them could "live longer without writing," and for suspecting that Johnson's silence signified neglect — "that when I do not write to you, I forget you." Given Boswell's general practice, it was not unreasonable for Johnson to expect a follow-up letter sometime in November. But since Boswell had not recently worried openly about Johnson's love, I suspect Johnson was expressing his own fear of being forgotten, projecting onto Boswell his worry that Hester Thrale would have him even less in mind once she left London.[35]

Though disappointed and even a bit angry that Boswell had not written since early October, Johnson was delighted that Margaret had invited him to Auchinleck, and responded that he had "not often received so much pleasure as from your invitation." Auchinleck could not make up for Streatham. But Margaret had finally accepted the "love" Johnson had often offered. "If my health were fully recovered," Johnson gallantly wrote, "I would suffer no little heat and cold, nor a wet or a rough road, to keep me from you." Then he graciously added that Auchinleck could be pleasant only if "its lady [were] well, and brisk, and airy": "For my sake, therefore, among many greater reasons, take care, dear Madam, of your health, and spare no expence, and want no attendance that can procure ease, or preserve it. Be very careful to keep your mind quiet; and do not think it too much to give an account of your recovery to Madam, your, etc." On 20 December, Margaret complied with this request: "I am better, and hope to have it in my power to convince you by my attention of how much consequence I esteem your health to the world and to myself." The two key grown-ups in Boswell's world now were fully allied.[36]

On the same day Margaret wrote Johnson, Boswell wrote Hester Thrale for the first time since July. Having just heard from Johnson that she and her daughters were in London for the winter, he asked her to let him know "from time to time" about Johnson's health. He also told her — and through her, Johnson — that he would be in London in March.

Boswell left for Auchinleck after Lord Kames died on 27 December. On 5 January, midway through his stay, he "was quite satisfied with [his] character and conduct at present": "It was what would have pleased my father and my grandfather." He hoped to please Johnson, too, with the "warmly respectful" letter he posted on 14 January.[37]

Johnson was indeed "delighted," especially since Boswell, following Johnson's advice to "be kind to . . . old servants," had moved an eighty-eight-year-old retired servant from a lonely cottage to a comfortable house near good neighbors. But almost everything included in the *Life* from this prompt reply repeats earlier advice, suggesting worry that Boswell would not persist: "You have now a new character and new duties: think on them, and practice them. Make an impartial estimate of your revenue, and whatever it is, live upon less. Resolve never to be poor." Gratified that Margaret Boswell "grows well," and hoping the couple would "long live happily together," Johnson also hoped that "to keep her well, no care nor caution will be omitted," suggesting that here, too, he did not trust Boswell to know or do what was right.[38]

Whether or not something in Boswell's letter elicited this implicitly critical advice, what Boswell wrote definitely prompted rebukes not printed in the *Life* but reported in Boswell's journal, where he noted that Johnson was "so rigorous against [his] drinking wine at all, and so discouraging to [his] settling in London, that [he] was a good deal hurt." Boswell's journals and letters make it is easy to imagine what he might have written on those topics; and Johnson's earlier letters and recorded comments suggest what he might have replied. This mostly effaced exchange foreshadowed key transactions during the next two years: Boswell repeatedly sought concessions from Johnson, especially concerning London, and Johnson lamented his friend's refusal to accept what Johnson saw as inflexible constraints.[39]

Concerning drinking, Boswell probably wrote Johnson what he reported to Paoli a few days later: that he was "now as moderate a Wine-drinker as your-self" — something Paoli applauded before Boswell got Johnson's response. Boswell might even have described having experienced what he called "constitutional sobriety," moments when he was happily "free of the rage of drinking" and drank "not from love of wine and intoxication . . . but from a desire to be cordial." Concerning London, Boswell almost surely wrote that since he no longer faced his father's opposition, he hoped to try his fortune at the English bar.[40]

Though Boswell himself was conflicted on both these issues, there were reasons he might have anticipated Johnson's endorsement. But Johnson's positions had not changed, even though he himself was now drinking occasionally. The question was not whether Boswell would be more comfortable socially if he could drink in moderation, but whether he could limit himself once he began. Having repeatedly seen how easily Boswell overindulged, Johnson continued to urge total abstinence. Concerning London, Johnson saw no harm in Boswell's seeking whatever help might come from Lord Mountstuart, Burke, and others. But if no additional funds turned up, London was simply unaffordable; and Johnson continued to fear that fixating on London would keep Boswell from enjoying all he had.[41]

What hurt Boswell "a good deal" was probably Johnson's exasperation that Boswell was unwilling to accept these constraints. Early in 1782, Boswell had not seen the danger of additional debts. In the fall, he failed initially to shoulder his new responsibilities or to recognize the importance of Margaret's health.

Now he ignored the core truth about his drinking and seemed bent on making himself miserable, despite his relative youth, his family, his career, and his substantial (though encumbered) inheritance. So Johnson's mostly positive letter included material Boswell later omitted from the *Life*.

"Hurt" by what Johnson wrote, Boswell did not reply. Instead, he sought support from Thomas Barnard, now the bishop of Killaloe in Ireland, who had been Boswell's "Father confessor" after his embarrassing drunkenness in 1781. But Barnard cordially refused to play his assigned role. He wrote facetiously of Boswell's "pretend[ing] to prefer" London, "that market of Beef and Pudding," to Edinburgh, "Musarum Sedes, Scientiarum Nutrix" [seat of the Muses, nursing mother of sciences], and wrote nothing about drinking.[42]

On 15 March 1783, five weeks after he had received Johnson's letter and five days after Barnard's arrived, Boswell left for London, where he and Johnson would reconnect after their longest separation since they had begun collaborating on the *Life*. Instead of taking a smaller, faster post chaise, as he usually did, Boswell took the "disagreeable and somewhat mean" stagecoach to Carlisle, where he visited Bishop Percy, and then to London, thinking it wise to be "rigidly economical" until he paid off all his debts. But he quickly resolved never again to submit to that punishing mode of travel.

Meanwhile, Johnson, who six months earlier had imagined traveling to meet Boswell at Ashbourne, had become seriously ill. Boswell had written Paoli on 18 February that Johnson was "much better," since his recent long letter said nothing about his health. So he was shocked on 21 March by his friend's appearance, and alarmed the next day to hear the physician Sir Lucas Pepys say he was afraid Johnson was dying.[43]

14

"Some Time Together before We Are Parted"
(March 1783 to May 1784)

"I am glad you are come," Johnson said once Boswell had located him at Hester Thrale's house; "I am very ill." Always eager for diversion, Johnson now was radically needy. Boswell as usual engaged Johnson by introducing topics and posing problems. Later, after Mrs. Thrale joined them, Johnson told Boswell, "You must be as much with me as you can. You have done me good. You cannot think how much better I am since you came in."

At Boswell's prompting, Johnson explained why "it is better to have five per cent out of land than out of money," and why "a man is not so much afraid of being a hard creditor as of being a hard landlord." He traced "the present anarchy in Government" back to the revolution of 1688, and he recited — "with an emotion which made them have full effect" — his verses on the death of Robert Levet. At dinner, Johnson was mostly quiet, then napped. But once awake, he resumed talking admirably about Burke, Sheridan, and Charles James Fox, who would soon form a coalition with Lord North, showing Boswell that "his mind was as vigorous and lively as ever." "I was all admiration," Boswell later reported, "and said, 'Oh, for shorthand to take this down!'" Hester Thrale, who had not seen Boswell since her husband's death two years earlier, and who would soon leave for Bath now that Boswell was in town, replied, "You'll carry it all in your head. A long head is as good as shorthand."[1]

But by the time Boswell recorded these words three days later (24 March),

Johnson's petulant opposition the night before to Boswell's ambitious plans as laird had left Boswell reluctant to engage with his housebound friend. Then, ten days later (3 April) Johnson further transformed the dynamics of the visit by calmly but decisively showing that Boswell simply could not afford to move his family to London.

Boswell in London (21 March through 30 May 1783)

On Boswell's second day in town (22 March), Johnson was "peevish," as he earlier feared he would have been had Boswell visited him while he was sick the previous spring. When Boswell said that General Oglethorpe planned to visit that evening, Johnson said, "Did not you tell him not to come? Am I to be hunted in this manner?" The next morning, when Boswell talked with Elizabeth Desmoulins, the widowed daughter of Johnson's godfather, about his friend's "not complaining" that he had not been "called to some great office, or was not richer," Johnson "flew into a violent passion and commanded [them] to have done; for nobody had a right to talk in this matter, to bring before a man his own character and the events of his life, when he did not like it should be done." Later, after Johnson wrote Hester Thrale that he was "recovering" but would not "venture" out the next day to meet Langton and his wife, he was irritated when Boswell asked whether he had been abroad: "'Don't talk so childishly,' said he. 'You may as well ask if I hanged myself today.'"

When first reconnecting with Boswell, Johnson had said he had "no objection" to his friend's residing in London, provided he spent at least four months a year at Auchinleck and "could secure a place the salary of which would pay the additional expense of living here." But now Johnson challengingly said, "I doubt if your fondness for London is so great as you talk." When Boswell then talked about building at Auchinleck on the site of the old castle, Johnson "raged against this": "It is too late to indulge fancy. It may do in a young man, but not at your age; not in a man with a wife and five children. . . . Talk no more in this way. People will only laugh at you, or be vexed, as I am."[2]

The next morning Boswell produced entries for 16–23 March, writing almost as much as he had ten years earlier, when he wrote all night after being elected to the Club. Then he had been elated. Now he was angry at Johnson's "check[ing] every ambitious wish which started from [him]," including the wish for a position that would let him afford to live in London, "and want[ing] to beat [Boswell] down to dull content with [his] present state." He recalled how in 1766 Johnson had "roughly" discouraged him from writing *Corsica*, even though Boswell had first achieved recognition by publishing it: "I raised myself twenty degrees higher in fame and in general advantage as a social man than I should have been had he been successful in repressing my generous ardour." So Boswell concluded his entry for the previous day (23 March) by asserting his ability to judge for himself, in defiance of the friend who testily insisted Boswell loved London less than he claimed. He conceded, however, that if he saw there was "little hope" of winning a position in London, despite his "family, talents, and conexions," he eventually would "set [his] mind to be satisfied with a judge's place in Scotland."[3]

After using the entire morning to write entries for the previous eight days, ending with a rejection of what Johnson had said the previous evening, Boswell called on Johnson after dinner, and "was not displeased that he was asleep," since Boswell was "not disposed to bear any checks." Having spent much time with Johnson on each of his first three days in London, Boswell dutifully visited on eight of the next ten — but only once each day. He planned a second visit on 25 March, but it rained heavily. On 27 March and 29 March, he did not even try.[4]

Meanwhile, on 31 March, Burke seemed to encourage the move to London, suggesting that Boswell's "estate, with the profession of the law in aid of it, might support [him] very well." But Burke also said Boswell "enjoyed London more by coming to it two or three months every year than if [he] lived in it." Later that day, Boswell and Langton "listened eagerly" as a learned woman "pointed out the economy by which living in London may be managed," after which Langton said, "This will put you again in the humour of it, and you'll have Dr. Johnson scolding you." "Ay," said Boswell, "It is setting up the poor cock to be thrown at again." Three days later (3 April), while writing the entry for 27 March, Boswell reported feeling "wonderfully steady in London," having "lost the idea of great distance between it and Auchinleck." But soon after writing those words, he went to Johnson's, accompanied by Langton, in whose company he now felt "easier" with Johnson, and discovered an unbridgeable chasm.[5]

Considerably healthier, Johnson was cordial and sympathetic, and Boswell finally took in what Johnson had assumed since he learned the terms of Lord Auchinleck's will. The debts that had kept Boswell home two of the last three springs, combined with unexpected limits on his income from Auchinleck, made moving to London unaffordable.

"I am unwilling to repress your ambition." Johnson said, with an affability Boswell had not heard eleven days earlier. "But it appears to me that as you would be obliged to maintain your family in some dignity here, you would find yourself embarrassed. When you come to London now and leave it because you cannot afford the expense of living in it constantly, people applaud your wisdom. Were you to settle here, they'd despise you as a man ruining himself."

Fig. 3: John Opie, portrait of Samuel Johnson, 1783, studio variant, Houghton Library, Harvard University, 82M-20.

This was "strong sense," Boswell wrote in his journal, "and it *did* repress [his] ambition." He now saw that trying the English bar was not like writing *Corsica*. Without additional income, relocating would be impossible.[6]

What Johnson said meshed with what Boswell had heard earlier that day from Henry Dundas, the lord advocate, who discouraged purchasing a seat in Parliament with borrowed money, but promised to "be friendly" should Boswell — "some time hence" — apply for a judge's place in Scotland. More impor-

Fig. 4: Sir Joshua Reynolds, portrait of James Boswell, 1785. © National Portrait Gallery, London; used by permission.

tantly, by the time Boswell wrote this entry, thirteen days later, Johnson's advice had been endorsed by many others. As soon as he left Johnson, Boswell tried to see Burke, who was out. But that night he had "some good conversation" with Paoli, who agreed with Johnson. So did Boswell's friend Dempster at breakfast the next day. That night, Colonel James Stuart's "firm, sensible remarks pressed down [Boswell's] foolish imaginations as lead or marble does fluttering leaves of paper." But on 16 April, despite what he had repeatedly heard from Johnson and others, Boswell confessed in the entry for 4 April that he still had "foolish imaginations," and was "not yet settled as to [his] choice of life." (*Rasselas* was originally titled "The Choice of Life.") While preparing to visit Burke's country estate on 22 April, Boswell planned to "make out [a] memorial of choice of life for Burke"; and on 29 May, his last full day in London, Boswell returned to this topic: first with Johnson and then with Burke. He also continued to cultivate Lord Mountstuart, hoping to find him at last a true patron.[7]

After hearing Johnson's "strong sense" on 3 April, Boswell waited a whole week before seeing his friend again, then saw him just once in the following week, five times in the next two weeks (18 April through 1 May), only twice in the next two weeks (2–15 May), and six times in his final two (16–29 May). Boswell also began drinking heavily, and seems to have written no letters to family or friends from 5 April until 17 April. On 20 April (Easter), he resolved against "too much drinking," and the next day cautioned himself to "be sober" at Burke's. But on 17 May, when Johnson again urged total abstinence, and Paoli seems to have concurred, Boswell defiantly resolved he "*would* enjoy wine" — "But not to excess."[8]

Meanwhile, Johnson worked at accepting his own severely narrowed range of reasonable hopes. Two days after he got Boswell to see why moving to London was impossible, he parted with Hester Thrale, who left for Bath. After Henry Thrale's executors, including Johnson, objected to her taking her daughters abroad, she declared, "If I did not leave England, I *would* leave London." It is unclear what Johnson knew or feared concerning Hester's attachment to Piozzi, from whom Thrale parted on 6 April, bending to the strenuous objections of her daughters. But as he anticipated, her departure marked a decisive change.

Since 1767, Johnson had written frequently whenever Hester Thrale was not nearby. But now he waited until she wrote first, more than three weeks later, perhaps in response to what he had posted to Queeney on 26 April. Then he waited until he received her second letter, which he thought "long in coming," before writing again. When letters to Queeney on 22 May and 2 June finally prompted a third letter from Hester, Johnson replied, "Why do You write so seldom? . . . Do not please yourself with showing me that You can forget me, who do not forget You."[9]

Slowly Johnson grew healthier, and was freely moving about by the end of May. But his social world had significantly narrowed. He had lost many "friends of easy conversation and familiar confidence," as he spelled out to Chambers on 19 April. Goldsmith, Garrick, Beauclerk, and Henry Thrale had died in the nine years since Chambers sailed for India. Others, such as Langton and William Scott, were often unavailable. In addition, as Johnson later complained to Hester Thrale, he now had to "go far for company, and at last come back to two sick and discontented women, who can hardly talk, if they had any thing to say, and whose hatred of each other makes one great exercise of their faculties."[10]

All That They Were, and More

Having seen Boswell just twice between 3 April and 18 April (Good Friday), Johnson was with him for dinner on Easter, and saw him on three of the next eleven days. Then Boswell was mainly occupied with his friend William Temple for two weeks. But Johnson saw Boswell (and sometimes Temple too) on six of his friend's final fourteen days in town.

When last with Boswell, eight years earlier, Temple had made his friend vow to limit himself to just six glasses of wine at dinner. In May 1783, after three weeks of frequent contact, he complained that Boswell was "irregular in his conduct and manners, selfish, indelicate, thoughtless, [with] no sensibility or feeling for others who have not his coarse and rustic strength and spirit. . . . Seems often absurd and almost mad . . . No composure or rational view of things." In sum, "years do not improve him." Johnson, too, was sometimes exasperated. But his assessment was more balanced. Boswell was selfish and manipulative, but also solicitous and kind, and his company was invigorating. After giving Chambers news of the Scot they had often discussed — "Boswels father is lately dead, but has left the estate incumbered; Boswel has, I think, five children" — Johnson enigmatically added, "He is all that he was, and more."[11]

Boswell's entries for some of the fifteen days he saw Johnson after 3 April, together with what he wrote in the *Life* about the others, show that Boswell's questions focused and animated Johnson, and Johnson's responses grounded Boswell. There was usually some edginess or worry, especially since both now saw that Johnson's health could not be taken for granted; also, Boswell now began to see Johnson as the major opponent of his moving to London. But there were no further angry outbursts, no insults, and no repressed resentments as they revived all the major motifs of their friendship.

On 10 April, their first day together after Johnson had shown why London was impossible, Boswell early in the conversation said that as fellow travelers, "[they] make it out together exceedingly well," adding, "Our journey to the Hebrides was very curious." Johnson emphatically praised the trip they had anticipated for ten years and were now recalling almost ten years later: "I got an acquisition of more ideas by it than anything I remember. I saw quite a different system of life." But when Boswell suggested they "must have a jaunt some-where" now that Johnson was feeling better, Johnson, who fifteen months earlier had wondered whether they would "ever have another frolick like [their] journey to the Hebrides," uncharacteristically did not imagine himself in mo-tion. When Boswell voiced a wish "to go and see some country totally different" from what he had been used to, "such as Turkey where religion and everything else are different," Johnson said nothing about longing to visit Egypt or China.[12]

On Good Friday, they got so caught up in conversation once others stopped by that they missed afternoon services. Boswell briefly left, perhaps sensing that Johnson wished some time alone, but then returned for coffee and private conversation before they went to church at seven. On Sunday, Boswell came for Easter dinner, as he had first done ten years earlier, though Johnson this time "seemed not to be well, talked little, grew drowsy soon after dinner, and retired."[13]

When he next saw Johnson, eight days later (28 April), after Margaret's nephew, Lieutenant David Cuninghame, had killed his antagonist in a duel, Boswell was delighted to hear Johnson decisively explain that dueling was compatible with scripture, which forbids revenge but not self-defense: "A man may shoot another who invades his character as he may shoot one who at-tempts to break into his house." Two days later, Boswell discussed two of his legal cases and planned "to get [Johnson] to dictate to [him] on both," but for some reason seems not to have arranged this. Since Johnson was too ill to dine at Paoli's the next day, Boswell afterward brought Burke's son Richard to Johnson's, then "just lay by and let him play the great organ." Later he got Johnson to agree that "young Burke did exceedingly well" in conversation: "He did very well indeed. I have a mind to tell his father." Boswell brought Temple and Johnson together, too, and tried to arrange another dinner with Wilkes and Johnson, as he had done in 1781. Also, when Boswell on 17 May mentioned having been with Thomas Sheridan, Johnson made a peace over-ture through his friend—"Tell Mr. Sheridan I shall be glad to see him and shake hands with him"—perhaps ending twenty-one years of estrangement.[14]

While Johnson and Boswell performed these well-practiced roles, including those that connected Johnson with others, they mainly constructed conversa-tions. In the Hebrides, Boswell had described himself for Johnson as the one who furnished materials for his friend's "great mill" to grind, the one who got his "locked up" fountain "a-going." Now he pictured himself to Langton as "an electrical eel," shocking Johnson into activity, or as "the boy in the bowling-green who gives him the bowls." Even when others were present, it was chiefly Boswell who kept talk moving: introducing new topics ("I said Horace had much thinking in him"), shifting focus ("I believe, Sir, a great many of the children born in London die early"), and inviting Johnson to expatiate ("I believe natural affection, of which we hear so much, is very small": "I mentioned the Doctor's excellent distinction between liberty of conscience and liberty of teaching").[15]

By asking about the management of his new estate, Boswell again encouraged Johnson to assume the role of laird. On Good Friday, when he mentioned his wish for "a good garden with walls," Johnson quickly explained why this made no sense, since a wall substantial enough to keep out deer would cost far more than a garden so far north could yield: "No, Sir, such a contention with nature is not worth while." But then — speaking both as Boswell's advisor and as laird — Johnson suggested an alternative: "I would plant an orchard, and have plenty of such fruit as ripen well in your country. . . . Cherries are an early fruit. You may have them; and you may have the early apples and pears. . . . For ground that would let for forty shillings, you may have a large orchard; and you see it costs only forty shillings. Nay, you may graze the ground when the trees are old. You cannot while they are young." When Boswell declared, "A hothouse [heated greenhouse] is a certain thing," Johnson agreed, continuing to imagine himself in Boswell's situation:

> JOHNSON. "A hothouse is pretty certain; but you must first build it; then you must keep fires in it, and have a gardener to take care of it." BOSWELL. But if I have a gardener at any rate?" JOHNSON. "Why, yes." BOSWELL. "I'd have it near my house. There is no need to have it in the orchard." JOHNSON. "Yes, I'd have it near my house. I would plant a great many currants. The fruit is good, and they make a pretty sweetmeat."

Musing about adventurous travel was no longer reasonable, but fantasies of "great estate" were timely, since what Johnson imagined with gusto and specificity was of immediate use.[16]

Boswell's questions engaged Johnson, and Johnson's talk energized Boswell. On 15 May, only the third time Boswell saw his friend that month, he was afraid to acknowledge his "dreary hypochondria," so simply said he was "over-fatigued." But to set Johnson in motion, he expressed his wish to be in Parliament. Boswell probably anticipated objections, and Johnson predictably said, "Unless you come, like your countrymen, resolved to support any administration, you'd be the worse for being in Parliament, because you'd be obliged to live more expensively." But when Boswell declared that he would never sell his vote and that "it would vex [him] if things went wrong," Johnson's spirited reply surprised and delighted him:

> JOHNSON. "That's cant, sir. It would not vex you more in the House than in the gallery. Public affairs vex no man." BOSWELL. "Have not they vexed your-

self a little, Sir. All the turbulence of this reign, and the House of Commons voting that the influence of the Crown has increased, etc.?" JOHNSON. "Sir, I have never slept an hour less or eat an ounce less meat. I'd have knocked 'em on the head, to be sure. But I was not vexed." BOSWELL. "I declare, Sir, upon my honour, I did imagine I was vexed, and I took pride in it. But I see it *is* cant, for I neither eat less nor slept less."

Then Johnson generalized for the friend he had been instructing for twenty years: "Nay, my friend, clear the bottom of your mind of cant. You may talk as other people do. You may say, 'I'm your most humble servant.' You're not his most humble servant. You may say, 'These are sad times. It is a melancholy thing to be reserved to such times.' You don't mind the times. You tell a man, 'I'm sorry you had such bad weather the last day of your journey, and were so much wet.' You don't care sixpence whether he was wet or dry. You may *talk* in this manner; it is a mode of talking in society. But don't *think* foolishly."

Johnson's energetic analysis brought "a return of animation, of manly spirit." Also, this analysis meshed with Boswell's recent insight that much of his depression was just "mouldy imagination." Margaret was really ill, his debts were large, and much of the income of Auchinleck was assigned to his stepmother. But Boswell was not really vexed when he thought and said he was, and his depression often disappeared when he turned his mind elsewhere.[17]

"Very Uncertain If I Should See Him Again"

On 29 May, the day before he left London, Boswell spent much of the morning with Johnson, who had seemed close to death ten weeks earlier, but now looked fine. Knowing this might be their final conversation, however, each friend expressed what he saw at the core of their friendship.

At the start of the visit, Boswell had "felt a steadiness as laird of Auchinleck which [he] never before experienced in London." But now he lamented "how absurd and weak" he was: not in his profession — "for I do very well when I come to an argument in law" — but "in conduct and in speculative opinions," where he lacked "force of mind." He needed Johnson. When he lamented "not having [Johnson] near . . . to consult upon all occasions of any difficulty," Johnson urged him "to get as much force of mind" as he could. Then, by addressing his friend's speculative and practical questions, Johnson modeled how Boswell could guide himself.

Besides repeating his general advice about spending — "Live within your income. Always have something saved at the end of the year" — Johnson demonstrated the power of computation. He asked "*how many* trees [Boswell] had sold for £70," and scolded him for not counting and for not measuring the girths of what he was selling. When Boswell replied that counting and measuring would take time, Johnson said, "I hope you have not sold more than 100 trees for £70, and 100 trees may be measured in a day." Then Johnson spelled out how to decide when to harvest a tree: "Consider whether the value of its yearly growth or the interest of the price is most, and then either cut or delay." As he had done earlier when urging Boswell to have an orchard rather than a garden, Johnson showed how careful attention to costs and benefits would produce sensible decisions.

When Boswell described a couple that lived in London for only £500 a year, Johnson replied, "But *your* family would not be kept in London for £500 a year, nor £1000 neither. You would wish to make a figure suitable to your rank. Your lady would wish to do it." Like Dundas and Burke earlier, Johnson urged Boswell to persist in his career: "Every new cause would teach me more law, and the more causes I had, the less surprising it would be that I was made a judge." In addition, probably in response to Boswell's report that his legal practice had declined after his father retired as judge, Johnson urged his friend to "court employment in all honest and liberal means, be still more civil to agents than before. . . . Have them to dine . . . and show them you are desirous of practice."[18]

Ten weeks earlier, Johnson had reported that Boswell's company did him much good. Now Boswell found himself "animated by [Johnson's] manly conversation." He now shared with Johnson the image he had first used seven years earlier to describe the energizing power of his talk: "I told him I was persuaded there was a transfusion of mind, like Hermippus Redivivus in body. I had experienced it from him." But each was about to be deprived of the other's conversation for at least a year, perhaps forever.[19]

To reconnect sooner, Boswell invited Johnson to Auchinleck, as he and Margaret had both done six months earlier, and Johnson responded with two complementary fantasies of returning to this estate. "I cannot come this year," he said, "But when I grow better, as I hope I shall, I should gladly come. I should like to totter about your Place, and live mostly on milk, and be taken care of by Mrs. Boswell." When Boswell later declared that no one "had a more sincere respect and affection" for Johnson than he had, Johnson seemed to endorse this claim by saying, "If I were in distress, there is no man I would come to so soon as to you. I should come to you and have a cottage in your park." While reaffirming Boswell's special status, Johnson replaced fantasies of adventurous travel, domestic intimacy, and collaborative island development with fantasies of Auchinleck as haven, as hospice.[20]

Johnson then embraced Boswell and said "with solemn fervour, 'God bless you for Jesus Christ's sake.'" Apprehensive about his health after two years of distressing symptoms, and anxious about his friendship with Hester Thrale, who had written just twice in eight weeks, Johnson feared bearing "the weight of time with unseemly, if not with sinful impatience," as he had written Chambers. He also worried about Boswell. Earlier he had seen Boswell in process: not yet at twenty-two the man he would be at thirty; not so "regular and useful" six years later as he would become once happily married; at thirty-four, not yet the man of "exemplary piety" Johnson hoped in time to reverence. But now at forty-two, married for more than thirteen years and newly installed as laird, Boswell still needed work. As Boswell was hastening off to Burke's, Johnson shouted a reminder to say good-bye to Mrs. Williams.[21]

Though Johnson was much stronger than at the start of the visit, Boswell walked away "with agitation and a kind of fearful apprehension of what might happen before [he] returned." (Mrs. Williams was also worried, and suggested that Boswell urge Johnson to write his will.) Far less confident than he had felt ten weeks earlier, Boswell feared being unable to function effectively in a world without Johnson. So at the end of the longest entry for the visit, having described his afternoon with Burke and others, and a "hearty" late supper with Dilly, Temple, and his brother David, Boswell returned an earlier moment when Johnson had warmly endorsed his behavior as laird.

After Johnson noted that people's "minds are more solemnly affected in places appropriated to divine worship than in others," and added that some people "have a particular room in their house where they say their prayers," Boswell said he had such a room at Auchinleck, where every morning he would "pray and read a part of the Holy Scriptures and a part of Thomas à Kempis": "I never fail to find myself calmed and elevated." Johnson encouraged his friend to keep the room "for that purpose"; and Boswell, after recording these words, added, "I intend to do so." By maintaining this approved ritual, he would be pleasing Johnson and perhaps keeping himself as free from melancholy as when he had last visited the estate that was now his.[22]

Boswell's Quest for Preferment, Johnson's Uncertain Health (1 June 1783 through April 1784)

On 30 May 1783, fearing he would be adrift without Johnson and Burke nearby, Boswell tried to convince himself he was truly "fixed" by what both men had told him the day before. But even as he recorded the arguments that had "satisfied [him] at the time," Boswell winced at being stuck in Scotland, with only occasional visits to London to look forward to. When he resumed his journal in Edinburgh two months later, he was in "very bad spirits," drinking "liberally, just to dissipate dreary dullness." Three weeks earlier, he had asked Colonel Stuart's "sagacious Advice if I shall offer myself as Member for

Ayrshire if Col: Montgomery does not stand." (A seat in Parliament, though unpaid, would justify his living in London.) Now (8 August) he wrote Burke, requesting that he be picked to replace Dundas as lord advocate of Scotland, or if Ilay Campbell was given that position, that he be chosen to replace Campbell as solicitor general.

Boswell justified seeking these enormously powerful positions by appealing to Burke's sympathy, hoping his "generous friendship" would relieve him "from a state of dulness and discontent." Burke explained that he had used up most of his little credit and would be "little consulted about the arrangements of Scotland"; but he promised to do what he could.[23]

Meanwhile, Johnson began experiencing a series of physical ailments, none anticipated, and each more serious than those of the previous two years. Early on 17 June, a stroke temporarily deprived him of speech, though he was still able to think and write. By mid-July he was well enough to visit Langton at Rochester. But early in September, during a visit to the Salisbury home of William and Dina Bowles, new young friends, a swelling of his left testicle became painful enough to demand painful, risky surgery. This was postponed only because gout invaded Johnson's feet "with violence," leaving him "helpless as an infant," unable to walk to church for six weeks, by which time the inflamed testicle, having been lanced, ceased to bother him. On 3 November, Johnson finally managed the walk to St. Clement's, and a week later wrote both Lucy Porter and John Taylor that his health had been "wonderfully restored." But on 14 December, while attending a meeting of the new Essex Head Club he had established to help fill his lonely evenings, Johnson suffered an acute asthmatic attack, and his difficulty breathing, combined with the swelling of his legs from congestive heart failure, kept him home indefinitely. On 19 February 1784, more than nine weeks into this confinement, Johnson received "sudden and unexpected relief" by a discharge of twenty pints of urine, and three weeks later he dressed in ordinary clothes for the first time in three months. But lingering cold weather kept him inside until 21 April: "a confinement of one hundred twenty nine days," as he later wrote, "more than the third part of a year, and no inconsiderable part of human life."[24]

During the last seven months of 1783, Boswell wrote four letters to Johnson, who sent three replies. Early in 1784 — especially in February and March — they wrote more frequently. As usual, Boswell initiated each exchange. He wrote as soon as he learned of Johnson's stroke, "anxious about his being worse, and begging to be relieved"; and Johnson promptly replied to Boswell's "very friendly" anxiety, reassuringly describing his almost complete recovery from the "very frightful blow" he had suffered. A month after Boswell heard from Johnson and a day after he wrote Burke about a position, Boswell again wrote — "in kind concern about him — inviting him to Auchinleck — that I am dreary." Now, however, Johnson was slow to reply.

"There has seldom been so long a time in which I have had so little to do with Boswel, as since he left London," Johnson wrote Queeney Thrale on 23 August, about ten days after he got Boswell's invitation. "He has written twice, and I have written once." Given how infrequently he and Boswell had corresponded recently, it seems odd that Johnson thought three letters in ten weeks was uncommonly little contact. But having remarked this, Johnson waited another five weeks before replying to Boswell: weeks when he sent three letters to Bowles (with whom he spent three of these weeks), and two each to Taylor and Langton. Probably, as in the summer and fall of 1778, Johnson was not eager to address Boswell's dejection at not being able to live in London. (Just before writing Johnson, Boswell had complained to Paoli of his "dreary dejection": "How hard is it that when so many people are raised to seats in Parliament and offices of consequence, I am wasting my days in provincial obscurity.") The only paragraph printed in the *Life* from what Johnson finally wrote on 30 September begins by complaining that Boswell "should not make [his] letters such rarities": "It is very long since I heard from you; and that I have not answered is a very insufficient reason for the silence of a friend." Anything Johnson wrote about visiting Auchinleck or about Boswell's dejection was omitted.[25]

Soon after writing to Burke, Paoli, and Johnson in early August 1783, Boswell reached Auchinleck, where he was not so contented as before, and "began to despair of acquiring any knowledge in country affairs." He found even entertaining to be "a laborious and anxious task," read little, was "quite averse to writing," and "was exact only in keeping my Book of Company and Liquors." While Johnson worked at keeping his mind in motion — explaining the construction of the hot-air balloons that had been launched in France and then in England, exploring Stonehenge with Burke and "confut[ing] two opinions which have been advanced about it" — Boswell "thought of appointing a faithful trustee and going to reside in London or in France." Early in October, Johnson's letter, with its wish for more time — "I hope God will yet grant me a little longer life" — led Boswell to think "with dreadful gloom" of his friend's death: "It appeared to me that if he were gone, I should find life quite vapid and myself quite at a loss what to do, or how to think."[26]

On 16 October, however, Boswell experienced "sudden relief from hypochondria," and three days later he asked Johnson, "Why should I not venture in London?" Soon afterward, he was chosen to preside at the quarter sessions at Ayr and was again asked to chair a general meeting of freeholders called to petition Parliament against "nominal and fictitious votes" — those created by temporarily assigning land to relatives and other dependents, making them eligible to vote. Boswell was clearly respected by his peers. So when he learned on 20 November that he had not been named to either position he sought, he sent an "indignant manifesto" to Burke: "You flattered me with hopes that they were to have no understrapping Manager of affairs on this side of the Tweed. But this appointment is a wretched proof to the contrary. I have an indignant feeling upon the occasion." Two days later, Boswell vented to Johnson as well.[27]

Johnson began to respond as soon as he read his friend's complaint of "neglected merit," trying to encourage patience while hoping Boswell had not written others: "Of the exaltations and depressions of your mind you delight to talk, and I hate to hear. Drive all such fancies from you." Having written this page, Johnson was interrupted by "one disease or another," and finished his letter only four weeks later, a week after Fox's coalition, with Burke as paymaster of the forces, had been replaced by a ministry headed by William Pitt the Younger. Johnson therefore urged Boswell to forget about politics and stay in Scotland:

> Wrap yourself up in your hereditary possessions, which, though less than you may wish, are more than you can want.
>
> As your neighbours distinguish you by such honours as they can bestow, content yourself with your station, without neglecting your profession. Your estate and the Courts will find you full employment; and your mind well occupied will be quiet.

In closing, Johnson answered two quite different questions Boswell had posed. He quickly judged the creation of "fictitious votes" a "fraud," which it was certainly "lawful, and perhaps [Boswell's] duty to resist." Deciding "what, in propriety and humanity, should be done with old horses unable to labour" gave Johnson "more perplexity." So he wrote at length, trying to help his friend derive the proper course of action from basic principles.[28]

A month before Johnson finished this letter, Boswell had "sincerely renewed [his] most affectionate vows to [his] valuable spouse," but then had so seriously violated them that entries for the seventeen days from 26 November through 12 December were later removed. When Johnson's letter arrived on 31 December, Boswell was completing a sober confinement to cure gonorrhea, during which his "mind . . . had, as it were, ease and elbow-room." He had also just completed *Letter to the People of Scotland on the State of the Nation,* intended "to rouse a spirit for *property* and the *Constitution* in opposition to the East India Bill." In attacking this bill, which had been proposed by Fox but largely written by Burke, Boswell explicitly realigned himself with Johnson, from whom he had heard nothing for almost twelve weeks, calling him "the man in the world for whom [he has] the highest respect," though Johnson had "not been able to convince [Boswell] that *Taxation was no Tyranny.*" Enormously pleased with this pamphlet, especially after he began receiving praise from those to whom he sent copies, and hopeful it might help him with Pitt's Tory administration, "and surely with the King himself," Boswell sent a copy to Johnson on 8 January. Boswell had opposed Johnson and the ministry on the Middlesex election and America, but he assured his friend that his "general principles of government are according to [Johnson's] own heart."[29]

Johnson's letter, especially its engaged analysis of how to treat old horses, had left Boswell hopeful that his friend "might live some time yet." But a letter from Charles Dilly on 7 January gave "bad accounts of Dr. Johnson's health," prompting Boswell to write the next day. Three weeks later, another "alarming" account from Dilly got Boswell to write directly to Dr. William Heberden and Dr. Richard Brocklesby, the physicians attending Johnson, "begging to hear particularly about Dr. Johnson's health." He also asked Francis Barber to write "at least once a week of his Master, but not to let him know, as it might alarm him."[30]

On 7 February, Boswell received a "not unfavourable account" from Dr. Heberden, and from Dr. Brocklesby's report he derived "hopes of [Johnson's] living some years." In his entry, Boswell wrote that these accounts gave him hope that he "should have the happiness of having some more of his admirable counsel in this world." On 14 February, the day his own body was deemed wholly cured from venereal infection, he reported to Johnson Pitt's praise of the East India *Letter,* and perhaps mentioned also what he had written Paoli five days earlier: that he was currently drinking no wine. The next day, however, Boswell received a deeply troubling report from Johnson, and for almost the first time heard his friend ask for advice.[31]

Up to this point, Johnson had written much less graphically to Boswell than to others concerning his many ailments. On 30 September, for instance, he mentioned having been "much harassed with the gout," but did not say that it "came upon [him] with violence, which [he] never experienced before," as he had written Langton a week earlier. He told Boswell nothing about probably needing surgery on the painfully swollen testicle, concerning which he wrote with some alarm to Bowles and Langton, Taylor and Chambers, and Hester Thrale. (After the stroke, Johnson had resumed regular correspondence with Hester Thrale, sending twelve letters in the following three weeks, then an average of three a month for the next year.) In December, Johnson explained that "one disease or another" kept him from finishing what he had begun weeks earlier; but instead of specifying what had happened, he simply reported being "a little better," "though sickness and solitude" weighed on him "very heavily." In contrast, Johnson had just written Taylor of being "very severely crushed by [his] own spasms"; and three days later he wrote Thrale that the convulsions of his breast had finally driven him to take prescribed narcotics: "Doctor Heberden recommends opiates, of which I have such horrour that I do not think of them but *in extremis.*" Whatever the reason — perhaps to model stoic fortitude when writing his biographer — Johnson's letters to Boswell were relatively restrained.[32]

On 11 February, however, after more than eight weeks of confinement, Johnson finally told Boswell what had happened on 14 December, when he "was seized with a spasmodick asthma so violent" that only "with difficulty" did he get home, where he had remained since. Dangerous as that was, he had more serious problems: "The asthma, however, is not the worst. A dropsy gains ground upon me; my legs and thighs are very much swollen with water, which I should be content if I could keep there, but I am afraid that it will soon be higher. My nights are very sleepless and very tedious. And yet I am extremely afraid of dying." Having five days earlier asked Dr. Heberden "if any hope of amend[m]ent remains, and by what medicines or methods it may be promoted," Johnson now asked Boswell to see what his own physicians thought of his case and to request a written opinion from Sir Alexander Dick. He also wrote that if he managed to survive till autumn, he would "be glad to try a warmer climate." He hoped to emulate the painter Allan Ramsay, who "recovered his limbs in Italy," rather than the writer Henry Fielding, who died shortly after arriving in Lisbon. But there were difficulties: "How to travel with a diseased body, without a companion to conduct me, and with very little money, I do not well see." So Johnson asked for Boswell's advice: "Think for me what I can do."

Johnson was relying on Boswell in an entirely new way. Instead of calling for energizing diversion or help in patching up a quarrel, he was asking for clearheaded, practical advice concerning seemingly insurmountable obstacles. Having listed the difficulties in getting to Italy, Johnson asked Boswell to think for him, as he often had thought for Boswell.[33]

Johnson almost surely told some of the friends who stopped by of his hope to be somewhere warmer if he survived till August, especially after 19 February, when his having been relieved of so much fluid left him guardedly optimistic. Paoli's writing to Boswell on 20 February about getting Johnson to Italy probably reflected such a conversation. But Boswell was the only friend Johnson wrote for advice. Having for years been both pleased and exasperated by Boswell's "troublesome kindness," and having noticed his current solicitude, Johnson asked his help in escaping the next English winter. By restricting what

Boswell knew about his ailments, Johnson had earlier withheld full intimacy. Now he fully empowered his friend.[34]

Boswell did what he could from Edinburgh. Having written just before this letter arrived, he wrote again eight days later, enclosing the comments of Sir Alexander Dick and of Dr. Thomas Gillespie, Lord Auchinleck's physician. When he received Johnson's thanks for these opinions, Boswell wrote to Drs. William Cullen, Alexander Monro, and John Hope, all on the faculty of medicine at the University of Edinburgh, seeking "advice upon Dr. Johnson's case." Cullen and Monro wrote letters Boswell later carried to London; Hope wrote directly to Brocklesby.[35]

Meanwhile, Johnson had recovered enough strength by 23 February to read Boswell's *Letter*, and for the first time in almost fifteen years praised one of Boswell's publications. He agreed with Boswell's argument and shared his "indignation at the indecency with which the King is every day treated." He also praised Boswell's learning, asserting that the pamphlet "contains very considerable knowledge of the history and the constitution, very properly produced and applied." Probably responding to Boswell's report that Dundas had quoted the pamphlet in Parliament and that Pitt had written with praise, Johnson added: "It will certainly raise your character, though perhaps it may not make you a Minister of State."[36]

Though healthy enough to read and critique this pamphlet, Johnson was far from fully recovered, as he explained on 18 March, when he responded to the invitation from Margaret enclosed in Boswell's letter of 9 March by saying he could not guess when he might be able to travel to Auchinleck, though "such a letter as Mrs. Boswell's might draw any man, not wholly motionless, a great way." It was only in this letter, as Johnson anticipated his friend's arrival in London, where an unusually cold spring still kept him housebound, that he reported what had happened four weeks earlier: how "the dropsy, by God's blessing," had "run almost totally away by natural evacuation." But Johnson did not write Boswell what he repeatedly told others: that the "natural evacuation" he had experienced on a day he had set aside for fasting and reflection was truly "wonderful" and "amazing." Dr. Heberden in years of practice had seen "but four examples" like it and did not suppose the relief "to be at all owing to medicine." Only on 30 March, after Boswell had asked about Dr. Brocklesby's description of how "Dr. Johnson was wonderfully relieved," did Johnson confirm that this was "by the blessing of God," as he repeated "with solemn earnestness" when he finally saw Boswell five weeks later.[37]

On 22 March, probably before he received Johnson's letter declining the invitation to Auchinleck and reporting the "natural evacuation," Boswell started toward London. But in York he heard that Parliament had been dissolved, and so returned to Ayrshire, hoping to be elected. Johnson, still housebound, wrote his approval: "You could do nothing so proper as to haste back when you found the Parliament dissolved." Having earlier explained why Boswell should not grumble when passed over (24 December), and should not expect much of the new ministry (18 March), Johnson now noted that his chance of entering government had much improved: "With the influence which your address must have gained you, it may reasonably be expected that your presence will be of importance, and your activity of effect." But securing a seat in Parliament required "much prudence." Drawing on his experience with Henry Thrale's campaigns and his knowledge of Boswell's inclinations, Johnson urged his friend to "endeavour to oppose without exasperating; to practice temporary hostility, without producing enemies for life." He especially warned Boswell "to be scrupulous in the use of strong liquors," since "one night's drunkenness may defeat the labours of forty days well employed." But he closed his paragraph of electoral advice with a rousing call to action: "Be firm, but not clamorous; be active, but not malicious; and you may form such an interest, as may not only exalt yourself, but dignify your family."[38]

Having written five letters each since the start of 1784, all but one during the previous seven weeks, Boswell and Johnson were significantly connected. As he waited for Boswell's arrival, Johnson took vicarious delight in thinking about his campaign. But he was uncertain, as he wrote Langton, whether winning the seat would truly benefit their friend.[39]

15

"Love Me as Well as You Can" (1784)

Having failed in his bid for Parliament, Boswell wrote Johnson from Lichfield on 30 April 1784, and arrived in London five days later. In anticipating the visit, he had written Reynolds, Dempster, and Barnard—and also the overseer James Bruce, who expected him at Auchinleck—that his goal was "chiefly to attend upon Dr. Johnson"; and he was with Johnson on most of the days when both were in London (or Oxford) between 5 May and 2 July.[1]

On 21 April, when it was finally warm enough to venture outside, Johnson reported walking "with a more easy respiration" than he had known "for perhaps two years past." But six weeks later, he felt "at a great distance from health, very weak and very asthmatick, and troubled with . . . nocturnal distresses": "I am little asleep in the night, and in the day too little awake." He therefore appreciated Boswell's company and attentive management, which he mentioned in four letters written during the visit. Also, because Johnson soon endorsed Boswell's resolve to try the English bar, their time together was remarkably harmonious.[2]

Practicing Law in England

Without a patronage position or a seat in Parliament, Boswell now planned to make the move to London entirely on his own. Anticipating John-son's death prompted him to act immediately. By "resolving" to move to

London, he was hanging a flag on his distressed fortress. Also, it meant doing something decisive, something he hoped he could control. Johnson still insisted that Boswell come only if he could finance the move without incurring new debts, living on what he earned from his legal practice and from Auchinleck. But there is no indication that Johnson pressed for details about Boswell's income and his debts. (At the end of 1783, Sir William Forbes had delicately hinted that Boswell's credit with his bank "was exhausted.") Also, Johnson seems not to have emphasized how difficult it would be for a forty-three-year-old Scot to succeed at the English bar.

Key conversations about the move seem to have occurred early. Johnson had not agreed by 14 May, when Boswell wrote Barnard that he was "almost resolved to remove to London for [his] Town Residence," then reported Johnson's objections and his rebuttals. Johnson clearly had withdrawn his objections by 31 May, when he wrote Hester Thrale that "Boswell is resolved to remove his family to London, and try his fortune at the English Bar," and added, "Let us all wish him success." I suspect Johnson had approved the plan two weeks earlier. For on 17 May, Boswell sent Temple a "*full* account of [his] *resolution* to establish [him]self at the English bar," and sent Langton a "*short* account of ditto." It seems unlikely Boswell would have firmly resolved what three days earlier he had only "*almost* resolved" unless Johnson had accepted the venture.[3]

On 7 August, Johnson would explain to Sir William Forbes that he withdrew his "prohibitions" because he found Boswell's "ardour for English Honour, and English Pleasures so strong that, he would have considered all open and declared opposition, as envy or malignity, or distrust of his abilities." Once Johnson endorsed the plan, he offered specific, cautionary advice: "Take care to attend constantly in Westminster Hall; both to mind your business, as it is almost all learnt there (for nobody reads now), and to show that you want to have business. And you must not be too often seen at public places, that those who wish to get the fees you may get may not have it to say, 'He is always at the playhouse or Ranelagh, and never to be found in his chambers.'" But Johnson also warmed to the project. "He tells me," Boswell wrote Temple, "If you only take care not to exceed your income you cannot be wrong. You have every chance in your favour. You will *certainly* improve your mind, and you *may* improve your fortune." The "loss of your Scottish business," Johnson wrote on 11 July, "which is all you can lose, is not to be reckoned as any equivalent to the hopes and possibilities that open here upon you. If You succeed, all question of prudence is at an end . . . ; and if after a few years You should return to Scotland, You will return with a mind supplied by various conversation, and many opportunities of enquiry, with much knowledge and materials for reflexion and instruction." ("To strive with difficulties, and to conquer them, is the highest human felicity," Johnson had written years earlier in *Adventurer* 111; "the next, is to strive, and deserve to conquer.")[4]

A Final Jaunt Together

Boswell's move to London having been accepted, both friends played their familiar roles with mutual satisfaction. Though weak and anxious, Johnson was seldom peevish. Boswell was constantly on duty. But he found relief when he visited Langton (31 May–1 June), and when he returned to London after first bringing Johnson to Oxford (4–8 June). Whether alone with Johnson or also with others, Boswell encouraged and sustained talk on a range of topics, including the misery of life, Burke's conversation, Milton's sonnets, and the difference between argument and testimony. As usual, Johnson volunteered stories about himself when relevant, revealing that he had once tried to learn knitting from Dempster's sister, for instance, and mentioning that at Oxford "he wrote his first exercise twice over, but never did so again."

Johnson and Boswell also traveled together for the last time, though not as far as either hoped. Johnson was so keen on confirming and consolidating his health by going to Oxford on 3 June—a trip he could not manage on his own—that Boswell was willing to miss a special performance of Handel on 5 June in order to indulge his "impatient and fretful" friend. But Reynolds suggested Boswell could accompany Johnson to Oxford, then return for the concert. Johnson was delighted to realize that Boswell made the journey "merely to keep him company," became irritated when Boswell lingered in London for a special dinner on 8 June, but perked up when Boswell returned.[5]

Johnson placed himself under Boswell's control without contesting his management. "How long we shall stay at Oxford, or what we shall do when we leave it, neither Bozzy nor I have yet settled," Johnson wrote Mrs. Thrale on 31 May; and on 7 June, with Boswell still in London, Johnson wrote Allen, "How long I shall stay, or whither I shall go, I cannot yet guess." On 11 June, Boswell wrote Mrs. Cobb in Lichfield, inquiring whether "it would be convenient for her to ask Dr. Johnson to her house," and he asked John Taylor on 22 June to inform him by return post when his house would be ready for Johnson. "Boswel has a great mind to draw me to Lichfield," Johnson wrote Taylor the next day, "and as I love to travel with him, I have a mind to be drawn if I could hope in any short time to come to your house, for Lichfield will I am afraid, not be a place for long continuance." Since Boswell would travel on to Scotland, however, Johnson was also "afraid of seeing [himself] so far from home," since he would have to "return alone."

Besides encouraging Boswell to manage the Oxford trip and to try arranging for Lichfield and Ashbourne, Johnson probably accepted his friend's final attempt in June to bring Johnson and Thomas Sheridan together—"by chance" —at Dilly's. But once Sheridan learned Johnson was coming, he left, refusing to perform in the scene Boswell hoped to produce.[6]

Johnson also applauded Boswell's efforts to find a way for him to reach Italy. In the *Life,* Boswell heightened the drama by having Johnson first ask about Italy only on 27 June, just before Boswell was about to return home. It seems unlikely, however, that Johnson would have waited that long. His persistent difficulty in breathing showed the need for warmer air, and his friends —especially Boswell, Paoli, and Reynolds—had started much earlier to work out how to get him to the Mediterranean. The Oxford trip showed that Johnson could manage travel if accompanied. By 16 June, when Johnson and Boswell had returned to London, an Italian friend had agreed to accompany Johnson in return for a lifetime annuity from Reynolds. The only remaining obstacle was money. Various friends, including Dr. Brocklesby, offered to help pay for the trip; but Johnson refused to accept funds from anyone but the king. So on 23 June, Boswell wrote to Lord Thurlow, the lord high chancellor, to see whether Johnson's pension might be increased. On 28 June, a day after Boswell reported Johnson's saying "he should wish much to go to Italy, and . . . dreaded next winter in England," Boswell received a positive response, and the next day he told Johnson the king would probably provide what was needed.

Johnson was deeply touched—"This is taking prodigious pains about a man"—moved to tears of joy and gratitude—"God bless you all for Jesus Christ's sake"—and rendered "unable to speak." The following day, their last day together, Boswell and Johnson dined with Reynolds to discuss Italy. Johnson explained how this trip would hardly compare to the one aborted in 1776: "Were I going to Italy to see fine pictures, like Sir Joshua, or to run after women, like Boswell, I might be sure to have pleasures in Italy. But when a man goes to Italy merely to feel how he breathes the air, he can enjoy very little." In Italy, however, Johnson would surely breathe with more ease. Though far from his friends, he would be accompanied by someone he respected. He could observe structures more interesting than Stonehenge and would have additional time to prepare for death. Boswell spent 1 July trying to confirm the increased pension, but left the final negotiation to Reynolds while he enjoyed an extended flirtation in Lichfield with the "enchanting" Anna Seward. At the time there seemed no reason to anticipate difficulties, nor is it clear that Boswell's staying longer in London would have helped. But later he must have wondered.[7]

Understanding Johnson's Anger

Though sad that Johnson was dying, and distressed that his resolve for London troubled Margaret and also Grange, Boswell seems to have been relatively free of melancholy. There is no evidence of heavy drinking or picking up prostitutes. At ease once Johnson endorsed the move, Boswell was open to a major new insight concerning behavior that had deeply troubled him since 1769: Johnson's angry, relationship-threatening outbursts at his friends, eruptions not arising from heated arguments and out of proportion to any evident provocation. "Dr. Johnson's harsh attacks on his friends," he told Sir Joshua on 5 June, "arise from uneasiness within. There is an insurrection aboard. His loud explosions are guns of distress."[8]

The immediate occasion for the insight was Johnson's account on 19 May of an episode that had occurred in March. He had asked Langton to tell him "in what he thought [Johnson's] life was faulty," and was surprised when Langton produced "a sheet of paper on which he had written down all the texts of Scripture recommending charity." Johnson refused to imagine being perceived as defective in charity. "I hope scar[c]ely any man has known me closely but to his benefit," he had written Hester Thrale the previous July, two weeks after his stroke, "or cursorily, but to his innocent entertainment." So he now called "out to his friend in a loud and angry tone, 'What is your drift, Sir?'" When Langton replied that Johnson "sometimes contradicted people in conversation," Johnson exploded. Two months later he was still exasperated; for "what harm does it do any man to be contradicted?"

This comic scene let Boswell see with detachment something he realized had been at play whenever he awakened Johnson's deepest fears. In fact, when Boswell in the *Life* described their conversation on 19 May 1784, it began with such an exchange. Boswell tried to get Johnson to imagine reconnecting with his friends in heaven, but Johnson rejected the idea "with heat," asking, "How did he know *where* his friends were, or whether they would be his friends in the other world? How many friendships have you known formed upon principles of virtue? Most friendships are formed by caprice or chance, mere confederacies in vice or leagues in folly." But the dynamics were easier to see in Johnson's earlier talk with Langton, with whom Boswell surely discussed the matter when they visited a few days before Boswell told Reynolds that he now understood Johnson's "harsh attacks."[9]

In the past, Boswell had pictured Johnson as a wild beast, tossing and goring people for sport, roaring and bellowing when angry or opposed, or as a force of nature, producing volcanic eruptions, violent thunder and lightning, or a terrible earthquake. Now, by combining Johnson's strong and ever-present fear of death with what Beattie had told him about Johnson's constant wrestling with "shocking impious thoughts," Boswell constructed a sympathetic explanation for many of Johnson's angry outbursts. Boswell remained critical of Johnson's sophistry and "spirit of contradiction," his inflexibility and occasional envy. But he now fully understood and forgave the behavior that had most shocked and frightened him.

Boswell's insight was rooted in felt affinity. In 1775, after his first sustained bout of melancholy since his marriage, Boswell wondered why he had not sent Temple "a few lines, merely as firing guns of distress"; and a year later, when telling Johnson of his efforts "to preserve a decent appearance" during his latest depression, he had used essentially the same metaphor: "Like a reduced garrison that has some spirit left, I hung out flags, and planted all the force I could muster, upon the walls." Johnson's fears seemed deeper and more sustained than Boswell's. Also Johnson seemed much less open to pleasure than Boswell and refused to anticipate being reunited with friends in heaven. But now Boswell understood Johnson's anger when he expressed this hope.[10]

This new insight, which eventually shaped how Boswell presented Johnson's angry outbursts in the *Life,* also affected Boswell's interactions with Johnson once he returned to Oxford. At breakfast on 11 June, when Johnson said he had thought of constructing a book of prayers, and all those present "joined in pressing him to execute the plan," Johnson "seemed to be a little displeased at our importunity, and in agitation said, 'Do not talk thus of what is so awful. I know not what time God will allow me in this world. There are many things I wish to do.'" When Adams and others persisted, Johnson replied, "'Let me alone! Let me alone! I am overpowered!' And then he put his hands upon his face and reclined for some time upon the table." At supper the next day, Johnson startled Adams by saying he feared he "'may be one of those who shall be damned' (looking down dismally)." When Adams asked what Johnson meant by "damned," Johnson—"passionate and loud"—replied, "Sent to hell, and punished everlastingly." After four more exchanges—two with Adams, one with Boswell, one with Adams's wife, Sarah—Johnson silenced them by declaring, "I'll have no more on't." Boswell's engagement in these scenes and his later descriptions were informed by his new sympathy with Johnson's inner turmoil.[11]

Collaboration Affirmed

The *Life* describes several intimate, poignant scenes toward the end of the visit, including the moment when Boswell told Johnson that the king was likely to increase his pension, dinner the next day at Reynolds's to discuss Italy, and their affectionate parting in Reynolds's coach, after which Johnson, "without looking back, sprung away with a kind of pathetick briskness." Boswell's text memorably brings each of these moments to life. Another scene, described in a letter to Temple but not included in the *Life,* should be added to this collection. Whenever it occurred, it contained Johnson's strongest praise of Boswell's achievement as an independent Johnsonian, his final endorsement of this now-mature friend. It also allowed Boswell to anticipate collaborating with Johnson beyond this visit.

According to the *Life*, when Boswell early in his 1783 visit offered to send Johnson some of his *Hypochondriack* essays, hoping he would "pick out the good ones," Johnson replied, "Nay, Sir, send me only the good ones; don't make *me* pick them." When Boswell read some of these essays aloud during this last visit, Johnson declared, "Sir, these are very fine things; the language is excellent, the reasoning good, and there is great application of learning. I may say to you what my wife said to me after I had published four or five of my *Ramblers*. 'I thought very well of you before. But I did not expect anything equal to this.' I should have you publish them in a volume and put your name to them."[12]

This praise was much stronger than what Johnson had written four months earlier about Boswell's *Letter to the People of Scotland*. In both tone and substance, it resembled his emphatic written praise for the published Corsica journal. Johnson's enthusiasm also recalls his comments on the even richer Hebrides journal: "The more I read of this, I think the more highly of you." What Elizabeth Johnson said about the *Rambler* also parallels what Johnson wrote Hester Thrale at the end of the Hebrides trip: "[Boswell] has better faculties, than I had imagined, more justness of discernment, and more fecundity of images."

In each case—Johnson with the *Rambler*, Boswell with the *Hypochondriack* (and earlier with the Hebrides journal)—the writer surpassed informed and loving expectations. By linking Boswell's essays to those he had written at Boswell's age, and by adopting words he had heard thirty-four years earlier from a woman whose judgment he respected, who knew his former writings well, and who at the time had known Johnson almost as long as he had now known Boswell, Johnson highlighted their deep alignment. In 1766, Johnson had dismissed some of Boswell's comments on religion as childish: "This . . . is just such stuff as I used to talk to my mother when I first began to think myself a clever fellow, and she ought to have whipped me for it." Now he suggested Boswell was like him at his best. "The praise given you by your Philosopher Guide is very encouraging," Temple noted. It was like a final blessing.

In reporting this praise to Temple, Boswell added that Johnson was to revise the *Hypochondriack* essays, and then Boswell would "bring them forth in two or perhaps three elegant volumes." Boswell seized on this chance to collaborate further. Picturing Johnson revising what he had already shown Forbes, Kames, and others was a concrete way of imagining their friendship continuing even with Johnson in Italy.[13]

Hopes Disappointed

As Johnson and Boswell parted on 30 June 1784, each held tight to a hope that soon proved impossible. By the end of July, Boswell realized that a lack of funds compelled him to postpone trying for the English bar. Six weeks later, Johnson learned that his pension would not be increased, ruling out his getting to Italy. A month before this second disappointment, the harmony produced by Johnson's endorsing Boswell's plans for London had ended. After steady interaction from late January through early August, including two letters from Boswell and four from Johnson in the first five weeks after Boswell left London, there was no contact at all for more than twelve weeks. In fact, Boswell might never have written again had Johnson not sent a final letter wondering at this long silence and urging Boswell to act while there was still time.

Having seen Boswell most days during the last three weeks of June, Johnson clearly had his friend in mind during July and early August. On 8 July, two days after his legs began once again to swell and the same day he wrote Hester Thrale for the last time, Johnson reminded Reynolds that the increased pension had not been confirmed, and explained what to say should the chancellor "continue his attention to Mr. Boswell's request." Two days later, he wrote Bowles that his "fellowtraveller Mr. Boswell" had replaced William Strahan in the Essex Head Club. Then on 11 July, a day when he started to church but found his legs tired and his breath obstructed, Johnson responded to a request Boswell had posted a week earlier, spelling out why trying for the English bar was reasonable—provided Boswell's "expence never exceeds [his] annual income." He also noted that Boswell's "kind negotiation" had not yet led to an enlarged pension, reported that his health had not improved, detailed his medications, and asked Boswell to check "how much of the vinegar [of squills] your Physicians generally consider as a powerful dose."[14]

About to see whether country air might provide some relief, Johnson told Boswell he was leaving final negotiations regarding the pension to Reynolds and would "try to go down with hope and tranquility." Struggling for health during a "frigid ungenial summer," Johnson longed for assurance that he might eventually "obtain some help from a softer climate." So two of the three letters that survive from the first ten days after he reached Ashbourne on 20 July were to the friends responsible for initiating and carrying on this negotiation. On 21 July, besides writing the first of many detailed reports for Dr. Brocklesby, Johnson also wrote Reynolds that he had not "made much progress in recovery." Five days later, while reporting to Boswell that he was "very feeble, and very dejected," and complaining of solitude, since Taylor was "busy in his fields, and [went] to bed at nine," Johnson wished that Boswell's "affairs could have permitted a longer and continued exertion of [his] zeal and kindness": "They that have your kindness may want your ardour."

Twelve days later, as he was explaining to Sir William Forbes why he had approved Boswell's plan to try for the English bar, Johnson got a letter from Boswell that probably reported his having just written Reynolds and certainly lamented that his "ambitious prospect of going to the English bar [was] impracticable at least for some time."[15]

Preparing to confront Margaret, Grange, and others, Boswell from Lichfield had asked Johnson for arguments supporting the move. While traveling home, he also described his plan at length to Temple, explaining how he hoped to overcome the chief obstacles: his ignorance of English law, his lack of sufficient income, and his debts. "It is amazing," he added, "with what avidity I read to fit me for trying what I wish for so much." He planned to "live in London upon a small scale for some time," which Burke approved as "very manly," and imagined it possible "to get [his] debts kept quiet and gradually cleared off."

By 17 July, however, after being "harassed by the arguments of relations and friends against [his] animated scheme of going to the English bar," Boswell had become deeply discouraged and "miserably melancholy," as he wrote Paoli. Three days later — the same day Johnson arrived at Ashbourne to find "a house half built, of very uncomfortable appearance" — Boswell imagined himself "incapable" of mastering English law. He also realized that interest payments on his debts left barely enough to maintain his family in Scotland. He would have to live "in penurious privacy" in London, which Margaret, "with her admirable good sense[,] observes would deprive [him] of all the felicity which London now yields." In addition, Margaret had spat blood the night before, underscoring how "the weakness of her lungs renders her very unfit to live in the smoke of London." So Boswell wrote Temple — *"in confidence"* — that his "airy scheme will not do." Two days later (22 July), however, Boswell added in a postscript that he was "rather better": "My scheme revives. O, would but *rex meus* [my king] patronize me!"[16]

On 3 August, responding to what Johnson had written on 26 July about his health and the pension, Boswell wrote both Reynolds and Johnson. To Reynolds, he crafted a letter designed to encourage "ardour" in pressing Lord Thurlow for what he had promised their "feeble and dejected" friend: "Let me then intreat you my Dear Sir to persevere in exerting yourself to obtain for him that Royal Bounty of which he has been flattered with such hopes that it would be mortifying should he be disappointed. I am truly astonished that there has been such a delay. Does it not hurt your generous mind?"

To Johnson, Boswell sent what he described as "a long melancholy letter quite in misery," what Johnson characterized to Forbes as "a gloomy account of his perplexity and irresolution." Boswell also expressed "anxious apprehensions" concerning Johnson, prompted by a dream, and he offered the comfort and companionship Johnson currently lacked by inviting him to Auchinleck. Boswell clearly wanted reassurance that Johnson was well. He also hoped for the sort of animation he had often experienced in Johnson's company. Johnson's letters had seldom pulled Boswell out of depression. But if Johnson came to Auchinleck, his vigorous conversation would surely enliven and steady him. Boswell also expected Johnson to sympathize with his disappointment.[17]

"Write to me often, and write like a man"

Because this letter arrived as Johnson was explaining to Forbes why he had endorsed Boswell's trying for the English bar, his reply was less sympathetic than it might have been. Johnson made clear to Forbes that he "withdrew [his] prohibition" of London only after Boswell agreed to contract no new debts. But having repeatedly seen how little Boswell could be trusted to keep such resolutions, and how easily he spent borrowed money, Johnson acknowledged the "very great" danger that he would "be driven by his passions beyond the bounds which he has consented to fix." Masking how enthusiastically, despite these fears, he had warmed to his friend's venture, Johnson reported having told Boswell—"with as much energy as I could call to my assistance"—"that He is too rich for an Adventurer, and by a game so hazardous and daring, he stakes more than he can win."[18]

After justifying himself to Forbes, Johnson wrote to Boswell. Embarrassed at having supported what he knew was risky, and worried that his friend would never learn, Johnson was relieved that Boswell needed to postpone London. ("To gain time is a great advantage," he had just written Forbes. "Reason and the advice of his Friends will probably prevail.") What Boswell later printed from this letter is supportive and considerate, but firm: "Write to me often, and write like a man. I consider your fidelity and tenderness as a great part of the comforts which are yet left me, and sincerely wish we could be nearer to each other. — * * * * * * * * *. — My dear friend, life is very short and very uncertain; let us spend it as well as we can. — My worthy neighbour, Allen, is dead. Love me as well as you can. Pay my respects to dear Mrs. Boswell. — Nothing ailed me at that time; let your superstition at last have an end." Instead of sympathizing with Boswell's "dejection and fretfulness," however, Johnson rebuked him for making himself miserable, "affecting discontent, and indulging the vanity of complaint."

Two days later, Johnson wrote again, as he had done in July 1776, after first scolding Boswell for sinking into depression. Then, Johnson had acknowledged that if Boswell were "really oppressed with overpowering and involuntary melancholy," he was "to be pitied rather than reproached," and coaxed him to busy himself with the books Johnson had sent. Now, even though Johnson knew how disappointed his friend felt, and how sad he was that Johnson was dying, he mainly blamed Boswell for dwelling on what he could not have. So he advised Boswell to buck up and get on with his life: "Make the most and best of your lot, and compare yourself not with the few that are above you, but with the multitudes which are below you. . . . Go steadily forward with lawful business or honest diversions." After additional words Boswell chose not to print, Johnson concluded: "This may seem but an ill return for your tenderness, but I mean it well, for I love you with great ardour and sincerity."[19]

Boswell was devastated by what Johnson said and by what he failed to say. The charge of "affecting discontent" seemed especially unfair, since Johnson knew how avidly Boswell longed for London, and surely realized that his eagerness to make the move now was a direct response to his friend's dying. Boswell also felt Johnson "abuse[d] [him] too harshly for complaining . . . of melancholy and discontent," as he wrote Grange in September. Though Johnson repeatedly asked for letters to compensate for the loneliness of Ashbourne, and had sent four in response to two from Boswell, Boswell did not write for more than three months and might have remained silent if Johnson had not written again.[20]

This failure to write prompted Percy Fitzgerald a century ago to argue that Boswell deliberately withheld letters to punish Johnson for his lack of sympathy and for his past "tyranny and insult": "I can find no plausible solution but one that is unfavourable to Bozzy — viz., that he cast his old friend off when he could do him neither good nor harm." Evidence not available to Fitzgerald, however, suggests that Boswell's shocking failure to connect with Johnson was mainly self-protective. Given his friend's grim prognosis, Boswell pulled into his shell.[21]

In March 1784, Boswell explained to Thomas Percy that he had delayed thanking him for his hospitality the previous March because the death of Percy's son soon afterward "made it so difficult for [him] to write." Writing to Johnson now was even more difficult, for it meant looking directly at the illness that was the fundamental cause of Boswell's depression. And Boswell clearly was deeply depressed. Soon after receiving Johnson's letters, he retreated spiritless to Auchinleck, where, after a momentary "cheerfulness," he "suffered in the most dismal manner." He lived "very privately," did not as usual attend the Ayr races, had many fewer guests than the year before, which at the time had already seemed bleak, and paid fewer visits to others. He was living out his recurring fantasy of retiring to some remote corner of the world.[22]

Boswell wrote hardly anything between 3 August, when he posted letters to Reynolds and Johnson, and 11 November, when he returned to Edinburgh. His journal had lapsed before he left London, and he did not resume it until 14 November, when he wrote no summary of the missing months. His register does not report letters received between 30 March and 19 November; and after a sketchy list of letters sent during the last half of July, it is blank from 3 August until 12 November, when Boswell noted: "In August September October and November 1784 sent a few letters and received several. But being under a cloud of inactivity did not mark them in my Book." Only one of Boswell's letters from these months survives, though it mentions another and promises a third, which seems to have been written. We know of seven that reached Boswell between 13 August and 10 November, mainly because they have survived.[23]

Boswell's listlessness after receiving Johnson's August letters—his writing no journal entries and only a few letters, and later his not writing the usual summary of those three months—suggests that he was experiencing the deepest and most sustained depression of his adult life. Six years earlier, two years after depression had become a recurring feature of his life in Scotland, Boswell in the sixth *Hypochondriack* essay had melodramatically described the paralysis he was now experiencing: "To pay a visit, or write a letter to a friend, does not surely require much activity; yet such small exertions have appeared so laborious to a Hypochondriack, that he has delayed from hour to hour, till friendship has grown cold for want of having its heat continued, for which repeated renewals, however slight, are necessary; or perhaps, till death has carried his friend beyond the reach of any tokens of his kindness, and then the regrets which pained him in the course of his neglect are accumulated, and press upon his mind with a weight of sorrow."

Boswell did not write Johnson, even though writing his dying friend was almost a duty, and writing "like a man" might have been good therapy. But Boswell did not write others either, including Percy, who on 29 July had replied to the upbeat letter Boswell sent early in July, and Temple, who on 3 August answered Boswell's call for "comfort" with a long supportive letter. Though Johnson's failure to sympathize clearly troubled Boswell, I doubt whether anything Johnson might have written would have kept Boswell connected. Since anticipation of Johnson's death had initially prompted his "resolution" immediately to try for the English bar, discovering that this plan was impossible called attention to his inability to prevent Johnson's death, after which he would lack clear direction. When his father died, Boswell felt he could neither act nor think until he had talked with Johnson. With Johnson himself now dying, Boswell had no one to turn to.[24]

So on 11 September, when he received Reynolds's news that the pension would not be increased and also a sad letter from Grange, Boswell wrote Grange — but not Reynolds or Johnson. What he wrote — our only sustained glimpse of Boswell's thoughts and feelings during this period — suggests a wish to detach or buffer himself from Johnson's experience.

> I have had two letters from Dr. Johnson from Dr. Taylor's at Ashbourne. He is rather better; but he abuses me too harshly for complaining to him of melancholy and discontent. . . . He seemed at a loss what to think of the state of my negociation for his getting to Italy, as Sir Joshua had never received an answer from the Chancellor. But last night I had a letter from Sir Joshua telling me that the Chancellor had called on him and told him that his application to a certain Person in favour of Dr. Johnson had not been received so warmly as he had expected; but he would apply again. The Chancellor spoke strongly; he said the journey should not be delayed, and desired that in the mean time Dr. Johnson should draw on him for five or six hundred pounds, and should mortgage his pension to him, which his Lordship explained to Sir Joshua was meant only that Dr. Johnson might not seem under an obligation in any greater degree than could possibly be. So I hope this matter will be adjusted pretty well.

Whatever Johnson had said about "his sufferings" in his second letter, which might have been written as late as 13 August, when his asthma "perceptibly remitted," allowing him to move "with more ease than [he had] enjoyed for many weeks," Boswell wanted to imagine Johnson getting better rather than worse. Though Boswell knew Johnson would accept money only from the king ("a certain person"), and was disappointed and angry that George III would not increase the pension, he still wanted to assume that "this matter" would somehow be "adjusted." He wanted to imagine a healthier Johnson soon on his way to Italy. By writing Grange instead of Reynolds or Johnson, he avoided hearing otherwise.[25]

This suggestion seems supported by what Boswell wrote after reading what Johnson reported in his November letter concerning his health: "I have this summer sometimes amended and sometimes relapsed, but upon the whole, have lost ground very much." In his entry for 12 November — the first in months — Boswell wrote, "I had received a letter from Dr. Johnson last night that the dropsy increased upon him. I was callous by reiteration of misery. Tonight I wrote a short letter to him in a kind of despair." The phrase "reiteration of misery" might simply mean that Boswell was absorbed by his own distress, as when he had described himself five years earlier as "very callous from melancholy." But here it seems to suggest that for a long time — certainly since Johnson's alarming letter in February — Boswell had been dwelling on his friend's relentless march toward death. He sought relief by not focusing on Johnson or by picturing him soon on the way to balmy Italy. When he finally did try to connect with the dying friend, who had refused Thurlow's offer, Boswell felt "a kind of despair," for he had nothing positive to anticipate. So earlier he had held back. After writing Grange on 12 September, Boswell spent eight more weeks at Auchinleck, during which he did not write Johnson — or anyone else. Then he went to Edinburgh for the start of winter session, received another letter from Johnson, and began to revive.[26]

Last Words

If it is possible to sympathize with Boswell during this period, it is difficult to respect him, especially since the dying Johnson was so patient and resilient, so determined to keep his mind alert and open as his body lost strength. While Boswell buried himself in Auchinleck, hardly writing anything, Johnson documented his symptoms in a detailed Latin journal, wrote frequent reports to Dr. Brocklesby, and regularly connected with various friends through letters. Sixty-six letters survive from the twelve weeks between his August and November letters to Boswell. While at Ashbourne, Johnson also completed copying many of his prayers and meditations — including a prayer "Against Inquisitive and Perplexing Thoughts," composed soon after his second August letter to Boswell — into a set of notebooks for George Strahan to edit and publish, a task that led him systematically to relive his sporadic efforts to narrate a different future by forming and keeping resolutions, a drama not central in the autobiographical narrative Johnson had constructed for Boswell.[27]

Johnson remained at Ashbourne until 27 October, then returned home, stopping at Lichfield, Birmingham, and Oxford before finally reaching London on 16 November. After 13 August, his asthma for a while was somewhat relieved, though he was "still restless, still weak, still watery." By mid-October, the asthma was again "very troublesome." "I have now spent the greatest part of the summer in quest of health, which, alas! I cannot boast of having found," he wrote on 30 September to William Strahan, who would himself die the following year. Especially during the early summer, Johnson had been "often deeply dejected," as he wrote Langton two weeks after his August letters to Boswell. But on 6 October, he reported that his mind was "calmer than at the beginning of the year": "I comfort myself with hopes of every kind, neither despairing of ease in this world, nor of happiness in another." On 9 September, Johnson replied to Thurlow's offer of a loan with a letter crafted in a masterly way to ensure that the lord chancellor would feel no guilt about the pension not having been increased. The same day, he assured Reynolds that he did "not despair of supporting an English winter." A week later, after telling Brocklesby why he still imagined that "a better climate may be useful," Johnson bravely added, "But I hope to stand another English winter."[28]

Johnson surely thought of Boswell when he wrote to Reynolds and Thurlow about Italy. When he reached Lichfield eighteen days later, friends probably asked about Boswell, who had been there in April and again in July. But there is no hint in anything Johnson wrote during this period of exactly what he thought and felt about his silent friend. Then on 3 November, midway through his final two weeks in Lichfield, Johnson sent another letter, ending the longest silence since early 1771 when it was Boswell's turn to write.

During this visit to Lichfield, after praising the Reverend Henry White for having so attentively cared for his dying father, "alleviating, as far as human Consolation is able, the Struggles of the Mind under the Ruins of the Body," Johnson confessed his remorse at pridefully refusing to set up his father's bookstall in the Uttoxeter market, and described his attempt in 1781 to atone for this obstinate "Breach of Duty." He arranged to have "massy, deep and hard" tombstones placed to "protect the bodies" of his father, mother, and brother, as he had earlier ordered a stone to "protect [his wife's] remains." He also wrote Boswell, giving him a final chance to escape remorse for having failed to write his dying friend.

Four months earlier, on the same day he ordered the stone for Elizabeth's grave (12 July), Johnson had used the imagery and analysis of the *Rambler* to jostle Langton out of a general inattentiveness that seems, like Boswell's later depression, a reaction to Johnson's condition and his perceived harshness. Langton had responded promptly, kept up regular correspondence while Johnson was in Ashbourne and Lichfield, and would be a constant companion once Johnson returned home. Writing now to Boswell, Johnson followed a restrained but grim account of his health by pointedly asking why Boswell had stopped writing: "In this uncomfortable state your letters used to relieve; what is the reason that I have them no longer? Are you sick, or are you sullen?" In reporting this letter in his register, Boswell noted only what Johnson had written about his dropsy. But most of the words printed in the *Life* addressed Boswell's puzzling silence. Having long appreciated Boswell's "fidelity and tenderness," and knowing Boswell was fully aware how ill and needy he was, how close to death, Johnson naturally expected him to write.[29]

Though Johnson at times had unfairly scolded Boswell for not writing, this rebuke was wholly deserved. Clearly, Boswell had not done all he could to divert and engage his dying friend. In a paragraph only paraphrased in the *Life,* Johnson "persevered in arraigning [Boswell] as before," presumably for "affecting discontent and the vanity of complaint." But Johnson chiefly tried to rally his friend to exert himself: "Whatever be the reason, if it be less than necessity, drive it away; and of the short life that we have, make the best use for yourself and for your friends." Johnson did not declare his "love," as he had in both August letters. But the whole letter was a loving gesture. Johnson was giving Boswell a final chance to act.

Boswell received Johnson's letter when he reached Edinburgh for the winter term, already to that extent in motion. A scolding letter from Temple ten days earlier had not energized him or prompted a response. Nor did Johnson's letter immediately banish Boswell's depression, as his talk so often had. But the morning after reading this letter, Boswell "awaked with the first *image* [his] mind ha[d] produced for a long time": " 'My spirits,' thought I, 'are worse now than ever. Formerly I could appear gay, though inwardly sad. Now I cannot. The garrison is now so weak that not only is there not a sufficient complement of men within it, but it cannot even furnish as many as to make a show upon the walls.' " That night, Boswell wrote perhaps his first two letters since 12 September; but the one to Johnson was so despairing that Margaret kept him from posting it. Boswell resumed his journal two days later, starting with an entry for the day after he read Johnson's letter. Then on 19 November, eight days after first reading Johnson's letter, Boswell finally wrote Johnson something he could post.

In his register, Boswell reported writing to "Dr. Samuel Johnson" of his own "sad illness," suggesting that he explained his "omission to write" had a "real cause": he had not been "sullen," but paralyzed by depression. With little hope of seeing Johnson alive, it was hard to avoid despair. But Boswell then wrote and posted a letter, something he might not have done had Johnson not written first. Johnson's caring gesture helped Boswell face his fears and begin to act dutifully. At some point, Boswell wrote again, perhaps when he finally wrote Temple on 2 December.[30]

On 16 November 1784, three days before Boswell posted his first letter to Johnson since 3 August, Johnson had returned to London for the most richly documented portion of his life. Boswell's first letter arrived too late to receive an answer. Johnson wrote his last full letter, warmly thanking John Ryland for his long and attentive friendship, on 4 November, a day after he wrote Boswell; afterward, he wrote only short notes. Boswell's second letter came too late to be read. Johnson surely had Boswell in mind when he read the first letter and whenever he bundled up the many letters Boswell had sent. But there is no way to tell how Johnson then viewed their friendship. He might have thought about Boswell's biography when he burned various private papers, including his "Annals" and much of his diary, or when he gave George Strahan the prayers and meditations he had copied. But Boswell and his biographical project were not obviously on Johnson's mind as he prepared to enter an uncertain future.[31]

Though Boswell had probably read about Johnson's "dangerous relapse" in the newspapers of 7 December, he was "stunned, and in a kind of amaze," when a letter from Dr. Brocklesby informed him on 17 December that Johnson had died four days earlier. "I did not shed tears," he wrote two days later; "I was not tenderly affected. My feeling was just one large expanse of stupor. I knew that I should afterwards have sorer sensations." "I have lost a Man whom I not only revered but loved," he wrote Reynolds on 23 December, "a man whose able and conscientious Counsel was ever ready to direct me in all difficultys." On 28 December, Boswell was "a little uneasy" to discover that when Johnson finally wrote his will, he appointed as executors Sir Joshua Reynolds, Dr. William Scott, and the scholar and magistrate Sir John Hawkins, who had known Johnson from when both wrote for the *Gentleman's Magazine*. The will named these executors and thirteen others to receive books "as a token of remembrance." It did not mention Boswell.[32]

When Boswell finally inherited the estate that Lord Auchinleck had often threatened to sell or assign to trustees, he received no paternal blessing and unexpectedly discovered that his father had allocated much of the income to his second wife. Now Johnson had left those private papers he had not burned in the hands of others and had not acknowledged Boswell as a special friend. Temple was "disappointed & angry," having "fully expected [Johnson] would have left his Papers to [Boswell's] care, & desired as the last act of a long friendship" that Boswell "would be his editor & historian." Boswell felt disinherited.[33]

From the beginning of their friendship, Johnson had warmly praised Boswell in conversations and in letters; and a week after leaving London in late June, Boswell had reported Johnson's high praise of the *Hypochondriack*. Eventually, Boswell also heard that on his deathbed, when too ill to reply to Boswell's letter of 19 November or even to read his next letter, Johnson had talked kindly of him. He also noticed that several other longtime friends, including Hector and Taylor, Adams and Charles Burney, were not mentioned in the will.

Still, Johnson's final letters clearly worry about Boswell's ability to cope. Boswell heard this anxiety much more fully than we can. For when he read and reread those letters, he saw not only the stern words eventually printed in the *Life*—"Write to me often, and write like a man"; "Love me as well as you can"; "Are you sick, or are you sullen?"—but also those words that Boswell made sure others would never read. Later, in October 1787, when Boswell was midway through drafting the biography he hoped would expiate his failure to write at the end of 1784, he received further evidence of Johnson's final reservations about his judgment and self-control: a copy of the letter Johnson had written Forbes, expressing his fear that if Boswell moved to London, he might "be driven by his passions beyond the bounds which he has consented to fix."

16

Rewriting the Hebrides Trip (1785)

Johnson's death authorized Boswell to write the *Life*. Five days before he read the will that failed to mention him, Boswell described to Reynolds the "peculiar treasure which [his] assiduity has secured": "A great number of his Conversations taken down exactly — scenes Which were highly delightfull at the time and will forever afford instruction and entertainment." He soon saw in the *London Chronicle* a notice that John Hawkins planned both to edit Johnson's works and to write a "Life of the Author, collected from a Diary kept by himself and other documents." But he also head from Charles Dilly that "the People at large will pay more respect to a life of Dr. Johnson by you than by any of his Executors."

Boswell feared, however, "that habits of indolence and dejection of spirit would probably hinder [him] from laudable exertion"; just as when his father died, he felt anxious about managing such a valuable inheritance. So he turned worry that he could not work energetically, and awareness that others would more quickly satisfy the hunger for biographies, into a conscious strategy. "I shall be in no hurry," he wrote Reynolds on 23 December; "I wish first to see many other lives of him that I may both receive additional information and correct Mistakes and Misrepresentations." In the meantime, Boswell would publish his "Journal of a Tour to The Hebrides in Company with him," a text he told Dilly would serve as "a good Prelude" to the *Life*. (On 21 January,

Forbes wrote Langton that their friend "proposes speedily to publish his own account of their tour to the Hebrides").[1]

In 1773, Boswell had written entries describing Johnson's first ten weeks in Scotland, and later he had added full entries for four additional days. But the text still needed material concerning the final weeks. Also, the initial entries were sketchy, and the whole lacked an introduction and a conclusion. Though Johnson had assured Boswell the journal was not "written in a slovenly manner," Boswell still planned to edit it carefully. He even briefly thought of "writing it anew," organizing the material by place, as in the *Journey,* rather than by date. But overall, the text Boswell had shared with Johnson as he wrote, had later shown others, and had again shown Johnson at some point in 1784, seemed close to publishable, as Boswell reconfirmed in February 1785 when he read portions to two different friends, both of whom agreed "it might be printed with little variation."[2]

It was therefore realistic to promise that it would be published "soon," "in the spring." But only at the end of April, after a key conversation with Edmond Malone, did Boswell finally begin completing and revising this text.

Postponed Revision

Boswell's reaction to Johnson's death was powerful. On 28 December, he could remember little or nothing concerning 19–24 December except his "sad spirits." Whatever he felt about Johnson's last letters and his own long silence, he was more than "a little uneasy" when he learned he was not mentioned in Johnson's will, while some who were hardly so close "had books left them."

When he reached Auchinleck on 30 December, Boswell "instantaneously was relieved of that wretchedness which had depressed" him. He was "wonderfully recovered," he wrote Grange on 8 January; and his "good spirits continued" when he returned to Edinburgh on 13 January, as he wrote Temple eight days later. But Boswell's failure to keep a regular journal until he reached London on 30 March suggests he was still depressed, especially before 23 February, when he finally began to summarize his activities from the start of the year. Also, despite his promises to publish soon a text that would satisfy the demand for Johnson's "wisdom and wit" and establish his claim as biographer, he did not begin revising his Hebrides journal. So late in February, Boswell resolved to "set [himself] down quietly in London and get the work executed easily," and he facetiously wrote Dilly on 11 March that he would "write out [his] Tour to the Hebrides in the *retirement* of London."[3]

After arriving in London on 30 March and dining at Dilly's the next day,

Boswell may have begun work on the *Tour*. But his journal does not mention Dilly again until 27 April; on 7 April, he wrote Temple he "hope[d] to settle to make out [his] Hebrides for the press"; and on 18 April, Temple voiced "surprise" at his friend's "indifference & indolence." As usual, Boswell was fully caught up in the activities that made London so attractive: regularly dining with friends, attending the Literary Club and the Essex Head Club (though now without Johnson), drinking heavily, and seeking out prostitutes. But it was not simply the bustle of London that kept Boswell from starting this work. In fact, Boswell managed to revise the text later in his visit, despite maintaining a busy social life. Something else blocked him.[4]

Two dreams of Johnson in the long period between Boswell's announcing that he would soon publish the Hebrides journal and his finally focusing on this project—dreams on 5–6 February and 20–21 March, described in the only full entries written between 28 December 1784 and 1 May 1785—suggest some of the feelings that might have made Boswell reluctant to return to the text that he had longed to publish in 1775.

Lustig and Pottle shrewdly interpret the first dream as an attempt to explain why a "hurried" Johnson in his will had failed to mention his biographer.

> Last night I dreamt that I was with my much respected friend, Dr. Johnson. I saw him distinctly, sitting in a chair opposite to me in his usual dress. He talked something which I do not perfectly recollect about his library not being in such order as he could have wished, and gave as a reason his being hurried as death approached. He then said in a solemn tone, "It is an aweful thing to die." I was fully sensible that he had died some time before, yet had not the sensation of horror as if in the presence of a ghost. I said to him, "There, Sir, is the difference between us. You have got that happily over." I then felt myself tenderly affected, and tears came into my eyes, and clasping my hands together, I addressed him earnestly, "My dear Sir! Pray for me."

This dream "made a deep and pleasing impression" and moved Boswell to seek his friend's intercession the next morning: "I . . . invoked him to pray for me if he heard me and could be of influence."[5]

Six weeks later, Boswell was self-consciously looking ahead to his own death. He drew up his will on 19 March. The next day, after writing Percy about the "shock" Johnson's death had given his mind, he added, "I gaze after him with an eager eye; and I hope again to be with him." The next evening, having begun his journey to London, Boswell "dreamt he was sitting with Dr. Johnson": "Did not recollect he was dead, but thought he had been very ill, and wondered to see him looking very well. I said to him, 'You are very well, Sir.' He called out in a forcible pathetic tone, 'O no!' He said, 'I have written the letter to Paoli which you desired.' He then expressed himself towards me in the most obliging manner, saying he would do all in his power (or words to that purpose) to show his affection and respect, and seemed to search his mind for variety of good words." Besides revealing a wish that Johnson were alive and well, and able to greet him when he reached London, this dream made up for Johnson's silence after his November 1784 letter by emphasizing his abiding "affection and respect." When Lord Auchinleck died, Boswell had longed to connect with Johnson. Now this longing was even stronger.[6]

In August 1782, while his father lay on his deathbed and Margaret was spitting up blood, Boswell had comforted himself by adding entries to those he had written in the Hebrides, entries he would later share with Johnson. But returning now to a text connected from the start with frustration at Johnson's failure fully to cooperate, and later associated with anger when Johnson resisted publication, would steadily remind Boswell that Johnson was no longer there. Describing for the first time what happened when Johnson met Lord Auchinleck would underscore that neither man was now alive. Reporting Johnson's hope to see Boswell's grandchildren would be sad. More importantly, writing the introduction would mean briefly considering the whole span of his friendship with Johnson, including his failure to write his dying friend and his not receiving a final blessing. So Boswell delayed revising until the end of April, when he found someone to accompany him as he retraced this significant journey.[7]

Finally in Motion

On Friday, 29 April — a "most agreeable day" — after dining with several others at the home of Edmond Malone, an Irishman who had abandoned law and politics in Dublin to become a literary scholar in London, Boswell "sat with [Malone] till two in the morning, full of bar scheme, and encouraged." A full entry would have described their talk about the English bar and fleshed out just what Malone "encouraged" — and how. The next day, Boswell stayed home "almost all forenoon writing Tour," and after dinner went to Dilly's. On Sunday, as usual, Boswell did not write. But on Monday, 2 May, he wrote "much Hebrides Tour," as he may have done on three of the next four mornings. Eighteen weeks after telling Reynolds and Dilly he would "soon" publish his journal, Boswell had finally begun working.[8]

Boswell's reconnecting with Dilly on 27 April suggests he was ready to start. But Malone's encouraging talk two days later seems the key to Boswell's actually writing. In February, a few days after Forbes had explained how Boswell might borrow the funds needed to finance a move to London, Boswell began summarizing his life since 30 December. Then, on the morning after talking with Malone about the bar, Boswell started work on the *Tour*. Though Boswell did not explicitly mention the Hebrides text in noting his talk with Malone, it seems almost certain that Malone offered to help with the revision, since later Boswell assumed he would do this. In fact, on 30 May, the next time Boswell reported seeing Malone, he added a codicil to his will appointing Malone — along with Forbes and Temple — as his literary executors, who were to review his papers and publish whatever seemed appropriate.[9]

The same day Boswell began working on the *Tour,* he "resolved" to write a second *Letter to the People of Scotland,* this one opposing Henry Dundas's bill to reduce the number of judges on the Court of Session from fifteen to ten. The defiant pamphlet was chiefly an attack on Dundas ("Harry the ninth"), who had promised to assist Boswell but provided no real help. Along the way, Boswell aligned himself with his father, whom Dundas (and his older half-brother Robert) had persuaded in 1774 to create nominal or fictitious votes for Sir Adam Fergusson, "against the old and real interest of the county." Boswell also alluded to Johnson's dictated essay on Whigs and Tories, "in which it is shewn, by the wonderous powers of that illustrious mind, that there is but a shade of difference between a moderate Whig and a spirited Tory — between reasonable men of each party." Until this letter was published on 26 May, it absorbed much of Boswell's time. But aggressively and boastfully asserting his principled independence energized Boswell when he began his collaboration with Edmond Malone.[10]

An Irishman a year younger than Boswell, Malone had moved to London in 1777, had met Boswell at Reynolds's in 1781, and in 1783 and 1784 mainly saw him at the Club. Pottle suggests that once Malone saw Boswell's journal in 1785, he realized "that this man had a great work of literature in all but publishable shape, but that his lack of self-confidence and his bent towards dissipation might rob the world of it." Also, Malone was "deeply and incurably fond of Boswell." Though Malone's edition of Shakespeare was being printed, he generously devoted considerable time to Boswell's project.[11]

At first, Boswell probably imagined showing Malone portions of his manuscript once he had completed the text and begun revising. On 4 June, he handed Malone thirty-four pages of the corrected journal describing 17–22 August 1773, presumably what he had "laboured at revising . . . all the forenoon," and Malone soon returned them with detailed comments. Six days later Boswell sent twenty-four additional revised pages, concerning which Malone the next day sent just "a few very hasty notes." On 3 June, however, Boswell and Malone had worked together in a different way, when Boswell spent "almost all the forenoon with Malone revising *Hebrides.*" Together they read Boswell's freshly written introduction, Boswell's "character" of Johnson, and the newly expanded entries for 14–16 August. On 22 June, after Boswell had lain in bed till one in the afternoon, ill from the excesses of the day before, he once again "went to Malone and corrected well," probably beginning with the pages on which Malone had barely commented. Either man might have suggested their doing this when they had met the day before at the Club. From then on, that sort of collaboration became their standard procedure. Only on 13 July would Boswell again work alone, synthesizing everything he and Johnson had heard about "Prince Charles's history in the Hebrides." The next day he and Malone revised that new material—together.[12]

From the start, the Hebrides journal had been a richly collaborative text. Boswell wrote in isolation, but mainly focused on what Johnson had said and done, keeping in mind how his friend might react to what Boswell was about to write. Now Boswell had Malone in mind as he added material at both ends of what he had earlier shared with Johnson. The revising was mostly done together—a mode of collaboration they would resume once Boswell had drafted most of the *Life*.

As Boswell and Malone read through the manuscript sentence by sentence, they took turns writing the changes they agreed on. (Since virtually every sentence of the original journal was modified, it was misleading for Boswell to claim in an early footnote that everything from the middle of the entry for 21 August through the second paragraph for 26 October was *the very Journal which Dr. Johnson read*.") The results are evident in the revised manuscript and on galley proofs, though usually it is not clear who initiated each modification. But the letters they later exchanged as Malone supervised the second edition while Boswell was in Scotland suggest the roles each generally played. Several of Boswell's questions—such as, "is *horsehirer* english for *locator equorum?*"—reveal worries about possible Scotticisms, concerning which Malone was the clear authority. But when the issue involved fact or emphasis—as when Malone suggested changing "It is a *terrible* steep to climb" to "*painful*"—Boswell's judgment was decisive, for he alone had been there. These letters also indicate the kind of negotiating that probably occurred when they revised together during the summer.[13]

The work went slowly, since Boswell and Malone both had other commitments. But their collaboration ensured that the task was completed. It is not clear, for instance, that Boswell did any revising at all in the eleven days between 10 June, when he sent pages to Malone, and 22 June, when they spent the afternoon together. But he spent long periods working with Malone on six of the sixteen days from 28 June through 12 July. On 17 August, Malone even got Boswell to work when he showed up drunk. By the end of September—

nine months after Boswell had promised to publish the journal "in the spring" — the entire 532-page text had been printed. Publication would surely have been even further delayed, and perhaps might never have occurred, without what Lustig described as Malone's "wholehearted and selfless" support — support Boswell acknowledged by dedicating the book to this new friend.[14]

Besides keeping Boswell on task, Malone's help was radically reassuring. A month into the process of collaborative revising, Boswell wrote Barnard, who had earlier urged Boswell to "give the World the Memorables of the Modern Socrates for his Honour as well as your own," that Malone, "the best critick of our age," was helping him winnow "the chaff " out of his original journal while suggesting "little elegant variations which though they do not alter the sense, add much grace to the expression." (Temple worried that Boswell's having "so scrupulous a critick" might "greatly diminish [his] journal," which "would please more, if [he] gave it with more freedom.") As Boswell constructed this first installment of his biography, claimed intimacy with Johnson, and presented himself as a warm admirer who nevertheless saw Johnson's limitations, Malone's close involvement convinced Boswell that it was proper to publish any material that survived their combined scrutiny. Boswell also sent sections of the *Tour* to Barnard as they were printed, hoping he, too, would endorse how this text presented their friend.[15]

Revising "Johnson," "Boswell," and Their Friendship

Johnson had provided a precedent in the *Journey,* in which he eliminated some of his pushiness, mocked his prejudices, dropped the exasperation with Boswell expressed in his letters, removed most hints of competition, and acknowledged Boswell's role as trip planner and censor. Boswell referred to Johnson's text at both ends of the *Tour* as well as in numerous footnotes. Like Johnson, Boswell cut much of Johnson's assertiveness, significantly reduced his own neediness, and mostly presented their friendship as less contentious, more comfortably complementary than it had sometimes seemed. But at moments, the revised text reveals Boswell's enduring anger.

The largest changes involved the presentation of "Boswell." In revising, Boswell omitted most of the hesitations and doubts, hopes and fears, prayers and resolutions he had earlier described for Johnson. He kept the first reference to his fear of ghosts, but dropped the more vivid later accounts, and also his report that he was comforted by reflecting that Johnson was in the next room. Boswell only slightly modified the passage describing how, when he "felt a return of spleen" at Armadale, he "should have been very sickly in mind" if he had not "Mr. Johnson to contemplate": "his firmness kept me steady." But since he removed most other descriptions of his melancholy, and most references to his worries and fears, including his frightening dreams, his need no longer seemed great. Boswell kept most of the vivid account of standing on deck during the violent storm that forced their boat to Coll, waiting for an order to pull the rope he had been handed to keep him focused while trying to compose his mind with prayer. But he cut his prayer and resolution, which he had reported for Johnson and other readers of the journal.[16]

Besides being less dependent on Johnson's mental strength, the "Boswell" of the *Tour* is more thoughtful and reasonable, more poised and self-assured than the one in the journal. Boswell kept his report that were it not for Johnson's "peculiar accuracy of investigation," he would have believed many stories that proved false. But he cut the specific examples of his credulity. He retained his earlier assessments of Johnson's opinions and observations, at times significantly augmented his role in conversation, and in footnotes further objected to some of Johnson's assertions. Having unsuccessfully tried in the journal to get Johnson to explain why "scenes through which a man has gone improve by lying in the memory," Boswell now let his own speculations stand as sufficient. In addition, the entries first written in 1785 included Boswell's reflections on several topics Johnson discussed while in Scotland and then in the *Journey,* including extempore prayer and "second sight."[17]

Boswell also downplayed Johnson's moral control. He still reported having stayed up drinking on 12 September, and Donald Macqueen's comment that "his governor's gone to bed." But Boswell in the *Tour* seemed to need little governing, and Johnson was not judgmental but "good-humoured," as he was two weeks later when Boswell woke up with a hangover. Boswell cut all later references to his drinking and all of Johnson's stern admonitions. Whatever he felt as he deleted those early warnings—and just ten days before he began revising, Boswell had once again resolved to stop drinking—Boswell kept from readers how alarmed Johnson had become at his binges.[18]

At the same time, the *Tour,* like the original journal, regularly described Boswell's getting Johnson in motion, often despite considerable inertia, and steering him to this or that place while letting him think he was in charge. The new entry for 1 November begins by noting, "Though Dr. Johnson was lazy and averse to move, I insisted that he should go with me and pay a visit to the Countess of Eglinton," and ends by reporting, "My friend was much pleased with this day's entertainment, and owned that I had done well to force him out." This was emblematic of the whole trip. At the start, Boswell described in detail how he got Hester Thrale to help "launch" Johnson from London, and how he engaged Lord Elibank, Dr. Robertson, and Dr. Beattie to help "attract" him north. And near the end he declared, "Had it not been for me, I am persuaded that Dr. Johnson never would have undertaken such a journey," and so would not have experienced what he later described as "the pleasantest part of his life" and would not have been able to write the *Journey to the Western Islands.*[19]

The "Johnson" in the *Tour* closely resembles the "Johnson" of the journal, but differs significantly from the "Johnson" constructed in the *Journey.* In the "character" added at the start, Boswell wrote that Johnson's mind was "stored with a vast and various collection of learning and knowledge, which he communicated with peculiar perspicuity and force, in rich and choice expression"; and what follows repeatedly illustrates Johnson's mental agility, his skill at assessing evidence and analyzing arguments, his ability to speak with energy and authority on virtually any subject. But Boswell also highlighted Johnson's "heterodox" opinions, such as his denial of Burke's "wit," his "contempt of tragick acting," and his "unaccountable prejudice against Swift."[20]

Though Johnson in the *Journey* mocked his own prejudices, suggesting that he had learned from his companion's "gentle remonstrance" at his "copious exaggeration," Boswell kept most examples of his friend's "fits of railing at the Scots." Having introduced himself at the start as a "citizen of the world" who humored certain English in their "outrageous contempt of Scotland" by self-consciously treating them like children, Boswell regretted that Johnson had not given him a chance to review the *Journey* before it was published so that he could have suggested changes in a few places where his friend "laid himself open to be attacked." Also, in the newly written entry concerning their Sunday at Auchinleck (7 November), Boswell faulted Johnson's stiff-backed unwillingness to accompany him and his father to the Presbyterian parish church: "Though we have there no form of prayer nor magnificent solemnity, yet, as God is worshipped in spirit and in truth, and the same doctrines preached as in the Church of England, my friend would certainly have shown more liberality had he attended."[21]

At times, Boswell followed the *Journey* in suppressing Johnson's pushiness. When they stopped for refreshment on 1 September, for instance, Boswell dropped Johnson's suspicion that his companion's serving "was better than his." But Johnson in the *Tour* remained fiercely competitive. Boswell called attention to his "spirit of contradiction" and his tendency to argue "for victory," both phrases added to the original journal, and flagged Johnson's ability to be "the greatest sophist that ever wielded a weapon in the schools of declamation." The avoidance of hostilities mainly depended on the goodwill of others. On 16 August, for instance, Boswell feared that a dispute between Johnson and Sir Adolphus Oughton concerning Ossian "would have run high"

—until "Sir Adolphus, who had a very sweet temper, changed the discourse, grew playful, laughed at Lord Monboddo's notion of men having tails, and called him a Judge, *a posteriori,* which amused Dr. Johnson; and thus hostilities were prevented." In the expanded entry for 21 August, when Monboddo greeted Johnson by saying, "In such houses . . . our ancestors lived, who were better men than we," Johnson's reply — "No, no, my Lord. . . . We are as strong as they, and a great deal wiser" — was such a direct "assault upon one of Lord Monboddo's capital dogmas" that Boswell feared "a violent quarrel." But Monboddo politely "made no reply," thus avoiding an altercation.[22]

Also both early and late in the book, labored-over passages that were not part of the journal Johnson had read emphasize that Johnson's verbal abuse at times was so extreme that Boswell was forced to omit what he had said. On 15 August, Johnson's first full day in Scotland, he made sure that David Hume would not be invited to meet him by saying "'*something much too rough,*' both as to Mr. Hume's head and heart." In 1777, after reading Adam Smith's eulogy for Hume, Boswell had challenged Johnson to "knock Hume's and Smith's heads together, and make vain and ostentatious infidelity exceedingly ridiculous." But now he self-consciously suppressed what Johnson had said in Edinburgh, since "violence" was, in his opinion, "not suitable to the Christian cause." Boswell deleted Johnson's words — "I know not indeed whether he has first been a block head and that made him a rogue, or first been a rogue and that has made him a blockhead" — but he emphasized that his friend was capable of voicing the harshest insult a reader could imagine.[23]

Something similar occurs in the entry for 6 November, which describes how, while defending the learning of Scottish ministers, Lord Auchinleck recalled from a catalogue the title *Durham on the Galatians* and asked Johnson, "Pray, sir, have you read Mr. Durham's excellent commentary on the Galatians?" Johnson had not. Boswell described his father's brief advantage: "By this lucky thought my father kept him at bay, and for some time enjoyed his triumph, — but his antagonist soon made a retort, which I forbear to mention." The draft reports that when Lord Auchinleck added, "You may buy [Durham's book] any time for half a crown or three shillings," Johnson replied, "Sir, it must be better recommended before I give half the money for it." By cutting those words, Boswell spared his father as he had earlier spared Hume. But he called attention to Johnson's willingness to use the most appalling insults imaginable to win arguments.[24]

As he began publishing his friendship with Johnson, Boswell retained his key descriptions of how they complemented each other, making the trip a true "copartnership," with each friend doing "all he could to promote its success."

But by reducing his own neediness and emphasizing his control, Boswell made the friendship seem more balanced than it appeared in the original journal. At both ends of the text, Boswell also emphasized their comfortable intimacy. After describing how Johnson "embraced [him] cordially" once he had arrived, Boswell added that he and Johnson "walked arm-in-arm up the High Street to [Boswell's] house in James's Court." When they finally reached Iona two months later, he and Johnson did not simply "cordially" shake hands, as in the original journal, but "cordially embraced."

Boswell dropped many instances of Johnson's gratuitous, aggressive teasing and his edging toward anger when Boswell was pleased by the dunes on Coll or when he taunted Johnson for not having seen China. Also, when he reported Johnson's ad hominem retort during *their* debate about the learning of the Scottish clergy — "I see you have not been well taught; for you have not charity" — Boswell now added that his own "exulting air" had virtually forced Johnson to retaliate with "warmth." But Boswell's revision of the two episodes that had most troubled him at the time — Johnson's relationship-threatening anger when Boswell started to ride toward Glenelg and their aggressive tussle after Johnson mentioned having often imagined keeping a seraglio — also indicate that anger persisted through the process of revision. In the *Life,* Boswell would sympathetically explain Johnson's remarkable roughness and seemingly excessive anger and would highlight Johnson's apologizing for hurtful, seemingly gratuitous insults. But in revising these key episodes from early in the trip, Boswell was not yet willing to empathize or forgive.[25]

In highlighting Johnson's passionate unpredictability after they had climbed Rattakin — his stopping Boswell from riding ahead with a "tremendous shout," and later declaring, "Sir, had you gone on, I was thinking that I should have returned with you to Edinburgh and then parted, and never spoke to you more" — Boswell did not greatly change his original account of what had happened. But he failed to report what could have explained Johnson's eruption. Boswell had written his original entry to explain behavior he had justified "lamely," hoping further to placate Johnson and to elicit an explanation, which Johnson eventually offered in the *Journey:* he reported having been terrified when his horse "staggered a little" on the steep descent. In revising, instead of using what he knew would help account for Johnson's "passion," Boswell let this episode stand in for all those moments when Johnson maintained control by judgmental, seemingly irrational anger.

After describing the "truly comick" scene when one of the guides tried to distract Johnson, "as one does a child," by calling his attention to the "pretty goats" on Rattakin, then whistling to make them jump, Boswell cut his having "laughed immoderately," perhaps because he learned later that Johnson had been terrified. But he did not mention Johnson's fear. Footnotes in the *Tour* quote from the *Journey* concerning the valley where they first stopped that day and the wretched inn where they spent the night. But even after Malone suggested substituting "*painful*" for "*terrible,*" and Boswell insisted "the steep is really *terrible; for there is danger,*" he did not insert a note reporting what Johnson had experienced when descending the "terrible steep." By adding that Johnson's "extraordinary warmth confounded [him] so much," Boswell helped readers appreciate why he initially failed to justify himself. But he made no comparable effort to explain Johnson's behavior.[26]

Boswell's refusal to sympathize became clear once Barnard challenged him to see the episode from Johnson's perspective. Assuming that Boswell, taking advantage of being "better mounted" than Johnson, had tried to "get to [their] Inn as fast as [he] Could, regardless of the Perilous Situation in which" he left Johnson," Barnard wrote, "If you had served me as you did your Fellow Traveller upon the Road to Glenelg, I should have calld after you as Loudly as he did." Boswell did not reply directly. But to clarify that Johnson's situation was not "perilous," he asked Malone in the second edition to add a further statement of extenuation: "Vass also walked by the side of his horse, and Joseph followed behind: as therefore he was thus attended, and seemed to be in deep meditation, I thought there could be no harm in leaving him for a little while." Clearly, Boswell wanted to emphasize Johnson's scary irrationality.[27]

In revising his account of what occurred after Johnson mentioned having often imagined keeping a seraglio, Boswell turned what in the journal was a key moment of mutual aggression and sexual rivalry into an example of Johnson saying the cruelest things to avoid being laughed at.

After heightening the comic impact of hearing "the grave Dr. Samuel Johnson, 'that majestick teacher of moral and religious wisdom,' while sitting solemn in an arm-chair in the Isle of Sky, talk, *ex cathedra,* of his keeping a seraglio, and acknowledge that the supposition had *often* been in his thought," Boswell explicitly reported what was implicit in the journal: "I could not but laugh immoderately" at the "ludicrous contrast." Presumably, it was this laughter that led Donald Macqueen to ask whether Johnson would admit Boswell into his seraglio, as Boswell reported in the original entry. Now, however, Boswell omitted Macqueen's question, Johnson's reply—"Yes . . . if he were properly prepared; and he'd make a very good eunuch. . . . He'd do his part well"—his own aggressive retort—"I take it . . . better that you would do your part"—and Johnson's response—"I have not told you what was to be my part"—as well as Johnson's continued elaboration of Boswell's "office as eunuch."

There is no hint in the *Tour* that Boswell deftly contrasted his own potency with Johnson's in a retort he had earlier seen as the chief reason Johnson "expatiated" so exuberantly on having him castrated. ("Though he treats his friends with uncommon freedom, he does not like a return.") Instead, Boswell simply described Johnson's excessive reaction to Boswell's irresistible laughter: "He was too proud to submit, even for a moment, to be the object of ridicule, and instantly retaliated with such keen sarcastic wit . . . that, though I can bear such attacks as well as most men, I yet found myself so much the sport of all the company, that I would gladly expunge from my mind every trace of this severe retort."

After "keen sarcastic wit," Boswell in galley proofs added, "and such a variety of degrading images, of every one of which I was the object," suggesting that the fantasy of Boswell as eunuch called to mind all the other "degrading images" Johnson had applied to Boswell throughout their long friendship, including most of those Boswell had deleted from the Hebrides journal and those he would eventually cut as he wrote the *Life*. Instead of being threatened with castration, Boswell castrated Johnson. [28]

The Applause of the "Jury"

The friends whom Malone assembled at dinner on 22 September— Reynolds and Langton, Dempster and Brocklesby, each of whom had received a copy of the newly printed *Tour* the day before — "applauded it much." The reviews, including those Boswell and Malone read together at breakfast on 1 December, two weeks after Boswell returned from preparing to move his family from Scotland to London, were mixed but substantial. The *English Review* asked, "Was it meritorious, was it right or justifiable in Mr. Boswell to record and to publish [Johnson's] prejudices, his follies and whims, his weaknesses, his vices?" But the *Gentleman's Magazine* admired Johnson for "suffering the occasional failings, and the little reprehensible peculiarities of his temper and character, to be recorded in the page which he knew was destined to the public, and would descend to posterity." More significantly, a correspondent thanked the reviewer in the *St. James's Chronicle* for calling attention to the book, noting that he had previously "read all the Doctor's writings with pleasure, and I hope with profit also," but that "Mr. Boswell has made me personally acquainted with a man to whom I was before a stranger; he has drawn his picture better than Sir Joshua could have drawn it." Impressed by Boswell's power of analysis, Sir Alexander Dick wrote, "You really are another edition of Sir Michal Montaine."[29]

When William Windham objected that Boswell did not "seem sufficiently warm and hearty towards Dr. J.," neither Reynolds nor Malone agreed. Boswell, too, was "sure affection as well as veneration ever attend our illustrious Traveller, though as one of his *school,*" he practiced "*discrimination.*" Boswell and Malone knew just how much had been cut to spare Johnson. But Boswell also knew that a few key episodes misrepresented Johnson's irrational anger and harshness. The *Life* would be different.[30]

17

Boswell Claiming His Inheritance (1786–1791)

Like *Corsica* seventeen years earlier, the *Tour* quickly captured readers' attention. All 1,500 copies were sold within two weeks. A second edition was published on 22 December, and a third ten months later. When Boswell read Hester Thrale Piozzi's popular *Anecdotes of Dr. Johnson* in March 1786, a month after being called to the English bar, and when he conferred with Sir John Hawkins four months later concerning Johnson's sexual conduct, knowing Hawkins would soon publish his *Life of Samuel Johnson, LL.D.*, Boswell knew the *Tour* had established his credentials to write the definitive biography. But he was slow to begin writing. Only on 5 June 1786, eight weeks after his first month on the northern circuit and six weeks after ending an intense, eight-month affair with the fascinating Margaret Caroline Rudd, did Boswell finally spend a morning "sorting materials for Dr. Johnson's *Life.*" He continued sorting during the next three weeks, but lamented having done "nothing yet . . . to Johnson's *Life.*" He resolved the next day "to fast and try to write," but still he "could do little." On Sunday, 9 July, however, Boswell "confined" himself to the London house he had rented for his family, "took only tea and dry toast to breakfast and boiled milk and dry toast at night," and finally "did the first part of Dr. Johnson's *Life,* and made arrangements for more of it."[1]

Troubled Progress

For the *Tour,* Boswell had a full journal for most of Johnson's time in
Scotland and notes for the remaining days. He had ample materials for the
Life, too, including full entries for many days with Johnson from May 1763
through June 1784, plus anecdotes, letters, and other documents he had begun
gathering even before he met Johnson. Revising his full entries and fleshing out
his notes would resemble what he had just done for the Hebrides trip. But
narrating Johnson's life before he met Boswell, and his life apart from Boswell
during their friendship, would be much more difficult. He had the list of
anonymous publications Johnson had corrected, and he spent a day with
Malone constructing a chronological list of what Johnson had written for the
Gentleman's Magazine. He also inventoried his entries describing conversations with Johnson or reporting anecdotes concerning him, noting where biographical stories were located. He constructed a list of biographical questions
and reminders, most of which he eventually checked off. He had many of
Johnson's letters, soon was given more, and continued to seek others, even
after the first edition was published. Boswell also continually supplemented
his extensive collection of anecdotes, but needed to decide how to treat stories
he could no longer confirm with Johnson and what to do when close friends of
Johnson disagreed about the details of an incident.[2]

Having heard complaints about the *Tour* from some he had never imagined
offending, including Langton, Burke, and Forbes, Boswell saw the need to
clear certain passages with those whose conversations he would be including
or on whom he would be reporting Johnson's remarks. Boswell would also
need to comment on each of Johnson's major works, offer a full and coherent
account of his friend's religious and political ideas and his literary criticism,
and assess all he had accomplished. Clearly, accounting for Johnson's entire
life would be harder than what Boswell had just done, and would take longer.
At first, however, Boswell did not anticipate how much harder or how much
longer.[3]

Boswell's journal and letters chart his progress: his sometimes writing steadily and sometimes not; later his spending long days revising, snatching just a
few hours on other days, and sometimes letting the whole process slide. In
addition, the journals and letters partly reveal Boswell's responses to two
competing works of Johnsoniana: Hawkins's *Life of Johnson* (1787), which
Boswell and other members of the Club formally declared "a false and inju-
rious account" of Johnson; and Johnson's "voluminous" correspondence with
Hester Thrale, published in 1788—playful, allusive, comfortable letters in
which Boswell and other friends were treated "much more lightly than [they]

had reason to expect"; letters that left Boswell feeing "degraded from the consequence of an ancient Baron to the state of an humble attendant on an author" and that initially "cooled [his] warmth of enthusiasm for '[his] illustrious friend' a good deal." (Boswell retaliated by publishing "Johnson's supposed Nuptial *Ode*," though the *Life* shows he eventually rose above resentment at how Johnson wrote about him to Thrale.) There is no record, however, of Boswell's reaction in 1787 when Sir William Forbes showed him Johnson's letter of August 1784 explaining that when he approved Boswell's moving to London, he doubted his friend's ability to manage himself.[4]

Having begun writing in July 1786, Boswell by the end of 1787 had narrated Johnson through 1777, helped greatly after he reached 1763 by his journal entries, many of which he used with only minor changes. Five months later he had reached the end of 1782. By January 1789, thirty months after he had begun, he had finished a "rough draft" of all but the end, which he delayed writing for two years, until most of the manuscript had been revised. As he carried the narrative forward and then began revising, Boswell also continued to insert newly discovered information, a layered process that can be tracked in the manuscript.[5]

From the start, Boswell anticipated finishing much sooner than he did, then guiltily adjusted his expectations. In May 1787, he had hoped the book would be at the press by August, and so in February 1788 was "ashamed" that he had "yet seven years to write." In January 1789, after writing the introduction and the dedication to Sir Joshua Reynolds, Boswell anticipated publishing in May. But the first pages were not sent to the printer until a year later, while Boswell and Malone were still revising. In December 1790, with Malone in Dublin and John Courtenay, an Irish-born MP who had become one of Boswell's closest friends, occasionally helping with revisions, Boswell imagined publishing early in March. In the end, he settled on 16 May 1791, the twenty-eighth anniversary of the day he and Johnson first met.[6]

Besides its enormous size — 1137 quarto pages in the first edition — there were other reasons why completing the *Life* took longer than anticipated. Following months of vacillation about moving to London, Boswell finally brought his family there soon after he started writing. Hoping to succeed at the English bar, he sought business by attending court sessions. He rode the home circuit three times in 1786–1787 and traveled the northern circuit in July 1788, each trip taking weeks from his writing. Boswell also took time in the fall of 1788 to canvass for the Ayrshire seat in Parliament. In addition, he spent December 1786 in Carlisle, "deciding on English election law" for the capricious and domineering Earl of Lonsdale, from whom he hoped for a seat in Parliament (Lonsdale controlled nine). A year later, Lonsdale made Boswell recorder of Carlisle, requiring him to be there on five different occasions before Boswell finally terminated this demeaning relationship.[7]

When not busy with work that took him away from the biography, Boswell often "led a life of dissipation and intemperance," as Margaret complained early in 1788 after what Boswell agreed was "a shameful interval of neglect." (A week later, Boswell had added fifty-two pages to the manuscript.) Since Margaret's consumption grew worse in smoky London, she returned to Auchinleck in May 1788 and died a year later, leaving Boswell remorseful at not having been there "to soothe her last moments." Lonely without his "cheerful comforter in all difficulties," the woman whom Johnson had called his "anchor," Boswell wrote Temple on 13 August 1789 of his "*avidity* for death," his eager "wish to be laid by [his] dear, dear wife": "*Why* should I struggle? I certainly am *constitutionally* unfit for any employment. The law life in Scotland amidst vulgar familiarity would now quite destroy me. I am not able to acquire the law in England. To be in Parliament unless as an independent Member would gall my spirit. To live in the country would either harass me by forced exertions or sink me into a gloomy stupor. Let me not *think* at present, far less *resolve*." He had only one consolation: "The *Life of Johnson* still keeps me up," he added. "I must bring that forth, and then I think I may bury myself in London in total obscure indifference."[8]

Two months later, when Boswell began steadily revising with Malone, he seems to have been more troubled and less secure than ever. There were periods of melancholy and dissipation, when he did little or nothing. In May 1790, when Temple claimed that "he had never seen anybody so idle," Boswell agreed: "I could scarcely take the necessary trouble of preparing my book for the press." But he still "dreamed of applying resolutely to the practice of the law, and of having it said, 'He never took fairly to the English bar till he was fifty.'" When depressed in July 1790, just before he finally broke free of Lonsdale, Boswell reported feeling "precisely as when in wretched low spirits thirty years ago, without any addition to [his] character from having had the friendship of Dr. Johnson and many eminent men, made the tour of Europe, and Corsica in particular, and written two very successful books": "I was as a board on which fine figures had been painted, but which some corrosive application had reduced to its original nakedness." At times he drank so heavily that friends and family became alarmed. In February 1791, having still not drafted the final pages, Boswell even feared his religious belief was "wavering," and Courtenay described him as "very low and dispirited and almost melancholy mad." But three months later the magisterial *Life* was published.[9]

The Life *as Autobiography, as Collaboration, as Brief*

By examining the journal entries and letters Boswell wrote as he drafted and then revised the *Life*, by studying how he modified entries describing his time with Johnson, by noticing what he cut from Johnson's letters and how he used his own, and by carefully attending to the many deletions and additions, changes and further changes throughout the long process of constructing this enormous biography, the following account explores what this extended activity meant for Boswell. Building on the substantial, illuminating work of many scholars and critics, I want to examine what this evidence suggests were Boswell's thoughts and feelings as he wrote and then revised his final account of a friendship he had earlier coproduced and at last made central to Johnson's experience, as he relived much of his own life from 1763 through 1784 and continued to engage with Johnson, holding tight to the teacher and friend who was no longer a living presence.

In November 1787, midway through drafting his narrative, Boswell "dreamt . . . of seeing Dr. Johnson cursorily but without having any conversation." But Boswell was in continual conversation with Johnson from the time he began sorting materials until the *Life* was published. The *Life* was their final collaboration, Boswell's final reflection on Johnson and their friendship, his final attempt to communicate with the man who still bulked large in his life. While revising the Hebrides journal, Boswell relived those fifteen weeks of travel. With the *Life*, he revisited all twenty-two years of their significant interactions.[10]

From early in 1787, when his narrative reached 16 May 1763, until January 1789, when he had drafted all but the end, Boswell reread—entry by entry—everything he had earlier written about Johnson, plus all their correspondence. Over those two years, he systematically encountered again every recorded moment of instruction or argument, of intimacy or gruffness, all the praise and rebukes he had recorded, all the affectionate teasing and judgmental anger, all the times when Johnson had seemed wise or outrageous, challenging or reassuring, open or evasive. He also recalled a few exchanges not fully recorded earlier, some of which he now fleshed out. As he decided what to use, what to modify, and what to omit, Boswell also remembered thoughts and feelings he had never directly expressed. As he reread the letters Johnson and he had exchanged, deciding which to use and which to excerpt or summarize—and only a few the letters not printed in the *Life* have survived independently—Boswell remembered and reexperienced his "disappointment" when Johnson failed to write, his delight when Johnson wrote wisely and affectionately, his frustration when Johnson ignored or refused a request, his anger or shame when Johnson scolded—all the feelings that sometimes had spurred him to act, sometimes had left him paralyzed. As he later revised his narrative and decided how much to print from each letter, Boswell lived through all that again.[11]

Reexperiencing each moment in this friendship inevitably led Boswell to reflect on all the ways he had performed himself with Johnson: how he had adopted many of Johnson's ideas (while rejecting or modifying others), had defined or measured himself against Johnson. In journal entries and letters, Boswell often contrasted his current self with what he had been, usually to the advantage of what he had become. But no other project had involved such thorough and sustained autobiographical retrospection. The *Life* is not Boswell's autobiography. The layered manuscript mainly reveals Boswell's complex thoughts and feelings about Johnson and their friendship. But it also entices us to wonder how Boswell connected with the "Boswells" he found in the entries he used and perhaps modified, in the letters he included, paraphrased, or omitted. Also, how did he distinguish himself from the "Boswell" he narrated from May 1763 through November 1784, and from the narrator he constructed for this text?[12]

By carefully supplementing what he had directly witnessed or heard from Johnson with information from many of Johnson's other friends, and with what he learned from various documents, and by repeatedly correcting the "errors" of Hawkins and Piozzi, Boswell established his authority to tell Johnson's story fully and accurately, to describe his character with assurance and sympathy, and to assess his life and works. He especially sought to show his friend's "superiority" in "the art of thinking, the art of using his mind": his "continual power of seizing the useful substance of all that he knew, and exhibiting it in a clear and forceful manner; so that knowledge, which we often see to be no better than lumber in men of dull understanding, was, in him, true, evident, and actual wisdom." By filling page after page with Johnson's engaged, wide-ranging, enlivening talk, Boswell helped readers experience what from the start had most impressed him in Johnson.[13]

But Boswell had other goals, too. By including most of the conversations described in his journals, and by printing most of the thoughtful, bracing letters he received from Johnson, Boswell thoroughly wrote himself into Johnson's life, affirming his special intimacy despite the potent rivalry of Beauclerk, Langton, and especially Hester Thrale. He also documented the many ways Johnson valued his friendship. By consistently downplaying his own neediness, and highlighting his critical detachment and collaborative independence, Boswell presented his friendship with Johnson as more balanced and mutually respectful than it often seems in the texts I have used to reconstruct it. By challenging Johnson on a range of topics — sometimes adding to what he had earlier reported saying, or offering new reflections on some of Johnson's claims — Boswell extended their engaged conversations while demonstrating his ability to function in a world without Johnson.

The *Life* manuscript also shows Boswell moving beyond exasperation and anger at behavior that had earlier troubled him, and sympathetically exploring the roots of Johnson's notorious harshness and unexpected rage. Also, by consistently sympathizing with his friend's heroic struggle against ingrained and at times paralyzing melancholy, Boswell provided a basis for reciprocal understanding. The text seems designed to demonstrate that Johnson should have acknowledged that Boswell, too, was "constitutionally" depressed, and in particular should have sympathized in August 1784, as he sometimes had earlier. An extension of the letters that Johnson had been too sick to answer or even read late in 1784, the *Life* appealed for the blessing Boswell's inertia had kept him from receiving.

Foregrounding Boswell

Boswell had embarked on the biographical project to connect securely with Johnson. Though Piozzi and Hawkins had each mentioned him only once, Boswell wrote himself fully into Johnson's life.

For the *Tour,* Boswell had journal entries or notes for most of the 101 days Johnson was in Scotland, all days when both friends were together. Boswell saw Johnson on fewer than 330 additional days during fourteen of Johnson's final twenty-two years. But because Boswell decided to write the *Life* "in scenes," presenting Johnson's wit and wisdom in dramatic context, and because he usually was "uncommonly assiduous in recording Johnson's conversation," the two friends are presented as being regularly together from 16 May 1763, when Boswell formally enters as a character, until their final parting on 30 June 1784. Their conversations in 1763 fill more pages than the narrative for the previous six years, suggesting that Boswell quickly became a major figure in Johnson's world. From that point onward, more than half the pages describe moments when Johnson was with his biographer. Occasionally, Boswell laments his "negligence" in preserving his friend's talk. But accounts of their conversations fill more than twice as many pages as those used to describe the first fifty-three years of Johnson's life. There is so much of this talk that one early reviewer mistakenly sensed that Boswell and Johnson had conversed "almost daily . . . for upward of twenty of the last years of [Johnson's] life."[14]

The *Life* makes clear that many others — especially Garrick and Reynolds, Langton and Beauclerk, Goldsmith and Burke — had been Johnson's friends for years by the time he met Boswell. Boswell also notes that soon after meeting Hester and Henry Thrale in 1765, Johnson "became one of the family," with rooms "both in their house in Southwark, and in their villa at Streatham," and he applauded the happy change their friendship provided Johnson, whose "melancholy was diverted and his irregular habits lessened by association with an agreeable and well-ordered family." But these and Johnson's other friends chiefly appear in the *Life* as actors in scenes Boswell helped produce. With few exceptions, what Johnson did and said when with the Thrales; when dining with Reynolds or Langton; when conversing at the Club with Goldsmith, Burke, and Beauclerk; when breakfasting with Levet; or when drinking late-night tea with Mrs. Williams appears in the *Life* only because Boswell, too, was present. Also, Boswell included just a few of Johnson's many letters to Hester Thrale and, for the first edition had none of Johnson's early letters to Langton.[15]

For most of Boswell's London visits, the specific dates indicate on how many days he and Johnson were *not* together. But though Boswell occasionally reports a few of his own activities when apart from Johnson, he does not invite readers to wonder what Johnson might have done before or after being with Boswell, or on the days he did not see Boswell. Also, because Boswell reproduced so much concrete, dramatic, and suggestive conversation, capturing with such specificity Johnson's mental energy, assurance, and wit, grateful readers may not notice how little they know about Johnson's life when away from Boswell.[16]

Though Boswell knew Johnson only during the last third of his life, the pages covering Johnson's life before meeting his biographer also demonstrate Boswell's centrality. Boswell introduces material he heard directly from Johnson in most of the first twenty paragraphs, and often afterward: "He told me that he remembered distinctly having been told"; "The fact was acknowledged to me by himself"; "He delighted in mentioning this early compliment: adding, with a smile, that 'this was as high a proof of his merit as he could conceive.'" Both Piozzi and Hawkins reported that at age three, after accidentally treading on a duckling, Johnson had composed a four-line epitaph — a story Johnson's stepdaughter had heard from Johnson's mother and "positively maintained" to Boswell. But Johnson had "assured" Boswell that his father made the verses. As Boswell charted Johnson's progress from Dame Oliver's school to Tom Brown's and then to Mr. Hunter's, readers learned also that he and Johnson had traveled to Scotland and visited Lichfield together in 1776, and that when he realized that Johnson "saw the romantick beauties of Islam in Derbyshire much better than [he] did," despite his seeing with only one nearsighted eye, he told Johnson "he resembled an able performer upon a bad instrument."[17]

When Boswell supplemented with anecdotes collected from others what

Johnson had authoritatively reported, he often inserted himself into key episodes, imaginatively participating in Johnson's early experiences. In describing the all-night "frisk" with Langton and Beauclerk, for instance, the first extended anecdote involving these major rivals, Boswell compensated for not having been there by entering more fully than usual into Johnson's thoughts: first when Johnson answered the violent knocking at his door with "a poker in his hand, *imagining, probably,* that some ruffians were coming to attack him," and later when those setting up their hampers in Covent Garden "stared so at his huge figure & manner . . . that *he soon saw* his services were not relished" (emphasis added). Also, though the narrative at that point had reached only 1752, eleven years before Boswell met Johnson and twenty years before he met Beauclerk, Boswell reaffirmed his own closeness to his subject by insisting that Johnson's puzzling attachment to "the gay, dissipated" Beauclerk was "a most agreeable association."[18]

Once Boswell formally meets Johnson in 1763, the *Life* is dominated by the scenes he helped produce. Also the Johnson-Boswell correspondence fills much of the space not devoted to their conversations. Boswell includes uncut seventy-six of the letters Johnson sent him, and deletes little from most of the others. Forty of Boswell's letters are also included in full or with just small cuts, another eighteen are partly quoted, and many others are paraphrased or mentioned. Much of the time, these letters are chiefly what carry readers from the end of one of Boswell's visits with Johnson to the beginning of the next.

Not at the start, however, when Johnson hardly wrote. Brief descriptions of Boswell's first two letters from Utrecht, the long letter Johnson finally wrote in December 1763, and a paragraph from Boswell's reply cover the first five months of what would be the longest gap between their meetings. But having put himself at the center of Johnson's life during 1763, Boswell was offstage for more than two years, until Johnson next wrote in January 1766. This letter, their conversations in February, and the letters they exchanged in August and November fill most of 1766. (The key letters to Langton in March and May were inserted only in later editions.) But then Johnson again fell silent for nineteen eventful months. Johnson's third long silence, from June 1768 to September 1769, is hardly noticed, however, since three pages after confidently remarking that Johnson "tossed and gored several persons" at supper the night before, Boswell is in back London, urging Johnson to return. But after Boswell left London in November 1769, "there was a total cessation of all correspondence between Dr. Johnson and [him]" for seventeen months.[19]

From April 1771, however, when Boswell ended this mutual silence, through December 1779 — more than two-fifths of the *Life* — Johnson's friendship with Boswell wholly takes over the narrative, with their letters mainly carrying readers from visit to visit. Even when Boswell includes additional material to flesh out key aspects of Johnson's life — excerpts from Johnson's fall 1775 journal in France, for instance, or Langton's account of Johnson's visit to his militia in the summer of 1778, or letters Johnson sent others — the Johnson-Boswell correspondence mostly fills the gaps between Boswell's visits.

Then there is a shift. Having spent time together in all but one year from 1772 through 1779, Johnson and Boswell did not see each other in two of the next three years; and with two key exceptions — the thirteen months from March 1782 through March 1783, and the first three months of 1784 — their correspondence no longer fills most of the space between visits. Johnson sent fewer letters — just three in 1780, only one in 1781 — and Boswell cut substantially from several Johnson wrote later. Boswell, too, wrote fewer letters, which were no longer quoted at length in the *Life* and sometimes not even mentioned. In addition, Boswell had significant material concerning some of the gaps between his final visits, especially letters in which Johnson bravely and resiliently narrated his struggles for health. So for long stretches during Johnson's final years, including the end, the narrative uncharacteristically focuses on Johnson's life apart from Boswell.[20]

Boswell as Valued Friend

Though Boswell's drawing heavily on his conversation with Johnson and on their correspondence risked exaggerating his significance to the older man, he had clear evidence that Johnson treasured his friendship. On 24 May 1763, Johnson delighted the young Scot he had just met by twice pressing him to stay; and the *Life* reports Johnson's often asking Boswell home for additional conversation. When Johnson seemed reluctant to talk on the night before their first shared Good Friday, and Boswell said it was midnight: "He cried, 'What's that to you and me?' and ordered Frank to tell Mrs. Williams that we were coming to drink tea with her, which we did." Especially when ill or depressed, Johnson found Boswell's presence an enlivening tonic. "Life admits not of delays; when pleasure can be had, it is fit to catch it," he wrote in 1777, urging Boswell to Ashbourne. "You must be as much with me as you can," he said after Boswell reached London in 1783; "You cannot think how much better I am since you came in." Fourteen months later, Johnson was "impatient and fretful" until Boswell agreed to accompany him to Oxford, "though with some inconvenience to [himself]," and six days later Johnson welcomed Boswell's return "with more than ordinary glee."[21]

Presumably to avoid charges of vanity, Boswell deleted from the draft Johnson's taking him "cordially by the hand" on 14 July 1763 and saying, "My dear Boswell! I do love you very much"; and he never included Johnson's saying in 1772, "I do love thee, I do love thee," and in 1781, "I love you better than ever I did." When he reported Johnson saying on 21 July 1763, "There are few people whom I take so much to as you," he self-consciously hoped his reporting this would "be ascribed to a better motive than to vanity." He retained Johnson's declaration toward the end of the Ashbourne visit in 1777: "My regard for you is greater almost than I have words to express." But in describing the following Good Friday, Boswell conveyed a sense of their mutual affection by calling attention to what he was *not* reporting: "Having fallen into a very serious frame of mind, . . . mutual expressions of kindness passed between us, such as would be thought too vain in me to repeat."[22]

To refute the claim by John Wolcot ("Peter Pindar") that Johnson did not really respect "Bozzy," Boswell included all the letters in which Johnson declared his love and esteem. He also cut, muffled, or redirected Johnson's aggressive teasing and most examples of his exasperation and criticism, whether in conversations or in letters. The demeaning birthday insult at Ashbourne, for instance, was deleted, as was what Johnson wrote in 1775 about Boswell's "disgusting and offensive" love of "publication," and the fear Johnson shared with Paoli that drinking would make Boswell mad ("for madness was in [his] family"). "How can you talk so like an ass?" first becomes "How can you talk so foolishly?" and then "How can you talk so?" And it is not Boswell but "one of the company" whom Johnson calls a "Dunce."[23]

Considerably different in age, the two men complemented each other. Boswell valued Johnson's mental prowess and assurance, and was delighted by his energetic encouragement, while Johnson enjoyed Boswell's flattering but challenging attentiveness, his conviviality and kindness. Boswell usually initiated and sustained the conversations that brought Johnson to life. In fact, Boswell sometimes reports posing questions simply to set Johnson in motion, as when he asked him to explain what Aristotle meant by catharsis, having assumed an "air of ignorance, to incite [Johnson] to talk, for which it was often necessary to employ some address." Also, from the start we regularly hear Boswell telling Johnson, who "loved praise, when it was brought to him; but was too proud to seek for it," what others said or wrote about him. Of course, most of the time others performed these functions for Johnson. But in the *Life,* we chiefly see Boswell fulfilling his friend's needs.[24]

The *Life* briefly mentions Johnson's short trips with Reynolds and Beauclerk, his visits to Percy and Langton, Bowles and George Strahan, his frequent visits to Lichfield and Ashbourne, his staying at Brighton with the Thrales and traveling with them to Wales; and it quotes at length from the journal Johnson kept while with the Thrales in France. But we regularly see Johnson traveling with Boswell or planning to travel. It was Johnson who suggested the day trip to Greenwich, proposed that they explore the Hebrides after Boswell returned from abroad, then volunteered to accompany Boswell to Harwich, and imagined touring Holland with his new friend. In March 1772, Johnson excitedly described in detail how, if Boswell purchased St. Kilda, they would "go and pass a winter amid the blasts there." Johnson also proposed that Boswell join him in 1776 on his "jaunt" to Oxford, Birmingham, and Lichfield; asked Boswell to come to Bath that April; and the following fall pressed him to come quickly to Ashbourne, where he showed Boswell the nearby sights. Johnson also repeatedly asked Boswell in letters about "some other little adventure": "Shall we touch the continent?" "I . . . hope you and I may yet shew ourselves on some part of Europe, Asia, or Africa." Boswell also added to the draft Johnson's praise of Boswell in 1778 as "the best traveling companion in the world."[25]

The *Life* also consistently shows Johnson living vicariously through Boswell. From conversations in 1763 about how his new friend might study and travel abroad to the letter in 1784 advising him how to stand for Parliament, Johnson energetically imagined what he would do in Boswell's circumstances. He expressed "great pleasure" in 1776 that Boswell at last was "on good terms" with his father, and anticipated "great delight" two years later if Boswell succeeded in "gaining ground at Auchinleck." Also, throughout their friendship, long before Boswell became laird as well as afterward, Johnson enjoyed explaining how he would manage an estate like Auchinleck. In addition—I suspect partly in response to Reynolds's and Temple's criticism of his passionate affair with Margaret Caroline Rudd—Boswell reported that Johnson had approved of his initially visiting her, "induced by the fame of her talents, address, and irresistible power of fascination," and even envied Boswell's acquaintance with this "celebrated" woman.[26]

Boswell is also the only friend shown directly helping Johnson produce texts. The major example was the *Journey to the Western Islands of Scotland,* based on the trip Boswell mainly produced, a book Johnson regularly referred to as "our travels." The *Life* also reports how Boswell assisted with the *Lives of the Poets,* including his arranging for Johnson to confer with Lord Marchmont about Pope. In addition, from April 1772 through June 1781, Boswell got Johnson to dictate a total of nine legal briefs, many of which he included in the *Life,* plus "On the Distinctions between Tory and Whig" and an explanation of the "atonement made by our Saviour"—dictations Boswell listed in the 1793 edition among Johnson's "prose works."[27]

Boswell also shows Johnson actively preparing Boswell to write the *Life.* He reports numerous occasions when Johnson told stories that mattered to him, confirmed or corrected the anecdotes of others, assembled everything he had written for William Dodd, and dictated his famous letter to Lord Chesterfield. Boswell retained Johnson's playful refusal in 1775 to tell even "his dearest friend" why he carefully collected orange peels, and described one additional time when Johnson protested Boswell's "pressing him with too many questions." But he dropped the other moments when Johnson grew angry at his questions, or else identified the questioner—even the person Johnson faulted for having "but two topicks, yourself and me"—simply as "a gentleman."

Whatever Boswell felt when including key information Johnson had not shared, such as how, during his first severe depression, "he was sometimes so languid & inefficient that he could not distinguish the hour upon the Town-Clock," or how he had stood for an hour in the rainy Uttoxeter market to atone for his earlier proud refusal, the *Life* suggests that Johnson generally supported the biographical project. In addition, having in the *Tour* repeatedly described Johnson reading his journal with pleasure, Boswell reported a moment in 1778 when Johnson corrected his account of their conversation the day before by putting him "in mind of some of it which had escaped [his] memory," and then added Johnson's gratitude for Boswell's diligence: "He was much pleased with my paying so great attention to his recommendation in 1763, the period when our acquaintance began, that I should keep a journal; and I could perceive he was secretly pleased to find so much of the fruit of his mind preserved; and . . . it delighted him, on a review, to find that his conversation teemed with point and imagery."[28]

Though Mrs. Piozzi cut from Johnson's letter of 19 June 1775 the statement that in the Hebrides journal Boswell "moralized, and found [his] faults, and laid them up to reproach [him]," Boswell presented himself as the friend who most fully helped Johnson recognize his failings, especially his excessive verbal aggression, cope with the consequences, and change his behavior.

A few pages before describing their first meeting, for instance, Boswell added to the draft Johnson's explanation of the "irreconcileable difference" that had just occurred between him and Thomas Sheridan, and reported his own repeated but unsuccessful attempts to restore harmony between these former friends—efforts he twice recalled later—and criticized Sheridan's "persevering resentment." He dramatized his remarkable achievement in bringing Johnson and John Wilkes together, though they had attacked each other "with some asperity in their writings," and quoted with satisfaction Johnson's declaration a year later that "the contest is now over." He also detailed his essential role in restoring peace in 1778 after Johnson and Percy exchanged angry, personal insults.[29]

It is also with Boswell that we see Johnson most fully reflecting on his argumentative excesses. The *Life* reports how Reynolds once got Johnson to apologize for a personally insulting remark, and how Beauclerk, by challenging Johnson's "uncivil" behavior, got him to desist. But Boswell does not report how Beauclerk the day before wished someone would "teach Johnson how to behave"; and neither Reynolds nor Beauclerk led Johnson to focus at length on his offensive behavior. Nor could Langton when Johnson asked that "worthy" friend to tell "sincerely in what he thought [Johnson's] life was faulty." But the *Life* shows Boswell regularly praising or criticizing Johnson for how he performed at dinner or supper the day before.

On 10 April 1778, for instance, right after Johnson had helped his biographer recall some of what he had said a day earlier at Reynolds's, Boswell said, "You were yesterday, Sir, in remarkable good humour; but there was nothing to offend you, nothing to produce irritation or violence. There was no bold offender. There was not one capital conviction. It was a maiden circuit. You had on your white gloves." Six days later, however, after Johnson had shocked those dining at Dilly's by calling the Americans "Rascals — Robbers — Pirates," whom he would "burn and destroy," Boswell told Johnson he was like "a warm West-Indian climate," where people enjoy "a bright sun, quick vegetation, luxuriant foliage, luscious fruits; but where the same heat sometimes produces thunder, lightning, and earthquakes." Two days later, Boswell exasperated Johnson by saying, in response to another "intemperate" attack on the rebellious colonists, that he "was always sorry when [Johnson] talked on that subject." Three weeks later, after Boswell had explained how "vexed and angry" he felt when Johnson — "upon some imaginary offence" — had attacked him rudely among those who did not know how fond he was of his future biographer, Johnson apologized profusely and promised to "make it up to [him] twenty different ways."[30]

Boswell also reported that in one of their final conversations, after asking Johnson whether he thought his rough manner "had been an advantage or not," he answered for Johnson: "Perhaps it has been of advantage, as it has given weight to what you said: you could not, perhaps, have talked with such authority without it"; to which Johnson added, "Obscenity and Impiety have always been repressed in my company." Perhaps, too, Boswell added, "Many people who might have been benefited by your conversation, have been frightened away," wary of being rebuked or attacked. But if so, the *Life* provided access to much that Johnson had said during the last third of his life, including this final conversation about his roughness.[31]

The *Life* also presents Boswell as the friend who best distracted Johnson from his inner turmoil and momentarily eased his enormous burden of guilt. In seven of the eleven years from 1773 through 1783, Boswell was with Johnson from morning through evening on Good Friday. Describing that day in 1775, Boswell expanded a brief statement in his journal — "we sat a long time in a sort of languid, grave state, like men watching a corpse; or nearly like that" — into this richly reverential passage: "We sat a long while together in a serene undisturbed frame of mind, sometimes in silence, and sometimes conversing, as we felt ourselves inclined, or more properly speaking, as *he* was inclined; for during all the course of my long intimacy with him, my respectful attention never abated, and my wish to hear him was such, that I constantly watched every dawning of communication, from that great and illuminated mind."

Early in the Ashbourne visit two and a half years later, Boswell led Johnson to talk calmly about what he had angrily resisted discussing in 1769: fear of death and people's "unhappy uncertainty as to [their] salvation." A week later, while he and Johnson "stood in calm conference . . . in Dr. Taylor's garden, at a pretty late hour in a serene autumn night, looking up to the heavens," he got Johnson to agree that the "strong" biblical texts concerning damnation might "admit of a mitigated interpretation." John Hawkins reported having been Johnson's confidant and "confessor," especially in 1784. But having seen Boswell lead Johnson to speak fully and with ease about "this awful and delicate question," readers are likely a few pages later to endorse Sir William Forbes's comment that "there is not a man in the world to whom [Johnson] discloses his sentiments so freely as to [Boswell]."[32]

Boswell's (Un)neediness

Besides showing how Johnson valued his friendship, Boswell made numerous changes to present their friendship as more balanced and collaborative than it had sometimes seemed. Johnson remains wise and authoritative, an energizing, stabilizing presence. But despite Boswell's self-doubt and guilt as he drafted and then revised the massive, semiautobiographical text, the "Boswell" who interacts with Johnson is less needy and insecure, more confident and poised, than in his original journal entries and letters. This is especially clear at the start.

During their first sustained conversation alone, Johnson still spoke with confidence of the "very strong evidences" for Christianity. But Boswell deleted his own thoughts in response: "Having felt the uneasiness of Scepticism, I listened to this great Oracle with much satisfaction, and had great comfort in hearing / thinking there was so able an Advocate for the truth / authenticity of Revelation." When Johnson a month later first offered to provide a plan of study, Boswell no longer asked, "Will you really take a charge of me?" At first he wrote, "My heart warmed at finding him seriously disposed to take a charge of me," but later he dropped this. After reporting Johnson's sustained defense of subordination four weeks later, Boswell initially wrote what was in his journal: "I was happy to hear my notions of subordination . . . so ably defended. My *zeal* I thought would after this be more '*according to knowledge.*'" But later he deleted this. When he quoted Johnson's advice about melancholy a few days later, Boswell did not reveal having introduced the topic by reporting he "was much afflicted with Melancholy, which was hereditary in [his] family." Nor did he add, "It gave me great relief to talk of my disorder, with Mr. Johnson." A week later, Boswell initially followed his journal in thanking Johnson for "confirming [him] in good principles." But this, too, he eventually cut.[33]

Comparable changes later continue to establish Boswell's strength and poise. Because Boswell included most of his requests for clarification and advice, we often hear Johnson telling him what to think or do — up to the very end. But Boswell usually toned down his delight at what Johnson said. In 1768, for instance, when he asked Johnson whether practicing law hurt one's "nice feelings of honesty," Boswell did not report that Johnson's reply "satisfied [him] as to a thing which ha[d] often and often perplexed [him]." Nor did Boswell report his satisfaction nine years later when Johnson "philosophically" clarified how being with those who filled him with "awe" also calmed "the uneasy tumult of [his] spirits," something Boswell had "often and often experienced," though he could not "clearly explain or account for it." Boswell also assigned some requests for advice and assurance to unnamed others, preserving Johnson's answers while hiding his own neediness. Having initially left open the option of acknowledging his worry in 1768 about the "superiour talents" of a lady he "greatly admired and wished to marry," for instance, Boswell eventually ascribed this fear to "a gentleman," as he did his wondering in 1776 "whether a man who had been guilty of vicious actions would do well to force himself into solitude and sadness."[34]

Boswell kept the key passage describing how Johnson's energetic conversation on 16 March 1776 "elevated" him "as if . . . into another state of being," reviving him "by transfusion of *mind*." Also, he still remarked how at Ashbourne eighteen months later he realized Johnson's mental strength: "Johnson's steady vigorous mind held firm before me those objects which my own feeble and tremulous imagination frequently presented, in such a wavering state, that my reason could not judge well of them." But he did not flag most of the other occasions when Johnson's companionship rescued and preserved him from melancholy. When Boswell wrote Johnson in April 1779 that he was "in great pain with an inflamed foot" and his spirits were "sadly sunk," his journal reported that "the very sound of Dr. Johnson's voice roused" him from his "dejection." But in the *Life,* Boswell focuses less on his "spirits" than his foot, reporting that the conversation of Johnson and Reynolds "was the most pleasing opiate to pain that could have been administered."[35]

To explain what Johnson was responding to in his letters, Boswell usually described or quoted what he had written. But he included few passages that expressed his needs. When Margaret fell ill in January 1778, we learn that Boswell told Johnson he "never stood more in need of his consoling philosophy"; but we do not see what he wrote in that "dismal state of apprehension." We can read some of what he wrote in December 1775 when worried that Johnson "may have somehow taken offence at some part of [his] conduct." But we cannot see his repeated questions the following summer about Hume's dying so cheerfully. At first, the manuscript revealed Boswell's "impatience/ disappointment" when Johnson failed to write in 1764–1765, and described his writing "anxiously" in 1767 when Johnson once again was silent. But Boswell later deleted those words and printed no letters in which he wondered whether Johnson had ceased to care for him. He also printed only one of his many complaints of melancholy.[36]

Boswell included most of the letters he wrote in 1777 when trying to arrange for a fall visit, including the long, comfortable letter of 9 June (misdated 9 July), which finally got Johnson's attention. For 1780, too, he quoted substantial portions of the three letters he wrote trying to coax Johnson to York for "solemn and . . . pleasant talk." But he quoted nothing from the two letters he wrote in September 1769 when he found that Johnson was not in London, or from what he wrote in April 1776 when Johnson had joined the Thrales in Bath and Boswell felt neglected. He cut from his letter of March 1772 his requiring "a renewal of that spirit which [Johnson's] presence always gives [him]"; and he did not even mention his long response after Johnson rebuked him for planning to visit London right after having been installed as laird—a letter in which Boswell wrote, "I felt myself drawn irresistibly. I imagined I could neither act nor think in my new situation until I had talked with you."[37]

The letters Boswell included in the *Life* chiefly demonstrate his energy and autonomy. He asks for news about the execution of Dodd, the *Lives of the Poets,* and Johnson's health. He provides information, advice, and even consolation. He also expresses frustration and anger. The first letter quoted almost completely (6 November 1766) rebuts at length Johnson's "correction" of Boswell's Latin and relies on what Johnson had earlier written Baretti about monasteries to challenge what Johnson had just written against "the utility of vows." Next, Boswell printed his letter defying Johnson's wish that he "empty [his] head of Corsica" (26 April 1768). Many of the letters included from 1774–1779 were not needed to explain Johnson's replies. Instead, Boswell corrects Johnson's claim that "the *Life* we have of Thomson is scanty," consoles him for the death of Harry Jackson and the illness of Mrs. Williams and Mrs. Aston, complains that Johnson had been "too rigid" in blaming Boswell's caution concerning Beauclerk, and gloats over Lord North's conciliatory offer to the Americans early in 1778.[38]

Boswell's Independence and Intellectual Collaboration

To demonstrate how well he could manage in a world without Johnson, Boswell — both as character and as narrator — regularly challenged Johnson's claims, criticized his arguments, and collaboratively modified his ideas. Despite his worries and fears as he constructed the enormous biography, and though Johnson no longer was an energizing, grounding presence, Boswell extended many conversations he had earlier produced and recorded.

At times, Boswell objected strenuously to assertions he had earlier protested mildly, such as Johnson's "very strange" violence against Rousseau in 1766, or had even endorsed, such as the comments on melancholy and madness that had delighted him in 1777, but that he later claimed "always" to have rejected. He explained Johnson's odd opinions and prejudices and accounted for curious judgments by contrasting his friend's deficient sensibility with his own. When reporting formal disputes on an array of topics, including whether the Scots should have a militia, whether loss of memory at seventy reveals "a diseased mind," how climate affects the mind, and whether "there *should* be some difference" between the conversation of the old and the young, Boswell regularly augmented what he had earlier reported saying, at times even adding speeches not hinted at in his journal.[39]

On three topics concerning which he usually relied on Johnson's authority — government, religion, and the happiness or misery of human life — Boswell used the *Life* to establish his independence while also showing how he and Johnson finally reached collaborative agreement.

In the "character" of Johnson printed at the end of the *Life,* Boswell added to what he had published in the *Tour:* in both politics and religion, his friend "had, perhaps, at an early period, narrowed his mind somewhat too much." When the narrative reaches 1738, he also added a passage aligning himself with reason and justice, and with what later events clearly showed to be correct policy, when he opposed Johnson's future "defence of the decision of the House of Commons upon Mr. Wilkes's election for Middlesex, and of the unconstitutional taxation of [their] fellow subjects in America." Though Boswell in his journal occasionally contrasted his own uninformed "notions" with Johnson's grounded, principled reasoning, he now associated Johnson with zeal and violence while presenting himself as the voice of large-minded tolerance. He dropped his account of how Johnson's "old Oxford eloquence" at Ashbourne revived his "venerable mysterious notions of the sacredness of monarchy"; and in reporting their talk a few days later about his desire to live mainly in London, despite his responsibilities to Auchinleck, Boswell contrasted Johnson's "old feudal notions" with his own "old feudal principles." Then, when introducing the brief that Johnson dictated in support of Joseph Knight's claim of freedom, Boswell described his friend's opposition to slavery as "zeal without knowledge." These changes prepare readers for the significantly modified account of their heated quarrel about America, in which a reasonable Boswell held his own despite Johnson's "violent agitation" and so deserved credit for courage as well as for good judgment. Nor will readers be surprised to learn that seven months later Boswell calmly rebuked Johnson in public for abusing Americans.[40]

Early in 1784, however, eight years after he had skillfully led Johnson and Wilkes to make peace and a year after hostilities with the American colonists had ended, Boswell sent Johnson his first *Letter to the People of Scotland,* reaffirming that his "general principles of government" were "according to [Johnson's] own heart." Johnson, once he finally read the pamphlet, replied that he was "very much of [Boswell's] opinion." Earlier, Boswell had declared his principled independence, but now he and Johnson were realigned.[41]

While Boswell pointedly opposed Johnson on the Middlesex election and taxation of the American colonies, he never rejected Johnson on religion. He always appreciated Johnson's thoughtful assessment of the "very strong evidences" for Christianity, even though they appear "in some degree strange to reason." Just as Johnson called attention to "great men" such as Hugo Grotius and Sir Isaac Newton, who became "convinced of its truth after a serious consideration of the question," Boswell used Johnson to show that strong-minded, fundamentally skeptical men could be believers, and he regularly quoted Johnson's arguments against Hume. He confirmed the rational basis for Johnson's authority by repeating from the *Tour* that Johnson "was prone to superstition, but not to credulity": "Though his imagination might incline him to a belief in the marvellous and the mysterious, his vigorous reason examined the evidence with jealousy." Boswell quoted—in a note—Johnson's "wise and energetic" late prayer titled "Against Inquisitive and Perplexing Thoughts." He also took for granted that whatever Johnson did as a Christian had to be reasonable, or at least not against reason. So he urged anyone "thoughtless enough" to suppose that thanking God for recovery from illness shows a "weakness" of understanding to "look up to Johnson, and be convinced that what he so earnestly practiced must have a rational foundation."[42]

As we have seen, however, Boswell had repeatedly been frustrated that

Johnson failed to explain the efficacy of prayer or to clarify how people can be free if God knows in advance what they will do. Having been delighted when Johnson, by "striking his foot with mighty force against a large stone till he rebounded from it," refuted Berkeley's "ingenious sophistry to prove the nonexistence of matter," Boswell wanted his friend to show as conclusively how it made sense to believe in human freedom while also believing in divine omniscience. There are three distinct phases of this process in the *Life*. Without claiming to match Johnson's power of mind, Boswell presented himself in 1769 and 1778 as bolder than Johnson in confronting this vexing issue, less fettered and confined. In 1784, he suggested a resolution both accepted.[43]

Early in October 1769, when Boswell first tried to get his friend to address "the perplexed question of fate and freewill," Johnson simply declared, "We *know* our will is free, and *there's* an end on't." Boswell revived the topic two weeks later: "Predestination . . . cannot be avoided if we hold an universal prescience in the Deity," adding, "If a thing be *certainly* foreseen it must be fixed and cannot happen otherwise, and if we apply this consideration to the human mind, there is no free will nor do I see how prayer can be of any avail." In response, Johnson mentioned texts by Samuel Clarke and John Bramhall and urged Boswell to "read [Robert] South's Sermons on Prayer," but again "avoided the question which has excruciated Philosophers and Divines beyond any other." Seeing that Johnson "shrunk from any abridgement of an attribute usually ascribed to the Divinity, however irreconcilable in its full extent with the grand system of moral government," Boswell did not persist. But he noted that Johnson's "supposed Orthodoxy here cramped the vigorous powers of his understanding": "He was confined by a chain which early imagination and long habit made him think massy and strong, but which, had he ventured to try, he could at once have snapt asunder."[44]

In contrast, Johnson more fully grappled with this problem on 15 April 1778. Many others were present, too, including Dr. Henry Mayo, a nonconformist minister. Mayo raised the topic by asking whether Johnson had read Jonathan Edwards's *On Grace* (Johnson said he had not), and by reflecting—after Boswell reported that the book "puzzled" him so much concerning "the freedom of the human will" that his "only relief . . . was to forget it"—that Edwards "makes the proper distinction between moral and physical necessity." Boswell and Johnson then took over, with three speeches each. Boswell used many more words than in the journal to explain how God's "universal prescience" implies "the moral necessity of human action." Instead of speaking once, and suggesting books to read, as in the journal, Johnson then attempted in two ways to show how God's prescience does not eliminate freedom; Boswell decisively rejected each argument. "All theory is against the freedom of the will," Johnson acknowledged, but "all experience is for it." As in the journal, Boswell reported that he "did not push the subject further," even though his friend was uncharacteristically "mild in discussing . . . theological tenets, which he generally would not suffer to be in any degree opposed." Boswell wanted a more substantial and satisfying response to the arguments he had deftly presented. But because Johnson addressed the problem seriously, Boswell was neither impatient nor critical.[45]

In their final discussion of this topic, added to the original draft for 23 June 1784, the problem was familiar but the dynamic wholly different. Boswell as usual raised the issue. But now he also suggested a solution, leaving Johnson only to concur and amplify.

Instead of pressing Johnson to explain how human freedom was compatible with divine foreknowledge, Boswell described having just witnessed "the shocking sight of fifteen men executed before Newgate." Then he explained that since there was so much wickedness and misery in the world, "human life was not machinery, that is to say, a chain of fatality planned and directed by the Supreme Being." For "were it machinery it would be better than it is in these respects, though less noble, as not being a system of moral government." In other words, if the human world ran as smoothly as a clock designed by a benevolent God, there would be no crime and no need for punishment, but also no virtue, no sacrifice, no self-control. By not mentioning divine prescience, which Johnson would not wish to curtail, but instead denying a divinely planned "chain of fatality," Boswell ensured harmony.

Johnson agreed with Boswell's analysis; and as he revised his draft, Boswell stressed that they "always" agreed "upon the great question of the liberty of the human will, which has been in all ages perplexed with so much sophistry." Johnson's initial comment — "But, Sir, as to the doctrine of Necessity, no man believes it" — resembles what he had said in 1769 and 1778. But now he offered a new analogy: "If a man should give me arguments that I do not see, though I could not answer them, should I believe that I do not see." Earlier, Boswell had complained that Johnson's "supposed Orthodoxy . . . cramped the vigorous powers of his understanding." But in reporting this final conversation, Boswell added, "Johnson at all times made the just distinction between doctrines *contrary* to reason, and doctrines *above* reason."[46]

Unlike the problem of human freedom, which was fully discussed at only a few discrete moments, though alluded to elsewhere, the unhappiness of human life was a constant concern. Boswell repeatedly challenged the author of *The Vanity of Human Wishes* and *Rasselas* to admit that some conditions were happy, and at times tried to make Johnson confess that he was happier than he claimed. But Johnson regularly insisted that "a man is *never* happy for the present"—except when drunk. When Boswell, recalling what he had just reported Johnson saying, suggested another exception—"when driving quick in a post-chaise"—Johnson replied, "No, Sir . . . you are driving quick *from* something or *to* something." When Boswell argued "that being in love, and flattered with hopes of success; or having some favourite scheme in view for the next day, might prevent that wretchedness of which we had been talking," Johnson replied, "Why, Sir, it may sometimes be as you suppose; but my conclusion is in general but too true."[47]

The central tension is evident in what Boswell reported for Easter 1778. Responding to Boswell's wish to "have the arguments for Christianity always in readiness," Johnson used the "very certain . . . unhappiness of human life" as a key step toward proving personal immortality. If there is "a First Cause," who "must be good as well as powerful, because there is nothing to make him otherwise, and goodness of itself is preferable," then only "a future state" will compensate for what we now experience, a world in which none are happy, though we could not be certain of that without "a positive revelation." Boswell accepted this argument. But he impishly added that *Rasselas* had often made him unhappy: "For it represented the misery of human life so well, and so convincingly to a thinking mind, that if at any time the impression wore off, and I felt myself easy, I began to suspect some delusion." Initially—as in his journal—Boswell noted that Johnson "did not seem to like this remark." Later he dropped the comment.[48]

Throughout the *Life,* Boswell continued to debate with Johnson—and with himself—about happiness. Concerning the *Rambler,* for instance, Boswell remarked that "Johnson had penetration enough to see and seeing would not disguise the general misery of Man in this state of being," something "men of reflection" will agree is the "true state of human existence." But he then stressed what had heartened him in Holland: how these essays "displayed every consolation which our state affords; not only those arising from the hopes of futurity, but such as may be attained in the immediate progress through life." Instead of depressing "the soul to despondency and indifference," Johnson "every where inculcated study, labour, and exertion."[49]

Concerning *Rasselas,* Boswell was more ambivalent. First, he diffidently questioned Johnson's gloomy assessment: "I will not maintain that the morbid melancholy in Johnson's constitution may not perhaps have made life appear more insipid and unhappy than it generally is, for I am sure that he had less enjoyment from it than I have." Then he leaned the other way: "Attentive observation and close inquiry have convinced me that there is too much truth in the gloomy picture." Later, Boswell added a short essay on happiness, which concludes, "If we walk with hope in 'the mid-day sun' of Revelation, our temper and disposition will be such, that the comforts and enjoyments in our way will be relished, while we patiently support the inconveniencies and pains." So even before he described meeting the man he later referred to as his "Imlac," Boswell filtered Johnson's central insight through his own sensibility. But in contrast with Johnson, Boswell advised readers not to "think too deeply," to "cultivate under the command of good principles, '*La Théorie des sensations agréeable*,' and as Mr. Burke once admirably counseled a grave and anxious gentleman, 'live pleasant.'"[50]

Hundreds of pages later, these thoughts are reinforced by an even longer reflection based on a collaborative entry Boswell had originally written ten days after boldly challenging Johnson on America: an argument that "happiness should be cultivated as much as [people] can," and that they should "guard against imagining that there is an end of felicity upon earth" when they "grow old, or are unhappy." In the account of Good Friday 1778, Boswell reinforced his central advice by introducing this key statement by Oliver Edwards: "You are a philosopher, Dr. Johnson. I have tried too in my time to be a philosopher; but, I don't know how, cheerfulness was always breaking in." Then Boswell added that all the "eminent men" to whom he had repeated this anecdote deemed Edwards's turn toward cheerfulness "an exquisite trait of character." While admiring Johnson's patience and persistence, Boswell clearly endorsed a stance that was not "so grave as to exclude all gaiety."[51]

Boswell reported a final conversation about happiness on 12 June 1784, three months after he had reaffirmed his fundamental agreement with Johnson on politics and shortly before their final discussion about freedom. When Johnson, as usual, claimed that human life is "upon the whole" more miserable than happy, Boswell now supported his friend, declaring "that no man would choose to lead again the life which he had experienced," a claim Johnson endorsed "in the strongest terms." (In the initial draft, "Johnson exclaimed, 'I would not lead my life over again though an Archangel should request it.'") Having reported their unqualified agreement, Boswell then added a Johnsonian answer to Burke's "very ingenious" argument that the universal wish to live longer is equivalent to a wish to relive our past lives. Though this might seem "plausible," Boswell imagined that "there is a deceitful hope that the next part of life will be free from the pains, and anxieties, and sorrows . . . already felt": "We are for wise purposes 'Condemn'd to Hope's delusive mine,' as Johnson finely says." Boswell concluded this final collaborative reflection on happiness by quoting the lines from *Aureng-Zebe* that Johnson had recently printed in the *Life of Dryden* — lines insisting that "life [is] all a cheat," though everyone hopes "from the dregs of life . . . to receive, / What the first sprightly running could not give."

Later, however, hoping to use Johnson as a witness against himself, Boswell added a passage subversively questioning whether Johnson was really as miserable as he claimed. First, he reported how when someone—probably Boswell himself—told Johnson "that it seemed strange that he, who has so often delighted his company by his lively and brilliant conversation, should say he was miserable," Johnson replied, "Alas! It is all outside; I may be cracking my joke, and cursing the sun, *Sun, how I hate thy beams!*" This parallels Johnson's response on being told that Dr. Adams had described him as "a gay and frolicksome" student at Oxford: "Ah, Sir, I was mad [rude] and violent. It was bitterness which they mistook for frolick"—a statement Boswell quoted without question early in the *Life*. But now Boswell wondered whether what Johnson said about his underlying misery was "a genuine picture of his mind, or . . . the effect of his persuading himself contrary to fact, that the position which he had assumed as to human unhappiness, was true." After all, the *Life* was filled with examples of Johnson's exuberance, and Boswell was unwilling to give up hope. So he concluded by applying to Johnson a passage from Fulke Greville's *Maxims, Characters, and Reflections* (1756): "Aristarchus is charming: how full of knowledge, of sense, of sentiment. You get him with difficulty to your supper; and after having delighted every body and himself for a few hours, he is obliged to return home;—he is finishing his treatise, to prove that unhappiness is the portion of man."[52]

Winning Johnson's Blessing

By masking his past and current neediness, and showing how well he could function in a world without Johnson, Boswell might have imagined earning Johnson's respect. But because he had not written during fifteen of Johnson's final nineteen weeks, he also needed his friend's understanding and forgiveness. So Boswell emphasized Johnson's "constitutional melancholy," which he had noted but used only once in the *Tour*. (The phrase was not in the journal Boswell showed Johnson.) By sympathetically explaining how this caused Johnson's notorious harshness and anger, by working to forgive the behavior that had most troubled him, and especially by applauding his friend's heroic struggle against ingrained and at times paralyzing melancholy, Boswell appealed for reciprocal understanding. The whole text—especially the final hundred pages—can be read as an argument that Johnson should have sympathized more fully with his biographer's "constitutional melancholy" and should embrace Boswell when they are reunited in heaven.[1]

"You tossed and gored several persons"

In writing and then revising the *Life,* Boswell worked at constructing a balanced assessment of his friend's verbal violence. Here, as in other early biographies, Johnson is depicted as intensely competitive, offended when challenged or even interrupted, often overbearing. Boswell added references to his friend's stunning loudness, his ability to "roar" down opponents, his tendency to start arguments from a "spirit of contradiction" and then grow "outrageous." Also, by sometimes changing "I said" to "I ventured to tell him" or "I ventured to ask," Boswell emphasized how risky it was even to mention certain subjects. At times, Johnson seems more like a bull or a bear than a gentleman, requiring Boswell to shift topics.[2]

But there are no moments in the *Life* when Boswell made Johnson seem harsher or more insensitive than in the original journal, none when he was willing to say the most brutal things imaginable to win arguments and avoid being laughed at, none when Boswell highlighted his friend's ungrounded, enduring, and excessively threatening anger. On the contrary, after describing his first evening with Johnson at the Mitre, Boswell asked whether Johnson's "frankness, complacency and kindness to a young man, a stranger and a Scotchman, does not refute the unjust opinion of the harshness of his general demeanour." Eighteen years later, Johnson's response when Boswell showed up drunk and obnoxious was clear evidence of his patience and "kind indulgence." Though Hester Piozzi's *Anecdotes* suggested that Johnson was always on the attack, "much the greatest part of his time he was civil, obliging, nay polite in the true sense of the word." Boswell suppressed many of Johnson's testy, aggressive comments, including gruff rebukes of Boswell, and twice insisted, with Malone as his primary witness, that "many gentlemen, who were long acquainted with [Johnson], never received, or even heard a strong expression from him."[3]

Boswell also sympathetically explored the roots of Johnson's excessive conversational roughness, seeking to understand and forgive behavior that had troubled him when he worked on the *Tour*. In a few sustained discussions supplemented by numerous examples, he distinguished three complementary and overlapping sources. Johnson had learned to approach every conversation as "a contest" in which he "could not brook appearing to be worsted" and if necessary would use "robust sophistry" — and even insult — to triumph. In addition, Johnson was a vigilant foe of "folly, impudence, or impiety," always ready, even eager, to attack what seemed wrongheaded or dangerous. Boswell also traced much of Johnson's harshness, including his "uttering hasty and satirical sallies, even against his best friends," to "his constitutional irritability of temper" and to his "constitutional melancholy, the clouds of which darkened the brightness of his fancy, and gave a gloomy cast to his whole course of thinking."[4]

Like Reynolds, and also Piozzi, Boswell carefully distinguished between Johnson's arguing for victory and his speaking to instruct. He quoted Johnson's claim that "the happiest conversation [is] where there is no competition, no vanity, but a calm quiet interchange of sentiments," and he reported much genial, instructive talk. But he also included many examples of Johnson's quick-witted, often insultingly ad hominem retorts. In June 1768, when Johnson was "highly satisfied with his colloquial prowess the preceding evening," Boswell's saying, "Yes, Sir, you tossed and gored several persons," seems more praiseful than critical. Boswell admired his friend's ingenuity. At times, however, Johnson was "too desirous of triumph in colloquial contest," and Boswell labeled some of his retorts "unjustifiable." So he approvingly quoted Reynolds's claim that "when upon any occasion Johnson had been rough to any person in company he took the first opportunity of reconciliation, by drinking to him or addressing his discourses to him."[5]

Boswell generally applauded Johnson's zealous attacks on immorality and on whatever threatened "to unhinge or weaken good principles." Having in the *Tour* criticized Johnson's "much too rough" comment on Hume, with whom Boswell had passed "many an agreeable hour," he reported in the *Life* how three years later he got Johnson to agree with him that Dr. Adams had treated Hume much too gently, both in print and in person. But Boswell thought that Johnson sometimes inappropriately expanded the domain in which personal abuse was justified. In Johnson's first three political pamphlets, "there was, amidst many powerful arguments, not only a considerable portion of sophistry, but a contemptuous ridicule of his opponents, which was very provoking"; and Boswell avoided discussing *Taxation No Tyranny* with Johnson because its "extreme violence" was "unsuitable to the mildness of a Christian philosopher." He also regretted his friend's gratuitous, ungentle, and ill-informed aggression concerning Quaker baptism in 1776, and his shocking severity two years later toward Jane Harry, a young woman "for whom he had shewn much affection" before she became a Quaker.[6]

Boswell also felt his friend was "too easily provoked by absurdity and folly." When Johnson, "smiling with much complacency," curiously claimed in 1775 to be "a good humoured fellow," Boswell, "also smiling," replied: "No, no, Sir; that will *not* do. You are good-natured but not good-humoured. You are irascible. You have not patience with folly and absurdity. I believe you would pardon them, if there were time to deprecate your vengeance; but punishment follows so quick after sentence, that they cannot escape."[7]

Boswell was generally more sympathetic with the testy comments and angry outbursts he attributed to Johnson's "constitution," even though some of these had greatly troubled him. When Johnson in 1778 claimed, "A man's being in good or bad humour depends upon his will," Boswell initially added, as he had in his journal, "If this be true, the Doctor is much to blame upon many occasions." Then he dropped this hypothetical criticism, insisting that a person's "humour is often uncontroulable by his will." Johnson was not in control. His angry assaults and "sudden explosions of satire" were like the eruptions of a volcano.[8]

Two memorable episodes in the *Life*—what happened in 1769 when Boswell pressed Johnson to explain his fear of death and what happened in 1778 when Boswell announced his having arranged for Johnson to discuss Pope with Lord Marchmont—illustrate Boswell's new appreciation of how Johnson was controlled by his "morbid constitution." In each case, Boswell's journal simply reported Johnson's reaction: his angry threat not to visit Scotland if Boswell continued to tease him with questions, and his petulant refusal to meet with Pope's executor. The images Boswell introduced show his ambivalent feelings about Johnson's "constitutional" outbursts, ranging from deep respect to enduring exasperation.

"Johnson's harsh attacks on his friends arise from uneasiness within," Boswell told Reynolds in 1784: "His loud explosions are guns of distress." In describing Johnson's anger when Boswell kept asking Johnson about his fear of death, Boswell in the *Life* created a dynamic, telling image to explain this unexpected and threatening response: "His mind resembled the vast amphitheatre, the Colisaeum at Rome. In the center stood his Judgement which like a mighty gladiator combated those apprehensions that like the wild beasts of the *Arena*, were all around in cells ready to be let out upon him. After a conflict he drove them back into their dens, but not killing them, they were still assailing him." By zooming in on this "insurrection," and his friend's unending vigilance against the beasts that Boswell's questions released, Boswell created informed sympathy for what earlier he had simply called "Johnson's gloomy horrour for death." Unlike Johnson's irrational and excessive passion when Boswell rode ahead to Glenelg, as Boswell had described it in the *Tour,* Johnson's outrage at Boswell's questioning—his being "thrown into such a state, that he expressed himself in a way that alarmed and distressed [Boswell]"—had a cause his biographer came to regard with admiration.[9]

In contrast, the two images Boswell eventually introduced to account for Johnson's surprising rejection of the interview with Lord Marchmont—"I shall not be in town tomorrow. I don't care to know about Pope"—express pity but also frustration. Initially, Boswell suggested three possible explanations without choosing among them: "Whether I had shewn an over-exultation, which provoked his spleen; or whether he was seized with a suspicion that I had obtruded him on Lord Marchmont, and had humbled him too much; or whether there was any thing more than an unlucky fit of ill-humour, I know not." Eventually, Boswell settled on the third, attributing Johnson's reaction to "something morbid in his constitution" with which "this great and good man had

occasionally to struggle." At the last stage of revision, Boswell added two anal-
ogies to help readers appreciate Johnson's "unaccountable caprice," images
much less heroic and sympathetic than the one that explained Johnson's angry
refusal to discuss his fear of death: "Let the most censorious of my readers
suppose himself to have a violent fit of the tooth-ach, or to have received a
severe stroke on the shin-bone, and when in such a state to be asked a question;
and if he has any candour, he will not be surprized at the answers which Johnson sometimes gave in moments of irritation, which, let me assure them, is ex-
quisitely painful." Understanding Johnson's "constitutional" eruptions clearly
did not entail respecting them.[10]

Johnson's "Injustice to Himself"

The *Tour* did not focus on Johnson's fear of death. When Johnson at
Dunvegan said he had been "trying to cure [his] laziness all [his] life, and could
not do it," and Boswell noted that "if a man does in a shorter time what might
be labour of a life, there is nothing to be said against him," Johnson replied,
"Suppose that flattery to be true, the consequence would be, that the world
would have no right to censure a man; but that would not justify him to
himself." But Johnson did not speak of the need to justify himself to God. The
Life, in contrast, twice reports Johnson describing his fear of being judged
unworthy. At Ashbourne in 1777, he told Boswell that "the better a man is, the
more afraid he is of death, having a clearer view of infinite purity," and at
Oxford in 1784, he shocked Dr. Adams and his wife by declaring, "As . . . I
cannot be *sure* that I have fulfilled the conditions on which salvation is granted,
I am afraid I may be one of those who shall be damned."[11]

To prepare readers for these anguished conversations, Boswell regularly
quoted from the *Prayers and Meditations,* in which Johnson expressed his
"pious anxiety" and resolved to change. He also added to the "character"
imported from the *Tour* another possible source of Johnson's unease: "The
solemn text, 'of him to whom much is given, much will be required,' seems to
have been ever present to [Johnson's] mind, in a rigorous sense, and to have
made him dissatisfied with his labours and acts of goodness, however comparatively great." ("In a rigorous sense" was inserted later into what was
already an addition to the "character" adopted from the *Tour.*) In addition,
Boswell argued that constitutional melancholy, besides limiting Johnson's
ability to labor, also warped his assessment of all he had accomplished. Faced
with Johnson's unreasonable fear of damnation, Boswell transformed him
into a heroic sufferer whose daily struggle against depression was sufficient
cause for applause.[12]

In early conversations reported in the *Life,* however, Boswell was as demanding and potentially judgmental as Johnson feared God would be. When they were first alone, for instance, and Johnson reported that he "generally went abroad at four in the afternoon and seldom came home till two in the morning," Boswell asked whether "he did not think it wrong to live thus, and not make more use of his great talents." Three years later, Boswell joined Goldsmith in urging Johnson to write more, insisting, "We have a claim upon you." Similarly at Oxford ten years later, Boswell told Dr. Wetherell and Johnson that though Johnson had always been "a great friend to the Constitution both in Church and State," he had "never written expressly in support of either," so there was "really a claim upon him for both."[13]

In addition, once he had narrated Johnson to London, Boswell started each year by noting what his friend had published, holding him to task much as Johnson did in his annual reviews. For those years with few or no publications, Boswell sometimes suggested Johnson was working on long-term projects. In 1745, for instance, when Johnson published only "Miscellaneous Observations on the Tragedy of Macbeth," Boswell conjectured that he was "occupied entirely" with the new edition of Shakespeare he had proposed. Similarly in 1757, when Johnson published nothing except some articles in the *Literary Magazine,* "He probably prepared a part of his Shakespeare." But Boswell eventually became more skeptical, more judgmental. For 1760, for instance, he initially wrote, "Johnson was either very busy with his Shakespeare, or very idle for not only can I find no other publick composition by him, but not even a private letter to any of his friends." For 1761, after noting that it was not known how much work — if any — Johnson had done on Shakespeare, and before listing the few short texts he published, Boswell introduced Johnson as a witness: "He certainly was at this time not active; for in his scrupulous examination of himself on Easter eve, he laments in his too rigorous mode of censuring his own conduct that his life since the communion of the preceding Easter had been 'dissipated and useless.'"

Johnson may have been "too rigorous," but Boswell used his assessment. Three years later, when "except what he may have done in revising *Shakespeare,* we do not find that he laboured much in literature," Boswell again quoted Johnson against himself, with no suggestion now that this judgment was too harsh: "My indolence since my last reception of the Sacrament has sunk into grosser sluggishness, and my dissipation spread into wilder negligence. My thoughts have been clouded with sensuality, and except that from the beginning of this year I have in some measure forborne excess of strong drink, my appetites have predominated over my reason. A kind of strange oblivion has overspread me, so that I know not what has become of the last year, and perceive that incidents and intelligence pass over me without leaving any impression."[14]

At this point, however, Boswell developed a new motif. In partial defiance of the expectations established by his own year-opening paragraphs, and despite Johnson's massive guilt, Boswell began shifting his focus from Johnson the producer — or nonproducer — of literary texts to Johnson the Christian warrior. The "Majestic Teacher of Moral and Religious Wisdom" who had written the *Rambler* was also a tormented melancholic who recorded his suffering in a private diary but seldom complained, who despite repeated failures still sought to change. Simply bearing up through adversity came to seem sufficient, especially since Johnson remained so intellectually alive, so quick to advise and help.[15]

Right after quoting what Johnson had written early in 1764 about the previous year's "sluggishness," Boswell remarked that at regular times each year his friend piously reviewed his past and resolved to improve. Then he introduced what Johnson movingly wrote on 18 September 1764, his fifty-fifth birthday: "I have now spent fifty five years in resolving; having from the earliest time almost that I can remember been forming schemes of a better life. I have done nothing; the need of doing therefore is pressing, since the time of doing is short." Since "such a tenderness of conscience, such a fervent desire of improvement will rarely be found," Boswell defended Johnson against those so "hardened in indifference to spiritual improvement" that they could "treat this pious anxiety of Johnson with contempt." He also added a key paragraph to the draft, describing how "about this time [Johnson] was afflicted with a very severe return of the hypochondriack disorder which was ever lurking about him," making him shun company, "the most fatal symptom of that malady." Dr. Adams found his old friend "in a deplorable state, sighing groaning talking to himself, and restlessly walking from room to room," and heard Johnson declare, "I would consent to have a limb amputated to recover my spirits."[16]

Boswell had never witnessed what Adams vividly described in 1784 — what Langton, who had also been present, never shared with Boswell. Nor had Boswell realized the full extent of Johnson's spiritual struggles until he read the *Prayers and Meditations* in 1785, then reread them year by year while constructing his narrative. I suspect Boswell's understanding of Johnson deepened over time as he tracked Johnson through the years following publication of the *Dictionary.* But once Boswell had described his friend's midlife depression, he used Johnson's mental state to explain any year when he published little, presenting a tormented Johnson with informed sympathy and appreciation.

In 1767, for instance, when Johnson's "diary affords no insight into his employment," he reported in August having "been disturbed and unsettled for a long time, and . . . without resolution to apply to study or to business, being hindered by sudden snatches." For 1768, Boswell added a paragraph noting that the "great perturbation and distraction" mentioned in Johnson's meditations explain why "nothing of his Writing was given to the publick this year except the Prologue to his friend Goldsmith's Comedy of '*The Good-natured Man*.'" In 1769, when Boswell discovered that nothing had been published, not even a dedication or a prologue, and could point to no project on which Johnson was working, Johnson's "'Meditations' too strongly prove that he suffered much both in body and mind; yet he was perpetually striving against *evil* and nobly endeavouring to advance his intellectual and devotional improvement." Johnson's resolutions to change were transformed into noble endeavors. Since Johnson's meditations revealed his inner turmoil, the proper response to his periods of inactivity was empathy and understanding: "Every generous and grateful heart must feel for the distresses of so eminent a benefactor to Mankind, and now that his unhappiness is certainly known must respect that dignity of character which prevented him from complaining." While not producing literary texts, Johnson himself became a text based on Boswell's sympathetic reading of the *Prayers and Meditations*.[17]

Boswell therefore shifted his mode of weighing Johnson's achievement. In 1772, when Johnson "was altogether quiescent as an Authour," Boswell added to the draft, "It will be found from the various evidences which I shall bring together, that his mind was acute lively and vigorous." Besides the first of many dictated briefs, these "evidences" included the "vigorous intellect and . . . lively imagination" that Boswell and Johnson's other friends "constantly found" when they were with him. On Good Friday that year, when Boswell for the first time saw his friend absorbed in solemn self-examination, "his large Greek Testament before him," Johnson's *Meditations* report his mind "unsettled" and his memory "confused." So Boswell applauded the "philosophick heroism" that allowed Johnson "to appear with such manly fortitude to the world, while he was inwardly so distressed," and found that his friend exemplified "the mysterious principle of being 'made perfect through suffering.'" In 1776, too, when "Johnson executed . . . no work of any sort for the Publick," Boswell added "that his mind was still ardent, and fraught with generous wishes to attain to still higher degrees of literary excellence," as is evident in "his private notes of this year."[18]

Of course Boswell reported and assessed whatever texts Johnson did produce, especially the *Lives of the Poets*. He applauded the first set as "a luminous proof that the vigour of [Johnson's] mind in all its faculties, whether memory, judgment, or imagination, was not in the least abated"; and in announcing the completion of the project in 1781, Boswell quoted Johnson's hope that they were "written . . . in such a manner as may tend to the promotion of piety." Still, the image of Johnson as tormented but eminently pious, heroically resolving to achieve all he thought was required, persisted.[19]

Boswell started narrating each of Johnson's final years by calling attention to his friend's mental energy and engagement, despite increasing sickness and pain. For 1782, "the history of his life . . . is little more than a mournful recital of the variations of his illness, in the midst of which, however, . . . the powers of his mind were in no degree impaired." In 1783, "he was more severely afflicted than ever . . . but still the same ardour for literature, the same constant piety, the same kindness for his friends, and the same vivacity both in conversation and writing, distinguished him." In 1784: "I am arrived at the last year of the life of Samuel Johnson, a year in which, although passed in severe indisposition, he nevertheless gave many evidences of the continuance of those wondrous powers of mind, which raised him so high in the intellectual world." What began as an annual listing of publications, then highlighted Johnson's struggles to improve despite often paralyzing depression, finally focused on his enduring mental vigor, his piety, and his patience.[20]

Boswell assumed readers would agree that Johnson's "numerous and various works" were more than sufficient. He was also certain that Johnson's "disturbances of mind" explained his not having done much more. Depression at least twice produced such extreme lassitude that Johnson literally could do nothing. Melancholy regularly obliged him "to fly from study and meditation to the dissipating variety of life," as he told Boswell soon after they met. Anyone afflicted with constitutional melancholy "must divert distressing thoughts, and not combat with them," Johnson constantly advised: "Let him take a course of chymistry, or a course of rope-dancing, or a course of anything to which he is inclined at a time. Let him contrive to have as many retreats for his mind as he can, as many things to which it can fly from itself." Clearly, therefore, Johnson's depression excused many "deficiencies." In addition, Boswell regularly described "indolence and procrastination" as "inherent in [Johnson's] constitution," so his writing anything substantial required enormous resolution.[21]

Johnson's writing so much, and so well, despite constitutional melancholy and constitutional indolence, was truly remarkable. But Boswell also documented how Johnson's "constitutional gloom" — a phrase that replaced "melancholy desponding view of himself" in final revisions — "together with his extreme humility and anxiety with regard to his religious state, made him contemplate himself through too dark and unfavourable a medium." Johnson's "injustice to himself" was evident in his diary for Easter 1777, for instance: "When I survey my past life, I discover nothing but a barren waste of time, with some disorders of body, and disturbances of the mind, very near to madness, which I hope He that made me will suffer to extenuate many faults, and excuse many deficiencies" — words Boswell assumes readers will find it "painful to think came from the contrite heart of this great man, to whose labours the world is so much indebted." So Johnson's living so resiliently and unquerulously, despite depression and fear of death, was also a major achievement.[22]

Renewing Their Friendship in Heaven

About thirty pages before narrating Johnson's death — right after describing the final letters he and Johnson exchanged, and just before relieving readers of "any farther personal notice of its authour" — Boswell added to the draft that he now "look[ed] forward with humble hope of renewing our friendship in a better world." Though Johnson had refused to enter into Boswell's fantasy that they would be reunited in heaven, Boswell hoped to reconnect with the friend who had been constantly on his mind as he worked on this expansive text. He longed for a cordial embrace like the one he and Johnson had shared — at least in the *Tour* — after landing on Iona. But for several reasons, Boswell was apprehensive.[23]

In Boswell's 1785 dreams, Johnson had been solemn but obliging, and Boswell dreamed late in 1787 that he saw his long-dead friend "cursorily but without any conversation." But in August 1789, two months after Margaret's death and just before Boswell began revising the almost-finished manuscript, he had a more disturbing dream: "Thought I was in a room into which Dr. Johnson entered suddenly with a very angry look at me. I said to him, 'My dear Sir, you certainly have nothing to say against me.' He answered sternly: 'Have I nothing to say against you, Sir?' I awoke uneasy and thought this applicable to my connection with E. M."

His anticipated revising with Edmond Malone ("E. M.") was the chief reason Boswell imagined Johnson angry. But Johnson's enduring reaction to an episode Boswell had not yet described and would not for a year and a half — his having not written to his dying friend — also surely worried him.[24]

In several letters, Johnson applauded Boswell's "kindness," his attentive helpfulness; and Boswell quoted him saying in 1783, "Were I in distress, there is no man to whom I should sooner come than to you." In February 1784, Johnson thanked Boswell for the "many enquiries which [his] kindness has disposed [him] to make" concerning Johnson's welfare; and five months later, after Boswell had begun arranging for an increase in the pension so his friend could travel to Italy, Johnson lamented Boswell's having to leave before the negotiations were completed, since Boswell could be an effective ally and advocate: "They that have your kindness may want your ardour." Clearly, Boswell was someone Johnson relied on. But as he included this evidence of Johnson's gratitude, Boswell surely wondered at his dying friend's feelings after he twice asked for letters in August 1784 — "I consider your fidelity and tenderness as a great part of the comforts which are yet left me" — and then for months heard nothing.[25]

Writing the biography reminded Boswell that Johnson — like Margaret but unlike Lord Auchinleck — regularly forgave his offenses. But what happened at the end might have been different. (Even Margaret had ceased to trust him after the affair with Rudd.) For instead of momentarily failing to sympathize, as when he pressed Johnson in 1769 to explain his fear of death or when he called attention to Johnson's birthday in 1777, Boswell for months failed to do what Johnson had earnestly requested. Rather than trying to distract or comfort his dying friend, he retreated to Auchinleck and wrote only after Johnson, in a puzzled third letter, asked, "Are you sick, or are you sullen?" Since Boswell received no answer to what he finally posted, he could not tell whether he had been forgiven, especially after discovering he was not mentioned in Johnson's will.[26]

So Boswell used the *Life* to argue for the same understanding and forgiveness for himself that he had given Johnson. When Johnson dismissed Boswell's paralyzing depression as his "hypocrisy of misery," his "affectation of distress," Boswell protested. At the same time, he uncharacteristically edged toward accepting some responsibility for this failure to write. Also, he embedded the account of his long silence within a narrative that contrasted his loyalty and gratitude, his respect and sympathetic understanding, with the behavior of others.

When describing how Johnson was first overwhelmed by "morbid melancholy," Boswell claimed to know "by dire experience" what his friend suffered, and therefore fully sympathized. Starting with his account of 1776, therefore, he handled Johnson's rebukes of his melancholy in a special way. He did not simply omit them, as he did with what Johnson wrote in 1775 about Boswell's "love of publication" or in 1783 about his drinking and the move to London. Nor did he include them completely, along with his spirited answers, as he did with what Johnson wrote in 1766 criticizing his Latin, or in 1768 wishing he would "empty [his] head of Corsica," or in 1777 insulting his "cowardly caution" concerning Beauclerk. Instead, Boswell printed enough of Johnson's complaints about his melancholy to show what about them troubled him, cut much that galled him, and used the *Life* to criticize Johnson for assuming that his friend's depression was "owing to [his] own fault, or that [he] was, perhaps, affecting it from a desire of distinction."[27]

Johnson's rebuking Boswell for depression in 1776 "seemed strangely un-reasonable in him who had suffered so much from it himself"; happily, John-son quickly acknowledged that his friend might be "really oppressed with overpowering and involuntary melancholy." But in August 1784, though Johnson knew exactly why Boswell felt so overwhelmed, he refused to sym-pathize in a follow-up letter, though he reaffirmed his love. Even what Johnson wrote twelve weeks later — his last letter to Boswell — contained a paragraph that "persevered in arraigning [Boswell] as before, which was strange in him who had so much experience of what" the younger man suffered.[28]

Having argued that Johnson *should* have sympathized, rather than charging Boswell with "affectation," Boswell initially attributed his failure to write to depression, combined with Johnson's demand that he "write like a man": "I unfortunately was so inexplicably ill during a considerable part of the year, that it was not in my power to write to my illustrious friend upon topics of entertainment as formerly, or without expressing such complaints as offended him." But though Boswell regularly — often outrageously — evaded respon-sibility by claiming he could not have acted otherwise, he eventually edged toward admitting some blame. He added the eight words I will italicize to the sentence just quoted: "it was not, *or at least I thought it was not,* in my power to write." Johnson was dying and wanted letters. Boswell, though depressed, anxious, and resentful, still had the "power" to write, since he had often proudly written *Hypochondriack* essays despite low spirits. But for more than three months he had done nothing, and finally wrote only after Johnson sent another letter.[29]

Boswell slightly offset this admission, however, by adding the emphasized phrase to the next sentence: "Having conjured him not to do me the injustice of charging me with affectation, I was *with much regret* long silent." To heighten readers' sympathy with his own feelings, Boswell later added that he "felt the force of Shakespeare's words, 'How weary stale flat and unprofitable / Seem to me all the uses of this world,'" though eventually he deleted this glimpse into his depression. Then, after quoting part of Johnson's November letter, Boswell complained that in a paragraph he omitted, Johnson persisted, despite having "so much experience of what [Boswell] suffered" — and at this point Boswell again thought of using the passage from Hamlet's first soliloquy — in "arraign-ing" Boswell. Finally, the biographer, despite having been absent from London and all but incommunicado as Johnson lay dying — "I, however, wrote to him two as kind letters as I could; the last of which came too late to be read by him, for his illness encreased more rapidly upon him than I had apprehended" — nonetheless tried to insert himself into Johnson's final moments: "I had the consolation of being informed that he spoke of me on his death-bed, with affection, and I look forward with humble hope of renewing our friendship in a better world."[30]

A few pages before he described Johnson's final three letters, and both justified and apologized for his long silence, Boswell added to the manuscript the poignant story Johnson had told Henry White during his final days in Lichfield. Though Johnson "could not in general accuse himself of having been an undutiful son," he had once out of pride "refused to attend [his] father to Uttoxeter-market." So years later Johnson tried to "atone for this fault" by going to Uttoxeter in the rain and standing "for a considerable time bare-headed . . . on the spot where [his] father's stall used to stand." In reporting this story of rebellious pride and expiation, Boswell did not mention that Johnson had praised White's loving solicitude toward his own dying father, behavior Johnson pointedly contrasted with his disobedience. But Boswell knew the complete story. In fact, I suspect Boswell saw how White's supporting his ailing father — "alleviating, as far as human Consolation is able, the Struggles of the Mind under the Ruin of the Body" — resembled the behavior of those who, like Langton, frequently wrote Johnson in the summer and early fall, and then regularly visited his deathbed. Boswell, in striking contrast, failed to write until it was too late. Though Boswell did not spell out the connection, I see his citing the Uttoxeter story at this point in the narrative as itself a gesture of confession and expiation. Immediately after describing the letters he finally wrote, Boswell pointedly "reliev[ed] the readers of this Work from any farther personal notice of its author," guiltily withdrawing after an episode where he was clearly deficient.[31]

While partly acknowledging his responsibility, however, Boswell embedded the account of his unsupportive silence within a narrative that highlighted the disappointing behavior of several others. Right after describing his last glimpse of Johnson, for instance, "as he sprang away with a kind of pathetick brisk-ness," Boswell told how Hester Thrale had abandoned Johnson to marry Gabriel Piozzi. Then, as "a sincere friend of the great man whose Life I am writing" — words added to the draft — Boswell chose this point in his narrative to de-scribe at length how this woman had misrepresented Johnson in her *Anecdotes*. Soon afterward, having already emphasized his tact and diligence in negotiating an increase in Johnson's pension, Boswell told how George III had refused — an "unexpected failure" concerning which Boswell self-consciously "ab-stain[ed] from presuming to make any remarks, or to offer any conjectures." Also, both before and after describing his own failure to write, Boswell de-fended his friend against Sir John Hawkins's "uncharitable" reflections about his fear of death, his using a knife to stab his swollen legs, and his designating Francis Barber as his heir.[32]

Boswell told two stories that sharply distinguished him from Hawkins. Near the end, Hawkins alarmed Johnson by pocketing one of the two quarto volumes that contained "a full, fair, and most particular account of [Johnson's] own life, from his earliest recollection," an act that probably prompted Johnson "hastily [to] burn these precious records, which must ever be regretted." At this point, Boswell reported earlier confessing to Johnson that he had read a good deal of those volumes, and asking Johnson whether he could have helped it, to which Johnson had "placidly" replied, "Why, Sir, I do not think you could have helped it." Boswell also admitted having been tempted "to carry off those two volumes, and never see him more"; and Johnson, when asked "how this would have affected him," had replied, "I believe I should have gone mad." Unlike Hawkins, however, Boswell had resisted the temptation.[33]

Boswell had neglected the dying Johnson for more than three months, and finally wrote too late to get a reply. But unlike Hester Thrale Piozzi, George III, and Sir John Hawkins, Boswell had not abandoned or betrayed or misjudged Johnson. Also though he had disappointed his needy friend, he had now expiated. The *Life* as a whole, with all its sympathy and understanding, ending with the words "admiration and reverence," was Boswell's atonement for what he had earlier failed to do. Near the end of his life, Johnson had written inscriptions for the graves of his wife, his father, his mother, and his brother. Boswell had written hundreds of pages of thoughtful, respectful, protective, and mostly loving biography. And he was writing "like a man."

Hester Thrale had shared many more of Johnson's days and had received the bulk of his letters. Hawkins had been named an executor in the will that failed even to mention Boswell. But the *Life* amply demonstrated that Boswell best understood Johnson, best loved him, and best deserved his love. Beauclerk was the young friend Johnson most admired, even envied, and regarded with "a tenderness more than common," as Boswell wrote in a passage he later cut — a person whom Johnson told Langton he "would walk to the extent of the diameter of the earth to save" from his final illness. Langton, the "worthy" friend Johnson most easily imagined in heaven, had been with Johnson in his deepest depression and during his final days; and (as Boswell reported) it was to Langton that the dying Johnson quoted from Tibullus, "*Te teneam moriens dificiente manu*" ("When I expire, let my trembling hand hold yours") — a gesture "saturated with a sense of strong yet delicate friendship," as David Womersley has noted. But though not as brilliant as Beauclerk or as virtuous as Langton, the "Boswell" presented in the *Life* surpassed both those rivals. He had much more energy, wit, and conversational courage than Langton. He was more earnestly religious than Beauclerk; and unlike Beauclerk, he shared and sympathized with Johnson's constitutional melancholy.

Having failed to receive a blessing in Johnson's final letter, and having not been mentioned in Johnson's will, Boswell could not formally receive a posthumous blessing. But when the *Life* pleased those best equipped to judge — longtime friends like Hector and Reynolds, Langton and Burke, and newer members of the Club who had known Johnson well, like Malone and Barnard — then it clearly was a worthy homage, a culminating gesture of friendship by someone who deserved to be embraced once Boswell and Johnson were reunited.[34]

The Life *after Boswell*

Despite Boswell's worry that interest in Johnson might have waned in the five years since he began sorting materials, and despite its high price (two guineas), the first edition of the *Life* in two quarto volumes sold briskly. So did the second, published in 1793 in three octavo volumes (priced at £1 4s.), with additional anecdotes, many newly found letters, and Johnson's brief against slavery. Even before Boswell died, in 1795, when he was a year older than Johnson had been when he first met Boswell, his biography foregrounding their friendship had clearly displaced Piozzi's *Anecdotes* and Hawkins's *Life*.

In the third edition (1799), carefully edited by Malone with help from Forbes and Boswell's son James, the substantial "addenda" of the second edition were properly woven into the larger narrative. Three more editions were published between 1804 and 1811, after which the revised text was regularly reprinted. In 1887, G. B. Hill produced a fully annotated edition of the *Life* together with the *Tour,* with extensive notes and many appendices; and this edition was later "revised and enlarged" by L. F. Powell (1934–1950), using for the first time the recently recovered Boswell Papers. Meanwhile, numerous lightly annotated editions and abridgments have been printed, offering most readers their first encounters with Johnson and Boswell. The collaborative biographical project, having significantly deepened and reconfigured the Johnson-Boswell friendship in the last years of Johnson's life, became a major source of Johnson's — and Boswell's — enduring fame.

Of course much more is now known about Johnson than was available to Boswell. Many documents deliberately withheld from him, such as those in the *Thraliana* as well as Johnson's letters to Frances Burney, have been published, along with others Boswell never suspected, such as Johnson's *Annals* and Burney's journal. Significant aspects of Johnson's experience that Boswell seems never to have imagined, such as his sustained collaboration with Chambers on the Vinerian Lectures, have been carefully studied, and additional facts about Johnson continue to be ferreted out. But despite its limitations, Boswell's *Life* remains a text all biographers of Johnson must use. It is there, for reasons Ralph W. Rader and others have helped clarify, that we most fully encounter Johnson as a dramatic presence, with a vitality and coherence found nowhere else. Boswell's accuracy has been contested, his incompleteness lamented, and his understanding of Johnson challenged. But with Johnson's cooperation, Boswell made himself a significant actor in Johnson's life; and Boswell's images of "Johnson," of "Boswell," and of their friendship cannot be ignored. The book Boswell wrote in part to win Johnson's forgiving embrace has guaranteed that he and Johnson will always be linked.[35]

Much more is now known about Boswell, too, and about the composition of the *Life,* than was available for more than a century after his death. In particular, we have most of the material Boswell entrusted to his literary executors (Temple, Forbes and Malone): documents eventually squirreled away in various houses owned by descendents of Boswell and Forbes but now recovered, catalogued, and in large part published. Boswell's journals, memoranda, and voluminous correspondence document his interactions with many of his most notable contemporaries, his wide-ranging engagement with ideas and events, as well as his persistent efforts at self-construction and self-documentation. The layered manuscript of the *Life* reveals his remarkable energy, imagination, and skill in constructing this groundbreaking biography.[36]

These documents, together with Johnson's diaries and letters, and the diaries and letters of others, have enabled me to construct an account of a friendship much less harmonious and static, and much more engaging, than the one presented in the *Journey,* the *Tour,* and especially the *Life.* By drawing on everything Johnson and Boswell wrote to and about the other, I have traced the psychological currents that flowed between them as they collaboratively negotiated and renegotiated their friendship, telling a story that I hope reaches through its specificity into the dynamics of most sustained friendships, with their breaks and reconnections, their silences and fresh intimacies, their continuities and transformations.

Appendix

Key Events in Lives of Samuel Johnson (SJ) and James Boswell (JB), Days They Were Together, and Letters They Exchanged

What follows lists a few key events in the lives of both men before they met in 1763, plus some of those described in this study.

The table of days they were together — whether briefly or at length, alone or with others — adds 20–26+ days to the total of 400 that Hitoshi Suwabe meticulously compiled from the *Life* and the Yale editions of Boswell's journals ("Appendix: Boswell's Meetings with Johnson, A New Count" [Lustig 246–57]).

The table of letters adds several by Boswell to the list compiled by R. W. Chapman (Chapman 3: 276–96).

Year	Major events	No. of days together	No. of letters: JB to SJ	No. of letters: SJ to JB
1709	SJ born.			
1728–1729	SJ at Pembroke College, Oxford; leaves without degree.			
1731	SJ's father, Michael Johnson, dies.			
1735	SJ marries Elizabeth Jervis Porter, a widow; opens a school.			
1737	SJ to London — with David Garrick.			
1740	JB born.			

Year	Major events	No. of days together	No. of letters: JB to SJ	No. of letters: SJ to JB
1744	SJ's *Life of Richard Savage*.			
1746	SJ's proposal for an English dictionary.			
1750–1752	SJ's *Rambler*.			
1752	SJ's wife, Elizabeth, dies.			
1755	SJ's *Dictionary* published.			
1756	Proposal for a new edition of Shakespeare.			
1759	SJ's mother, Sarah, dies; *Rasselas* published. JB studies with Adam Smith at Glasgow.			
1760	JB abandons college for London; brought home to study law.			
1762	SJ receives annual pension of £300. JB to London with allowance of £200.			
1763	SJ & JB meet on 16 May. JB to Holland to study law.	22	3	1
1764	SJ and Sir Joshua Reynolds found the Club. JB begins grand tour; meets Rousseau, Voltaire.	0	3*	0
1765	SJ meets Thrales, publishes edition of Shakespeare. JB in Italy; in Corsica meets General Paoli.	0	1	0
1766	JB's mother dies. JB writes thesis in civil law, begins practicing law in Edinburgh.	4+	5	2
1767	SJ helps Robert Chambers with Vinerian Lectures on English law, a project that continues through 1770.	0	3–5	0
1768	JB publishes *An Account of Corsica*.	7+	3–4	1

Year	Major events	No. of days together	No. of letters: JB to SJ	No. of letters: SJ to JB
1769	JB marries Margaret Montgomerie; JB's father (Lord Auchinleck) remarries.	14–15	3	2
1770	SJ's *False Alarm* (on expulsion of Wilkes as MP).	0	0	0
1771	SJ's *Falkland Islands* (against war with Spain).	0	3	1
1772		23	3	2
1773	Veronica Boswell born; JB elected to Club.	16 (spring)	7	7
	SJ & JB travel through Highlands to Hebrides.	101 (fall)		
1774	SJ travels to Wales with the Thrales.	0	11–13	11
1775	SJ publishes *Journey to Western Islands of Scotland, Taxation No Tyranny*; visits France with the Thrales.	27	13*	11
1776	David Hume dies cheerfully, despite nonbelief.	38–39	13–14**	14
1777	JB begins monthly *Hypochondriack* essays (continued until August 1783).	11	14	13
1778	Boswell's "best London visit ever."	36	10–11	4
1779	SJ publishes first set of *Lives of the Poets*.	28 (spring) 5 (fall)	13	6
1780		0	8	3
1781	Henry Thrale dies. SJ publishes second (larger) set of *Lives*.	32–34	3	1
1782	JB's father dies; JB becomes laird.	0	8	7
1783	SJ suffers stroke in July; is very ill in December.	26	5	4
1784	Hester Thrale marries Gabriel Piozzi. SJ dies 13 December.	30–32	10	10
Total		420–426+	142–149	100

Year	Major events	No. of days together	No. of letters: JB to SJ	No. of letters: SJ to JB
1785	SJ's *Prayers and Meditations*. JB's *Journal of a Tour to the Hebrides*.			
1786	Hester Piozzi's *Anecdotes of the Late Samuel Johnson*. JB moves to London to practices law and write *Life*.			
1787	John Hawkins's *Life of Samuel Johnson*.			
1788	Piozzi's *Letters to and from the Late Samuel Johnson*.			
1789	JB's wife, Margaret, dies in Auchinleck on 4 June.			
1791	JB's *Life of Johnson* published on 16 May.			
1793	Second edition of *Life of Johnson*.			
1795	JB dies in London on 19 May.			

*One of these letters was sent to Johnson only in June 1777.

** The letter written on 8–9 April may not have been sent to Johnson.

Cue Titles and Abbreviations

Anecdotes	Hester Lynch Piozzi, *Anecdotes of Samuel Johnson,* ed. S. C. Roberts (New York: Arno, 1980)
Applause	*Boswell: The Applause of the Jury, 1782–1784,* ed. Irma S. Lustig and Frederick A. Pottle (New York: McGraw-Hill; London: Heinemann, 1981)
Bate	W. Jackson Bate, *Samuel Johnson* (New York: Harcourt Brace Jovanovich, 1977)
Biographer	*Boswell: The Great Biographer, 1789–1795,* ed. Marlies K. Danziger and Frank Brady (New York: McGraw-Hill, 1989)
BP	*The Private Papers of James Boswell from Malahide Castle in the Collection of Lt.-Colonel Ralph Heyward Isham,* ed. Geoffrey Scott and F. A. Pottle, 18 vols. (Privately printed, 1928–1934).
Catalogue	Marion S. Pottle, Claude Colleer Abbott, and Frederick A. Pottle, *Catalogue of the Private Papers of James Boswell at Yale University,* 3 vols. (Edinburgh: Edinburgh University Press; New Haven, Conn.: Yale University Press, 1993)
Chapman	*The Letters of Samuel Johnson with Mrs. Thrale's Genuine Letters to Him,* ed. R. W. Chapman, 3 vols. (Oxford: Clarendon Press, 1952)
Clingham	*New Light on Boswell,* ed. Greg Clingham (Cambridge: Cambridge University Press, 1991)

Corr.1	*The Correspondence of James Boswell and John Johnston of Grange,* ed. Ralph Walker (London: Heinemann; New York: McGraw-Hill, 1966)
Corr.2	*The Correspondence and Other Papers of James Boswell Relating to the Making of the 'Life of Johnson,'* ed. Marshall Waingrow, 2nd ed. (Edinburgh: Edinburgh University Press; New Haven, Conn.: Yale University Press, 2001)
Corr.3	*The Correspondence of James Boswell with Certain Members of the Club,* ed. Charles N. Fifer (New York: McGraw-Hill, 1976)
Corr.4	*The Correspondence of James Boswell with David Garrick, Edmund Burke, and Edmond Malone,* ed. Peter S. Baker, Thomas W. Copeland, George M. Kahrl, Rachel McClelland, and James Osborn (London: Heinemann; New York: McGraw-Hill, 1986)
Corr.5	*The General Correspondence of James Boswell, 1766–1769,* Vol. 1, *1766–1767,* ed. Richard C. Cole, with Peter S. Baker and Rachel McClellan (Edinburgh: Edinburgh University Press; New Haven: Yale University Press, 1993)
Corr.6	*The Correspondence of James Boswell and William Johnson Temple, 1756–1795,* Vol. 1, *1756–1777,* ed. Thomas Crawford (Edinburgh: Edinburgh University Press; New Haven, Conn.: Yale University Press, 1997)
Corr.7	*The General Correspondence of James Boswell, 1766–1769,* Vol. 2, *1768–1769,* ed. Richard C. Cole, with Peter S. Baker and Rachel McClellan (Edinburgh: Edinburgh University Press; New Haven, Conn.: Yale University Press, 1997)
Corr.8	*The Correspondence of James Boswell with James Bruce and Andrew Gibb, Overseers of the Auchinleck Estate,* ed. Nellie Pottle Hankins and John Strawhorn (Edinburgh: Edinburgh University Press; New Haven, Conn.: Yale University Press, 1998)
Corr.9	*The General Correspondence of James Boswell, 1757–1763,* ed. David Hankins and James J. Caudle (Edinburgh: Edinburgh University Press; New Haven, Conn.: Yale University Press, 2006)
Corsica	James Boswell, *An Account of Corsica, The Journal of a Tour to That Island, and Memoirs of Pascal Paoli,* ed. James T. Boulton and T. O. McLoughlin (Oxford: Oxford University Press, 2006)
Defence	*Boswell for the Defence, 1769–1774,* ed. William K. Wimsatt and Frederick A. Pottle (New York: McGraw Hill, 1959)
Diaries	Samuel Johnson, *Diaries, Prayers, and Annals,* ed. E. L. McAdam, Jr., with Donald and Mary Hyde (New Haven, Conn.: Yale University Press; London: Oxford University Press, 1958)

Earlier Years	Frederick A. Pottle, *James Boswell: The Earlier Years, 1740–1769* (New York: McGraw-Hill, 1966)
Experiment	*Boswell: The English Experiment, 1785–1789*, ed. Irma S. Lustig and Frederick A. Pottle (New York: McGraw-Hill, 1986)
Extremes	*Boswell in Extremes, 1776–1778*, ed. Charles McC. Weis and Frederick A. Pottle (New York: McGraw-Hill, 1970)
GT1	*Boswell on the Grand Tour: Germany and Switzerland, 1764*, ed. Frank Brady and Frederick A. Pottle (New York: McGraw-Hill; London: Heinemann, 1953)
GT2	*Boswell on the Grand Tour: Italy, Corsica, and France, 1765–66*, ed. Frank Brady and Frederick A. Pottle (New York: McGraw-Hill; London: Heinemann, 1955)
Hebrides	*Boswell's Journal of a Tour to the Hebrides with Samuel Johnson, LL.D., 1773*, ed. Frederick A. Pottle and Charles H. Bennett (New York: McGraw-Hill; London: Heinemann, 1961)
Holland	*Boswell in Holland, 1763–1764*, ed. Frederick A. Pottle (New York: McGraw-Hill, 1952)
Hypochondriack	James Boswell, *The Hypochondriack*, ed. Margery Bailey, 2 vols. (Stanford, Calif.: Stanford University Press, 1928)
Impossible Friendship	Mary Hyde, *The Impossible Friendship: Boswell and Mrs. Thrale* (Cambridge, Mass.: Harvard University Press, 1972)
JM	*Johnsonian Miscellanies*, ed. G. B. Hill, 2 vols. (New York: Barnes & Noble, 1966)
Journey	Samuel Johnson, *Journey to the Western Islands*, ed. Mary Lascelles (New Haven, Conn.: Yale University Press, 1971)
Laird	*Boswell: Laird of Auchinleck, 1778–1782*, ed. Joseph W. Reed and Frederick A. Pottle (New York: McGraw-Hill; London: Heinemann; Edinburgh: Edinburgh University Press, 1993)
Larsen	*James Boswell as His Contemporaries Saw Him*, ed. Lyle Larsen (Madison, N.J.: Fairleigh Dickinson University Press, 2008)
Later Years	Frank Brady, *James Boswell: The Later Years, 1769–1795* (New York: McGraw-Hill, 1984)
Letters	*The Letters of Samuel Johnson*, ed. Bruce Redford, 5 vols. (Princeton, N.J.: Princeton University Press, 1992–1994)
Life	*Boswell's Life of Johnson, LL.D. Together with Boswell's Journal of a Tour to the Hebrides*, ed. G. B. Hill, rev. L. F. Powell, 6 vols. (Oxford: Oxford University Press, 1934–50)
Life ms 1	*James Boswell's "Life of Johnson": An Edition of the Original Manuscript in Four Volumes*, Vol. 1, *1709–1765*, ed. Marshall Waingrow (Edinburgh: Edinburgh University Press; New Haven, Conn.: Yale University Press, 1994)
Life ms 2	*James Boswell's "Life of Johnson": An Edition of the Original Manuscript in Four Volumes*, Vol. 2, *1766–1776*, ed. Bruce Redford, with Elizabeth Goldring (Edinburgh: Edinburgh University Press; New Haven, Conn.: Yale University Press, 1999)

Life ms 3	*James Boswell's "Life of Johnson": An Edition of the Original Manuscript in Four Volumes*, Vol. 3, *1776–1780*, ed. Thomas F. Bonnell (Edinburgh: Edinburgh University Press; New Haven, Conn.: Yale University Press, 2012)
Lives	Samuel Johnson, *The Lives of the Poets*, ed. Roger Lonsdale, 4 vols. (Oxford: Oxford University Press, 2006)
London	James Boswell, *London Journal, 1762–1763*, ed. Gordon Turnbull (London: Penguin Classics, 2010)
Lustig	*Boswell: Citizen of the World, Man of Letters*, ed. Irma S. Lustig (Lexington: University Press of Kentucky, 1995)
Newman	*James Boswell: Psychological Interpretations*, ed. Donald J. Newman (New York: St. Martin's, 1995)
Note Book	*Boswell's Note Book, 1776–1777*, ed. R. B. Adam (London: Oxford University Press, 1925)
Ominous	*Boswell: The Ominous Years, 1774–1776*, ed. Charles Ryskamp and Frederick A. Pottle (New York: McGraw-Hill; London: Heinemann, 1963)
Redford	Bruce Redford, *Designing the "Life of Johnson,"* (Oxford: Oxford University Press, 2002)
Register	Boswell's Register of Letters: Yale M 251 (1763–1764), M 252 (1764–1766), M 253 (1769–1777), M 254 (1778–1782), M 255 (1782–1790)
Thraliana	*Thraliana: The Diary of Mrs. Hester Lynch Thrale (Later Mrs. Piozzi), 1776–1809*, ed. Katharine C. Balderston, 2 vols. (Oxford: Clarendon Press, 1951)
Tinker	*The Letters of James Boswell*, ed. C. B. Tinker, 2 vols. (Oxford: Clarendon Press, 1924)
Vance	*Boswell's "Life of Johnson": New Questions, New Answers*, ed. John A. Vance (Athens: University of Georgia Press, 1985)
Wife	*Boswell in Search of a Wife, 1766–1769*, ed. Frank Brady and Frederick A. Pottle (New York: McGraw-Hill; London: Heinemann, 1956)
Yale J (C, L, M)	The Papers of James Boswell at Yale University, as described in *Catalogue*
Yale-SJ	*Yale Edition of the Works of Samuel Johnson*, 23 vols. (New Haven, Conn.: Yale University Press, 1958–)

Notes

Introduction

1. *London* 54, 63, 220–23; Bate 359 (see also 268–69). In the spring of 1760, encouraged by the Irish actor Francis Gentleman, Boswell had unsuccessfully attempted to meet "Dictionary Johnson" through the Irish poet Samuel Derrick (*Life* 1:384–85). For talk about Johnson shortly before Boswell came to London in November 1762, see *BP* 1:70, 84, 128–29.

2. *London* 250–51, 261, 271, 289, 294, 297; *Life ms* 1:331–32. For Boswell's sword, see *London* 20–21, 114, 168. For an informed and suggestive reflection on the unlikelihood of "a close personal attachment . . . between two men so different as Johnson and Boswell in character and experience," see Bertrand H. Bronson, *Facets of the Enlightenment* (Berkeley and Los Angeles: University of California Press, 1968), 210–40.

3. For Johnson's writing when first in London, see Thomas Kaminski, *The Early Career of Samuel Johnson* (New York: Oxford University Press, 1987). For his plan to seek a new wife, see *Diaries* 52. For Johnson's lassitude and the delay on Shakespeare, see *Yale-SJ* 7:xvi–xxvi and Bate 341–47.

4. *Earlier Years* 46–50, 107–10; *London* 218, 178–79; *Corr.*9: 394–96.

5. For Johnson as mentor, see Anthony W. Lee, *Mentoring Relationships in the Life and Writings of Samuel Johnson: A Study in the Dynamics of Eighteenth-Century Literary Mentoring* (Lewiston, N.Y.: Mellen, 2005).

6. *Hebrides* 243–44.

7. For a wide-ranging survey and astute analysis of recent reflections on literary collaborations, see two chapters in Marjorie Stone and Judith Thompson, *Literary Coup-*

lings Writing Couples, Collaborators, and the Construction of Authorship (Madison: University of Wisconsin Press, 2006), 3–37, 309–33.

8. *Boswell's London Journal, 1762–1763*, ed. Frederick A. Pottle (New York: McGraw-Hill, 1950), 339–40; *London* 269.

9. For the limits of memory, see Sue Halpern, *Can't Remember What I Forgot* (New York: Harmony, 2008). For Boswell on the limitations of any journal, see *Wife* 242, 292–93. For a sense of how much is said during any long dinner conversation — much more than could be contained in even the longest of Boswell's entries — see Deborah Tannen, *Conversational Style: Analyzing Talk among Friends* (Norwood, N.J.: Ablex, 1984). For a few moments when Boswell noted giving Johnson's meaning but not his exact words, see *Defence* 46, 87, 105. To see how their full accounts of 1 September 1773 present what is obviously the same day, though with different details and different emphases, see *Hebrides* 106–12, *Letters* 1:73–77, and *Journey* 37–49. For a journal that corroborates and expands on conversations Boswell reports, see Thomas Campbell, *Dr. Campbell's Diary of a Visit to England in 1775*, ed. James L. Clifford (Cambridge: Cambridge University Press, 1947). For Boswell's and Charlotte Burney's nonoverlapping accounts of 7 April 1781, see *Laird* 309–12.

10. *Idler* 84 (*Yale-SJ* 2:263).

Chapter 1: Taking Charge of Boswell (1763)

1. *London* 112.

2. *Corr.9:* 111, 208 (see also 159); *London* 104 (see also 42), 139.

3. Pottle, *London Journal*, 286n2, 342; *London* 190, 198, 231, 218, 240.

4. *London* 229–30, 243–44.

5. *Life ms* 1:276; *London* 245. For Johnson as celebrity, see *Corr.9:* 222, 257; *BP* 1:128–129; *London* 50.

6. *London* 250–51.

7. *London* 267, 269–71.

8. *London* 220, 261, 283, 243, 272.

9. *London* 230, 243, 259–60; Tinker 1:16. For Sheridan's playfulness, see *Corr.9:* 134.

10. *London* 251, 270–71, 299; Yale L1421; Tinker 1:38–39; *Corr.6:* 43, 48.

11. *London* 273; Pottle, *London Journal*, 338; *London* 317 (see also 130); Tinker 1:30. A few days after hearing Johnson's encouragement, Boswell read Temple's praise of "the candour, the humanity and reflection" of the journal he had kept for ten weeks before coming to London (*Corr.6:* 44). For Johnson's resolves to keep a journal, see *Diaries* 71, 73. For analysis of Boswell's journal, see *Earlier Years* 86–94 and *Later Years* 145–53.

12. Tinker 1:12; *London* 287, 265. For advice to Grange, see *Corr.1:* 81. On 15 July, when Boswell felt the port he had drunk with Johnson the night before "boiling in [his] veins," Dempster told him he "had better be palsied at eighteen than not keep company with such a Man as Johnson" (*London* 272). For eighteenth-century British explanations of "melancholy," see the introduction to *The English Malady: Enabling and Disabling Fictions,* ed. Glen Colburn (Cambridge: Cambridge Scholars Press, 2008).

13. *London* 244, 250, 271, 289; *Corr.6:* 42, 48; Tinker 1:24, 31; Yale L528; Pottle, *London Journal*, 340.

14. *London* 293, 297; Pottle, *London Journal,* 342.

15. *London* 216 (catches), 225–26 (Macheath); Tinker 1:17, 24, 29–30.

16. *London* 257 (Ogilvie), 273 (burning journal), 286 (Dempster), 264 ("perambulate"—see also Tinker 1:24); *Corr.6:* 48.

17. *London* 229, 244, 251, 294.

18. *London* 255 (see also *GT1* 304–5), 220–23, 243 (see also 240–41), 270–71.

19. *London* 229, 251, 289; Yale C1424; *Corr.6:* 42–43; Yale L528.

20. *London* 230, 274, 258–62.

21. *London* 296. For a vivid description of the Thames and Greenwich in 1763, and a suggestive fantasy involving Johnson, Boswell, and Boswell's deranged brother John, see Philip Baruth, *The Brothers Boswell* (New York: Soho Press, 2009).

22. *London* 250, 283, 286, 269, 284. For Bowles, see *Corr.2:* 192–96. See Sandra K. D. Stahl, "Personal Experience Stories," in *Handbook of American Folklore,* ed. Richard M. Dorson (Bloomington: University of Indiana Press, 1983), 268–76.

23. *London* 250–51, 270, 293–94; Tinker 1:23–25. For examples of Johnson's living through other friends, see *Letters* 1:160–62, 164–66, 171, 192–93, 196–98, 200, 205–7, 213–14.

24. *London* 287–89, 293; *Letters* 1:224–25.

25. *Yale-SJ* 4:167 (*Rambler* 99); 16:57, 98–99, 123–28, 163–64 (*Rasselas*); 2:72 (*Idler* 23); *London* 289, 297; *Life ms* 1:331 (Johnson's plan to come to Holland was added to the original draft).

26. Without comparable journal entries, it is impossible to say whether Johnson expressed his liking and love to other young friends as emphatically as he did to Boswell. But surviving letters to Chambers and especially to Langton suggest he might have. See *Letters* 1:107, 112, 162, 165–66, 195. None of Johnson's letters to Beauclerk survive.

27. *London* 299, 529; *Life ms* 1:327; *BP* 1:128, 130. There are numerous references to Hume's *History* from the end of 1762 (*London* 71) through July (*London* 258). For Anna Williams, see *London* 294 and 299.

28. *London* 301, 303; *Life ms* 1:332.

29. This dialogue about "forgetting" was added to what Boswell originally drafted (*Life ms* 1:332).

30. *Corr.1:* 112–13; *Corr.6:* 61–62; *London* 299. See Susan Manning, "'This Philosophical Melancholy': Style and Self in Boswell and Hume" (Clingham 126–40).

31. *Holland* 16; *Corr.1:* 113; *Corr.6:* 62–64 (see also 80), 69n2.

32. *BP* 1:69–70; *Corr.6:* 65–66, 69–70; *Corr.1:* 114.

33. *Corr.6:* 74; *London* 300; *Corr.6:* 72, 45, 58; Yale L528.

34. *Corr.1:* 116, 115, 111; *Corr.6:* 72.

35. *Holland* 42–43. For Boswell's earlier anger at not hearing from Grange, see *Corr.1:* 42, 55, 81.

36. Boswell's letter to his father on 7 October has not been found, but in reply Lord Auchinleck was delighted with his son's progress (Yale C223). For requests to help keep him on track, see *Corr.6:* 74 and *Holland* 47.

37. *Holland* 17, 47, 389. For examples of battle imagery, see *Holland* 49, 61, 67, 92, and Allan Ingram, *Boswell's Creative Gloom* (Totowa, N.J.: Barnes & Noble, 1982), 39–43.

38. *Letters* 1:230, 232–37, 231–32, 225. For Strahan's fear that he had somehow

offended Johnson when, after receiving patient, encouraging letters in February, March, and April, he heard nothing for two months, see *Letters* 1:209–10, 217–21, 224–25.

39. *Letters* 1:237–40; *Diaries* 77. For Johnson on his negligence as a correspondent, see *Letters* 1:174, 192. For Johnson's genially scolding Langton in March 1766 for not writing letters, and lightly chiding Chambers nine months later for failing to produce lectures in his first term as Vinerian Professor, see *Letters* 1:264–66 (compare 171) and 276–78 (compare 164). My discussion of Johnson's first letter complements Lance Wilcox's astute analysis in "Edifying the Young Dog: Johnson's Letters to Boswell," in *Sent as a Gift: Eight Correspondences from the Eighteenth Century*, ed. Alan T. McKenzie (Athens: University of Georgia Press, 1993), 135–40.

40. *Holland* 92–94.

41. Yale C223; see *Life* 1:384–85, *Holland* 40–41, and Yale L221–26.

42. *Holland* 92–93, 96–97; *Life ms* 1:335n9.

Chapter 2: "Perpetual Friendship"? (1764–1767)

1. *Letters* 1:261–62, 328–29; *Wife* 145–56, 163–64.

2. *Letters* 1:362–63.

3. *Holland* 164–67. Boswell showed Johnson "a specimen" of this dictionary in 1769 (*Wife* 322). For a full discussion of this project, the manuscript for which has recently been discovered, see James J. Caudle, "James Boswell (1740–1795) and His Design for *A Dictionary of the Scot[t]ish Language*, 1764–1825," in *Dictionaries* 32 (2011): 1–32.

4. *Holland* 174, 121, 177, 211; *Corr.*6: 87; *Holland* 202, 205, 231, 240. For the child Boswell had named after the martyred king Charles I, see *Earlier Years* 98 and *London* 292, 353n4, 522n1, 522–23n3.

5. *Earlier Years* 148–49; *GT1* 29–30, 29n2; *Corr.*6: 108–9. For Boswell's travels in 1764, see the introduction to *James Boswell: The Journal of His German and Swiss Travels, 1764*, ed. Marlies K. Danziger (New Haven, Conn.: Yale University Press; Edinburgh: Edinburgh University Press, 2008), xxix–lviii.

6. *London* 272–73 (see also 186–87, 299); *Corr.*6: 111; *Holland* 50, 95, 222, 237: *GT1* 19, 19n9, 41n2, 46n8, 48. For Frederick Calvert, the sixth proprietor of Maryland, see *GT1* 48n2.

7. *GT1* 53–54; *London* 304.

8. *GT1* 64, 64n2; *GT2* 23. For Boswell's anxiety in writing to Temple, too, see *Corr.*6: 104.

9. *GT1* 118–19.

10. *Life* 3:118; see also Kevin Hart, *Samuel Johnson and the Culture of Property* (New York: Cambridge University Press, 1999), 32. *GT1* 117, 111; *Life ms* 2:3.

11. *GT1* 258 (see also 262), 280; Tinker 1:40; *Corr.*6: 54; *GT2* 54 (see also 56–57), 101. For Boswell's meeting Wilkes in 1763, see *London* 229, 231, 245.

12. *Letters* 1:196–201, 205–6, 212–15; Yale C72.

13. *GT1* 254; *Earlier Years* 5; *Corr.*6: 123; *GT1* 231, 254, 265 (see also 251–52 and *GT2* 340.

14. *GT2* 81 (see also Tinker 1:77), 5–6, 10, 19–20. The long letter dated 3 October 1765 exists in three versions: Yale L1117, 1116, and 1115 (see also *Catalogue* 1:343–44).

15. *GT1* 225, 275–76, 246, 260; *Corsica* 120–21; *GT2* 182–83, 20. For Boswell's earlier plan to visit Spain in April 1765, see *Holland* 227. For Paoli, see Marie-Jeanne Colombani, "Paoli, (Filippo Antonio) Pasquale (1725–1807)," *Oxford Dictionary of National Biography.*

16. Yale L30; *GT2* 194; Yale C72.

17. *GT1* 231; *GT2* 7, 178, 239, 50, 225. For episodes of depression, see *GT2* 38, 56, 65, 74–76, 83, 138.

18. *Life ms* 2:2n7 (see also notes 3 and 4); *Letters* 1:261.

19. *Holland* 231; *Diaries* 77–78; *GT1* 100, 81; *GT2* 65; *Diaries* 92–93; *Letters* 1: 249–50.

20. *Letters* 1:261–63, 265.

21. For Lord Auchinleck's exasperation when Boswell stayed well beyond the allotted time, see Yale L227–29.

22. *GT2* 270, 277–81.

23. *GT2* 283.

24. *GT2* 281–83; see 85, 92–93 (Mallet); 268–69, 270–72, 275 (Wilkes in Paris).

25. *GT2* 322–27, 287, 283.

26. *GT2* 326, 285–87; *Yale-SJ* 16:74. For Johnson's "constantly" reading the *London Chronicle,* see *Wife* 330; for his rising early, see *Diaries* 99–103, 109, and *Letters* 1:265, 267. Boswell had naively imagined introducing Rousseau to Johnson (*GT2* 261 and Tinker 1:87); but Rousseau knew Johnson "would detest" him (*GT1* 258).

27. *GT2* 287; *Life ms* 2:6. Boswell curiously did not report talking with Johnson about his mother's death.

28. *GT2* 295–96; *BP* 1:129–30; *Diaries* 99–100, 103; *London* 230.

29. *Diaries* 106, 109; *Letters* 1:265; *Applause* 246; see Bate 407–12.

30. *Earlier Years* 291; *Corr.5:* 16, 34–35.

31. *Life ms* 2:10; *Corr.6:* 150; *Corr.5:* 57.

32. James L. Clifford, *Hester Lynch Piozzi (Mrs. Thrale)* (Oxford: Clarendon Press, 1941), 64–65; Bate 412.

33. *Letters* 1:271–73; *GT2* 283 ("court").

34. *Corr.6:* 159; *Corr.5:* 119; *Wife* 322; Sanford Radner, "James Boswell's Silence" (Newman 157); *Wife* 13. For Boswell's recollection in 1783, see *Applause* 83.

35. *Corr.6:* 159; *Life* 2:22–25; *Earlier Years* 291; *Letters* 1:200 (monks).

36. *Corr.6:* 192 (busy); *Wife* 96–97 (David's oath); Frederick A. Pottle, *The Literary Career of James Boswell* (Oxford: Clarendon Press, 1929), 27–50, 236–65. For Miss Blair, see *Earlier Years* 311–17, 325–28, 335–37, 341, 343–51; for Zélide, see *Earlier Years* 318, 337, 344, 348; for the Douglas case, see *Earlier Years* 311–17. Hume agreed to manage publication (*Wife* 28, 35, 46); Gray (through Temple) was in favor (*Wife* 11, 91); Hailes offered encouragement and detailed suggestions (*Wife* 13–14, 73, 75, 93, 104), as did Temple (*Wife* 73, 91, 93–94, 98, 100, 103–4, 108).

37. *Corr.5:* 108–9, 110, 111, 151, 178, 249.

38. *Diaries* 111; *Letters* 1:276–77. For Johnson's mind-stretching collaboration with Chambers, see Robert Chambers, *A Course of Lectures on the English Law,* ed. Thomas M. Curley (Madison: University of Wisconsin Press, 1986), 1:11–29, and Thomas M. Curley, *Sir Robert Chambers* (Madison: University of Wisconsin Press, 1998), 84–127.

39. *Corr.*5: 249; *Letters* 1:274–93; see *Diaries* 114–15.

40. Boswell nurtured interest in Corsica with paragraphs in the *London Chronicle* (*Corsica*, 223–25).

41. *Corr.*6: 142, 169, 205–6.

42. Yale M6, 9.

43. *Corsica* 193–94, 178.

44. *Corsica* 195–96; *Corr.*6: 214. Boswell asked Pitt about including what he had said to Boswell praising the Corsicans (*Corr.*5: 139), and Paoli about publishing one of his letters (*Corsica* 216), so Hailes probably assumed he had asked Johnson, too.

45. *Corsica* 207–8.

46. *Corsica* 130, 161, 197–98; *GT*2 298, 326; *Corsica* 209, 161–63, 182, 14, 17–18; see *Corr.*7: 25.

Chapter 3: Jostling for Control (1768–1771)

1. *Letters* 1:298; see *Earlier Years* 375.

2. *Wife* 145–49. By April 1, 3,500 copies had been sold, and a second edition was depleted early in 1769. The book was soon translated into Dutch, French (twice), German, and Italian. For its reception, see *Earlier Years* 357–58, 367–68.

3. *Wife* 152–53, 148, 150, 156.

4. For Johnson's guilt, see his letter of 9 September 1769 (*Letters* 1:329), discussed shortly.

5. *Wife* 150. In the *Life*, Boswell dropped Harwich (*Life ms* 2:27).

6. *Wife* 147, 156.

7. *Wife* 153–56; *Corsica* 182.

8. *Letters* 4:125 (see also *Letters* 1:302, 1:304–5, 2:147–48); *Wife* 164–65, 141. For Boswell's later assisting Paoli, see *Wife* 181, 181n3.

9. *Wife* 165–66; *Corr.*7: 28; *Corr.*6: 236. Early in 1763, Boswell had called Garrick "Thou Greatest of Men" (*London* 112). See William Ober, *Boswell's Clap, and Other Essays* (Carbondale: Southern Illinois University Press, 1979), 41–43, for Boswell's nineteen infections, and 2–25 for the changing treatments.

10. *Corr.*6: 236; Tinker 2:313; *Life ms* 2:12 (see also Bate 424 and *Impossible Friendship* 12).

11. *Wife* 176–77; *Life ms* 2:32–33. See *Corr.*2: 223–24; *BP* 6:139 (Langton "tost" in 1773).

12. For discussion of Kenrick's *Epistle to James Boswell, Esq., occasioned by his having transmitted the moral Writings of Dr. Samuel Johnson, to Pascal Paoli, General of the Corsicans* (July 1768), see *Corr.*7: 58–59, 60n13; *Wife* 167–68; *Life* 2:61.

13. *Corr.*7: 84; *Diaries* 120; *Letters* 1:328.

14. *Letters* 1:318; *Diaries* 119, 122–23.

15. *Earlier Years* 395–96; *Letters* 1:261, 328.

16. *Letters* 1:329.

17. *Life ms* 2:31.

18. *Wife* 122, 180, 197–98 ("inconstancy"); *Wife* 281–82 ("profligacy"); *Corr.*7: 110–11. For discussions of Margaret Montgomerie, see *Corr.*6: 245–47, 248, 250–51, and *Corr.*7: 171–72, 187–88.

19. *Corr.*6: 164; *Wife* 108, 216–17, 225–26.

20. *Wife* 230 (see also 217), 233–37, 240–41.

21. *Wife* 218, 225, 230, 235, 246.

22. *Wife* 248–54. For concern about venereal infections, see *Wife* 226; *Earlier Years* 428; Ober, *Boswell's Clap*, 40–41. For Margaret's relationship with Johnson, see *Wife* 197, 335, and Irma S. Lustig, "'My Dear Enemy': Margaret Montgomerie Boswell in the *Life of Johnson*" (Lustig 228–45).

23. *Corr.*7: 228; *Wife* 262, 247, 249, 269.

24. *Corr.*6: 255, *Corr.*7: 218–19, 222; *Wife* 269; *Letters* 1:329. Both Greg Clingham ("Double Writing: The Erotics of Narrative in Boswell's *Life of Johnson*" [Newman 200]), and Thomas A. King ("How [Not] to Queer Boswell," in *Queer People: Negotiations and Expressions of Homosexuality, 1700–1800*, ed. Chris Mounsey and Caroline Gonda [Lewisburg, Pa.: Bucknell University Press, 2007], 127), curiously assume Johnson was referring to himself — not Margaret — when he teased Boswell about his absent "Mistress."

25. *Wife* 301.

26. Boswell's spending the night of 6 October at Streatham is established by his entry for 12 May 1778 (*Extremes* 344). In an otherwise undocumented meeting on 23 or 24 October, Boswell shared with Johnson what Margaret had written about the *Rambler* in a letter he received on 23 October, as he reported to her on 24 October (*BP* 8:239). The *Life* describes Boswell's bringing Paoli and Johnson together on 10 October (*Life* 2:80–82), just before Paoli left for a brief tour. But this remarkable event is not noted in his memorandum for 11 October (Yale J20.1). Also, newspaper articles, at least one of which seems to have been written by Boswell, report this meeting occurring on 30 or 31 October (*Earlier Years* 563–64; Heather Klemann, "Boswell and the Un-diaried Month of October 1769," *Johnsonian News Letter* 61 [September 2010]: 30–33).

27. *Wife* 316 (see also 331), 310, 312; Yale J20.1. For Boswell's persistence, see *Corr.*1: 259, *Corr.*6: 262, and *Earlier Years* 347.

28. *Wife* 313–14. This attack on the Corsicans was added to the draft (*Life ms* 2:41–42).

29. *Wife* 318–21. "With a disdainful look" was added to the first version (*Life ms* 2:44). Goldsmith had introduced Boswell to Reynolds on 24 September (*Earlier Years* 430–31).

30. *Wife* 321–25.

31. *Wife* 327–32. Presumably, all those present recognized Johnson's allusion to Pope's *Essay on Man*: "Imagination plies her dangerous art, / And pours it all upon the peccant part" (2:143–44).

32. *Wife* 322–23; see *Letters* 1:272.

33. *Wife* 327–28; Bate 433. For earlier collaborations — all mainly Johnson's creations, even when Boswell was involved — see *London* 259, *Wife* 148.

34. *Wife* 323, 332, and Yale J20.1; *Extremes* 155 and *Applause* 246; see also *Wife* 302, 332. See *Life ms* 2:48 for the key addition Boswell made for 19 October 1769, drawing on what Johnson said in 1777. On 26 April 1768, the same day Boswell answered Johnson's letter about *Corsica,* the *Publick Advertiser* published his reflection on the first execution he had seen without being "haunted with frightful thoughts" (*Hypochondriack* 2:277–82).

35. *Wife* 332–33; *Life ms* 2:56–57; Yale J20.1, 59–60.

36. *Wife* 333–34.

37. See *Extremes* 254–55 for their next full discussion of fear of death.

38. On 31 October, Paoli and Johnson witnessed Boswell's marriage contract (Yale M21); *Wife* 342–43; *Life ms* 2:61–62.

39. *Corr.6*: 273, 282–83; *Remarks on the Profession of a Player* (Suffolk: Elkin Mathews & Marrot, 1929), 14–15; *Corr.4*: 30–34; *Wife* 343. Boswell and his father were soon reconciled (*Corr.7*: 262n2 and *Earlier Years* 442); but because of something that happened during Margaret's first visit to Auchinleck in October 1770, she never returned there until Lord Auchinleck died (*Later Years* 19).

40. *Letters* 1:237 (1763), 261 (1766), 329 (1769).

41. *Life ms* 2:66.

42. *Diaries* 142; *Letters* 1:362–63, 273. For Johnson's deep longing for mind-filling, off-duty experiences, see *Yale-SJ* 5:3 (*Rambler* 207) and *Extremes* 162.

43. *Letters* 1:107, 358. For news, see *Letters* 1:264–65, 267, 352, 356; for confessions, *Letters* 1:171, 192, 200; for health, *Letters* 1:336, 352, 358, 367.

44. *Defence* 83; Hart, *Johnson and the Culture of Property,* 32; *GT1* 118–19; *GT2* 101; *Life ms* 2:31; *Wife* 165–66 and Yale J15; *Critical Memoirs of the Times* 5 (25 March 1769): 386–88; Yale J20.1. For Boswell's desire to emulate William Drummond of Hawthornden, who recorded Ben Jonson's conversation, see Yale L1261. James J. Caudle explored this connection fully in "O Rare Sam Jo[h]nson: Boswell's Drummond and Johnson's Jonson," a paper delivered at "Johnson at 300: A Houghton Library Symposium," Harvard University, Cambridge, Mass., August 27–29, 2009.

45. *Holland* 120, 137, 162–68; *Wife* 322.

46. For writing projects, see *Wife* 322, *Corr.6*: 294n1. For Paoli's visit to Scotland, see *London Magazine* 40 (1771): 433–34.

Chapter 4: New Collaborations (1772)

1. *Defence* 41; *Letters* 1:382; *Diaries* 146–47; *Defence* 44 (see also 80), 68 (see also 59, 84), 104–7 (see also 118). See Cor. 4:39 and *Defence* 81. For Boswell's persistent longing for London, see James J. Caudle, "James Boswell (*H. Scoticus Londoniensis*)," in *Scots in London in the Eighteenth Century,* ed. Stana Nendic (Lewisburg, Penn.: Bucknell University Press, 2010), 109–38.

2. *Defence* 25–26.

3. *Letters* 1:388–90. For Johnson's health, especially his difficulty sleeping, see *Diaries* 142–43, 146–47.

4. *Defence* 55, 39, 52. For journal writing, see *Defence* 67, 81, 101, 126.

5. *London* 271; *Defence* 44, 63.

6. *Defence* 50–52, 84–85.

7. *Defence* 58, 75.

8. *Defence* 44, 55, 68, 46–47, 72–74, 102.

9. *Defence* 55, 121–23 (see also 69–70), 129. For Goldsmith, see *Defence* 109–110 and *BP* 9:264.

10. *BP* 9:258 (Spain); *Defence* 96 (Fielding); *BP* 9:265 (Garrick — see also *Wife* 322–23);

Defence 94–95 (preacher), *BP* 9:258 (brother). When he met Boswell's brother eight years later, having in the meantime traveled to Scotland, Johnson wrote he would "find Scotland but a sorry place after twelve years residence in a happier climate" (*Letters* 3:280).

11. *Defence* 122–23.

12. *Defence* 56–57.

13. *Defence* 107–9 and n6, 355–56; *Life* 2:183–85, 143. For Crosbie, see *Earlier Years* 309, and *Later Years*, 26.

14. *Defence* 84–85; *Life ms* 2:78–79; *Life* 2:184. Curley suggests Johnson and Chambers just talked, after which Chambers wrote lectures (*Course of Lectures* 1:22). In 1754, Johnson dictated at least one *Adventurer* essay to John Hawkesworth, and perhaps others to Richard Bathurst (*Yale-SJ* 2:333–35; Bate 292).

15. *Life* 2:185; *Defence* 112–13. In contrast, Johnson's friend Taylor simply read the sermons Johnson wrote for him.

16. *Defence* 113–14, 126.

17. *Defence* 116–120 (see also 58), 123 (see also 125).

18. *Defence* 40–42, 57 and n8a.

19. *Defence* 91 (Foote), 118–19 (Garrick); *BP* 9:256 (Johnson and Burke), 263–66 (May 7–11).

20. *Defence* 102, 119, 126. See Bate 455–60.

21. *Defence* 83; *Corr.2*: 5–8; *Life* 3:321–22; *Corr.3*: 16. For Levet, see *London* 311 and James L. Clifford, *Young Sam Johnson* (New York: McGraw-Hill, 1955), 304–5. David Nokes suggests that Johnson consciously sought a biographer, someone "sufficiently close, as he had been to Savage, and yet sufficiently detached to write from his own point of view" (*Samuel Johnson: A Life* [New York: Holt, 2009], 186). If so, the best candidate before 1772 was Bennet Langton, whom Johnson consistently regarded as a lenient judge (*Letters* 1:106–7, 171, 192, 265, 267), and to whom he gave key manuscripts. See Lyle Larsen, "Dr. Johnson's Friend, the Worthy Bennet Langton," *Age of Johnson* 20 (2010): 145–72.

22. *Defence* 83; *Thraliana* 1:173; *Hebrides* 374.

23. *Defence* 40, 71, 95. See *Diaries* 146–47.

24. See Richard B. Schwartz, *Boswell's Johnson: A Preface to the "Life"* (Madison: University of Wisconsin Press, 1978), 74–81, on autobiographical reflections in Johnson's published writings and private Latin poetry. For Johnson's account of the meeting with George III, see *Letters* 1:278–79 and Hyde MS 10 (749), Houghton Library.

25. *BP* 9:257–58; *Hebrides* 300. "Duert" seems the only possible reading of what Boswell wrote. Up to this point and most of the time afterward, Boswell wrote his often detailed entries from notes written soon afterward, but not during conversations—as he insisted when Garrick later accused him of doing this (*Extremes* 257). See, however, *Anecdotes* 31, *Corr.4*: 314, and what Boswell first wrote at the bottom of *Life ms* 2:36.

26. *Diaries* 142–43, 146–67.

27. *Yale-SJ* 2:264 (*Idler* 84)—see also 2:314 (*Idler* 102). *Diaries* 14, 20–21, 9–10. In 1734, perhaps in anticipation of his marriage, Johnson succinctly reported in Latin, under the title "ANNALES," a series of key events, starting with his birth in 1709, then his extended stay with Cornelius Ford in the autumn of 1725 and ending with his recent proposal to edit Politian's *Poems* (*Diaries* 24–29).

28. *Diaries* xv, 146, 119, 121; *Thraliana* 1:173; *Life* 4:375; *Hebrides* 300. When he first published the *Annals*, Richard Wright concluded from Johnson's "enumerations of particular dates in the blank pages of the book, that he intended to have finished these Annals, according to this plan, with the same minuteness of description in every circumstance and event" (*Diaries* xiv). Wright also noted after the first paragraph that "this was written in January, 1765," without explaining how this was known. (The manuscript has not been reported since it was sold at Sotheby's in 1819.) If Johnson began in 1765, he worked at this text over time, since there are references to 1767 and 1768, seemingly written even later (*Diaries* 5, 8).

29. On Johnson's "desire to protect his privacy," see John A. Vance, "The Laughing Johnson and the Shaping of Boswell's *Life*" (Vance 221–23).

30. *Diaries* 161. For a later example of autobiographical remembering directly prompted by Boswell's project, read first Johnson's answer on 18 April 1783 to Boswell's question about walking (*Applause* 100), then what he wrote Chambers the next day (*Letters* 4:125).

31. *BP* 9:264; *Corr.2*: 5–8; *Thraliana* 1:173. The texts Johnson struck were "Preface to the Translation of Sully's Memoirs" and "Remarks on the Chaplain Lindsey's Account of the conquest of Goree." Percy's original list is part of the Donald & Mary Hyde Collection of Dr. Samuel Johnson at the Houghton Library.

32. *BP* 9:266; *Defence* 134.

Chapter 5: Embracing the Biographer (1772–1773)

1. *Defence* 96; *Life ms* 2:83; *Later Years* 40–41.

2. *Letters* 1:392–93, 397.

3. *Letters* 1:394; *Wife* 322; *Letters* 1:272, 363.

4. *Letters* 2:8.

5. *Corr.6*: 316; Yale L52; *Corr.4*: 16, 44–45, 49; *Defence* 139; *Corr.3*: 17.

6. *Later Years* 40–41; *Life* 2:203–4; *Life ms* 2:82–83.

7. *Letters* 2:25, 8, 8n5.

8. *Corr.6*: 326; *Defence* 160–68. For Boswell's supping, dining, or breakfasting with Lord Mountstuart on almost half the days from 14 April through 4 May, see *BP* 6:118–22, 124, 131.

9. *Diaries* 130, 148. For forgetting resolutions, see *Diaries* 147, 157–58. See also Greg Clingham, *Johnson, Writing, and Memory* (New York: Cambridge University Press, 2002), 31–32.

10. *Diaries* 80, 146–50; *Defence* 126–29; *Letters* 1:391.

11. *Defence* 171–75; *Diaries* 153–57.

12. *Defence* 171–77.

13. *Defence* 73, 102, 169; *BP* 6:123.

14. *Defence* 95; *Extremes* 302; *Laird* 470; *Diaries* 153–157, 225; *Letters* 4:27.

15. *Letters* 2:28.

16. *Diaries* 155–56; *Defence* 174–75.

17. *Defence* 57–58; *Corr.3*: 27; *BP* 6:119; *Letters* 2:27. Boswell met Garrick in 1760; Goldsmith and Johnson in 1762–1763; Chambers, Langton, and Percy in 1768; Reynolds and George Colman the elder in 1769; Burke and Beauclerk in 1772. He corre-

sponded with Garrick, Goldsmith, Johnson, Langton, and Percy. Though Boswell first mentioned the Club in his journal for 1772 (*Defence* 58), he surely had heard about it earlier, and perhaps noticed on 16 October 1769 that Johnson, Reynolds, and Goldsmith all went to a meeting after dining with him.

18. *Corr.*3: 27; *Hebrides* 53n2; *BP* 6:120–24.

19. *Life ms* 2:100–3.

20. *Life ms* 2:100; *BP* 6:130–31; *Hebrides* 53.

21. *BP* 6:132–39. The words in brackets were not in Boswell's detailed notes, but were added for the *Life* (*Life ms* 2:105). The next day, Johnson wrote Hester Thrale, "I dined in a large company at a Dissenting Booksellers yesterday, and disputed against toleration, with one Doctor Meyer [Mayo]" (*Letters* 2:30).

22. *BP* 6:140–41. Curley focuses on this scene from Chambers's perspective (*Sir Robert Chambers,* 148–49); Bruce Redford describes the revisions (Redford 148–49). See also Bate 486–88, and Greg Clingham, *James Boswell: The Life of Johnson* (Cambridge: Cambridge University Press, 1992), 52–55.

23. *Hebrides* 5; *BP* 6:126. For Johnson's health, see *Diaries* 154; *Letters* 2:9–11, 14, and 16.

24. *Life* 2:262; Chapman 1:332; *Letters* 2:41–42.

25. *Letters* 1:41–44; *Life ms* 2:117. For Johnson's "impatience" to see Boswell, though old men "seldom" feel this, see *Hebrides* 307. Boswell added "arm-in-arm" in revising. For Beattie's absence from Scotland during Johnson's visit, see *Letters* 2:44, 42n8.

Chapter 6: Cooperation and Rivalry in Scotland
(14 August to 22 November 1773)

1. *Letters* 2:52–53.

2. Yale J33, 7; Yale L996; *Hebrides* 79.

3. Boswell's original journal (apart from pages 507–64) and Johnson's letters are easily accessible. Johnson's *Journey* and Boswell's *Tour* are regularly printed together; and *Johnson and Boswell in Scotland: A Journey to the Hebrides,* ed. Pat Rogers (New Haven: Yale University Press, 1993), allows readers easily to compare all three surviving accounts, though for the first two months, Rogers prints the edited *Tour* rather than the journal Johnson read.

4. *Hebrides* 255, 127–28, 78–79.

5. For additional talk about common friends, see *Hebrides* 69, 104, 242, 345 (Goldsmith); 53, 209, 272 (Beauclerk); 64, 272, 292 (Langton); 53, 171–72, 234, 321, 345 (Burke); 73, 208, 255 (Reynolds).

6. *Hebrides* 192, 173–74, 299–300. For seeking time apart, see *Letters* 2:73; *Hebrides* 110–11, 137–40 (see also *Letters* 2:88); 160, 222, 303, 345; for gallop, see *Hebrides* 285; for shells, 321. On 16 September, Johnson went without Boswell to see "Rorie More's cascade in grand fullness" (175), and the next day Boswell explored a ruin without Johnson (178–82).

7. *Hebrides* 215–16 (clergy—see also 233–34). For challenges, see *Hebrides* 107, 263, 302.

8. *Hebrides* 107 (milk); 265 (posts); 58 (macaroni).

9. *Hebrides* 227 (adventure); 217 (foxes); Pat Rogers, *Johnson and Boswell: The Transit of Caledonia* (Oxford: Clarendon Press, 1995), 23; *Letters* 2:62, 75, 98, 102 (health). Though John J. Burke, Jr., has suggested that Boswell "simply chose not to record" Johnson's complaints ("The Documentary Value of Boswell's *Journal of a Tour to the Hebrides,*" in *Fresh Reflections on Samuel Johnson,* ed Prem Nath [Troy, N.Y.: Whitston, 1987], 356–57), I think it more likely that Johnson competitively resisted complaining.

10. *Hebrides* 37n9, 64, 344; for Johnson's resistances, see *Hebrides* 236, 290, 302, 314–15.

11. Brian Finney, "Boswell's Hebridean Journal and the Ordeal of Dr. Johnson," *Biography* 5 (1982): 332. Finney's illuminating article is worth reading along with this chapter and the next.

12. Rogers, *Transit of Caledonia,* 139–70; *Hebrides* 35 (see also *Letters* 2:54), 72 (see also *Letters* 2:62), 99. Even before they left Edinburgh, Boswell persuaded Johnson to leave behind the pistols he had brought from "an erroneous apprehension of violence" (*Hebrides* 33); but at Montrose, Johnson grew angry when Boswell suggested he bring lemons, since he did not want to be thought a "feeble man who cannot do without anything" (*Hebrides* 50). Some overlap with the flight after Culloden was inevitable, but Johnson and Boswell eagerly solicited firsthand accounts of what had occurred.

13. *Letters* 2:54–57, 88; *Hebrides* 35–36, 42, 141–48, 84, 96.

14. *Hebrides* 106–13; *Letters* 2:72–77; *Journey* 48 (on Johnson's fear). I agree with Finney that Johnson's behavior "reveals his deep-seated feelings of dependence on his young travelling companion," but not that "through this disturbing incident Boswell is made to realize . . . the changing nature of their relationship" ("Boswell's Hebridean Journal," 324).

15. *Hebrides* 114–17, *Defence* 96–99, and *Letters* 2:77 (Sir Alexander and his wife); *Hebrides* 133–35 and *Letters* 2:87 (Raasay); *Hebrides* 143 (bones; see also 319); *Hebrides* 75, 84 (ghosts; see also *Letters* 2:92).

16. *Hebrides* 159–61 and *Letters* 2:90–91 (Flora Macdonald); *Hebrides* 165–66 and *Letters* 2:91 (to Dunvegan); *Hebrides* 166–67 (Norman and Lady MacLeod); *Hebrides* 199 and *Letters* 2:93 (Ullinish); *Hebrides* 212 and *Letters* 2:93 (Talisker); *Letters* 2:85, 87 (waiting).

17. *BP* 1:128 (Boswell's source was Hume, who heard the story from Wilkes). Irma Lustig first suggested to me that Johnson's aggressive teasing—see *Wife* 156, *Defence* 87—might indicate envy of the pleasure Boswell got from freely exercising his sexual potency.

18. *Hebrides* 100. Johnson did not mention this episode in *Letters* 2:65 and did not report this conversation in *Journey* 32. See also John B. Radner, "Johnson's and Boswell's Sexual Rivalry," *Age of Johnson* 5 (1992): 201–46.

19. *Hebrides* 159–61, 165; *Letters* 2:67, 72.

20. *Hebrides* 176–77 (see also 167–68). For Boswell's fear of castration, see *Later Years* 116–18.

21. *Hebrides* 165; Finney, "Boswell's Hebridean Journal," 323; *Later Years* 74. For Boswell's writing the entry for 13 September after the "seraglio" episode, see Radner, "Sexual Rivalry," 208–9 and note 10.

22. *Hebrides* 226 (see also 229–30). For an earlier complaint that Johnson lacked good humor, see *Hebrides* 68.

23. *Hebrides* 293–94; *Letters* 2:116 (see also *Hebrides* 368).

24. *Hebrides* 183, 169, 174–76, 192; *Letters* 2:75; *Diaries* 160, 157.

25. *Hebrides* 185, 236, 314–15 (see also 290, 302).

26. *Letters* 2:100–1 (see also 93–94); *Hebrides* 247–51; *Journey* 132 (see also *Hebrides* 431–32).

27. *Hebrides* 107 (see also Bate 469), 267.

28. *Hebrides* 263–64. Nine days later Johnson faulted Boswell for not observing that their room on Mull was "the prettiest room we have seen since we came to the Highlands" (*Hebrides* 302).

29. *Hebrides* 285 (see also 240, 133), 160, 222–23, 173–74. On 9 October, when Boswell "was fatigued" from an uphill climb, he judged a scalck "a reasonable indulgence" (*Hebrides* 285). See J. S. Madden, "Samuel Johnson's Alcohol Problem," *Medical History* 11 (1967): 141–49.

30. *Hebrides* 324–38 (see also 201), 363–64, 347 (see also 112); *Letters* 2:106–7 (see also 77).

31. *Hebrides* 344–45, 336. Boswell wrote just brief notes for the nineteen days from 22 October to 9 November, then wrote brief entries for 10–11 November, their first days in Edinburgh.

32. *Hebrides* 365 (see also 65–66), 374–76 (see also 369); *Letters* 2:102–3, 110, 115; *Journey* 161.

Chapter 7: Negotiating and Competing for Narrative Control (14 August to 22 November 1773)

1. For the Wales journal, see *Diaries* 163–222; for France, for which only the second of three volumes survives, see *Diaries* 228–56.

2. *Letters* 2:73; *Hebrides* 333, 241–42, 270, 315; Rogers, *Transit of Caledonia*, 112–13, 136–37. J. D. Fleeman, ed., *A Journey to the Western Islands of Scotland* (Oxford: Clarendon Press, 1985), xxxviii.

3. Yale J33, 7, and Yale L996. For memories, resolutions, and longings or regrets in Johnson's later journals, see *Diaries* 176, 201, 238.

4. *Corr.*4: 55. Surviving entries and notes for Boswell's previous eighty-six (or more) days with Johnson fill about 163 pages in print, but surviving entries for the first sixty-five days of this trip fill more than 300 pages.

5. *Hebrides* 45, 62, 121; *Letters* 2:95; Gordon Turnbull, "'Generous Attachment': The Politics of Biography in the *Tour to the Hebrides*," in *Dr. Samuel Johnson and James Boswell*, ed. Harold Bloom (New York: Chelsea House, 1986), 228. For a description of Boswell's journal, see *Catalogue* 1:16–18.

6. *Hebrides* 411–12. For Boswell's "amorous constitution," mentioned in a passage written in 1782 and shown Johnson in 1784, see *Hebrides* 353, 353n2. For a nuanced analysis of this "ordeal," see Finney, "Boswell's Hebridean Journal," 319–34.

7. For blanks, see *Hebrides* 97, 234, 294, 304, 307, 342; for topics, see 153, 188, 193, 329 (see also 60, 165, 219); for Chesterfield, see 97–98. Boswell's many references to Samuel Ogden's *Sermons on Prayer* (*Hebrides* 46, 63, 249–50, 317–18, 330) also invited Johnson to engage with a topic he had refused to consider at length in 1769 or 1772 (*Hebrides* 46, 63, 249–50, 317–18, 330, 336; see also Robert C. Walker, "Boswell's Use

of 'Ogden on Prayer' in *Journal of a Tour to the Hebrides*," *Age of Johnson* 19 [2009]: 53–68).

8. See *Hebrides* 211–12 (see also 433), 297–98, 298n1.

9. *Hebrides* 183, 322 (see also *BP* 9:265), 235.

10. *Hebrides* 183, 121–22, 188 (see also 193), 243.

11. *Hebrides* 110–13. See *Extremes* 49–50 and 50n.6 for Boswell's consciousness that he was addressing those not privy to what he would automatically know or recall.

12. *Hebrides* 176–77. Also see *Hebrides* 263 for Boswell's response to the dunes on Coll—a reaction that angered Johnson.

13. *Hebrides* 294–96, 320–22; *Corr.*3: 33. See Finney, "Boswell's Hebridean Journal," 228.

14. *Hebrides* 162–63, 63, 105, 112, 118.

15. *Hebrides* 231, 243. Boswell shows Johnson taking the lead in conversations more often than in the past (*Hebrides* 47–48, 96–97, 229, 374; see also *Letters* 2:73, 83–84, 91, 105).

16. *Hebrides* 36, 127, 199, 256–57, 232, 236; see also 47, 170, 244, 299.

17. *Hebrides* 167–70, 165.

18. *Hebrides* 174, 103, 293, 208, 287–88, 322; 99, 80, 233, 64 (see also 218, 236, 257, 301–2, 341). For critical detachment in earlier journals, see *GT2* 287; *Wife* 153–54; *Defence* 119, 126. Also see William C. Dowling, *The Boswellian Hero* (Athens: University of Georgia Press, 1979), 108–9.

19. *Hebrides* 188.

20. *Hebrides* 244–45, 106, 64; *Corr.*3: 49. For a suggestive discussion of the active role played by readers of journals, see Margo Culley, introduction to "A Day at a Time: Diary Literature of American Women from 1764 to 1985," in *Women, Autobiography, Theory,* ed. Sidonie Smith and Julia Watson (Madison: University of Wisconsin Press, 1998), 218–21.

21. *Hebrides* 241–42,188, 271, 293, 302, 226; *Letters* 2:115.

22. For Wilkes—and also Garrick—reacting to what they heard from those who had read Boswell's Hebrides journal in 1775, see *Extremes* 242, 257. For a suggestive account of how Boswell was translating "Johnson's private oral culture . . . into a written system," see Stuart Sherman, *Telling Time: Clocks, Diaries, and English Diurnal Form, 1660–1785* (Chicago: University of Chicago Press, 1996), 205.

23. *Hebrides* 244–45 (see also 216). The page (or pages) describing the "little house" is missing.

24. *Hebrides* 106, 218 293–94, 245 (see also 216), 298n3, 300. For autobiographical sharing, see 45, 50, 169, 174, 176, 192, 252.

25. *Hebrides* 226; *Letters* 2:95; *Hebrides* 45, 177.

26. *Ominous* 102; *Letters* 2:209, 223, 228, 239; *Hebrides* 257. For Langton, see *Letters* 1:106–7, 164. When Johnson linked Boswell and his journal with "such a faithful Chronicler as Griffith" (*Letters* 2:95)—alluding to lines from Shakespeare's *Henry VIII* (IV.ii.69–72) that Boswell later quoted at the start of the *Life* (1:24)—he came close to alerting Mrs. Thrale to his young traveling companion's new role (see Sherman, *Telling Time,* 221).

27. *Hebrides* 299.

28. *Letters* 2:54; *Hebrides* 271, 302. For a discussion of Johnson's extensive correspondence with Hester Thrale, see Bruce Redford, *The Converse of the Pen: Acts of Intimacy in the Eighteenth-Century Familiar Letter* (Chicago: University of Chicago Press, 1986), 206–44.

29. *Hebrides* 79, 93, 136, 175, 302. Johnson at least twice rebuffed Boswell's attempts to compromise Mrs. Thrale (*Hebrides* 105, 348–49); and when Boswell asked Johnson for an ode he had composed for her on Skye, Johnson responded, "I'd as soon give you my ears" (136).

30. *Hebrides* 114 (see also 148), 111; *Letters* 2:73 (see also 66), 62–67, 81–84, 75–77.

31. *Letters* 2:54, 65, 103, 73, 94–95, 71.

32. *Letters* 2:72–73, 78, 95, 104–105, 100, 102, 103, 108, 117, 119.

33. For the trip's self-consciously becoming memory even before completed, see *Letters* 2:94–95, *Hebrides* 329.

34. *Letters* 2:50; *Yale-SJ* 16:118 (*Rasselas*, ch. 32); *Letters* 2:86, 72, 94–95; *Diaries* 238; *Letters* 2:114, 3:66.

35. *Hebrides* 307, 188, 375–76 (see also 443). "I know Mrs. Boswell wished me well to go," Johnson wrote after reaching London (*Letters* 2:120).

36. *Hebrides* 391, 341. For early anticipations of Johnson's book, see *Edinburgh Examiner* 20:309 and *Corr.*3: 37n31.

Chapter 8: Collaboration Manqué (November 1773 to May 1775)

1. *Letters* 2:119–20; *Defence* 197–98, 200–2; *Corr.*6: 338.

2. *Tinker* 1:196; *Life* 2:269–70; *Yale* L996; Register (Yale M253 for December 1773 and January 1774); Yale C2308 (see also Yale C2306, quoted in *Defence* 197); *St. James's Chronicle* or *British Evening Post* for 29 January–1 February 1774 (see *Corr.*3: 45n3).

3. *Letters* 2:123–25, 127–28.

4. *Life* 2:275; see *Life ms* 2:120n1.

5. *Letters* 2:133–34, 128.

6. *Corr.*3: 42–44; *Corr.*4: 59–61; *Tinker* 1:203; *Letters* 2:140, 142. Forbes's letter to John Forbes (15 February 1775) is quoted in *Journey to the Western Islands of Scotland*, ed. Fleeman, xxvii.

7. *Letters* 2:144.

8. *Defence* 216. Boswell opened the entry for the day he received Johnson's letter (25 June)—an entry probably written after he replied but before he heard again from Johnson—by recalling how "Mr. Samuel Johnson has often recommended to me to keep a Journal," confirming that he was a true disciple (215).

9. *Letters* 2:145–46 (see also 147–48, 170); *Corr.*3: 44–45. Four of the nine children born to Hester Thrale in the previous ten years had already died, and Ralph Thrale would die in July 1775, two months after the birth of another daughter (Mary Hyde, *The Thrales of Streatham Park* [Cambridge, Mass.: Harvard University Press, 1976], xii).

10. *Letters* 2:150 (see also 166); *Life* 2:283; *Diaries* 191; *Defence* 225, 228–31, 235–36.

11. *Life* 2:283–84, 285n1. The letter dated 30 August in the *Life* is surely the one listed in the Register (Yale M253) for 30 July. It responds to what Johnson wrote on 4 July; and its leisurely tone does not fit Boswell's mood from 10 August through 10 September,

when he wrote many letters hoping to get Reid's sentence commuted (see Yale L505, 1206, 1029–30, 1092, 380, 1103).

12. *Defence* 227, 235–36. Gordon Turnbull, "Boswell and Sympathy: The Trial and Execution of John Reid" (Clingham 112).

13. *Letters* 2:149–50.

14. *Defence* 315–16, 322 (see also *Later Years* 106–7); *Ominous* 12–13; *Letters* 2:153–56; *Caledonian Mercury*, 30 October 1773, 3.

15. *Journey* 119, 97 (compare the famous passage in Tacitus's *Aricola: ubi solitudinem faciunt, pacem appellant* ["they make a wilderness and call it peace"]), 58, 91–92. For Johnson's inner debate, see John B. Radner, "The Significance of Johnson's Changing Views of the *Hebrides*," in *The Unknown Samuel Johnson*, ed. John J. Burke, Jr., and Donald Kay (Madison: University of Wisconsin Press, 1983), 131–49.

16. For a wish not to be forgotten, see *Journey* 37. Hester Thrale reported regularly telling Johnson that his letters "were better than the printed book" (*Anecdotes* 106). For a comparison of these letters with the *Journey,* see Rogers, *Transit of Caledonia,* 108–39.

17. *Journey* 130, 49–50, 161, 148.

18. *Journey* 49 (see also *Letters* 2:77), 119–20 (see also *Letters* 2:100, *Hebrides* 250–51). Boswell, however, thought Johnson still treated the storm "too lightly" (*Hebrides* 250n8).

19. *Journey* 3, 11 (see also 138, 144, 145), 125 (see also 133), 117 (compare 51), 153.

20. *Journey* 12. On being in charge, compare *Journey* 20 (on the Buller of Buchan) with *Hebrides* 72 and *Letters* 2:62, and compare *Journey* 42 (on distributing coins at Glensheals) with *Hebrides* 108 and *Letters* 2:74.

21. *Journey* 48.

22. *Journey* 66, 71 (see also 145). For Johnson's identification with Odysseus, see *Letters* 1:92 and Lawrence Lipking, *Samuel Johnson: The Life of an Author* (Cambridge: Harvard University Press, 1998), 49, 32.

23. Edward Tomarkan, "Travels into the Unknown: *Rasselas* and *A Journey to the Western Islands of Scotland,*" in Burke and Kay, *Unknown Samuel Johnson,* 150–67. Compare *Letters* 2:73 with *Journey* 40–41, on the moment when Johnson decided to write his book; *Letters* 2:166, 170.

24. For Boswell's letter of 3 January 1775, see *Life ms* 2:123.

25. *Letters* 2:170, 166, 172, 182; *Ominous* 64; *Life* 2:291; Yale L998; Yale C946, 1450. For Boswell's comments and corrections, see Mary Lascelles, *Notions and Facts: Collected Criticism and Research* (Oxford: Clarendon Press, 1972), 161–68.

26. *Letters* 2:171 (see also 178); *Life* 2:293–94; Yale L997.

27. *Letters* 2:168; *Ominous* 67. Readers wishing to sample the ongoing debate about Johnson and Macpherson might start with two articles in *The Age of Johnson* 17 (2006): Thomas M. Curley's "Samuel Johnson and Truth: The First Systematic Detection of Literary Deception in James Macpherson's *Ossian*" (119–96), and Nick Groom's "Samuel Johnson and Truth: A Response to Curley" (197–202).

28. *Letters* 2:171; *Hebrides* 317 (see also *Letters* 2:106); Niall Rudd, *Samuel Johnson: The Latin Poems* (Lewisburg, Penn.: Bucknell University Press, 2005), 58–59; *Ominous* 63–64 (see also 146); *Letters* 2:182 (contrast 146, 150, 154, 166–67, 171, 178). Initially Boswell considered including Johnson's entire letter and parts of his reply (*Life ms* 2: 124n8, 2:130n1).

29. *Corr.*3: 49; Yale C1267 (Forbes); *Hebrides* 378.

30. Yale C1451; *Ominous* 87.

31. *Ominous* 157. Based on Boswell's journal (*Ominous* 87–161), his correspondence with Temple (*Corr.*6: 356–79), Johnson's letters to Hester Thrale (*Letters* 2:205–9), and *Life ms* 2:168–69, Johnson and Boswell were together on fifteen of Boswell's first thirty days in London (21 March through 19 April), and on twelve of his final eighteen (5–22 May).

32. *Ominous* 102 (Boswell is quoting from the end of Pope's *Essay on Man* [4:385–86]—lines he quoted on the title page when he finally published his journal, ten years later); Yale C1074 (Dilly); *Corr.*6: 364, 372, 403. For Kames, see *Ominous* 68.

33. *Ominous* 102, 136. Stuart Sherman noted Boswell's initial defiance, which Boswell masked by describing Reynolds's reaction before he reported Johnson's request that he not share the journal (*Telling Time*, 214). For Boswell's wish for reciprocal sharing from Hester Thrale, see Clifford, *Hester Lynch Piozzi*, 125, and *Impossible Friendship* 29.

34. *Ominous* 103–5; *Journey* 55 (see also *Hebrides* 285); *Ominous* 99, 111. Similarly, Boswell expressed anger at Margaret mainly when drunk (*Later Years* 122–23; *Ominous* 178, 195).

35. *Ominous* 116–17, 127–28, 134; *Life ms* 2:158. Johnson's advice about journals is not reported in the journal.

36. *Ominous* 99, 111–13, 104–5 (see also *Applause* 101–2). Just before describing what had happened at the Club, Boswell "counterbalance[d]" Johnson's roughness by reporting how Johnson had told Blair and others that the day he met Boswell was "one of the happiest days in his life" (*Ominous* 110).

37. *Ominous* 128 (see also 95), 116–17, 147–48, 99–100. Boswell recorded only a single "rough" remark (134), and just one moment of embarrassing public teasing (151–53).

38. *Corr.*6: 364, 403; *Ominous* 103.

39. *Defence* 233; *Ominous* 77.

40. *Life* 3:122–123n2; *Ominous* 155, 146–47, 147n6 (see also 139 for the "lascivious" fondness described in entries for 10–11 April); *Diaries* 225; Samuel Johnson, *Dictionary of the English Language*, 2 vols. (London, 1773; reprinted Beirut: Librarie du Liban, 1978), 2:2103. Johnson had used "viaticum" in describing the last days of Father Paul Sarpi (*Works* [London, 1825], 6:269), and in writing to Bennet Langton when his sister, Elizabeth, thought she was dying (*Letters* 1:387). He would do so again at the end of his own life (*JM* 2:155).

41. *GT1* 119.

42. *Corr.*6: 372 (see also *Ominous* 102); *Ominous* 132 (see also *Defence* 118–19); *Corr.*6: 377, 403.

43. *Letters* 2:192, 205; *Life ms* 2:167; *Corr.*6: 375. On 18 May, Hester Thrale sent Boswell "a thousand Thanks" for his "entertaining Manuscript" (Yale C2265), but on 20 May, Johnson seems not yet to have known she had seen it, as he did two days later (*Letters* 2:207–9).

44. *Letters* 2:203; *Corr.*6: 375; *Ominous* 100, 157, 157n7; *Letters* 2:156 (see also *Hebrides* 175–76), 223n12 (see also *Impossible Friendship* 88). For discussion of the English bar in 1775, see *Ominous* 77–78, 88, 99–100, 103, 114, 153–54. Even Sir John Pringle no longer simply opposed the move, assuming that Lord Auchinleck agreed (*Ominous* 139; see also Yale C2308). Lord Mountstuart and the Duke of Queensberry

both claimed they would help secure an office to help compensate for the income Boswell initially would lose (*Ominous* 108, 139). For Boswell's getting new anecdotes from Johnson, gathering stories about Johnson, and hearing assessments, see *Ominous* 93, 98, 113–16, 130, 132–33, 135.

Chapter 9: Renegotiating the Friendship, Part 1 (1775–1777): Depression, Defiance, and Dependency

1. *Letters* 2:213–14; *Corr.*6: 392, 394; *Ominous* 158.

2. *Corr.*6: 379–80, 386, 396.

3. *Ominous* 158; *Corr.*6: 375–76, 392 (see also 378).

4. *Corr.*6: 392; *Life* 2:381 (see also *Life ms* 2:170n8); *Letters* 2:267. In the *Life*, Boswell did not quote from his July letter.

5. *Letters* 2:228, 265–67. Six years earlier, Johnson had simply assumed that marriage would make Boswell "more regular and useful" (*Letters* 1:329).

6. *Letters* 2:270; *Lives* 4:72.

7. *Corr.*3: 60, 64; *Life* 2:386–87; *Ominous* 163–64.

8. For drinking, see *Ominous* 173, 178; for gambling, *Ominous* 169–70, 173, 178, 191, 196, 199; for violence, *Ominous* 178, 195, 196.

9. *Life* 2:293–94; *Corr.*6: 358–59 (see also *Ominous* 80); *Public Advertiser* no. 14,178, 2; *Corr.*6: 394; *Corr.*3: 65; *Ominous* 172.

10. *Corr.*6: 403.

11. *Hebrides* 17n10; *Ominous* 179, 197, 200–1. For Boswell's earlier arranging to write the life of Lord Kames, as he would soon arrange to gather material concerning Sir Alexander Dick and others in his father's generation, see Richard B. Sher, " 'Something That Put Me in Mind of My Father': Boswell and Lord Kames" (Lustig 64–86, especially 78–79), and Yale L1081. For Johnson's contact with Hume, see Ernest Campbell Mossner, *The Life of David Hume* (Oxford: Clarendon Press, 1954), 393–94, 438, 586.

12. *Ominous* 201–2.

13. *Life* 2:410–11; *Letters* 2:280.

14. *Ominous* 177, 180, 187–88. For the Ayrshire election, see *Later Years* 92–95 and *Ominous* 184; for Pringle, see Yale C2314–2315.

15. *Ominous* 184–86 (see also 53–54 and *Defence* 137–38). For Boswell's sense that Johnson supported his "firmness" on male succession, see *Defence* 234, *Ominous* 59, and *Corr.*6: 396.

16. *Ominous* 205–6. See also *Ominous* 59–60 (Monboddo) and Yale C2308 (Pringle).

17. *Ominous* 206, 206n7, 209, 211, 214. Boswell also asked his brother David "what [he] should do as to the entail" (*Ominous* 210–11).

18. *Letters* 2: 284–85; *Ominous* 221 (see also 241). We have Johnson's letters complete except a portion of the fifth (24 February), but only a few sentences from Boswell's, plus paraphrases.

19. *Letters* 2:284, 287, 291–92, 294. For Johnson's awareness of helping Margaret, see *Letters* 2:289, 296.

20. *Letters* 2:298; *Life* 2:422; *Ominous* 232–33, 237, 240–41, 243, 245–48, 270; Register (Yale M253 for February–March 1776).

21. *BP* 11:276; *Ominous* 303 (see also 248, 263–71, 339–41, 343). For Boswell's contacting Lord Mountstuart in 1775, see *Ominous* 107–8, 110–11, 136–37, 139.

22. *Ominous* 256–60, 256n4, 262; *Life* 2:427. For Boswell's similar experience a year before, when he read excerpts from *Taxation No Tyranny*, see *Ominous* 80. In December 1775, Boswell wrote David Garrick that he would visit his brother Peter in Lichfield on his way to London (*Corr.*4: 69).

23. *Ominous* 290, 297. At Birmingham, Johnson "sent Mr. Boswel with Hector to Bolton's, while [he] sat with Mrs. Careless," as he wrote Hester Thrale when he also wrote Taylor that he was bringing Boswell, but "will take care that he shall hinder no business, nor shall he know more than you would have him" (*Letters* 2:309–11).

24. *Note Book* 7–8; *Ominous* 277, 287, 292. For more on Jones and "Fludyer" (really Fludger), see Clifford, *Young Sam Johnson*, 117–19.

25. *Ominous* 303; *Diaries* 105–8 (doubts and scruples; see also 64, 70, 83, 266, 276); *Thraliana* 1:384–85 (fear of insanity; see also *Hebrides* 174).

26. *Ominous* 295 (see also 298 and *Extremes* 264), 132; *Note Book* 10, 3–4.

27. *Ominous* 93, 116; *Hebrides* 64; *Ominous* 277. For Johnson's resolutions to attend public worship, see *Diaries* 57, 71, 73–74, 78, 106, 267–68, 309–10. For writing to support Christianity, see *Diaries* 294 and *Applause* 234.

28. *Letters* 3:79; *Ominous* 265. For Boswell's snatching other moments to write, see *Ominous* 253, 259, 263–64, 266.

29. *Ominous* 276–77, 286–87, 303 (see also 251).

30. *Ominous* 283, 263, 263n1, 286–87; *Corr.*6: 359 (see also *Ominous* 74, 81–82, 95).

31. *Ominous* 293, 298, 303–6, 315; Ober, *Boswell's Clap*, 18, 36–38. For "seraglio," see *Hebrides* 176–77; for "fucking," see Ominous 114 and *Dr. Campbell's Diary*, 68–69.

32. *Ominous* 303–7, 139.

33. *Ominous* 303–4, 306, 307n9, 319, 321, 322–23. For Charles Ryskamp and Frederick A. Pottle on this episode, see *Ominous* 323n5.

34. *Ominous* 322, 332, 337–38, 341, 343, 352–61; *BP* 11:273–75; *Corr.*6: 375–76, 382, 410, 415. For examples of later speculation about sexual conduct, see *Extremes* 107, 116, 129–30, 133, 135. For Boswell's evolving relationship with Mrs. Rudd, see Gordon Turnbull, "Criminal Biographer: Boswell and Margaret Caroline Rudd," *Studies in English Literature* 26 (1986): 511–35.

35. *BP* 11:265–66, 270, 272–75, 283–87, 290–91; *Extremes* 174, 322; *Letters* 2:332, 328. For Johnson's contentious relationship with Wilkes, who always was playfully friendly with Boswell, see Arthur H. Cash, "Samuel Johnson and John Wilkes," *Age of Johnson* 18 (2007): 67–130.

36. *BP* 11:272, 280; *Ominous* 352. For Boswell's laments about abstinence, see *BP* 11:270–71, 275–76.

37. *Letters* 2:329–30 (see also *Letters* 1:378), 334; *Diaries* 260; *Impossible Friendship* 40 (see also *Corr.*3: 71).

38. *Extremes* 5–10; *Ominous* 323; Register (Yale M253 for June 1776).

39. *Life* 3:86–87; *Ominous* 322, 223.

40. *Diaries* 257; *Ominous* 234, 241; *Extremes* 11–13.

41. *Life* 3:88–89; Register (Yale M253 for July 1776).

42. *Ominous* 265 ("Of a Particular Providence" immediately follows "Of Miracles" in *An Enquiry Concerning Human Understanding*), 278 (see also *Hebrides* 238); *Extremes* 24–27; *Life* 3:91–92; Tinker 1:255–56; *Corr.*3: 74. See *Later Years* 150–55, and Ernest Campbell Mossner, *The Forgotten Hume* (New York: Columbia University Press, 1943), 180–83, 206–7.

43. *Letters* 2:360–61, 364–66; Register (Yale M253 for November 1776; see also *Extremes* 57).

44. *Ominous* 270, 276, 290.

45. *Corr.*6: 419 (see also *Extremes* 13); *Extremes* 27–28. For religious and philosophical reflections, see *Extremes* 21–22, 32, 41–42, 54, 80, 82–84, 92–95, 99–100, 102–3, 109–15, 117–18; see also *Corr.*6: 422–32, Yale L1081, and Yale C2320.

46. *Ominous* 167, 167n2; *Extremes* 41, 54, 122; *London Magazine* 45 (1775): 570–71; *London Magazine* 46 (1776): 593–94; *London Chronicle,* 23–25 November 1776, 509.

47. *Life* 3:105; *Extremes* 67, 61–65, 69, 84, 89, 107. For a repeat of this pattern with Margaret in the first half of 1782, see *Laird* 419–20, 429, 437, 462.

48. *Extremes* 80, 82; *Letters* 3:8–9; *Corr.*6: 430–32.

49. *Extremes* 69, 78, 83; *Life* 3:101–2; Yale L665. See also *Hebrides* 311–12, 269, 428; *Letters* 2:365; Letters 2:104–5, 104n7, 104n11, 105n17.

50. *Letters* 3:7–10.

51. *Life* 3:105. Johnson was "much pleased" with Boswell's letter, which speculated at length about the English bar, and reported Margaret's promise to send a jar of orange marmalade as a token of friendship (Register: Yale M253 for February 1777).

52. *Extremes* 89–90, 93–94, 96, 100. For Boswell's "very agreeable dream" six years later of finding the diary in which Hume revealed he was "in reality a Christian and a very pious man," see *Applause* 176–77.

53. *Ominous* 232, 240–41; *Extremes* 100, 104.

Chapter 10: Renegotiating the Friendship, Part 2 (1777–1778): Confrontation, Collaboration, and Celebration

1. *Life* 3:106–7, 118; *Letters* 3:35, 39–40.

2. *Letters* 3:45, 47, 49, 55; Chapman 2:188; *Extremes* 134–35.

3. *Extremes* 138; *Letters* 3:56–57; Register (Yale M253 for August 1777). See also *Diaries* 268–69; *Letters* 3:51, 64–65; *Impossible Friendship* 45.

4. *Extremes* 142; *Letters* 3:48; *Life* 3:133.

5. *Extremes* 149–83: *Letters* 3:65–77; *Diaries* 275–77. For a fuller discussion, see John B. Radner, "Pilgrimage and Autonomy: The Visit at Ashbourne"(Lustig 203–27).

6. Chapman 2:207; *Letters* 3:68, 74.

7. *Note Book* 15–17, 19–20 (compare *London* 250); *Anecdotes* 7–11; Lustig, "The Friendship of Johnson and Boswell: Some Biographical Considerations," *Studies in Eighteenth-Century Culture* 6 (1977): 210. For other accounts of Johnson's initial turn to religion, see *Corr.*2: 192, 300, and *Applause* 123. For Johnson's refusal in 1775 to let Boswell copy his Diploma as Doctor of Laws from the University of Oxford, see *Life* 2:332n1.

8.*Extremes* 155 (see also 178 and *Wife* 332); *Life* 3: 208 See also *Ominous* 145, *Applause* 176, and Helen Deutsch, *Loving Dr. Johnson* (Chicago: University of Chicago Press, 2005), 122–24.

9. Chapman 2:209; Letters 3:57; see also *Letters* 2:156, 361, and *Impossible Friendship* 208–9.

10. *Life* 3:133–35; *Letters* 3:66, 74; *Extremes* 182, 163 (see also *Ominous* 284).

11. *Extremes* 169–71, 183; see also *Ominous* 99–100.

12. *Extremes* 173–77; Register (Yale M253 for October 1777); *Extremes* 165, 178, 181. For parallel encouragement in letters, see *Letters* 2:360, 364–65, and *Letters* 3:19. As he left Edinburgh in August, Lord Auchinleck vexed Boswell by saying, "You may be dead before this time twelve month" (*Extremes* 138).

13. *Extremes* 168–69, 166, 181, 173, 68–69.

14. *Extremes* 154–55; *Note Book* 22–23.

15. *Extremes* 157–58 (see also *Letters* 3:68 and *Diaries* 276). For 1773, see *Letters* 2:75 and *Hebrides* 183.

16. *Note Book* 23; see also *Letters* 3:103 and *Extremes* 297. For 1769, see *Wife* 332–34.

17. *Extremes* 182–84 (see also Life 3:205). See also *Extremes* 175–76 (a recent argument) and 165 (a warning about drinking). For Boswell's heavy drinking in the previous months, see *Extremes* 127–135, 138–39, 142.

18. *Life* 3:209–10. See also *Hebrides* 329 and *Extremes* 187.

19. *Extremes* 188, 185, 190–91; Register (Yale M253 for October 1777).

20. *Extremes* 181–82, 156–57; Radner, "Pilgrimage and Autonomy," 210–11. Boswell differed from Johnson on Ilam (*Extremes* 178), female "modesty" (180), and the power of music (183).

21. *Extremes* 155, 155n1. For earlier collaborative entries, see Boswell's report of their talk about entails (*Ominous* 256–57), and the fifth and eleventh paragraphs for 22 March 1776 (*Ominous* 287–88, 290). Compare what Boswell earlier wrote about "promiscuous concubinage" (*London* 272–73), which seems simply a paraphrase of Johnson. See also the many "Johnsonian" journal passages Boswell hoped his companion would applaud in his shared Hebrides journal (*Hebrides*, 63–64, 122, 137–51, 153, 178–80, 219–20, 224, 237, 241–42, 259–60, 329).

22. *Extremes* 158–59, 158n6. Boswell owned André-François Boureau Deslandes's *Réflexions sur les grands hommes qui sont morts en plaisantant* (1712).

23. *Extremes* 163–64 (compare to *Ominous* 146 and *Extremes* 80, 91, 102). For collaborative reflections on a range of other topics, see *Extremes* 163, 166, 168–71.

24. For a full discussion of these essays, see Margery Bailey's introduction (*Hypochondriack* 1:3–99).

25. *Diaries* 279; *Letters* 3:20, 74–98.

26. *Letters* 3:66, 98–100; *Life* 3:211; *Thraliana* 1:205.

27. *Letters* 3:101–4; Register (Yale M254 for February 1778); *Life* 3:219–21; *Extremes* 209; Yale L2082, 2038. See *Hypochondriack* 1:142–49.

28. *Extremes* 209–10, 217.

29. *Extremes* 215–16, 220, 350. I have added two days to the list compiled by Hitoshi Suwabe (Lustig 252–53): 16 April (see *Extremes* 288, top line, and 292, first full para-

graph), and 14 May (see Yale M144, 758). For descriptions of this journal (Yale J54 and J55), kept on loose sheets, see *Catalogue* 1:24–25.

30. *Life* 3:104–5; *Extremes* 221–22. For Johnson's sometimes-alarming poor health throughout 1777 and into 1778, see *Extremes* 211n6, and *Letters* 3:19, 21, 24, 52, 60, 68, 73, 93, 94, 99, 102. For a similar fantasy of Lord Auchinleck in heaven, see *Extremes* 100, 117–18.

31. *Life* 3:221; *Extremes* 225.

32. *Extremes* 168–69, 223, 225; 1 Corinthians 13:12; Register (Yale M254 for March 1778). A year earlier, Boswell had written that he "felt more agreeably when under parental awe than when unrestrained" (*Extremes* 34) — but not when his father was sarcastic and dismissive (*Extremes* 190; *Ominous* 270, 338).

33. *Extremes* 219, 181, 301–02. For 1777, see *Ominous* 256, 265, 278.

34. *Extremes* 224, 250, 290, 297.

35. *Extremes* 246, 250, 261. Much of the entry for Good Friday was not written until ten days afterward (294, lines 5–6); but the remarkably full entry for the 15th might have been written the following day, for which no entry has survived (291n8).

36. *Diaries* 287–92; *Extremes* 291–97; *Life* 3:302n3. For 1776, see *Diaries* 258; *Ominous* 315–16. For shared autobiographical anecdotes in 1778, see *Extremes* 245–46, 248, 251, 264, 273–74, 288, 299, 320, 327, 339–40. For Johnson's earlier and later reactions to Boswell's talk of rejoining his friends in heaven, see *Defence* 73 and *Applause* 215.

37. *Ominous* 352; Yale L665; *Extremes* 165, 128–29, 132; Yale C2779; *Extremes* 218, 279, 310, 318. For Johnson's support of Boswell's sobriety, see *Extremes* 225, 247–48, 251, 257 (Garrick), 300, 320–22 (Reynolds), 350.

38. *Ominous* 116 (1775); *Extremes* 165 (1777).

39. *Extremes* 287–88, 261. Felicity Nussbaum notes that both Boswell in the *Life* and Mary Knowles in the *Gentleman's Magazine* (61 [1791]: 502) flag Johnson's "unprecedented and irrational violence" at this dinner ("Boswell's Treatment of Johnson's Temper: 'A Warm West Indian Climate,'" *Studies in English Literature* 14 [1974]: 432n20). For a discussion of Mrs. Knowles's report of this conversation, including material Boswell did not include in his entry and later could not recollect, see Judith Jennings, "'By No Means in a Liberal Style': Mary Morris Knowles versus James Boswell," in *Women Editing, Editing Women: Early Modern Women Writer and the New Textualism,* ed. Ann Holinshead Hurley and Chanita Goodblatt (Newcastle upon Tyne: Cambridge Scholars Publishing, 2009), 227–56.

40. *Extremes* 299–301; see *Hypochondriack* 1:150–55.

41. *Diaries* 290; *Corr.*2: 195–96. For the quarrel with Percy and the reconciliation, see *Extremes* 274–75, 302, 311, 317, 319; also *Life* 3:272–78. For Boswell's help with earlier quarrels, see *Ominous* 133 and *Life* 1:385–88 (Thomas Sheridan); *Ominous* 345–50 and *Extremes* 174 (Wilkes); *Note Book* 18 and *Life* 4:431, 115n4 (Thomas Barnard, dean of Derry).

42. *Extremes* 328–29.

43. For Johnson's testiness to Langton, and Boswell's efforts to reconcile them, see *Defence,* 186; *Corr.*3: 35–37, 44–46; *Life* 2:279; *Letters* 2:147–48, 170. For the entries written on 7 May, see *Extremes* 278–79, 322–28.

44. *Extremes* 3 2 8–3 0, 3 1 7.

45. *Extremes* 3 3 1 (see also 2 4 8). For "No. 3 6," see *Extremes* 2 3 4, 2 5 2, 2 6 0, 2 6 2, 3 0 8, 3 1 1, 3 7 7, 3 2 7. For 1 7 7 6, see *Ominous* 3 2 2. For Boswell's "sanitized" account of this conversation, see Clingham, "Double Writing" (Newman 1 9 1–9 2).

46. *Extremes* 3 3 8, 3 3 6, 3 3 9; *Laird* 1 0 1–2.

47. *Extremes* 3 4 1–4 2; in the *Life*, Henry Thrale is not present (*Life* 3:3 4 9–5 1).

48. *Extremes* 2 9 2–9 3 —quoted by Anthony W. Lee at the start of "Mentoring and Mimicry in Boswell's *Life of Johnson*" (*Eighteenth Century* 5 1 [2 0 1 0]: 6 7–8 5).

Chapter 1 1: "Strangers to Each Other" (May 1 7 7 8 to March 1 7 8 1)

1. Yale L6 0 9.

2. *Extremes* 3 4 7; *Life* 3: 3 5 9–6 0. Boswell confessed to both Langton and Temple his own "unaccountable procrastinating indolence" in failing to write, despite his constant esteem and love (*Corr*.3: 9 4; Tinker 2:2 0 3). But early in 1 7 7 9, he still feared a "diminution of . . . affection & esteem" when Temple failed to write (Yale C2 7 9 5).

3. *Letters* 3:1 1 8–1 9; *Extremes* 2 9 2, 3 0 0.

4. All three letters are briefly described in the *Life* (3:3 6 6), though "dreary dejection" is used only in the Register (Yale M2 5 4 for August 1 7 7 8).

5. *Letters* 3:1 2 5, 1 1 8–1 9, 1 4 1–4 2; Samuel Johnson, *Dictionary* (1 7 7 3), 2:1 1 8 0 ("lune"); *Laird* 4 2–4 3; Register (Yale M2 5 4 for November 1 7 7 8). Johnson's "exhorting abstinence" is not mentioned in the *Life*.

6. Register (Yale M2 5 4 for January 1 7 7 9); *Laird* 4 7–4 9; *Life* 3:3 7 1–7 2.

7. *Letters* 3:1 5 6–5 7; *Laird* 5 6. See also *Corr*.2: 1 3.

8. *Life* 3:3 7 6.

9. *Laird* 9 8, 5 6, 7 1, 9 3; *Diaries* 2 9 3–9 4. Compare *Diaries* 2 2 4–2 5 and *Ominous* 1 4 5 (1 7 7 5); *Diaries* 2 8 8 and *Extremes* 2 9 7 (1 7 7 8).

10. *Laird* 6 9; *Life* 3:3 8 2. For heavy mid-April drinking, see *Laird* 7 5, 7 8, 8 0, 9 1, 9 3.

11. *Laird* 8 2–8 3, 9 0–9 2, 1 0 0. For Johnson's earlier and later praise of Beauclerk, see *Hebrides* 5 3; *Corr*.3: 1 0 4; *Letters* 3:2 3 1. For Hackman, see *Laird* 7 3–7 5.

12. *Laird* 1 0 2–3; *Life* 3:3 9 1–9 2; Tinker 2:2 8 4.

13. *Laird* 1 2 1–2 2; *Life* 3:3 9 5; *Letters* 3:8–9, 1 7 8. Compare what Johnson wrote a silent Langton in 1 7 6 6 (*Letters* 1:2 6 4–6 6).

14. *Life* 3:3 9 5–9 6; *Laird* 1 2 2–2 3.

15. *Letters* 3:1 8 1; *Laird* 1 3 5; *Life* 3:3 9 9; Yale L6 7 1.

16. *Laird* 1 3 7, 1 3 9–4 5; *Letters* 3:1 8 5–8 6, 1 8 9; Tinker 2:2 9 9–3 0 0.

17. *Laird* 1 2 6, 1 3 0–4 5; *Letters* 3:1 8 5.

18. *Life* 3:4 1 1–1 7.

19. *Letters* 3:1 9 9–2 0 0. For earlier praise of Burton, see *Letters* 1:3 9 4 and *Ominous* 2 7 7.

20. *Life* 3:4 1 3–1 7; *Letters* 3:2 1 5, 2 1 5n2 (Johnson is quoting Horace's *Epistles*, I.xiv.1 3); see also *Letters* 3:2 1 8. The four definitions of "fond" in the 1 7 7 3 edition of Johnson's *Dictionary* are the following: "Foolish; silly; indiscrete; imprudent; injudicious"; "Trifling; valued by folly"; "Foolishly tender; injudiciously indulgent"; "Pleased in too great a degree; foolishly delighted" (1:7 7 6).

21. Tinker 2:296–97; *Life* 3:418; *Letters* 3:220 (2 December 1779).

22. Register (Yale M254 for December 1779, January and March 1780); Yale C1269; *Life* 3:418. For Boswell's finances, see *Later Years* 194–95. Starting at the end of 1774, Boswell regularly took stock of each year's income and expenses, and planned, with Sir William Forbes, what needed adjusting (*Ominous* 49–51).

23. *Letters* 3:230–33; see *Hypochondriack* 1:136–37.

24. *Extremes* 223; *Hypochondriack* 1:148–49, 329; *Laird* 199.

25. Register (Yale M254 for May 1780); *Laird* 209.

26. *Letters* 3:280, 303–4; *Laird* 75.

27. *Laird* 177, 223, 237. For Dr. Dunbar, see *Letters* 3:282n5, 304; also *Hebrides* 65. For David's challenges, see *Laird* 230, 246–47. Boswell's Register (Yale M254) reports fifteen letters sent in April and twenty in May, but only ten in June (six announcing the birth of Elizabeth), six in July, and only one in the first twelve days of August. Entries for 18–19 May and 25–27 May are now missing, as are those for 6–11 June, 20–26 June, and 3–13 July.

28. *Laird* 223, 232–33; *Hebrides* 345n1, 436; *Laird* 230; Register (Yale M254 for August–October 1780). See also *Laird* 246–47, 256–57; Chapman 3:291.

29. *Laird* 241, 256; *Letters* 3:303; *Life* 3:438–39. Earlier, Boswell had promised Grange "excellent wit and wisdom" from his Ashbourne journal (*Corr.*1: 289).

30. *Letters* 3:317–18; *Life* 3:438; see *Defence* 73.

31. *Laird* 263, 267–72 (see also *Corr.*3: 110–11 and Tinker 2:309). Entries for 1–6 November, 15–16 November, 22 November–1 December, and 16–26 December are missing, along with the final eight pages of the Review (*Laird* 268, 269, 272, 276, 283).

32. *Laird* 272–73; see *Extremes* 221.

33. *Laird* 274–76. The letter to Johnson on 16 December is reported—but not described—in the Register (Yale M254: page 6 of loose leaves for December 1780), and is not mentioned in the *Life*.

34. *Yale-SJ* 4:245. For earlier collaboration with Johnson on depression, see especially the eighth and final paragraphs of no. 5 (*Hypochondriack* 1:136, 141) and the third and final paragraphs of no. 6 (1:143–44, 148–49).

35. *Hypochondriack* 2:40–46.

36. *Hypochondriack* 1:148–49, 2:46; *Laird* 279–83; Yale C159.2. For the essays Blair praised, see *Hypochondriack* 1:198–220.

37. Yale L1009; *Corr.*3: 113 For Johnson on free will, see *Extremes* 289–90; for Temple, see Yale C2803.

38. *Letters* 3:328; *Laird* 292.

Chapter 12: The Lives of the Poets *and Johnson's (Auto)biography (1777–1781)*

1. *Letters* 3:156. See *Lives* 1:14–50 and William McCarthy, "The Composition of Johnson's Lives: A Calendar," *Philological Quarterly* 60 (1981): 53–67. In composing the *Lives,* Johnson used his early *Savage* and Goldsmith's *Parnell,* and got Herbert Croft to supply a biography of Edward Young.

2. *Life* 3:108, 117, 96; *Laird* 141. For manuscripts and proofs, see *Extremes* 350;

Letters 3:156, 156n2, 328. For talk about the project and specific *Lives,* see *Extremes* 150, 230–231 and *Laird* 58, 71, 98–99.

3. *Lives* 1:248 (see also 253), 3:75, 3:1, 1:262, 4:31. For explicit or implied references to Boswell, see *Lives* 4:101, 179, 58.

4. *Lives* 4:68, 126, 172–73; *Extremes* 182.

5. *Lives* 2:148 (see also 122); *Life* 4:45; *Lives* 2:107, 2:125, 2:152–53, 2:62–63, 4:103, 3:200, 4:56.

6. *Lives* 3:38, 3:209, 3:20, 4:40–42, 3:18, 4:58 (see also *Letters* 3:89–90).

7. Robert DeMaria, Jr., *The Life of Samuel Johnson* (Cambridge, Mass.: Blackwell, 1993), 284–87.

8. *Letters* 3:248; see *Lives* 3:341; see also *Diaries* 111, 272–73. For Johnson's reliance on Nichols, see Frederick W. Hilles, "Johnson's Correspondence with Nichols: Some Facts and a Query," *Philological Quarterly* 48 (1969): 226–33.

9. *Lives* 2:8–9, 3:1, 3:100, 3:16.

10. *Lives* 2:178–79, 3:90–91, 4:11, 4:99, 4:103, 2:192, 2:200, 3:189.

11. *Defence* 175; *Lives* 2:101, 187–88.

12. *Lives* 2:399; 3:100 (and 351); 4:165 (and 452); 4:87 (and 355). See *Extremes* 330–31. Hester Thrale knew the identity of the other two women (*Anecdotes* 106); Boswell never reported asking.

13. *Lives* 4:36. For references to Sarah Johnson, see *Diaries* 111, 113, 272 and *Letters* 2:190–91. For an illuminating discussion of this passage concerning Pope's mother, written less than a year before the Uttoxeter visit, see Julie Crane, "Johnson and the Art of Interruption," *Age of Johnson* 19 (2009): 33.

14. *Life* 3:46; Gay W. Brack, "Tetty and Samuel Johnson: The Romance and the Reality," *Age of Johnson* 5 (1992): 168; *Diaries* 292, 319 (see also 127, 238).

15. *JM* 2:426–27 (see also *Corr.2:* 300); Rudd, *Johnson: Latin Poems,* 121–22, quoted in Nokes, *Samuel Johnson,* 332. See Clifford, *Young Sam Johnson,* 135; Bate 129. Jeffrey Meyers connects the Uttoxeter episode with the death of Henry Thrale (*Samuel Johnson: The Struggle* [Philadelphia: Basic Books, 2009], 418–19).

16. *Letters* 3:298, 3:318, 3:320, 4:443. For Nathaniel, see Clifford, *Young Sam Johnson,* 165–72, and Bate 162, 524. See also *Diaries* 8, 19, 67.

17. See Isobel Grundy, "Samuel Johnson: A Writer of Lives Looks at Death," *Modern Language Review* 79 (1984): 257–65.

18. *Diaries* 264; *Letters* 3:60. For Johnson's reviewing his whole career while writing these *Lives,* see Lipking, *Life of an Author,* 286.

19. *Letters* 3:236–37, 264, 280, 290, 296–97, 308.

20. *Diaries* 267, 300. For more on Johnson's health, see *Letters* 3:181–83, 189, 190, 221.

21. *Letters* 3:303, 324–25, 328; *Lives* 1:44.

22. *Diaries* 291–92, 294–96; compare *Diaries* 264; see also *Letters* 3:285.

23. *Diaries* 303–5.

24. *Diaries* 298–99, 301–2 (see also 144); *Thraliana* 1:454–55; Chapman 2:398.

25. *Diaries* 298, 302, 309–10 (see also 228 [18 September 1775]); *Yale-SJ* 16:156 (ch. 45). Johnson celebrated his birthdays with small dinners in 1782 (*Diaries* 332) and again in 1783 (*Letters* 4:199).

26. *Letters* 3:328–29.

Chapter 13: Reconnecting (1781–1783)

1. *Laird* 292–94, 304, 308, 301; *Life* 4:74; *Later Years* 208–10.

2. *Diaries* 304–6; *Letters* 3:299, 305–6, 330–32, 334, 337, 341. See Clifford, *Hester Lynch Piozzi*, 187; *Thraliana* 1:486–87; *Impossible Friendship* 60–61.

3. *Laird* 324; *Diaries* 52. For Thrale's and Johnson's thoughts about marriage, see Clifford, *Hester Lynch Piozzi*, 206–7, and Bate 554. For Hester Thrale's need "to divorce herself personally from Johnson," see William McCarthy, *Hester Thrale Piozzi: Portrait of a Literary Woman* (Chapel Hill: University of North Carolina Press, 1985), 107–8.

4. *Laird* 322–23 (from the *Life* ms). Already in 1776, Boswell had found Johnson "rather laxer in his notions [concerning religious orders] than in *The Rambler* and *Idler*" (*Ominous* 262).

5. *Laird* 316–21; *Later Years* 214. For a nuanced analysis of why Boswell composed this poem, which Bate found "in appalling taste" (Bate 554–55) and Brady thought "embarrassing" but also "exceptionally clever" (*Later Years* 211–12), see Lustig, "Friendship of Johnson and Boswell," 207–10.

6. *Life* 4:96; *Laird* 328–29.

7. *Laird* 329–330; 301n3; Larsen 86. That spring, Boswell probably speculated with Reynolds about whether Johnson "would yield to the amorous solicitations of the beautiful Duchess of Devonshire" (see *Applause* 113). For Boswell's attractiveness to women, see *Laird* 309–12, 314, 330–31, 338, 340–41, 361–62. For his anger at Lady Auchinleck's control of his father, see *Corr.6*: 396 and *Extremes* 118.

8. *Laird* 330–68. Boswell recorded no talk for 2 May, for instance, when he and Johnson were together before, during, and after dinner, but spent pages describing conversations with the Earl of Bute on 5 and 13 May, including some talk about Johnson's pension (*Laird* 344–45). I have added two meetings to those listed by Hitoshi Suwabe (Lustig 254–55): dinner at Paoli's on 16 April (*Letters* 2:335) and at Allen's on 22 May (*Laird* 361).

9. *Laird* 347, 361–62; *Life* 4:117–18. Boswell reported no heavy drinking after Johnson—and Paoli, too (*Laird* 346n8)—had rebuked him.

10. For Johnson's wish that Hester Thrale keep the brewery, see Gay W. Hughes, "The Estrangement of Hester Thrale and Samuel Johnson: A Revisionist View," *Age of Johnson* 14 (2003): 158–59.

11. *Laird* 370–76.

12. *Diaries* 298; *Laird* 374.

13. *Life* 4:123–24 (see also *Hebrides* 63–64), 128–31 (see also *Laird* 407n5). The dictated letter is Yale C1596.

14. Register (Yale M254: loose sheets for June–November 1781); *Laird* 392–93, 407–8, 407n5; Tinker, 2:314–15.

15. *Laird* 415n2, 416.

16. *Letters* 3:377, 4:3–4, 3:345 (see also 3:336: "When I am out of order I think it often my own fault").

17. *Corr.3*: 122; *Laird* 433–34; *Impossible Friendship* 69. To Burke, Boswell was quoting Addison's *Cato* (V.i.7), which in turn echoes *Hamlet* (V.ii.10–11).

18. *Diaries* 317; *Letters* 4:27–28. See also *Letters* 4:45, 72, 90, 112.

19. *Laird* 450, 439; Yale L1012 and Yale C2158; *Hypochondriack* 2:173–74, 178. For Boswell's emulation of Burke, see *Defense* 253, *Applause* 19, and Elizabeth Lambert, "Boswell's Burke: The Literary Consequences of Ambivalence," *Age of Johnson* 9 (1998): 210–11, 218–22.

20. *Impossible Friendship* 70; see *Thraliana* 1:535.

21. *Letters* 4:44–45.

22. *Laird* 451–52, 454–55; *Impossible Friendship* 73.

23. Chapman 3:293; *Letters* 4:70; *Impossible Friendship* 72; Register (Yale M254 for August 1782).

24. *Laird* 470. Boswell never reported asking Johnson.

25. *Diaries* 325; *Thraliana* 1:540–41, 528 (see also Bate 566–68); *Letters* 4:23, 38–39, 70–71.

26. *Later Years* 106; *Laird* 454, 474–75.

27. *Corr.3*: 126; *Laird* 476–77. See *Laird* 290, 467–68, 472–73; *Hypochondriack* 2:90–91.

28. Register (Yale M254 for September–October 1782); *Letters* 4:72 (see also *Letters* 2:364); Yale C2807. For Boswell's ambivalence about becoming a proper laird, see *Extremes*, 22, 42, 46, 67, 121, 171; *Laird* 402.

29. For the decision by 9 September, see *Corr.3*: 124–25.

30. *Laird* 481–82; *Applause* 6. For Boswell's finances as he became laird, see *Corr.8*: xli–xlii.

31. *Letters* 4:73 (see also 77); *Laird* 481. See *Corr.3*: 124–25.

32. *Laird* 480–82; *Applause* 11–12. See Lustig, "'My Dear Enemy,'" 233–34.

33. *Applause* 11–12, 22, 30–33, 37; *Laird* 108, 225, 232, 479; Yale L1086. See Sher, "Boswell and Lord Kames" (Lustig 64–86). When closer to death ten days later, Kames disappointed Boswell by saying "nothing edifying, nothing solemnly pious" (*Applause* 43; see also 45).

34. *Diaries* 337–42, 348 *Letters* 4:83. For Metcalfe, see *Letters* 4:75. Johnson did not mention finding letters from Boswell and his wife when he returned home, though he did report writing them on 7 December (*Diaries* 352, 354). But had Johnson seen their letters before he left for Streatham and Brighton, it would be difficult to explain his delay in writing.

35. *Letters* 4:90–91. For Johnson's fear a year earlier of being neglected, see *Letters* 3:379.

36. *Life* 4:157. For Johnson's earlier overtures, see *Letters* 2:329–30, 2:360, 3:42–3; 3:79, 3:99, 3:304, 3:318.

37. Tinker 2:314; *Applause* 50.

38. *Letters* 4:112 (see also *Letters* 4:73 and *Life* 4:163).

39. *Applause* 58.

40. For sobriety, see Yale L1014, 1015; Yale C2158, 2159; *Applause* 9, 29, 53. For thoughts of London, see *Corr.3*: 127 and *Applause* 10, 33.

41. For Johnson's drinking, see *Laird* 297.

42. *Corr.3*: 129–30, 133. See *Laird* 338–39, 351, 360–61, 364.

43. *Applause* 70–74, 77; *Letters* 4:113, 116; Yale L1015.

Chapter 14: *"Some Time Together before We Are Parted"*
(March 1783 to May 1784)

1. *Applause* 73–75 (see also *Corr.*1: 298). Johnson's often anthologized "On the Death of Dr. Robert Levet" is included in *Life* 3:137–38. In 1778, Boswell firmly rejected Garrick's claim that he wrote notes as people were speaking (*Extremes* 257). But when Hester Thrale Piozzi later suggested that Boswell regularly went to the other end of the room to write down what had just been said (*Anecdotes* 31), he admitted sometimes doing this — with Johnson's approval (*Corr.*4: 314). See Adam Sisman, *Boswell's Presumptuous Task* (London: Hamish Hamilton, 2000), 146–51.

2. *Applause* 74, 77–79, 82–83; *Letters* 4:45 ("peevish"), 118–19 ("venture").

3. *Applause* 83–84.

4. *Applause* 84–93.

5. *Applause* 90–91, 87. In the *Life,* Boswell reported Johnson's saying early in the visit, 'Boswell, I think, I am easier with you than with almost any body'" (*Life* 4:194).

6. *Applause* 90–91, 87, 96.

7. *Applause* 94, 96–97, 108; *Corr.*1: 298. For contact with Lord Mountstuart on days with entries, see *Applause* 81, 84, 86–87, 92–93, 121, 135, 144–46.

8. *Applause* 107, 113, 143–44 and 144n3 (see also 147–49); for letters, see Register (Yale M255 for April–May 1783). Boswell's adding a note on 25 May to what Johnson had written Wilkes the day before indicates contact otherwise undocumented (*Letters* 4:139n3). After Boswell realized on 11–12 April how little he could remember of talk ten days earlier (*Applause* 91–92), he seems to have kept full notes.

9. *Diaries* 358–59; *Thraliana* 1:558–61; *Letters* 4:135–37, 145.

10. *Letters* 4: 124–27, 133–34, 137 (see also 139, 160).

11. *Diaries of William Johnston Temple, 1780–1796,* edited with a memoir by Lewis Bettany (Oxford: Clarendon Press, 1929), 41; *Letters* 4:126.

12. *Applause* 98; *Letters* 4:4.

13. *Applause* 100, 106, 110.

14. *Applause* 117–18, 123–24, 128, 143, 146; *Diaries of Temple,* 40; *Laird* 348–51 (Wilkes in 1781).

15. *Hebrides* 231, 244; *Applause* 108, 109–10, 123–24.

16. *Applause* 102–3. See Johnson's rejection of "what is called hospitality," in which he also dramatically entered into Boswell's circumstances (*Applause* 101, 142; see *Defence* 84).

17. *Applause* 141.

18. *Applause* 151–54.

19. *Applause* 74, 152, 152n2 (see also *Ominous* 156n4).

20. *Corr.*4: 130; *Applause* 152; *London* 331.

21. *Applause* 154; *London* 284; *Letters* 1:329, 2:267, 4:127.

22. *Applause* 157–58.

23. *Applause* 158, 157; *Corr.*4: 135–38.

24. *Letters* 4:148–53, 173–74, 179, 196–97, 209, 211, 214–16, 218, 236–37, 276–77, 290, 319. For the visit to Bowles, see Bate 580–82. For Bowles's account of what Johnson said, see *Corr.*2: 192–96.

25. Register (Yale M255 for August 1783); Yale L1016 (see also *Corr.*1: 302); *Letters* 4:164, 189, 209.

26. *Applause* 160–63, 173; Register (Yale M255 for October–November 1783); *Letters* 4:180, 204, 221–22.

27. *Applause* 164, 167; *Corr.*4: 137–39 (see also 139n2).

28. *Letters* 4:262–64; *Life* 4:248.

29. *Applause* 170–71,172–76; *Life* 4:259, 259n1 (see also *Applause* 172 and *Later Years* 249–50). Boswell worried, however, that the pamphlet might offend Burke and Lord Mountstuart (*Applause* 203, 217).

30. *Applause* 174; Register (Yale M255 for January 1784).

31. Register (Yale M255 for February 1784); *Applause* 184–85; Yale L1097.

32. *Letters* 4:182–84, 196–97, 200–1, 205, 207–11, 214, 260, 265.

33. *Letters* 4:282, 285. For earlier references to Ramsay in Italy, see *Letters* 4:133, 189.

34. Yale C2161. See *Letters* 4:260.

35. *Applause* 191n7, 195–96. See Yale C984–5, 988 (Dick), 1374 (Gillespie), 867 (Cullen), 2045 (Monro), 578 (Brocklesby), 579 (Brocklesby to Hope), 1551–53 (Hope).

36. *Letters* 4:291. The paragraphs Boswell did not wish to have printed in the *Life* from this letter and from the one Johnson wrote on 18 March probably concerned Pitt, who was still prime minister in 1791, when the *Life* was published.

37. *Letters* 4:294–96, 300 (see also 323–24), 306; Hawkins, *The Life of Samuel Johnson, LL.D.*, ed. O. M. Brack (Athens: University of Georgia Press, 2009), 340–42; *Applause* 195; *Life* 4:271–72 (added to the original draft). For the lingering cold, see *Letters* 4:308, 310. For a careful review of the medical literature that might illuminate this "wonderful" evacuation, see William W. Fee, "Samuel Johnson's 'Wonderful' Remission of Dropsy," *Harvard Library Bulletin* 23 (1975): 271–88.

38. *Applause* 200; *Letters* 4:306.

39. *Letters* 4:310, 306. In the seven weeks from 11 February through 30 March 1784, Johnson wrote many more letters to Boswell (five) than to Bowles (one) or Taylor (one) or Langton (one) — even more than to Hester Thrale (three).

Chapter 15: "Love Me as Well as You Can" (1784)

1. *Corr.*3: 152, 149; *Corr.*8: 89. On 6–8 May, Johnson visited George Strahan in Islington; on 31 May and 1 June, Boswell was with Langton in Rochester; and on 4–8 June, Johnson remained in Oxford while Boswell returned to London. Boswell's journal and the *Life* report him being with Johnson on twenty-eight of the remaining days. They also both dined at Hoole's on 11 May (*Applause* 211) and at Taylor's on 12 May (*Letters* 4:325). The *Life* suggests that Boswell saw Johnson on several days from 21 to 29 May (*Life* 4:281; see *Applause* 217n8) and saw him "frequently" on 17–21 June (*Life* 4:311).

2. *Applause* 174, 174n9 (see also *Later Years* 267); *Letters* 4:319, 328–329 (see also 327, 332, 335–36).

3. *Corr.*4: 159–60; *Letters* 4:329, 362; Register (Yale M255 for May 1784). Temple objected in detail on 27 May and wondered what Burke and Johnson thought: "If they approve, I have nothing to oppose" (Yale C2823). A week later, having reread Boswell's

letter, he wrote, "If you really have Dr Johnsons approbation, I have no more objections; but take care you did not surprise or cajole him into consent. I know he likes flattery & that you can submit to avail yourself of it to him" (C 2824).

4. *Letters* 4:362; *Applause* 242, 259; *Letters* 4:347; *Yale-SJ* 2:455.

5. *Applause* 220, 226–27, 230, 232–33, 237–42, 250–51; *Letters* 4:332; *Diaries* 370.

6. *Applause* 231, 250; *Letters* 4:329, 332, 336; Register (Yale M255 for June 1784).

7. *Applause* 248, 253–57. See *Letters* 4:354 and *Life* 4:339; see also Donna Heiland, "Swan Songs: The Correspondence of Anna Seward and James Boswell," *Modern Philology* 90 (1993): 286–88.

8. *Applause* 229.

9. *Letters* 4:166; *Applause* 215–16.

10. *Laird* 470; *Corr.* 6: 392; *Life* 3:89.

11. *Applause* 234, 238. We do not have Boswell's original notes or journal entries for these scenes.

12. *Life* 4:179–80; *Applause* 261. In 1781, Boswell had shown some of his essays to Forbes (Yale L541.3, Yale C1271), and in 1782 had shown some to Kames (*Laird* 463–65). In the *Life* (1:210), Boswell quoted Elizabeth Johnson's praise as he introduced the *Rambler,* but did not report Johnson's later applying these words to the *Hypochondriack.*

13. *Applause* 213, 242; *GT2* 286; Yale C2827. After Johnson's death, Boswell asked Reynolds about "a half bound Volume of printed Essays, which [Johnson] undertook to revise" (*Corr.* 3: 176–77).

14. *Letters* 4:341–45, 347. On 1 July, a day after he parted from Boswell, Johnson heard from Thrale that she was marrying Piozzi, and the next day wrote a harsh letter (*Letters* 4:338) in which (as Bate put it) "all the pain of the last year and a half suddenly expresses itself" (Bate 589). On 8 July, after Thrale firmly rejected his characterization of her marriage as "ignominious," Johnson wrote more kindly, but for the last time, though Thrale replied on 15 July (Chapman 3:184). See McCarthy, *Hester Thrale Piozzi,* 37–38.

15. *Letters* 4:342, 354–55, 401 (see also 357); Register (Yale M255 for August 1784).

16. *Corr.* 3: 169–171; *Applause* 258–62; *Letters* 4:355. Though opposed to Boswell's trying the English bar, Temple dismissed his friend's "pusillanimous" worry that he was incapable of mastering English law (Yale C2827).

17. *Corr.* 3: 172; *Letters* 4:362; *Life* 4:379. Two weeks earlier, Boswell had invited Paoli (see Yale L1018 and Yale C2163).

18. *Letters* 4:361–63. Bruce Redford, following R. W. Chapman (who did not have access to what Johnson wrote Forbes on 7 August), dates Johnson's letters to Boswell as c. 5 August and c. 7 August (*Letters* 4:354n1, 358, 360). But Johnson noted that Boswell's "gloomy" letter arrived as he began writing Forbes. So his first reply was written no earlier than 7 August, and perhaps later, since Johnson's first words (according to the *Life* manuscript) were, "I was in no haste to answer your letter, for it" (Yale M144, 1010). Johnson's second letter was posted two days after the first.

19. *Letters* 4:358–60; see *Letters* 2:348–50.

20. *Corr.* 1: 304.

21. *Boswell's Autobiography* (London: Chatto & Windus, 1912), 250.

22. *Corr.* 3: 154; *Corr.* 1: 304–6; *Applause* 268, 265. *James Boswell's Book of Com-*

pany at Auchinleck, 1782–1795, ed. Viscountess Eccles and Gordon Turnbull (London: Roxburghe Club, 1995), documents the decline in social activity. In 1783, Boswell dined elsewhere ten times in September, six times accompanied by Margaret; but now he dined away only twice, both times alone. In October 1784 there were many fewer guests at dinner than in the previous October (39 rather than 117) and correspondingly fewer staying over (31 rather than 102).

23. Boswell enclosed a letter to the Reverend Joseph Fergusson in his letter to Grange and promised "to write earnestly to Mr. Dundas" about him as well as about himself (*Corr.* 1: 306) — a letter he seems to have sent (*Applause* 369n1). For the seven received, see Yale C990–91, 1362, 2355, 1637, 2828, 2215.

24. *Hypochondriack* 1:146; *Applause* 262; Yale C2827.

25. *Corr.* 1 304–5; *Letters* 4:368 (see also Diaries 381–82, 384).

26. *Applause* 263 (see also *Laird* 135: "callous from melancholy").

27. For *Prayers and Meditations*, see *Diaries* xvi–xvii; Michael Bundock, "The Making of Johnson's *Prayers and Meditations*," *Age of Johnson* 14 (2003): 83–89; and Katherine Kickel, "'Occasional' Observations of a Quiet Mind: Meditative Theory and Practice in Samuel Johnson's *Prayers and Meditations* (1785)," *Age of Johnson* 20 (2010): 35–60.

28. *Letters* 4:374–75, 420, 411, 383, 416, 400, 398, 405.

29. *Corr.* 2: 389; *Letters* 4:348–50, 443–44. Compare these letters jostling silent friends into activity with Johnson's lament two years earlier that he and Langton were both unwisely letting their long friendship "dye away by negligence and silence" (*Letters* 4:22–24).

30. *Applause* 263–64 (see also 265–71).

31. For accounts of Johnson's final days, see Hawkins, *Life of Johnson,* 349–58; John Hoole, "The Narrative of John Hoole" (*JM* 2:145–60); and *Life* 4:415–18. For Boswell's concern about his letters and their return, see *Corr.* 3: 175 and *Experiment* 19n1.

32. *Applause* 271–74; *Corr.* 3: 174–75.

33. Yale C2829.

Chapter 16: Rewriting the Hebrides Trip (1785)

1. *Applause* 271–72; Register (Yale M255 for December 1784); *Corr.* 3: 179.

2. *Hebrides* 188 (see also 242), 411–12; *Applause* 277.

3. *Applause* 272–77 (the final entries were written on 23 February); Register (Yale M255 for March 1785).

4. Yale C2830, 2831; *Applause* 285–88; Register (Yale M255 for April 1785).

5. *Applause* 276–77n6; see also Yale L1019.

6. *Corr.* 3: 186; *Applause* 283–84.

7. *Hebrides* 369–76.

8. *Applause* 287–90.

9. *Applause* 277–78 (Forbes), 303n6 (codicil). See also *Applause* 291, 300.

10. *Applause* 288n4, 289–302; James Boswell, *A Letter to the People of Scotland* (London, 1785), 59, 92, 104. See Michael Fry, "James Boswell, Henry Dundas, and Enlightened Politics" (Lustig 87–100). Once Boswell's *Letter* "catalyzed the opposition," the bill was withdrawn (*Later Years* 280).

11. *Hebrides* xviii–xix (see also *Corr.*4: 165–72 and Peter Martin, *Edmond Malone: Shakespearean Scholar* [Cambridge: Cambridge University Press, 1995], 96–102). For Boswell's earlier contact with Malone, see *Laird* 323–24, 336, 347, and *Applause* 217n6, 248.

12. *Corr.*4: 189–95; *Applause* 306, 313, 323.

13. *Corr.*4: 222 (see also 233), 256, 264. See *Corr.*4: 189–266. For Boswell's claim to be publishing exactly what Johnson had read, see *Hebrides* 54n4 and *Corr.*4: 210.

14. *Applause* 306, 315, 317, 322, 338; *Life* 5:1. In December 1785, after having worked with Malone on the first and second editions of the *Tour*, Boswell added a second codicil naming Malone as sole literary executor for the publication of the *Life of Johnson* (*Applause* 304n6).

15. *Applause* 336; *Corr.*3: 196 (see also 181, 174); Yale C2835.

16. *Hebrides* 75 and *Life* 5:105 (ghosts—but see *Hebrides* 202, 317, 84); *Hebrides* 247–51 and *Life* 5: 280–83 (storm). Boswell still included his worry on 21 September at not having heard from his wife (*Hebrides* 194 and *Life* 5:232); but he dropped most fearful reflections, including all those based on dreams (*Hebrides* 37n9, 87–88, 122, 149, 220, 270, 289–90, 303–4). He kept his report that on 7 September "a kind of lethargy of indolence" kept him from exerting himself to get Johnson to talk (*Hebrides* 122 and *Life* 5:159); but he dropped the seven lines describing the return of "spleen or hypochondria." He included a veiled allusion to his prayers on Raasay (*Hebrides* 142 and *Life* 5:169), and a more explicit account of his private devotions on Iona (*Hebrides* 336 and *Life* 5:336–37); but he dropped three other reports of private devotions, and his comment that he was "so much a disciple of Dr. Ogden's" that he ventured "to pray even upon small occasions" if he felt himself "much concerned" (Yale J33, 7; *Hebrides* 317, 324, 330). Boswell kept his report that on 28 August "a sentence or two of the *Rambler's* conversation gave [him] firmness," but greatly toned down the fears that made him needy (*Hebrides* 95 and *Life* 5:128).

17. *Hebrides* 335 and *Life* 5:336 (credulity). For an early argumentative footnote, see *Life* 5:32n3. For augmented Boswell, see *Life* 5:154 (also *Hebrides* 118) and 205–6 (also *Hebrides* 164). For the effect of memory, compare *Life* 5:333 with *Hebrides* 329. For new, semicollaborative reflections, see *Life* 5:365, 390–91 (compare *Journey* 107–10 on "second sight").

18. *Hebrides* 222–23 and *Life* 5:258–59; *Hebrides* 344 and *Life* 5:342. See also *Hebrides* 240, 246, 285, 344–45. Boswell cut his reference to drinking "too much" on 5 September (*Hebrides* 119), no longer specified drinking "three bowls" of punch at Kingsburgh, nor reported that the "jovial bout disturbed [him] somewhat" (*Hebrides* 160 and *Life* 5:159). Also, in the revised entry for 17 October, Boswell suggested—diffidently—that drinking might change a man "for the better" (*Life* 5:325; the original pages for this part of the entry are missing). For Boswell's resolve on 20 April 1785 to curb excessive drinking, see *Applause* 287 (also *Later Years* 282); for later heavy drinking as he continued revising, see *Applause* 290, 292–94, 312, 325–27, 334, 336, 338, 340–42.

19. *Life* 5:373, 375, 14–16, 405.

20. *Life* 5:32 and 32n3 (Burke's "wit"), 38 (actors), 44 (Swift).

21. *Life* 5:19–20, 70, 130, 248–49, 384 (see also *Hebrides* 443–44). Boswell did not highlight Johnson's self-mockery concerning the innkeeper at Montrose (*Life* 5:72). Concerning Banff, where Johnson wrote that windows in Scotland "are seldom accommo-

dated with weights and pullies" (*Journey* 22), Boswell remarked Johnson's overgeneraliz-ing (Life 5:109–10n6). For a suggestive analysis of Boswell's strategy, see Evan Gottlieb, *Feeling British: Sympathy and National Identity in Scottish and English Writing, 1707–1832* (Lewisburg, Penn.: Bucknell University Press, 2007), 123–33.

22. *Hebrides* 107 and *Life* 5:142 (serving); *Life* 5:387 ("contradiction"), 324 ("vic-tory"), 17 ("sophist"); *Life* 5:45 (Sir Adolphus); Yale J33, 28, and *Life* 5:77 (Monboddo).

23. *Hebrides* 17, 17n10 and *Life* 5:29–32; *Life* 2:441–42; 3:119.

24. *Hebrides* 376, 443 and *Life* 5:383.

25. *Hebrides* 243–44 and *Life* 5:278 (copartnership); Yale J32, 1, and *Life* 5:21–22 (arm in arm); *Hebrides* 331 and *Life* 5:334 (Iona). Omitted teases: *Hebrides* 293 and *Life* 5:305 (courting); *Hebrides* 322 and *Life* 5:329–30 (Inch Boswell). For suppressed anger: *Hebrides* 263 and *Life* 5:291 (dunes on Coll), *Hebrides* 291 and *Life* 5:305 (Pekin). For the debate about Scottish clergy, see *Hebrides* 216 and *Life* 5:252 (also *Hebrides* 265 and *Life* 5:292, as well as *Life* 5:396). Boswell kept, however, Johnson's complaint that Boswell's "bustling and walking quickly up and down" as they waited to sail from Coll was like "getting on horseback in a ship" — "All boys do it; and you are longer a boy than others" — and also what he himself had written to express his irritation with this demean-ing insult: "He himself has no alertness, or whatever it may be called; so he may dislike it, as *Oderunt hilarem tristes* [Gloomy people hate a merry fellow]" (*Hebrides* 294–96 and *Life* 5:307–8).

26. *Hebrides* 110–14 and *Life* 5:144–46; *Journey* 48 ("endangered"); *Corr.*4: 256, 264 (*terrible*). For Boswell's sense that his laughter might have contributed to Johnson's anger, see *Life* 5:216–17. Boswell also knew that Johnson "did not like to be left alone" (*Life* 5:302). Johnson originally spelled the name of the formidable hill "Rattiken" (*Letters* 2:76), then "Ratiken" (*Journey* 48); Boswell, having earlier used "Rattachan" (*Hebrides* 109), now used "Rattakin."

27. *Corr.*3: 209, 211–13; *Corr.*4: 222.

28. *Hebrides* 176–77 and *Life* 5:216–17 (see also *Hebrides* 424–25). For Boswell's enhancement of this "comic" scene, see William Siebenshuh, *Form and Purpose in Bos-well's Biographical Works* (Berkeley and Los Angeles: University of California Press, 1972), 37.

29. *Applause* 342; *Experiment* 10; *Applause* 346–50 (see Larsen 103–37 and *Later Years* 323–25); Yale C999.

30. *Corr.*4: 200, 207.

Chapter 17: Boswell Claiming His Inheritance (1786–1791)

1. For Boswell reading Piozzi's *Anecdotes*, see *Experiment* 53; for its rapid sale, see McCarthy, *Hester Thrale Piozzi*, 50–51. For circuit, see *Experiment* 50–58; for Haw-kins, *Experiment* 81. For Rudd, see *Applause* 335–40; *Experiment* 8, 32–35, 37–40, 42–47, 50–51, 51n6, 59–61; *Later Years* 294–95, 319–20, 322, 325, 335–36; and Turnbull, "Criminal Biographer," 522–31. For sorting, see *Experiment* 67–72, 74, 76; for initial writing, *Experiment* 81–83. For earlier *Lives* of Johnson, see *The Early Biogra-phies of Samuel Johnson*, ed. O. M. Brack, Jr., and Robert E. Kelley (Iowa City: Univer-sity of Iowa Press, 1974).

2. Yale M153 and M158.

3. *Corr.*3: 231 (Langton), 147–48 (Burke); Larsen 123–24 and *Corr.*2: 179 (Forbes). For negotiation with Percy, see *Corr.*2: 304–7. For later objections by others, see *Corr.*3: 317–19, 325–26, 336–38, 342–43, 372.

4. *Experiment* 156, 194, 199; 223; Larsen 97. For Boswell's rising above resentment at what Johnson wrote in these letters, see *Life* 3:134 and 134n1, where, instead of protesting Johnson's insulting comment ("in the phrase of *Hockley in the Hole,* it is a pity he has not a *better bottom*"), Boswell praised his friend's "ardour of mind, and vigour of enterprise."

5. For a detailed chronology, see *Corr.*2: xlix–lxix. For a description of the manuscript and the "Papers Apart," see *Catalogue* 1:85–88 and Redford 23.

6. *Corr.*2: lv–lxvii, 175, 306, 218; *Biographer* 127; Tinker 2:388.

7. For vacillation, see *Experiment* 8, 16, 64–65, 69–70, 135, 146–47, 190. For the bar, see 136, 270. For Parliament, see *Experiment* 250–51. For Lonsdale, see *Experiment* 87–88, 101–2, 106–9, 156–57, 161–62, 164–84, 256–57, 280–85.

8. *Experiment* 190, 192–93, 286; *Biographer* 11–12. For lingering remorse and later longings for Margaret, see *Experiment* 253, 274 and *Biographer* 70, 82, 136. See Ingram, *Boswell's Creative Gloom,* 187–93 on the "consolation" of working on the *Life.*

9. *Biographer* 56 (see also 108), 86, 100–1, 122, 125. See also *Experiment* 130, 144, 148, 153, 159, 164, 188–89, 194, 203, 205, 219–20, 224, 232, 237, 241, 247–48, 280; *Biographer* 61–62, 124, 130; *Corr.*4: 408–9.

10. *Experiment* 157.

11. See Frederick A. Pottle, "The Power of Memory in Boswell and Scott," in *Essays on the Eighteenth Century Presented to David Nichol Smith* (Oxford: Clarendon Press, 1945), 168–89, and William R. Siebenshuh, "Boswell's Second Crop of Memory: A New Look at the Role of Memory in the Making of the *Life*" (Vance 94–109).

12. For examples of retrospection, see *Defence* 44, 104 (1772) and *Laird* 237 (1780). For Marshall Waingrow on inferring from Boswell's omissions and changes, see *Corr.*2: xxxiv–xxxix.

13. *Life* 4:427–28. For a few of Hawkins's "errors," see *Life* 1:125n4 (added to draft), 141, 192n3, 204–5, 208n1, 340–41. "Sir John's carelessness to ascertain facts is very remarkable" (*Life* 4:327n5). Also see Herbert Davis, *Johnson Before Boswell* (New Haven, Conn.: Yale University Press, 1960), 96–125. For Mrs. Piozzi's "unintentionally" deviating "from exact authenticity of narration," see *Life* 3:226, 228–29 — both additions to the original manuscript (see *Extremes* 246–47) — and *Life* 4:340–47. On the "slippery techniques by which Boswell insinuates his own centrality and authority," and the complicity of later scholars, see John Wiltshire, *The Making of Dr. Johnson: Icon of Modern Culture* (Westfield, UK: Helm, 2009), 46–82.

14. *Life* 1:26. *Monthly Review,* quoted in Larsen 178. For days together, see Appendix. For "negligence," see *Life* 2:372, 375; 4:100, 182; also 3:376, 4:166, *Life ms* 2:192.

15. *Life ms* 1:345–46; 2:23.

16. For 23 March 1772, when the journal reported Johnson's going to the Club after dining with Boswell, the *Life* simply moves to their next meeting, four days later (*Defence* 58; *Life* 2:157).

17. *Life ms* 1:15–19, 22, 38–40, 21–22; *Life* 1:60n3; *Life ms* 1:41. Also see *Life ms* 1:76, 107, 139, 153, 169, 351–54.

18. *Life ms* 1:177–79 (see also *Life ms* 2:20–21). For Boswell's using anecdotes from a range of Johnson's friends, see *Life ms* 1:38, 44–48, 58, 68, 98–99, 111, 170–75; see also John J. Burke, Jr., "But Boswell's Johnson Is Not Boswell's Johnson" (Vance 172–203). Boswell significantly changed the story of Johnson's idling in a churchyard on Sunday, which Beauclerk had told to prove that Johnson "did not practice religion" (*Life ms* 1:178 and *Ominous* 93); and he removed Langton from the significant scene where Adams discovered Johnson in deep depression (*Applause* 246 and *Life ms* 1:339).

19. *Letters* 1:473–76; *Life* 2:20–25, 66–68, 116.

20. Having earlier cut major parts of only the two letters from July 1776, Boswell now cut all but a short paragraph from the letter of 21 September 1782, much of what Johnson wrote on 30 September 1783, and much of the final three letters.

21. *Life ms* 1:273, 275 (see also 314); *Life ms* 2:158; *Life* 3:269 (additional talk); *Life* 2:213–14; *Life* 3:131; *Life* 4:166, 226, 283, 286.

22. For 14 July 1763, see *Life ms* 1:303. Johnson's declaration of "love" in 1772 (*Defence* 52) was in the journal that became the copy text for the *Life*, but on a page not used; his declaration of love in 1781 (*Laird* 293) was never in the draft. For "regard," see *Life* 3:198; for "serious frame," see *Life* 3:312 (compare *Extremes* 197).

23. *Corr*.2: 111–12 (Pindar); *Life* 1:450, 2:70, 3:135, 3:216, 3:442 (for declarations of love and esteem in letters); *Extremes* 158 and *Life ms* 3:103n1 (birthday insult); *Ominous* 63 and *Life* 2:295–96 ("publication"); *Life ms* 3:112 ("madness"); *BP* 6:258 and *Life ms* 2:78n5 ("like an ass "); *Life ms* 2:44 ("Dunce").

24. *Life* 3:39, 4:427.

25. *Life ms* 1:314, 327, 331 (added to the draft); *Life* 2:149 (St. Kilda); *Life* 3:294 (see also *Extremes* 290); *Life ms* 2:98 (Hebrides); *Life* 3:131, 288, 435 (another adventure). For trips with others, see *Life ms* 1:341 (Cambridge with Beauclerk); *Life* 1:377–79 (Devon with Reynolds); *Life* 1:476–77, 3:360–63, 4:8, 4:22 (visits to Langton); *Life* 4:235–39 (visit with Bowles); *Life* 2:389–404, 3:93–94, 3:132 (with the Thrales, including France).

26. *Life* 2:3–4, 140, 168; 4:204–6; 2:202; 3:93–94, 368, 79–80, 342–43. On Rudd, see also *Life ms* 2:197 and 197n6, *Life* 3:330. For Reynolds and Temple on Rudd, see *Applause* 339 and Yale C2835.

27. *Life* 3:116–17, 418, 342–44; *Life of Samuel Johnson, LL.D.* (London, 1793), 1:xxix–xxxi.

28. *Life* 1:260; 2:444, 455, 459–60, 464–65; 3:140–48; 2:330–31 (orange peels [added — see *Life ms* 2:144]), *Life* 3:268 (questions in 1776); *Life ms* 2:212 and *Life* 3:57, 268 ("a gentleman" instead of Boswell in 1776 and 1778); *Life ms* 1:41 (town clock); *Life* 4:372–73 (Uttoxeter); *Life* 3:260 (Johnson seeing journal).

29. For Piozzi's cut, see Chapman 2:228–29, 229n8. For Sheridan, see *Life* 1:387–89; *Life ms* 1:267; *Life* 4:222, 330. For Wilkes, see *Life* 3:64–79, 3:183, 4:107. For Percy, see *Life* 3:271–78.

30. *Life* 3:329 (Reynolds); *Life* 3:384–85 (Beauclerk — see also *Laird* 83 and Redford 155–56); *Life* 4:280 (Langton). *Life* 3:260, 290, 300, 315, 338 (Boswell). For other discussions of previous days' conversations, see *Life* 1:443–44, 2:66.

31. *Life* 4:295. See also *Hebrides* 257 and *Life* 5:288.

32. *Ominous* 145; *Life* 2:357 (see also *Life* 4:148); *Life* 3:153–54, 200 (compare *Note*

Book 23, where Boswell infers that "Johnson seemed inclined to mitigate" what in the *Life* Johnson openly states might be "mitigated"), 208. Hawkins, *Life of Johnson,* 341.

33. On skepticism, see *Life ms* 1:275 (but see also *Life ms* 1:280 and *London* 250). On "charge," see *London* 251 and *Life ms* 1:284. On subordination, see *Life ms* 1:309 (see also *London* 283). On melancholy, see *London* 287 and *Life ms* 1:312 (see also *Ominous* 276 [and 286] and *Life* 2:440, *Ominous* 303 and *Life* 3:5). On principles, see *Life ms* 1:317 and *London* 293.

34. *Wife* 147 and *Life ms* 2:25 (law); *Extremes* 168 and *Life* 3:175–76 (awe); *Life ms* 2:30 ("Lady"); *Life* 3:27 ("solitude"—see also *Ominous* 322). Also compare *Life ms* 2:155 to *Ominous* 140–41, and *Life* 3:49 to *BP* 11:267. See also *Life* 4:223, where I think the "gentleman [who] talked of retiring" was not Burke but Boswell.

35. *Life* 2:427 (see also *Ominous* 256); 3:193 (see also *Extremes* 181). *Applause* 101 and *Life* 3:391 (food and spirits); see also *Extremes* 165, 178 and *Applause* 141 (for moments not mentioned in the *Life* when Johnson's conversation "had an immediate cordial effect" on Boswell's spirits); also compare *Extremes* 173 to *Life* 3:180 (on attending church with Johnson).

36. *Life* 3:122n2; 3:215; 2:411; *Life ms* 2:1–3 (see also Redford 124–25), 23. For Boswell's anxiety, disappointment, and complaints, see *Life* 2:381 and *Life* 3:89–92, 211, 362, 368, 372, 418. For a few of Johnson's responses to fears that he no longer cared, see *Life* 2:3, 383–84 and *Life* 3:135, 216, 362.

37. *Life* 3:118, 3:438–39, 2:68–69, 3:44; *Defence* 26 and *Life* 2:144–45; *Laird* 481 (see also *Life* 4:155–56).

38. *Life* 2:2–24, 58–59; *Life* 3:116–17,133, 211, 221.

39. *Life ms* 2:8 (Rousseau); *Life ms* 1:41–42, *Life* 3:175–76 and *Extremes* 168–69 (melancholy and madness). For odd opinions or prejudices, see *Life ms* 1:122–23 (disparaging actors); *Life ms* 2:126–30 and *Life* 4:168–69 (disliking Scots); *Life* 4:61–62 (denigrating Swift). For Johnson's deficiency in taste, see *Life ms* 2:147–48, 191 (added to *Ominous* 276). *Life ms* 2:187, 274 (Scottish militia, and Boswell's hesitation in stating that Johnson was "*certainly*" in the wrong); *Life* 3:191 and *Extremes* 180 (memory); *Life ms* 1:234 (climate); *Life* 3:336–37 and *Extremes* 327 (conversation). For Boswell's adding what he might have said but had not reported, compare *Life* 3:296 with *Extremes* 291. For his quoting—as if spoken *to* Johnson—what his journal described as a long "digression from Dr. Johnson," see *Extremes* 171 and *Life* 3:178.

40. *Life* 4:426; *Life ms* 1:92; *Life ms* 1:309; *Life ms* 3:101–03, 123–24, 145, 147–49; *Life* 3:225, 315. On the Middlesex election, see *Corr.6:* 264. See also *Life ms* 1:90–91, on "the flaming heat of patriotism and zeal for popular resistance" in *London,* which Boswell oddly calls a "juvenile poem," though Johnson was twenty-eight when it was published.

41. *Life* 4:259, 261.

42. *Life ms* 1:274; see also *Life ms* 1:280, 317–18. For Hume, see *Life* 1:444–45, 2:106, 3:153, 4:422n1. For "vigorous reason," see *Life* 4:426, 370, 370n3. For prayers on recovery, see *Life ms* 1:218, 218n1; see also *Life* 4:271–72 (added).

43. *Life ms* 1:331–32. Freedom is also mentioned in 1772 (*Life* 2:178), 1778 (*Life* 3:335), 1781 (*Life* 4:71, 122–23), and in a footnote to 1783 (*Life* 4:238n1).

44. *Life ms* 2:43, 54–55. The word "supposed" was added to the draft. See *Defence*

102—a passage not used in the *Life* (*Life* 2:178). See *Life ms* 1:340; also *Life ms* 2:28 and *Wife* 153.

45. *Life* 3:290–91 (see also *Extremes* 289–90). Though based on Boswell's entry, this passage was inserted on the verso of page 691.

46. *Life* 4:328–29. No entry survives for this discussion. For what Boswell first drafted, see *Applause* 249. For background, see *Applause* 190. Boswell probably had in mind the argument in letter 69 of Montesquieu's *Persian Letters*, which suggests that although God can know whatever he wishes about what people will do, he usually does not seek this knowledge, leaving his creatures free to behave well or badly—a letter to which Boswell referred readers of the conversation about freedom in 1778 (*Life* 3:291n3; see also *Laird* 283 and *Corr.2:* 319–22).

47. *Life ms* 2:154; *Life* 3:5; *Life* 2:453 (see also *Ominous* 138, 303); *Life* 3:199. See also *Life* 1:457; *Life* 2:169, 451–52; *Life* 3:242, 378.

48. *Life* 3:316–17; see *Extremes* 301–2 and *Life ms* 3:230.

49. *Life* 1:213.

50. *Life ms* 1:240–41. Boswell is alluding to Étienne Bonnot de Condillac's *Traité des sensations* (1754); the "grave and anxious gentleman" was Langton (*Corr.4:* 143).

51. *Life* 3:164–66 (see also *Extremes* 163–64); *Life* 3:305.

52. *Life* 4:300–5; Yale M144, 956; *Life* 1:48–49. Curiously, Boswell cut from the draft for October 1779 his telling Johnson during a discussion of the *Dictionary,* "You have had more happy days since that time than you ever had before" (*Laird* 142; *Life* 3:405).

Chapter 18: Winning Johnson's Blessing

1. *Life* 5:17, 380.

2. Easily offended: *Life* 2:253–54; *Life* 3:273, 315, 337, 384–85. Loud voice: *Life* 3:139, 150, 155–56. "Ventured": *Life* 3:153 (compare *Extremes* 155), 155 (compare *Note Book* 22). Bull and bear both (*Life* 2:66); bear (*Life* 2:347–48); bull (*Life* 3:156). Diverting (*Life* 3:290, 315). For widespread reports of Johnson's roughness, see Wiltshire, *Making Dr. Johnson,* 13–38.

3. *Life* 1:410; *Life* 3:81 (an added passage); *Life* 4:109–10, 341. Felicity Nussbaum charts how Boswell consistently balances Johnson's temperamental moments with his benevolence ("Boswell's Treatment of Johnson's Temper," 423). Bruce Redford, having described how Boswell eliminated most of Johnson's hostility and petulance during the 1776 visit, astutely sees Boswell's adding two paragraphs on Johnson's politeness as evidence of his "arguing with himself" (Redford 152–54).

4. *Life* 1:410; *Life* 2:450 (added to draft); *Life* 3:80–81 (added); *Life* 4:111, 429 (added).

5. *Life* 4:111 (victory); *Life* 2:359 ("quiet interchange"); *Wife* 153 and *Life ms* 2:28; *Wife* 327 and *Life ms* 2:52; *Defence* 122 and *Life ms* 2:73–74, 76 (insulting retorts); *Life* 2:66 ("tossed and gored"); *Life* 3:80 and *Life* 4:274 ("unjustifiable"); *Life* 2:109 (apologize—see also *Anecdotes* 97). See *Life* 3:335–36, 408, where Johnson pulls back from insults; and *Life* 4:168, where Johnson mused, "I wonder how I should have any enemies; for I do harm to nobody"—a comment concerning which Boswell added to the draft, "This reflection was very natural in a man of a good heart, who was not conscious of any

ill-will to mankind, though the sharp sayings which were sometimes produced by his discrimination and vivacity, and which he perhaps did not recollect, were, I am afraid, too often remembered with resentment."

6. *Life* 5:30 *Life* 2:12–14; *Life* 4:295; *Life* 2:443; *Life* 3:80; *Life* 2:286 (completed in revises: see *Life ms* 2:121n1); *Life ms* 2:131; *Life* 2:203 and *Life* 3:298–99 (compare *Ominous* 288 and *Extremes* 288–289, where Johnson seems less violent). Frances Reynolds also noted that whenever "Religion or morality" was challenged, Johnson "totally disregarded all forms or rules of good-breeding" (*JM* 2:257).

7. *Life* 2:362–63.

8. *Extremes* 324–35; *Life* 3:335, 80.

9. *Applause* 229; *Life* 2:106–7. For an intimate confession that Boswell moved from 1778 to 1769 in order to prepare for this new image a week later, see *Extremes* 155 and *Life ms* 2:48.

10. *Life* 3:344–45 (compare *Extremes* 338–39); see *Corr.* 2: 395.

11. *Life* 5:231 (see also *Hebrides* 192); *Life* 3:154; Life 4:299–300.

12. *Life* 4:427.

13. *Life ms* 1:275; *Life ms* 2:9, 193.

14. *Life ms* 1:129–130, 230, 247–48 (and nn4–6), 250, 338–39.

15. *Life ms* 1:147. See *Life ms* 1:40–41, 339 (and *Applause* 246). Concerning "that melancholy, which the public now too well knows was the disease of [Johnson's] mind," Hawkins wrote, "no cause can be assigned; nor will it gratify curiosity to say, it was constitutional" (*Life of Johnson*, 173).

16. *Life ms* 1:338–39.

17. *Life ms* 2:23–24, 34; see *Corr.* 2: xlv–xlvi.

18. *Life ms* 2:67; *Life* 2:189–90, 412.

19. *Life* 3:370; *Life* 4:34. In the first edition, Boswell followed Hawkins in mistakenly assigning publication of the first set of *Lives* to 1778 rather than 1779.

20. *Life* 4:136 (see also 149), 163 (see also 253 — "Notwithstanding . . . Thrale's" — a passage added to draft), 257 (see also 374).

21. *Life ms* 1:312; *Life ms* 2:192; *Life ms* 3:5, where Boswell has Johnson apply to himself what the journal has him prescribing for Boswell (*Ominous* 303). For "constitutional" indolence, see *Life ms* 1:25, 59, 217–18. For Johnson's insistence that idleness was "a disease which must be combated," that we must "burst the shackles of habitual vice," see *Life* 1:428, 475; *Yale-SJ* 5:63 (*Rambler* 155); *Life* 4:9.

22. *Life* 4:381; *Life* 2:119; *Life* 3:98–99 — a passage originally added on verso of page 626 of the manuscript, then modified by Malone during revision (see also *Life ms* 3:72–73, 73n6).

23. *Life* 4:380. For Johnson's resistance, see *Life* 2:162 (*Defence* 73); *Life* 3:312 (*Extremes* 297); *Life* 4:279–80 (*Applause* 215). But see also *Life* 2:43–44, *Corr.* 2: 107.

24. *Biographer* 9. For earlier dreams of Johnson, see *Applause* 276–77n6, 284. On 10 February 1791, Boswell would write Malone that 923 pages of "the Copy" had been printed, "and there remain 80, besides the Death" (*Corr.* 4: 400). Page 1003 of the manuscript (923 plus 80) describes the negotiation concerning the pension, which is continued through page 1006. Page 1008 has Johnson for the last time in Lichfield, with the Uttoxeter anecdote. What Boswell wrote about Johnson's final letters and his eventual response

comes on 1012–13. The movement toward death begins on the second page numbered 1019, which corresponds to *Life* 4:398.

25. *Life* 4:226 and *Applause* 152, 152n8 (Auchinleck); *Extremes* 297 and *Life* 3:312; *Life* 4:379–80. See also *Life* 3:105, 135, 417, 421 and *Life* 4:259, 266.

26. *Life* 3:157 (compare *Extremes* 157–58; see also *Life* 2:106–9); *Life* 4:380. For Margaret and Rudd, see *Experiment* 253, 274.

27. *Life ms* 1:40–41; *Life* 2:295; *Life* 4:163; *Life* 2:20–25, 58–59; *Life* 3:210–12. In 1786, Boswell wrote Margaret, "My constitutional melancholy has been grievous" (*Experiment* 77).

28. *Life* 3:86–87, *Life* 4:379–80.

29. Boswell later replaced "inexplicably ill" with "ill," then with "much indisposed." For a standard evasion, see the entry where he justified copying Johnson's diary at Ashbourne: "Perhaps it was not quite right in me to *take* the liberty of copying out of a little paper-book in his open desk a prayer composed by him on his last birthday, and some short notes of a journal. But my veneration and love of him are such that I could not resist" (*Extremes* 181–82; see also *Experiment* 214, 221).

30. See Deutsch, *Loving Dr. Johnson*, 212–14, which includes an image of page 1012 of the manuscript, showing the lines from *Hamlet* that were twice included and later deleted.

31. *Life* 4:372–73; *Corr.2*: 300; *Life* 4:352–53, 361–62, 407, 380. George Strahan sent the complete story on 4 March 1791, perhaps just before Boswell wrote this portion of the *Life* (*Corr.2*: 300). But Boswell might have earlier heard it from White (see *Corr.2*: 76, 79), and could have read it in the *Political Magazine* for December 1787, which Strahan transcribed. See Deutsch, *Loving Dr. Johnson*, 203–6, and Donna Heiland, "Remembering the Hero in Boswell's *Life of Johnson*" (Clingham 196).

32. *Life* 4:339 (Thrale), 349–50 (George III), 370–71, 395, 399, 399n6 (Hawkins). See Irma Lustig, "Boswell at Work: The 'Animadversions' on Mrs. Piozzi," *Modern Language Review* 67 (1972): 11–30. Hawkins dedicated his edition of Johnson's works to George III (see Hawkins, *Life of Johnson*, 482).

33. *Life* 4:405–6, 406n1. See also *Corr.3*: 175–76; Hawkins, *Life of Johnson*, 355–56; and Michael Bundock, "Did John Hawkins Steal Johnson's Diary?" *Age of Johnson* 21 (2011): 77–92.

34. *Life ms* 2:140; *Life* 4:10, 406–7; David Womersley, introduction to *The Life of Samuel Johnson* (New York: Penguin, 2008), xviii. For Beauclerk's freedom from depression — "except when ill and in pain" — see *Life* 3:5, 192. Anecdotes inserted for 1783 in the second edition helped keep Beauclerk in mind long after his death in 1780 (*Life* 4:180, 197).

35. Vance includes Rader's illuminating study "Literary Form in Factual Narrative" (25–52), along with several key articles by Donald Greene and Frederick A. Pottle debating the accuracy and completeness of the *Life*. For discussion of this continuing debate, see Vance 1–23 and Hart, *Johnson and the Culture of Property*, 92–100. See also Wiltshire, *Making Dr. Johnson*, 145–255.

36. David Buchanan, *The Treasure of Auchinleck: The Story of the Boswell Papers* (New York: McGraw-Hill, 1974) and Frederick A. Pottle, *Pride and Negligence: The History of the Boswell Papers* (New York: McGraw-Hill, 1982).

Index